Implementing SAP® Business Planning and Consolidation

 **PRESS**

SAP PRESS is a joint initiative of SAP and Galileo Press. The know-how offered by SAP specialists combined with the expertise of the Galileo Press publishing house offers the reader expert books in the field. SAP PRESS features first-hand information and expert advice, and provides useful skills for professional decision-making.

SAP PRESS offers a variety of books on technical and business-related topics for the SAP user. For further information, please visit our website: *www.sap-press.com*.

Peter Jones

Implementing SAP® Business Planning and Consolidation

Bonn • Boston

Galileo Press is named after the Italian physicist, mathematician, and philosopher Galileo Galilei (1564–1642). He is known as one of the founders of modern science and an advocate of our contemporary, heliocentric worldview. His words *Eppur si muove* (And yet it moves) have become legendary. The Galileo Press logo depicts Jupiter orbited by the four Galilean moons, which were discovered by Galileo in 1610.

Editor Katy Spencer
Copyeditor Julie McNamee
Cover Design Graham Geary
Photo Credit iStockphoto.com/shahrohani
Layout Design Vera Brauner
Production Kelly O'Callaghan, Graham Geary
Typesetting Publishers' Design and Production Services, Inc.
Printed and bound in the United States of America, on paper from sustainable sources

ISBN 978-1-59229-422-0

© 2013 by Galileo Press Inc., Boston (MA)

1st edition 2013

Library of Congress Cataloging-in-Publication Data
Jones, Peter, 1953 Oct. 9–
Implementing SAP business planning and consolidation / Peter Jones.—1st ed.
p. cm.
ISBN 978-1-59229-422-0—ISBN 1-59229-422-7 1. SAP ERP. 2. Business
planning—Computer programs. 3. Business planning—Data processing. I. Title.
HD30.28.J663 2013
658.4'01028553—dc23
2012034690

Contents at a Glance

Dear Reader,

When I look at the cover of *Implementing SAP Business Planning and Consolidation*, I'm reminded that writing a book is like navigating a winding road: the trip is filled with hairpin turns, smooth straight-aways, and the occasional yielding to fellow drivers. Exploring new vistas and views of the world, we continually realign ourselves to an ever-changing landscape, with hopefully minimal cursing of the GPS along the way. We arrive at our final destination, all the better for having taken our road trip and learning incredible lessons.

So get your roadtrip playlist ready and join Peter Jones and contributor Tim Soper as they expertly guide you through the implementation process of Business Planning and Consolidation (BPC). Learn to develop effective business solutions, aggregate data, and save time with SAP's BPC tool. From start to finish, this comprehensive book guides you through configuring and implementing the necessary dimensions, master data, and hierarchies for both the Planning and Consolidation components.

We at SAP PRESS are always eager to hear your opinion. What do you think of *Implementing SAP Business Planning and Consolidation*? Because your comments and suggestions are our most useful tools to help us make our books the best they can be, we encourage you to visit our website at *www.sap-press.com* to share your feedback.

Thank you for purchasing a book from SAP PRESS!

Katy Spencer
Editor, SAP PRESS

Galileo Press
Boston, MA

katy.spencer@galileo-press.com
www.sap-press.com

Contents

5 Data Loading in BPC 263

6 Forecasting, Planning, and Budgeting in BPC 369

7 Consolidation in BPC 427

9 Business Process Flows (BPF) 577

10 Migration Process to BPC V10.0 621

Acknowledgments

It has been four or five years since I wrote my last technical book, and when considering the opportunity to write this book on SAP Business Planning and Consolidation Version 10.0 (BPC), I remembered the challenges that came along with a task of this nature. Having been involved with writing three other SAP books, one on FICO configuration and two on BW reporting and data modeling, I'm aware of the importance of accurate and consistent information in a book of this nature. I realize that many functional, application, and IT consultants, as well as anyone who just wants a better idea of the functionality and application of BPC V10.0, will be looking to this book for answers and ideas to help with the implementation or even the decision to implement BPC V10.0. Because we all participate in some sort of SAP-based project activity, we are aware of the many challenges of completing a project on time, on budget, and with a successful approval rating from the customer. Writing a technical book is very similar to that experience but only to a much larger audience. Writing a technical book for an SAP product, which is, by nature, changing and shifting as we speak, presents the most significant challenge of making sure we deliver the most up-to-date and consistent information possible at the current time as well as we position the information we provide for future possible changes. In many cases, a task like this takes from seven to nine months; during that time, the SAP systems are changing on an ongoing basis. By the time this book is available, some of the functionality discussed will have evolved. However, an understanding of the underlying basics and the application of the concepts will always work no matter what upgrades have occurred. We are able to reference during this book the specific support packages (SPs) and patches so you have some point of validation or reference for the material presented in this book. This way, after reading this book, you don't have to go back through the book and realign the process we've been talking about to reflect any future SPs or patches.

The opportunity to write for SAP PRESS about the latest and greatest BPC version is definitely an honor, privilege, and challenge all at the same time. One of the challenges in writing this book is the surprise factor. We all know that BPC as an integrated component of SAP NetWeaver is relatively new, and with the advent of BPC V10.0 for SAP NetWeaver, the integration has become very robust and has changed by leaps and bounds from BPC V7.5. That being the case, we've found frequent surprises while working with the new product, especially because it's recently in ramp-up, and many different aspects of this product have emerged as we worked our way through system configuration, projects and documentation. There have also been times when we have had questions about the impact or effect of tweaking certain parameters, so we spent time testing every inch of the process just to be sure everything is covered. I guess we wouldn't be in this business if we didn't have that sense of curiosity for the new and interesting. It would just get downright boring if everything worked as expected and correctly all of the time. Like us, you probably love those times when you finally understand and say to yourself, "so, that's how it works," and then savor the success for a moment before moving on to the next challenge.

Another challenge we all face with a new product is the amount of documentation that is available. For BPC V10.0 for Microsoft and NetWeaver, the volumes of documentation are growing quickly and will continue to grow for all of the new functionality coming out in the next series of SPs and patches. As you know having as many options available for documentation and knowledge transfer is always helpful. With this BPC product we have several challenges and this book looks to offer an additional source of information to overcome those challenges. With the evolution of the product, as we move from SP to SP and patch to patch, it is critical to understand the core functionality and the concepts behind the functions. Once this is understood no matter what new tweaks are added to the features or functionality we should be in good shape to address them, understand how we can use them and quickly integrate them into a current environment and architecture.

This book strives to answer many of your questions and to help make the search for value in the functionality of BPC V10.0 both for SAP NetWeaver and Microsoft a little easier. I hope you find at least one of those surprise moments that will help you configure, implement, or just understand the activities and processes involved in BPC. Be sure to reference this book during your projects, or, if you have a serious work/life balance issue like I do, you might just read this type of documentation in your spare time.

This book also presented another challenge in that we are working with several new products all at the same time. One is SAP NetWeaver Business Warehouse (BW) 7.3, which just finished ramp-up around the middle of last year, so the tires have been kicked, and we can feel pretty good about the stability and consistency of the system. The second is SAP Enterprise Performance Management (EPM) add-in version 10.0, which is delivered as the standard frontend reporting component with this product. It is also a new product with more SPs and patches coming out than the core BPC V10.0 has. The distribution cycle for the EPM add-in patch is every three to four weeks, and a SP increase is in line with a SP change process being assigned to BPC. Finally, of course, the BPC V10.0 itself has changed dramatically, and also the underlying platform was changed to reflect a more integrated suite to SAP NetWeaver. So we'll be working and describing multiple system functionalities and architectures all together in this book.

As everyone knows, there are always many, many people that help support an endeavor like this one, and the person that has helped me in many a situation is my incredible wife. After the last book I wrote for SAP NetWeaver BW, my comment was "I'm done writing books," but after writing several articles for BI Expert, I caught the bug again and was very thankful when this opportunity came along. My wife, Lisa, has dealt with the numerous deadlines and milestones, that always come with juggling your day job, and writing a book with great patience and commitment. Lisa, thank you many times over for all of your help, support, patience, and giving up all of those weekends while I sat and typed away.

I would also like to thank another group of people who have made it possible to help me hone my skills on BPC V10.0 for SAP NetWeaver by graciously letting me work on their BPC project. Initially they were going with BPC V7.5, but after a series of discussions, they decided to forgo the safe route of BPC V7.5 and go headlong into the BPC V10.0 product with all of the gotchas that we know will come with a product that is in ramp-up as we go live. Thanks to Timothy Daley, Samuel Mathai, and Antoinette Lepre for their patience during this BPC project and dealing with the numerous issues that come with a very new BPC product and platform.

I would also like to thank Bill Miller for his help with my efforts in the SAP world. He offered me the opportunity to expand my scope of knowledge and experiences with the SAP software, and I thank him for the effort and risk he took to support my interests.

A special thanks to Tim Soper who has worked tirelessly in helping as a supporting author on this book. His efforts, professionalism, and commitment have been invaluable to the success of this book and the information available. I know this took significant amounts of time from your schedule and weekends. In addition to your sacrifices, I know that Jazmin has also dealt with those deadlines and milestones. Jazmin, thanks for your understanding and patience during this process.

There are so many people's efforts that go into a book like this from the software developers at SAP who create a software product of this caliber, to everyone that I've worked with when it came to fixing bugs and investigating that interesting parameter that showed up on a screen and had to be investigated, as well as everyone on the multiple BPC V10 projects that I've been involved with that have exchanged ideas and concepts to make this product a better and more effective component for a corporation to use and benefit from over time.

One of my main goals in writing this book is to offer some ideas, concepts, and a roadmap around the development and implementation of a BPC V10.0 project for either SAP NetWeaver or Microsoft. I believe from a conceptual point of view as well as a system point of view we have successfully achieved this goal.

One of my other goals in writing this book is to have everyone that reads it come away with ideas and methods but also additional questions as to how they can improve the approach they are currently using to work with BPC V10.0. If we constantly question our own ideas and approaches, then we'll definitely have many of those surprising moments in our SAP careers.

This introduction provides an overview of what you'll find in this book. You'll get an idea of what the various chapters will help you achieve, and develop practical scenarios showing the use of the functionality and approaches in configuring and implementing Business Planning and Consolidation.

Introduction

During the course of this book, we'll give you a good idea of the process used in Business Planning and Consolidation Version 10.0 (BPC V10.0) for planning, budgeting, forecasting, and consolidation, as well as enhancing the reporting activities associated with BPC and the underlying SAP NetWeaver Business Warehouse (BW) objects.

In the initial chapters, we'll discuss the building blocks of BPC, including the architecture and data modeling process, and then work through the tasks and activities in each of the areas for BPC. Each chapter will build upon the previous one in terms of configuration of a planning and forecasting (P&F) process as well as the approach to consolidation. We'll also build from chapter to chapter on the initial dimensions, and then cover the master and transactional data that we load in Chapter 5. As we work our way through these phases in a project, we'll be using the word "planning" quite a bit, but remember that many, if not all, of the activities we'll be developing can also be used for forecasting and budgeting as well.

This approach will help develop a roadmap for each of the aspects of BPC while working with it in a project. We'll incorporate as much of the new functionality and features of the BPC V10.0 for both SAP NetWeaver and the Microsoft platform, as well as BW 7.3 and the Enterprise Performance Management (EPM) add-in V10.0. This will provide the most up-to-date understanding of the future features that will be available in all of the different components involved in BPC, which will help you develop a roadmap to take advantage of these enhancements in any strategy that your customer is interested in implementing in the future.

We'll also incorporate as much as possible the differences and similarities of the SAP NetWeaver and Microsoft versions during the discussion and demos of each aspect of BPC V10.0.

Software Specifications and Coverage

This book is based on the specific support packs (SPs) available for BPC, SAP NetWeaver, and EPM. In this case, we'll be working with BW 7.3 SP5, BPC SP5 (Microsoft and SAP NetWeaver; we'll include as much as possible of the new Equity Pick Up [EPU] functionality for financial institutions), and EPM SP10 patch 2 (including the Large Volume Patch).

As you know, the implementation and configuration of any product is a combination of system configuration and subjective viewpoint. Basically, it's not all straightforward configuration, and sometimes you have to rely on your subjective views versus exactly what the system can offer to accommodate the required results for your customer. We'll offer our viewpoint based on the project and product experience we bring to the table. In some cases, we'll develop multiple scenarios to suggest other approaches. Some of these approaches may not work for your company, but this will give you some good ideas of how to architect, configure, and implement BPC.

Target Audience

This book is written in a way that makes it useful to many different consulting and business users. For example, this book can take a starting BPC consultant through the entire project cycle of a BPC project, making it an indispensable part of a beginning consultant's reference information.

For the senior application consultant, this book offers time-saving tips and tricks during each phase of the BPC cycle, so the consultant doesn't have to search all over for detailed process descriptions (such as changes to transports for BPC V10.0) and screenshots or even understand some of the unique concepts and approaches to uploading data from source systems to BPC. There are so many aspects to this process that it's difficult to be aware of and knowledgeable about everything and even more challenging to remember it all. It's essential to be able to refresh your memory on different aspects of the many processes involved.

For the IT consultant, this book provides a good idea of what to expect and be aware of during the install process, through the maturity of the project, and to go live and production support. We'll also offer some tips on performance aspects of BPC V10.0 as we work through each of the areas.

For management, this book describes the different options available using BPC V10.0 for planning, consolidation, or even reporting options using both BPC and BW objects. This will offer insight into using BPC to make critical decisions during the project planning phases as well as enhancing the implementation and configuration process for those options.

Finally, for the business user at a corporation that has just implemented BPC, this book is an excellent reference guide. As you know, SAP has its own terminology, and knowing the terminology specific to BPC and BI is vital to deciphering and grasping the information that your BPC consultant offers. The terminology in this book will allow the business user to communicate better and more effectively with the BPC consultants and other groups outside of the financial department.

Chapter Breakdown

This section will give you a high-level overview of each chapter and what to expect as you read through the material. The material incorporated into each chapter consists of hands-on information, activities, concepts, and issues that you may encounter during the implementation of the BPC products.

Chapter 1: Overview of Planning and Consolidation

Before we start working with the actual BPC components and processes, you need to understand some of the concepts behind planning and consolidation. This chapter provides the background information you need to understand some of the approaches to planning, forecasting, and budgeting as well as consolidation. This will give you a high-level overview of the generic processes that will be discussed throughout this book with a focus on the functionality rather than the system processes. This overview won't offer you the level of knowledge of a planner or a consolidation accountant if you aren't already in these fields, but it will help you put together a framework around the aspects of the fields of knowledge that we'll discuss in this book.

Chapter 2: The Fundamentals of BPC

This chapter starts out by going through the initial setup of the systems: BW, BPC, and EPM. This will cover the application or functional side of the set up activities and not the Basis portion. We'll discuss the additional steps you have to execute depending on whether you're working with a Microsoft or SAP NetWeaver version system. Some of the topics that we'll discuss in detail include the settings in the Implementation Guide (IMG) for BPC for SAP NetWeaver, BPC for the Microsoft Platform, and the different installation options for the EPM add-in.

After completing the initial setup, we'll move into the use of the numerous starter kits that are available and their installation processes. These are excellent "accelerators" for your project because in a very short time, you can be demoing and reporting with the functionality available for planning, forecasting, and consolidation.

Next, we'll discuss the functionality and improvements in the new BPC administration screens. This portion will help set you up for the navigation required within the WEB ADMINISTRATION screens. We'll cover the features in the START PAGE, workspace, web reporting, FAVORITES LIBRARY, and other activities that can be executed from the web HOME screen.

Chapter 3: BPC Architecture

After getting accustomed to the new look and feel of the BPC frontend, we can start getting into the details of the initial architecture and modeling required to accommodate any of the other activities—planning and consolidation. As in any of the other components, such as BPC's predecessors SEM-BPS/BCS and BI-IP, there are critical decisions that need to be made concerning the architecture and structures of the data modeling for BPC. In a number of cases, after these objects are created and installed, there's no going back, and if a change is required, the change process is as time intensive as if you configured the change from scratch.

We'll discuss some concepts about the overall architecture and review the issues that you may have to overcome over time. This discussion will help you navigate through these critical decisions and understand the options as well as the pros and cons of each. This architecture will incorporate the initial source systems—BW or Microsoft—as well.

After laying the groundwork for a consistent and manageable architecture, we move into working with the core objects required in BPC: EnvironmentShell, models, dimensions, properties, members, and hierarchies. This represents another series of very crucial decisions for the BPC project. We'll review and discuss the multiple different activities to develop each one of these objects. In conjunction with this, we'll discuss some of the questions around currency translation, data loading activities, and required properties for consolidation and/or planning. Some new features in these areas help support activities such as simulation of currency translation or intercompany matching, and some features have been around for some time. Because the objects in the BPC world are different from the objects in the BW world, we'll discuss these differences and offer options for a solution.

If you've been working on the BPC V7.5, you know that properties in BPC V10.0 are being used very aggressively, so we need to identify the individual responsibilities for each property so that the standard delivered program will work accurately. In this chapter, we'll look at and configure the standard delivered properties as well as others that will be useful for different processes.

Chapter 4: Reporting in BPC

In this chapter, we'll discuss the completely new and restructured reporting frontend for BPC V10.0 and all of EPM. This component, as you might expect, will be demonstrated in most of the following chapters because executing reports for any of the source system information you want to analyze requires the reporting frontend. In this chapter we will work with the EPM add-in and not specifically with the web-based reporting options within the BPC component. Even though the Web-based reporting option is quite functional the EPM add-in is the tool of choice when it comes to reporting for both external and internal users.

We'll start from scratch and work our way through the different features for both the reporting process and some of the activities that you'll use in the planning, forecasting, budgeting, and consolidation processes. Remember, although all of the features discussed look more like reporting capabilities, they are also very useful in the planning aspect of the component.

We'll work through the initial process of accessing the BPC cubes either via the standard BPC process or with the OLE DB (Object Linking and Embedding database) approach to ensure that you are aware of the current differences in the two activities. Working our way through the EPM ribbon tab in the Excel worksheet to explain all of the available features and their functions, this section will include both new and familiar favorite features that you may have used in reporting toolsets in other SAP reporting components. Some of the concepts we'll discuss in detail include the use of member recognition, report editor, local members, global members, hierarchies in the EPM add-in, and much more. During the discussion on navigation in the EPM add-in, we will stress certain aspects of the add-in that are similar to the EvDRE (Everest Data Range Exchange) functions and those that are similar to the BEX Analyzer functions. This will be very helpful based on your background in BW and BPC and will allow you to quickly understand how to use many of the features.

After you understand the basic functionality available in the initial screen of the EPM add-in, we'll start to expand on these concepts with some much more detailed features that are available. Building on your confidence in setting up reports and templates with the foundation of navigating the EPM add-in, we'll explore advanced concepts, including advanced formulas, EPM functions, report sharing, other reporting and worksheet options, VBA, and macros. This will allow you to create the enhanced reports or input templates that your customers are looking for in a project.

After the advanced topics, we'll move on to the use of the EPM add-in with the SAP BOBJ Dashboard Designer (referred to as the Dashboard for short) component and the additional integration that the EPM add-in has with the other Microsoft tools such as Word and PowerPoint.

Because we'll be accessing the features in the Data Manager portion of the EPM add-in, we'll review the navigation process within this tab on the EPM ribbon, but a more detailed discussion of the features in this area will be handled during the use of the Data Manager in Chapters 5 and 6.

As a final review, we'll look at the development of EPM add-in reports for planning and forecasting (P&F), and consolidation. With all of the information discussed in this chapter, you'll be able to create finished reports for each of the areas.

In this chapter, we'll work with some already loaded basic demo data because we won't get to the actual loading process until the next chapter; however, it's important to have a strong grasp of the reporting functionality for the remaining chapters in this book.

Chapter 5: Data Loading in BPC

In this chapter, we'll discuss and configure multiple approaches to maintaining the master and transactional data in BPC, starting with an overview of the basic system architecture needed to support both the SAP NetWeaver and the Microsoft versions of the BPC systems. Because the Microsoft version is based more on SQL tables, much of the conversation is based on SAP NetWeaver version but due to the fact that the MS version uses the flat file upload process we will cover this as well. We'll diagram the data flow process from the source systems—SAP ERP systems, flat files, or other sources—through to the integration occurring in the BW environment between BW and BPC InfoCubes/InfoObjects. The data modeling required to make everything work correctly is a bit tricky, so we'll discuss how to handle aspects of this such as compound InfoObjects, additional attributes that are different between BW and BPC, whether to use standard content objects, and other core decisions that need to be made for this process to work correctly.

A number of BW-based activities have crept into BPC, such as multiple tables, useful transactional codes, ABAP programs, use of the process chain, and data loading activities. We'll discuss and configure each data flow activity—master data and transactional data—to offer a view of the effort and functionality. A number of BPC-specific programs such as the Script Logic tester and the validation of standard content programs are very important in several scenarios, so we'll describe and configure these during the appropriate phase of BPC development. Working with hierarchies is another tricky data loading activity, so we'll work through several scenarios with the different types of hierarchies—text, internal, and external—to offer some suggestions as to how to upload each.

Then, we'll look at the differences between the data loads for consolidation and P&F. There can be differences between the starting points in terms of data for each, so we'll focus on the uploading process similarities as well as the differences. Moving from basic data loading of master data and transactional data, we take on a more unique transactional data flow focusing on the rate model. We'll discuss and configure the data flow for the exchange rates from Table TCURR in SAP ERP through to the BPC Rate model with stops in BW. Much of this will require the use of the BW process chain, and we'll review all of the aspects of this process. For the BW core consultant, this may be second nature, but for the Microsoft BPC consultant, this is new functionality. As of V10.0, there are fewer times when you'll need to create, from scratch, a Business add-in (BAdI) for use with BPC calculations, but there are still times where it will be required to understand and know how to integrate a BAdI into the BPC process. We won't go through detailed ABAP or BAdI architecture, but we'll demonstrate a basic setup of these components. A large amount of options are available in this area in terms of data flow around the use of Script Logic, calculations, and other manipulation of data. However, we won't be able to configure all of the options, but we'll configure some of the options and describe many others.

Chapter 6: Forecasting, Planning, and Budgeting in BPC

In this chapter, we'll continue the scenario that is laid out throughout the initial five chapters of the book and use these components to build out a fully functional planning, forecasting, and budgeting process. Now that we've uploaded some data from SAP ERP and/or a flat file, we can start the planning process.

Starting with the development of the initial plan information and following through with multiple cycles of different planning techniques, we'll arrive at a fully loaded plan version that can be used for tracking the overall progress of the corporation through the year's activities.

We'll discuss moving the data through multiple copies from version to version to provide the business user multiple versions of the plan data for what-if scenarios, working versions, and the final version. As we move through the chapter, we'll show some planning processes a corporation might experience. These activities can be used to assemble a series of plan steps that each area of the corporation can use to arrive at the results required. In each phase of the planning cycle, BPC has a number of approaches to accommodate the business user's needs.

We'll discuss the movement of the data through a top-down and bottom-up approach to simulate a typical planning process, we'll work our way through a planning process that will require additional manipulation of the data using calculations, that are both executed by the system and executed via business user processing. We'll show some unique calculations that you may see during a P&F process such as the use of allocations in BPC.

At this point, quite a bit of reporting and analysis are going on, so we'll see several reports and input templates that will help facilitate the display and processing of the planned data. This comparison of actuals to plan isn't as straightforward as it may seem, so we'll focus on the reporting and analysis process during this chapter.

You can choose from a number of different types of planning, so we'll explain, discuss, and configure a few of them to give you an idea of the process and complexity of the configuration. Some of the types of planning that we'll discuss include sales volume, cost center, strategy planning, and HR planning. We'll then discuss the concept and use of retraction in BPC to SAP ERP functionality.

Chapter 7: Consolidation in BPC

We shift a bit of the conversation to consolidation in this chapter. Our data set will be a bit different, and the audience will be different for these tasks. We'll discuss all of the aspects of the consolidation process in BPC. We start with the initial set up of the ownership process by setting up the ownership information such as ownership percentages, control percentages, and methods. Following this, we'll work through the different types of consolidation methods such as equity, proportional, and purchase. These high-level discussions won't necessarily turn someone who is not an accountant into an accountant overnight. Instead, the chapter's purpose is to describe what the system will be using as a concept to structure the business rules and processes to calculate the appropriate consolidation approach. One of the other initial steps in setting up the consolidation process is to configure the use of journal entries (JE). We'll configure this task and later demonstrate the use and result of posting information using JEs.

After everything is configured for consolidation, we then go step by step through the different aspects of consolidation. By following the general tasks, we'll work through the currency translation process, which we've set up in a previous chapter, and then configure the functions to regroup and reclassify the data. This can be very useful in a situation where a restatement is required after the period has been closed. We can then direct our attention to the configuration and execution of the inter-unit eliminations process, and follow this up with the automatic adjustments (EPU and inter-unit elimination) process in BPC. In each case, we'll show the different accounting consolidation methods with the appropriate BPC configuration and process.

Even though we execute some of these directly in the system, we'll also show the use of the Consolidation Monitor, which is a feature new to BPC V10.0 but an existing consolidation toolset in other SAP modules. This allows you to manage and execute the consolidation process centrally. Rather than having to execute the activities via Data Manager Packages and process chains, the Consolidation Monitor does that for you, and you can manage the results based on a green/yellow/red light system. This also offers some features to support the analysis and investigation of the errors. In addition, this chapter will go into the use of the incremental consolidation process as well as a discussion of the new EPU options for finance and banking. We wrap this chapter up with the configuration of the Intercompany Matching feature and show the flexibility of this process.

Chapter 8: Management of the BPC Process

In this chapter, we look to wrap up all of the configuration and processes that you've gone through with system components. We start with an always needed aspect of security in the BPC environment. Because security in BPC is unique, you need to have a firm understanding of the functionality and options available for securing different activities, including reporting, data loading, consolidation-specific tasks such as JEs, and the activities in the Consolidation Monitor. In conjunction with this topic, several other areas need to be configured. One area is the use of the controls component in BPC. This feature is new to BPC V10.0, but it replaces the validation processes used in the previous BPC systems. We'll go through the process of setting up and implementing the controls, including the configuration of the different rules for controls both driven by transactional data as well as master data for validation purposes. After the configuration is complete, we can then view and execute the controls activities from the Control Monitor, which we'll also see configured as well. Validation is also still available, so we'll show that configuration as well. We follow this up with the use of work status, which is somewhat integrated with security and definitely integrated with the controls. We'll show the setup and use of work status to manage the data loading, JE entries, and other processes during planning and consolidation. The combination of work status, controls, and security create a very interesting matrix of functions, and understanding the process will help you with your configuration of each individual component.

Finally, the use of the audit process is discussed, which will allow the different tasks and activities for both data loading as well as data changes to be audited and tracked. We'll discuss the use of both types of auditing activities.

Chapter 9: Business Process Flows (BPFs)

After the entire configuration is completed, we'll then move onto the discussion and development of the Business Process Flows (BPFs) component. The overall concept here is to have everything available for the business user in one place so that the process is consistent and repeatable and some emailing and *some* workflow activities can be incorporated. We'll go through the step-by-step process of building out the features of the BPFs from the different filtering options to the execution process. We'll take into account the integration required to build out the steps, activities, and tasks, and then the activation of the instance and the execution of the BPFs from the workspace.

Chapter 10: Migration Process to BPC V10.0

Another event that is a normal occurrence in the life of any company using SAP is the migration from one version to another. Many times, the migration is a result of new functionality or increased improvement in performance, but in any case, these types of activities are normal. We'll look at the process of migrating from BPC V7.5 to the current BPC V10.0. This discussion will take you through both the migration of the backend application as well as the frontend reporting component by moving from the EvDRE reporting options to the EPM reporting component. This can be accomplished in several different ways, so we'll discuss the options and work out some of the pros and cons of each.

This overview of the chapters included in this book will help the reader work through the material in this book in a consistent manner and direct you to the appropriate section of this book that may be of use to you. In the next chapter we will discuss the concepts of planning, budgeting, forecasting, and consolidation that will be used in this book.

This chapter will provide a strong foundation for using BPC effectively with a high-level look at the concepts of planning, forecasting, budgeting and consolidation. This chapter will prepare you for the system activities that we will be discussing in this book.

1 Overview of Planning and Consolidation

The planning, budgeting, and forecasting concept is critical to the success of the corporation. Many studies show that the majority of all corporations that fail do so because the planning process was not consistent or designed correctly. Another study asked CEOs of these failed corporations why they failed. The one thing that came to their minds collectively was the fact that they didn't plan enough and didn't plan proactively. It's very difficult to plan, budget, or forecast in an accurate, timely, and consistent way. Often the process of planning (in the following scenarios and discussions when "planning" is mentioned it actually refers to all three of the different activities, although there are nuances to the different types) has so many moving parts that many people just give up trying to plan correctly from the beginning.

1.1 Concepts of Planning

Planning is not like consolidations, where someone else (GAAP or IFRS rules and regulations from the government) is telling you how to do it and when to do it, and even sometimes have someone on-site such as a federal government representative to oversee the consolidation process. No, your planning process is done all on your own and is somewhat unique to the different industries. For the financial industry, the focus is on growth based on fees and services, whereas for a manufacturing industry, the focus is all about inventory and production.

The planning process is the lifeblood of the short-term and long-term revenue stream of a corporation and the overall income/expense process within a corporation. Without the planning process, a corporation would be unable to understand its market and its internal mechanics. In this current industrial environment, planning is more critical than ever before. We need to be able to manage and plan our overall expenses and revenues whether those areas are related to production of a product or the activities of a service-oriented industry. What is important to one corporation in the finance area, for example, may not be as important for a company in the service industry. Regretfully, when the economic environment gets difficult such as occurred between 2007 and 2010, the planning process is sometimes lost in translation, whereas the consolidation process is required by the government so it's always looked after and updated consistently. What we need to realize is that this is the perfect environment to improve and upscale your planning processes, and this additional effort will pay you back in full during the course of a recovery.

Besides all of the questions around how to plan, whether it's better to plan from the bottom up or from the top down, and what information is incorporated into the planning cycle, the one critical area for successful planning is the ability to integrate the planning process into the corporation's activities. It's a great accomplishment to plan and integrate the planning processes across all areas and aspects of a corporation. Many times during a planning cycle, the areas of a corporation are on very different pages of the planning process, so being able to integrate them is normally the lion's share of the effort. Full integration of the planning process will make the overall effort much more straightforward. Having sales forecast data available and in the appropriate format for logistics to use or for human resources to review would be helpful for any business. Not only will this allow easier and more useful reporting but you will be able to run a report and physically see the information across modules. You can also merge the information into your actual planning process to enhance the information you have and make your plan even better. For example, after the planning process is complete in the logistics area being able to drive the enhanced information back into the Material Requirements Planning (MRP) or the Material Production Supply (MPS) to improve the planning process is invaluable. Figure 1.1 shows an example of an integrated approach to planning.

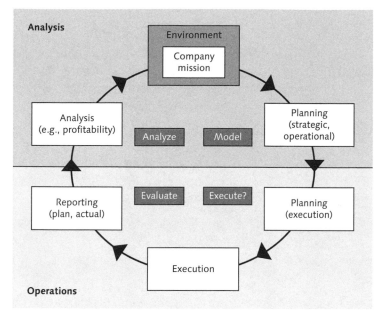

Figure 1.1 Integrated Planning Process

In Figure 1.1, all areas of the business are fully integrated into the planning process. Starting with the overall Company Mission Statement and moving through the initial planning process and then into the execution of the planning activities, the company is looking at both operational and strategy information. All along this process, evaluation and validation activities are performed to make sure that the operational and strategy planning activities are in sync. The outcome of example might be that all departments—finance, sales, human resources, logistics, manufacturing, and inventory—are looking at the same planning information but in their respective languages. In conjunction with this process comes the effort to make sure you transition from just operational planning, which gets you only part of the way, to the strategic planning, which takes into account information that doesn't exist in the operational layer, such as marketing issues, governmental impact, industry performance indicators, and other events that will impact your planning process. Figure 1.2 shows some of the topics covered in each of the planning activities. Each has its own responsibilities and tasks in the process of validating the projected costs that will be incurred by the corporation.

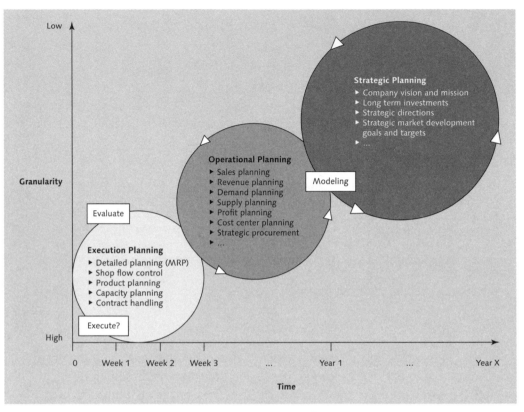

Figure 1.2 Planning Levels: Execution, Operational, and Strategic

Now that we have Sarbanes-Oxley (SOX) compliance, the planning information that is distributed to the stakeholders is more important than ever to make sure it is consistent with the expected results of growth and revenues of your company.

1.2 Concepts Of Consolidation

Consolidation refers to merging many things into one. Financial consolidation is the aggregation of the financial statements of a group of companies into one as a consolidated financial statement. This seems, on the surface, fairly straightforward, but going down to the next level of understanding is where it gets more interesting. There are several ways to consolidate financial information for a group of companies. If you think about this in more basic terms, you can understand the consolidation concepts. Let's assume you have ownership in a store and that ownership grants you the right to over 75% of the value of the store (any ownership of over 50% would be classified in this group). In this case, you have quite a bit at stake, and you're sharing in the overall activities of the store. During consolidation, you need to take into account the underlying financial postings of this store so that you truly reflect your risk/reward and income/expense. This is done using the *purchase method* (you'll see other names for this, such as subsidiary of the company, but the result is the same). Another approach to ownership of over 50% is called *proportional*. In this case, the ownership is over 50%, and the controlling company collects the items of the subsidiary's balance sheet and income statement and integrates them into the consolidated statements to the extent of the investor's percentage of ownership rather than at the full amount (what the purchase method would do). So this only shows the percentage that is an accurate portion of the ownership percentage.

Of course, if looking at the opposite side of this picture, you see the situation where you only own 10% of the store (or less than 50%), which is called the *equity method*. In this case, you don't take into account any data from the store in the consolidated statement. The only items that you take into account are the changes in the stakeholders' equity of the company. This in turn only impacts the investment value and possibly goodwill stated on the consolidated statement.

If you look at this in an overview sense, you see that several factors and components are working together for financial consolidation to be correct and effective. In Figure 1.3, the components that are working together to successfully accomplish a validate consolidation include a hierarchy, the ownership model, a method definition, and method assignment.

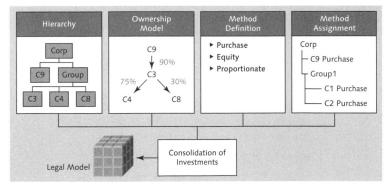

Figure 1.3 Overview of Consolidation

These are all aspects of consolidation that we will discuss and review in Chapter 7. Now, of course, there's more to this process than just this but these are the core activities that are required for consolidation. If you have two or more companies, but each is in a different country, you also have to take care of any currency difference. If one company is doing business in U.S. dollars, and the other is doing business in euros, before you start this consolidation process, you must take care of the currency translation differences. You also have to take into account any transactions that would have occurred between the two companies. For example, if one company sells to the other company, and they are both owned by another company, then any transactions between the two companies have to be eliminated before the consolidation process starts. This eliminates any double counting of the financial information.

The end result is that the parent company can now show a consolidated financial statement with data that will show revenues and expenses that are truly consistent with the GAAP and SOX requirements. This is critical for stakeholders so they can see a clean financial statement—apples to apples so to speak—and this would help them if they are looking to invest or purchase stock.

1.3 Summary

After you've worked through this book, you should be comfortable with all of the different aspects of BPC during a planning or consolidation cycle. In this chapter, we have discussed a high level overview of the concepts involved in planning, forecasting, budgeting and consolidation. This offers a general alignment of some of the system activities that we will be discussing in this book.

This chapter covers the basics of the system architecture for all of the components—from the initial setup of the systems to accessing SAP NetWeaver BW, the Microsoft platform, BPC, and EPM add-in at a high level. Also, the standard content delivered with the system and available starter kits also help accelerate the implementation process. We'll pay particular attention to IFRS Starter Kit.

2 The Fundamentals of BPC

This chapter provides information about the basics of SAP NetWeaver Business Warehouse (BW) system and the SAP Business Planning and Consolidation (BPC) version for the Microsoft platform system as well as NetWeaver BPC. It covers the basics of the system architecture for all of the components at a high level and then explains the initial setup of the systems and how to access BW, Microsoft, BPC, and EPM. From there, we'll move into the standard content that is delivered with the systems to help accelerate the implementation process, including the IFRS Starter Kit.

2.1 System Architecture

Significant changes have been made to the overall architecture to support the BPC V10.0 system, but instead of muddying the water with an analysis of the two different versions, we'll focus on the enhancements within the system platforms. Many of the changes in the architecture of the BPC systems have to do with increased performance and stability. Rather than having several different levels of architecture, the BPC V10.0 has minimized the number of layers that the data needs to travel through. This allows stronger integration between levels and faster processing of the information both during the uploading and the reporting/input template process.

Let's start this process by reviewing the BPC version for the Microsoft platform. Looking at this architecture, we find that the changes have reduced the amount of reads that the system requires during the processing of data. Figure 2.1 offers a diagram of the current system architecture of the Microsoft version of BPC V10.0. In this architecture, we end up with fewer components to function and execute the read/write process. Based on these components, we've enhanced the process by using the following:

▶ Only the .NET 3.5 component

▶ Pure 64-bit process

▶ Single process/no com + service architecture

▶ .NET impersonation program

▶ Configurable platform with `Web.configuration`, which allows the `MaxConcurrentSessions` parameters to increase the total number of concurrent users possible

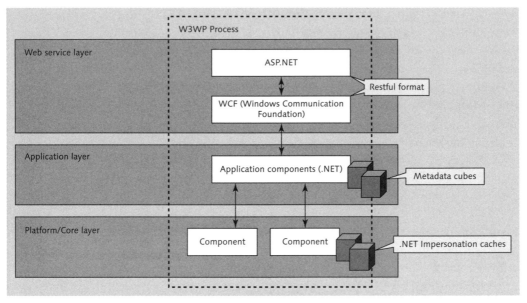

Figure 2.1 Architecture of BPC V10.0 for Microsoft

As you can see in Figure 2.1, the architecture starts with the Platform/Core layer that supports the actual data storage for BPC for Microsoft. This will store all of the master data, transactional data, and configuration for any objects or functions in the system. The application layer supports the rollup of the information required to execute the current activities within the system. For example, if you're executing a report, and all of the metadata is reflected in this layer as cache (memory) than it is available for the report to run more efficiently. The Web service layer is the presentation layer that allows the user to have access to the information stored in the platform/core layer. With this approach, the frontend or user view is a thin web-based presentation view. This is supported by the Windows Communication Foundation (WCF), which is a part of the .NET Framework for all windows based components.

If you look at just one portion of this system architecture to see the differences between the versions, you'll find that in BPC V10.0 for Microsoft, there is an implementation of a cache mechanism that improves the performance for the retrieval of the data. In BPC V7.x, however, queries were used to retrieve the metadata. The cache mechanism helps pass the data across the platform more efficiently and consistently. This caching component is displayed in the Figure 2.2.

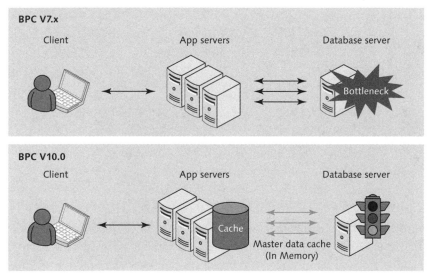

Figure 2.2 Comparison of Data Retrieval between BPC for Microsoft V7.x and V10.0 – Global Cache

In terms of BPC V10.0 for SAP NetWeaver, the changes are as dramatic as the Microsoft version. The first aspect that everyone will notice is that there's no .NET layer in the system. Having one less layer improves system maintenance and performance significantly. This change also helps, as a by-product, the integration between the SAP NetWeaver platform and the BPC frontend. This also requires that the Web services are embedded in the SAP NetWeaver layer of the system architecture, allowing for maintenance to reside with SAP NetWeaver rather than a separate third layer within BPC. This is displayed in the Figure 2.3.

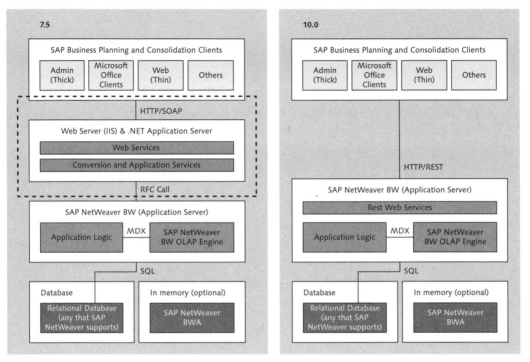

Figure 2.3 Comparison of BPC V7.5 and BPC V10.0 System Architectures

Reviewing specifically the system architecture of the BPC V10.0 for SAP NetWeaver, you see more integration than before with the BW portion of the SAP NetWeaver system (see Figure 2.4). The processing of information for all activities is more direct using the Web services processing based on this new system architecture. The improvements in the Business User Console (top portion of Figure 2.4) help integrate all of the different parts of BPC together so that the user experience is more consistent across the planning and forecasting and the consolidation components of the SAP NetWeaver version. The addition of the Consolidation Central component, which incorporates the new Consolidation Monitor, helps with the centralization of all consolidation activities in the SAP NetWeaver version. The reduction in layering also helps integrate all of the Microsoft Office Suite components and provides a more direct and complete connection between all of the tools within this suite. Another important by-product of this architecture is the closer integration with the security and authorization approaches in the SAP NetWeaver system. Although BPC still has its own security and authorization process, we can see improvements and linkage back into the BW authorizations.

After the Basis group completes their process, they will hand the system over to you for the initial setup process on the functional side. At that point, you and possibly others will have access to the BPC and BW systems, but prior to starting any configuration, make sure that you validate and test the system for general functionality and features. Report any concerns or issues to the Basis team for troubleshooting and fixes. It's much easier to get these issues taken care of now before adding more objects and configuration to the system.

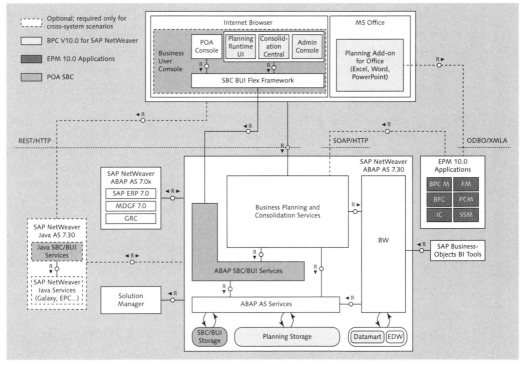

Figure 2.4 BPC SAP NetWeaver v10.0 System Architecture

Now that we have a fully functional BPC and BW system, we can review the access process.

2.2   Accessing the System

The BPC process of accessing the systems is very similar to that of any of the SAP environments. For the two different BPC versions, the frontend access is very similar because they both access the BPC functionality via the WEB ADMINISTRATION link. On the other hand, the access to the backend processes for both is different due to the fact that the SAP NetWeaver version uses BW as the core component to store all of the data, objects, and configuration, whereas the Microsoft version uses a Microsoft-based system to do the same. Realize that access to both areas of BPC, frontend and backend, is based on the responsibilities and tasks that you are assigned based on the position you have: IT, report user, BPC developer, BW developer, manager, and so on. Each position will have specific BW, Microsoft version, and BPC roles assigned, and this will alter the views of the different systems that we'll discuss. That being said, you initially need a user name and password, which is normally set up by the Basis or IT department. During the installation process, the Basis or IT group will take care of setting up the system architecture to support the BPC component as well as installing the standard content for BPC, including a copy of the EnvironmentShell and some initial user name/password information.

Note: Terminology Overview

The EnvironmentShell references the initial standard content that is installed for your use during the configuration of BPC. This EnvironmentShell contains a set of objects that makes up the basic configuration for either the planning or consolidation processes. We'll revisit this for a more detailed explanation in Chapter 3 during the initial architecture phase of your BPC project.

2.2.1   SAP NetWeaver Business Warehouse (BW) System

For BPC V10.0 for SAP NetWeaver, we have the support of the BW system. This is where all of the data, programs, and tables are stored for use by BPC V10.0 for SAP NetWeaver. To access the BW system, you need to have loaded the SAP GUI onto your laptops or have some sort of sharing option such as Citrix to access the BW system. The nice thing about the setup of the user/password for BW is that it's also the same user/password in the BPC system. Assuming that you already have your system information available, you can execute the process of accessing the backend BW system. We'll cover more of the BW activities in Chapters 3 and 5, but let's just navigate a bit to get used to what is available via the BW system.

Figure 2.5 shows the initial screen of the BW system after you've executed the Transaction code RSA1. The initial DATA WAREHOUSING WORKBENCH: MODELING screen defaults to display your FAVORITES folder. You may see a slightly different screen depending on how you set up the initial view of Transaction RSA1, but it will be very similar to this.

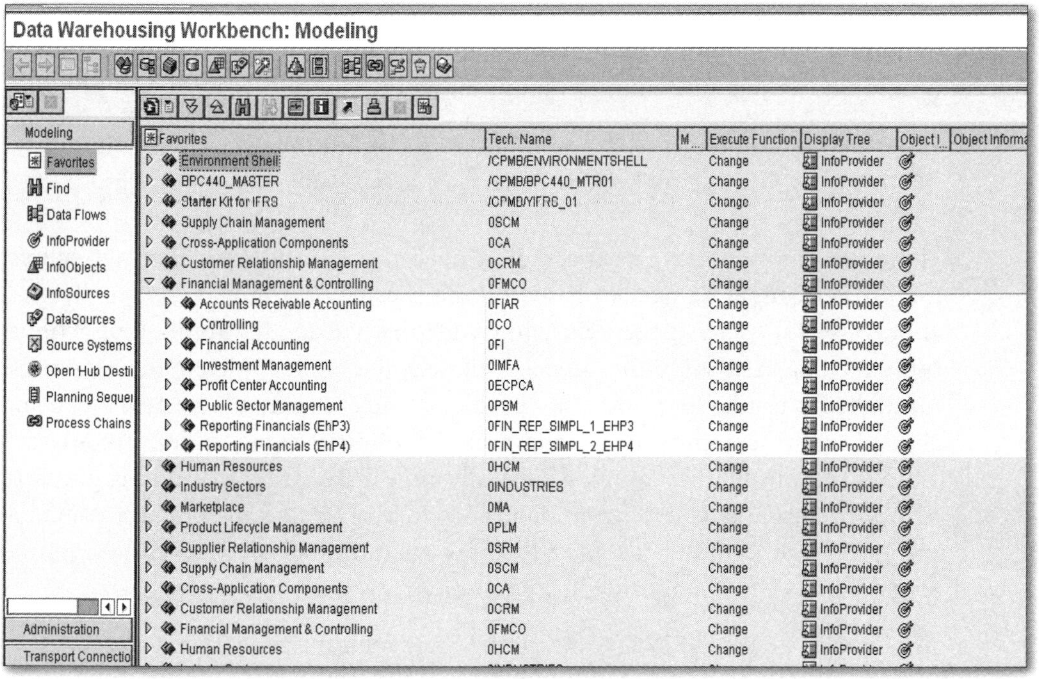

Figure 2.5 Initial BW Administration Workbench Screen – Favorites Folder

From here, you can gain access a number of different areas within the BW landscape, but normally you need to ask your BW security group for access to several specific activities, such as the following:

► The ability to access any transaction codes, programs, tables, and function modules that start with "UJ*". Currently all of the different activities and tables within BW that support BPC start with "UJ".

► The ability to access Transaction code RSA1 but only have a "display" activity type in security. This will help ease the nerves of the BW developers that the BPC developers are not coming into the BW system to create anything.

▶ The ability to access within Transaction code RSA1 the objects that are specific to BPC. These objects normally start with "/CPMB/", so you can request to have display access to these objects.

▶ The ability to access within Transaction code RSA1 the objects that you may have to use for the data flow process to BPC, for example, the use of some standard content DataSources from BW to BPC. (A DataSource in BW is used to process data from a source system such as SAP ERP to BW.)

> **Note: Best Practice**
>
> It is best business practice *not* to change anything directly in BW for any BPC objects. All BPC changes would be configured from the BPC Web Administration screens.

These are the most important activities needed within BW for BPC. Of course, more access might be needed based on the specific data flow activities that you are involved in, such as the ability to switch the BPC model from a transactional InfoCube to a basic InfoCube. This will allow you to remove/delete the data in the InfoCube for testing purposes. The specifics of each process will be developed and aligned with the appropriate group during the initial conversations about each group's responsibilities. You will normally have a BW team or support group to help with the backend configuration needed to upload the data, both transactional and master, to BPC, but it's good to know what they need to do from both the configuration and the data loading point of view.

After you've accessed BW in transaction RSA1, you can see that there are different types of objects (covered in Chapter 3); notice the differences between the core BW objects that start with a Z, 0, or Y, and the ones that start with a /CPMB/. This, generally speaking, will define the BPC objects. In Figure 2.5, you can see the InfoAreas (icon that looks like a green double diamond) that show the different objects based on where they were configured.

> **Note: Terminology**
>
> An InfoArea is a component of BW that allows the grouping of objects for use during configuration. The InfoArea can be found in two views: InfoProviders and InfoObjects.

Also in Figure 2.5, you can see that a number of different types of objects are available. One that we'll discuss in detail in Chapter 5 is Process Chains shown in the

MODELING list (at the left side of the screen). In this system, there are a number of process chains, but the ones specific to BPC show up with a technical name starting with /CPMB/, as mentioned earlier (see Figure 2.6). To get to this view of the BW ADMINISTRATION WORKBENCH, you click on the PROCESS CHAINS option in the left-hand navigation pane. Approximately 40 standard process chains are available for use to support the movement of data from multiple source systems to BPC.

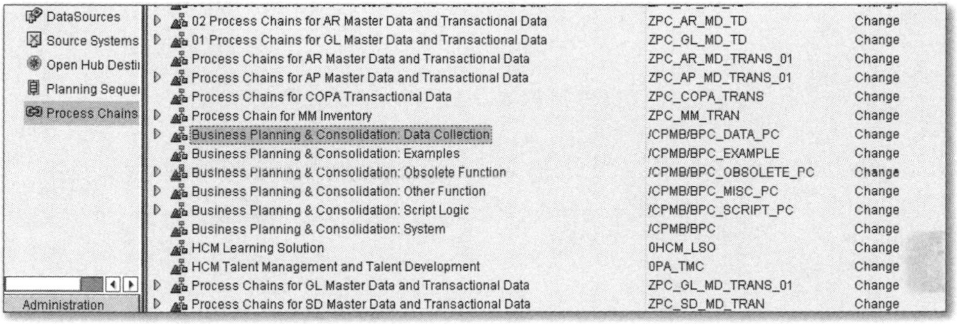

Figure 2.6 View of the Process Chains in BW for BPC Data Manager Activities

As mentioned earlier, in BW, all of the different programs, function modules, and transaction codes for BPC start with "UJ*". To see a list of one of these groups, and the transaction codes, execute Transaction SE16 and view Table TSTC. This table holds all of the transaction codes available in BW. In Figure 2.7, we've accessed transaction SE16 and entered the TABLE NAME "TSTC". After this screen is executed, then use the filter UJ*, and you'll see that there are 15 transaction codes available for BPC in BW, as shown in Figure 2.8.

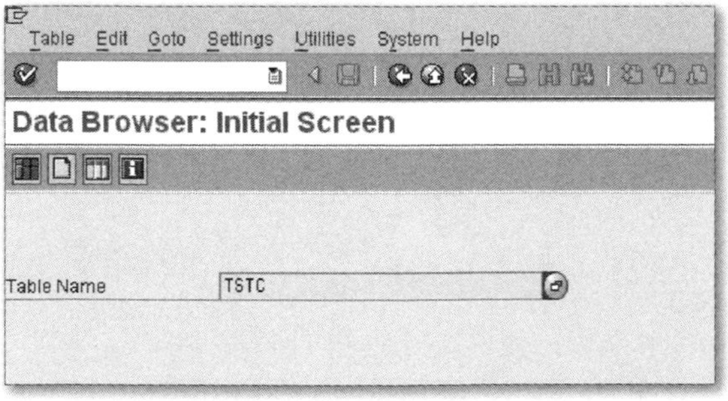

Figure 2.7 Data Browser: Initial Screen

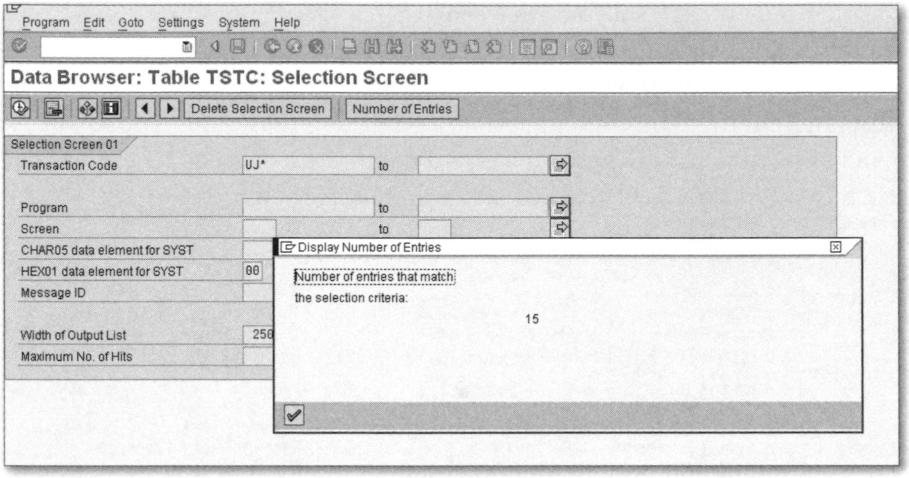

Figure 2.8 Access to the Transaction Codes for BPC in BW

Two initial setup activities that you should review before starting any configuration or testing are the EnvironmentShell parameters and the Model parameters. This is important because these parameters can help support some of the reporting and programming activities. As you'll see, they can help define the number of columns/rows on your reports and also help with the setup of activities within the BPC system such as email availability, Journal Entries (JEs), and consolidation parameters. These can be found in the BW Implementation Guide (IMG). In BPC V7.5, these were found in the WEB ADMINISTRATION screen. To review and tweak the parameters available, you use another Transaction, SPRO, to access this IMG. Execute this transaction, and then choose the SAP REFERENCE GUIDE to open a screen that looks like Figure 2.9.

From the CONFIGURATION PARAMETERS line, you can access the parameters for applications and environments for use in consolidation and in planning and forecasting. Figure 2.10 shows the environment parameters that are commonly defined at the time of installation. Follow these steps to set up the parameters:

1. Open the CONFIGURATION PARAMETERS node using the arrow to the left of the description.

2. Execute the SET ENVIRONMENT PARAMETERS using the EXECUTE button.

3. Choose the ENVIRONMENT that you want to affect with additional parameters, and use the EXECUTE button.

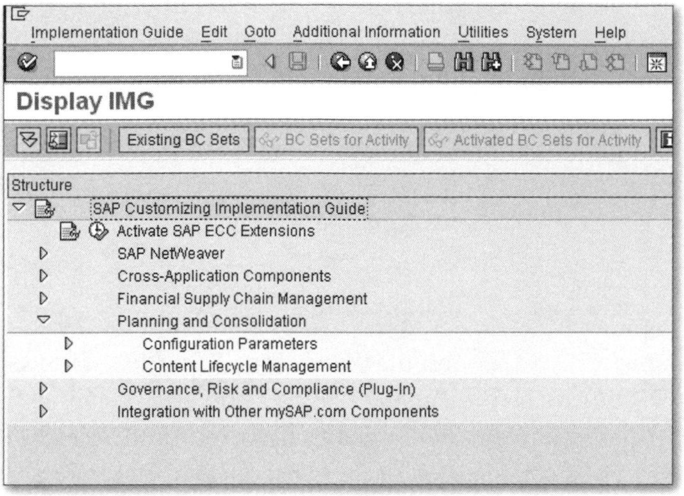

Figure 2.9 Display IMG – Configuration of Parameters

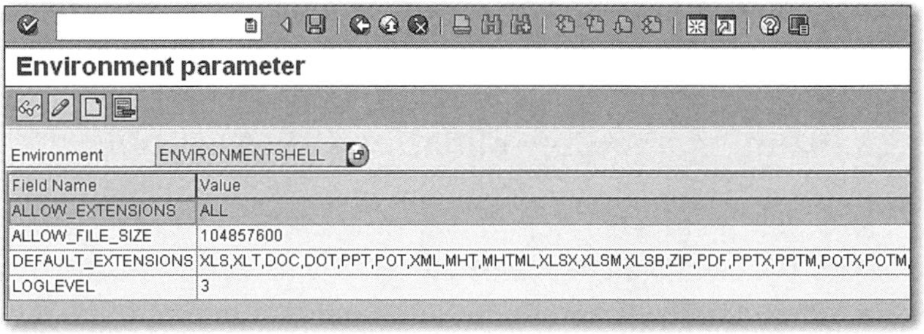

Figure 2.10 Environment Parameters for BPC for SAP NetWeaver in the IMG

There are well over 75 different system parameters for both the environment and models (the APPLICATIONS header was used in BPC V7.5) that can be used to help control and manage different aspects of the system for both performance and functionality. In BPC V10.0, there are approximately 45 different environment parameters. Following is a small sampling of the commonly used parameters:

- MAXLRCOLUMNS
  Defaulted to 30 columns for an EPM report.

- MAXLRROWS
  Defaulted to 10,000 rows in an EPM report.

- ALLOW_FILE_SIZE
  Allowed file size to be loaded to the server.

▶ ALLOW_EXTENSIONS
Normally uses ALL as a value. This is the allowable extensions on a file format.

▶ DEFAULT_EXTENSIONS
Default file types that can be used in BPC.

▶ CLR_COMMENTS_HISTORY
Controls the ability to clear the comments from the BPC tables.

▶ ALLOW_SSO_HTTP
Allows the use of the Single Sign-On (SSO) functionality in BW.

To access the Model parameters, you click on the option SET MODEL PARAMETERS, which is found under the CONFIGURATION PARAMETERS node (refer to Figure 2.9). From there, you assign the environment and model to the screen and access the model parameters. If you want a complete list of these parameters, go to the SAP help website for BPC: *http://help.sap.com/epm*. Now that you've viewed the BW backend system and checked the parameters, you're ready to access the BPC web-based screens.

2.3   Business Planning and Consolidation (BPC) System

By using the BPC web link to the WEB ADMINISTRATION screen, you can execute all of your activities for both configuration and data loading processes. Again, this will be based on your security access, but for now, let's just look at the full picture and assume that you have full authorizations. The website links will be supplied by the Basis group after installation. The link will look something like this:

http(s)://<server name.com>:8000/sap/bpc/web

The user/password is generally the same as your user/password as the backend system, either BW or Microsoft. You also have to make sure that these links are available in your driver folders so that they can be accessed by others on the team. Go to *C/WINDOWS/Drivers/etc/hosts* to find a file that supports the URL files for SAP BPC. Figure 2.11 shows the resulting file to store these links. By following these links, you'll be able to set up the initial connections for the BPC Web service to communicate with BPC.

There are other approaches to accomodating the different URL connections versus accessing the user HOST files. You will need to work with your Basis group to align the appropriate approach that will support the central maintenance of this component.

Figure 2.11 Drive Folder for Storage of HOST Web Links

Now that the URL is set up, you can access the BPC Web Client START PAGE screen. When you log on to the BPC Web Client START PAGE screen, you'll see something similar to Figure 2.12. This screen is made up of a number of different sections. Quite a bit of functionality is available in each area, so we'll touch on each here briefly and go into more detail in later chapters that are directly related to each menu option. We'll reference the callout number as shown in Figure 2.12 in the following subsections.

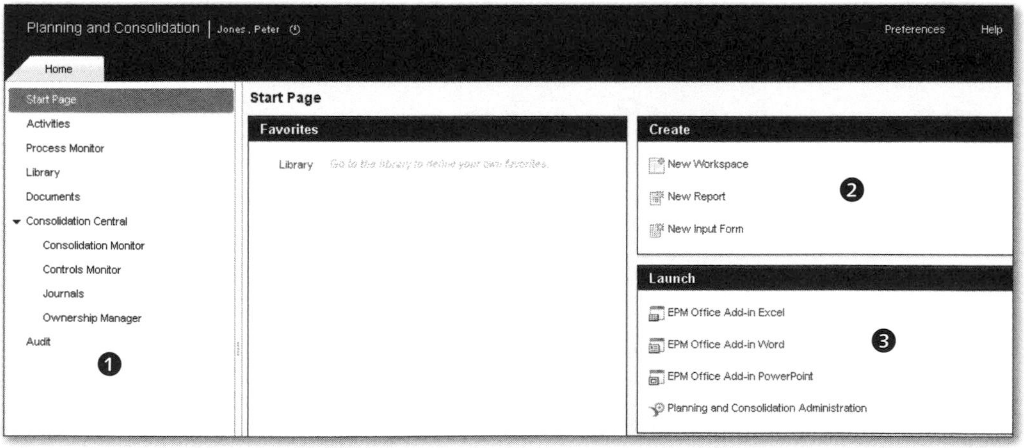

Figure 2.12 Initial Web Client Start Page for BPC

Navigation Pane (❶)

When you log in to the Web Client of PLANNING AND CONSOLIDATION, the first screen that you see is the START PAGE, which is the first node in the HOME tab navigation pane. In the START PAGE, you'll find the following features:

▶ FAVORITES
This can be set up as a list that contains quick links to, for example, the workspaces, reports, input forms, and books that you access frequently during your normal activities. You can define your own list of favorites. You can add an object to this list by clicking the ADD TO FAVORITES link from many of the Web Client pages.

▶ CREATE
The CREATE area contains shortcuts to the processes to create a new web-based report, input templates, or workspace.

▶ LAUNCH
When you first access the Web Client, the LAUNCH area contains links to install the SAP EPM solutions, add-in for Microsoft Office, and the Administration area. After these components are installed, the LAUNCH area contains links to the EPM add-in and a link to the ADMINISTRATION area.

From this START PAGE, you can also do the following:

▶ Change the environment, which means changing from one set of data to another (e.g., changing the view from a set of consolidation data to a set of planning data).

▶ Set preferences that allow you to change the view of the information, for example, switching language, format of the dates, amounts, and time zones.

▶ Access help, which, if set up, takes you to the *http://help.sap.com* website for further information.

The next option in section one is ACTIVITIES. This function displays the processes that contain steps requiring specific action by you as the currently logged-on user. When you first open the ACTIVITIES view, the upper part of the view displays all processes that have activities requiring action by you. Selecting a process populates the DETAILS window with all of the activities for that process that require action by you. Select the next activity that requires action by you, and choose OPEN. This opens the activity workspace where you perform the required tasks; you indicate that you've completed the actions required by choosing COMPLETE in the activity workspace. This modifies the status in the ACTIVITIES view and the status changes to SUBMITTED if a review is required, and it changes to COMPLETED if no review is required. You can see only the activity contexts for which you are an owner or a reviewer. If you are the responsible reviewer for an activity context, you can choose to APPROVE or REJECT an activity that is ready for review. APPROVE sets the activity context to the status COMPLETED. REJECT causes the activity context to remain open until the responsible user resubmits it for approval.

The PROCESS MONITOR is the next option on the list. If you've been assigned access to the process monitor, you can see a complete list of processes and display the full set of information available for individual process instances. The process instance owner can finalize and reopen steps from the process monitor. When you open the process monitor, it displays the process name, process context, status (completion percentage, number of steps completed, in progress, pending), start date, and owners for each process instance. You can filter the processes displayed using SHOW PROCESSES or STATUS. When you select a business process flow from the list, it opens the instance monitor to allow you to see the status of all steps and activity instances in that process instance. You can use GROUP BY to group by step, process context, status, and action required. You can also filter using SHOW ACTIVITIES.

The LIBRARY option listed next enables you to view, edit, and create planning and consolidation objects, such as workspaces, reports and input forms, SAP Crystal Dashboards, and books. The objects in the LIBRARY view are sorted by folders. You can select a folder to see the objects saved to it:

▶ GROUPS
Users with the appropriate role assigned can create a folder under the top-level folder GROUPS. After an object is created below GROUPS, it depends on the creator as to which access rights they grant to others.

▶ PUBLIC
This folder contains content that can be accessed and modified by all users depending on the permissions in place. It is possible to restrict access to this folder. Users with the task profile UPDATE COMPANY FOLDERS can add and manage the content.

▶ SAP
This folder contains predefined content, such as templates, provided by SAP. No users can write to this folder, but everyone has access to this folder.

▶ PRIVATE
You can create your personal folder and save content in it that you don't want to share with other users. The content of this folder can't be accessed by other

users. If you have more than one personal folder, you can move content from one folder to another. You can share content stored in your personal folder with other users. Simply, select the users and the roles you want to provide access.

▶ FAVORITES
You can add objects to this folder to group to together the objects that you use frequently. The FOLDER column shows the folder in which the object is stored.

You can also create new folders under the GROUPS, PUBLIC, SAP, and PRIVATE folders.

DOCUMENTS is the next option in the list. This is a central repository for storing or sharing files and websites. You can use the features of the DOCUMENTS view to post, share, and retrieve files or the contents of a website, and to manage the display of content.

The CONSOLIDATION CENTRAL module in the Planning and Consolidation functionality enables you to generate and manage consolidated data, giving you an accurate view of the financial situation of your organization. It consists of four components:

▶ CONSOLIDATION MONITOR
Execute, generate, and monitor consolidated data from data reported by group and entity members.

▶ CONTROLS MONITOR
Execute and monitor controls used to validate the reported data.

▶ JOURNALS
Create and manage journal entries containing adjustments and eliminations used for correcting reported data.

▶ OWNERSHIP MANAGER
Create and manage ownership-based hierarchies used for performing statutory consolidations.

The CONSOLIDATION MONITOR, JOURNALS, and OWNERSHIP MANAGER options will be covered in detail in Chapter 7, and the CONTROL MONITOR will be covered in detail in Chapter 8.

The final executable function in this section is AUDIT. This function allows you to prepare reports that contain system information and a history of administration and business user activities. As shown in Figure 2.13, audit reports enable you to report on any topics included in the SECURITY section, such as USERS, TEAMS, TASK PROFILES, and DATA ACCESS PROFILES. In the GENERAL section, you can execute reports to review DATA CHANGES, COMMENTS, WORK STATUS, and ADMINISTRATION ACTIVITY. Finally, in the BPF section, you can run reports changes and statuses for OPERATION, INSTANCE, and ACTIVITY.

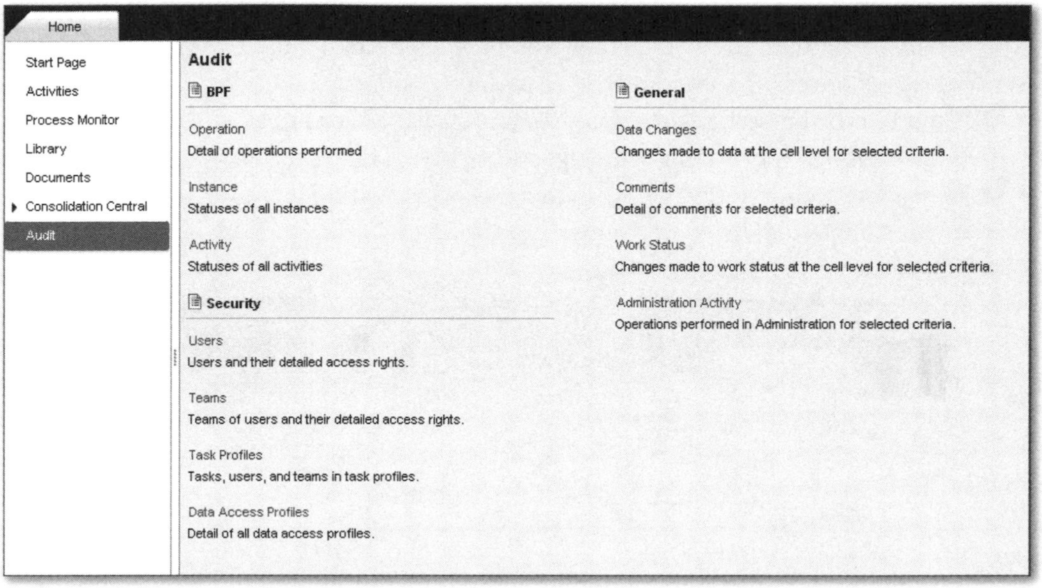

Figure 2.13 Audit Screen from the BPC Home Page

Create Pane (❷)

Now that we have discussed the Navigation pane, we will move on to the CREATE PANE. The CREATE area contains the NEW WORKSPACE, NEW REPORT, and NEW INPUT FORM options for creating workspaces, reports, and input forms.

A *workspace* is a grouping of specific content that behaves like a folder and contains planning and consolidation items, such as reports, input forms, SAP Crystal Dashboards, and so on. In a workspace, you can include content from the library or create new reports or input forms. Content that you include is available both in the workspace and in the library. Reports or input forms that you create are part of the workspace and are not available outside the workspace. To create a new workspace, follow these steps:

1. Choose CREATE A NEW WORKSPACE from the START PAGE.

2. Click on the plus sign to specify the dimensions and members of the additional global context.

3. Click on ADD CONTENT to add to your workspace.

4. You can choose from the list of items (e.g., reports or SAP Crystal Dashboards) available in the LIBRARY view. Select an item, and then click OK.

The other two components of the CREATE section—NEW REPORT and NEW INPUT FORM—allow the user to create web-based reports or input forms for use. The process of creating these reports is as easy as dragging and dropping the dimensions into the sections for columns and rows. An example of the initial screen for creating reports is show in Figure 2.14. We'll cover the creation of reports via the EPM add-in in Chapter 4, so much of what you do there will be transferrable knowledge to these components.

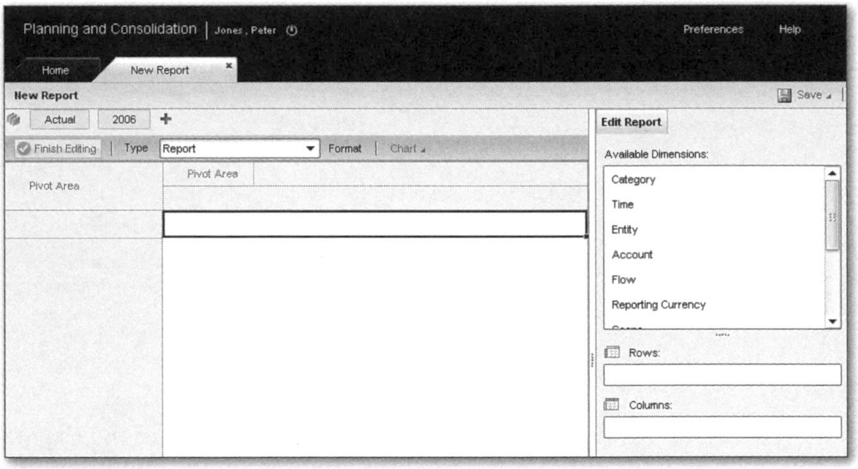

Figure 2.14 Initial Screen for Creating a Web-Based Report in BPC

Launch Area (❸)

The last area we will discuss in the webclient Start Page is the LAUNCH Area. When you first access the Web Client, the LAUNCH area contains links to install the SAP EPM solutions add-ins for Microsoft Office and the ADMINISTRATION area. After these components are installed, the LAUNCH area contains links to the EPM add-in and a link to the ADMINISTRATION area. Each of these links directs you to a very different aspect of BPC. The first three links for the Microsoft components —BPM OFFICE ADD-IN EXCEL, BPM OFFICE ADD-IN WORD, and BPM OFFICE ADD-IN POWERPOINT— offer the initial screens for creating, changing, and formatting the different reporting components. In this case, we'll defer the discussion of the add-ins until Chapter 4.

One thing to note, however, is that much of the development of the reports and input templates, as well as execution of the data loading process for BPC, is done in the Excel add-in. Any information or reports generated in this component can be displayed in a Word or PowerPoint document.

The other item in this list, the PLANNING AND CONSOLIDATION ADMINISTRATION link, will open an additional tab on this screen to allow the user to configure BPC dimensions and models to the business rules and Script Logic. The businesss rules and Script Logic will be both explained and configured in later chapters in this book. In Figure 2.15, you can see some of the different tasks included in the ADMINISTRATION link after you execute it.

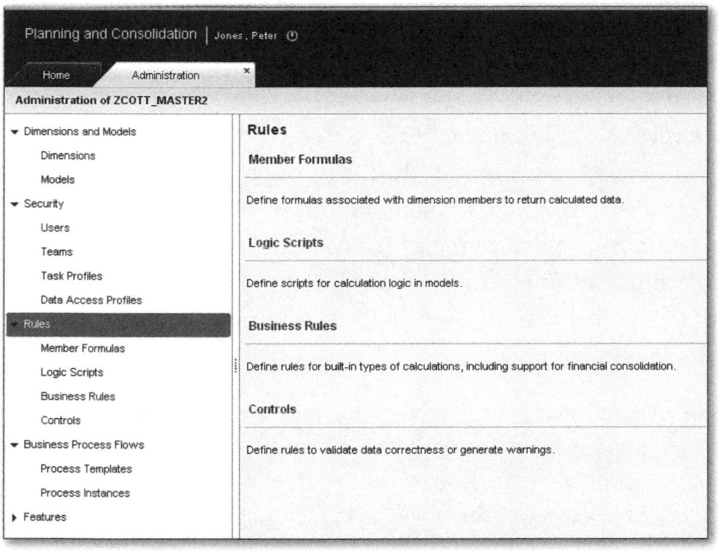

Figure 2.15 BPC Administration Screen with Components

2.3.1 Enterprise Performance Management (EPM) Add-In

If you've worked with the EPM products in the past, you probably realized that each of the toolsets had its own user interface (UI); however, with version EPM V10.0, that approach has changed. There are reporting options within each of the products that are inherent to the specific component, but the focus should be on using the Excel interface of the EPM V10.0 add-in for reporting on all components within this suite. If your focus is BPC, then this UI is required for the reporting and input functionality, as well as the direct access to the Data Manager portion to execute BPC-specific activities.

One of the significant by-products of the EPM V10.0 reporting component is that it not only supports the EPM products—including both the Microsoft and SAP NetWeaver versions of BPC, Strategy Management, Profitability and Cost Management, and Financial Information Management—but it also offers the ability to execute reports and templates using the core Business Intelligence InfoProviders in BW as well as database tables from other third-party systems.

Note: BW InfoProviders

BW InfoProviders are any objects within BW that are used for reporting purposes. There are several types of InfoProviders, including some that are very familiar to many such as Basic InfoCubes, Data Store Objects (DSOs), and others that are unique such as VirtualProviders and RemoteProviders. We'll be focusing on InfoCubes in this book and will discuss these in more detail in Chapter 3. BPC can use either MultiProviders, DSOs, or InfoCubes to support the uploading of data from BW InfoProviders.

We now have another very useful reporting toolset to use against the BW InfoProviders, as well as the BEX suite and the SAP BusinessObjects components. As in all cases, we have to identify the group that will benefit from this reporting component. As you'll see, this fits a wide range of users from hard-core Excel-based report users who want to use all of the functionality within Excel to help support the reporting from both the BW and the BPC sides, to the users who are used to Excel and want that same look and feel.

Note: BEx and SAP BusinessObjects BI Suite

The Business Explorer Web Analyzer (BEx Web Analyzer) as well as the SAP BusinessObjects Suite of reporting tools are available and have been the mainstay of the BW system for reporting purposes. These consist of a set of reporting components that are normally used to execute reports from BW.

From a reporting point of view, you now have to include the EPM V10.0 add-in into the mix of what component to use for reporting. You can choose from an impressive lineup of toolsets, including SAP Crystal, Analyzer, SAP BusinessObjects Web Intelligence, SAP BusinessObjects Dashboard Designer, BEx Analyzer/BEx Web Analyzer, or Business Explorer. Even though the Analyzer and BEx Analyzer support the use of the Excel component of the Microsoft Office suite, you'll find that the EPM add-in separates itself from the rest in a number of different ways that might be of some interest to you. Figure 2.16 offers a view of the positioning of the EPM add-in with the rest of the reporting components. As you can see, this component crosses over multiple groups of users as well as types of reports and as such will be discussed throughout multiple chapters in the book.

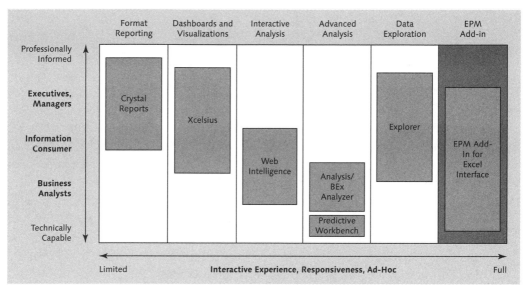

Figure 2.16 EPM add-in as a Part of the Reporting Strategy

To access the EPM add-in, you must download and install the most current version from the SAP Service Marketplace website. You'll find it in the Software Download section. You may need to have the Basis team do the installation depending on the authorizations you have for your company laptop. You may also want to run the EPM add-in cleanser, which is also found on the SAP Service Marketplace website, to collect any programs on your laptop from a past install process that might have an impact on the EPM add-in installation. At the end of the cleansing run, you can choose to delete or retain the files that may cause you installation issues.

After you've completed the installation of the EPM add-in, you need to set up a folder that will store the server connections after you create them for the EPM add-in. You need to be aware of the different connections so that during this discussion, you've identified the appropriate link. If you've installed the EPM add-in correctly, you should see something similar to Figure 2.17 after you open a basic Excel spreadsheet. Notice that EPM and DATA MANAGER tabs have been added to the end of your Excel ribbon. Generally speaking, the DATA MANAGER tab is used during the BPC process, so we won't discuss this option here, but it will be covered extensively in Chapters 4 through 7. In this situation, we are interested in the EPM tab.

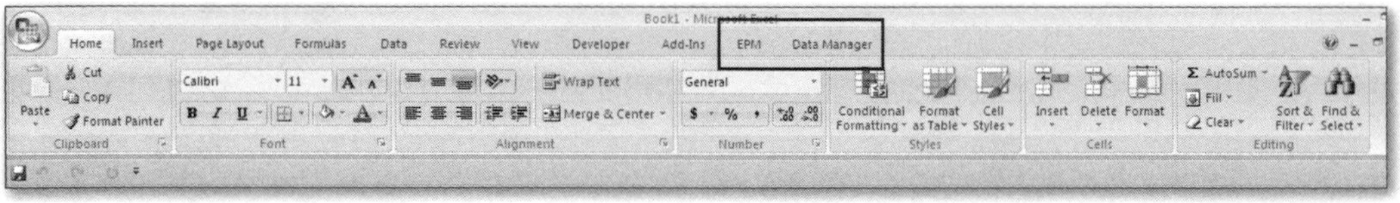

Figure 2.17 Excel Ribbon with EPM Tabs

Let's open the EPM tab from the Excel ribbon to see what is available. In Figure 2.18, the initial set of options is shown. We haven't logged on to the EPM add-in yet, so much of the ribbon is grayed out. Let's now work through the process of logging onto a BW InfoProvider and note the different approaches for the BW InfoProviders versus the BPC-based InfoProviders. Just remember that this process is exactly the same whether you are using the BPC link to access your BPC cubes or you are using the BW Link (OLE DB Link) to access basic BW cubes. If you click on the LOG ON button, you'll see a screen that is similar to Figure 2.19. You can use the button to the right of the CONNECTION field to access the connection options.

Figure 2.18 EPM Ribbon Tab Parameters

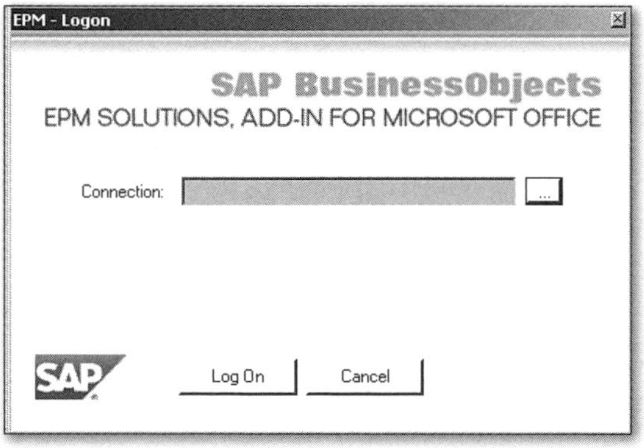

Figure 2.19 Connection Screen for EPM

After you execute that option, you'll see the screen shown in Figure 2.20. Now, you might see something slightly different depending on your authorization and EPM support patch level. As you can see, there are links to INFOCUBES that are available. You'll also notice that there are connections to both true base BW cubes (the ones that start with either 0, Y, or Z) and the BPC-based cubes (the ones that start with CPMB). This means that even though you normally access the BPC cubes via other connections such as the WEB SERVICES link, you can also get to a BPC cube using the OLE link. On the right-hand side, you'll see the CREATE button, which you can choose to display all of the available connections (see Figure 2.21). The initial option for the different links—PLANNING AND CONSOLIDATION, VERSION FOR SAP NETWEAVER, PLANNING AND CONSOLIDATION, VERSION FOR MICROSOFT, and LOCAL—will dictate what other fields will be available to you during the creation process. In our case, we want to take a look at the LOCAL connection. (We'll be referencing the two different connections throughout this book, so we can name them the LOCAL link and the BPC link.)

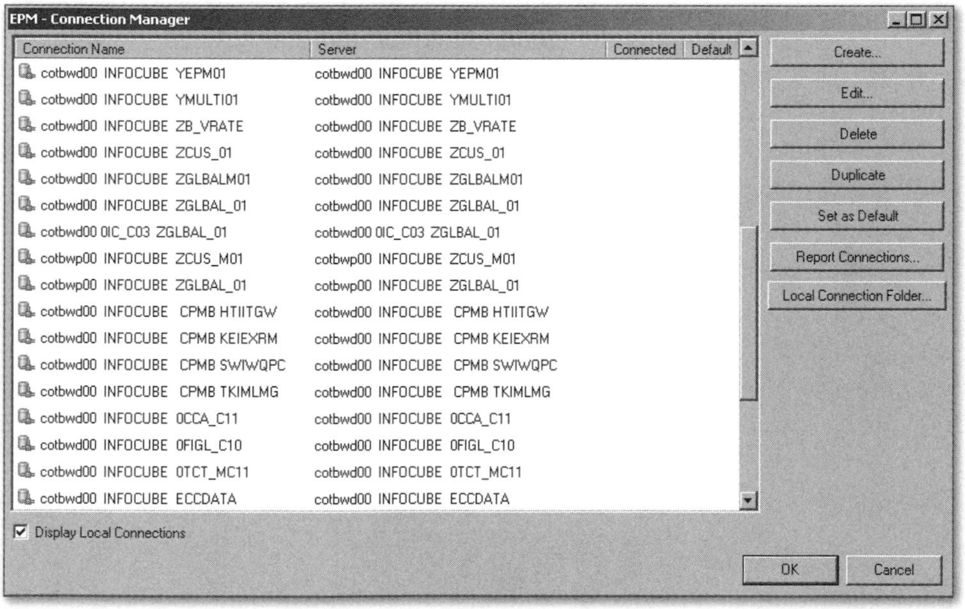

Figure 2.20 Connections to InfoProviders via EPM Connection Manager

After you access the LOCAL connection, you see several parameters. Figure 2.22 shows that the next option is to access a system based on one of the different connections. You can get to the BW-based cubes either with the BAPI PROVIDER FOR

BW NW (if you don't have the SAP GUI loaded onto your laptop) or the SAP BW OLE DB PROVIDER; we'll use the latter. Also, note that the DO NOT LOAD MEMBERS AT CONNECTION checkbox is new to the EPM add-in SP07 for the high data volumes (see Figure 2.22). If you know that the specific InfoCube you are linking to will have high data volumes whether it's transactional or master data, check this parameter. This manages the amount of data that is uploaded into the local cache of the Excel component during the initial execution of the Excel document. If you have significant amounts of data, the ability to access the Excel frontend will be impacted. To avoid very long wait times, you can use this parameter and only upload the data required for the initial query to execute.

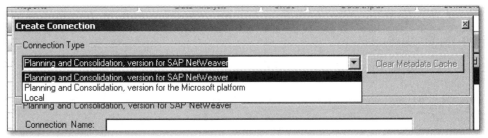

Figure 2.21 Connection Types Available via the Connection Manager

> **Note:**
>
> The SP levels are referenced throughout this book because currently BPC is issuing ongoing SPs for both BPC and EPM.

This parameter works well with the combination of the SAP NetWeaver BW Accelerator (BWA) to help with all of the data. This is the enhancement in EPM add-in SP07 that allowed the use of the EPM add-in against the BW InfoProviders. Without that option, it would be very difficult to sell your business users on the EPM add-in because the report runtimes would be impacted. This feature will also be available for use with access to BPC InfoCubes via the Web services approach to access.

After you choose the SAP BW OLE DB PROVIDER option, shown in Figure 2.22, the rest is straightforward. Clicking the CONNECTION button in the middle of the screen opens a dialog box that shows all of the connection information to the server (see Figure 2.23). After you fill this in, the connections are stored, and you don't have to do this again for the same cube. The information for these fields is the same as you would do for the setting up access to enter the SAP system via the SAP GUI.

After you set this up, you'll automatically be delivered to a screen that shows the link to an INFOPROVIDER. Choose this, and the system will take you back to the original screen where you can then choose whatever cube or InfoProvider you like.

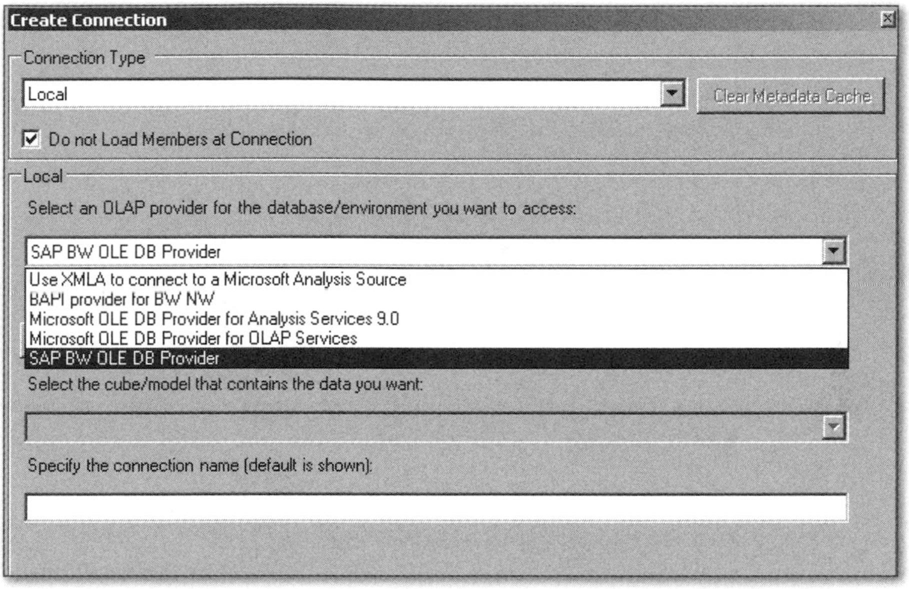

Figure 2.22 Local Connections Available in the Create Connection Screen

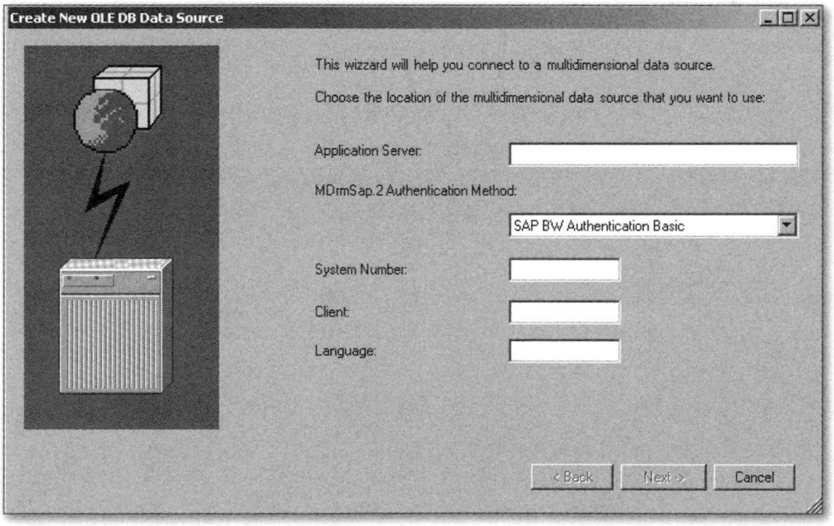

Figure 2.23 Create New OLE DB Data Source Screen for Connection Information

Figure 2.24 shows the final step in this process and the available InfoProviders. Remember that the InfoProviders are listed alphabetically based on the description and not the technical ID. You've now create the connection to a BW InfoProvider using the OLE link. After you identify the InfoProvider, you can log on just as you log on to an SAP system. Don't forget about the Do not Load Members at Connection parameter for the high data volumes.

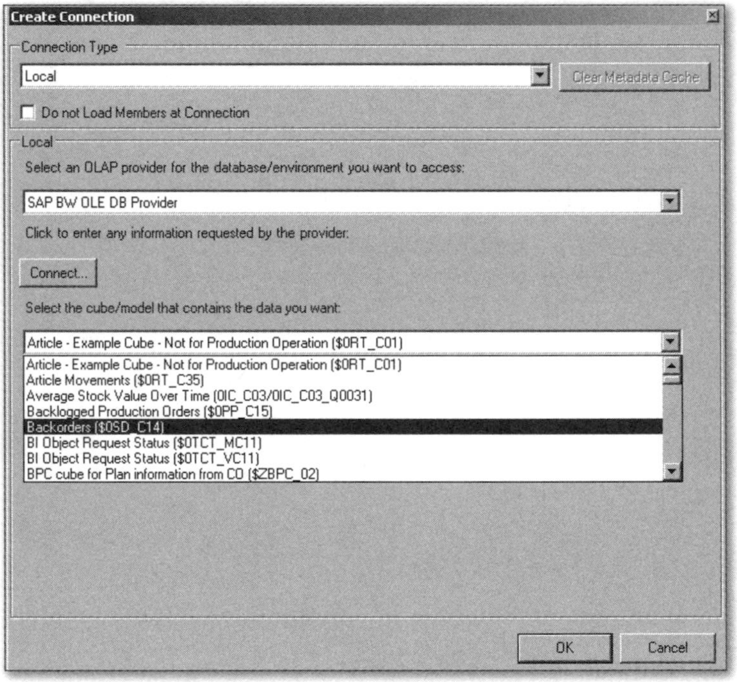

Figure 2.24 Available InfoProviders in the Create Connection Screen

After you've finished and logged in to your EPM add-in, it will show your characteristics and key figures for the InfoCube, and you're ready to create your report. This view is very similar to what you would see after you log on to your BPC InfoCube. Some minor differences appear in the view of the list of objects in the Reports pane, but overall, you won't have any issues transitioning from using BPC or BW InfoCubes. In Figure 2.25, you'll see that most of the EPM tab options are now available.

Some of the options are specific to a BPC process, so those will still be grayed out, such as the Save Data option. As you can see, this is an entirely new component with quite a bit of functionality. We'll cover much of this functionality in Chapter

4, but to show everything in-depth would require another book just on the EPM add-in.

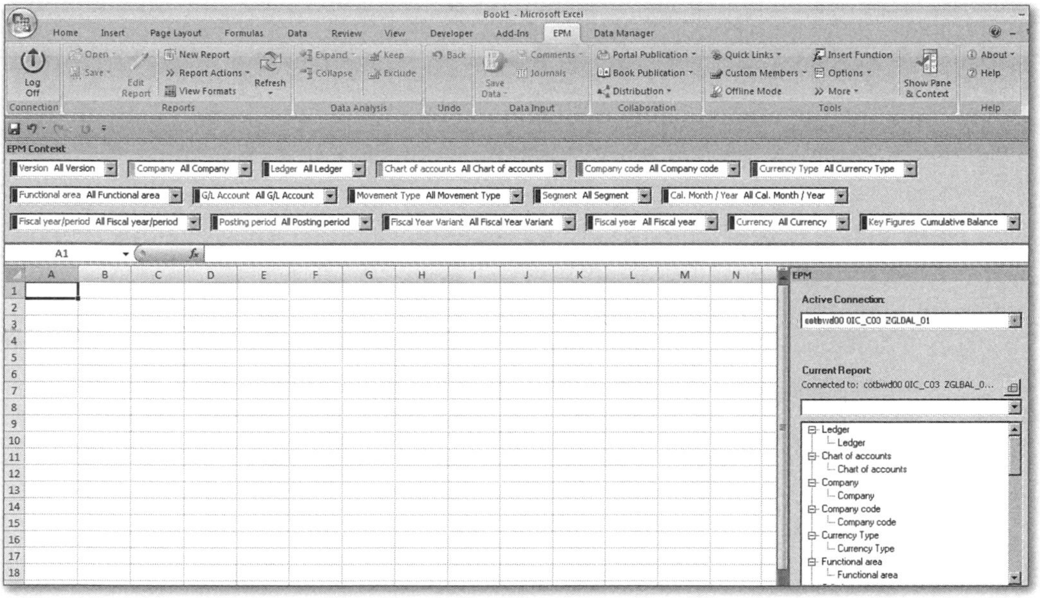

Figure 2.25 Sample of the Initial Screen for the EPM add-in

EMP Add-In Test Case

A recent comparison testing process for a company performed a side-by-side comparison of Essbase (Essbase is another reporting toolset that will help create reports for the user in Excel) and the EPM add-in. After the smoke cleared on a weeklong testing process with approximately 27 multiple-step test cases, the decision was made that the EPM add-in stood up to Essbase and in some cases exceeded Essbase in functionality in each test case. Not only did the functionality work to a satisfactory level, but testing was also done for performance, and some of the data volumes were extremely large, for example, the report testing was done on more than 1.2 billion records and more than 1 million values for all of the characteristics. More than 300 hierarchies were also included, and the reports ran in under 10 seconds.

In this section, we've just touched on the initial setup of the EPM add-in and the process of linking to it via the different InfoProviders in BW, but the process is very similar in the BPC version for Microsoft as well, except that in the BPC version for Microsoft, we aren't linking to BW InfoProviders but to Microsoft tables. In Chapter 4, we'll take this information and expand on it in detail.

2.4   BPC Starter Kit Information

SAP has delivered a series of starter kits that can be used for getting your BPC environment up and running in a short period of time. These starter kits have quite a bit of configuration already completed and can be of significant help in the overall process of setting up your BPC architecture. We'll cover the standard objects that SAP delivers to give you some good ideas on processes and also best practices. The one area where standard information isn't provided is in the master data (member) tables, which makes sense because everyone's master data is a bit different. After you upload some master data and transactional data, you'll have a fully functional sample environment. This will help in your ability to create demos and presentations for the business users, get early adopters on the system, and show the improved functionality of BPC. Although there are quite a few starter kits for the BPC V7.5, at this time, there is only one fully migrated starter kit for BPC V10.0: the IFRS Starter Kit. SAP will probably convert the other starter kits to the BPC V10.0 functionality in the future. If you have the luxury of having a BPC V7.5 system hanging around, you can install the starter kits and migrate them to the BPC V10.0 version based on the information in Chapter 10. This means you need to migrate your BPC V7.5 to BPC V10.0 and have already installed the starter kits you want. In any case, let's take a look at some of the components you get with the IFRS Starter Kit in BPC V10.0.

Installing starter kits into your environment is very straightforward. After you access the website for all of the starter kits, you simply execute the download from the site and into a folder or some sort of drive. Then you access the BW system that supports your BPC and use Transaction UJBR to EXECUTE the RESTORE option to install the EnvironmentShell for the specific starter kit.

> **NOTE: Website for Starter Kits**
>
> ▶ To access the starter kits for Healthcare and Public Sector go to *https://service.sap.com/swdc*
>
> ▶ To access the starter kits for Banking and Sales & Operations go to *https://websmp106.sap-ag.de/swdc*
>
> ▶ To access the starter kit for IFRS go to *https://www.sdn.sap.com/irj/bpx/ifrs*
>
> ▶ To access the accelerators for Human Capital, P&L, Sales Planning, and Legal Consolidation go to *http://help.sap.com/bp_bpc70/html/BPC/BP2_EN_DE.htm* to access each change the number after the BP to either 2, 3, 4, or 5 to get to the best practices for each module respectively.

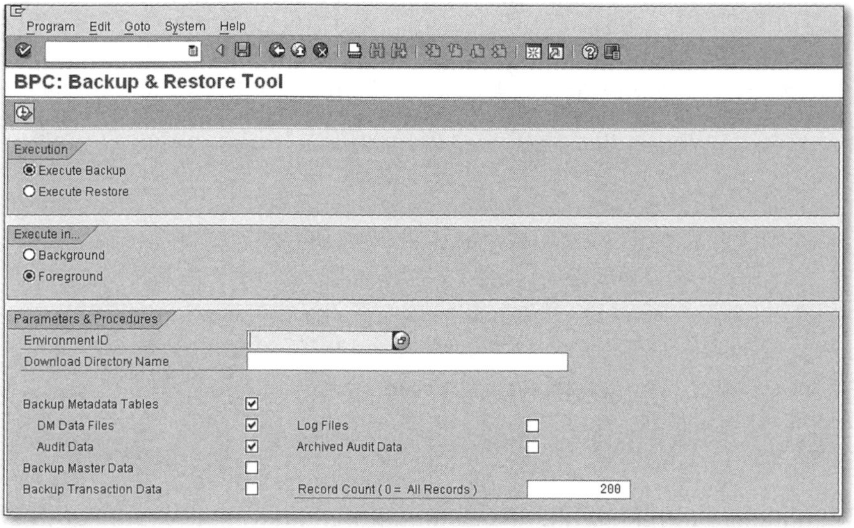

Figure 2.26 BPC Transaction UJBR – Backup & Restore Tool

Follow these steps to use the parameters shown in Figure 2.26:

1. In the Execution area, select Execute Restore.

2. In the Execute In... area, select Foreground.

3. In the Parameters & Procedures area, enter the EnvironmentShell name (uppercase) in the Environment ID box, and then click the search button at the end of the file field to search for the file that is storing the starter kit EnvironmentShell.

4. In the additional parameters in the Parameters & Procedures area, identify the information you want to have restored into your BPC system, including Backup Master Data, DM Data Files, Audit Data, and other items. Then Execute the process by using the execute button. After this is complete, a notification will appear that the installation was successful accompanied a green signal light.

After this is complete, the only remaining activity is to set up any missing security objects and then upload some transactional data. Now let's take a look at the individual starter kits.

2.4.1 IFRS Starter Kit

The IFRS Starter Kit, as mentioned, is the only one that has currently been switched over to the BPC V10.0 format, and it has significant amounts of objects and material. After the installation of the starter kit has completed, you can review the components that are standard delivered for this purpose. If this is about a 50-60% fit to what you need, then you have a very good start on your configuration and implementation. The basic material for the IFRS Starter Kit can be found on the wiki site for SAP:

http://wiki.sdn.sap.com/wiki/display/CPM/SAP+BusinessObjects+and+Consolidation+Content+Solutions

The wiki site will give you links to download these starter kits as well as some generic information about the different kits. SAP also provides eight nicely done PDFs on the IFRS Starter Kit that offer detailed information on configuration, available data entry objects, installation, and two case studies for your review. To access these PDFs you can use any search site, and search for PC100NW_IFRS*.

The installed version of the IFRS Starter Kit shown in Figure 2.27 shows that it's delivered with three Models: Consolidation, Ownership, and Rates. These are the required models for the implementation of the consolidation process for IFRS. This could also help in the process of setting up other consolidation models such as GAAP-related processes. The business rules and other Script Logic must be reviewed based on any changes required due to the differences between the two processes. Remember that a model in BPC is the view of an InfoCube in BW. Basically, when you create a model in BPC, you're creating an InfoCube in BW. We'll discuss this in more detail in Chapter 3.

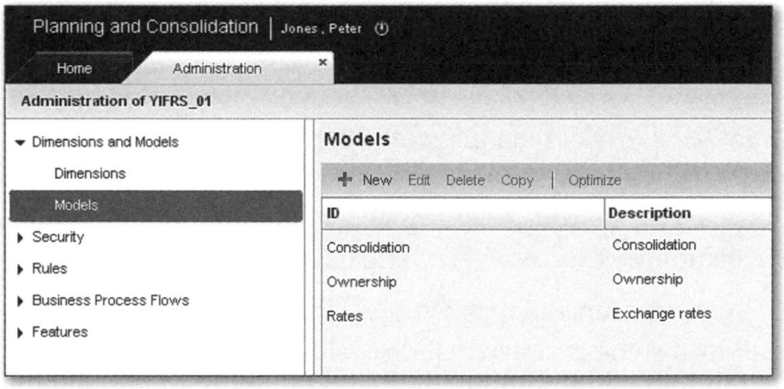

Figure 2.27 Web Client Administration Tab of BPC – IFRS Model

Within the business rules for consolidation, a number of components are already set up and available. Figure 2.28 shows that there are 12 methods, 42 method-based multipliers, 13 currency translations, and 29 eliminations and adjustments available to be aligned for your specific accounts and requirements. Also, more than

25 different reporting templates are provided for the basic consolidation reports, that is, trial balance, P&L, balance sheet, and comparison reports.

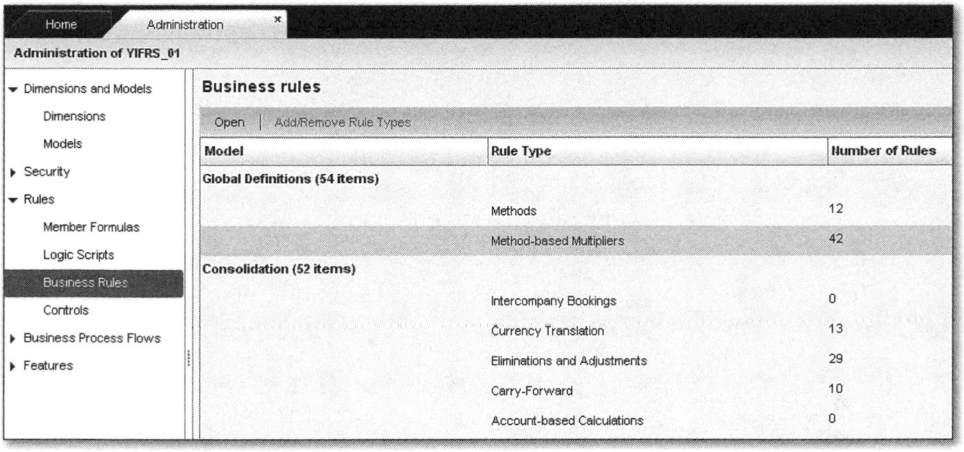

Figure 2.28 Delivered Business Rules for the IFRS Starter Kit

A quick review of a small portion of the method-based multipliers shows that much of the standard processes have been already designed (see Figure 2.29).

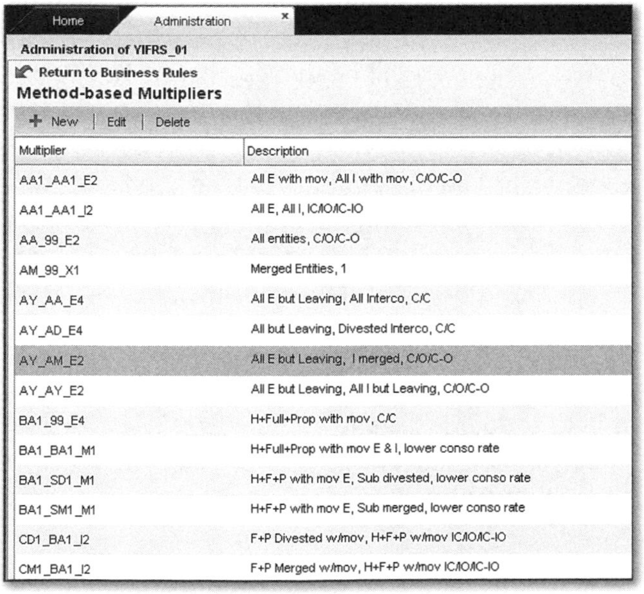

Figure 2.29 Method-Based Multipliers for the BPC IFRS Starter Kit

2.4.2 Other Starter Kits

Other starter kits are being migrated to the BPC V10.0 for the SAP NetWeaver as well as MS versions. As in the case of the IFRS Starter Kit, all of the others are helping to support the core functionality within a specific planning process. For example, the Capital Expenditure Planning Starter Kit helps you manage your capital expenditures based on your strategic goals. The key here is to offer the core dimensions or characteristics required to support a CAPEX (capital expenditures) planning process. Others that are available include a Liquidity Planning solution, a Sales Volume Planning solution, and Sales and Operation Planning Rapid Deployment Solution. Even though some of the starter kits might not be in the BPC V10.0, there are approaches that can be used to help install and implement them in your environment.

A number of others are also available specifically for the BPC version for Microsoft such as the Health Care solution, Public Sector solution, and Human Capital solution. For the most up-to-date information, additional contacts are listed on the SAP Community Network website to address more detailed questions about the availability of these other starter kits.

2.5 Summary

This chapter introduced the system architecture of BPC for both the SAP NetWeaver version and the Microsoft version. We also discussed the process of accessing the BPC systems both at the user frontend and the backend of the SAP NetWeaver BPC system, specifically BW. Then we logged on to both the frontend and backend to the BPC system using the SAP GUI for the backend and the BPC Web Client for the frontend. We discussed the three sections of the screen: START PAGE, CREATE, and LAUNCH. In each area, there were a series of links available to access other tasks within BPC.

We also reviewed and walked through a step-by-step process of setting up the EPM add-in for multiple different links to source systems. We specifically focused on the sequence to link a BW InfoProvider to the EPM add-in component, but all of the steps involved are required for any other connection as well.

In the final portion of this chapter, we discussed the starter kits that are available for BPC to get an accelerated start on your projects. Although starter kits are rarely an exact fit, they definitely help with questions concerning best practice and features.

For each of these topics, there is a huge amount of detailed information available that can't all be covered in this book; however, we'll discuss as much as possible in the upcoming chapters.

This chapter starts to develop the concepts around the initial architecture for BPC, including concepts for the version for SAP NetWeaver and the version for Microsoft. The architecture works through the configuration of the EnvironmentShell, applications, dimensions, properties, and members. We also introduce the integration between the BW and BPC objects.

3   BPC Architecture

In the previous chapter, we discussed the foundational backend and frontend of BPC architecture. Here, we'll expand on those concepts and focus on some of the past issues and concerns in the process of architecture in BPC as well as data loading questions for specific functionality, such as InfoObjects with compounds from SAP NetWeaver Business Warehouse (BW), hierarchies, and unique properties. Finally, the chapter discusses the standard content offered within the BPC architecture.

3.1   Terminology and Objects in BPC

Before we head into the more detailed discussions around the BPC process, you need to understand where all of these different objects align in the BPC environment. We've mentioned the EnvironmentShell in the previous chapter, and basically this is the component that supports and groups all of the objects together that you need for your process. One EnvironmentShell is specifically delivered as standard content, so we'll go through, in more detail, the objects available in that EnvironmentShell in the next section of this chapter. For now, though, let's talk about the other environments that you create based on the standard one. Figure 3.1 shows an overview diagram of the components in the BPC architecture. We'll start from the top and explain each object one at a time.

The first item in the list at the top-middle is the EnvironmentShell (environment), which contains dimensions that are shared among the different models associated with the environment. This is a standalone set of objects that are used within this environment and not shared with any other environment.

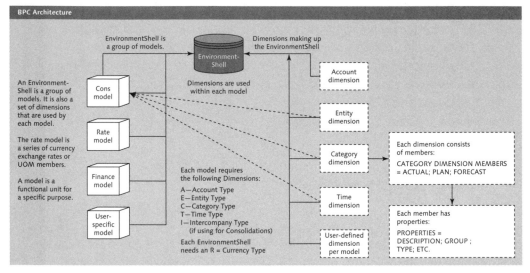

BPC Architecture

EnvironmentShell is a group of models.

Dimensions making up the EnvironmentShell

Environment-Shell

An Environment-Shell is a group of models. It is also a set of dimensions that are used by each model.

The rate model is a series of currency exchange rates or UOM members.

A model is a functional unit for a specific purpose.

Cons model

Rate model

Finance model

User-specific model

Dimensions are used within each model

Each model requires the following Dimensions:

A—Account Type
E—Entity Type
C—Category Type
T—Time Type
I—Intercompany Type
(if using for Consolidations)

Each EnvironmentShell needs an R = Currency Type

Account dimension

Entity dimension

Category dimension

Time dimension

User-defined dimension per model

Each dimension consists of members:

CATEGORY DIMENSION MEMBERS = ACTUAL; PLAN; FORECAST

Each member has properties:

PROPERTIES = DESCRIPTION; GROUP ; TYPE; ETC.

Figure 3.1 Overview of the Components of an Environment

Any copies of the standard EnvironmentShell are called by the appropriate naming convention based on what they are intended to be used for such as Planning, Sales, or Financial. For example, in many cases, it's just called the corporation's name. The next items on the right-side in Figure 3.1 are called dimensions. *Dimensions* are objects, or more precisely, a table or set of tables, that make up the functional information required for BPC to execute a specific process. They support the storage of master data; for example, a Category dimension stores the master data such as the Actual, Plan, Forecast, and Budget objects. If you were looking at a consolidation process, some of the dimensions in the environment would be Company Code, GL Account, Intercompany, Time, Category, and Currency. As you'll see, some dimensions are required for each of the standard structures used in an environment, but, overall, dimensions identify the coding block that you need to accommodate the process. These dimensions are different if the objective of the model is HR planning or CAPEX planning. You have to identify exactly which dimensions are required to support your process. This is another very important task that should be defined and validated by the business user groups that the process is being developed to support. Some dimensions are always going to be used, such as Time and Category (version), but others will be unique to specific activities, such as Customer, Segment, or Product. After you've identified the dimensions required, you can create your model. The model is a combination of different dimensions that make up the coding block for the transactional data, and as mentioned, these dimensions are unique to the process that the model is responsible to support. The models are shown in Figure 3.1 on the left side of the diagram. Different models that are available range from Consolidation to Planning. You and your business users define the purpose of each model. If you're looking at a planning scenario, then you might have a set of models such as the following:

▶ **Sales Planning**
This model might reflect the sales volumes and pricing required.

▶ **Inventory Planning**
This model might reflect the supporting product costs required for the overall planning process.

▶ **Rate**
This model is required for the foreign exchange (FX) translation of currencies.

▶ **HR Planning**
This model might reflect the labor information required to support the cost calculations.

▶ **Cost Center**
This model might support the required costs to calculate the rates for different activities during the production process.

As you can see, the model reflects the appropriate transactional activity required. A model has multiple dimensions and one key figure called SignData. This SignData object supports the transactional data values that are either posted to manually or uploaded to the BPC model. This means that the architecture of the BPC model reflects a view based on accounts rather than key figures.

> **Note**
>
> An account-based view of transactional data is structured with one key figure, and the accounts help support the unique values. For example, if you have statistical key figures (SKFs) such as headcount in this architecture, generally speaking, you would create a GL Account object to reflect headcount and use that to post the information into the cube.

However, if you're viewing an architecture based on key figures, you could have multiple key figures reflecting the different values. To follow the headcount example further, if you were to have a headcount required in this scenario, you would have two key figures: one for the currency-based values and another reflecting the need for the assignment of the SKF to store the headcount value. In this case, the values for headcount would not have a GL Account object associated with them. BW supports both architectures, but BPC models are strictly account based.

We've talked about the BPC architecture, and basically the version for Microsoft only has these objects, dimensions, the sign data objects, models, and other objects to worry about, whereas the version for SAP NetWeaver has additional objects that you need to understand. These objects are the BW based objects that mirror image the BPC objects. The BW objects are created at the same time that the BPC object is created and support the storage of both transactional data and master data. Table 3.1 shows the objects side by side for BPC and BW and how they match up. Not to say that these are exactly alike but during the creation process the BW objects and tables that are created are shown here.

SAP NetWeaver BW Objects	SAP NetWeaver BPC Objects
InfoArea: A folder that incorporates BW objects.	Environment
InfoCube: Transactional data tables.	Model
MultiProvider: Union of other InfoProviders.	Model
Characteristic InfoObjects: Fields that reflect functional values such as COMPANY CODE, CUSTOMER, GL ACCOUNT.	Dimensions
Attributes : Characteristics that add descriptive information or related information to another characteristic, for example, company code and currency attribute.	Properties
Characteristic Values: The ID of the characteristic, for example, Company Code 1000, 2000.	Members
Key Figure InfoObject: Field that supports quantitative values, such as transactional data.	SignData
Calculated Key Figure for Time: Period, YTD, QTD information.	Measure

Table 3.1 Comparison of BW and BPC Objects

This shows the tight integration between the SAP NetWeaver BW and the BPC components. You won't have one without the other. We'll investigate more about the different objects involved with the models and dimensions later in this chapter and cover in detail the concepts behind properties, measures, and members. Now, however, let's dive into more of the details around the data model in BPC.

3.2 Overview of Data Modeling for BPC

In the process of implementing, developing, and configuring BPC, you have to take a step back to do some initial data modeling. This can be anything from the basic setup and discussion concerning what a dimension is, all the way to the actual data modeling process of understanding and diagramming the system architecture. This task is as challenging as any portion of the configuration or setup because you have to actually think about a number of aspects of the project in terms of the results. Many times, a project immediately starts in with configuration, but a configuration process without a strategy or goal of an understood and known architecture is just work that will have to be redone.

> **Note: BPC Terminology**
>
> This chapter will refer to a number of terms such as dimensions, models, and so on, and we'll define all of them as we go along. For now, a *dimension* is a characteristic (e.g., Customer or Company Code) used in the data modeling of BPC.

You can never spend too much time on the data modeling task, and it normally is a dynamic process through a number of phases of the project. It's very easy to flush out architecture for the current state of the customer. Just get the current data flow process, do the old lift and shift approach, and you're done. The hard part about this is looking both down the road at what the customer might need in the future and also looking to offer some return on investment (ROI) on the project by a reengineering process. This is probably compounded by the time available to finish the project, but after you're finished, and the business users are working with BPC for either the consolidation or the planning and forecasting (P&F) process, you want to know there has been some improvement for all of this hard work. The improvement may be as simple as a reduction in the consolidation runtimes or as complex as a completely revamped approach to planning that offers the customer additional information to run their business more effectively.

This process definitely requires that you find a balance and then drive the approach based on those ideas and concepts. Many times, suggestions and recommendations offered on a project are realigned to the next phase, but that phase isn't quite scheduled quite yet. Then, over the course of the next several quarters, the issue that those recommendations addressed comes up again but the cost to reengineer is twice what it would have been to configure it initially. These components of the project process can take several iterations to resolve and their discussion could easily fill many chapters, but, for this book, we'll touch on these issues and leave the longer conversations to you and your implementation teams.

3.2.1 Key Data Modeling Questions

When considering the overall data model, you'll definitely encounter the question of how many Environments you need. An *Environment* is the critical component that supports all objects needed to configure BPC. This component incorporates all of the objects, tables, and programs required to develop a BPC scenario.

> **Note: BPC Best Practice**
>
> Normally we see only one Environment being used but I have seen up to three Environments in use. The question that needs to be asked is why more than one Environment. If there are specific needs to warrant more than one Environment then using more than one is best practice.

For this topic, let's just assume that we're only working with one landscape and one, either BW or Microsoft, system. That being said, what factors should you look at to determine how many shells to use? Generally speaking, you want to accommodate everything in one environment system. So the capability to have consolidation, P&F, and reporting all work out of the same environment is optimal. We haven't yet discussed the different objects within the EnvironmentShell, but the questions you need to answer on this topic come from basic concerns about the objects being used and how they will be integrated going forward, as well as a strategy to develop BPC and the functionality being used in the system. Some aspects to this decision may require more time for discussion, such as security, but overall, most of these other questions have a system answer. There are two areas that have no real system answer, so you have to address these questions as objectively as possible. The first question is really at the core of having one or a number of Environments. Business decision makers looking to implement BPC should ask themselves the following two questions:

► Are we sharing dimensions, activities, and/or processes?

► Are we using the same dimensions, the same master data, the same approach to security, and definitely the same approach to data flows or sources of information?

To answer these questions, you need to have done your homework about the impacted aspects of the project. If any of these areas—dimensions, master data, and reusable activities—are found to be inconsistent between groups (P&F and consolidation), then a good discussion about having more than one Environment is in order. Further discussion might be needed, for example, if a company has very different dimensions for consolidations versus P&F. If you are in a situation where the dimensionality of these two activities is very different, then sharing an Environment may be questionable. If this is not an issue, you can move to the next topic and review the concerns on using the same processes as well as the same data sources. If these topics result in a similar answer, then the split of Environment architecture has to be discussed in earnest and a decision concerning sharing an environment is needed. This doesn't mean that you should definitely use a dual Environment approach, but the issue needs to be discussed. Normally if you will be using both aspects of BPC—consolidation and P&F—you should get some data from the same sources at least for the start of the process so there will be some inherent links. Also, in terms of the dimensions, you can probably always share the dimensions of Time and possibly Category, Entity, and a few others. These areas of the project plan lend themselves nicely to a matrix of pros and cons. This conversation will then drive out the topic of the total number of models required for each of the Environments. This topic normally resolves itself by the functions and reporting activities that are required for each of the BPC activities.

> **Note: BPC Terminology**
>
> *Models* in BPC are the objects that all of the P&F, consolidation, and reporting activities are using to support the process. Models in a nut shell support transactional data for BPC. This means that they are made up of dimensions and the signdata key figure. We'll discuss models in more detail later in this chapter.

Generally speaking a good fit for the models will fall out of the different aspects of the processes being developed. For example, if a P&F is being developed in BPC, and the areas being integrated are Headcount, Cost Planning, and Sales Planning, then you'll probably see three different models, or at least two, to support the different aspects of each of these planning approaches.

Data volume is another aspect of a project that may lend itself to more than one Environment architecture. In the recent past, a number of companies have had very large data volumes. Based on an analysis of this BPC process, you might find that sharing would be more of a hindrance than an advantage. In this case, we're talking about data volumes in the hundreds of millions of records over a short length of time such as one calendar month or fiscal period. To accommodate different service level agreements (SLAs) that might be required, such as shorter times for data flow or calculations, it might be an option to split the data into two Environments and upload it more effectively via two data flows rather than one.

Another aspect of a BPC project that will help mold the architecture and data modeling is the data flow into BPC. This can vary but for a Microsoft BPC project, the focus is normally on the flat file approach, whereas if with a SAP NetWeaver BPC project, you can use many sources of data, including BW, flat files, and third-party sources. Depending on the approach to the data loading process, you can develop your overall BPC architecture diagram, which will include everything from the source system to the BPC objects. One of the significant concerns is how the master data will be uploaded. This can be a bit of a challenge because a number of properties and attributes of the dimensions are unique to BPC.

> **Note: BPC Terminology**
>
> A *property/attribute* of a dimension is an additional object that is added to the dimension for use with reports, calculations, or descriptions. Customer Location is an example of a property used with the Customer dimension. Properties will be discussed further later in this chapter.

For example, if you take something like Account as a dimension, you'll see that it has several required properties such as Account Type and Rate Type that aren't standard in the BW GL Account object. Therefore, if you get the information from BW, you either have to add these properties to the BW object or create a Z object (ZACCOUNT) to accommodate these new properties. In this way, you can avoid changing the standard delivered object for Account (0GL_ACCOUNT), but if you do that, you now have another dilemma: the existence of two account objects—0GL_ACCOUNT and ZACCOUNT. The standard object—0GL_ACCOUNT—is used in all of the standard InfoCubes and other objects for everything from reporting to data loading. On the other hand, you have a ZACCOUNT that's supporting the master data loading into BPC. This can cause issues with everything from creating a MultiProvider for reporting purposes to validation of the master data on the way into the system.

> **Note: BPC Terminology**
>
> A MultiProvider is a BW-based object that can be used to create a union of two or more BW objects for reporting purposes. For example, your sales information is in two different InfoCubes. One InfoCube supports Sales Order Create information, and another supports Sales Order Delivery information. Creating a MultiProvider of these two InfoCubes will allow you to see the sales order information from creation to delivery.

Another approach might be to either derive these values somehow as the master data is loaded or just use a flat file approach to uploading into BPC where the flat file supports all of the properties directly into the BPC object. Again, there are a number of questions with this approach, such as having inconsistent objects between BPC and BW for reporting purposes and business users who will be switching from a BPC object for reporting to a BW for reporting and wondering why certain properties have disappeared.

Reporting requirements also will impact the data modeling view. Many areas of reporting need to be addressed during this process so that the data modeling and architecture of the system will be consistent with the required final results. For example, if the requirement is to be able to match up actuals against plan data (a P&F scenario) on a real-time basis, then you must make sure that the required actual data is available in the right format and location to make this happen. Due to the differences in the structures of the InfoCubes between BW and BPC, the ability to marry up the data on a real-time basis is a bit more challenging than in a core BW scenario (two BW cubes) due to several components of BPC and BW (we'll address these more detailed topics later in this chapter). Needless to say, the reporting requirements in terms of timeliness — that is, whether real time or not — will impact the overall architecture and data modeling of your BPC project.

As you can see, starting from the core data flow options all the way to the reporting process, all of these topics will definitely alter and define portions of the data modeling process within both your core BW system as well as the BPC add-on. These discussions will confirm what is necessary and be followed by what the system can actually do. If you look at a generic diagram of an SAP NetWeaver BPC architecture, you can see that the data model, based on the topics previously discussed in terms of data volumes and data flow, need to be developed prior to the initial configuration so that the architecture has a focus (see Figure 3.2). This seems obvious because you have to understand where you're going before you can get there. Figure 3.2 shows that the sources of data have been identified and they range from flat files for some information to direct connections to the SAP ERP system for core operational information (❶). From there, the data moves from a "staging" InfoCube and manual loading process into the BPC model (❷). Additional postings are assigned to the BPC model via a manual budget/plan process (❸) and at the same time might be needed in the SAP ERP system as well (❹) possibly via a "retraction" process. This also depicts the need to do some drill-through reporting into the core SAP ERP system. So after executing the reports in BPC, a drill through into either BW InfoCubes or SAP ERP system tables is available (❺).

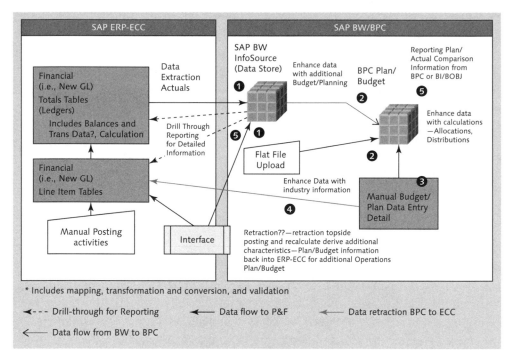

Figure 3.2 Overview of the Data Modeling and Flow of a SAP NetWeaver BPC Process

This discussion of data modeling and architecture appears at this point in the chapter to stress a point. The point is that sometimes you won't have a full grasp of the functionality or of the requirements in a project, but you still have to work through a good, maybe not complete, diagram of both the data modeling and the data flow. This gives you a good roadmap to work with and will drive out quite a bit of the details around the next several topics we'll discuss in this chapter concerning structures in BPC. As you can see, we're bumping into terms and terminology that you need to understand before moving forward.

3.2.2 EnvironmentShell

Now that we've looked at the overall architecture of BPC, let's get into the details around the EnvironmentShell itself. An EnvironmentShell is a starting point for the BPC process whether working on a consolidation project or a P&F project and is the standard delivered component for BPC. All other copies of the EnvironmentShell are noted as Environments. The core of an EnvironmentShell consists of models and dimensions as you saw earlier in Figure 3.1. Dimensions are used to build the model within an Environment. After the Basis team has finished installing BPC, you should be able to view the EnvironmentShell or at least view a copy of the EnvironmentShell. Depending on the security approach, you may find that the actual EnvironmentShell is secured and isn't available to anyone; in that case, the Basis team will, upon request, make a copy and allow access to the copy of EnvironmentShell. EnvironmentShell has four models supplied standard in the process. Along with these models, all of the different objects, such as templates, business rules, and some Script Logic, are delivered with this Environment. The four models that are delivered are Consolidation, Ownership, Planning, and Rates, as shown in Figure 3.3. This is a great start for the configuration process and should be used for the basic "create" process of any other EnvironmentShell or model within that shell. Again, the reasoning behind this is that all of the standard objects are delivered and will be copied over so you don't have to start from scratch.

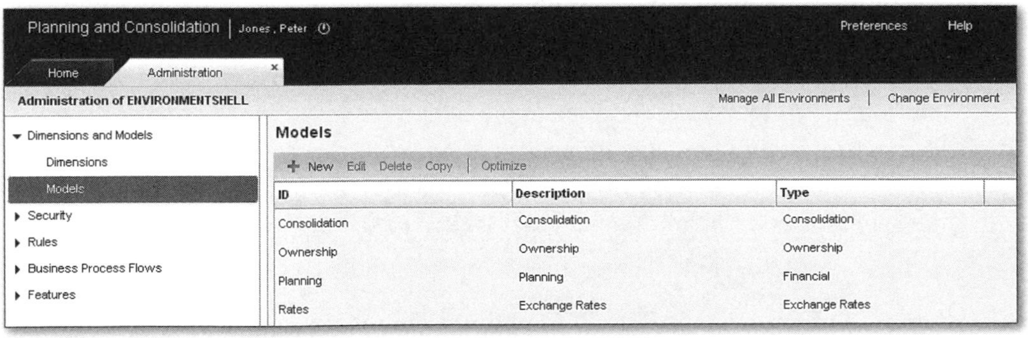

Figure 3.3 View of the Four Models Delivered with EnvironmentShell

Following is a basic definition for each model:

▶ **Consolidation model**
This model contains the architecture to complete the consolidation process within a corporation. This data is modeled with the financial process in mind, so it contains or will contain balance sheet and income statement information.

▶ **Ownership model**
This is a "supporting" model for the Consolidation model and stores information for use with the consolidation process. This information consists of consolidation methods, ownership percentages, and a rollup of data using a hierarchical view of the information for legal consolidation.

▶ **Planning model**
This is a financial model that can be aligned with the budgeting and P&F process within a corporation. It's designed by default to accommodate the currency translation process.

▶ **Rates model**
This model is also a supporting model for a financial process. This supports the currency translation process within the BPC structure. It contains exchange rates that are supplied to BPC from either BW or a flat file of exchange rates.

> **Note: EnvironmentShell Alterations**
>
> EnvironmentShell should not be changed or altered. This pristine copy of the BPC standard should be protected, and only a copy should be offered to the business for use. Normally you will see that Basis will lock down this standard content set of objects after creating a copy that can be used in its place.

Clearly, most companies won't fall into an exact structure as offered by these standard delivered models. If necessary, you can make a copy of the EnvironmentShell and then adjust the architecture as required by adding additional models, dimensions, and logic. Figure 3.4 shows an example of the EnvironmentShell to give you an idea of the dimensions that are available. As you can see, the standard delivered dimensions cover many of the core requirements. Figure 3.5 shows an example of the standard Consolidation model that is delivered.

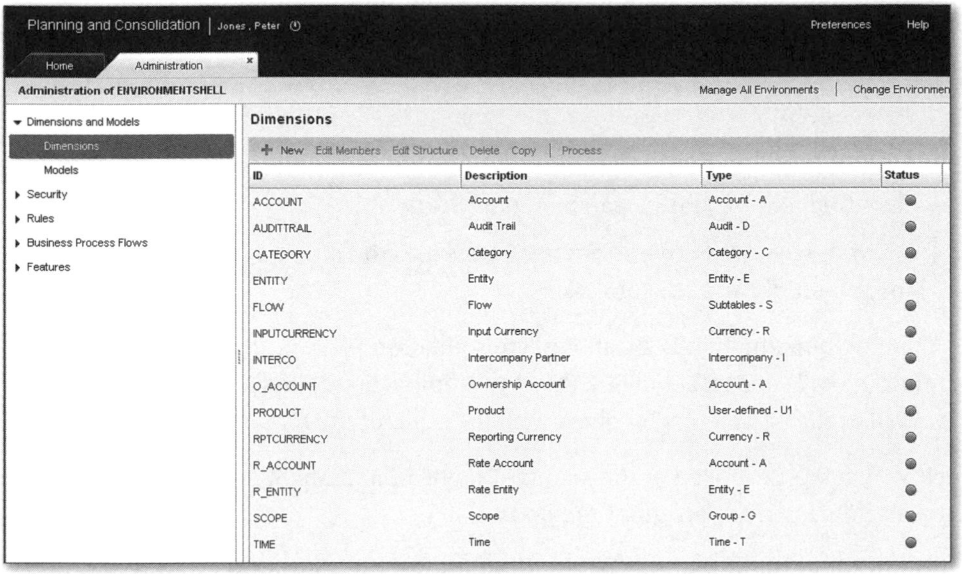

Figure 3.4 View of the Delivered Dimensions for EnvironmentShell

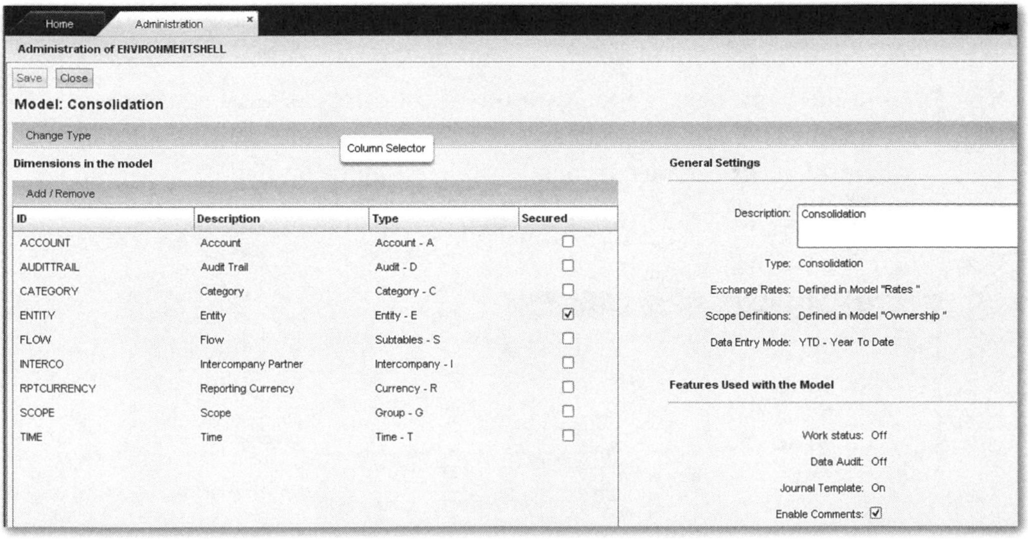

Figure 3.5 View of the Standard Delivered Consolidation Model

Following are the other objects and functionality that come along with the standard EnvironmentShell:

▶ Generic members for each dimension

▶ Business rules

83

- ▶ Script Logic
- ▶ Report and input templates
- ▶ Basic security roles
- ▶ Data Manager packages
- ▶ Required administrative parameters
- ▶ All of the required dimensions and properties to set up basic models for budgeting, planning, and consolidation

Again if your situation is a standard consolidation process, and you start with this model, it will support about 60-70% of your initial build. We'll discuss the indicators and all of the parameters involved with the build of the model later in this chapter.

Now that we've looked at the standard EnvironmentShell, let's make a copy of it for use during this portion of the book.

3.2.3 Configuration/Copy of EnvironmentShell

The process of creating a copy of the EnvironmentShell is fairly straightforward. Follow these steps:

1. From the home page, go to PLANNING AND CONSOLIDATION ADMINISTRATION • MANAGE ALL ENVIRONMENTS as shown in Figure 3.6. This will be the screen where all of the parameters mentioned here can be found.

2. Choose ENVIRONMENTSHELL • COPY, as shown in Figure 3.6.

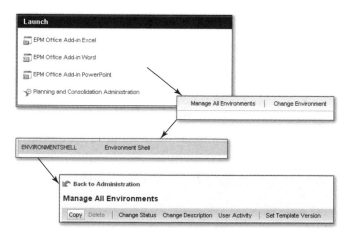

Figure 3.6 Copy Process for the EnvironmentShell

3. When a dialog box appears, enter an ID (no spaces) and a description (see Figure 3.7) in the appropriate fields. Then choose what you want to copy from the EnvironmentShell. Either DATA IN MODELS, WEB DOCUMENTS, or DOCUMENTS.

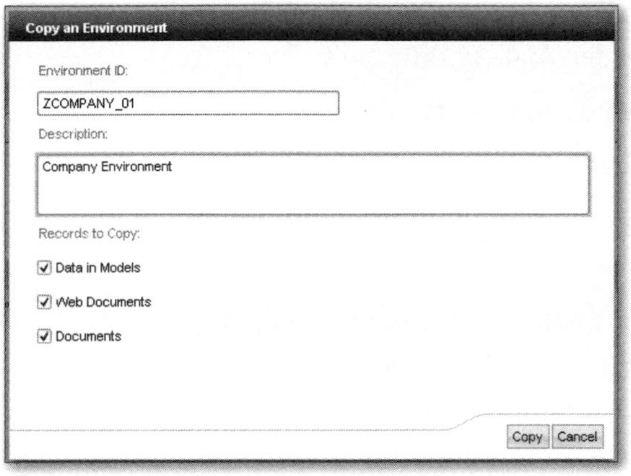

Figure 3.7 Details of the Copy Process for the EnvironmentShell to ZCOMPANY_01

4. After you've decided which items to copy, click COPY. A dialog box appears, and the system generates all of the models, dimensions, and other objects required as well as whatever you've chosen to copy based on the initial screen. Figure 3.8 shows a partial list of the copying activities.

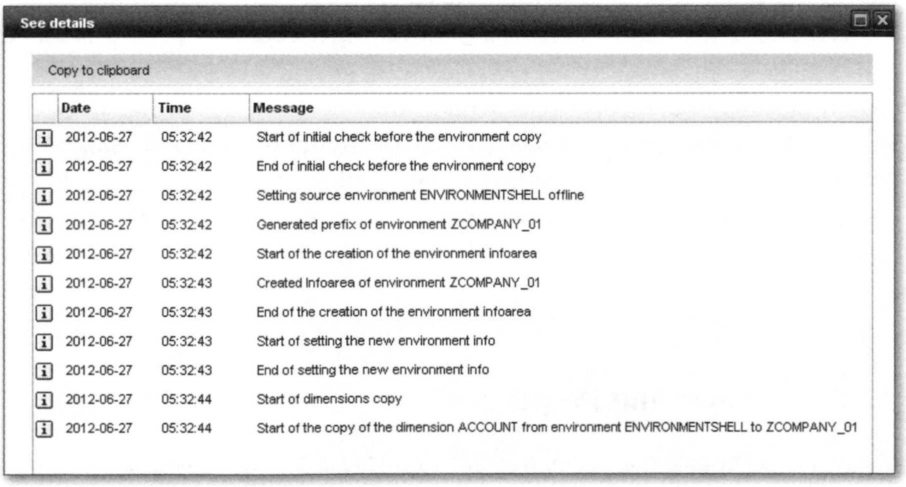

Figure 3.8 Example of the Steps the System Executes during the Copy Process

When this is complete, you can access the new Environment by going back into the home page, choosing the ENVIRONMENT link at the bottom of the page, and then choosing your new EnvironmentShell (in this case, named ZCOMPANY_01).

When you create a new environment, BPC does the following:

1. Copies the environment Web folders/data within file services
2. Creates a copy of all SAP NetWeaver BI objects
3. Copies all transactional and master data from the source environment to the new environment, if you choose to check the parameters
4. Copies security, planning, and consolidation metadata

If the system encounters an error when copying an Environment, it rolls back to clear the objects created during the failed copy. Because it's a shell, after you make a copy, it must be populated with publications and reports to become a fully functioning environment. The Environment sample environment doesn't contain any data except Time dimension information, and it has only a limited amount of master data in the form of dimension members. The dimension master data is limited to default members in most dimensions, so the environment works when an administrative task is run.

As a final comment on the functionality of a parameter, let's discuss the CHANGE STATUS parameter found in the MANAGE ALL ENVIRONMENT tab. An environment can have a status of either ONLINE or OFFLINE. A newly created environment has a status of OFFLINE until an administrator makes it available for use by giving it a status of ONLINE. When an environment is offline, users may be restricted from performing data retrieval, reporting (all of the current data may not be available), and export tasks. You can manually set the status of an environment by choosing MAN-AGE ALL ENVIRONMENTS • CHANGE STATUS, which allows the administrator of the Environment to manage what activities can be executed against the Environment. This parameter will also come in handy during the transport process, which we'll discuss in Chapter 8.

3.3   Dimensions and Properties

All of the aspects of BPC that we'll discuss in this book are important to an implementation, but if the core objects aren't configured correctly and the data model and architecture aren't thought out properly, then the rest of the activities in this process won't perform correctly or effectively. You may need to come back to this process to revisit or realign your approach at times, but overall, the core objects need to be firmed up and signed off in the very beginning stages, and the development and configuration of the dimensions and properties is critical. Let's now get into the details of these building blocks of the BPC process.

3.3.1 Definition of Dimensions

As we mentioned earlier, dimensions are the cornerstone of the architecture in BPC. You need to understand exactly what dimensions you need to accommodate your process. Some dimensions are required, and other dimensions will be user defined. Earlier, Table 3.1 showed that a dimension in BPC is the same as a characteristic in BW. There's definitely a similarity and always a mirror image of a dimension created in BPC as a characteristic in BW with all of the associated tables and links for master data, text, and hierarchies.

If you review any process or transaction that occurs, you'll get a very good idea of what a dimension represents. For example, a basic financial posting consists of an amount, and probably a number of these other dimensions such as a GL Account, Company Code, Currency, Posting Date, Profit Center, and Functional Area—and possibly more. All of these dimensions make up the coding block of the transaction. Now, when you're working with something as strictly regulated as consolidation, the dimensions are about 80% fixed, although others are available; for example, you may want to add something like Profit Center to get some matrix consolidation views. When you're working with P&F, the variations are much more based on the management approach to executing the business strategy. For example, if your company looks at the P&F based on a product point of view, Product and all of the accompanying dimensions will come along. If your company looks at the P&F based on the Customer point of view, however, then the architecture of the model is quite different with Customer being the focus, and all of the other dimensions related to this approach, such as Region, coming along.

Another very important aspects of dimensions is the use of hierarchies in the BI environment. Hierarchies are structures that align specific members in groups to reflect a view of the dimension. For example, if you look at the dimension Regions, you might see that there's a different view of Regions based on the group that is executing the report or analysis. If you're dealing with the tax department, the idea of Regions is organized around the tax requirements, whereas if you're working with a sales department, the idea of Regions is organized around the areas of responsibility specific to regions of the country and have no resemblance to a tax view of the Regions. You end up with a number of hierarchies reflecting the version of the view required. In this case, the tax group has one hierarchy to view, and the sales group has another. Everyone is happy with their own views as long as they don't have to integrate them into one. The real fun begins when you are faced with the challenge of aligning the different hierarchies. We'll come back to hierarchies later in this chapter (Section 3.6.2) to discuss this in more detail.

A final task in the dimension area is the assignment of the properties to the dimension. A property is an additional description incorporated into the dimension to offer more information on the member itself. For example, the Customer dimension offers a number of additional pieces of information that are critical to the success of the company's link to the customer, such as the customer contact, the sales person responsible for that customer, the address, phone number, email, and on and on. These are all properties of the dimension and can be added as needed for reporting or P&F requirements.

These components of the dimension are shown in Figure 3.9; specifically, this shows the dimension ACCOUNT (which for BW folks is the GL account).

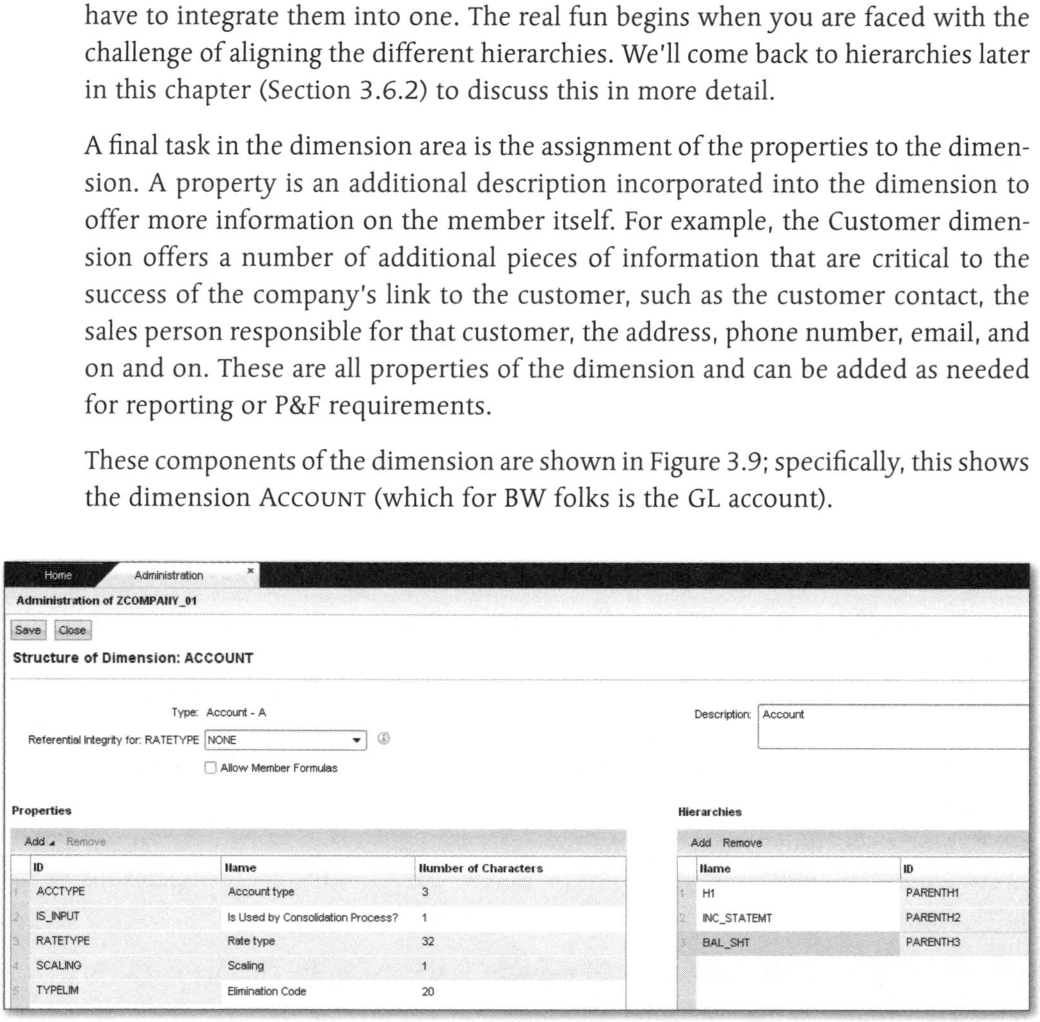

Figure 3.9 View of the Structure of a Dimension

The properties shown are all standard delivered, but in the case of the hierarchies, only H1 is delivered, and the other two are user defined to accommodate the different views of the GL accounts for the income statement and balance sheet reports.

3.3.2 Dimension Types

To start creating dimensions, you have to decide on what dimension type the object will be. You use dimension types to organize data within a dimension based on the type of information involved. An environment can have multiple dimensions of one type. Each model within the environment can have only one of each of the required types but, you can have more than one dimension type 'user-defined.' For example, the environment might contain the entity dimensions EntityB and EntityF, with the Budgeting model using EntityB, and the Forecasting model using EntityF. Again, to keep the standard content in focus, after you copy the EnvironmentShell, you'll have a copy of each of the required dimensions within your environment. Remember the dimension type is one thing, and the dimension itself is another, so in some cases, the dimension type matches the dimension name (e.g., dimension type C and the dimension Category), and in others, it doesn't (e.g., dimension type D and the dimension AuditTrail). When you create your own dimensions, you'll also follow whatever naming convention you've developed and match those dimensions with the appropriate dimension type.

Table 3.2 describes the types of dimensions within the system.

ID/Description	Definition
A – Account	Usually contains chart of accounts and other planning assumption measures. The dimension is normally represented by a hierarchy of accounts.
C – Category	Represents the versions or scenarios based on which data is tracked. It contains the types of data you're going to track, such as actual, budget, and forecast. You can set up categories to store versions, such as BudgetV1, BudgetV2, and so on.
D – Audit	Represents the various data sources that can be used to manage the main data and adjustments, if any. This can be used very effectively in calculations and in business rules of a reporting consolidation model to segregate input data.
E – Entity	Represents the business units that are used to drive the business process. Depending on your model design, the Entity type can be an operating unit, a cost center, a geographic entity, and so on. This represents the organization unit, whether defined for legal purpose or from a business angle. This can be cost center, profit center, legal company, or region. The dimension is normally represented by a hierarchy of entities. The Entity dimension type is also the normal dimension to assign security.

Table 3.2 Dimension Types and their Descriptions

ID/Description	Definition
G – Group	Reports consolidated results in multiple group currencies within a single entity structure. Group provides multiple currencies for a group member. Assign both an R and a G identifier to a consolidation model, but assign only the G identifier to the Ownership model referred from the Consolidation model. You can't assign both an R and a G identifier to the same Ownership model.
I – Intercompany	Contains the intercompany codes for the entities. This represents the intercompany codes for the purposes of legal consolidation intercompany matching and elimination.
R – Currency	Contains the currency rates for all currencies in which your company does business. For validation purposes, all environments must contain a Currency dimension; however, each model within an environment isn't required to have a Currency dimension. The Currency dimension in a Reporting model must contain the REPORTING property; the Currency dimension in a Rate non-reporting model doesn't need to contain the REPORTING property.
S – Subtables	Breaks down the account activity or flow. For example, some accounts, such as fixed assets, have a Subtables dimension containing Opening, Additions, Deletions, Transfers, and Ending Balances. The Subtables-type dimension is important for writing business rules that require currency translation amounts to be calculated by account.
T – Time	Contains the time periods for which you store data. This represents the time periods based on which data are stored. The time periods can be customized in various forms or represented as weekly, monthly, or quarterly.
U – User-defined	Represents a user-defined dimension. This can represent any character the business requires. Some examples include Customer, Product, Cost Center, Profit Center, and Region.

Table 3.2 Dimension Types and their Descriptions (Cont.)

Now that we've covered the dimension requirements and types, we can discuss the dimensions themselves.

3.4   Create a Dimension

Let's start by understanding the process of creating a dimension. This portion of the process is an afterthought after all of the work goes into the validation of what dimensions are needed, but you need to understand some basic requirements as well as some best practices while setting up the dimensions. To start the process, go to the home page, and then follow these steps:

1. Click on the PLANNING AND CONSOLIDATION ADMINISTRATION link.

2. From there, click on DIMENSIONS, and then click on +NEW (Figure 3.10).

Figure 3.10   View of the Dimension Screen

3. After the NEW screen opens, you'll see a dialog box as shown in Figure 3.11.

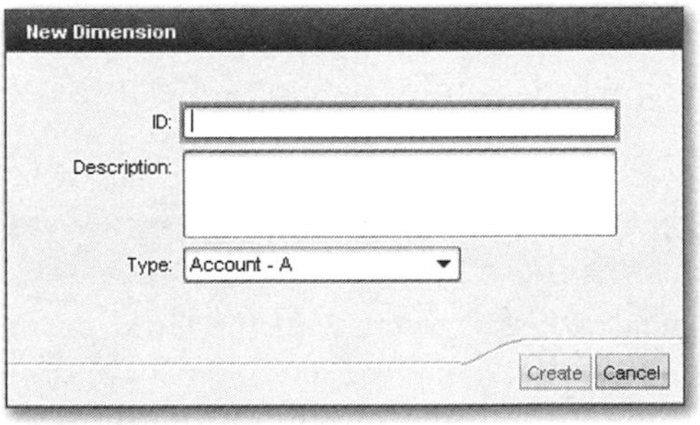

Figure 3.11   Dialog for Creating a New Dimension

4. Fill in the ID and DESCRIPTION fields, and then identify choose which dimension type is to be assigned from the TYPE dropdown list. In this example, Customer is the dimension, and User-Defined is the dimension type. Depending on the dimension type you choose, additional information will either be requested or

delivered. For example, if you choose the dimension type ACCOUNT-A, you'll be asked to accept several properties such as ACCTYPE, RATETYPE, and SCALING. SCALING is a generic property that is normally assigned to the dimension during the create process.

5. After the dimension has been generated, the option to add additional properties is offered as shown in Figure 3.12.

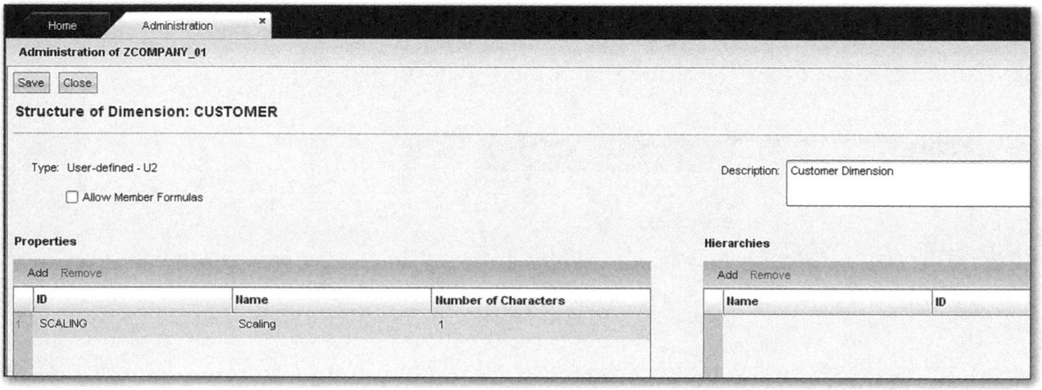

Figure 3.12 View of the Structure Screen for Creating a Dimension

The property SCALING has been added, and you can now add any additional dimensions needed. For this example, we'll add an additional property named IMPORTANCE. This will provide additional information on the customer as to whether they are high-, medium-, or low-volume customers, which is information you can use to improve the reporting process.

> **Note: BPC Confirmation of Environment Connection**
>
> Make sure you're in the appropriate Environment to start by checking the lower-right corner and confirming that the Environment is correct. If not, use the hyperlink to the right of the Environment label at the lower right corner of the screen to switch the environments. Click on this hyperlink and you will see a list of the different Environments.

6. Click the ADD link under the PROPERTIES label, and add the property requirements. Figure 3.13 shows the result.

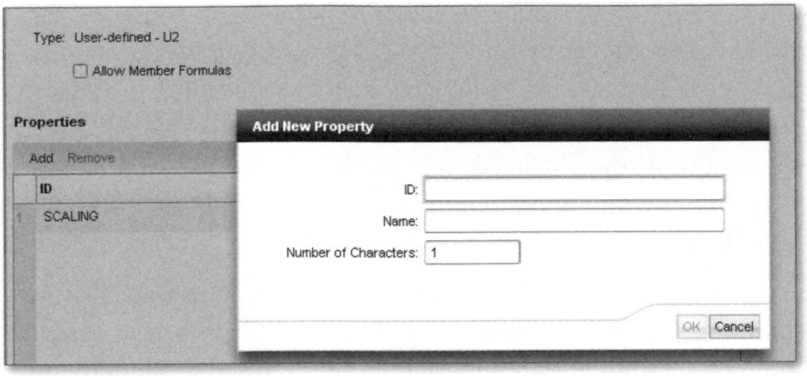

Figure 3.13 Add New Property Screen

7. Enter the information in the three fields required to support the member set. In this case, we'll enter "IMPORTANCE" in the ID field, "Level of Importance" in the NAME field, and "3" in the NUMBER OF CHARACTERS field. The results are shown in Figure 3.14.

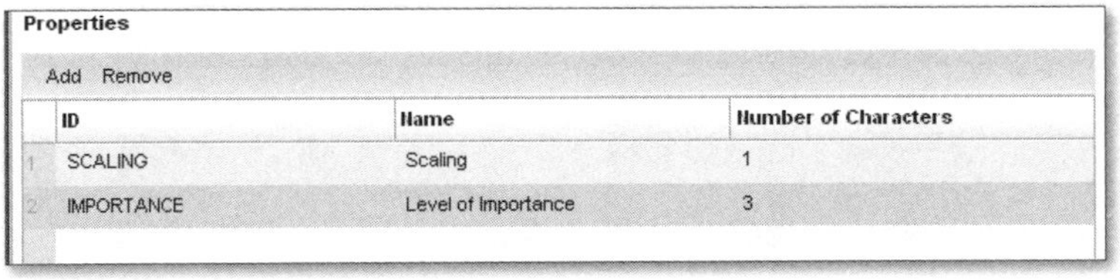

Figure 3.14 Results of Adding an Additional Property to Dimension

Following are some tips concerning this creation process that might come in handy when you are configuring dimensions and properties in the future:

▶ Enter your IDs in all uppercase. This isn't required, but it helps with the overall use of the properties in the logic coding and reporting. Look at how the standard objects come into the system, and try to keep that trend going.

▶ Dimensions are 32 characters long and will accommodate just about all of the standard lengths in BW for characteristics. There was an issue in previous versions of BPC. For example if the Project System (PS) IDs were going to be used because they could be any length up to 32 characters in length as well.

▶ Properties that are longer than 60 characters (in the BPC version for SAP NetWeaver) will still be accommodated, but the characters over 60 will be stored differently in BW, so the property won't support the use of their property ID's in programs and other reporting activities.

▶ Before you finish with a dimension, update it with at least one value such as NONE, or some other identifier that will be used for a blank field in a transaction. If you don't add at least one dimension member you will not be able to use the dimension in a model. Once you attempt to process a model you will get an error that one of the dimensions do not have a member and therefore the model will not be processed and activated until you add at least one member to the dimension.

Although you've just created a property by a user-defined approach, there are other approaches available. You can have the system generate properties based on the dimension type, or you can have the system generate properties based on the model that is to be created as well. You can also just copy an existing dimension, and with that copy, all of the properties will be assigned. The COPY option is on the same toolbar as the NEW option. You'll be prompted for the same basic information as though you were creating a dimension.

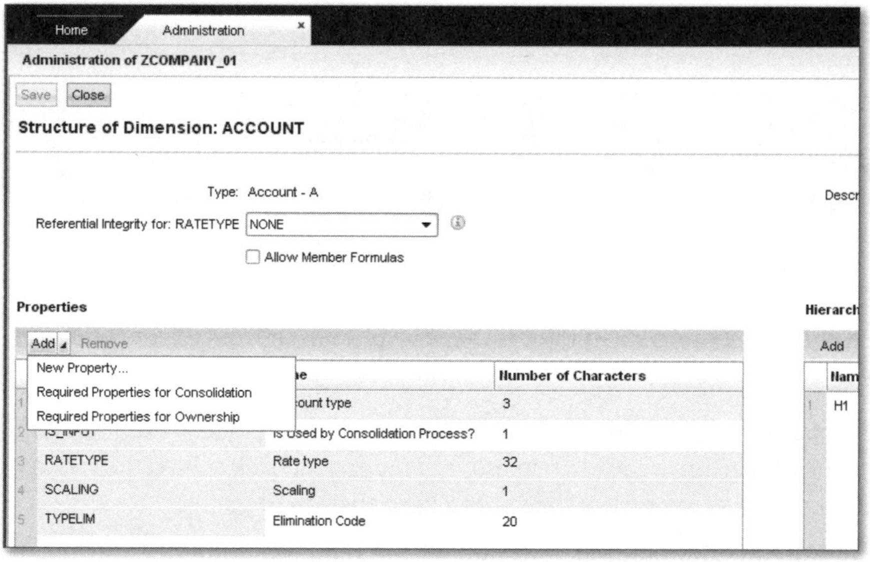

Figure 3.15 Edit Screen for the Dimension ACCOUNT

Several other options are also available to you during the creation of a dimension. Figure 3.15 shows the dimension edit screen for the ACCOUNT dimension. On this screen, you can set up referential integrity. This option offers you the ability to validate the member values of another property during the uploading process. For example in this case, we are able to validate the RATETYPE property that is being applied to the dimension members that are being either uploaded or manually added to the list to another RATETYPE property being used in another dimension of type A. This can be used to make sure that any RATETYPE being used is consistent with a standard list of RATETYPES from another dimension.

In addition, you can also click on ALLOW MEMBER FORMULAS to allow the use of the dimension logic on this specific dimension. Dimension logic is the ability to fill a specific member with a value based on a formula assigned to the specific member. For example, in most cases, a GL account showing net income is a calculation or a rollup of a number of other accounts in a hierarchy. If you like, you can use this ALLOW MEMBER FORMULAS checkbox to apply a specific formula directly to the GL account net income and have it show up in a report. Using this approach does raise a number of concerns, including performance of these formulas in a report as well as the configuration. However, if you do use these formulas, remember you can only use base values in the calculation during formula creation. For example, to calculate net income, you might be able to use a subtotal to make the calculation easier, but that isn't possible because you have to use all base level members for this dimension logic to work. You also need to realize that the total length of the formula can't be longer than 500 characters. Taking these two comments into account, you can see that this approach is challenging. If you have to use all base level members to calculate something like net income from a full GL account hierarchy, you'll probably bump up against the 500-character limit quickly.

You can also see in Figure 3.15 that there is another option for adding properties. You can either add a new property, a required property for Consolidation, or a required property for Ownership.

3.5   List of Dimensions and Properties

The view and setup of the different dimensions is very similar if not exactly the same as what we discussed in the previous section. Therefore, we won't go through each dimension here and show the same process over again. However, some dimensions offer a view of the dimension that will be beneficial, so we'll discuss those here. The following dimensions are those that you normally see and, in many cases, are required for the creation of a BPC model. The required properties for each of the dimensions are also incorporated in the following subsections. When these required properties are for specific models, it will be noted in the discussion.

3.5.1 Time Dimension

The time dimension defines the units of time for your model and how those units aggregate. Any dimension that is assigned the type T is a Time dimension. Each model can have only one Time dimension. Generally speaking the Time dimension will have all of the required properties as well as members assigned and available directly from the installation process. Table 3.3 lists the Time dimension's required properties.

Property Name	Description
BASE_PERIOD	A system-generated property, used by the query engine for calculations and by the consolidation process.
LEVEL	Time can be a year, quarter, month, week, or day. The LEVEL property is important in defining your time periods. You must have the correct level for each member. You must follow the chronological format throughout the Time dimension. The following is the correct format: ▸ YEAR ▸ QUARTER ▸ MONTH ▸ WEEK ▸ DAY
PERIOD	The PERIOD property allows you to filter, sort, and report based on the period.
YEAR	The YEAR property allows you to filter, sort, and report based on the year. You should place the YEAR properties in chronological order in the file, in order for the EPMMemberOffset function to give offsets correctly.
MONTHNUM	If the Time dimension is used in a Consolidation model, then this property is required. This provides a sorting order to the leaf members of the Time dimension within a year. The leaf members would be those that are at the next level down.
TIMEID	If used in a Consolidation model, then this property is required. This property is used to determine the current versus prior month. This is a numeric ID used for identifying the time member, for example, 1 for 2012.JAN.

Table 3.3 Required Properties for the Time Dimension

3.5.2 Category Dimension

The Category dimension (sometimes referred to as the Version dimension) defines the groupings in which you store information in your model. Typical categories include Budget, Actual, Forecast, and so on. The Category dimension can also be used as a type of holder for specific planning activities. For example, you can have working, final, what-if, most pessimistic, and most optimistic versions. Just be aware of what the responsibility and intent of your "categories" are and what they are being used for; you don't want to mix up the members and intention of those members too much. Any dimension that is assigned the type C is a Category dimension. Each model can have only one Category-type dimension. Table 3.4 shows the required property for the Category dimension.

Property Name	Description
YEAR	Used to assign a year to the category, to be used with the EPMRetrieveData and EPMMemberOffset functions in reporting.

Table 3.4 Required Property for Category

The properties in Table 3.5 are required only if the Category dimension is used in a Consolidation or Ownership model and if simulations in translation are required.

Property Name	Description
CATEGORY_FOR_OPE	Category of source data to use when performing carry forward (CopyOpening is the name of the Script Logic program used to execute the carry forward process).
FX_DIFFERENCE_ONLY	Specifies whether the translation result is calculated normally (blank or N) or if only the translation difference with the source category is computed (Y).
FX_SOURCE_CATEGORY	Category of source data to be used when running currency translation on a simulation category.
OPENING_PERIOD	Opening period number of source data to use when performing carry forward (CopyOpening). This can be absolute (e.g., 12 for December) or relative (e.g., −1 for prior period).

Table 3.5 Required Properties for Category in the Consolidation and Ownership Models or Using the Simulation Option for Currency Translation

Property Name	Description
OPENING_YEAR	Year offset of source data to use when running carry forward (CopyOpening). This is relative (e.g., –1 for prior period).
OWN_CATEGORY	Category of source ownership data to be used when running consolidation on a simulation category.
OWN_YEAR	Period number of source ownership data to be used when running consolidation on a simulation category. This can be absolute (e.g., 12 for December) or relative (e.g., –1 for prior period).
OWN_PERIOD	Year offset of source ownership data to be used when running consolidation on a simulation category. This is relative (e.g., –1 for prior year).
RATE_CATEGORY	Category of source exchange rate data to use when running currency translation on a simulation category.
RATE_PERIOD	Period number of source exchange rate data to use when running currency translation on a simulation category. This can be absolute (e.g., 12 for December) or relative (e.g., –1 for prior period).
RATE_YEAR	Year offset of source exchange rate data to be used when running currency translation on a simulation category. This is relative (e.g., –1 for prior year)
STARTMNTH	Starting month for the year.

Table 3.5 Required Properties for Category in the Consolidation and Ownership Models or Using the Simulation Option for Currency Translation (Cont.)

3.5.3 Account Dimension

The Account dimension defines the chart of accounts for your model and how those accounts are calculated and aggregated. Any dimension that is assigned the type A is considered an Account dimension. Each model can have only one Account-type dimension. This is one of the critical dimensions in the model. It normally is a strong dimension, which means that it's linked to all of the transactional data as it's posted into the model. This is also one of the dimensions that takes advantage of using a number of properties for reporting, calculations, and processing. The properties in Table 3.6 are required for the Account dimension.

Property Name	Description
ACCTYPE	Account type. Can be INC for Income, EXP for Expense, AST for Asset, and LEQ for Liabilities and Equity. The account type can't be blank. This is a critical property because it controls the signage of the transactional data that is uploaded. It's used to control the sign display and aggregation in reporting
RATETYPE	Used by the currency conversion business rules. If currency conversion isn't required, this property will be blank. If this is used for currency conversion, then the values assigned will help in executing FX calculations. Examples of the values in this property are END, AVG, and HIST.
SCALING	Scaling options are Y or N. Used by EvDRE, EPMScaleData, and Library view. Value is optional, but if a value isn't defined, scaling is unavailable for the associated member ID.
TYPELIM	Specifies that automatic adjustments details are created based on a generic value, rather than mentioning the member itself. Allows you to apply the same processing to several accounts having the same property value. This is required if the Account dimension is used in the Consolidation model.
IS_INPUT	Flag for ownership accounts to be used in method-based multipliers. This is required if the Account dimension is used in the Ownership model.
DIMLIST(1, #)	This property is used in the selection criteria for business rules or other Script Logic calculations. You'll possibly see multiples of DIMLIST for varying uses. This isn't a required property, but it's very useful and normally available.
ELIMACC	This is used in the U.S. elimination process to identify the offset accounts.

Table 3.6 Required Properties of the Account Dimension

Table 3.7 shows optional properties that you'll find in the Account dimension.

Property Name	Description
FORMULA	This can be used in any dimension to store dimension logic.
GROUP	This is used to identify accounts as Profit & Loss (P&L) or Balance Sheet (BS) accounts for reporting purposes.
USER DEFINED	There can be many different properties used by the Account dimension for reporting purposes or Script Logic calculations.

Table 3.7 Optional Properties for the Account Dimension

Additional information is needed to explain the inherent functionality of the ACCTYPES property. This property is automatically added by the system when creating an Account-type dimension. It's used to manage the reporting and posting of transactions and to make sure that the appropriate signage is allocated to the record. There are four Account types as listed in Table 3.8.

ACCTYPE ID	GROUP	SIGN IN DATABASE	SIGN IN REPORT
AST – ASSETS	BS	+	+
EXP – EXPENSE	PL	+	+
INC – INCOME	PL	–	+
LEQ – LIABILITY & EQUITY	BS	–	+

Table 3.8 Account Types Available for the ACCTYPE Property

The example results of this property are explained in Table 3.9 and 3.10.

ACCTYPE	Value in Database	Value Displayed in a Report
AST	$125.00	$125.00
EXP	$125.00	$125.00
LEQ	–$125.00	$125.00
INC	–$125.00	$125.00

Table 3.9 Results of the ACCTYPE Property on Transactions

ACCTYPES also control the aggregation behavior of balance sheet accounts as shown in Table 3.10.

ACCTYPE	Values stored in Database set to Periodic Storage			Values Displayed in Report set to YTD		
AST	125	125	125	125	125	125
EXP	125	125	125	125	250	375
LEQ	–125	–125	–125	125	125	125
INC	–125	–125	–125	125	250	375

Table 3.10 Aggregation Behavior for the ACCTYPE Property

These examples show how important accuracy is during the assignment of the values of this property. You'll also find that this extends to the values that will be used as nodes of the Account hierarchy. Not only is this property required, but it also must have an entry for all values, including the values used as nodes on the hierarchy.

Figure 3.16 shows the properties assigned to a typical Account dimension.

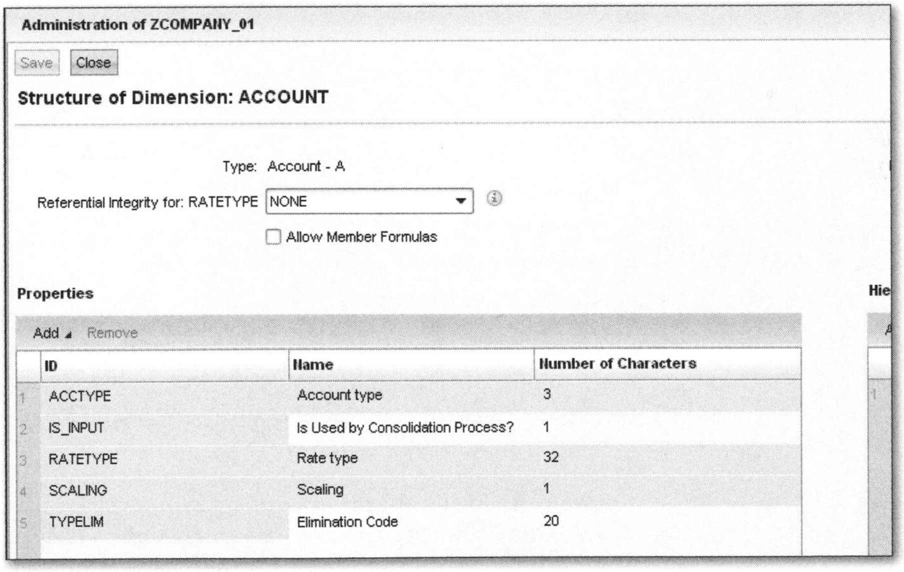

Figure 3.16 Structure of the Account Dimension Property View

3.5.4 Entity Dimension

The Entity dimension defines the organizational structure of the business units for your model and how the units aggregate. Any dimension that is assigned the type E is an Entity dimension. Each model can have only one Entity-type dimension. The Entity dimension is normally the central character that drives the business process. In a Consolidation model, the Entity dimension is the legal entity. This is one of the more critical dimensions that you'll need to define and a strong character across the transactional data. Table 3.11 shows the properties for the Entity dimension.

Property Name	Description
CURRENCY	The currency used by the entity. This is used to store the local or functional currency for each entity.
CTRL_CURRENCY_NOT_LC	Specifies the Reporting Currency dimension member against which a data control is performed. A control is an individual check for data accuracy and consistency. Controls are enabled or disabled at the model level. Valid values are as follows: ▶ Y: The generic LC (local currency) member is used. ▶ N: The entity currency property is used, for example, EUR. This can be used when loading pre-translated data from a source system where currency translation has already been performed. If no value is set, the default value is Y.
CONTROL_LEVEL	Specifies the controls that are relevant to an entity when a control set (a group of controls) is executed. Valid values are as follows: ▶ LEVEL 1: Basic controls ▶ LEVEL 2: Standard controls ▶ LEVEL 3: Advanced controls ▶ LEVEL 4: Comprehensive controls If 4 is selected, all controls having a level from 1 to 4 are executed. If blank or 0, no control is applicable.
ELIM	This property is required for the Consolidation model and defines whether the entity is used to store the intercompany elimination for a given node in the hierarchy. Valid values are Y or N. This is used normally by U.S. eliminations for identification purposes.

Table 3.11 Required Properties for the Entity Dimension

Property Name	Description
FX_TYPE	This property is required for the Consolidation model and defines the subset of currency conversion rules to apply to the entity, where FX_TYPE matches the Entity FX Type property of the rules.
INTCO	This property is required for the Consolidation model and defines the corresponding intercompany member for an entity.
SCALING	Scaling options are Y or N. Used by the Library view. Value is optional, but if a value isn't defined, scaling is unavailable for the associated member ID.

Table 3.11 Required Properties for the Entity Dimension (Cont.)

Table 3.12 shows additional properties that can be used with the Entity dimension.

Property Name	Description
OWNER	This property is used to store the user ID for work status activities. This is also required if additional options are used such as email notifications.
REVIEWER	This property is used to store the user ID for Business Process Flow (BPF) reviewers. This is also required if additional options are used such as email notifications.
USER DEFINED	In numerous situations, it's required that the Entity dimension Entity be enhanced with additional properties. Some of the more common reasons are for reporting purposes or filtering for Script Logic.

Table 3.12 Additional Properties Used with the Entity Dimension

3.5.5 Interco Dimension

The Intercompany dimension defines the base members associated with the level at which intercompany balances are tracked and executed to post the intercompany eliminations. This dimension is sometimes referred to as the Trading Partner dimension. If a Consolidation model is being created, this is a required dimension. Table 3.13 shows the properties that are required.

Property Name	Description
ENTITY	A 32-character field that can either be left blank or contain a valid member name of the entity dimension associated with the current model. The ENTITY property is validated against the Entity dimension, and blank fields are allowed.
SCALING	Scaling options are Y or N. Used by the Library view. The value is optional, but if a value isn't defined, scaling is unavailable for the associated member ID.

Table 3.13 Required Property for the Interco Dimension

3.5.6 Subtable/Flow Dimension

Subtable dimensions break down account activity or flow. For example, some accounts, such as fixed assets, have a Subtable dimension containing opening, additions, deletions, transfers, and ending balances. The Subtable-type dimension is important for writing business rules that require currency translation amounts to be calculated by account. Because the subtable information can be used for multiple accounts, it requires its own dimension. It's also sometimes thought of as a Consolidation type. Table 3.14 shows the properties included in the Subtable dimension.

Property Name	Description
FLOW_TYPE	These can come in many different groups. Defines the type of flow of the dimension, some examples are as follows: ▶ OPENING: Opening ▶ TRANSLOPE: Change difference on opening ▶ ALLOCINC: Allocation ▶ MERGER: Merger ▶ INCOME: Net income from the period ▶ CHANGE: Variation ▶ TRANSFER: Transfer ▶ TRANSFLOW: Translation change on flow ▶ VARSCP: Variation in scope (generic) ▶ VARSCPMETH: Variation in scope method ▶ VARSCPPERC: Variation in scope percentage ▶ VARSCPNEW: Variation in scope new company

Table 3.14 Required Properties for the Flow Dimension

Property Name	Description
	▶ VARSCPLEAV: Variation in scope sold company
	▶ CLOSING: Closing
	▶ NONE: No flow
	▶ BLANK: All other flows
SCALING	Scaling options are Y or N. Used by EvDRE, EPMScaleData, and Library view. The value is optional, but if a value isn't defined, scaling is unavailable for the associated member ID.

Table 3.14 Required Properties for the Flow Dimension (Cont.)

3.5.7 DataSource/Audittrail Dimension

The Audit dimension is user defined and tracks the source of input data. The Audit-Trail dimension, for example, will have the INPUT member assigned to any records uploaded into a financial or consolidated model. Another member, ADJ, might be assigned for any adjusting entries based on a journal entry in consolidation. Table 3.15 shows the properties included in the Audit dimension and, in some cases, only if the Audit dimension is used in a consolidation model.

Property Name	Description
SCALING	Scaling options are Y or N. Used by EvDRE, EPMScaleData, and Library view. Value is optional, but if a value isn't defined, scaling is unavailable for the associated member ID.
DATASRC_TYPE	Specifies whether a data source is used for input (I), manual adjustments (M), or automatic adjustments eliminations (A).
IS_CONSOL	Specifies whether data is consolidated or not. Typically, this is set to yes (Y), but set it no (N) for data sources used in group-specific adjustments (e.g., post-consolidation adjustments entered against a specific group).
IS_CONVERTED	Specifies whether data is translated or not. Typically this is set to yes (Y), but set it to no (N) for data sources used in currency-specific adjustments (e.g., adjustments in EUR, USD, etc.).
DATASRC_ORIG	Property used to create a grouping of data sources that can be used later as filters in automatic adjustments and eliminations business rules.

Table 3.15 Required Properties for the AuditTrail Dimension (Cont.)

Property Name	Description
DATASRC_STAGE	Defines which Audit member consolidation adjustments from lower groups are inherited in higher groups (parent groups).
DIMLIST	Property used to create a grouping of data sources that can be used later as filters in automatic adjustments and eliminations business rules.
COPYOPENING	Flag used to filter data sources when running carry forward (CopyOpening).
OPENING_DATASRC	Specifies a different destination data source, to which the corresponding amounts are carried forward. For example, this can be used where certain entries are posted to a data source that specifically identifies these adjustments as audit adjustments in the current year, but in future years, it might be required to simply include in another standard data source (i.e., Input).

Table 3.15 Required Properties for the AuditTrail Dimension (Cont.)

3.5.8 Scope Dimension

The Group-type dimension represents the relationship of entities for a given consolidation result or consolidation point. This group is consolidated in a single currency, so there is no need to have another dimension. You can continue to use the Currency-type dimension for this purpose, or you can split it into a Group-type dimension (type G) and use a pure Currency-type dimension (type R) to allow reporting in multiple group currencies. A Group dimension must be assigned to an Ownership and a Consolidation model. You should assign both a Currency and a Group dimension to a Consolidation model, but you should assign only the Group dimension to the Ownership model referred from the Consolidation model. You can't assign both a Currency and a Group dimension to the same Ownership model. Table 3.16 shows the properties required when using the Scope dimension in consolidation.

Property Name	Description
CONSO_TYPE	Specifies which set of rules to apply to a group. Refers to a group type filter in adjustments and eliminations.
CURRENCY_TYPE	Used for the currency conversion. ▸ N: Non-group ▸ G: Group

Table 3.16 Required Properties for the Scope Dimension in the Consolidation Model

Property Name	Description
DATASRC_LEVEL	Stores the consolidation differences resulting from different % or methods along the group hierarchy.
ENTITY	Blank or a valid entity ID. This is used to define the link between the group and the entity or to indicate the entity where the aggregation should be stored.
	If this property is filled with a valid entity ID, and the property STORE_ENTITY is set to Y, the results of the currency conversion for the current group are also copied into this entity (length = 32).
	This can be any valid reporting currency and is used for currency conversion.
GROUP_CURRENCY	This property can only be used on currency members with the property CURRENCY_TYPE of G and, in this case, it must contain a valid ID from the Currency dimension with the property CURRENCY_TYPE value of R (length = 50).
PARENT_GROUP	Must be a valid ID from the Group dimension. If you want to do the consolidation by level, you must indicate here the higher level from the group. If you want to use this property to define the hierarchy, enter the same code as the ID for your top group. If this property is blank, the dynamic hierarchy from the ownership application is used (length = 32).
STAGE_ONLY	This is used to control the storage of currency translation by group and base level members.
STORE_ENTITY	Specifies whether to store the ID entered in the Entity property.
	Y: If you want to store the ID entered in the Entity property.
	Blank: If you don't want to store the ID entered in the Entity property.
STORE_GROUP_CURR	Used for currency conversion.
	Y (or blank): By default the results of the conversion into a group currency are written in both the group member and in the currency member of the Currency dimension.
	N: If only the group member is to be stored, set this property to N (length = 1).

Table 3.16 Required Properties for the Scope Dimension in the Consolidation Model (Cont.)

Figure 3.17 shows the list of properties assigned to the Scope dimension.

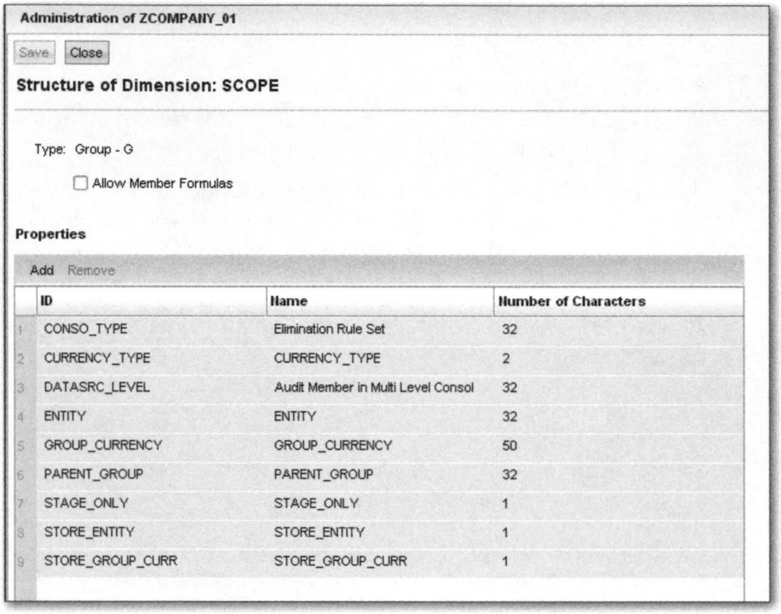

Figure 3.17 Structure of the Scope Dimension Property View

3.5.9 Rptcurrency Dimension

The Currency dimension is required if your company reports on local currency and translated values. These dimensions store the reporting and input currencies for your organization. Any dimension that is assigned the type R is a Currency-type dimension. Table 3.17 describes the required properties for a Currency dimension. If you're using the legal consolidation functionality of planning and consolidation, the Currency-type dimension requires additional properties.

Property Name	Description
ENTITY	A 32-character field that can either be left blank or contain a valid member name of the entity dimension associated to the current model. The ENTITY property is validated against the Entity dimension, and blank fields are allowed.
REPORTING	Specify your reporting currencies. If Y, this member is used for reporting purposes.

Table 3.17 Properties for the Report Currency

Property Name	Description
CURRENCY_TYPE	Used if the currency is used in the Consolidation model. Identifies the local currency member (L) versus reporting currency members (R) or transaction currency member (T).
MD	If the currency is used in the Rate model, then this property is required. This defines whether the currency exchange rate for that currency is used to multiply or divide with the local amount.

Table 3.17 Properties for the Report Currency (Cont.)

3.5.10 Inputcurrency Dimension

This currency is very similar to the Rptcurrency dimension but, as the name suggests, this is used in situations where there is a need to input information with a currency attached, for example, in a Rate model.

3.5.11 List of Additional Dimensions and Properties

The dimensions and properties listed in the previous sections are the ones that you'll encounter on a normal and consistent basis, but there are others that you'll see as well. These are incorporated into the other models such as the Ownership, ICMatching, or Rate models. They are very similar to the dimension types that are assigned to their primary dimensions. The additional dimensions are listed in Table 3.18.

Dimension	Description
O_ACCOUNT	This is a dimension type A and is very similar to the Account dimension found in the financial models. This particular dimension is used specifically for the Ownership model. The assigned members are system defined and used for the integration of the Ownership and Consolidation models. The use of this dimension will be explained in more detail in Chapter 7.
ICACCOUNT	This is a dimension type A and is very similar to the Account dimension found in the financial models. It's used in the ICMAtching model. The use of this dimension will be explained in more detail in Chapter 7.

Table 3.18 Additional Dimensions

Dimension	Description
ICDATASOURCE	This is a dimension type D and is very similar to the Audittrail dimension found in the financial models. It's used in the ICMatching model for specific datasource members used in the ICMatching business rules. The use of this dimension will be explained in more detail in Chapter 7.
R_ACCOUNT	This is a dimension type A and is very similar to the Account dimension found in the financial models. This is used in the Rate model for storing the rates for use in FX translation. The members assigned are similar to END, CLO, AVG, HIST, and FCST. These are assigned as formulas in the currency translation process.
R_ENTITY	This is a dimension type E and is very similar to the Entity dimension found in the financial models but normally used in the Rate model. Normally there is only entity included in this dimension—global—unless there is a need for multiple rates assigned to one GL account. In that case, it's possible to have multiple values so that this one-to-many relationship between GL account and rate can be accommodated.
User-defined dimensions	This is a dimension type U and is used for many different reasons in all of the different types of models. You'll probably not see this dimension as much in the Consolidation model but definitely in the Financial, Planning, and other generic models. Some examples of a user-defined dimension are Functional Area, Cost Center, Customer, Product, Region, Segment, and Profit Center.

Table 3.18 Additional Dimensions (Cont.)

In each case, the additional properties required are added to the dimension. The only property that is system assigned in this case is SCALING.

3.6   Additional Topics in the Development of Dimensions

Some additional aspects of dimensions are associated with other objects that are sourced and assigned to the dimension. They are critical in the overall process and incorporate aspects of the configuration such as security, formulas, members, and hierarchies.

3.6.1 Dimension Security

The security of dimensions is at the model level, and you secure a dimension within a model. We'll look at the creation of a model in the next section, but this is associated with the dimensions assigned to the model. Dimension security allows access to dimensions and their members. You can use the following features to secure dimensions.

Secured and Unsecured Dimensions

You can have a mixture of secured and unsecured dimensions in a model. Securing dimensions allows you to control which users (or teams) have read, write, or deny access to dimensions and their members. You need to define a dimension as secured if you want to control member access by specific dimensions. All users can access unsecured dimension members. Member access profiles are used to grant model access. At least one dimension in a model should be secured to ensure control over model and data access. When defining member access for secured dimensions it is important to be sure to define access for all secured dimensions of the model. Failure to do so results in the inability to access that model for any users or teams assigned to the member access profile. Security will be covered in more detail in Chapter 8.

Security for Member-level Dimensions

In addition to defining dimensions as secure for individual models, you can assign write access to members within the dimension using member access profiles. By default, users don't have access to any members of a secured dimension, so member access profiles must be set up for the users you want to give read-only, write access, or no access at all by using the denied options.

The parameter to set dimension security is shown in Figure 3.18. On the far-right side of the screen, notice the check box under the SECURED column.

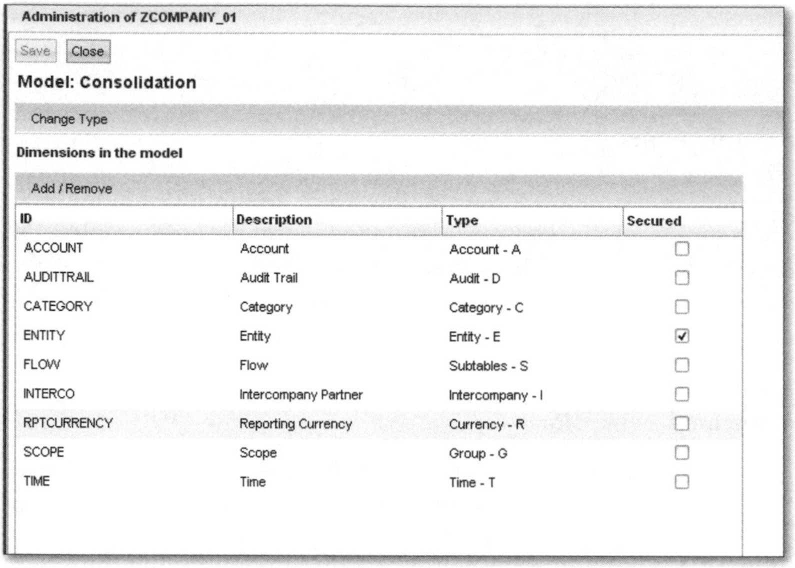

ID	Description	Type	Secured
ACCOUNT	Account	Account - A	☐
AUDITTRAIL	Audit Trail	Audit - D	☐
CATEGORY	Category	Category - C	☐
ENTITY	Entity	Entity - E	☑
FLOW	Flow	Subtables - S	☐
INTERCO	Intercompany Partner	Intercompany - I	☐
RPTCURRENCY	Reporting Currency	Currency - R	☐
SCOPE	Scope	Group - G	☐
TIME	Time	Time - T	☐

Figure 3.18 View of the Dimensions in the Consolidation Model with the Secured Parameter for ENTITY

3.6.2 Hierarchies on Dimensions

Hierarchies in dimensions are very important components that will be used in likely many implementations of dimensions to enhance reporting and calculations. It's important to measure the use of hierarchies because these structures can have an impact on performance in the program execution as well as in reporting. Using some combination of properties and hierarchies will normally help support any required reporting involving groups of members. Some hierarchies are required, such as the ownership hierarchy used during consolidation, but the use of hierarchies is optional. The ownership hierarchy will be revisited in Chapter 7 on consolidation. The hierarchies that you can assign have the following characteristics:

- They can be defined for any dimension.
- They can be automatically loaded or manually added.
- They are time independent, therefore, at this time, only the current view of the hierarchy is available. There may be additional enhancements in this area with SP08.

▸ They are used for rollups in a report and are very useful in the member selection screens, as well as being used within business rules and Script Logic for grouping information together.

3.6.3 Custom Measure Formulas

Custom measure formulas are used if you need to add additional time components to the Measure dimension. You use the UJA_MAINTAIN_MEASURE_FORMULA program to create and maintain custom measure formulas. Maintaining measures have the following restrictions:

▸ Pre-delivered measures can't be deleted.

▸ Pre-delivered PERIODIC on a periodic cube and YTD on a YTD cube measures can't be changed. Other pre-delivered measures can be changed, but best practice is to avoid any changes. Changes made in pre-delivered measures are overwritten when you make any changes to that model from the ADMINISTRATION screen. The recommendation is to create your own custom measures instead of changing the pre-delivered measures.

▸ Formula names can't be duplicated.

▸ Formula names must be entered in uppercase letters.

▸ Parent nodes of a hierarchy can't be used in measure formulas.

It's important to make sure that you use the same formula names during the configuration process that you defined in the FORMULA NAME field. This would be the technical name that you created and assigned as a name in the [MEASURES]. If your formula has to refer to another measure, enter the other formula name and new formula together in the FORMULA STATEMENT section. For example, refer to the formula statement of the periodic and QTD measures on a model with a YTD storage type. Also if you want to use a property of a dimension within the measure formula, you must include the technical name of the BW object. You can find this name using Transaction MDXTEST, in the BW system. In this transaction, choose INFOPROVIDER as the catalog, and then choose your model (cube). The system displays the list of dimensions. Expand the dimension and then its properties to view the property list. `[%TIME%].CURRENTMEMBER.PROPERTIES("2/CPMB/XXXXXX ")` is the syntax for using the `TIMEID` property of the Time dimension.

After identifying all of the required information, follow these steps to create a custom measure formula:

1. Go to Transaction SE38 in the BW system, and enter "UJA_MAINTAIN_MEA-SURE_FORMULA" in the PROGRAM field (see Figure 3.19).

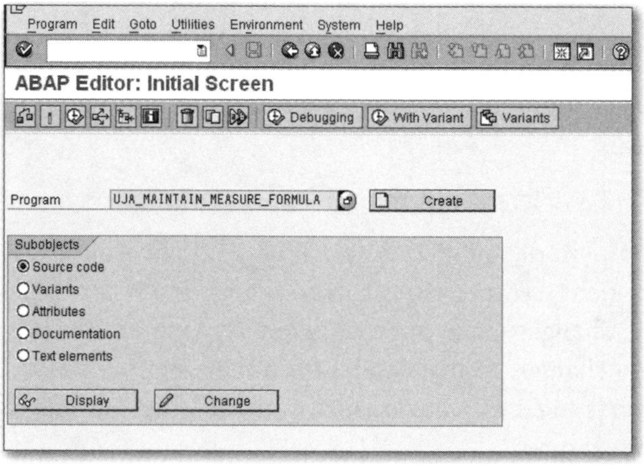

Figure 3.19 ABAP Editor: Initial Screen to Execute the ABAP Program

2. Click the EXECUTE button. In the MAINTAIN MEASURE FORMULA screen, enter the ENVIRONMENT ID, MODEL ID, and USER ID, as shown in Figure 3.20.

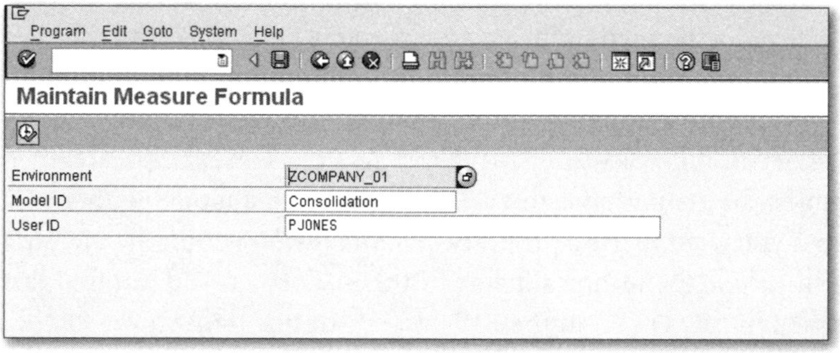

Figure 3.20 Maintain Measure Formula Screen

3. Execute the maintain measure formula program, and the results are shown in Figure 3.21.

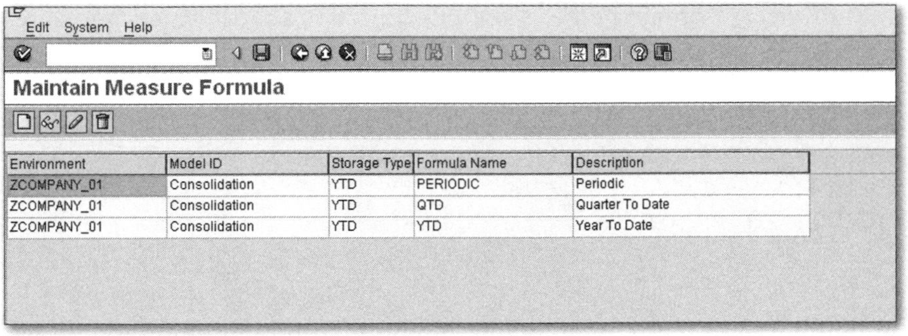

Figure 3.21 Maintain Measure Formula Program Results

4. In the MAINTAIN MEASURE FORMULA screen, the options are CREATE, DISPLAY, CHANGE, or DELETE (see the four buttons on the top left of the screen). To display the QTD formula, double-click next to the last line. The results are shown in Figure 3.22.

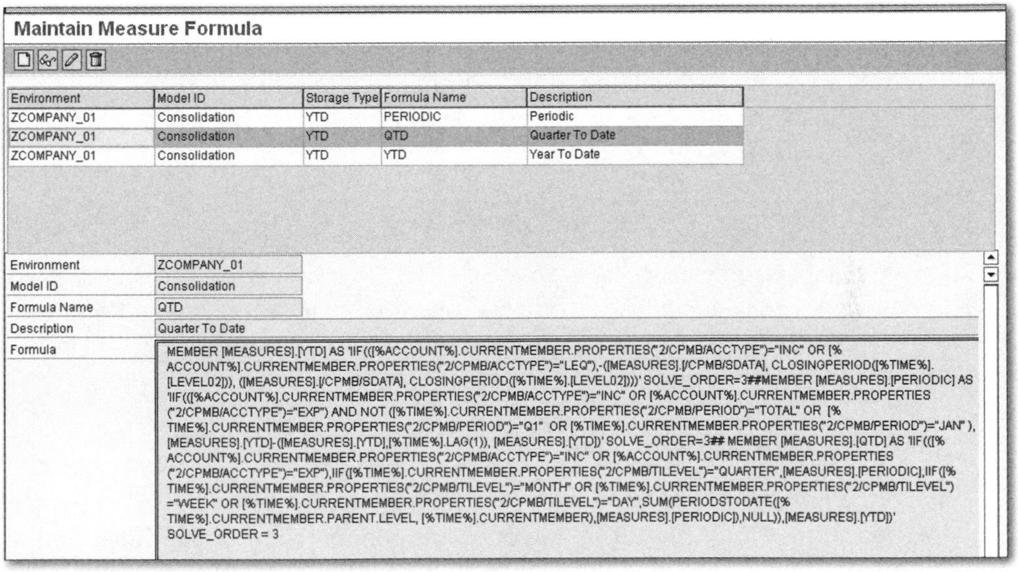

Figure 3.22 Maintain Measure Formula – Display QTD Formula

To create additional measure formulas, use the CREATE option, and fill in the appropriate formula for the measure required.

Following are some examples of the formulas required to add additional measures to the model:

▶ YTD on YTD model

```
MEMBER [MEASURES].[YTD] AS 'IIF(([%P_ACCT%].CURRENTMEMBER.
PROPERTIES("2/CPMB/ACCTYPE")="INC" OR [%P_ACCT%].CURRENTMEMBER.
PROPERTIES("2/CPMB/ACCTYPE")="LEQ"),-([MEASURES].[/CPMB/SDATA],
CLOSINGPERIOD([%TIME%].[LEVEL02])), ([MEASURES].[/CPMB/SDATA],
CLOSINGPERIOD([%TIME%].[LEVEL02])))' SOLVE_ORDER=3
```

▶ PERIODIC on YTD model

```
MEMBER [MEASURES].[YTD] AS 'IIF(([%P_ACCT%].CURRENTMEMBER.
PROPERTIES("2/CPMB/ACCTYPE")="INC" OR [%P_ACCT%].CURRENTMEMBER.
PROPERTIES("2/CPMB/ACCTYPE")="LEQ"),-([MEASURES].[/CPMB/SDATA],
CLOSINGPERIOD([%TIME%].[LEVEL02])), ([MEASURES].[/CPMB/SDATA],
CLOSINGPERIOD([%TIME%].[LEVEL02])))' SOLVE_ORDER=3||MEMBER
[MEASURES].[PERIODIC] AS 'IIF(([%P_ACCT%].CURRENTMEMBER.
PROPERTIES("2/CPMB/ACCTYPE")="INC" OR [%P_ACCT%].CURRENTMEMBER.
PROPERTIES("2/CPMB/ACCTYPE")="EXP") AND NOT ([%TIME%].CURRENTMEMBER.
PROPERTIES("2/CPMB/PERIOD")="TOTAL" OR [%TIME%].CURRENTMEMBER.
PROPERTIES("2/CPMB/PERIOD")="Q1" OR [%TIME%].CURRENTMEMBER.
PROPERTIES("2/CPMB/PERIOD")="JAN" ), [MEASURES].[YTD]-([MEASURES].
[YTD],[%TIM[%].LAG(1)), [MEASURES].[YTD])' SOLVE_ORDER=3
```

> **Note: Formula Mapping**
>
> In these formulas, the mapping to your individual formulas may be slightly different. For example, P_ACCT = ACCOUNT, There may also be a slight difference in the use of filters such as "INC".

3.6.4 Dimension Formulas

We discussed dimension formulas during our conversation on dimension properties. Recall that you turn this option on in the configuration of the dimension. If this is turned on, then you can add a formula to a member of the dimension and execute a calculation to fill that specific member.

Figure 3.23 shows the parameter turned on in the dimension of type ACCOUNT – A.

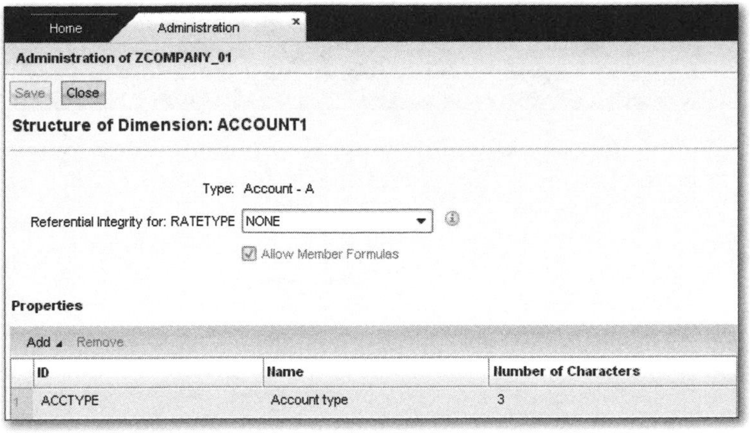

Figure 3.23 Structure of ACCOUNT1 Dimension with Allow Member Formula Turned On

After this is available, you can use the option under RULES • MEMBER FORMULAS to access the formula editor, as shown in Figure 3.24.

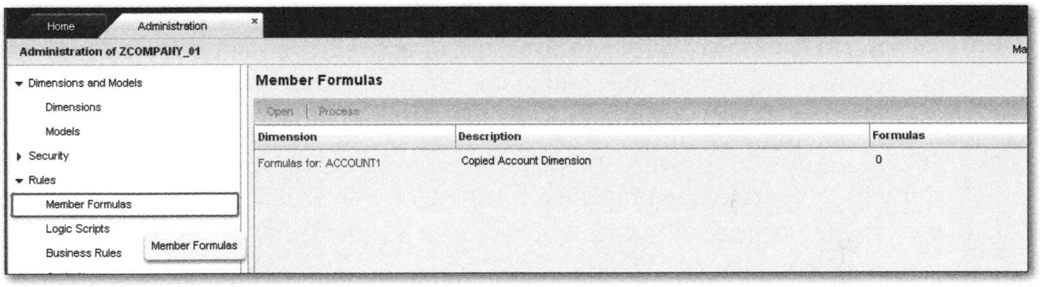

Figure 3.24 Member Formulas for the ACCOUNT1 Dimension

Now, choose the dimension, and click on OPEN to access the formula editor. In the editor, identify the member to assign the formula to, and create the formula required using the appropriate MDX (MultiDimensional eXpressions) syntax along with the base level members for the values (see Figure 3.25).

Remember to use the dimension formulas sparingly due to performance on the reporting process via the EPM add-in frontend. It is known that using the dimension member formula will have an impact on the performance of the report due to the calculations required during the execution of the report.

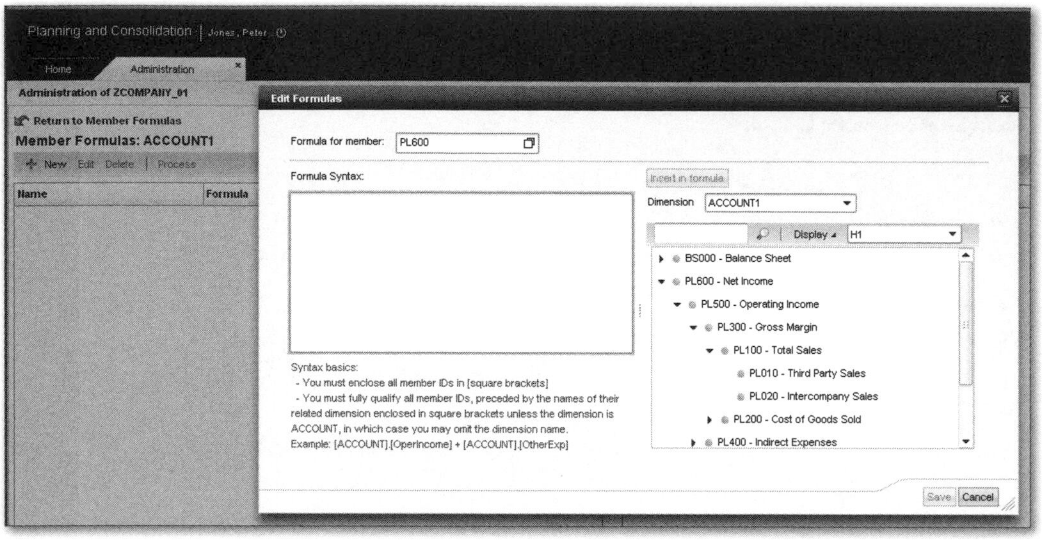

Figure 3.25 Edit Formula Screen for Dimension Formulas

In this process, an additional property is available to help with issues around the collision between two different formulas. For example, you might have a formula in a row and in a column that collide in a report, and one cell in the report needs to be calculated using one of the two different formulas. The SOLVE_ORDER property defines the order in which the system solves calculated members when they intersect with other calculated members. SOLVE_ORDER determines the order in which the system evaluates and calculates dimensions, members, calculated members, custom rollups, and cells. The system evaluates the members with the highest solve order first and calculates it last. Zero is the highest priority. Some guidelines for using SOLVE_ORDER follow:

▸ You can specify up to three measures and five members within a SOLVE_ORDER property.

▸ Specify dimensions by dimension name, making sure that the case level is correct. For example:

[ACCOUNT].[Account1] / [ACCOUNT].[Account2]

[PRODUCT].[Product1] + [PRODUCT].[Product2]

▸ The only exception to this rule is that you don't need to specify an Account dimension by name.

3.6.5 Owner Properties

The OWNER dimension property is created just as any property, but it holds a more significant position than other properties. Using the OWNER property as the designated property, the system recognizes and aligns the dimension as a driving dimension for a Business Process Flow (BPF) This dimension is usually the Entity dimension or the dimension with a dimension type E. You add the property to the dimension with any name. Therefore, the property doesn't have to be called OWNER but it's good to align the technical name with the responsibility. A dimension can have one or more owner-designating properties as long as each is unique. For example, if your business process dictates that an entity is the differing factor when it comes to entering data, then the E type dimension is the driver of that activity.

If your business process dictates that a profit center name is the differing factor, the Profit Center dimension would have a unique owner-designating property that drives the owner of the activity context. The BPF owner properties must be given unique names. The dimension you select to drive must have at least an Owner-type dimension property, which means that the members assigned to that property must be either a team of people or a person. The Owner-type dimension wouldn't make sense if the owner member was a region or an indicator. When more than one exists, you choose the appropriate property to use in the BPF. Both users and teams can be used as the OWNER property. Using teams offer additional flexibility to this property because they allow multiple people to be owners, and having several people versus one avoids any issues with coverage during the closing process or P&F activities. You can enter multiple names and teams separated by commas, but this requires additional maintenance by assignment based on the movement of the members or people from position to position. You must also include the domain or server name in the path. The steps to set up the OWNER property follows the same process as described previously for any property assigned to a dimension. When assigning members to this property, you can enter multiple names and teams separated by commas. We'll also run into an owner issue during the discussion of work status, but this is a different owner-based field and not a property.

> **Note: Business Process Flow (BPF)**
>
> The BPF component is used for easier access to all of the reports, input templates, and executable programs. This is a user-friendly frontend process that offers additional integration between users. BPF will be covered in detail in Chapter 9.

3.6.6 Reviewer Properties

The REVIEWER property is similar to the OWNER property in that it's used in a similar manner and the setup is exactly the same. Rather than the team of people or a person being designated as the owner with the responsibilities of the owner of a process, the reviewer has the responsibilities of receiving the information or documentation and validating that it has been processed successfully. This person or team member can approve or reject the action taken by the user. A reviewer can also reopen the previous step of a BPF. The REVIEWER property must be defined prior to creating a BPF template; the positioning of the reviewer assignment is at the same time as the owner in a BPF template.

The rules that apply to the REVIEWER property are consistent with the OWNER property as well. One of the differences between the owner and reviewer is that the reviewer can reopen the previous steps of a BPF. Before this can happen, however, the BPF must be configured to allow the reopening process to occur.

To define a REVIEWER property, open the dimension that you want to designate as the driver dimension of the BPF, and then add a REVIEWER property and its property values. When creating a BPF, choose ENABLE REVIEWERS, and then set a REVIEWER property when defining the step region criteria for a new step.

3.7 Models

Now that we've laid the groundwork of the building blocks, including dimensions, properties, and members, for BPC, we can move up the ladder to take those dimensions and combine them into models. As we mentioned, the model is a grouping of dimensions that are going to be used for a specific purpose such as consolidation.

There are two general groups of models:

▶ **Reporting**
These models are used for analysis and user activities. This category of models is the primary focus in consolidation, financial, and standard models. The standard models incorporate any sorts of budgeting and P&F processes.

▶ **Drivers and rates (formerly known as non-reporting)**
These models support the reporting category of models. These store reference information used during different calculations and analysis. They include information such as currency exchange rates and ownership information.

Each of these categories has three different models, as shown in Table 3.19.

General Category	Model Type	Main Use
Reporting	Standard	Planning, budgeting, and forecasting with no currency translation
	Financial	Planning, budgeting, and forecasting with currency translation
	Consolidation	Consolidation with currency translation and all activities involved with eliminations
Drivers and rates	Rates	Stored exchange rates for any activity requiring FX translations
	Ownership	Stores ownership information required for elimination and adjustments
	Generic	Stores any additional cost drivers required or SKFs required to support calculations such as allocations

Table 3.19 Category and Type for BPC Models

Other requirements during the creation of BPC models include the following:

▶ When creating a model, they must include four dimension types:

  ▶ Category – C

  ▶ Account – A

  ▶ Time – T

  ▶ Entity – E

  This is a requirement. During the creation process, it will confirm if all of the required dimensions are included prior to attempting to save and generate.

▶ When creating a Finance type model, Currency is also required.

▶ When creating a Consolidation type model, Currency – R, Audit – D, Scope (Group) – G, and Intercompany – I are also required

▶ When creating an Ownership type model, both Scope (Group) – G and Intercompany – I are required.

▶ In terms of dimension types used in the creation of a model, only the User-Defined – U is available more than once in a model.

Tables 3.20 through 3.24 give the required dimensions by model and model type. This will help validate your models as you enhance the configuration with additional dimensions.

Type ID	Dimension ID	Description	Planning	Cons	Rate	Ownership
C	CATEGORY	Category	X	X	X	X
T	TIME	Time	X	X	X	X
E	ENTITY	Entity	X	X		X
A	ACCOUNT	Account	X	X		
D	AUDITTRAIL	AuditTrail/ DataSource	X	X		
R	RPTCURRENCY	Report Currency	X	X		
I	INTERCO	Intercompany/ Trading Partner	X	X		X

Table 3.20 Dimensions Required by Planning and Consolidation Models

Type ID	Dimension ID	Description	Planning	Cons	Rate	Ownership
G	SCOPE	Scope/Group		X		X
F	FLOW	Flow/Subtable		X		

Table 3.21 Dimensions Specific to Consolidation

Type ID	Dimension ID	Description	Planning	Cons	Rate	Ownership
U	PRODUCT	Product	X			
U	SEGMENT	Segment	X			
U	COSTCTR	Cost Center	X			

Table 3.22 Dimensions Specific to Planning Models

Type ID	Dimension ID	Description	Planning	Cons	Rate	Ownership
U	CUSTOMER	Customer	X			
U	OTHER DIM	Other Dimensions required to support budget/plan/forecast	X			

Table 3.22 Dimensions Specific to Planning Models (Cont.)

Type ID	Dimension ID	Description	Planning	Cons	Rate	Ownership
A	R_ACCOUNT	Rate Account			X	
E	R_ENTITY	Rate Entity			X	
R	INPUT-CURRENCY	Input Currency			X	

Table 3.23 Dimensions Specific to Rate Models

Type ID	Dimension ID	Description	Planning	Cons	Rate	Ownership
A	O_ACCOUNT	Ownership Account				X

Table 3.24 Dimensions Specific to the Ownership Model

3.7.1 Configuration of Models

The generic steps to create a model don't really change from model to model, but, in some cases, unique parameters are required before completing the model configuration. To start, you either decide to copy an existing model or create the model from scratch. For a Consolidation model, you should always copy to start the creation process because of all of the standard programs and coding available from the existing Consolidation models. If, on the other hand, you were creating a Budgeting model, you could start by creating from scratch without incurring additional work after you start to work through different business processes or Script Logic.

After the work you've completed prior to this, the actual configuration is very straightforward, as you'll see. Again remember that if you don't copy from an existing model that uses the EnvironmentShell models then, you will probably be missing some standard delivered objects such as Data Manager packages, programs and report/input templates.

3.7.2 Create a Model

To create a model, follow these steps:

1. Go to the starting page of the BPC WEB ACCESS screen, and then choose PLAN-NING AND CONSOLIDATION ADMINISTRATION • DIMENSIONS AND MODELS • MOD-ELS (Figure 3.26).

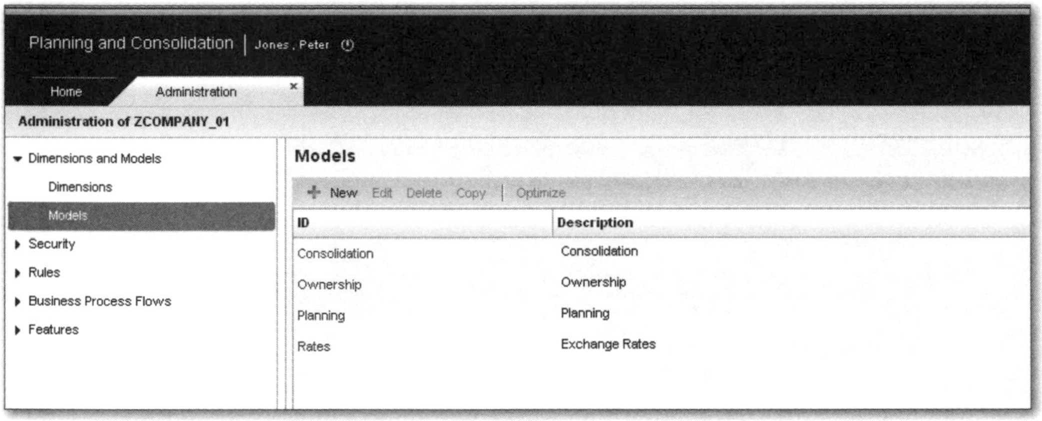

Figure 3.26 View of the Models Screen

2. Choose NEW, and fill in the model ID and DESCRIPTION fields (Figure 3.27). A wizard will take you through the process, and after Step 6, you'll be able to generate your model.

3. Step 2 MODEL TYPE (Figure 3.28) is critical in the process because additional parameters will inherently be included if the model type is either REPORTING or DRIVERS AND RATES as well as if this is a FINANCIAL or CONSOLIDATION model. In this instance, we'll define a FINANCIAL model.

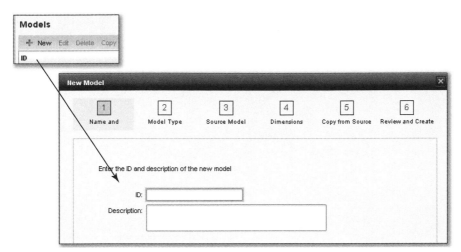

Figure 3.27 Filling in the ID and Description

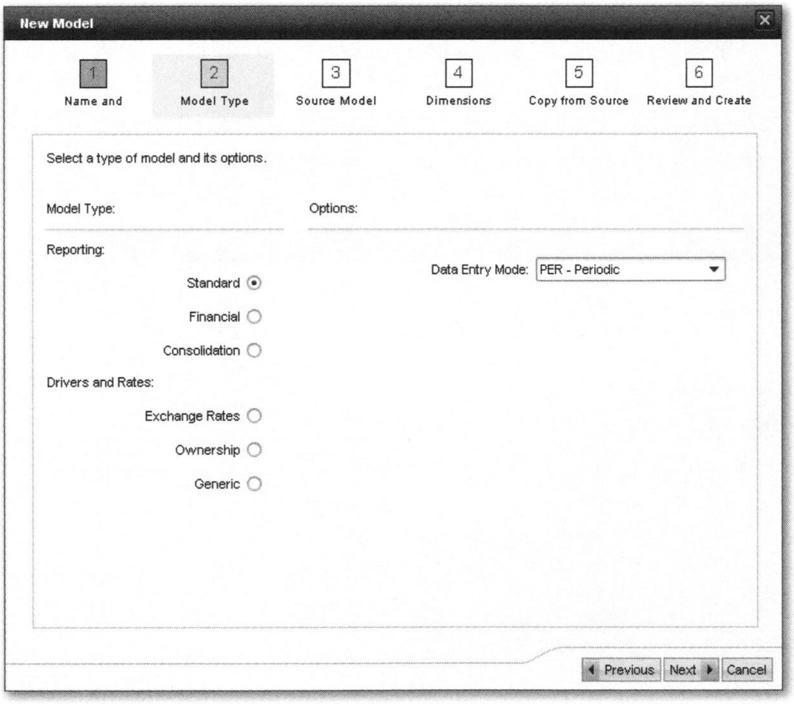

Figure 3.28 Step #2 – Define the Model Type

4. After this has been defined, additional information is displayed on the screen. Select the PER-PERIODIC option and also a RATES model link (Figure 3.29).

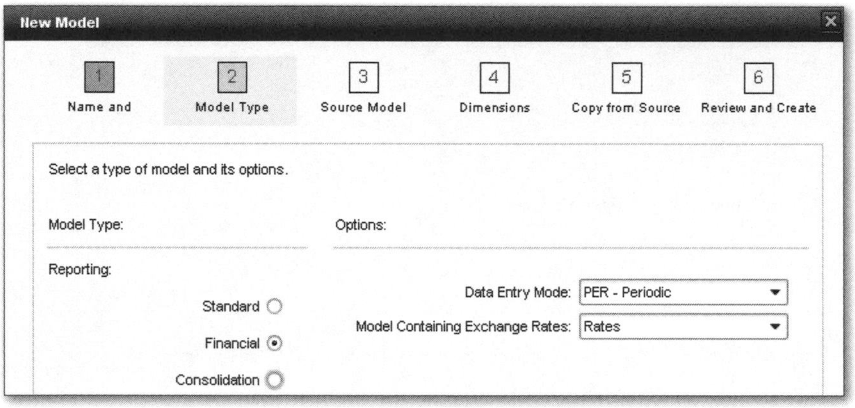

Figure 3.29 Parameters for Data Entry Mode and Exchange Rate

5. In Step 3 SOURCE MODEL (Figure 3.30), you decide to either start from scratch by choosing A BLANK MODEL or make a copy by choosing AN EXISTING MODEL, which incorporates all of the objects and additional features available in the supporting model. In this instance, select A BLANK MODEL.

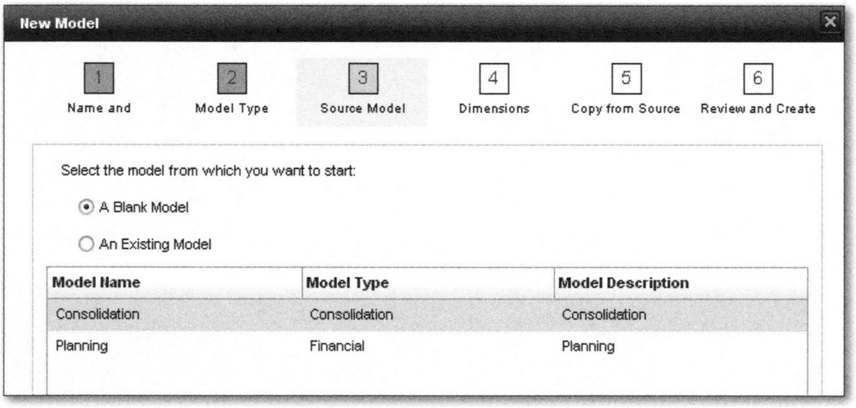

Figure 3.30 Use Either a Blank or Existing Model Process

6. In Step 4 DIMENSIONS (Figure 3.31), the system prompts you to confirm at least the required dimensions: ACCOUNT, CATEGORY, ENTITY, CURRENCY, and TIME (CATER).

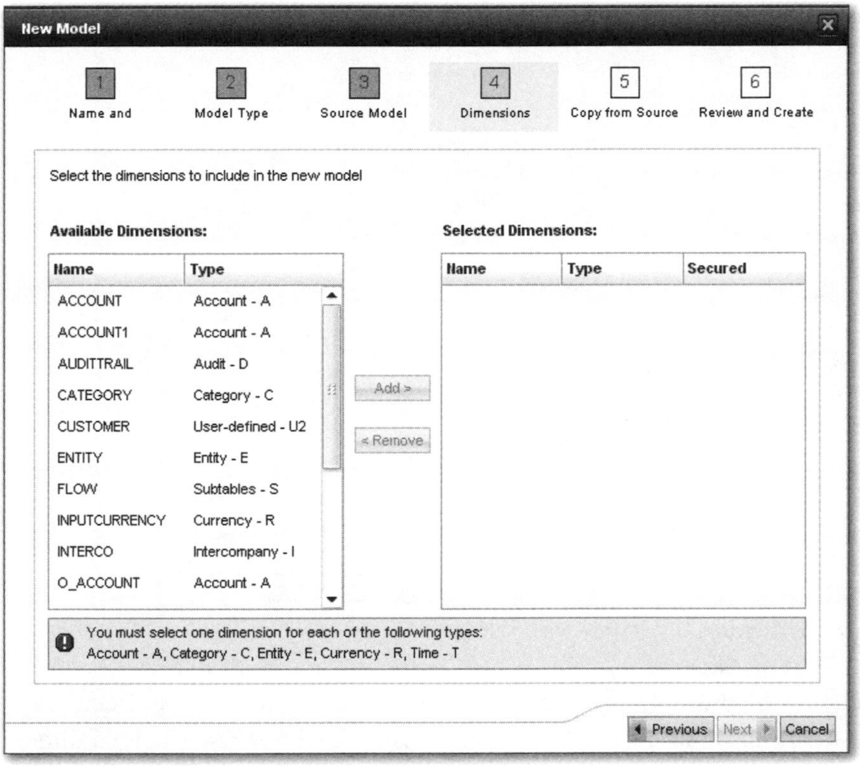

Figure 3.31 Choose the dimensions for the Model

Note: Required Dimensions

In this case, the R for currency is required because this is a Financial model that has a Rate model attached and therefore needs a Currency dimension or dimension type R included.

After you've chosen the appropriate dimensions, you'll see that a green prompt is generated (Figure 3.32) that states all required dimension types are included.

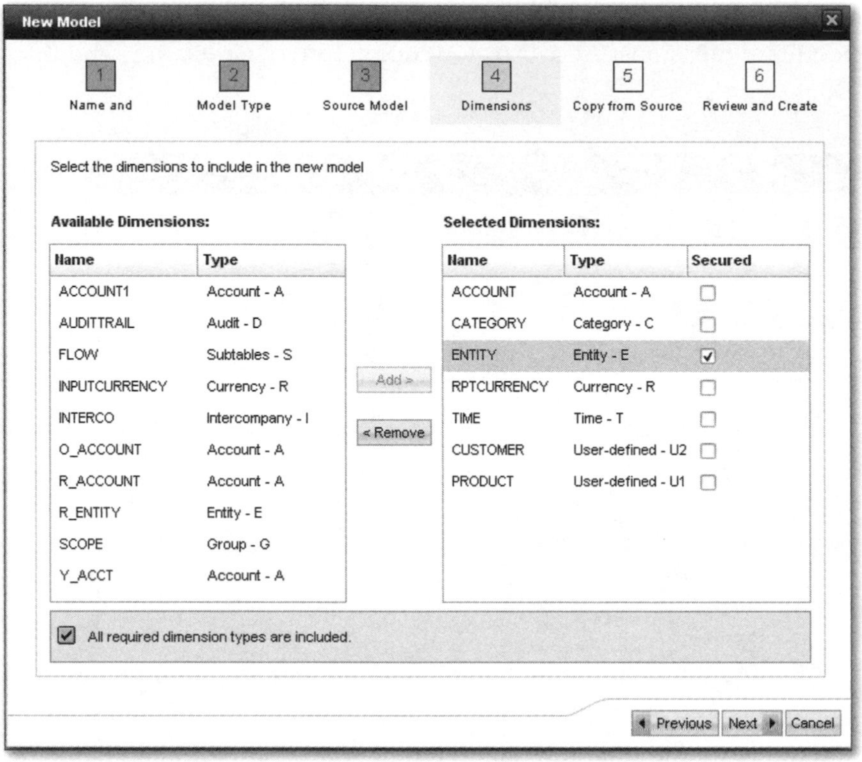

Figure 3.32 All Required Dimension Types Included

Notice that the prompt offered by the system confirms that the required dimensions are available in the model. We have also added two user-defined dimensions: PRODUCT and CUSTOMER. This will help you execute the budgeting process for the company. We've also assigned security to the Entity dimension.

> **Note: Secured Dimension**
>
> Remember that assigning the appropriate secured dimensions early on is critical. If any activities requiring a secure dimension are used, such as audit and workstatus, the ability to change the secured dimensions will be more complex. This is due to the records that are generated by the audit tables and the assignment of workstatus to the secured dimensions.

7. In Step #5 COPY FROM SOURCE, if we were using a source model, we would be prompted to choose what features and functionality should be incorporated into

the new model. In this case, we're starting from scratch, so the screen is empty (Figure 3.33).

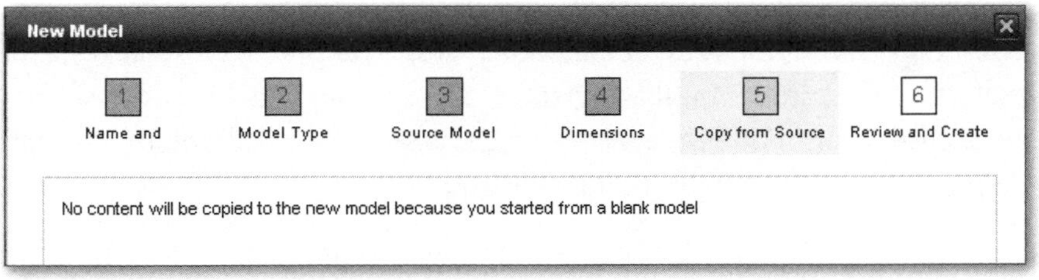

Figure 3.33 Copy from Source

8. In Step 6 Review and Create, you can verify the settings and configuration (Figure 3.34).

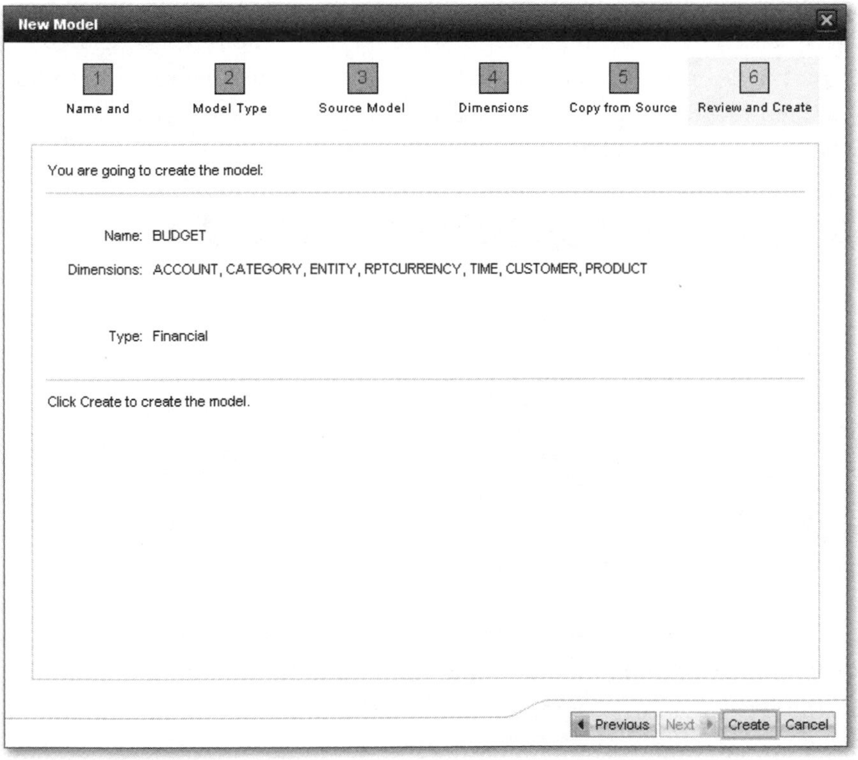

Figure 3.34 Review and Create

After you click CREATE, the system will build all of the required tables, fields, supporting programs, and code required for the availability of the model.

Of course, this is just the beginning of the process because to execute budgeting, you need to set up input templates, upload processes, Data Manager packages, and a number of other functions. You'll also need to set up some basic security so that you can get access to this model. We'll complete this set up but will follow through with the explanation and configuration in Chapter 8.

Now that we have the BPC dimensions and models completed, let's review the setup and supporting objects from the BW side of the fence. In terms of the BPC version for Microsoft, the Microsoft database mirror images the objects and tables created on the BPC side, but the BW side of BPC generates a bit more of a unique table structure.

One of the unique models to generate is Consolidation in this case. As mentioned, you can make a copy of the standard Consolidation model to help you with all of the functions that are set up behind the scenes. Most of the steps are exactly the same as we described earlier, but Step 2 MODEL TYPE requires an additional parameter for the OWNERSHIP MODEL. Figure 3.35 shows this requirement.

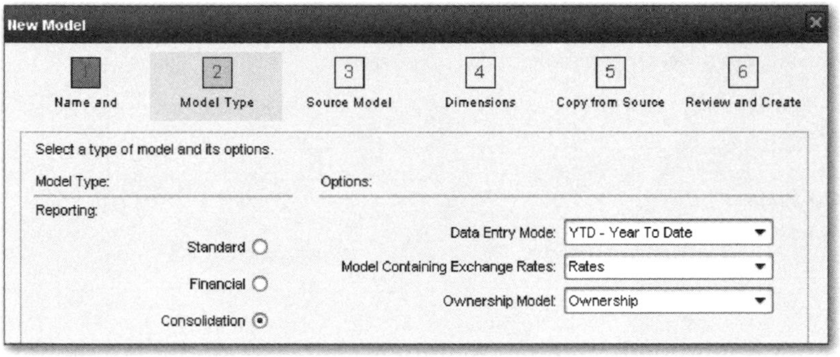

Figure 3.35 Step 2 Creating a Consolidation Model

The link between the Consolidation model and the Ownership model supports the ability to use the group/entity hierarchy to create the consolidation points. This will be further explained in Chapter 7.

There are unique parameters for the different Driver and Rate models, but, in most cases, the parameters will be straightforward and consistent with the type of model you would be developing.

3.8   Business Warehouse Objects

Now that the BPC structure is set up, we can consider what happened behind the scenes on the BW side. We won't try to make you a BW expert just as we won't be able to make you a consolidation expert during the course of this book, but it's important that you understand some of the basics that are involved in the BW architecture that relate to BPC. We'll focus on just the objects at this point and worry about the data flow objects in Chapter 5 when we discuss data loading.

3.8.1   Architecture of BW objects

Quite a few objects, tables, and programs are generated during the activation of the Environment. Let's see what happened when we generated the ZCOMPANY_01 environment. Understanding what is available in the BW system is important not only because the data flow is impacted but also because you need to make sure that you're able to take advantage of the options available. Remember that just about all of the data generated by BPC, including comments, transactional data, master data, and documents, are supported and stored in BW somewhere. Having to do some research on these items requires some basic understanding of the BW architecture. We won't cover the use of the different transaction codes, tables, or programs as well as anything involving the data flow such as the process chains, or data loading from/to BW and BPC. We'll show a few transaction codes here, but the majority of the BW activities will be covered in Chapter 5. Let's take a look at what was generated in BW for our environment.

3.8.2   BW Objects Support for the BPC Version for SAP NetWeaver

The diagram in Figure 3.36 shows the links that are generated between the different BW objects used for supporting the processing of data from/to the BPC platform.

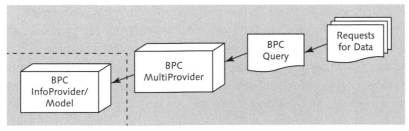

Figure 3.36   Data Flow from BPC to BW/BPC InfoProvider/Model

If you look at this data flow from right to left, you see that the Requests for Data are being generated by the BPC frontend whether for a reporting or input process. This request is then transmitted through a BPC transparent query, then into the BPC MultiProvider, and finally to the BPC InfoProvider that is storing the data. All of these objects are generated during the creation process of the dimensions and the models. If you look at the BW system via the SAP GUI view, you can see that the BPC ZCOMPANY_01 environment was generated and created a number of objects in the BW system (see Figure 3.37).

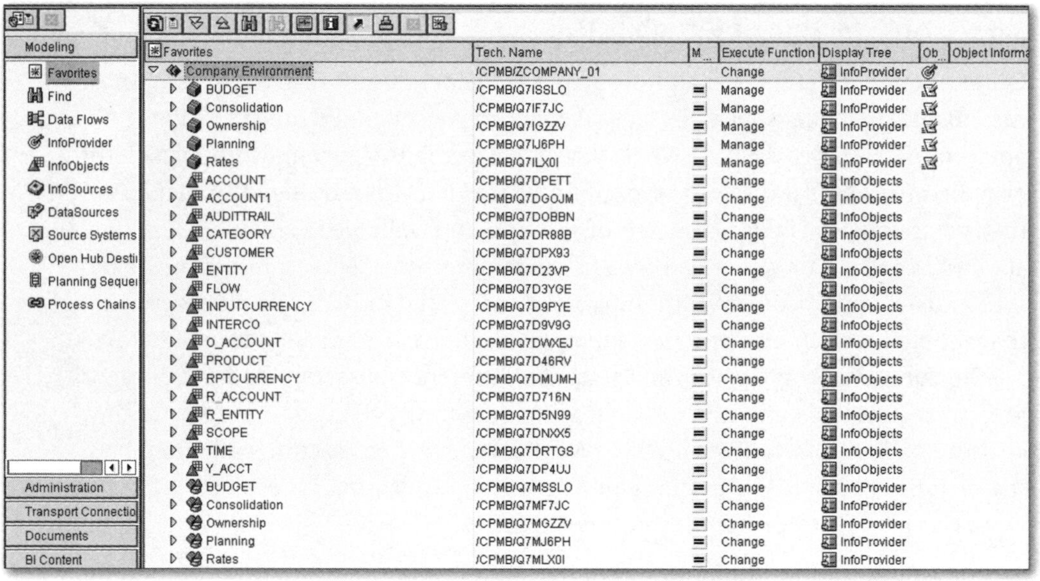

Figure 3.37 Display of the Company Environment in the BW System

As you can see, the different objects are created starting with the MultiProvider, dimensions, and InfoCube. The only other object that isn't shown here is the BPC query, and we'll show you where that is stored in a moment. There are definitely a number of books and documents available to describe and explain to you the different objects in BW and their responsibilities. The most important thing to remember is that you *do not* change anything via the BW side of the fence. This means that you should be able to display these objects, but having the ability to change these objects isn't necessary. This might seem a bit dramatic because there are specific fields that you can change on the dimensions, but the best practice is to do 100%

of your changes directly from the BPC side of the fence and then see the results on the BW side. This is also not to say that you should only have display available for all objects on the BW side. For example, the use of the process chains requires that you be able to both change and create new process chains. So talk with your security person and give them all of the appropriate information to support the different levels of security needed. You can support quite a bit of your work if you just have full access to any of the different transaction codes, programs, function modules, tables, or objects that start with a UJ*. It's useful that everything related to BPC in BW starts with a UJ* (except for the actual objects).

This view of the company environment is from the FAVORITES folder so that you can focus the view directly to the appropriate environment, but if you were to go into the INFOPROVIDER folder, you would see that all of the BPC objects are stored and located under one InfoArea called the BUSINESS PLANNING AND CONSOLIDATION INFOAREA (see Figure 3.38). This is automatically generated during the installation process.

Figure 3.38 InfoProvider Screen with Business Planning and Consolidation InfoArea

There are a number of unique aspects to the BPC objects, including the following:

- All objects on the BW side that are related to BPC start their technical names with a /CPMB/, which makes the analysis and search for these objects very straightforward.

- Partitioning isn't available in BW for BPC objects because the Time dimension is very different from what is available in standard BW.

- You can't permanently change the database performance parameters due to the fact that they change until you execute your next optimization process for BPC.

- Near Line Storage (NLS) isn't available in BW for BPC objects due to the difference in the Time dimension.

Note: Near Line Storage

The issues with the Time dimension and NLS is that the NLS will work *only* with the standard time used by a basic BW InfoCube. These are 0FISCPER, 0CALMONTH and others that are similar to this versus the TIME dimension in a BPC specific Model. This limitation is being reviewed, and there is a possibility in a future SP that this will be changed to accommodate the use of NLS with the TIME dimension from a BPC Model.

► You can find the technical names for the InfoProviders in Table UJA_APPL.

► The InfoProvider is generated in the namespace /CPMB/ with the following naming convention:

/CPMB/<Environment Prefix>I<Model Prefix><1Generatedchar>

► The MultiProvider is generated in the namespace /CPMB/ with the following naming convention:

/CPMB/<Environment Prefix>M<Model Prefix><1Generatedchar>

► The query is generated in the namespace /CPMB/ with the following naming convention:

<MuliprovName>!!O<MultiProvName>

This can be seen in Figure 3.39 from Transaction RSRT.

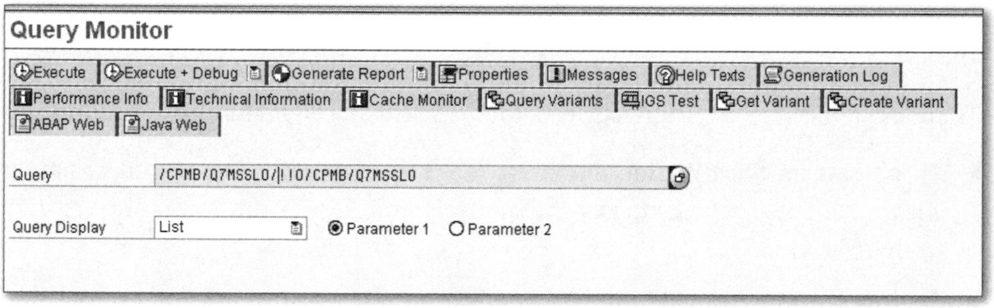

Figure 3.39 Query Monitor from Transaction RSRT

► The query technical name is found by using Table UJA_APPL. In the Data Browser, the technical name of the MultiProvider is in column MULTIPROV, as shown in Figure 3.40.

Data Browser: Table UJA_APPL			5 Hits			

MANDT	APPSET_ID	APPLICATION_ID	INFOCUBE	MULTIPROV	APPL_PREFIX	BE
100	ZCOMPANY_01	BUDGET	/CPMB/Q7ISSLO	/CPMB/Q7MSSLO	SSL	
100	ZCOMPANY_01	Consolidation	/CPMB/Q7IF7JC	/CPMB/Q7MF7JC	F7J	
100	ZCOMPANY_01	Ownership	/CPMB/Q7IGZZV	/CPMB/Q7MGZZV	GZZ	
100	ZCOMPANY_01	Planning	/CPMB/Q7IJ6PH	/CPMB/Q7MJ6PH	J6P	
100	ZCOMPANY_01	Rates	/CPMB/Q7ILX0I	/CPMB/Q7MLX0I	LX0	

Figure 3.40 Data Browser: Table UJA_APPL with the ZCOMPANY_01 Environment

This may come in handy when it's time to performance tune the EPM reports because there are some parameters that are available to be changed via the RSRT view.

▶ A BPC InfoProvider can be changed without using the re-modeling toolbox in SAP NetWeaver BI. Therefore you don't need to obey the underlying SAP NetWeaver restrictions on removing/adding dimensions.

▶ The MultiProvider and query are always created automatically and are both in the data flow, but the real-time InfoProvider is exchanged if you do a full optimization. You would then have to add the new cube to the MultiProvider after the optimization.

3.8.3 BW/BPC InfoObject

The InfoObject that BPC creates during the save and processing activities from the BPC frontend is a bit different from the normal InfoObject that is created directly from the BW Administration Workbench. If you look at one of the InfoObjects that was created from the ZCOMPANY_01 shell, you can see some differences. Again, you should not be changing anything from the BW side of the fence, but it's good to have some understanding of the structure of these objects. Figure 3.41 shows the InfoObject CUSTOMER from the BW side. You can immediately see that the technical name is different. They will always start with a /CPMB/ prefix and then add the additional characters to generate the full technical name. So, unlike the normal BW InfoObjects that get created from the BW system and the technical names can be assigned by the person creating the object. These InfoObjects are assigned a system generated technical name.

Another difference is that all of the attributes except for the standard delivered will immediately be assigned as navigational attributes rather than display attributes. This can be seen from the property/attribute IMPORTANCE, which is a user-defined property and is immediately assigned the navigational attribute type. The two standard properties that are listed here are the HIR, which a technical property generated by the system to support the different hierarchies that may be assigned to this InfoObject, and the SCALING property, which allows the display of the values to scale in the report and show values in the thousands or other scales of 10. Both of these properties are DISPLAY.

Also there is no concept of compounding in a BPC InfoObject. *Compounding* is the addition of another InfoObject that is required for the purposes of defining another InfoObject. For example, if you had an InfoObject such as city, you would need a compound of state so that you would know where to look for this value. Because there are cities that can be found in multiple states (e.g., there are six cities named Philadelphia in the United States, so to find the appropriate Philadelphia, you need the state), you need a compound of state. This causes additional issues when it comes to InfoObjects such as cost center because they will be compounded with the controlling area, and you need to understand what to do with this during the process of uploading the master data to the BPC object for cost center. We'll discuss this more in Chapter 5 on data flow. Finally, the length of the field that supports the ID of any BPC object is 32 characters. It has been extended since version 7.5 due to some SAP ERP objects having field lengths of more than 20 characters. As you know, the building blocks of the InfoCubes are the InfoObjects. Let's look at the InfoCube next.

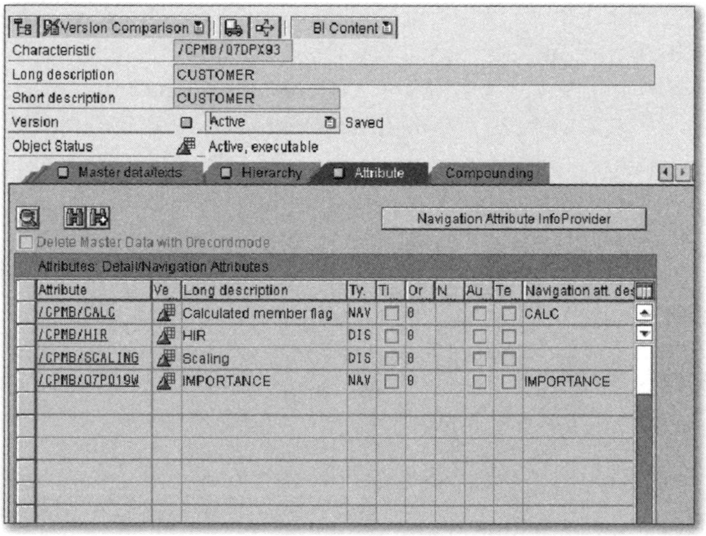

Figure 3.41 View of the CUSTOMER Dimension for BPC in BW

3.8.4   BW/BPC InfoCube

The save and processing activities in BPC not only create InfoObjects but they also generate a BW InfoCube and MultiProvider during the generation of a BPC model (see Figure 3.42). There are definitely differences between this InfoCube and other standard InfoCubes created in the BW environment. Some of the differences are listed here:

▶ The BPC InfoCube assigns the dimensions to individual nodes in the InfoCube. As you can see the dimensions are in a one-to-one relationship with the node that they are assigned to. The only time there is a difference is if the model has more than 13 dimensions. In that case, the final dimensions are grouped together in a 13th folder called OTHER and are grouped together. In this case, a full optimization process in BPC will help sort these dimensions out by organizing them based on the level of transactional data that is being supported.

▶ Each of the dimensions starts with a /CPMB/ as well as the technical name of the InfoCube. The technical names are system generated and not user defined.

▶ The MultiProvider is automatically generated as well to support the interface between the EPM add-in reporting and the InfoCube itself.

▶ Only one key figure is created—SignData—and there is no intervention by the developer. This is automatically set up during the processing of the model.

▶ All of the navigational attributes are turned on in the BPC model. Normally these navigational attributes are turned on based on requirements, whereas, in this case, they are automatically turned on by the system.

▶ The data storage for the BPC models hasn't changed since the SEM approach. Therefore, the records that are posted to the InfoCube via consolidation or P&F will accumulate in one request or package in the InfoCube until more than 50,000 records have been posted to that one package. At that point in time, the package will be closed by the system, and another request will be opened. There are approaches to automatically close the packages and specific times as well, but that is customized configuration.

If you review any objects on the BW side at all, the one that you should become familiar with is the InfoCube. This not only supports the BPC models but, generally speaking, the BW InfoCubes will be supporting the data uploads into the BPC models. Therefore, understanding the mechanics of the InfoCube is very important.

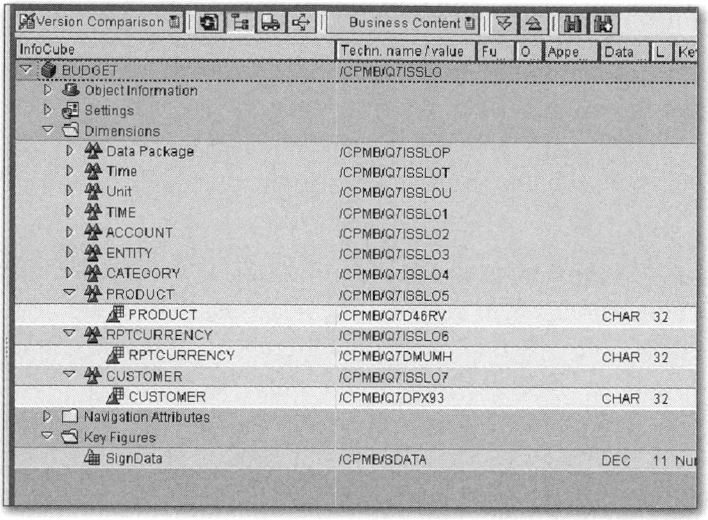

Figure 3.42 View of the InfoCube That Supports the BPC Model – Budget

At this point in the process, refer to Table 3.1 that we reviewed earlier in this chapter, as it has all of the different BW objects related to the BPC objects, and the BW objects have similar features as do the BPC objects. Again, if you want to investigate the BW architecture in more detail, there are a number of books, articles, and educational materials that will help you understand all of the architecture of BW. We'll revisit different areas of BW specifically when they come into play during the BPC process.

3.9 Summary

In this chapter, we covered quite a bit of material, from the concepts and discussion around data modeling and architecture of the BPC implementation to the details around the member values. It's safe to say that without a strong foundation of models, dimensions, and members the rest of the process will be more complex than required. It's also always good to look at the results that you are trying to achieve for both the reporting, consolidation, and P&F activities. We discussed, configured, and offered screenshots of all of the detailed steps to do each of the tasks involved. When implementing BPC, it's very important to make sure that all aspects of the process are reviewed, and the architecture of the dimensions and models are integrated together. This will help with the actual act of configuration because you know where you need to go and what is required to get there.

We started by showing the standard content EnvironmentShell, which includes the models, dimensions, members and some configuration around the business rules and Script Logic. We also found that with this standard content, we get three models: the Consolidation, Rate, and Planning. Then we worked our way through the use of this content by making a copy of the EnvironmentShell and using it as a starting point of our other activities. Following the process that we might use during an implementation, we moved to a more detailed discussion of each dimension and identified those that are required versus optional as well as the optional and required properties for each dimension. This discussion included an analysis of some of the user-defined properties are used for on the dimensions. During this analysis, we also covered the use of hierarchies and some of the more unique features available in the dimension configuration, such as the dimension logic and security.

After the dimensions were defined, we moved to the configuration of the models. These models are either inherited from the standard content and need tweaking, or they are new models that are created from the ground up. Remember that it's normally a good idea to start a new model with a copy of an existing model because all of the standard programs, processes, and features are copied over during this process.

We closed out this chapter with a discussion based on the BW InfoObjects that are the support network for the version of BPC for SAP NetWeaver. These objects are as critical as the frontend process in BPC. It's important to understand, to a point, the details behind the BW side of these activities to take advantage of whatever functionality is possible from the BW side, such as performance, storage, and reporting.

This chapter covers the new SAP Enterprise Performance Management (EPM) add-in reporting component, which will then be referenced throughout the rest of the book. This robust reporting toolset can be used for both reporting and input templates for all of the BPC-specific models as well as for the other third-party source systems and BW-based InfoProviders. It's an easy-to-learn, user-friendly component that offers extensive functionality specific to EPM and Excel-based functions.

4 Reporting in BPC

Several options are available for reporting in BPC, but the main reporting component is the SAP Enterprise Performance Management (EPM) add-in for Microsoft Excel, Word, and PowerPoint. In this chapter, we'll go over the basics of the EPM add-in, the functionality, and the navigational process. Then we'll move into more complex activities for both the reporting and input templates. After this discussion and configuration, the chapter reviews the advanced functionality of the Excel add-in, such as the development of asymmetric report/input templates, member recognition, multiple reports on one worksheet from multiple source systems, and other features. At this point, the integration between Excel and Word/PowerPoint is not as commonly used, but we'll review this information to make you aware of the enhancements in this process. Finally, we'll cover the use of VBA, macros, EPM add-in and FPML functions, and the inherent use of these EPM functions in reporting. This topic could also fill another book on its own with all of the information and material involved in the EPM add-in functionality, but here we'll provide a good, solid foundation covering the features and options available to get you moving in the right direction. Starting to work on a new reporting component without the basics to fall back on can be unnerving at best. After you start working with this toolset, you'll find that it's very functional and consistent, which is good because we can definitely say that the EPM add-in is the component that will be used against the BPC product for reporting purposes. That being said, we have to step back a bit and align ourselves with the reporting process overall and in BPC first before starting to discuss the features and functionality.

> **Note: EPM Add-In SP Level**
>
> We're working with the EPM add-in at SP10 P2. SAP is delivering a patch about every three to four weeks at this time and a SP consistent with the SP strategy for BPC itself. Even though the patches change on just about a monthly basis, all of the functionality that we review will be available and relevant in future patches or SPs. You, of course, will find enhanced functionality available based on future SPs and patches.

4.1 Report Considerations

As with any project, you need to make sure you keep your eye on the prize and that means being aware of the reporting requirements. You definitely have to set up the system correctly with whatever processes are required, but if you can't get the data out to the business user correctly, then the possibility of an unsuccessful completion of a project is much higher. Reporting requirements are critical to the overall success of the project and implementation. So, even though we're focusing on the configuration of the planning and forecasting (P&F) or consolidation processes, we have to get the reporting requirements as soon as possible in the overall project timeframe to accommodate the build. Depending on the complexity of the reporting requirements, this can add significant time to the project or require additional resources. A bit of an advantage here is that more often than not, you'll be looking at a majority of financial reports whether they are consolidation type or P&F type reports. You can definitely guess what types of reports you need, but it's always good to have the actual blueprints or functional/technical specifications to get everything accurate.

A final type of report that is easy to lose track of is the validation report. These reports are very important and in some cases the most difficult to accommodate because they validate the movement of both master data and transactional data across multiple systems. For BPC, the master data becomes even more important because if the master data isn't there during an upload of transactional data, the record will fail, and you'll have to go back, load the missing master data, and then load or reload the failed record(s). This type of report will most definitely be required in a financial scenario because you want to know that the data in the source system has actually gotten to the BPC model for P&F and consolidation.

For BPC, the integration between the frontend reporting and the backend configuration requires a bit more than just a basic BW reporting process. For example, as we've discussed, the use of properties on the dimensions is incorporated into reporting much more than in basic BW reports. An example of this difference is the use of navigational attributes. In the case of BW, the navigational attributes are available for reporting just the same as a characteristic, whereas in the BPC environment, the navigational attributes are available but more for display purposes rather than navigational purposes. To use the attributes/properties in the BPC model, you have to use an EPM function, which you'll see a bit later in this chapter. In BW reporting, you just have to make sure that it's turned on in the presentation layer and then it's available for reporting in the query. In other cases, such as validation reports, this integration is critical and without it, the ability to validate is almost impossible. This is due to the requirement to be able to read two tables—the source data and the target data—using one report. To do that, the backend system has to align the models and InfoCubes correctly to accommodate the report needs. An advantage that the EPM add-in has in this case is the ability to have multiple reports from different sources on either the same worksheet or different worksheets in the same workbook. This will help with the development and management of validation reports.

Note: Navigational Attribute Terminology

A *navigational attribute* has been designed to be used in a BI report as though it's a characteristic. Therefore, you can navigate and slice/dice a report based on a navigational attribute. In a BPC model, the navigational attributes aren't available for reporting in the same way as in a BI InfoCube due to basic core system functionality, which can't be changed. This may change in a future SP.

There are other aspects of what is developed in the BW backend and how it impacts BPC reporting, such as the development of the hierarchy options (time dependent versus versioning), member naming conventions, and compounding of InfoObjects. These impacts mean that it's very important to coordinate meetings between the report builders and the system configuration group to help each other succeed. This will also be very helpful when testing for performance and the ability to tweak the reports with the help of additional structure items such as hierarchies and properties to accommodate additional reporting requirements. Let's not forget that these BPC models are, in fact, transactional InfoCubes, which by nature aren't as strong for reporting as the basic InfoCubes. So, it's always good to try and improve the efficiency of the presentation layer and the reports to help the cause. You may even find that it's a good thing to add a few models to your

BPC architecture and label a "reporting layer" where all of the reporting will be sourced from. This way, you can avoid any impact on the models that are doing the actual work of the data processing for P&F or consolidation. This, of course, requires that you have an immediate process to move the completed data from the working models to the reporting models, but it may be worth it. This is a consideration during the architecture phase of the project. Some of the tricky areas where some additional support from the presentation layer might come in handy are for comparison reports or blended reports, that is, when you have a requirement to blend planned and actual data into one report.

If your data is in two separate models, then you have to make sure that the granularity and consistency of dimensions is available. You may not be able to create a MultiProvider and make a union of the data work due to this inconsistency of dimensions, so it is good if the BW backend can integrate the two into one model for reporting to support faster and more effective reporting options. You need to make sure that all of the information you need is actually in the presentation layer. If you lose sight of the requirements and find that not everything is available, you'll be forced to cobble things together to make the reporting process work. For example, it's always good to get a sample of each report to make sure you have all your dimensions and characteristics such as profit centers or segments incorporated into your BPC models in case you need them in the report.

You may also find that if the granularity or master data is not consistent across the different InfoCubes or Models then you might need to use a Virtual InfoCube to help support the integration of the data. Look at the functionality supplied with the Virtual InfoCube with Services to help with this. This option will help to integrate the levels and master data by use of a Function Module that can be accessed during the read process from the base InfoCube to the Virtual InfoCube. An example of this functionality might be that in your InfoCube the dimension Category has a value of ACTUAL but the other dimensions have the value of 001. This scenario is not uncommon. The Function Module can read the value for ACTUAL and map it to the integrated value of 001 to allow the data to be read from an InfoCube that has different master data. This can come in handy during the process of setting up validation reports but watch the performance impact of using this approach.

Finally, you may need to be concerned about the formatting requirements. This may not be as significant as it might be if using Crystal Reports in our project, but there may be some requirements for static, formatted reports that need to support using the EPM add-in. Note, however, that the EPM add-in can accommodate formatted reports with the generation of PDF type reports or using the formatting options either via Excel or EPM to accommodate the requirement. In any case, if complex formatting is required, you need to incorporate that into the project plan. Having 50 reports that are format intensive requires a significant amount of time to complete.

4.2   Other Reporting Components in BPC

The majority of this chapter is devoted to the EPM add-in component, but there are other options for reporting in BPC. We commented about them in Chapter 2 but didn't really get into using them. You can find them in the CREATE portion of the HOME screen of the BPC web screen. The ability to create both reports and input templates is available.

In this case, you'll build out a basic report using the NEW REPORT prompt. After you click on this prompt, you see the screen displayed with the dimensions broken up into rows and columns. From here, you can also see that you can switch the BPC Model that you're using as well by clicking on the MANAGE CONTEXT link and then using the dropdown menu to switch the model.

You can also change the type of display to either a REPORT or INPUT TEMPLATE using the toggle for the TYPE of view. Finally, you can add some formatting to the report via the FORMAT link. In this case, changing the look is limited to SCALING and DECIMAL PLACES. This option for reporting is very useful in a number of situations especially if you are looking to quickly create a report on the fly and review data as well as assigning it to your personal workspace.

To start, if you want to add some dimensions to the header area of the report, you use the ADD DIMENSION (the plus sign) option to extend the list that will be filters on the whole report. (see Figure 4.1). We've added several dimensions to the header, including Category, GL Account, Unit of Measure/Currency, Measure – Periodic, Product – All Products, and Entity – All Entities.

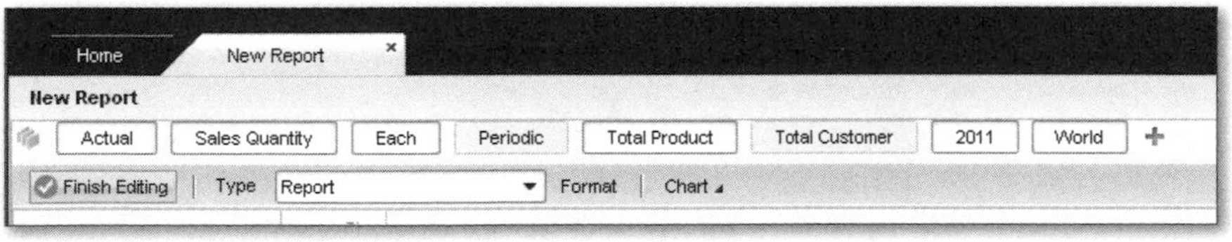

Figure 4.1 New Report with Dimensions in the Header of the Report

Now, right-click on the dimension CUSTOMER and select ADD TO ROW as shown in Figure 4.2.

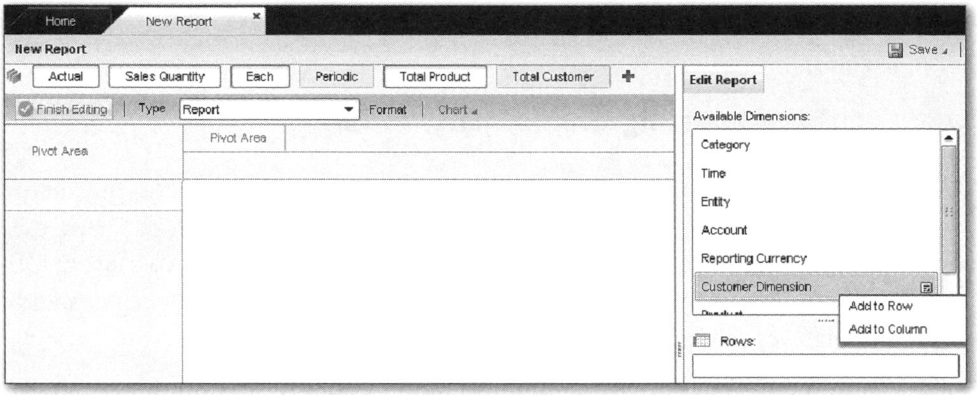

Figure 4.2 Add Customer Dimension to Row

If you add the Time dimension to the columns, you'll see that a basic report is available that contains some data (see Figure 4.3).

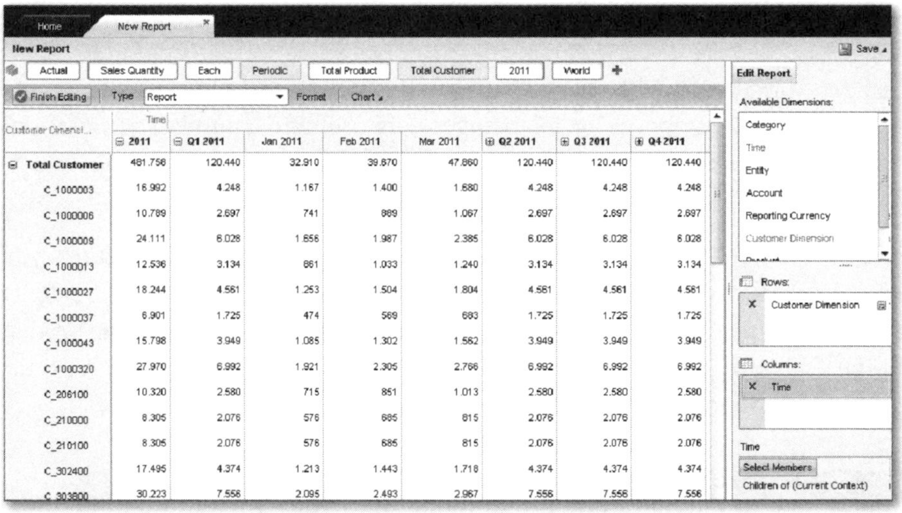

Figure 4.3 New Live Report Built in BPC

As you can see, the flexibility of this frontend is a bit limited, but it's great for a quick report to see results or validate information. When you're finished with this report, you can click on the FINISH EDITING button, and the navigation pane will disappear; you can change filters at this point, but the format is set. Then if you're interested in saving this report and being able to execute it in the future, you can click on SAVE or SAVE As to incorporate it into your workspace for future reference. Then choose PRIVATE • MY REPORTS • TOTAL CUSTOMER RPT (saved naming convention). After this is complete, go back to the HOME page, and click the LIBRARY option in the navigation pane to see the saved report as shown in Figure 4.4. You can execute the report via this screen as well.

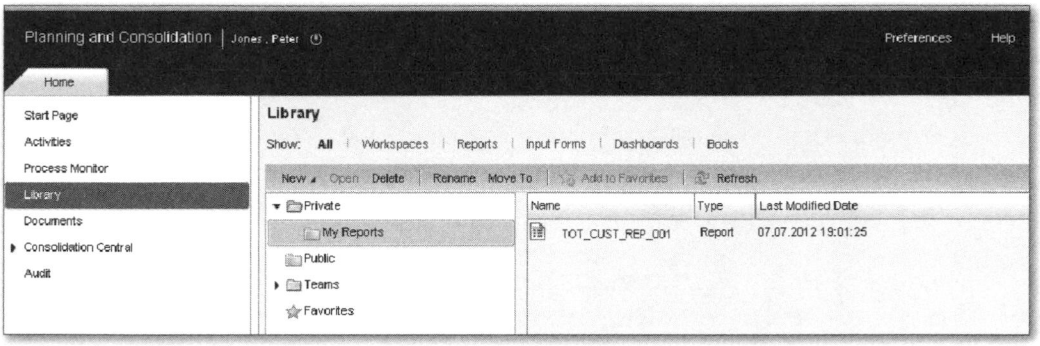

Figure 4.4 Library View of the Folder My Reports: TOT_CUST_REP_001

This approach can also generate an input template as well as new workspaces.

Although this is an option in some situations, overall this isn't a usable report for a standard template or a dynamic report that requires extensive formatting, dynamic functionality, or the use of Excel functionality.

4.3 Standard EPM Reports

EPM does have some standard reports and input templates, but without any idea of the underlying models, the standard delivered reports and templates require some work to be usable. Even so, let's not rule them out completely. We'll review the reports and input templates available. With an understanding of the standard reports and templates, you'll be able to copy and reuse some parts of these reports. To view the standard templates that are available and installed when the initial standard content is installed, you have to use a BPC model and access the EPM add-in. We'll discuss this process next, but first take a look at Figure 4.5 to see the EPM add-in being opened in Excel.

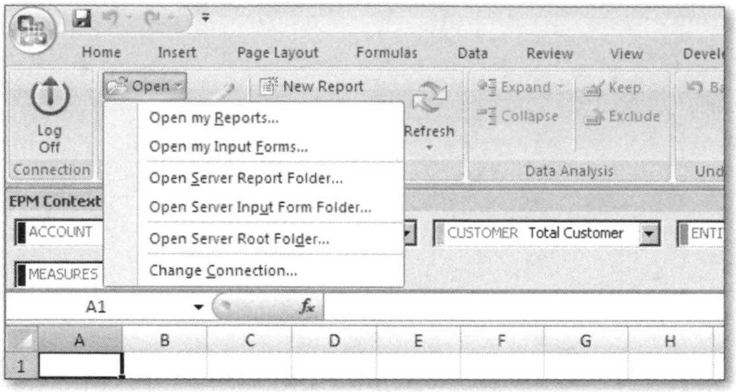

Figure 4.5 Opening the EPM add-in in Excel

From the OPEN SERVER ROOT FOLDER, go to the COMPANY (PUBLIC) folder to see the templates that are available. You'll notice that there are templates in the REPORTS, INPUT SCHEDULES, and BOOKS folders, as shown in Figure 4.6.

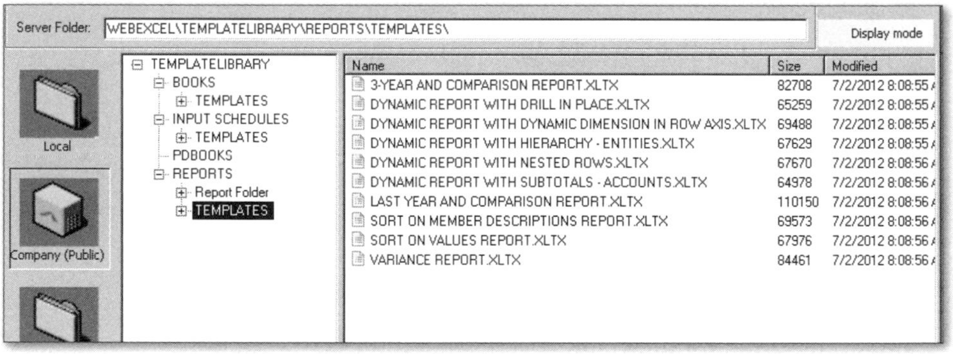

Figure 4.6 Templates in the Company (Public) Folder

There are templates for the Finance, Rate, and Ownership models that are part of the EnvironmentShell delivered with BPC. The templates are listed here:

▸ Finance model:
  ▸ 10 templates for reporting
  ▸ 5 templates for input forms

▸ Rate model:
  ▸ 4 templates for reporting
  ▸ 3 templates for input forms

▶ Ownership model

  ▶ 2 templates for reporting

  ▶ 0 templates for input forms

Just by reviewing the first report in the Company (Public) folder—3-YEAR AND COMPARISON REPORT—you see that it will execute, but there will probably be an inconsistency in the members and dimensions, so these reports have to be tweaked to be usable. You can also see that the report logo has to be changed. One of the nice extras about these template reports is that they all use the EPM formatting template, which is a good way to understand what features are available via this formatting template. In Figure 4.7, notice the additional first tab—EPM SAP TEMPLATE 1 at the bottom of the screen. This shows that the EPM formatting sheet is active for this report template.

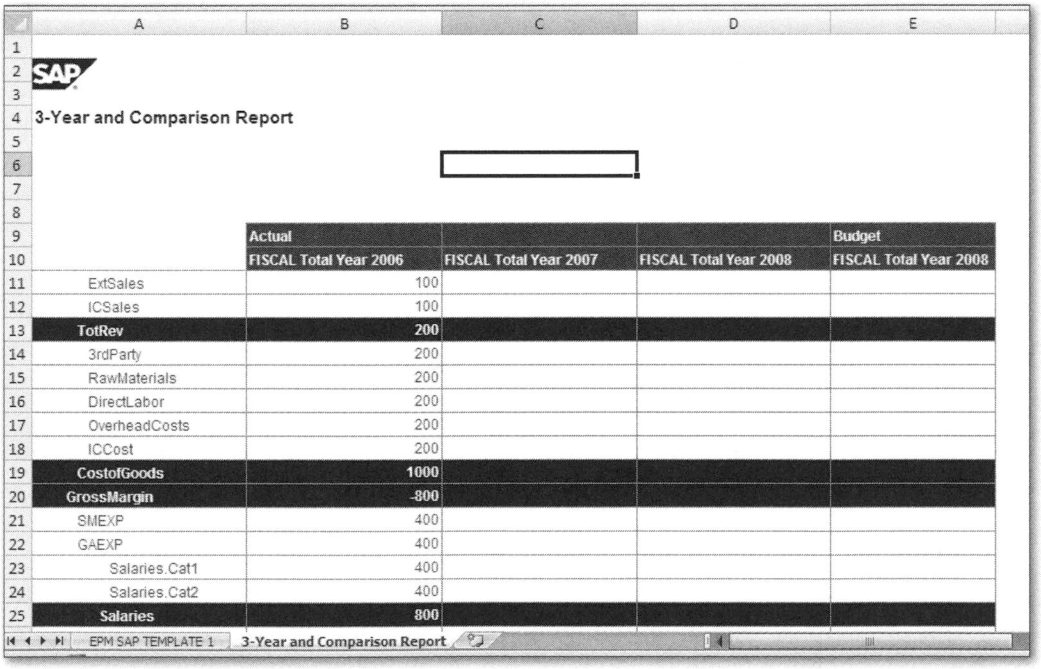

	A	B	C	D	E
2	SAP				
4	3-Year and Comparison Report				
9		Actual			Budget
10		FISCAL Total Year 2006	FISCAL Total Year 2007	FISCAL Total Year 2008	FISCAL Total Year 2008
11	ExtSales	100			
12	ICSales	100			
13	**TotRev**	**200**			
14	3rdParty	200			
15	RawMaterials	200			
16	DirectLabor	200			
17	OverheadCosts	200			
18	ICCost	200			
19	**CostofGoods**	**1000**			
20	**GrossMargin**	**-800**			
21	SMEXP	400			
22	GAEXP	400			
23	Salaries.Cat1	400			
24	Salaries.Cat2	400			
25	**Salaries**	**800**			

EPM SAP TEMPLATE 1 | 3-Year and Comparison Report

Figure 4.7 Template for the 3-Year and Comparison Report

There are some very good examples of asymmetric reports as well as reports that use the butterfly format of reporting. In addition, a few reports include customization, such as the report that is sorted based on the member description. Included in that report, you'll see the use of one of the advanced features—FPMXLCLIENT.TECHNI-CALCATEGORY.EPM—which offers a look at how the EPM reporting supports some of the EvDRE features such as the vertical line to support a series of member filters. The FPMXLCLIENT is shown in Figure 4.8.

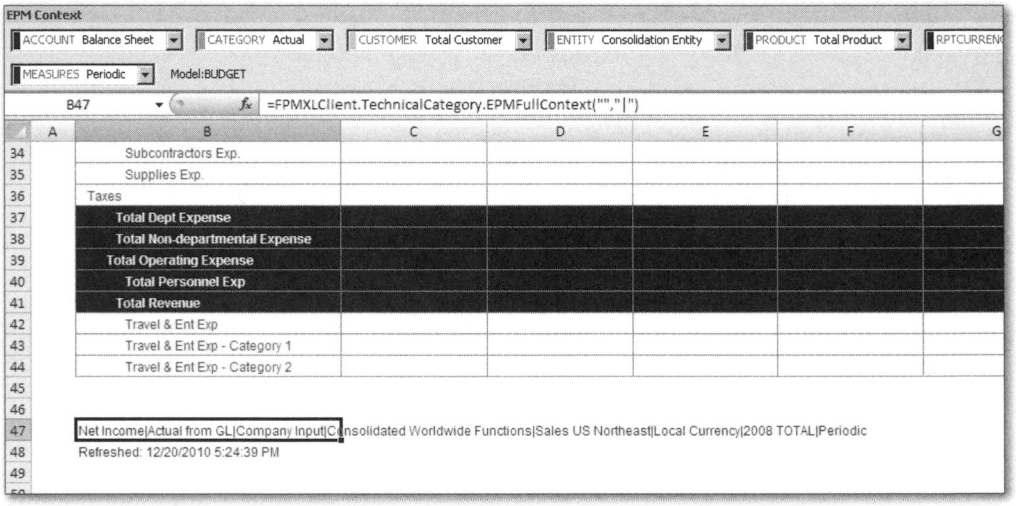

Figure 4.8 Sorting on Member Descriptions by Using FPMXLClient Features with Vertical Line to Support Filter Members

You can add report or input templates to the list of available templates for the business users. This is a reasonable option based on a possible method of distribution where you are supporting the business user with a series of standard templates. The business user makes a copy of the template that is the closest fit for the requirements. From there, the user alters and aligns the report to fit his needs. Remember to make sure that the connection feature is turned off. The connection is stored so that the report is specifically linked to one model, but because this is a template, we expect a number of people to use it so we need to disconnect it by choosing DO NOT STORE CONNECTION. This option can be found if you go to the EPM ADD-IN • EDIT REPORT • OPTIONS • REFRESH OPTIONS • PARAMETER (see Figure 4.9).

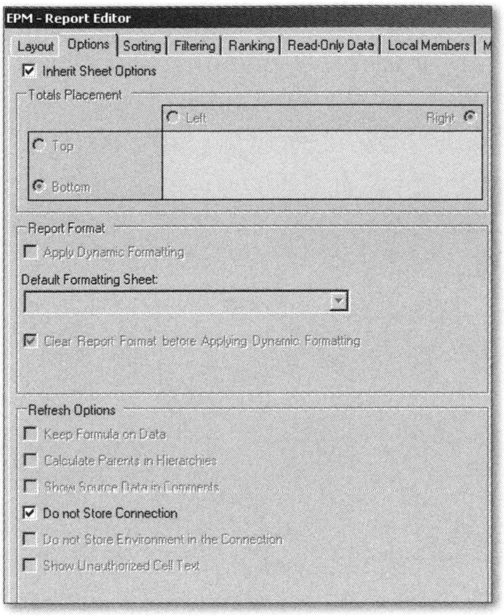

Figure 4.9 Choosing the Do Not Store Connection Option

After you've finished this process and added whatever logos or formatting you need, save the template to the TEMPLATE folder in the appropriate node either as an input form, report, or book. Remember as you save the template, you assign a .XLTX to the end so that it can be identified as a template version.

All in all, the standard reports are a good place to start and investigate some of the features and functionality available in the EPM add-in.

4.4   Overview of the EPM Add-In Component

Now that we've looked at the reporting options in the BPC component and reviewed the standard delivered reports and input forms, we can focus on the EPM add-in toolset and understand what that brings to the table for reporting purposes. If you review the use of the EPM add-in across the whole EPM suite, you see that the approach in the EPM V10.0 suite is to connect the frontend of all of the systems to one reporting component. Figure 4.10 shows that the EPM add-in supports all of

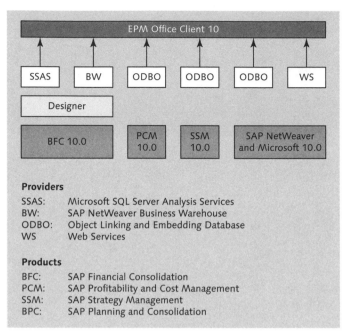

Providers
SSAS: Microsoft SQL Server Analysis Services
BW: SAP NetWeaver Business Warehouse
ODBO: Object Linking and Embedding Database
WS   Web Services

Products
BFC: SAP Financial Consolidation
PCM: SAP Profitability and Cost Management
SSM: SAP Strategy Management
BPC: SAP Planning and Consolidation

Figure 4.10 EPM Office Client V10.0 Integration with the EPM Suite

the components in the EPM environment, including the BPC version for Microsoft. If you're using any of the other components, you'll also run into the EPM add-in as a reporting tool. For the Business Financial Consolidation (BFC) product, there is an additional integration component required called the Designer, which is a view of the information so that either SQL Server Analysis Services (SSAS) or BW can support the data and pass it to the EPM add-in for reporting purposes. The two other components—Profitability and Cost Management (PCM) and SAP Strategy Management (SSM)—use the Object Linking and Embedding Database (OLE DB) connection, which we talked about earlier in Chapter 2. The two BPC products give you the ability either to create the OLE DB link or the Web services link. The Web services link is the one we'll be focusing on during the course of this book because it offers the ability to both execute reports as well as execute data input to be written to the BPC models.

This approach offers a number of advantages:

▶ Incorporating all of the reporting requirements and needs for all of the components into one central toolset.

- Switching from one component to another without having to revisit the reporting toolset and learn yet another option for reporting. This supports a reduction in training costs and learning curve from component to component and also consistency of the user experience.

- Integrating between the different systems and executing reports, as well as possibly integrating multiple sources of information onto one workbook, assuming that the data modeling will support this option.

- Incorporating links to multiple third-party systems into one central location.

- Enhancing the reporting capabilities of the EPM add-in to benefit all of the different EPM products.

As mentioned, the number of reporting frontends is significant, so having a strong knowledge base in one report system will enable you to use multiple other systems.

The EPM reporting tool can cross multiple user groups, but the main focus is on the hard-core financial users that are interested in having the capabilities of Excel as well as the integrated backend to the SAP systems. The EPM add-in can either be used as an ad hoc reporting toolset with access to many different options to enhance the final result of the report, or it can generate formatted reports that are print ready and can be distributed via email or hardcopy. An example of a formatted report is shown in Figure 4.11. In this formatted report, we've generated a CONSOLIDATED STATEMENT OF EARNINGS AND COMPREHENSIVE INCOME. As you can see, some additional formatting and alignment of the information for each cell needs to be performed.

One of the benefits of a formatted report is that it's normally a static report and not dynamic, so you don't have to worry about someone slicing and dicing the report. If that were the case, this report would be 100% more difficult to configure. All of the font, formatting, and display features making up this report are available in the EPM add-in. This is also an example of a butterfly report where the dimension members are shown in the report flanked by amounts or values, rather than the dimension members being linked to the left of the report and all of the key values to the right side of the report. This report also supports the ability for the column headings to be linked to the DATE field with which the user assigns a date. This way the column headings reflect what is available in the column and offer the appropriate column heading as well.

Period 2010.MAR

EXECUTIVE SUMMARY

Three months ended March 31				Three months ended March 31			Year ended December 31			Zero months ended		
2010 Actual	2010 Budget	2009 Actual		2010 Actual	2010 Budget	2009 Actual	2010 Forecast	2010 Budget	2009 Actual	2010 Actual	2010 Budget	2009 Actual
			Operations' earnings									
$ 425,800	$ (148,870)	$ (1,571,024)	Çayeli	$ (1,223,456)	$ 17,031	$ (1,571,024)	$ 11,520	$ 1,150,371	$ (339,320)	$ (1,649,256)	$ 165,901	$ -
(439,657)	6,038	(4,167,980)	Las Cruces	(4,974,982)	22,137	(4,167,980)	11,520	1,561,557	(1,784,883)	(4,535,325)	16,099	-
25,724	8,159	(2,371,342)	Pyhäsalmi	(2,553,039)	16,771	(2,371,342)	11,520	744,031	(985,265)	(2,578,763)	8,612	-
54,848,189	16,722	129,125,772	Other	201,833,940	-	129,125,772	23,040	2,266,680	89,403,572	146,985,751	(16,722)	-
54,860,056	(117,951)	121,015,426		193,082,462	55,939	121,015,426	57,600	5,722,639	86,294,103	138,222,406	173,890	-
1,428,840	5,010	(3,411,360)	Corporate development and exploration	(2,017,080)	(1,650)	(3,411,360)	34,560	3,444,270	34,560	(3,445,920)	(6,660)	-
11,814,270	1,637	(28,098,540)	General and administration	(16,554,990)	(2,268)	(28,098,540)	270,720	28,366,992	270,720	(28,369,260)	(3,905)	-
(4,793,122)	(38,866)	11,482,170	Investment and other income	6,794,168	(4,863)	11,482,170	(105,120)	(11,592,153)	(105,120)	11,587,290	34,003	-
120,377	248	(286,680)	Stand-by charges	(169,183)	-	(286,680)	2,880	289,560	2,880	(289,560)	(248)	-
60,275	-	(143,250)	Asset impairment	(84,415)	-	(143,250)	1,440	144,690	1,440	(144,690)	-	-
36,310,440	595	87,225,212	Finance costs	135,420,478	(787)	87,225,212	8,640	866,093	59,450,050	99,110,038	(1,382)	-
185,088	44,922	(574,080)	Income taxes	(394,752)	(11,540)	(574,080)	5,760	568,300	5,760	(579,840)	(56,462)	-
45,126,169	13,545	66,193,472	**Net income from continuing operations**	122,994,227	(21,108)	66,193,472	218,880	22,087,752	59,660,290	77,868,058	(34,653)	-
(67,050)	-	159,510	Income from discontinued operation (net of taxes)	93,900	-	159,510	(1,440)	(160,950)	(1,440)	160,950	-	-
$ 45,059,119	**$ 13,545**	**$66,352,982**	**Net income**	**$ 123,088,127**	**$ (21,108)**	**$66,352,982**	**$ 217,440**	**$ 21,926,802**	**$ 59,658,850**	**$ 78,029,008**	**$ (34,653)**	**$ -**
			Net income attributable to:									
$ 44,998,669	$ 13,545	$ 66,496,652	Inmet equity holders	$ 123,172,787	$ (21,108)	$ 66,496,652	$ 216,000	$ 21,781,692	$ 59,657,410	$ 78,174,118	$ (34,653)	$ -
60,450	-	(143,670)	Non-controlling interests	(84,660)	-	(143,670)	1,440	145,110	1,440	(145,110)	-	-
$ 45,059,119	$ 13,545	$ 66,352,982		$ 123,088,127	$ (21,108)	$ 66,352,982	$ 217,440	$ 21,926,802	$ 59,658,850	$ 78,029,008	$ (34,653)	$ -
			Earnings per common share									
			Income from continuing operations									
$ 70.72	$ 0.02	$ 103.88	Basic	$ 190.77	$ (0.03)	$ 102.81	$ 0.35	$ 34.84	$ 94.60	$ 120.05	$ (0.05)	$ (1.06)
$ 16.89	$ 0.01	$ 24.81	Diluted	$ 45.59	$ (0.01)	$ 24.57	$ 0.08	$ 8.32	$ 22.59	$ 28.70	$ (0.01)	$ (0.24)

Figure 4.11 EPM add-in Formatted Report – Executive Summary Report

Figure 4.12 is another example of a formatted report using the EPM add-in. In both this report and the one in Figure 4.11, you can see that these are asymmetric reports where the columns aren't consistently one set sequence of a category. In both reports, the categories of ACTUAL, BUDGET, and FORECAST are switched from set to set.

DATE (MM/DD/YYYY) 7/7/2012

CORPORATE SUMMARY

Three months ended As at September 30				Seven months ended AS AT JULY 31			Year ended December 31			Six Months ended APRIL 30		
2012 ACTUAL	2012 BUDGET	2011 ACTUAL		2012 ACTUAL	2012 BUDGET	2011 ACTUAL	2012 FORECAST	2012 BUDGET	2011 ACTUAL	2012 ACTUAL	2012 BUDGET	2011 ACTUAL
			Operations' earnings									
			Entity A			$ 165,901			$ 165,901	$ -	$ -	$ 165,901
			Entity B			$ 16,099			$ 16,099	$ -	$ -	$ 16,099
			Entity C			$ 8,612			$ 8,612	$ -	$ -	$ 8,612
$ -	$ -	$ -	Other	$ -	$ -	$ (16,706)	$ -	$ -	$ (16,706)	$ -	$ -	$ (16,706)
-	-	-		-	-	173,906	-	-	173,906	-	-	173,906
			CORPORATE DEVELOPMENT AND EXPLORATION			(6,660)			(6,660)	$ -	$ -	$ (6,660)
			GENERAL AND ADMINISTRATIVE EXPENSES			(3,905)			(3,905)	$ -	$ -	$ (3,905)
-	-	-	INVESTMENT AND OTHER INCOME	-	-	33,987	-	-	33,987	$ -	$ -	$ 33,987
			STAND-BY CHARGES			(248)			(248)	$ -	$ -	$ (248)
			ASSET IMPAIRMENT							$ -	$ -	$ -
			INTEREST EXPENSE			(1,382)			(1,382)	$ -	$ -	$ (1,382)
			INCOME TAX EXPENSE (RECOVERY)			(56,462)			(56,462)	$ -	$ -	$ (56,462)

Figure 4.12 Corporate Summary Report – by Entity

During most of this chapter, we'll discuss the ad hoc view of the data using the EPM add-in, but in the latter section of this chapter, we'll discuss and demonstrate some of the formatting features available in the EPM add-in.

4.4.1 BPC Access via the Web Services to the Excel Add-In

You need to be aware of the different connections available using the EPM add-in so you know that you're using the appropriate connection to achieve the results required. The flexibility of the EPM add-in to link to other third-party toolsets is limited, but you always have the option to move the data through the BW environment, and then the add-in can display the data via either a Basic InfoCube or a Virtual InfoCube. The additional connections to other third-party sources of data can be viewed by choosing LOCAL from the CONNECTION TYPE list as shown in Figure 4.13.

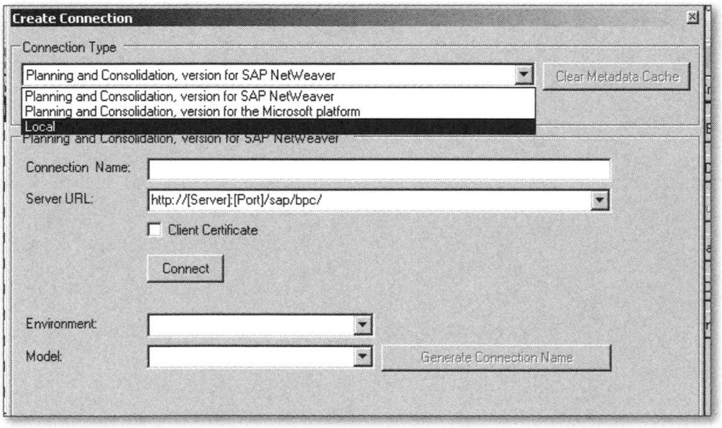

Figure 4.13 Creating a Local Connection

After this link is created, select the USE XMLA TO CONNECT TO MICROSOFT ANALYSIS SOURCE and click on CREATE to access the dropdown of the different source systems that are available, including Oracle, Siebel, and other databases (see Figure 4.14). Of course, there will be additional setup on both sides to accommodate the connection, but these are available standard from the EPM add-in.

In addition, notice the parameter DO NOT LOAD MEMBERS AT CONNECTION in Figure 4.14. This is to support large data volumes but is only available using the Local connection approach. This is definitely something to remember during the performance testing process. If, for example, you're reporting off of the standard BPC model using the Web services connection, and the performance isn't up to what you expected, then you can see if creating a local connection with this parameter turned on will help with the processing of the master data and transactional data for faster reporting times. The file path to do so is CREATE CONNECTION • LOCAL • SSA AUTHENTICATION METHODS.

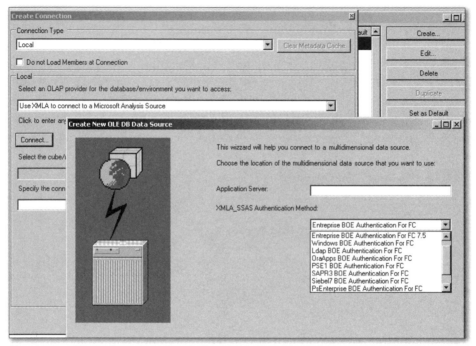

Figure 4.14 SSA Authentication Methods

Generally, you won't have to do all of this if the security set up in BPC is consistent with what you should be able to access. In other words, if you use the Web services connection directly from the BPC HOME page, you should see the BPC models that you have access to and can execute reporting and other data processing activities. From the HOME page, you execute the link to the EPM Office add-in for Excel to use the Web services connection. After the initial screen appears, you should see all of the BPC models that you have access and authorization to execute activities against. This executable is shown in Figure 4.15.

Launch
EPM Office Add-in Excel
EPM Office Add-in Word
EPM Office Add-in PowerPoint
Planning and Consolidation Administration

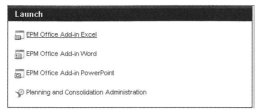

Figure 4.15 Launch Link for EPM Office add-in Excel

The available links are displayed in Figure 4.16. If your screen doesn't look like Figure 4.16, you may have to use the CREATE button to create the links. Then, if you follow the process explained in Chapter 2, Section 2.2 you'll be able to generate the connections. After the connections are initially displayed, you won't have to go through the create process again.

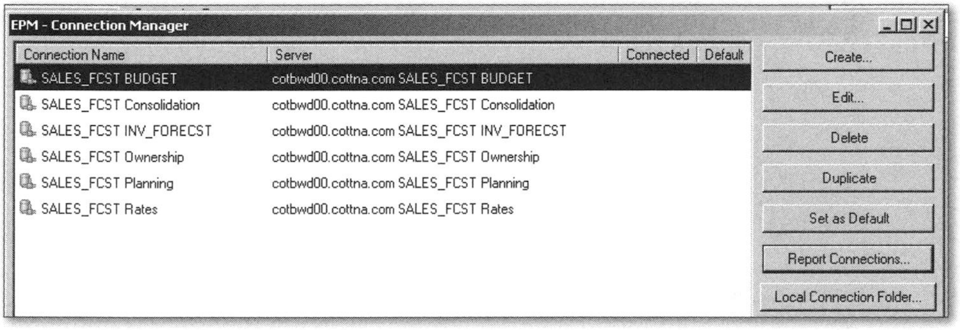

EPM - Connection Manager
Connection Name
Server
Connected
Default
SALES_FCST BUDGET
cotbwd00.cottna.com SALES_FCST BUDGET
SALES_FCST Consolidation
cotbwd00.cottna.com SALES_FCST Consolidation
SALES_FCST INV_FORECST
cotbwd00.cottna.com SALES_FCST INV_FORECST
SALES_FCST Ownership
cotbwd00.cottna.com SALES_FCST Ownership
SALES_FCST Planning
cotbwd00.cottna.com SALES_FCST Planning
SALES_FCST Rates
cotbwd00.cottna.com SALES_FCST Rates
Create...
Edit...
Delete
Duplicate
Set as Default
Report Connections...
Local Connection Folder...

Figure 4.16 EPM – Connection Manager View of BPC Models

Now that we have access to the BPC models via the Web services for BPC, we can review the features available in the EPM add-in.

4.5 Navigation in the EPM Add-In

Your initial view of the EPM add-in should give you some feeling of comfort because it looks like and acts like an Excel spreadsheet. In fact, you may decide to use only the Excel-based features to create useful and functional reports. You can also save your work, and all of the Excel features that you inserted into your report are available the next time you execute the report. But the EPM add-in has its own ribbon, which is displayed after the EPM add-in is installed on your laptop, and this is what we'll discuss and review in this section.

There may be times where either your EPM add-in isn't working or you want to deactivate it for some reason. To accomplish this, go to the START button on the Excel worksheet, and click EXCEL OPTIONS as shown in Figure 4.17.

Figure 4.17 Accessing the Excel Options Dialog Box

In the EXCEL OPTIONS dialog box, select ADD-INS on the left side to see the EPM add-in files as shown in Figure 4.18. Notice the COM ADD-IN entry in the TYPE column to the right of the selected EPM add-in line. Change the MANAGE option at the bottom of the page to COM ADD-IN, and click on GO. This will take you to the COM ADD-INS screen where the EPM ADD-IN FOR MICROSOFT OFFICE is checked as being active (see Figure 4.19).

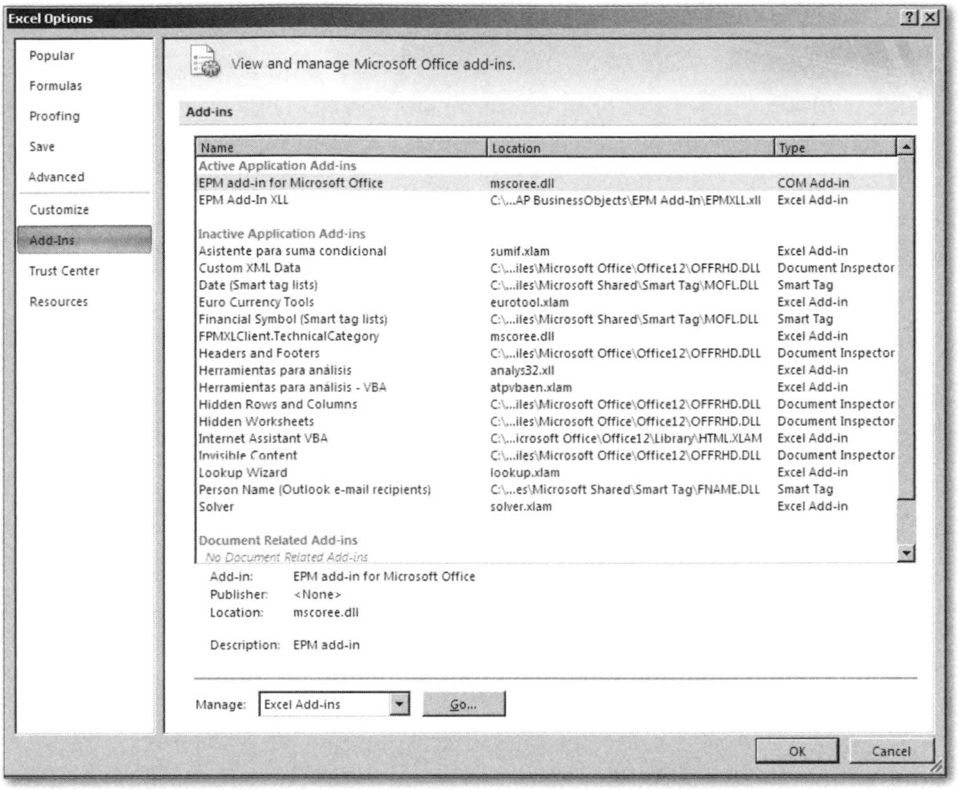

Figure 4.18 EPM add-in File for Microsoft Office

Figure 4.19 Selecting the EPM add-in for Microsoft Office

From here, you can uncheck the add-in to deactivate it as well. If you find that the add-in is deactivated, you come here to reactivate it. This may occur if you encounter an Excel error that generates a critical Excel error and automatically deactivates the Excel add-in.

4.5.1 Initial EPM Add-In Screen – Context and Current Report Panes

After you access the EPM add-in, you want to start to quickly get a feel for and understand what all of the options are on the screen. Let's start with the basic information to quickly understand what is useful and how to use it. The first items to understand are the different context and navigation panes that are available. Figure 4.20 shows that there are really two different portions of the screen with the lists of the dimensions available.

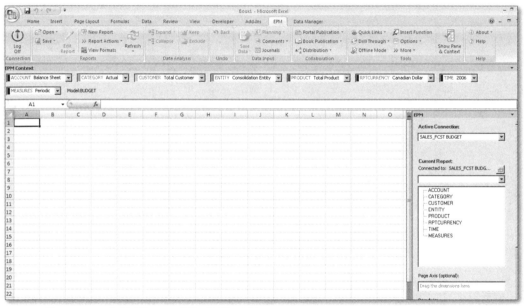

Figure 4.20 Initial Screen of the EPM add-in

You can use the arrow to the far right to move the EPM Context menu from the horizontal view above the worksheet to a vertical navigational pane view as shown in Figure 4.21. You can see that the list of dimensions is the same as the MODEL: BUDGET. The difference here is that the EPM CONTEXT menu (on the left) controls the entire workbook and all of the worksheets, while the CURRENT REPORT navigation pane (on the right) controls the report that is currently being displayed in the worksheet. This means that if you have multiple reports in this workbook, then you can manage the filters for all of the dimensions on all of the worksheets in the workbook based on the EPM CONTEXT menu and therefore assign the filter just once to impact all of the reports. This, of course, is if all of the reports are sourced from the one Budget model. A very good option if, for example, you were to create a series of reports with another option under the REPORT ACTIONS link, which would generate a set of reports with different filters for company codes. Then if you wanted to filter *all* of the worksheets by a specific category member, you could use the EPM CONTEXT menu.

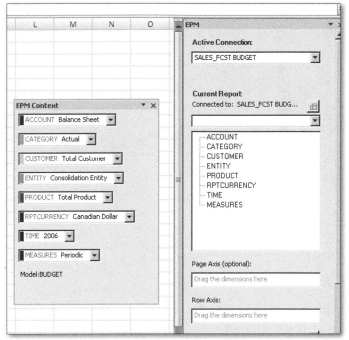

Figure 4.21 EPM Context Menu and Current Report Navigation Pane

In many cases, you'll work more from the CURRENT REPORT navigation pane to create your report, but the EPM CONTEXT menu may come in handy. The ability to show or display these objects can be controlled by the parameters in the OPTIONS link, which you'll see later in this chapter.

4.5.2 Build a Basic Report

Before we head into the actual EPM ribbon with all of the options available, let's create a basic report. We need to show some of the features to get a better idea of their effect, and to do that, we need an ad hoc report. We start by choosing OPTIONS • SHEET OPTIONS, and then selecting the ACTIVATE MEMBER RECOGNITION and ACTIVATE LOCAL MEMBER RECOGNITION checkboxes, as shown in Figure 4.22. This allows you to type in members of the dimensions into your report, and the report will attempt to recognize the values and assign them the EPM link to the member values in the system. After these parameters are checked, click OK to close the EPM – SHEET OPTION screen.

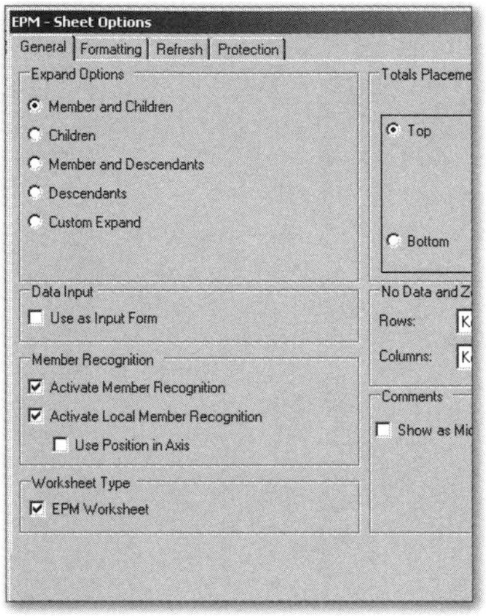

Figure 4.22 EPM – Sheet Options: Activate Member Recognition

You'll see that there are several different approaches to creating reports. We'll present all of the options in this chapter, and you can choose the one that works for you. To complete the build of a basic report, follow these steps:

1. Type in the member value "Total Customer" in one of the cells of the worksheet (Figure 4.23).

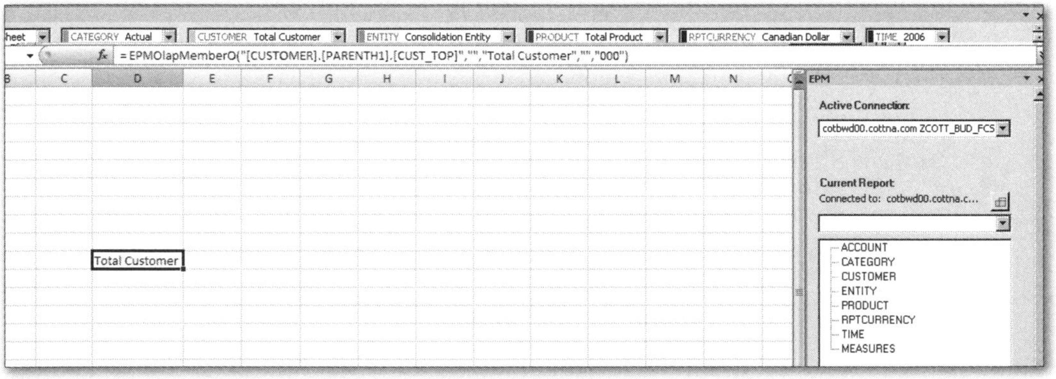

Figure 4.23 Typing in "Total Customer" in Cell D10

2. Type in the member value "2011" in one of the cells of the worksheet (Figure 4.24).

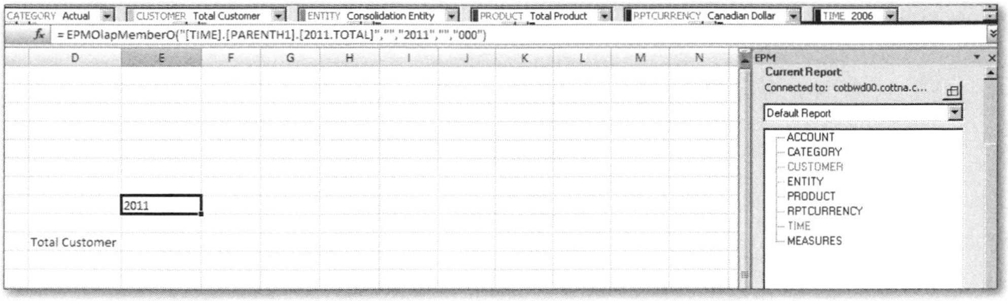

Figure 4.24 Typing in "2011" in Cell E8

3. Continue to type in dimension member values into the Excel worksheet in cells A1 through A8. These additional members are specific to the dimensions in the CURRENT REPORT pane: SALES QUANTITY, ACTUAL, WORLD, TOTAL PRODUCT, and EACH (see Figure 4.25), which correspond with the Account, Category, Entity, Product, and Rptcurrency dimensions. This creates the navigation pane in the report where you can adjust the filters that will impact the report information.

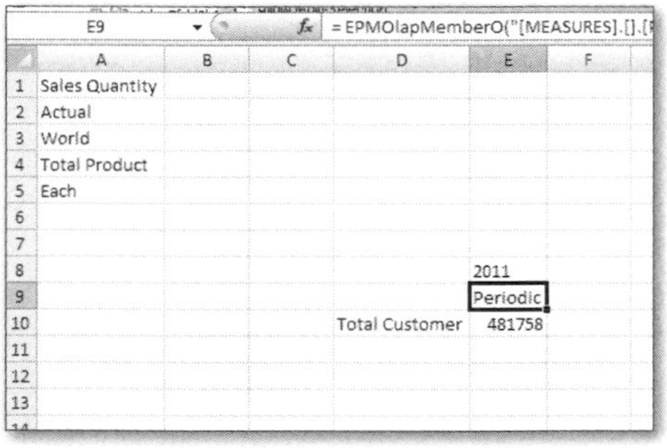

Figure 4.25 Additional Dimension Members in Cells A1 through A5

4. After this is complete, double-click on the value, a member selection sheet will be displayed, and you can switch between members. In cell E9, type in the value "Periodic" for the Measure.

As you can see, this immediately generates a value in the intersection cell of the Time dimension—2011—and the TOTAL CUSTOMER value for the Customer dimension. The TOTAL CUSTOMER value is a hierarchy of all of the customer values, so the result is a summary level sales quantity for all of the products and all of the entities.

You can also double-click on the value TOTAL CUSTOMER and expand this to the full list of customer values. This is available because we turned on the option to allow double-clicking for our reports (see Figure 4.26). You can access this option by choosing USER OPTIONS • NAVIGATION • ENABLE DOUBLE-CLICK.

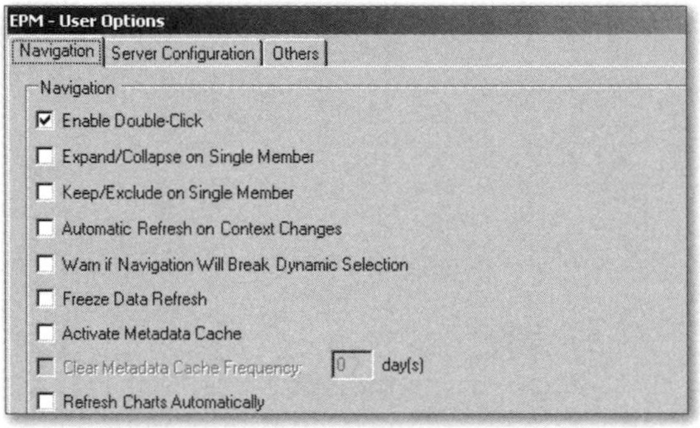

Figure 4.26 Enabling the Double-Click Option

5. Once you double-click on the TOTAL CUSTOMER, the EPM is processing the request, which allows you to see that during the execution of the drilldown process, you can also cancel the execution process. This not only cancels the execution from the frontend but also cancels the processing at the SQL level. This is a true cancel option and not just a cancellation of the frontend process.

The final view of the results of the drilldown process is shown in Figure 4.27.

As you can see, the top node of the hierarchy is still visible, and again, this is an option during the building of your report. You can either keep the intermediate nodes or remove them from the display and only see the members that make up that node. You've now created a basic ad hoc report in the EPM add-in.

This option requires that you have an idea of the member values of your dimensions. This may or may not be something that you feel comfortable with. Over time, as you get more comfortable with this toolset, you'll be looking to do more and more of this type of processing. If you're coming from an Essbase or an EvDRE background, you'll feel very comfortable with this approach.

The other two approaches are more aligned with those who have a BEX Analyzer background because it doesn't require you to know the actual member values to type them in—you can just pick them from a list or selection screen. These other approaches to the creation of a report are more wizard based, where the system steps you through the process by offering a wizard-like format or screen and the use of the NEW REPORT option from the EPM ribbon.

	A	B	C	D	E	F	G
1	Sales Quantity						
2	Actual						
3	World						
4	Total Product						
5	Each						
6							
7							
8					2011		
9					Periodic		
10				Total Customer	481758		
11				C_1000003	16992		
12				C_1000006	10789		
13				C_1000009	24111		
14				C_1000013	12536		
15				C_1000027	18244		
16				C_1000037	6901		
17				C_1000043	15798		
18				C_1000320	27970		
19				C_206100	10320		
20				C_210000	8305		
21				C_210100	8305		
22				C_302400	17495		
23				C_303800	30223		
24				C_307900	5799		
25				C_309100	43442		

Figure 4.27 Drilldown on the Hierarchy Total Customer

The initial one that you can immediately see on your EPM add-in is the drag-and-drop process on the CURRENT REPORT navigation pane shown in Figure 4.28. The CURRENT REPORT pane has been moved to the center of the screen to give you the full view of the navigation pane. The comment DRAG THE DIMENSIONS HERE gives you the hint to click on a dimension and drag it either to the ROW AXIS, COLUMN AXIS, or PAGE AXIS text boxes. The ROW AXIS and COLUMN AXIS are straightforward, and the PAGE AXIS is creating a navigation pane in the report for any dimensions that filter the data in the current report. The results are the same as those displayed using the member recognition process, but this may be a bit easier and user friendly. After the values are assigned to the correct axes, you can double-click on them to open the member selection screen and switch values.

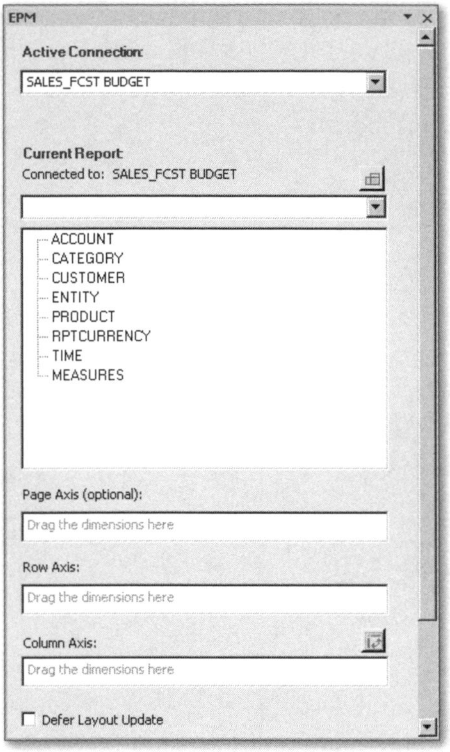

Figure 4.28 Current Report Navigation Pane

The completed view of this CURRENT REPORT screen is displayed in Figure 4.29. Notice the DEFER LAYOUT UPDATE option is selected. If you don't select this checkbox, the system will execute a refresh every time you add a dimension to either the rows or columns, causing significant time to be lost waiting for the report to refresh. If you have 20 or so dimensions to move, it can be very time consuming. After you're finished, just click on UPDATE at the bottom, and your report is refreshed once.

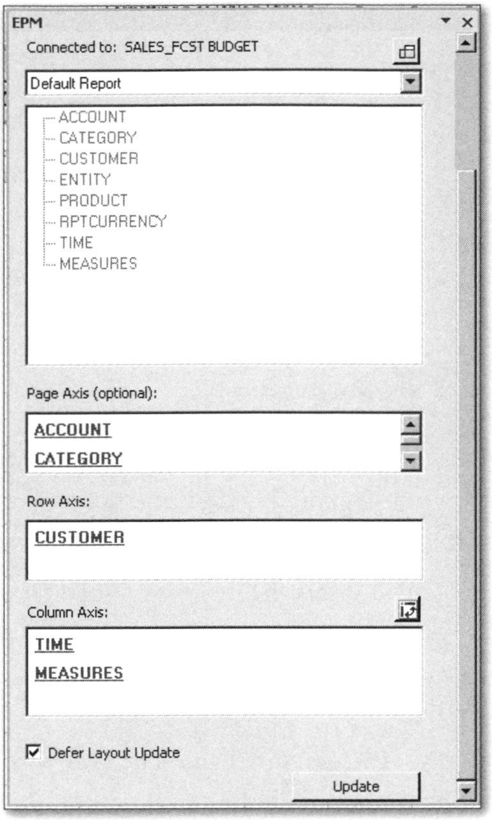

Figure 4.29 EPM Current Report Pane Filled in Using Drag and Drop for Dimensions

One other comment to be made with this approach is in reference to the member selection screen that appears if you double-click on the dimension (see Figure 4.30). This shows the default values in the EPM CONTEXT view. You can see the CONTEXT (ACTUAL) menu value at the very top of the list.

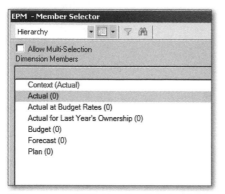

Figure 4.30 EPM Member Selector Screen – Context (Actual) Member Value

The final approach to creating a report is to use the NEW REPORT option in the REPORTS section of the EPM ribbon as shown in Figure 4.31. This method offers everything in one place and offers the following options:

▸ The ability to use the drag and drop process to insert the dimension members into the report.

▸ The ability to move the report around using the Shift arrows and align the report on the worksheet in the exact cells required.

▸ An automatic RESET REPORT option to allow the user to reset and start over with the build.

▸ Access to the member selection screen from the dimension.

▸ Report doesn't refresh while using this approach, so no need to activate the DEFER LAYOUT UPDATE option.

▸ All of the other options available in a report on the nine different tabs on this dialog box.

We'll dive into all of the other tabs in EPM Report Editor a bit later in this chapter.

Now that you understand the differences between the report creation methods, you can choose whatever approach you feel more comfortable using to create reports.

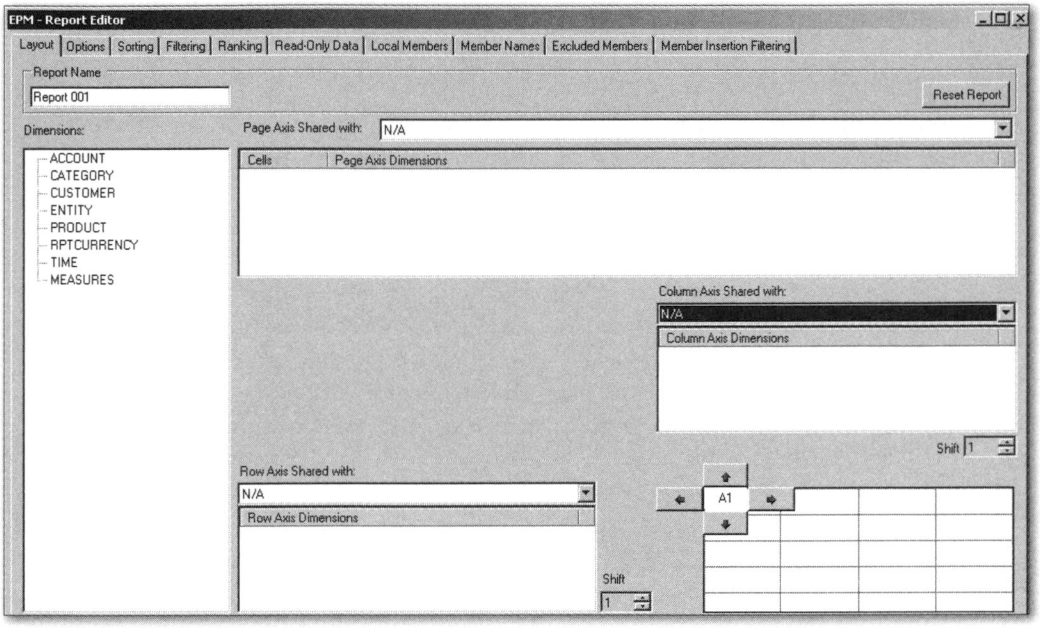

EPM - Report Editor
Layout
Options
Sorting
Filtering
Ranking
Read-Only Data
Local Members
Member Names
Excluded Members
Member Insertion Filtering
Report Name
Report 001
Reset Report
Dimensions:
Page Axis Shared with:
N/A
ACCOUNT
CATEGORY
CUSTOMER
ENTITY
PRODUCT
RPTCURRENCY
TIME
MEASURES
Cells
Page Axis Dimensions
Column Axis Shared with:
N/A
Column Axis Dimensions
Shift
1
Row Axis Shared with:
N/A
Row Axis Dimensions
A1
Shift
1

Figure 4.31 The EPM – Report Editor

4.6 Review of the EPM Ribbon

Now that you can see how easy it is to create a basic report, let's look at some of the features that will help you enhance the reports that you're creating as well as add additional functionality that will support the functional specification requirements. The best place to start is with the EPM ribbon. The ribbon has specific sections that contain quite a few valuable options (see Figure 4.32). We'll briefly look at a couple of options located in the SHEET OPTIONS and the USER OPTIONS portion of the ribbon.

Home
Insert
Page Layout
Formulas
Data
Review
View
Developer
Add-Ins
EPM
Data Manager
Log Off
Open
Save
Edit Report
New Report
Report Actions
View Formats
Refresh
Expand
Collapse
Keep
Exclude
Back
Save Data
Planning
Comments
Journals
Portal Publication
Book Publication
Distribution
Quick Links
Drill Through
Offline Mode
Insert Function
Options
More
Show Pane & Context
About
Help
Connection
Reports
Data Analysis
Undo
Data Input
Collaboration
Tools
Help

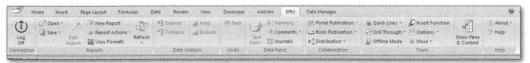

Figure 4.32 EPM add-in Ribbon

You'll likely find that when working with the EPM add-in, the options available in the different areas of the ribbon will be helpful for 60% of your requirements.

These options range from different levels for the refresh of your data to the creation of local members that can be used for combining information and executing calculations (similar to a Calculated Key Figure in BW). The features will support requirements around the ability to distribute your reports as well as create a book of reports for distribution via a printer or PDF. There are also options to create links between reports so that the business user can go from a summary view of the report to a more detailed report with additional information and functions.

> **Note: Calculated Key Figure Terminology**
>
> A calculated key figure (CKF) is a term used in the BEX Query Designer. A CKF is a combination of multiple other key figures and characteristics to create a result or calculation. For example, a CKF can be used to sum up a series of periods to create a quarterly YTD value to be displayed in a report. This can be accomplished by creating a local member or global member for use in your reports.

We'll be looking at each area of the EPM ribbon to understand what options are available and to provide examples where required to clarify the feature and results.

4.6.1 Reports

The REPORTS portion of the EPM ribbon offers tasks dealing with the initial creation of the report, opening and saving existing reports, report actions, the formatting features for EPM, and the refresh options. The EDIT REPORT and NEW REPORT dialog boxes as well as the formatting features offer a significant amount of information and options. We'll go into detail around these three functions in Section 4.8 when we discuss the advanced functions. For now, we'll focus on the other activities in this section.

Open and Save

Figure 4.33 shows the dropdowns for the OPEN and SAVE options. These two options are fairly straightforward and reference the location of where the reports and input templates are saved if you're working with a Web services connection in BPC. If you access the EPM add-in via the OLE DB link, these two options won't be available, and the only save is to a SharePoint site or a local drive. So this option is only available via the Web services connection. You'll notice that there are two distinct options in this list: opening and saving my reports/input forms or server based reports/input forms.

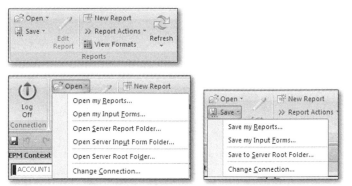

Figure 4.33 Reports Section of the EPM Ribbon: Open and Save

Table 4.1 shows the different levels of SAVE and OPEN with a description of the functionality.

Feature Name	Description
OPEN	
OPEN MY REPORTS	This allows the business user to open reports from a local drive or SharePoint.
OPEN MY INPUT FORMS	This allows the business user to open input forms from a local drive or SharePoint.
OPEN SERVER REPORT FOLDER	This allows the business user to open reports that have been saved to the server.
OPEN SERVER INPUT FORM FOLDER	This allows the business user to open input forms that have been saved to the server.
OPEN SERVER ROOT FOLDER	This allows the business user to open reports or input forms found on the server. This ROOT folder is a combination of both REPORT and INPUT FORM folders.
CHANGE CONNECTION (OPEN and SAVE)	This allows the user to change connections from the current report connection to others. This supports the ability to have multiple source system connections to one workbook. This is for both OPEN and SAVE.

Table 4.1 Save and Open Options in the Report Portion of the EPM Ribbon

Feature Name	Description
SAVE	
SAVE MY REPORTS	This allows the business user to save reports from a local drive or SharePoint.
SAVE MY INPUT FORMS	This allows the business user to save input forms from a local drive or SharePoint.
SAVE TO SERVER ROOT FOLDER	This allows the business user to save reports or input forms found on the server. This ROOT folder is a combination of both REPORT and INPUT FORM folders.

Table 4.1 Save and Open Options in the Report Portion of the EPM Ribbon (Cont.)

Figure 4.34 shows the results of choosing the OPEN SERVER ROOT FOLDER option. As you can see, the access is to all of the different folders. You'll also notice that you see the folders LOCAL, COMPANY, and ADMIN. This is due to security that is assigned. Based on the task profile that is assigned, you may see a specific number of folders but the LOCAL folder will always be available.

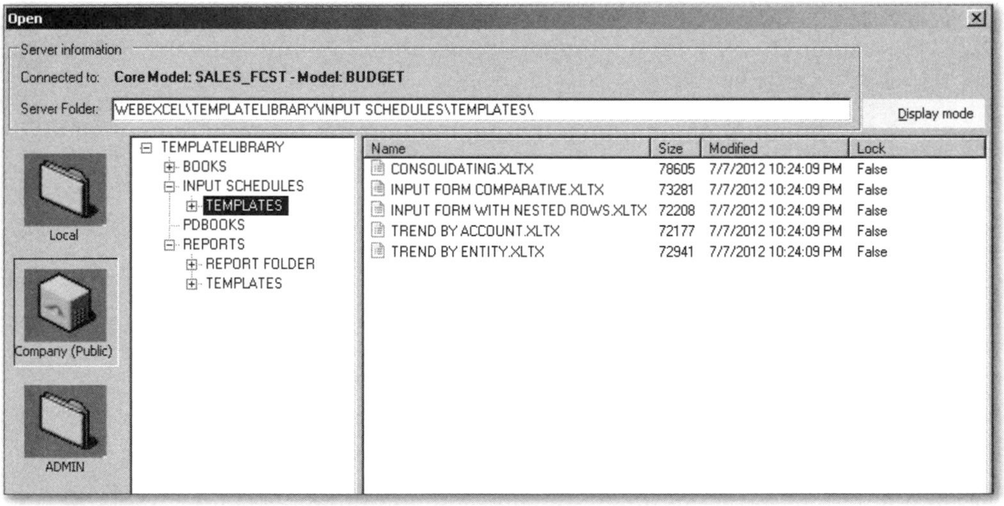

Figure 4.34 Open Server Root Folder Option

Report Action and Format

The next section of the Reports portion of the EPM ribbon is the Report Actions and Format options. As mentioned, the formatting of the Report portion will be covered later in the chapter in Section 4.8. In the Report Actions dropdown, there are a number of options available (see Figure 4.35).

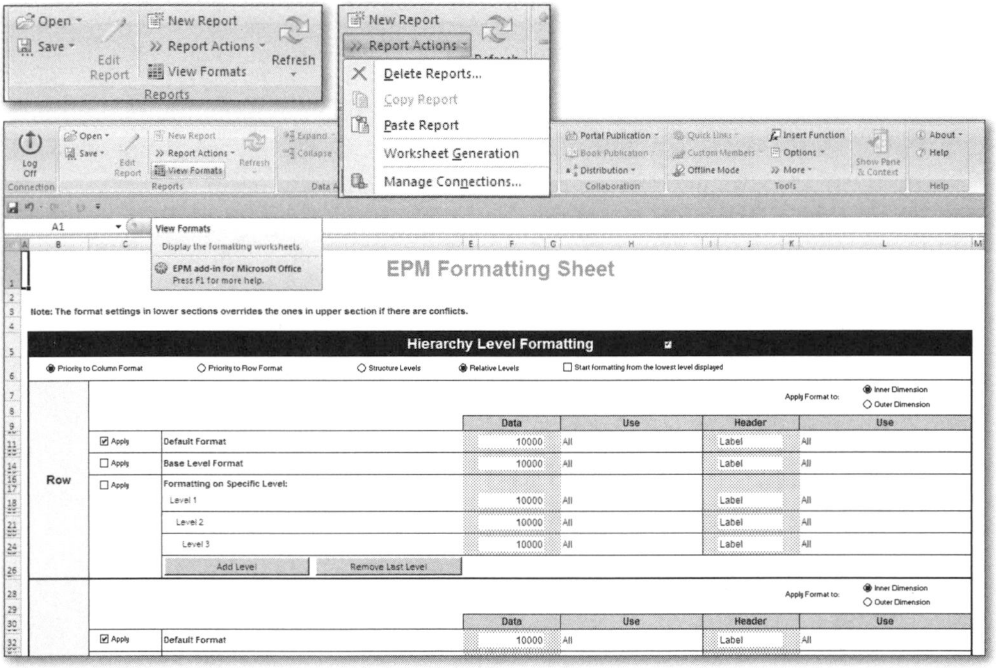

Figure 4.35 Reports Portion of the EPM Ribbon – View Formats and Report Actions

Table 4.2 shows the feature name and description of the use of the function.

Feature Name	Description
Delete Reports	Allows the business user the ability to delete reports.
Copy Report	Allows the business user the ability to copy reports. This feature can also use the Excel option to copy and paste reports.
Paste Report	Allows the business user the ability to paste reports. This feature can also use the Excel option to copy and paste reports.

Table 4.2 Report Action Features and Descriptions

Feature Name	Description
WORKSHEET GENERATION	Allows the business user to take a report, and based on a member selection, add multiple worksheets with the same report but filtered by the selected members.
MANAGE CONNECTIONS	Allows the business user to display the different connections that he has set up or is available to execute.

Table 4.2 Report Action Features and Descriptions (Cont.)

Of this group of features, the one that is most interesting and the most popular to business users is WORKSHEET GENERATION. This feature allows the business user to burst out a series of reports with a specific filter dimension. For example, if you use the basic report you created, you can choose to execute the worksheet generation based on the entities as shown in Figure 4.36. Here, we've chosen the WORKSHEET GENERATION option and chosen to use the PRODUCT as the selection dimension. As you can see, there are three products: PRODUCT A, PRODUCT B, and PRODUCT C.

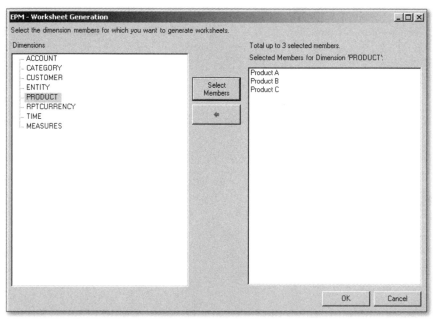

Figure 4.36 EPM – Worksheet Generation: Product

After this is complete, click on OK, and execute the worksheet generation process. Initially, we had only one worksheet with information, now we have three based on the three different products, as shown in Figure 4.37. The data is distributed to the three different tabs based on the driver: PRODUCT.

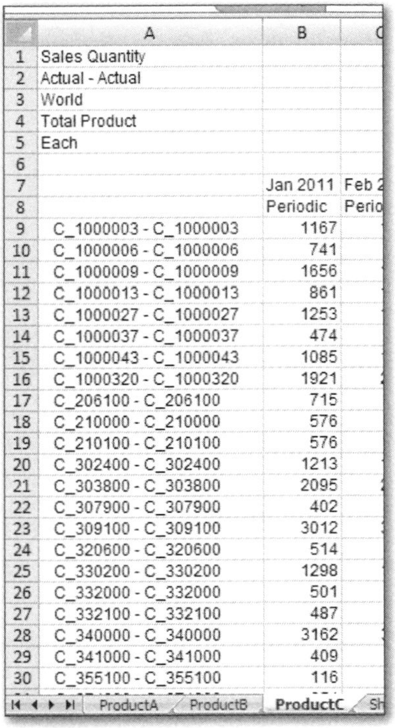

	A	B	C
1	Sales Quantity		
2	Actual - Actual		
3	World		
4	Total Product		
5	Each		
6			
7		Jan 2011	Feb 2
8		Periodic	Perio
9	C_1000003 - C_1000003	1167	
10	C_1000006 - C_1000006	741	
11	C_1000009 - C_1000009	1656	
12	C_1000013 - C_1000013	861	
13	C_1000027 - C_1000027	1253	
14	C_1000037 - C_1000037	474	
15	C_1000043 - C_1000043	1085	
16	C_1000320 - C_1000320	1921	
17	C_206100 - C_206100	715	
18	C_210000 - C_210000	576	
19	C_210100 - C_210100	576	
20	C_302400 - C_302400	1213	
21	C_303800 - C_303800	2095	
22	C_307900 - C_307900	402	
23	C_309100 - C_309100	3012	
24	C_320600 - C_320600	514	
25	C_330200 - C_330200	1298	
26	C_332000 - C_332000	501	
27	C_332100 - C_332100	487	
28	C_340000 - C_340000	3162	
29	C_341000 - C_341000	409	
30	C_355100 - C_355100	116	

ProductA / ProductB / **ProductC** / Sh

Figure 4.37 Results of the Worksheet Generation Process

Refresh

The next feature in the REPORTS portion of the EPM ribbon is the REFRESH option. In this dropdown, there are several refresh options, which can be significant depending on the total data volume in the report. For example, in a report using millions of records to generate the results, it's faster to only refresh a specific portion of the report instead of the entire report. Figure 4.38 shows the dropdown options.

Figure 4.38 Report – Refresh Option Dropdown

Table 4.3 gives an explanation of each of the REFRESH options.

Feature Name	Description
REFRESH REPORT DATA ONLY	Refreshes only the data for all of the reports in the worksheets, except the data for local members.
REFRESH SELECTED REPORT	Refreshes the data of the selected report and the report itself (including local member data, formatting, etc.).
REFRESH WORKSHEET	Refreshes everything that is in the current worksheet: the data of the reports, the data of the EPM functions, all of the reports (including local member data, formatting, etc.) and all EPM functions.
REFRESH WORKBOOK	Refreshes everything that is in the current workbook: the data of the reports, the data of the EPM functions, all of the reports, and all EPM functions.
REFRESH SELECTED DATA	Refreshes the selected data. For a report, you can refresh one cell range at a time and all of the cells of that range must belong to the same report. You can also refresh the EPM functions selected.

Table 4.3 Refresh Options and Descriptions

There is a distinct separation of these refresh options based on the data itself and the EPM functions/format. Review this list and make sure you're comfortable with the outcome of the refresh that you're using.

Edit and New Report

We mentioned that these features will be discussed late in this chapter because of the amount of functionality available in these two components. If you just look at the initial screen for both of these options, you can see that there are significant tasks that can be accomplished using these two options (see Figure 4.39). This definitely requires additional detailed discussion, which will lay out the multiple features.

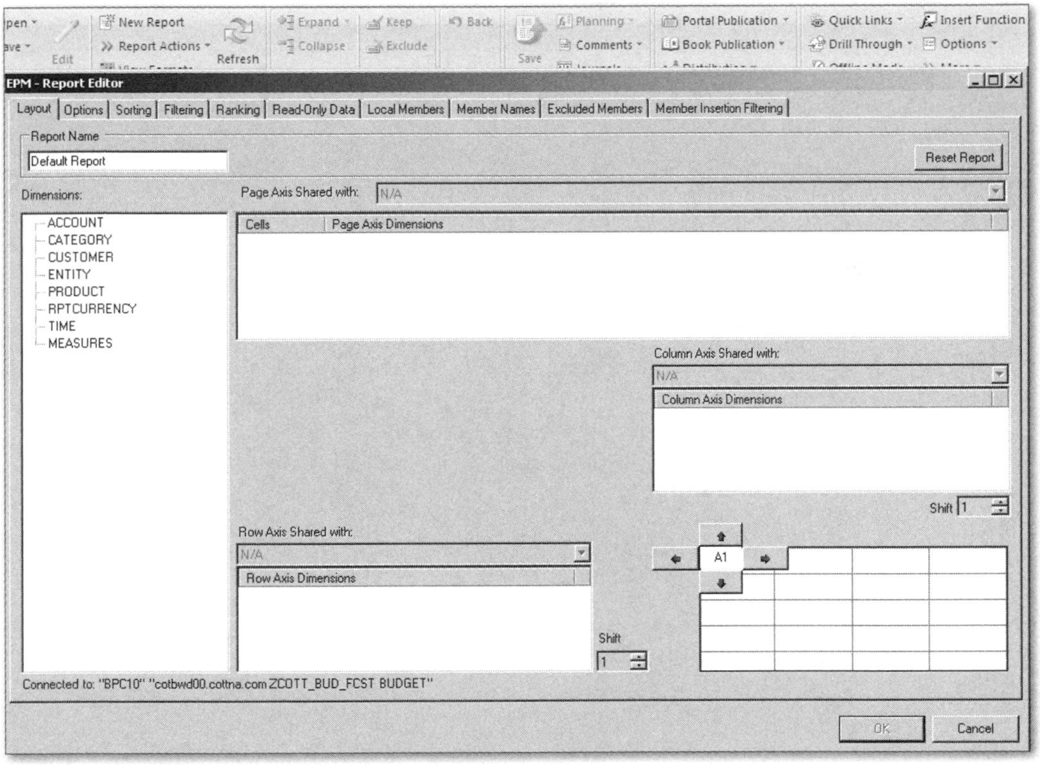

Figure 4.39 EPM – Report Editor and New Report Initial Screen

4.6.2   Data Analysis

The DATA ANALYSIS portion of the EPM ribbon focuses on the drilldown and filter process within the report. There are several drilldown options: EXPAND/COLLAPSE and KEEP/EXCLUDE, shown in Figure 4.40 that we will review further.

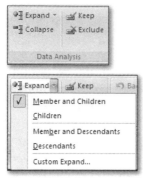

Figure 4.40 Expand/Collapse and Keep/Exclude Options

Expand/Collapse

The EXPAND option offers additional details around the level of expansion that is required. The options available for EXPAND/COLLAPSE are described in Table 4.4.

Feature Name	Description
EXPAND	
MEMBER AND CHILDREN	This expansion displays the member that you identified as the initial expansion point as well as the children of that member.
CHILDREN	This expansion displays the children of that member that were identified as the initial expansion point. It doesn't keep the member itself.
MEMBER AND DESCENDANTS	This expansion displays the member that you identified as the initial expansion point as well as the descendants of that member.
DESCENDANTS	This expansion displays the descendants of that member that were identified as the initial expansion point. It doesn't keep the member itself.
CUSTOM EXPAND	When you select this option, a dialog box opens, and you can define the levels you want to display and whether you want to include the selected member or not, for example, only level 3, the children of the selected member only, from/to specific levels, and only base members.

Table 4.4 Expand/Collapse Features and Description

Feature Name	Description
COLLAPSE	
COLLAPSE	This option allows the user to collapse a hierarchy from a specific lower level to an upper level. This can also be accomplished by double-clicking on the upper-level node as well.

Table 4.4 Expand/Collapse Features and Description (Cont.)

Keep/Exclude

The options available for the KEEP/EXCLUDE are shown in Table 4.5.

Feature Name	Description
KEEP	This option will keep all occurrences of the selected members, including all occurrences in an inner nested dimension. All other members are excluded.
EXCLUDE	This option will take away all occurrences of the selected members, including all occurrences in an inner nested dimension. All other members are kept.

Table 4.5 Keep and Exclude Options in the EPM Ribbon

An example of this feature is the ability to select specific values to keep in the report. Rather than having to open the member select screen to accomplish this, you can do this directly from the report screen. Figure 4.41 shows that we've selected two different sets of values in the report. This includes values C_1000006 and a group from C_206100 to C_302400 (rows 17 through 20 in Figure 4.41.)

Figure 4.41 EPM Report with Sections Highlighted for the "Keep" Feature

After executing the KEEP feature, the report reflects only the kept values, as shown in Figure 4.42.

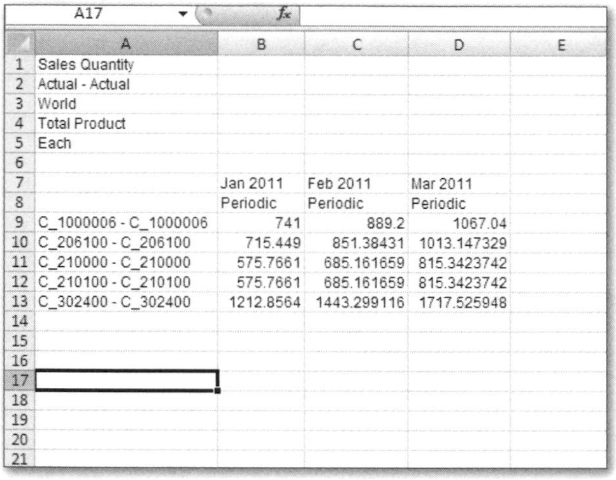

	A	B	C	D	E
	A17		fx		
1	Sales Quantity				
2	Actual - Actual				
3	World				
4	Total Product				
5	Each				
6					
7		Jan 2011	Feb 2011	Mar 2011	
8		Periodic	Periodic	Periodic	
9	C_1000006 - C_1000006	741	889.2	1067.04	
10	C_206100 - C_206100	715.449	851.38431	1013.147329	
11	C_210000 - C_210000	575.7661	685.161659	815.3423742	
12	C_210100 - C_210100	575.7661	685.161659	815.3423742	
13	C_302400 - C_302400	1212.8564	1443.299116	1717.525948	
14					
15					
16					
17					
18					
19					
20					
21					

Figure 4.42 Results of Executing "Keep" on the Initial Report

4.6.3 Undo

There are two UNDO' functions: one that you use for the EPM features and one for the Excel features. This section discusses the UNDO that is specific to the EPM features, which can be found in the UNDO portion of the ribbon as shown in Figure 4.43.

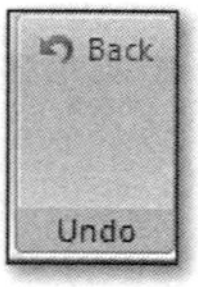

Figure 4.43 Undo in the EPM Ribbon

You might, for example, execute the UNDO feature on the last EPM KEEP feature to cause the report to revert to the view of all of the customers in the list.

The additional UNDO using the Excel features can be found at the very top of the EPM screen to the far left. An example of this is if you were to add some formatting using the Excel functions such as changing the font or size of the print or any other Excel feature, including the use of formulas. You could then use this UNDO feature to revert back to the original format or cell definition in the case of a formula.

4.6.4 Data Input

The DATA INPUT portion of the EPM ribbon deals with a series of activities that execute the process of writing information back to the BPC models. The process of writing back information can be either master data, transactional data, or basic comments, or calling the JOURNAL ENTRY screen for posting JE entries to the system. As you can guess, the options for PLANNING and SAVE DATA have to do with an EPM add-in that's an input template versus a report and are more aligned to a planning process, whereas the option of executing a JV entry is specific to the consolidation process. The only option that is aligned to all of the different activities is the ability to save a comment to the BW database for future display. These components are shown in Figure 4.44.

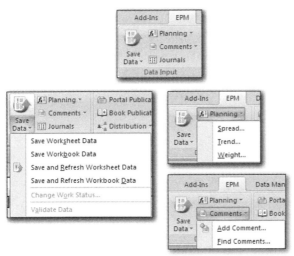

Figure 4.44 Data Input Portion of the EPM add-in Ribbon

Planning

The PLANNING portion has three different options to use during the planning process from the EPM approach. You have all of the different options available using basic Excel, but these three are specifically prompted from the EPM ribbon. To accommodate this, you need to have an input template open to activate these options. To show this feature, we'll use a basic input template and make sure that the USE AS INPUT FORM option in the SHEET OPTIONS dialog box is turned on, in Figure 4.45.

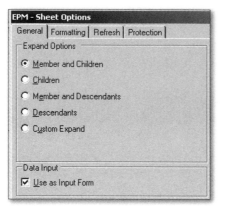

Figure 4.45 EPM Sheet Options – Use as Input Form

Now we'll add some data to the input template in the BUDGET category. Remember that when using an input template for planning, you must be posting at the base level member—the actual value itself. The inputted data is shown in Figure 4.46.

	A	B	C	D	E	F	G	H	I
1	Balance Sheet								
2	Budget								
3	Total Product								
4	Canadian Dollar								
5									
6			Jan 2011	Feb 2011	Mar 2011	Apr 2011	May 2011	Jun 2011	Jul 2011 A
7			Periodic	Periodic	Periodic	Periodic	Periodic	Periodic	Periodic P
8	C_1000003	Consolidation Entity	50	40	30	40			
9	C_1000006	Consolidation Entity							
10	C_1000009	Consolidation Entity							
11	C_1000013	Consolidation Entity							
12	C_1000027	Consolidation Entity							

Figure 4.46 EPM add-in as an Input Template with Data

Access the option to use spread for the data in the input form, as shown in Figure 4.47. As you can see, the fields that require information are SOURCE VALUE, DESTINATION, and WEIGHTS (OPTIONAL). You can also decide what to do with the results by choosing either OVERWRITE EXISTING VALUES or ADD TO EXISTING VALUES.

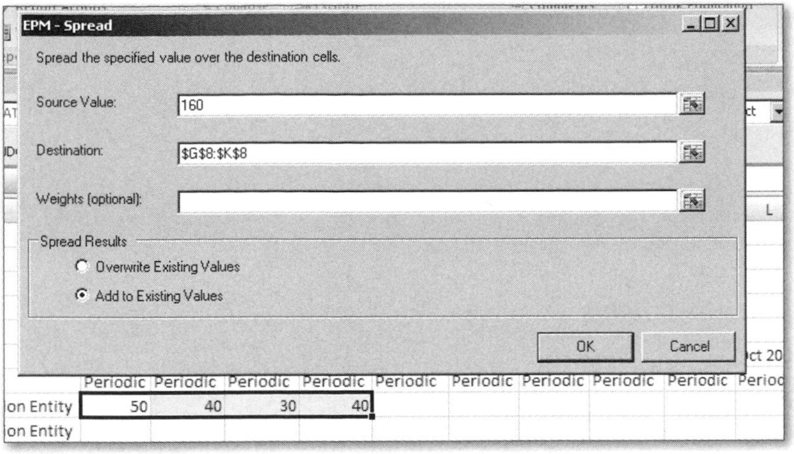

Figure 4.47 EPM – Spread Screen for the Data Input Process

In our situation we'll use the total values of the amounts entered which is "160", and spread these evenly over the next five periods. After all of the information is entered, click OK (see Figure 4.48).

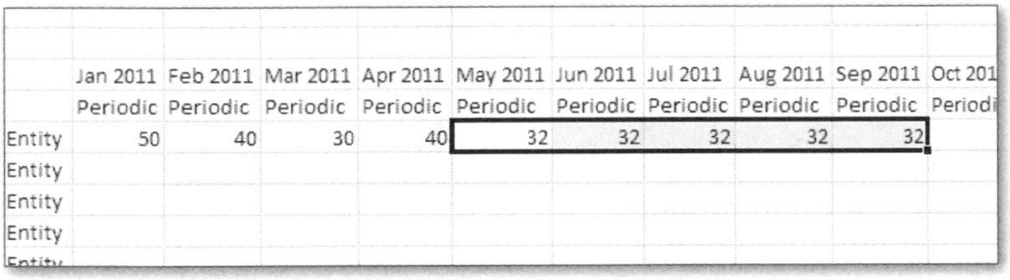

Figure 4.48 Results of Executing the Spread Feature for Planning

This can be a very useful tool to quickly enhance the data that you have in the input form. Assume that the information for JAN through APR is actuals, and you want to spread the average of the actuals over the next several months to use as the initial planning set of data. The other two options TREND and WEIGHT offer slightly different methods; for example, in the TREND option, the additional feature is the ability to trend BY PERCENTAGE or BY VALUE, and for the WEIGHT option, the offerings are BY PERCENTAGE, BY VALUE, or NONE. These options are shown in the TREND and WEIGHT PARAMETERS screens, Figure 4.49.

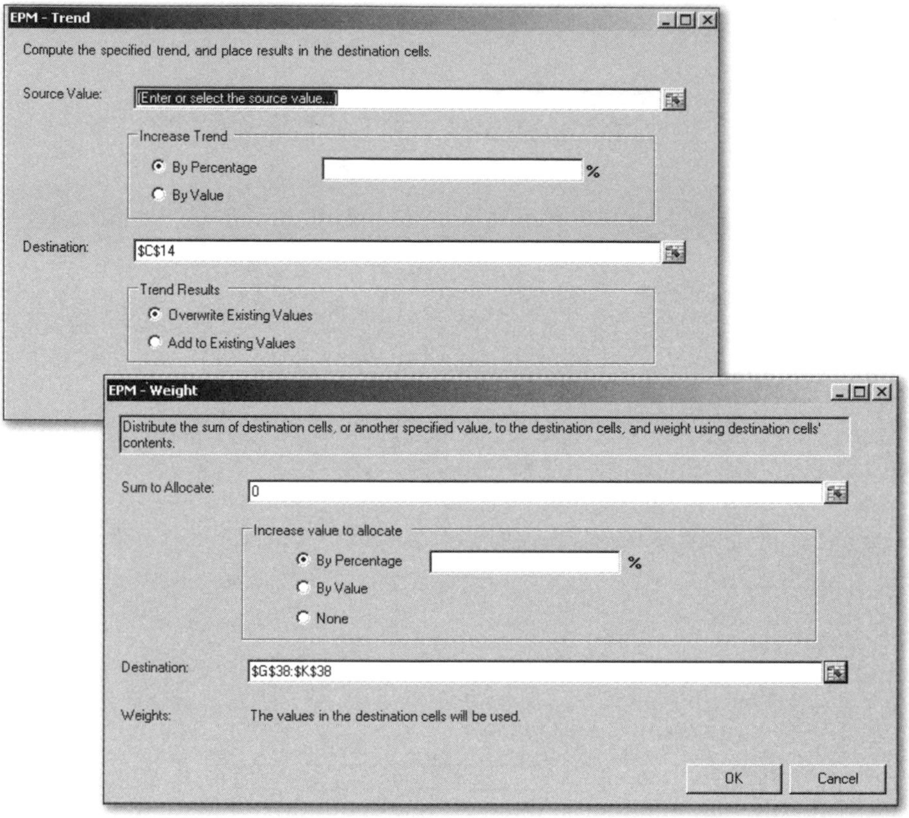

Figure 4.49 EPM – Trend and Weight Parameter Screens

Save Data

The SAVE DATA section of the DATA INPUT portion of the EPM ribbon is a logical follow-up discussion to the multiple planning options available because after you've executed the function, you then need to save the data. Using the first option in the SAVE DATA dropdown—SAVE WORKSHEET DATA—a notice is shown with the records of data you'll be saving (see Figure 4.50).

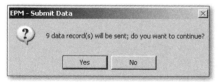

Figure 4.50 EPM – Submit Data for a Save process

The subsequent notice should be that the data has been saved as in Figure 4.51.

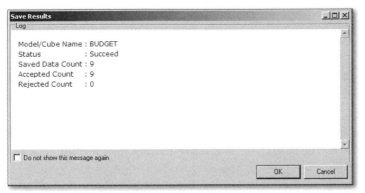

Figure 4.51 Save Results from the EPM Submit Data Process

The several SAVE options to choose from are listed in Table 4.6.

Feature Name	Description
SAVE WORKSHEET DATA	This option saves the data on the current worksheet.
SAVE WORKBOOK DATA	This option saves the data for the entire workbook.
SAVE AND REFRESH WORKSHEET DATA	This option saves the data in the worksheet to the server, and then the data are refreshed in the input form. This takes into account the data that you've saved and recalculates the amounts to be displayed. This option is the default option if you were to execute the SAVE DATA directly from the initial button.
SAVE AND REFRESH WORKBOOK DATA	This option saves the data in the workbook to the server, and then the data is refreshed in the input form. This takes into account the data that you've saved and recalculates the amounts to be displayed.

Table 4.6 Save Options Available from the EPM Ribbon

Note: Additional Save Feature

If the REFRESH ONLY DATA on SAVE & REFRESH DATA is selected in the USER OPTIONS screen, then during the refresh process, only the data for all EPM functions and all the reports in the worksheet are refreshed except for the local members. If this isn't selected, then the difference is that the local members and format will also be refreshed.

The final two options in this list—Change Work Status and Validate Data—are specific to BPC and require the WORK STATUS, CONTROLS, and VALIDATION features to be turned on in BPC to be available in the EPM add-in.

Comments

Comments can be very useful for both users that are viewing reports as well as those that are using BPC for P&F to document or track information as it's changing or to note something that looks inconsistent. To enable comments, you first need to activate it in the BPC model. If you look at the model configuration, you'll see that the ENABLE COMMENTS parameter is turned on for the Budget model in the FEATURES USED WITH THE MODEL portion of the screen (see Figure 4.52). You access this option via the ADMINISTRATION screen in the WEB ADMINISTRATION view of BPC. Then choose DIMENSION AND MODELS • MODELS • BUDGET • EDIT.

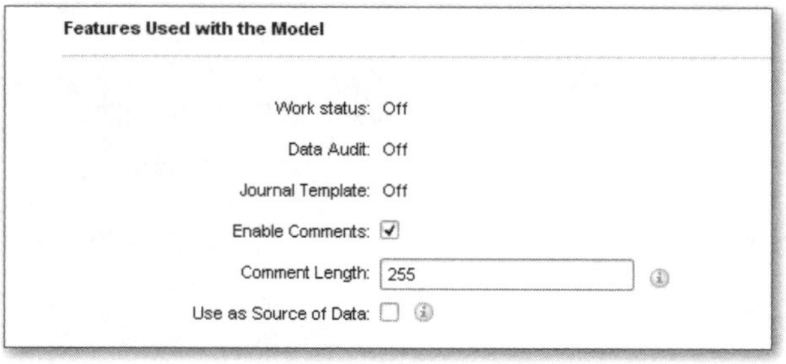

Figure 4.52 Enabling Comments

In the EPM add-in process, you can either use the BPC feature or the Excel feature to use comments. The difference between the two features is that the BPC option will allow you to link to the intersection of the information in the backend. So, if you attach a comment using this approach, your comment will follow the intersection of the data, whereas the Excel feature will be linked to the cell that you embed the data into and will only be viewed from that cell. So if you slice and dice your data, the comment may not follow the data as it moves around the screen. We'll highlight the BPC feature here because the Excel feature will work just about the same as you've been use to with Excel.

> **Note: Excel Feature**
>
> The Excel comments feature in the EPM add-in will work much better if you insert a column within the body of the report and use that as an option to insert a comment. If you attempt to use a column outside of the body of the report, the ability to link the comment to the data won't work as well as the former.

In the Comments feature, there are two options—ADD COMMENT and FIND COMMENT—as shown in Figure 4.53.

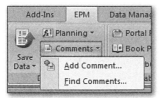

Figure 4.53 Add and Find Comments from the EPM Ribbon

To start, you click on a cell in the report, and then click on ADD COMMENT to open the EPM – ADD COMMENT dialog box as shown in Figure 4.54. The comment will automatically link to the intersection of the data in the EPM report. The following parameters are required:

▶ PRIORITY
  Assign a priority to the comment of CRITICAL, HIGH, MEDIUM, LOW, or NONE.

▶ COMMENT
  Insert a comment to attach.

▶ KEYWORD
  To search based on a keyword, you can assign a prompt in this field.

▶ CONTEXT OF COMMENT
  This will define the process of linking the comment to the data in the report.

▶ ACTIVE CELL: Assign the comments to the individual cell that has been identified.

▶ ACTIVE CONTEXT: The comment is applied to the context displayed in the EPM CONTEXT bar.

▶ CUSTOM CONTEXT: This option allows you to specify a different context than the current one to which to associate the comments. If this parameter is chosen, a list of dimensions will appear, and you can select a member or none of the members for each dimension.

In this case, we'll assign a priority of HIGH to the comment, add a comment, use the keyword "Validation" to allow a search for this comment, and use the ACTIVE CELL option to link the comment to the data intersection.

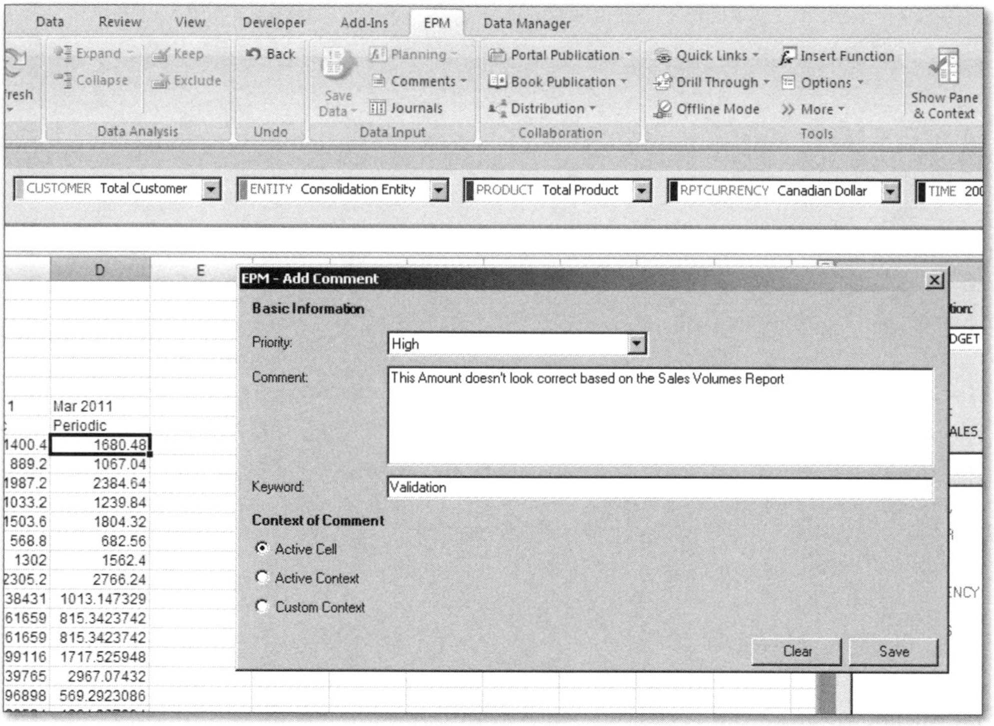

Figure 4.54 EPM – Add Comment Parameter Screen

After all of the appropriate parameters are assigned to the screen, you click on SAVE to save the information to the server. To retrieve the information, you choose COM-MENTS • FIND COMMENTS from the ribbon and then fill in the parameters to allow the search to occur. In this case, you can use the KEYWORD "Validation" to find the comment as shown in Figure 4.55. You can use all or just one of the parameters to find the comment.

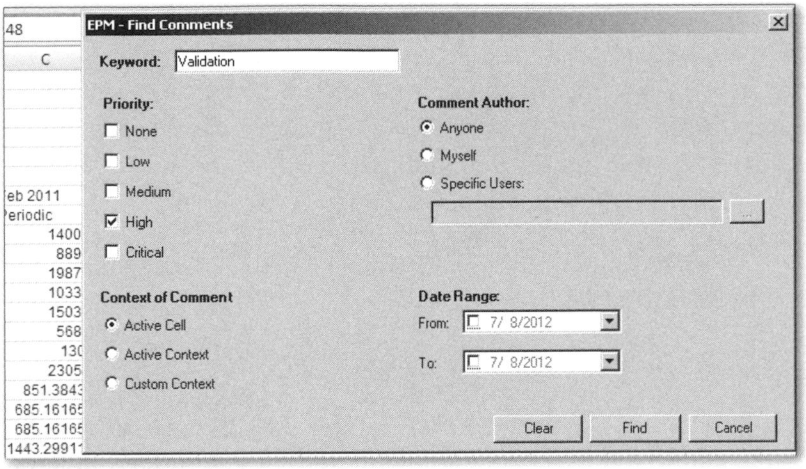

Figure 4.55 EPM – Find Comments

The comment itself doesn't show up directly in the report but on a separate report. After all of the parameters are chosen, and you click on FIND, you'll be taken to another tab on the Web Client frontend of BPC for the results (see Figure 4.56).

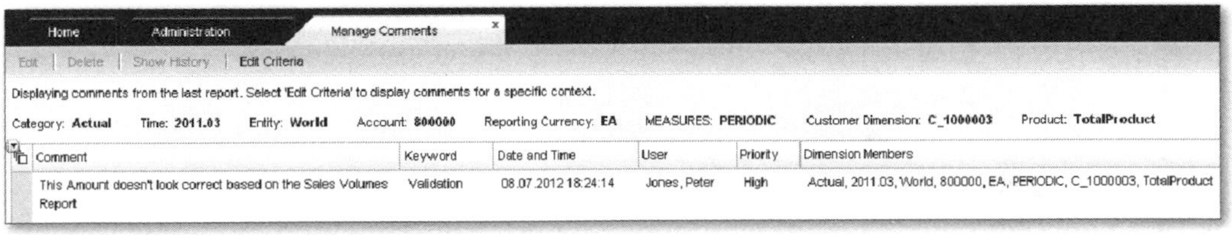

Figure 4.56 Manage Comments Tab in BPC

You can also manage the comment from this screen, which means that you can adjust the assignments of the dimensions and members for this comment. As you can see, this offers additional information such as date and time to offer additional perspective of when the comments were assigned. Depending on the approach you use to access the comments historically, you can set up a process to move the historical comments to another table in BW and use the normal reporting features to execute a report of historically saved comments. This is something of interest if you want to track the planning process historically. The Excel comment process is the same as you're use to with a normal Excel spreadsheet. You just use the context menu after a cell is clicked and insert a comment.

Several different comment parameters are available in the SHEET/USER OPTIONS dropdown. The SHOW AS MICROSOFT EXCEL COMMENTS in the EPM – SHEET OPTIONS dialog box provides you with the ability to see the BPC comment as though it's an Excel comment in the report. The familiar link in the corner of the cell appears, and you can scroll across the cell and see the information. A bit later in this chapter, we'll show how you can see all of the comments assigned to a specific cell by using an EPM function (EPMCommentFullContext).

The results of activating this parameter are shown in Figure 4.57.

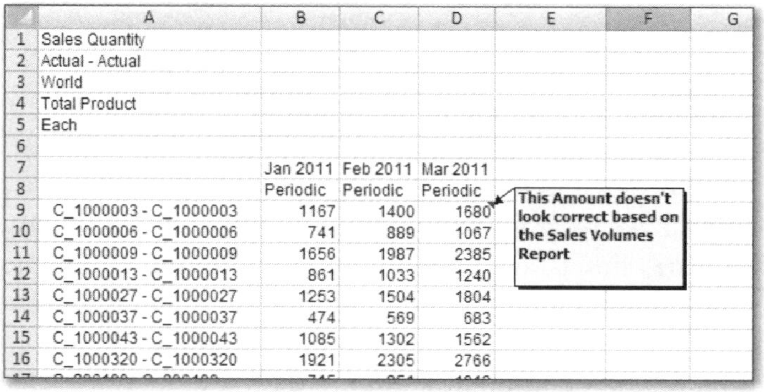

Figure 4.57 EPM add-in Report with BPC Comments Available via the Excel Link

This feature is definitely an asset during budgeting and planning activities when you're assigning comments and need to retrieve them via the specific report or input form.

Journals

The JOURNALS link in the EPM ribbon takes you directly to the JOURNAL ENTRY screen normally used for consolidation processes. If this option is turned on in your model, you can use this as an access point for your consolidation process as well. You can still execute the link, but it takes you to a web-based screen showing that the feature isn't turned on. Click on the option, and it will generate the additional tab on the BPC Web Client screen for this task as shown in Figure 4.58.

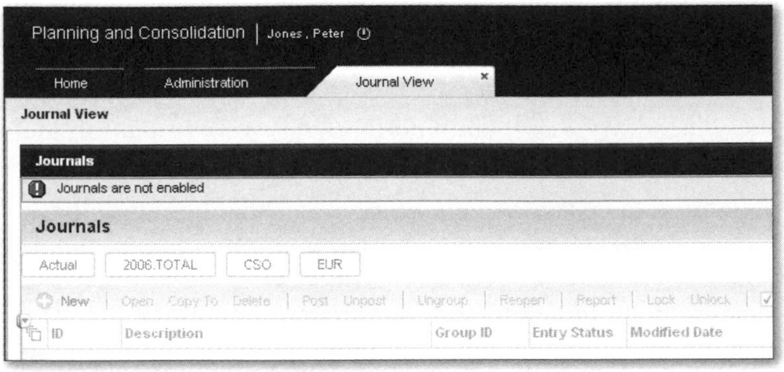

Figure 4.58 Journal View Tab via the Link in the EPM add-in Screen

We'll see this in action in Chapter 7 on consolidation.

4.6.5 Collaboration

The COLLABORATION portion of the EPM ribbon offers multiple approaches to the collection and distribution of the data from EPM. The different options are shown in Figure 4.59.

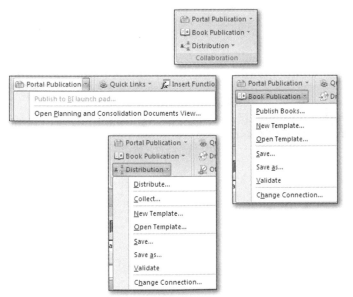

Figure 4.59 Collaboration Section of the EPM Ribbon

The PORTAL PUBLICATION option allows you to link other documents to the different models and dimensions. These documents can be accessed via the user's workspace as well as other reporting options. The two other options available are BOOK PUBLICATION, which links a series of reports so that you can publish these reports in a book format, and DISTRIBUTION, which pushes the reports to the business users. The DISTRIBUTION process includes two sublevel options: DISTRIBUTE and COLLECT. Based on the names, it's clear that they are exact opposite functions. The collect process allows the user to pull or collect information into BPC, whereas the distribution process pushes the information out to the different groups or business users. As you can see from the dropdowns, they all have something in common. That is, they need a template to support the process; unfortunately, if you create a template for one, it doesn't support the other options. We'll go through the process of setting up one of the different templates to give you an idea of what is required. The process is the same for all of the functions.

Portal Publications

PORTAL PUBLICATION offers the option to enhance the documents that are available from the BPC reporting views. To start this process, just click on the OPEN PLANNING AND CONSOLIDATION DOCUMENTS VIEW to go back to the Web Client frontend of BPC, as shown in Figure 4.60. Here you link additional documents to the models by dimensions. The generic ADD, OPEN, EDIT, and DELETE functions are available. If you use the ADD feature to execute the next set of screens, you'll see that this is a wizard type of process (see Figure 4.61).

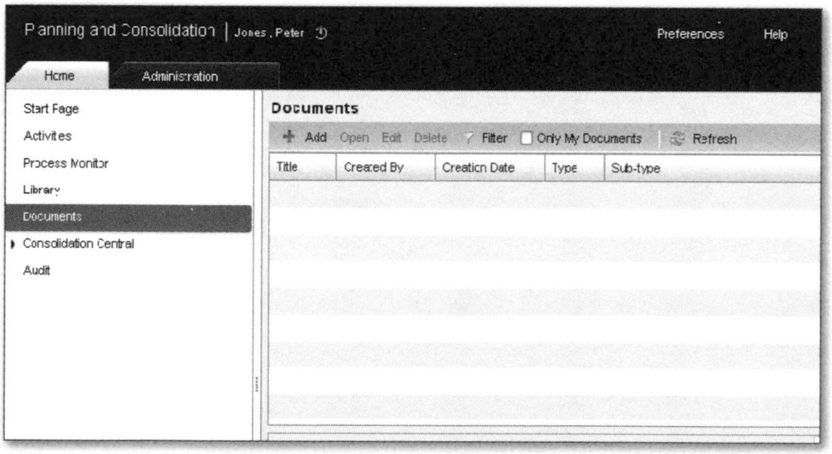

Figure 4.60 BPC Documents View of the Web Home Page

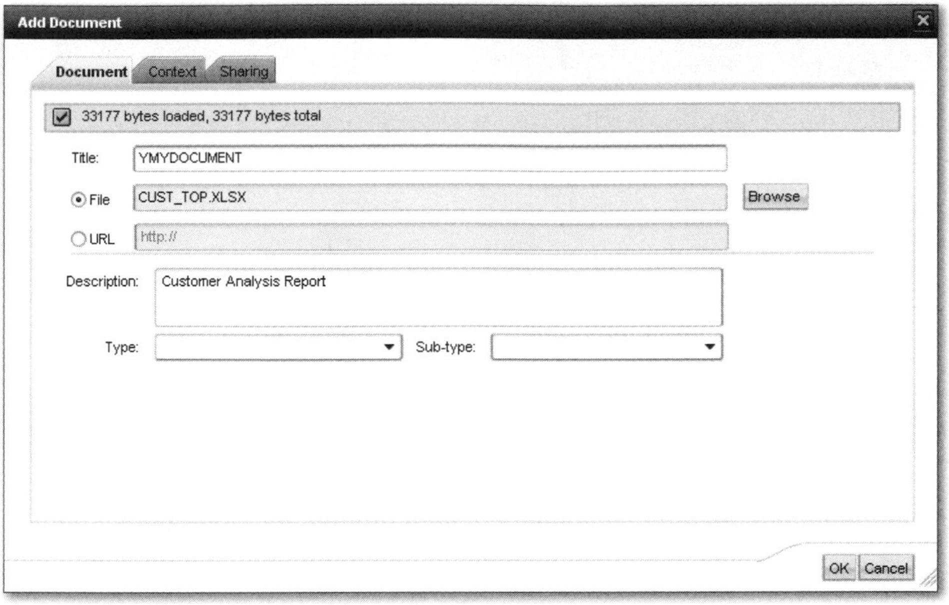

Figure 4.61 Add Document Screen in the BPC Web-Based Home Page

The Excel document that we distributed to the C drive—CUST_TOP.XLSX—has been attached and will be assigned to the BUDGETING MODEL. In this screen, you attach the document or URL, and you can also add an additional DESCRIPTION as well as a document TYPE and SUB-TYPE. These two additional links can be used as a search word to show all documents with a specific document type or sub-type. The document types are configured in the ADMINISTRATION screen under the FEATURES section of the page. These are only descriptive in nature and don't impact the actual data. In the CONTEXT tab, you can assign a MODEL as well as dimensions to the document for additional filtering effect (see Figure 4.62).

Finally you can use the SHARING option to assign specific users to have access to this document, as shown in Figure 4.63.

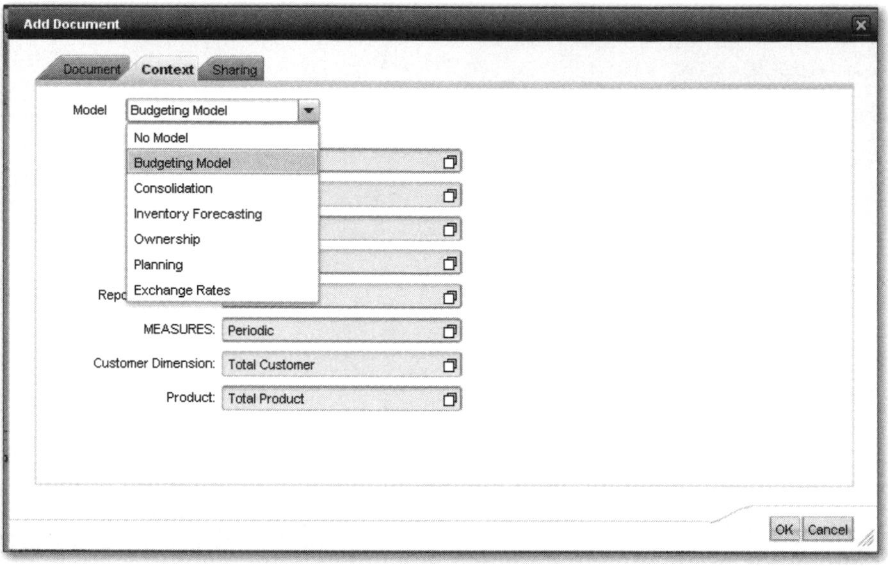

Figure 4.62 Add Document – Context Tab

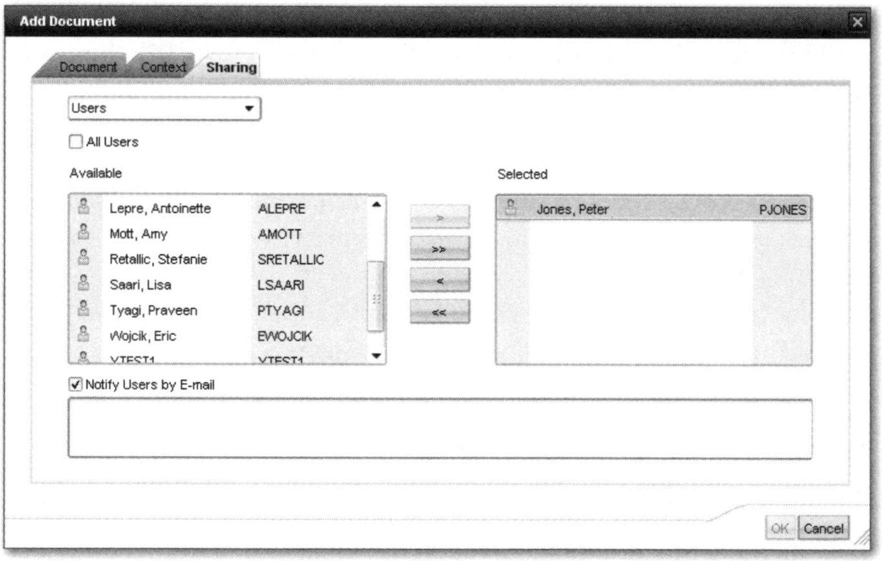

Figure 4.63 Add Document – Sharing Tab to Assign Users

The result is a document that is cataloged for your retrieval in the future, as shown in Figure 4.64.

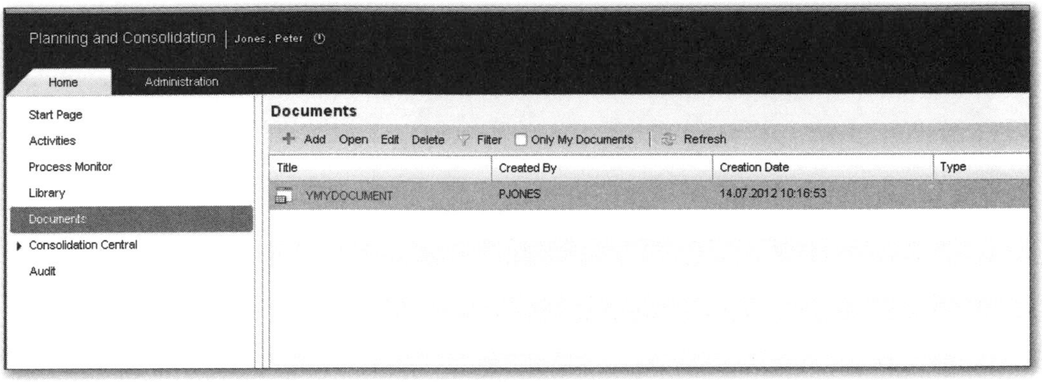

Figure 4.64 Documents Screen with Attached Document

Book Publication and Distribution

As you can see from the dropdown menus on each of the Publication and Distribution features, the process is very similar. Follow these steps:

1. Create a report or input form that you want to use for the initial dimensions of the template.

2. Open the TEMPLATE option and choose NEW TEMPLATE.

3. Create the new template using the report or input form created in step 1.

4. Click on SAVE.

5. Execute the publication or distribution process. This requires the formatting process for use in the publication and/or distribution of the information.

6. Either execute or schedule the process, whichever the user wants to use to process the information.

Let's review the distribution process to understand how it's applicable to all of the different options in this section. Initially, we need a report to use as a base for the template, so let's use the report we've been working with as starting point in the creation of the new template for distribution. Now that you have a report, you can start the process. If you use the context menu from the DISTRIBUTION link and choose NEW TEMPLATE, you'll see a screen similar to Figure 4.65. We've filled in the Template Name, the Variable Time, Section Name, workbook description, and default our INITIAL_REPORT into the report workbook section. These are all filled into the template and can be descriptions and naming conventions with whatever you're using for your project.

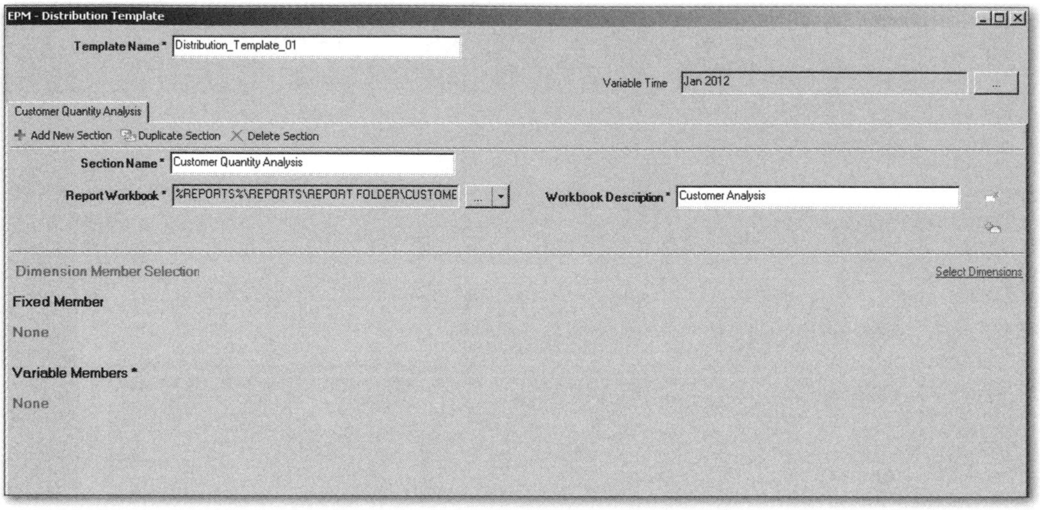

Figure 4.65 EPM – Distribution Template

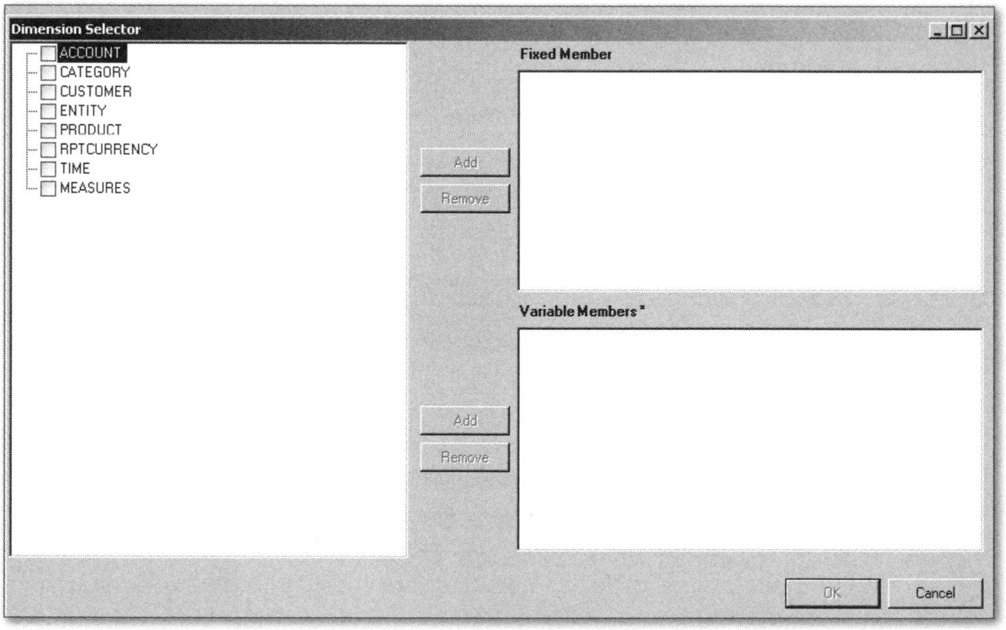

Figure 4.66 Dimension Selector from the Distribution Template Screen

After this is complete, you then click the SELECT DIMENSIONS link to pull in the dimensions found in the INITIAL_REPORT that you're using (see Figure 4.66). In this screen, you identify the dimensions that are FIXED MEMBERS, which are automatically listed in the report, and you identify the VARIABLE MEMBERS, which you'll need to assign, if you want, during the execution of the distribution process. Choose the checkbox to the left of each dimension and move them to the appropriate section of the DIMENSION SELECTOR screen.

For this example, we've split up the dimensions and moved all of them into the FIXED MEMBER field except for CUSTOMER, and we assigned that to the VARIABLE MEMBERS field (see Figure 4.67).

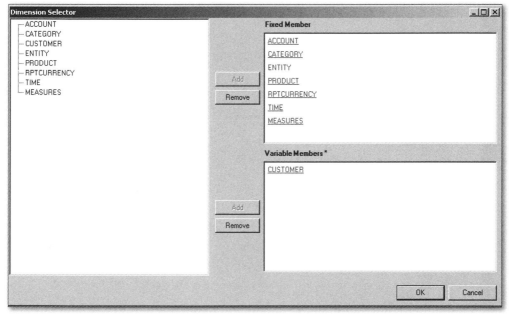

Figure 4.67 Dimension Selector Screen with Dimensions Assigned

After this is complete, click OK and go back to the DISTRIBUTION TEMPLATE as shown in Figure 4.68.

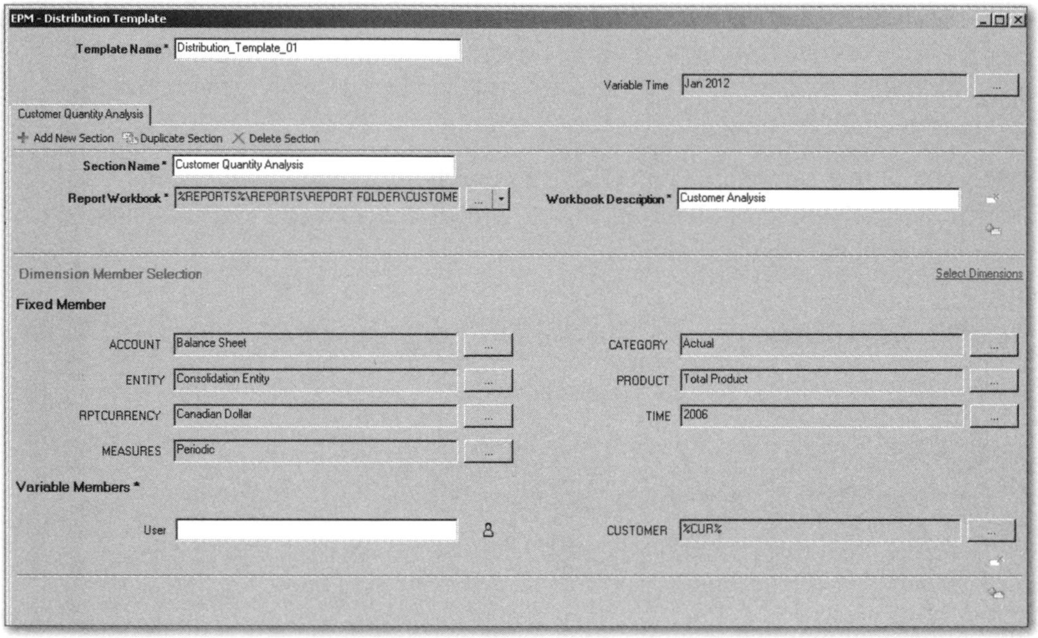

Figure 4.68 EPM – Distribution Template

You can tweak the dimensions for both fixed and variable fields by clicking on the link to the right of each field to identify the specific member value for each of the dimensions. For this example, adjust the ACCOUNT to "Sales Quantity", ENTITY to "World", RPTCURRENCY to "Each", and TIME to "Jan 2012". Also, fill in the USER to reflect the user that will be executing the process. These adjustments are shown in Figure 4.69.

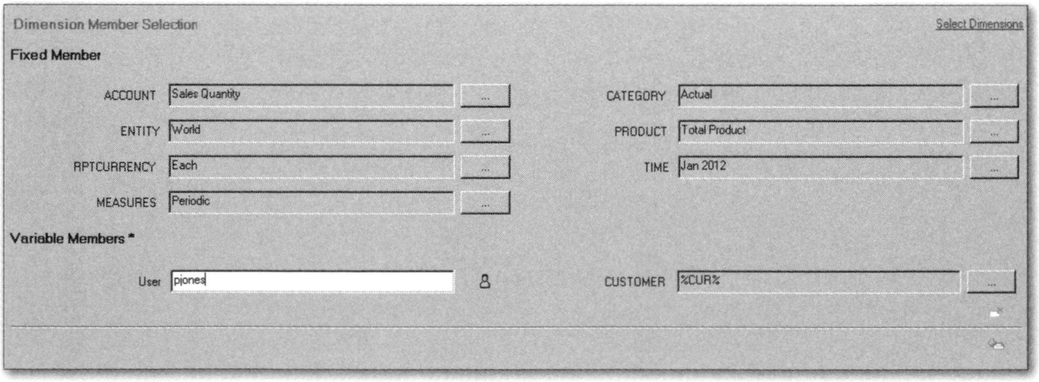

Figure 4.69 Dimension Member Selection with Appropriate Members Assigned

Now click on the SAVE option to see a display of the distribution template that will be used to align the information based on the requirements. Our only requirement, in this case, is the distribution of the information by customer, as shown in Figure 4.70.

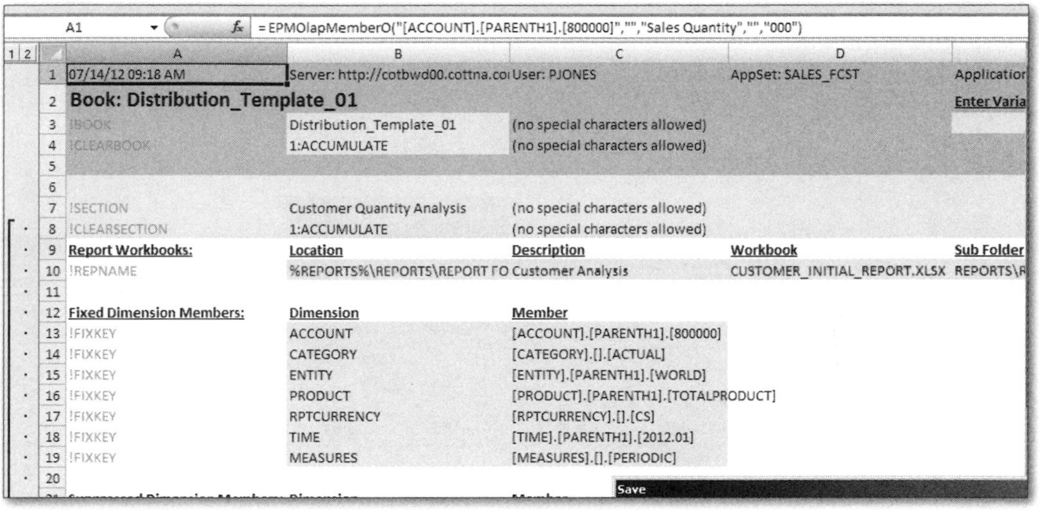

		A	B	C	D	
1	07/14/12 09:18 AM		Server: http://cotbwd00.cottna.co	User: PJONES	AppSet: SALES_FCST	Application
2	**Book: Distribution_Template_01**					Enter Varia
3	!BOOK		Distribution_Template_01	(no special characters allowed)		
4	!CLEARBOOK		1:ACCUMULATE	(no special characters allowed)		
5						
6						
7	!SECTION		Customer Quantity Analysis	(no special characters allowed)		
8	!CLEARSECTION		1:ACCUMULATE	(no special characters allowed)		
9	**Report Workbooks:**		**Location**	**Description**	**Workbook**	**Sub Folder**
10	!REPNAME		%REPORTS%\REPORTS\REPORT ΓO	Customer Analysis	CUSTOMER_INITIAL_REPORT.XLSX	REPORTS\R
11						
12	**Fixed Dimension Members:**		**Dimension**	**Member**		
13	!FIXKEY		ACCOUNT	[ACCOUNT].[PARENTH1].[800000]		
14	!FIXKEY		CATEGORY	[CATEGORY].[].[ACTUAL]		
15	!FIXKEY		ENTITY	[ENTITY].[PARENTH1].[WORLD]		
16	!FIXKEY		PRODUCT	[PRODUCT].[PARENTH1].[TOTALPRODUCT]		
17	!FIXKEY		RPTCURRENCY	[RPTCURRENCY].[].[CS]		
18	!FIXKEY		TIME	[TIME].[PARENTH1].[2012.01]		
19	!FIXKEY		MEASURES	[MEASURES].[].[PERIODIC]		
20						

Figure 4.70 Distribution Template 01 for the Customer Quantity Analysis

You can view some of the basic information that is being used in this case, such as the following:

▶ The APPSET is SALES_FCST

▶ REPORT WORKBOOK

▶ LOCATION

▶ DESCRIPTION

▶ SUB FOLDER

After this process is complete, save the template (see Figure 4.71) and start the actual distribution process.

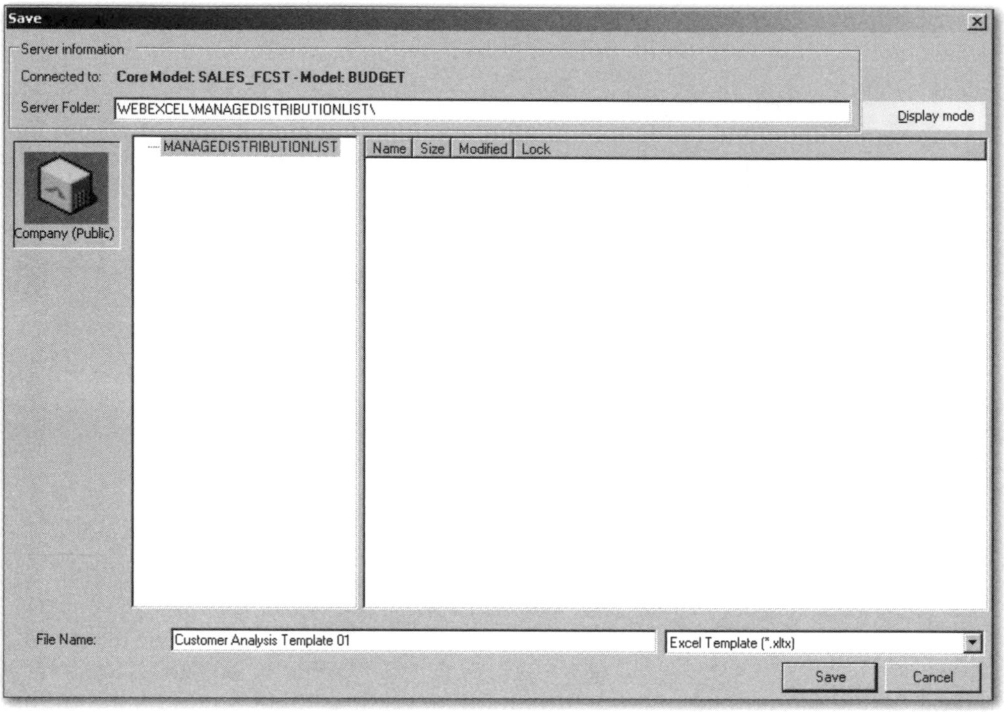

Figure 4.71 Save the Distribution Template – Customer Analysis Template_01

You start the process of distribution by clicking on the DISTRIBUTE link from the context menu under DISTRIBUTION. Upon clicking on this option, two options are available: DISTRIBUTE NOW and SCHEDULE THE DISTRIBUTION, as shown in Figure 4.72. Choose the DISTRIBUTE NOW option. If you choose the SCHEDULE THE DISTRIBUTION option, the next dialog box shows options to schedule the distribution by TIME, an EVENT, or SCHEDULE ONLY ONCE. After that screen, the options are very similar in both approaches. This is another wizard screen process, so you can easily step through the different screens and complete the parameters required.

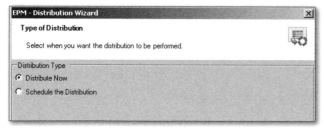

Figure 4.72 EPM – Distribution Wizard

The next step in the sequence is the identification of the distribution process either by email or by saving to a folder. For this example, you'll switch to offline mode and save to a folder. If you were to use the email process, the sequence of steps would require information for the sender and receiver of the file, whether to use the option to zip the file, and an email confirmation after it's received (see Figure 4.73).

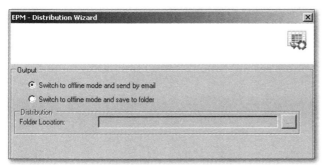

Figure 4.73 EPM – Distribution Wizard: Output

After you switch the output option to save to folder, you need to identify the folder that the reports will be saved to, as shown in Figure 4.74.

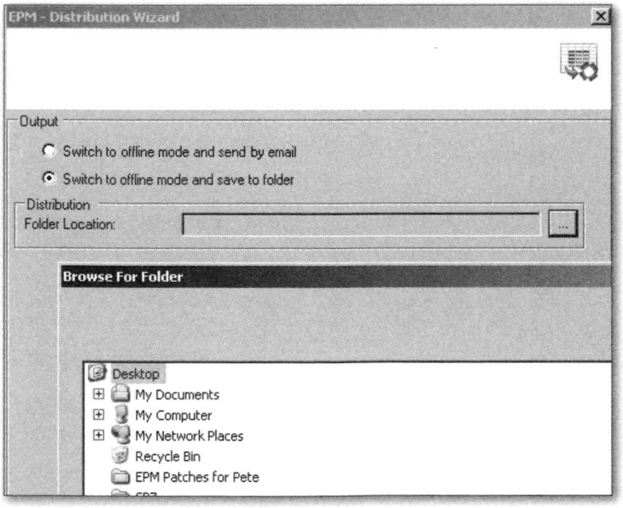

Figure 4.74 EPM – Distribution Wizard: Identify Folder Location

The result is shown in Figure 4.75.

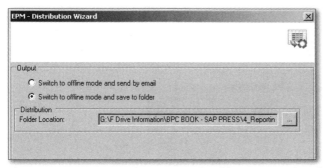

Figure 4.75 EPM – Distribution Wizard: Folder Location Identified

The next step in the EPM – DISTRIBUTION WIZARD is to identify the distribution template that you created previously for this purpose (see Figure 4.76).

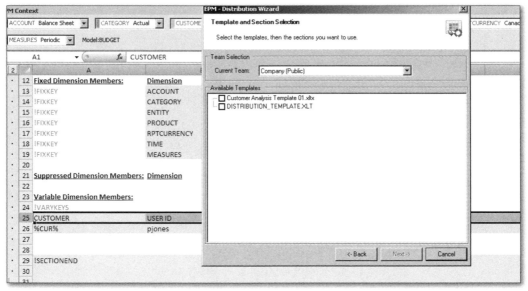

Figure 4.76 EPM – Distribution Wizard: Template for the Distribution Process

Choose the template and then click NEXT (see Figure 4.77).

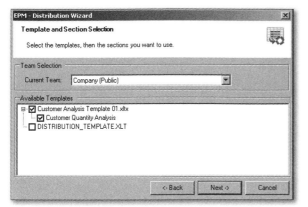

Figure 4.77 EPM – Distribution Wizard – Template for Distribution Checked

You can now view a summary of the information to be used for the distribution (see Figure 4.78).

Figure 4.78 Summary of the Information for the Distribution Run

Click NEXT to execute the distribution run (see Figure 4.79).

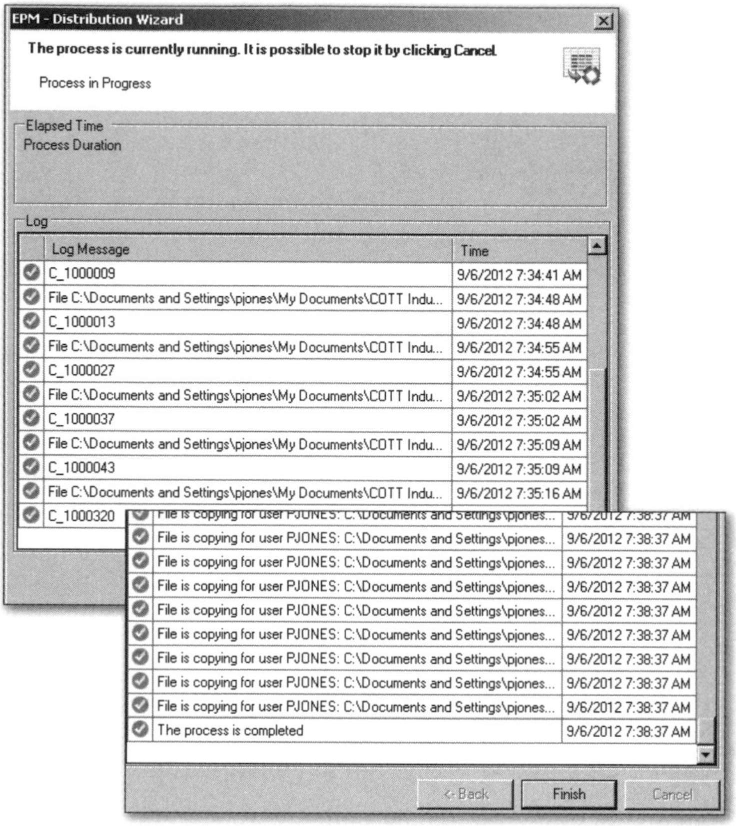

Figure 4.79 EPM – Distribution Wizard with Results of the Distribution Run

After this is complete, you can view the results of this process in the directory identified in the initial setup to store the reports (see Figure 4.80). As you can see, this generates a folder for each of the customers available in the report. This was requested during the creation of the template based on the dimension designated as the variable: Customer. These folders store individual reports for each customer based on the filters identified in the distribution template.

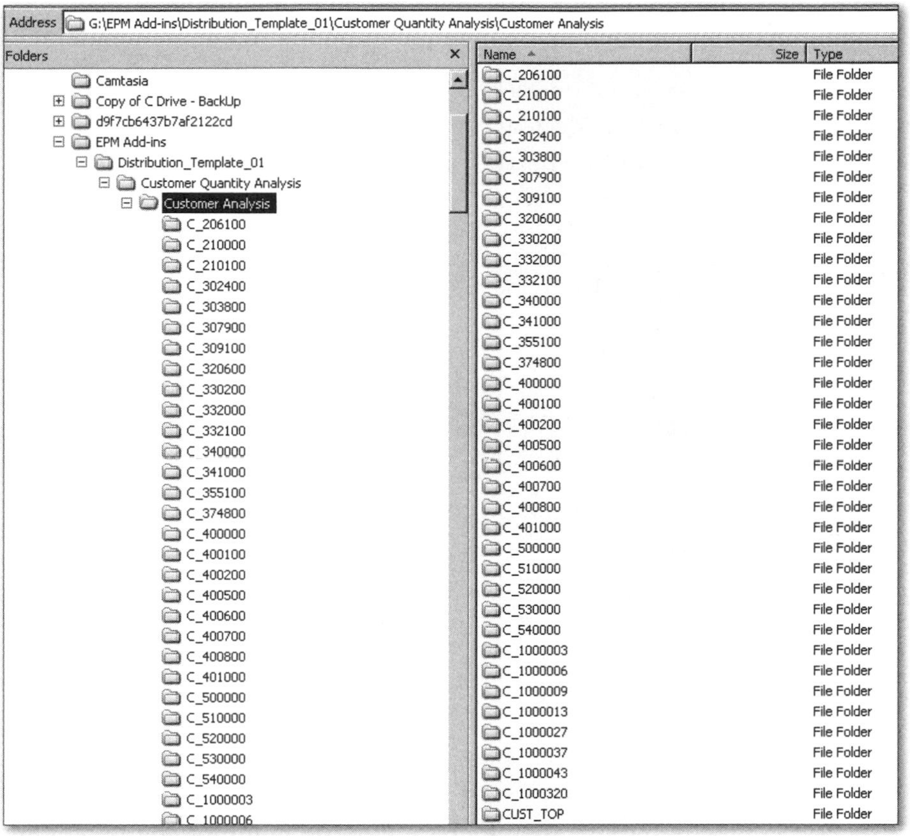

Figure 4.80 Results of the Distribution Run with Individual Folders for Each Customer

As we mentioned, the other available option, BOOK PUBLICATION, offers the ability to link a series of reports so that you can publish these reports in a book format. The same steps are used for this option, but you identify the reports that you want to group together in a book rather than a single report. As far as the COLLECTION option goes, you need to identify the location or folder that you use to collect the information from. After the source of the data folder is identified, you execute the collection process and display the results in the EPM add-in. The initial screen is shown in Figure 4.81. For the collection process, you create a collection template or input template that will be used as an upload template during this process. This is used during a planning process to collect information from a third-party source system. For example, if you have information for your planning process that must be collected from a retailer or customer, you might want to send them this collection template to have them enter the information, and then use the collection process to upload the information back into the BPC system. This is a very useful component especially if you're dealing with only small portions of data to collect. If larger data volumes are to be uploaded, you'll probably want to use the normal data uploading process via a Data Manager package.

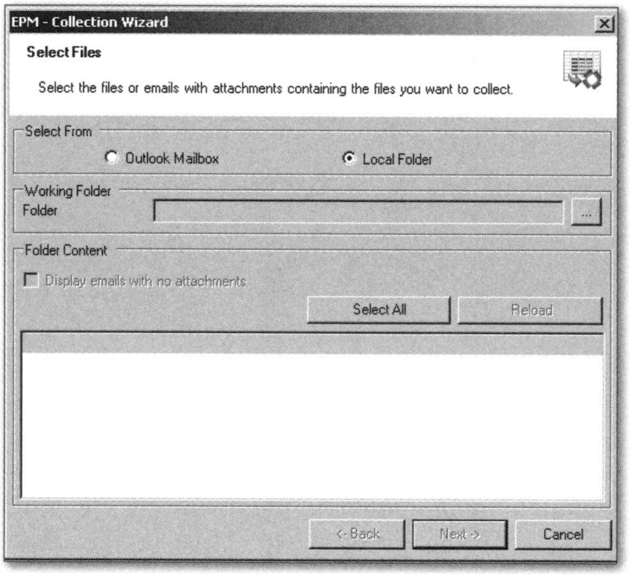

Figure 4.81 EPM – Collection Wizard

4.6.6 Tools

The TOOLS portion of the ribbon is probably the most important in the process of building your reports and input forms (see Figure 4.82). This section offers many features for reporting that can be found under the OPTIONS link. You also have the INSERT FUNCTION link to insert functions into your report. This allows the user to embed additional functions to help with calculations, accessing other features, accessing master data of the dimension members, and other activities. Two options are also available for generic DRILL THROUGH functions: QUICK LINKS and DRILL THROUGH components. These features allow the user to access other sources of information, possibly more details or additional reference data, from the original report just by using a dropdown with the additional links connected. The difference between the two options is that the DRILL THROUGH option requires the setup in BPC, whereas the QUICK LINKS option can be created from the EPM add-in without any additional configuration.

The OFFLINE MODE option offers the ability to remove the link from the server to the current report and to have static report information, if necessary, to do additional research before refreshing the data by switching the offline mode back. The features under the MORE button are a combination of additional features from the prompt to execute the migration of the EvDRE reports to the clearing of the metadata cache. We'll discuss each of these in this section.

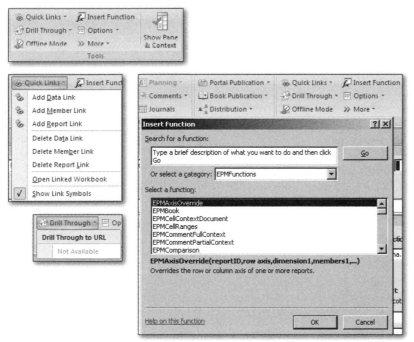

Figure 4.82 Tools Section of the EPM add-in Ribbon and Resulting Screens

Quick Links

The QUICK LINKS option is an enhancement to another option that's available—the DRILL THROUGH feature. If you look at the requirements to use the DRILL THROUGH option, you'll likely agree that QUICK LINKS might be of some use; however, the look and feel of QUICK LINKS might be a deterrent to using this as a mass solution to close any gaps around the drill through process. You can see that the context menu is the same series of prompts, and the only difference is that you're either creating or deleting the QUICK LINK connection (see Figure 4.83). You definitely want to make sure that the parameter to SHOW LINK SYMBOLS is turned on, so you can identify the cells that have a report connection. As far as the three different link options, they address how the Quick Link report will be connected to the source report. Basically, as in the use of comments, they are assigned based on indexing the data in the report:

▶ ADD DATA LINK
This is defined on a specific set of data. The linked workbook or report inherits the definition of the selected data cell. More specifically, the connection occurs with the members in the page axis, context menu, and cell intersection.

▶ ADD MEMBER LINK
This is defined on the specific member. The linked workbook or report inherits the definition of the member cell. In detail, it connects to the selected member(s) if multiple dimensions are in the column or row, the context menu, and the page axis.

▶ ADD REPORT LINK
This is defined on the definition of the report. Basically, this is linked to the members in the page axis and the context menu.

Figure 4.83 Quick Links Context Menu

To start, let's use the INITIAL_REPORT that we've been using and choose a cell in the report. Figure 4.84 shows this step.

	A	B	C	D
1	Each			
2	Total Product			
3	World			
4	Actual - Actual			
5	Sales Quantity			
6				
7		Jan 2011	Feb 2011	Mar 2011
8		Periodic	Periodic	Periodic
9	C_1000003 - C_1000003	1167	1400	1680
10	C_1000006 - C_1000006	741	889	1067
11	C_1000009 - C_1000009	1656	1987	2385
12	C_1000013 - C_1000013	861	1033	1240
13	C_1000027 - C_1000027	1253	1504	1804
14	C_1000037 - C_1000037	474	569	683
15	C_1000043 - C_1000043	1085	1302	1562
16	C_1000320 - C_1000320	1921	2305	2766
17	C_206100 - C_206100	715	851	1013

Figure 4.84 Initial Report View with Cell Identified

Next, select the QUICK LINKS • ADD DATA LINK option from the dropdown. You'll see the SERVER screen with the reports or input forms available to link directly to the cell (see Figure 4.85).

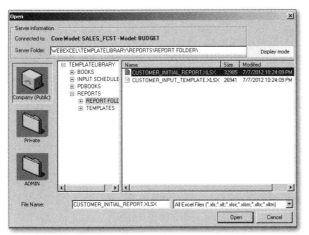

Figure 4.85 Open Dialog Box for Server Reports and Input Forms

After a report is chosen, click the OPEN option, and you'll see an arrow identifying that a Quick Link report has been assigned to this information (see Figure 4.86).

Return to the report, and use the link to access the additional report. In this case, we didn't make the linked report more detailed or specific than the one we're using as a source, but, in general, there are some specific requirements to link the two reports together for a more detailed report—possibly a report with comments, more information, or a different format. The results are shown in Figure 4.87.

	A	B	C	D	E
1	Sales Quantity				
2	Actual - Actual				
3	World				
4	Total Product				
5	Each				
6					
7		Jan 2011	Feb 2011	Mar 2011	
8		Periodic	Periodic	Periodic	
9	C_1000003 - C_1000003	1167	1400	1680	
10	C_1000006 - C_1000006	741	889	1067	
11	C_1000009 - C_1000009	1656	1987	2385	
12	C_1000013 - C_1000013	861	1033	1240	
13	C_1000027 - C_1000027	1253	1504	1804	
14	C_1000037 - C_1000037	474	569	683	
15	C_1000043 - C_1000043	1085	1302	1562	

Figure 4.86 Report with a Quick Link Assigned to the Data Level

B9		f_x	1804.32

	A	B	C
1	Sales Quantity		
2	Actual - Actual		
3	World		
4	Total Product		
5	Each		
6			
7		Mar 2011	
8		Periodic	
9	C_1000027 - C_1000027	1804	
10			
11			
12			
13			
14			

Figure 4.87 Results of a Data Linked Quick Report

Insert Functions

The INSERT FUNCTIONS feature is used in reporting to enhance the report capabilities by allowing the use of additional attributes, properties, and calculations. We'll be using this feature in Section 4.8 on advanced features, but for a basic example, we'll add the description of the customer member to a separate column. In this case, the description and the member value are the same, but you'll probably have a better description of your customer list in reality. This has been discussed quite a bit because those coming from the BEX background view the information as a standard option. In this case, you only have to enter the information and assign it to the connecting column. To do this, take your report, and insert a column next to the customer member column (see Figure 4.88).

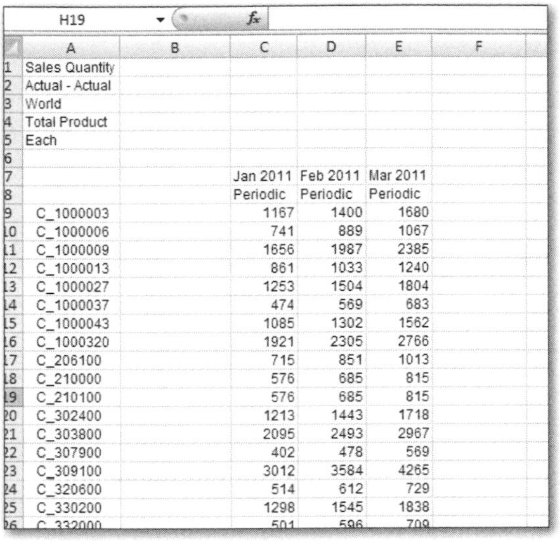

Figure 4.88 Report with Inserted Column Next to Customer Number

Note: Member Recognition

To allow the Member value to cascade to all of the members in the report, make sure that you have the MEMBER RECOGNITION option turned on in your report. You choose the parameter in the SHEET OPTIONS dialog box.

Next click the INSERT FUNCTION link to open the INSERT FUNCTION dialog box as shown in Figure 4.89.

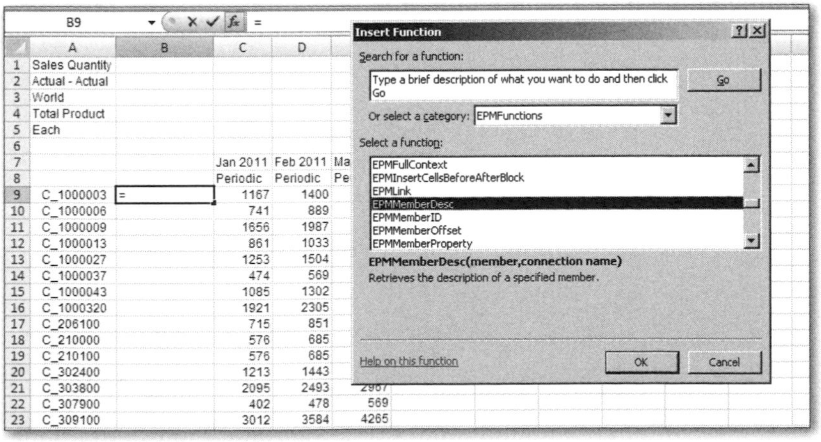

Figure 4.89 Insert Function – EPMMemberDesc Function

If you scroll down this list, you'll see that there are about 50 different EPM functions available and about 50 different FPMXLCLIENT functions available as well in the INSERT FUNCTIONS option. Both offer the ability to enhance the reports by using the properties and other parameters of the dimensions in the report as well as add additional features to help with calculations and display options. You'll probably use these in many of your reports to help support the business requirements for additional information.

After you choose an EPM function from the dropdown and click OK, the parameter screen appears for the information required to fill in the inserted column. In this case, you only need the dimension member you're looking to get the descriptions for (in this case, it's found in column A). This is shown in Figure 4.90.

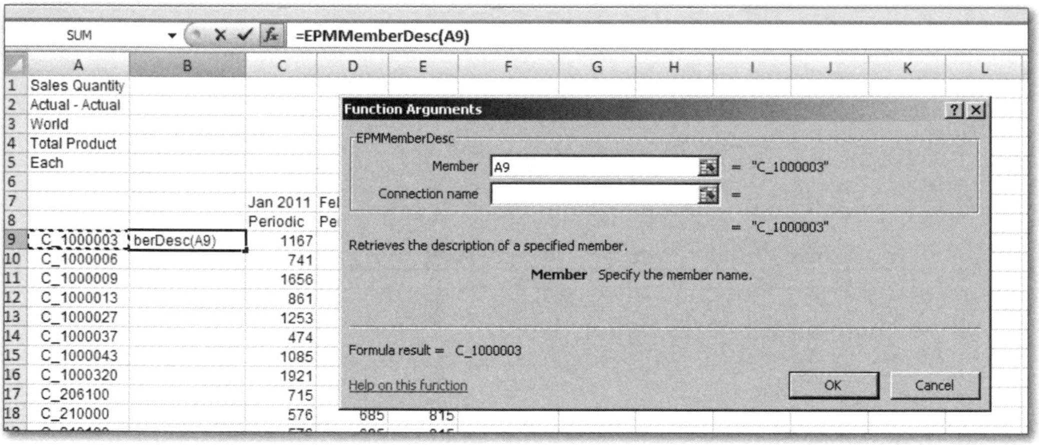

Figure 4.90 Function Arguments with Member Entered

Click the OK button, and the results will be displayed in the report. In this case, the descriptions of the customer numbers are actually the same as the numbers (see Figure 4.91). You can also clean up the header to show the title of CUSTOMER DESCRIPTION and hide the (FN) description title. This title is generated based on the member recognition process.

	SUM	▼	*fx*	=EPMMemberDesc(A9)		
	A	B	C	D	E	F
1	Sales Quantity					
2	Actual - Actual					
3	World					
4	Total Product					
5	Each					
6						
7			Jan 2011	Feb 2011	Mar 2011	
8		(fn) CUSTOMER	Periodic	Periodic	Periodic	
9	C_1000003	C_1000003	1167	1400	1680	
10	C_1000006	C_1000006	741	889	1067	
11	C_1000009	C_1000009	1656	1987	2385	
12	C_1000013	C_1000013	861	1033	1240	
13	C_1000027	C_1000027	1253	1504	1804	
14	C_1000037	C_1000037	474	569	683	
15	C_1000043	C_1000043	1085	1302	1562	
16	C_1000320	C_1000320	1921	2305	2766	
17	C_206100	C_206100	715	851	1013	
18	C_210000	C_210000	576	685	815	
19	C_210100	C_210100	576	685	815	
20	C_302400	C_302400	1213	1443	1718	
21	C_303800	C_303800	2095	2493	2967	
22	C_307900	C_307900	402	478	569	
23	C_309100	C_309100	3012	3584	4265	
24	C_320600	C_320600	514	612	729	
25	C_330200	C_330200	1298	1545	1838	
26	C_332000	C_332000	501	596	709	
27	C_332100	C_332100	487	580	690	
28	C_340000	C_340000	3162	3762	4477	

Figure 4.91 Report with the Customer Description Assigned in Column B

Drill Through

The DRILL THROUGH option offers the ability to "jump" from one BPC model to a target object. These objects include a transaction code in SAP, a URL link to a website, or a report in either SAP ERP or a BW cube. This is done by setting up the links from the source report to the target report. Remember that the jump from the BPC/EPM screen to any of the other target systems is done via a Web link or URL. Therefore, to drill through to an SAP ERP transaction code, you need to have the Web link to the system available so you can incorporate it into the configuration for a drill through.

> **Note: Drill Through**
>
> The drill through process from a BPC model report to a BW InfoProvider report uses the BW query connection. The setup of the DRILL THROUGH option is done in the BPC ADMINISTRATION screen. If you want to drill through from one BPC model to another BPC model, you have to use the QUICK LINK option, unless you create an OLE DB link for your BPC model, create a BEX Query, and then configure the links as usual. This has significant risks because the use of the BEX Query component against the BPC model doesn't read the data using the transparent query designed to support the report signage of the account-based data. Therefore, using a BEX report on a BPC model isn't suggested.

Because this function is set up and configured in the BPC ADMINISTRATION screen, the business user will need to understand what the source and target reports are and give that information to the BPC developers. The set up and use of variables as prompts to supply the parameters of the source report to the target report is very similar to what you might use in either BEX Analyzer and other reporting components that use this 'drill through' concept. The current approach is that the drill through is to a web-based BEX report or a report/transaction code in SAP-ERP.

The important components of this process are the URL link to the target report and making sure you use the appropriate variable prompts for the dimensions that you want to use as filters to pass the values from the source to target reports as well as the use of the BPC prompts of FILTER_IOBJNM and FILTER_VALUE to assign the InfoObject technical name and the filter value to the pass through during the drill through. One issue that normally comes up with this process is the fact that the master data is inconsistently between the source and target reports/systems. To accommodate this issue you will need to add a PROPERTY to the dimension and this property will store the appropriate master data that can be used during the drill through to match up with the target information. This way you can use the members that are consistent with BPC as well as link to the members from another BW InfoObject seamlessly.

Because this function is mostly set up in the BPC ADMINISTRATION screen, we'll cover this in more detail in Chapter 6 on planning, budgeting, and forecasting.

Offline Mode

The OFFLINE MODE option allows any user to read the workbook or reports even if the user doesn't have the EPM add-in installed. When offline, a workbook behaves like a standard Excel workbook. The context bar and the pane are automatically hidden. To assign the report back online just click the OFFLINE MODE option again, and the report will be linked, and the context bar and navigational pane will reappear.

Options

The options that are available in this section of the TOOLS portion of the ribbon are broken down into four topics: SHEET, CONTEXT, USER, and COMMAND DISPLAY. SHEET and USER options are very useful during the creation of your reports, so it's critical to make sure that you have them setup as according to what you want to accomplish. For example, we've been using the MEMBER RECOGNITION option in some of our reports. If this feature isn't turned on prior to creating Excel formulas or setting up some of the EPM functions, the it's not possible to have the results linked directly to the report. As you use this process, you may want to start each report by confirming these settings, and then move into the creation of the report. We'll look at each list of features and show what they do in terms of the display on a report. We'll comment on some of the features and how they impact the results of the reports in Section 4.8 where we build out some examples of reports.

Sheet Options

The component that has the most features involved is the SHEET OPTIONS. There are four different tabs for this component: GENERAL, FORMATTING, REFRESH, and PROTECTION. Within each, there are additional breakouts of parameters dealing with different aspects of the report structure. This option component is definitely one that you'll get very familiar with as you create your reports. Figure 4.92 shows a view of the SHEET OPTIONS screen. These settings will impact the navigation processes within the current worksheet.

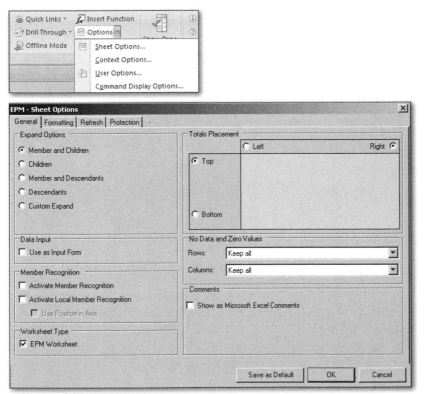

Figure 4.92 EPM – Sheet Options Screen with General, Formatting, Refresh, and Protection Tabs

Table 4.7 shows all of the parameters and a description of what each will support in a report.

Feature Name	Description
GENERAL TAB	
Expand Options	
MEMBER AND CHILDREN	Children of the parent and the parent itself.
CHILDREN	Only the children of the parent.
MEMBER AND DESCENDANTS	The descendant of the parent and the parent itself.
DESCENDANTS	Only the descendant.
CUSTOM EXPAND	This option allows the customization of the EXPAND option. You can either include or not include the parent and expand based on a custom level. You can also pick a specific level to start the expansion from and to.
Data Input	
USE AS INPUT FORM	Change the report to an input form. If this parameter is to be used, make sure you turn it on before starting the process of populating the worksheet. If not, all of the data will be lost after the parameter is turned on, and a refresh is executed.
Member Recognition	
ACTIVATE MEMBER RECOGNITION	This activates the member recognition for individual members; therefore, the business user will type in a member, and the system will attempt to recognize it and insert it into the report.
ACTIVATE LOCAL MEMBER RECOGNITION	This activates the local member recognition. This operates on calculated members and expands any calculation to the entire column or row that it's inserted.
USE POSITION AXIS	Activates when the LOCAL MEMBER option is turned on. This applies the calculation to the location in the axis where the calculation was created.

Table 4.7 EPM Sheet Options and Definitions

Feature Name	Description
Worksheet Type	
EPM Worksheet	This activates the worksheet to be an EPM worksheet. To disconnect from the EPM component, deactivate this parameter, and the workbook will not be connected to the server.
Totals Placement	
Top	Position of the hierarchy: Top.
Bottom	Position of the hierarchy: Bottom.
Left	Position of the hierarchy: Left Justified.
Right	Position of the hierarchy: Right Justified.
No Data and Zero Values	
Rows – Keep All, Hide Empty, Hide Empty and Zero Values, Remove Empty, Remove Empty and Zero Values	This option allows you to alter the display of the values that are either zero or empty in the rows. Empty cells are intersections that have no postings. Zero cells are intersections that have postings but sum to zero.
	The use of the different options will define what the business user sees. Note that the use of Hide Empties and Zeroes will still include them in the total line count for the report.
Columns – Keep All, Hide Empty, Hide Empty and Zero Values, Remove Empty, Remove Empty and Zero Values	This option allows you to alter the display of the values that are either zero or empty in the columns. Empty cells are intersections that have no postings. Zero cells are intersections that have postings but sum to zero.
	The use of the different options will define what the business user sees. Note, the use of Hide Empties And Zeroes will still include them in the total line count for the report.
Comments	
Show as Microsoft Excel Comment	If this parameter is active, the BPC comments will be displayed as an Excel comment; as you scroll over the cell, the comment will be incorporated into a popup.

Table 4.7 EPM Sheet Options and Definitions (Cont.)

Feature Name	Description
FORMATTING TAB	
Row Header Information	
NO INDENTATION	No indentation of the hierarchy nodes.
INDENT CHILDREN	Indent the children of the hierarchy.
INDENT PARENTS	Indent the parents.
Display Name	
CAPTION	Basic description of the member values.
FULL UNIQUE NAME	This will display the technical naming convention of the member with all of the EPM function links as well. This isn't something that is normally used due to the cryptic format.
AUTO FIT COLUMN WIDTH	Will adjust the column widths automatically. This is something you'll want to turn off after you've formatted the report.
REPEAT ROW HEADERS	Allows the display of the repeat row values.
REPEAT COLUMN HEADERS	Allows the display of repeat column values. This is very useful if you download the information to an Excel spreadsheet outside of the EPM add-in.
Report Format	
SET DEFAULT VALUE IN EMPTY CELL	Allows the user to define the value that will appear in an empty cell.
SET DEFAULT VALUE WHEN MEMBER NOT FOUND IN SHARED AXIS	If you have two reports that share an axis, the system will validate the shared members. If a member isn't available, then the value listed here will be used to fill the cell. The default is #NOMEMBERFOUND.
APPLY DYNAMIC FORMATTING	This parameter allows the application of the dynamic formatting sheets.
DEFAULT FORMATTING SHEET	This will be the assigned default formatting sheet. This can be a user-defined format sheet.

Table 4.7 EPM Sheet Options and Definitions (Cont.)

Feature Name	Description
CLEAR REPORT FORMAT BEFORE APPLYING DYNAMIC FORMATTING	To keep the existing formatting and override it with the dynamic formatting, you deselect this parameter. For the opposite, you check this parameter.
REFRESH TAB	
KEEP FORMULA ON DATA	This allows a formula to be kept in a cell even though the rest of the cells in the column or row are being calculated in another way. This is important if you're using a local member, and a specific cell is required to be calculated in another way.
SHOW SOURCE DATA IN COMMENTS	If the initial source of data for a cell is from the database, but you change the cell to a formula, then the result in this cell is the formula result and not the database value. This will allow the source data to show as a comment on that cell.
CALCULATE PARENTS IN HIERARCHIES	For simulation purposes, this allows the sum on each parent in the hierarchies included in a report. The data on each of the parents in a hierarchy are replaced by a sum formula.
REFRESH DATA IN WHOLE FILE WHEN OPENING IT	This will execute a refresh of all of the data in a workbook when opened.
CLEAR DATA IN WHOLE FILE WHEN OPENING IT	This will execute a CLEAR of all of the data in a workbook when being saved.
SHOW UNAUTHORIZED CELL TEXT	This will show text in a cell if you're not authorized to see it based on security. The text that will be displayed is found in the USER OPTIONS.
APPLY ONLY REPORT EDITOR DEFINITION FOR FASTER REFRESH	If this parameter is chosen when executing a refresh on a large report, the refresh will only be executed on the format and functions found in the Report Editor. Therefore, all manual formatting or Excel calculations aren't refreshed.
RESTORE DYNAMIC SELECTION ON REFRESH AFTER NAVIGATION	During a collapse or expand, the dynamic selection is broken, and the report selection becomes static. If this parameter is checked, the report will continue to be dynamic in nature.

Table 4.7 EPM Sheet Options and Definitions (Cont.)

Feature Name	Description
Protection	
NO PROTECTION	No protection is given to any of the worksheets or workbook.
PROTECT ACTIVE WORKSHEET	Protection is assigned to the current active worksheet.
PROTECT WORKBOOK	Protection is assigned to the workbook and all worksheets included.
PASSWORD PROTECTION	Create a password that will support the protection type that is chosen from this list.

Table 4.7 EPM Sheet Options and Definitions (Cont.)

Context Options

The CONTEXT OPTIONS refer to the CONTEXT menu that controls the entire workbook. These options help support some filtering and security options. Figure 4.93 shows the different parameters in this option. As this figure shows, the parameters will impact if you can lock or display the Context menu dimensions.

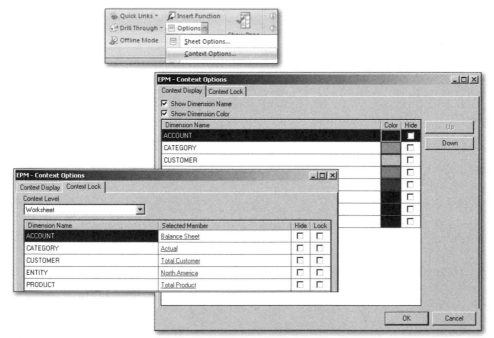

Figure 4.93 EPM – Context Options: Context Display and Lock

This will come in handy during the process of setting up standard parameters for the standard reports for the corporation. In the CONTEXT DISPLAY tab, the ability to show or hide the name and assigned color is available. The color that is assigned is for display purposes only and doesn't impact any functionality of the EPM CONTEXT menu. In the CONTEXT LOCK tab, the options are to either HIDE or LOCK the dimensions. You're also able to set the selected member values by clicking on the link of the dimension and selecting the members. If you LOCK the dimension, it will show up as a grayed out dimension. As you can see in Figure 4.94, two dimensions—ACCOUNT and CATEGORY—are locked and the corresponding fields are grayed out at the top of the screen. After you set up the parameters in this EPM – CONTEXT OPTIONS dialog box, this will control what the user sees in the display of all worksheets unless the CURRENT REPORT pane is used to override the assignments.

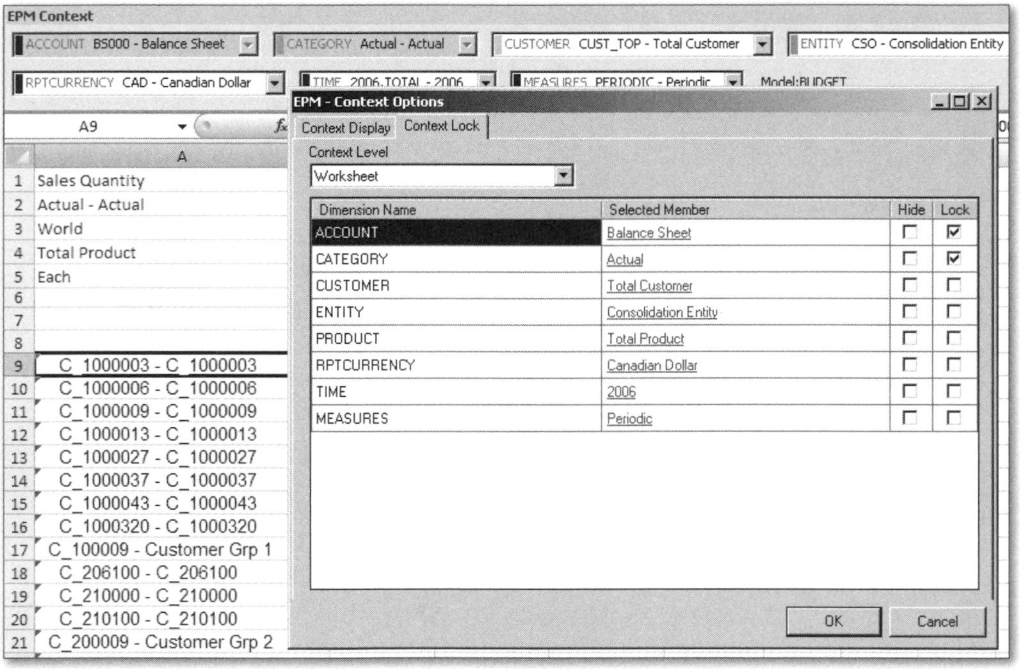

Figure 4.94 EPM – Context Options with Locked Dimensions

User Options

The EPM – USER OPTIONS screens are broken into three different tabs: NAVIGATION, SERVER CONFIGURATION, and OTHERS. The NAVIGATION and OTHERS tabs are the important ones when it comes to managing the functionality on a report. The SERVER CONFIGURATION tab is specific to the SAP BusinessObjects Enterprise Server information. Connections usually immediately return the SMTP server information, so you likely won't have to fill in any parameters on this tab. This information is important if you'll be using some communication processes in the distribution of workbooks via email. If you need to fill in these parameters, please discuss this with your Basis support team for the appropriate information to use. The NAVIGATION tab, on the other hand, has a number of parameters that impact the processing of information and the functionality during the build of the report. Figure 4.95 shows the parameters available in this tab.

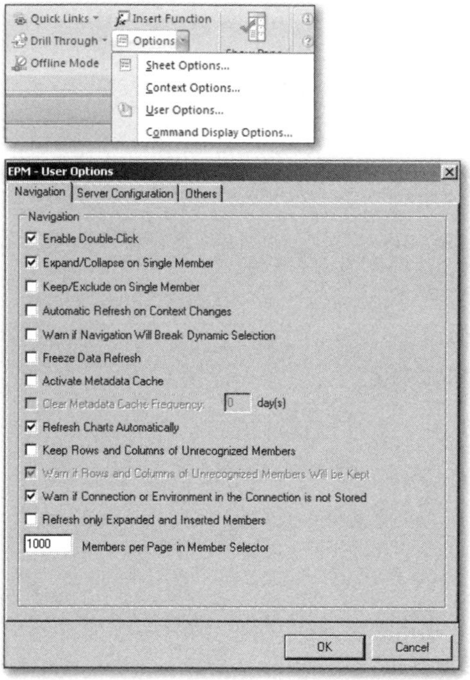

Figure 4.95 EPM – User Options: Navigation Tab

As you can see, some parameters come defaulted such as ENABLE DOUBLE-CLICK and MEMBERS PER PAGE IN MEMBER SELECTOR. These default parameters are basic settings that don't impact the performance of the report or workbook. We'll list the remaining options in Table 4.8 a bit later in this section with descriptions of what each will effect.

The OTHER tab offers parameters more specific to the features that are available on the report screen and panes (see Figure 4.96). Most of these are defaulted due to the initial display that the user will have after entering into the EPM add-in. For example, the options to DISPLAY EPM CONTEXT BAR and the DISPLAY EPM PANE are automatically selected. In the initial EPM SPs, these were not automatically turned on, and new users always questioned where to activate these options. Most of these seem reasonable to have available from the start when creating a report.

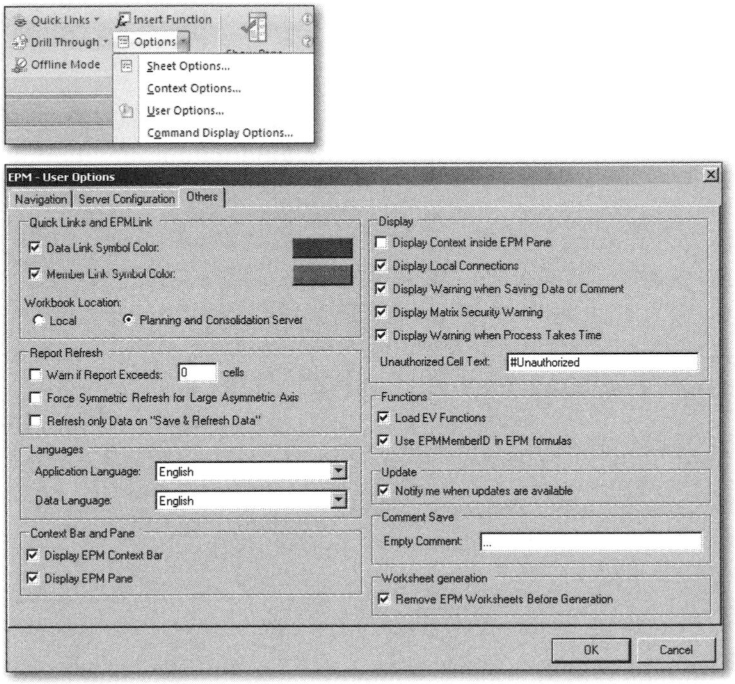

Figure 4.96   EPM – User Options: Others Tab

The parameters in both the Navigation and Others tabs are described in Table 4.8.

Feature Name	Description
NAVIGATION	
ENABLE DOUBLE-CLICK	Allows the ability to double click on the cells in the report and expand and collapse the data.
EXPAND/COLLAPSE ON SINGLE MEMBER	Allows the ability to execute an EXPAND/ COLLAPSE on a single member rather than a complete list of members.

Table 4.8   List of Parameters in the EPM – User Options Dialog Box

Feature Name	Description
KEEP/EXCLUDE ON SINGLE MEMBER	Allows the ability to execute a KEEP/EXCLUDE on a single member rather than a complete list of members.
AUTOMATIC REFRESH ON CONTEXT CHANGES	Allows an automatic refresh if a change to a context menu dimension occurs.
WARN IF NAVIGATION WILL BREAK DYNAMIC SELECTION	During the navigation process, certain processes will cause the dynamic navigation to break. This will offer a warning if the dynamic selection will break based on a specific process. For example, if you execute a KEEP on a specific member, then the dynamic selection will break, and the report will be more static then dynamic.
FREEZE DATA REFRESH	Freezes the data refresh on each selection process. If the report is very large, this eliminates the multiple refresh activities during a filtering process. This allows you to filter several dimensions and make changes to the report, and then execute a refresh for all of the changes rather than one at a time.
ACTIVATE METADATA CACHE	Activates the metadata cache so that the metadata doesn't have to be loaded every time you access the report. The metadata is stored in the local cache and allows the report to be executed faster during the access process.
CLEAR METADATA CACHE FREQUENCY	Allows the clearing of the metadata cache at a specific frequency. This parameter should be set up if ACTIVATE METADATA CACHE is turned on to allow any new members of the master data to be loaded on the next access process.
REFRESH CHARTS AUTOMATICALLY	Allows any charts that have been created to automatically refresh while accessing the report.

Table 4.8　List of Parameters in the EPM – User Options Dialog Box (Cont.)

Feature Name	Description
KEEP ROWS AND COLUMNS OF UNRECOGNIZED MEMBERS	If the members of a dimension have changed and there are members that have been removed or deleted, this keeps the unrecognized members available in the current report view.
WARN IF ROWS AND COLUMNS OF UNRECOGNIZED MEMBERS WILL BE KEPT	Generates a warning to tell the business user that some members of the report may be stale or members that have been removed.
WARN IF CONNECTION OR ENVIRONMENT IN THE CONNECTION IS NOT STORED	Generates a warning if a connection isn't stored. The connection for a template report or input form may not be stored because others will copy the template and link it to their own models. This parameter generates a warning to tell the user that the template will be saved but the connection will not be stored.
REFRESH ONLY EXPANDED AND INSERTED MEMBERS	Only allows a refresh on members that are new in a column or row. This helps when there is a large data volume associated with a report, and the refresh time can be long.
MEMBERS PER PAGE IN MEMBER SELECTOR	Determines the total number of members to display in the member selection view.
OTHERS	
DATA LINK SYMBOL COLOR	Identifies the color for the symbol that is assigned to the report for the QUICK LINK – DATA LINK option.
MEMBER LINK SYMBOL COLOR	Identifies the color for the symbol that is assigned to the report for the QUICK LINK – MEMBER LINK option,
WORKBOOK LOCATION – LOCAL	Determines that this workbook is to be assigned a local connection.
WORKBOOK LOCATION – PLANNING AND CONSOLIDATION SERVER	Determines that this workbook is to be assigned a planning and consolidation connection.

Table 4.8 List of Parameters in the EPM – User Options Dialog Box (Cont.)

Feature Name	Description
WARN IF REPORT EXCEEDS # OF CELLS	Generates a warning if the report is exceeding a total number of cells; the total number is assigned in this field.
FORCE SYMMETRIC REFRESH FOR LARGE ASYMMETRIC AXIS	Allows the ASYMMETRIC AXIS option to execute. This option can be useful if you have very large asymmetric reports and an out-of-memory message appears when a refresh is executed.
REFRESH ONLY DATA ON 'SAVE & REFRESH DATA"	Manages the information that is refreshed during a SAVE AND REFRESH DATA process. If this parameter is turned on, then everything that is in the current workbook is refreshed: only the data for all EPM functions and all reports (except the data for local members) in the workbook is refreshed. If it isn't turned on, then everything including the local members is refreshed.
APPLICATION LANGUAGE	Language that is defaulted for the application used in the report.
DATA LANGUAGE	Language that is defaulted for the data in the reports.
DISPLAY EPM CONTEXT BAR	Automatically displays the EPM CONTEXT bar when checked. When not checked, the EPM CONTEXT bar isn't displayed.
DISPLAY EPM PANE	Automatically displays the EPM pane when checked. When not checked, the pane isn't displayed.
DISPLAY CONTEXT INSIDE EPM PANE	Displays the EPM CONTEXT bar in the EPM pane rather than horizontally across the top of the Excel spreadsheet.
DISPLAY LOCAL CONNECTIONS	Automatically displays the local connection when checked on.
DISPLAY WARNING WHEN SAVING DATA OR COMMENTS	Automatically displays a message when the data or comments are saved.

Table 4.8 List of Parameters in the EPM – User Options Dialog Box (Cont.)

Feature Name	Description
DISPLAY MATRIX SECURITY WARNING	Automatically displays a message when a report containing unauthorized cells is refreshed.
DISPLAY WARNING WHEN PROCESS TAKES TIME	Automatically displays a message when the total number of row/column combinations are generated. The default is 5,000. This warning is displayed after a refresh, drag and drop members into a report, or member expansion.
UNAUTHORIZED CELL TEXT	Text that will show in the unauthorized cell values based on security.
LOAD EV FUNCTIONS	Allows the use of the EV functions in the EPM add-in. This supports the previous EV functions available in BPC V7.5.
USE EPMMEMBERID IN EPM FORMULAS	If you're referencing a member of a dimension in a report with an EPM function formula, you'll need to use the EPMMEMBERID feature if you're using either the ID and DESCRIPTION or just the DESCRIPTION in the display. These two settings will not support the use of the member in a calculation. If you activate this feature, you can reference any OLAP member (any member used in a report either in the axis, rows, or columns) in an EPM formula.
NOTIFY ME WHEN UPDATES ARE AVAILABLE	Generates a message on log on when an update is available for the EPM add-in.
COMMENT SAVE – EMPTY COMMENT	If you're using a mass process to update a comment, and specific members don't have the comment assigned, this will fill in the COMMENT field with a value. In this case the default is ..., but you can adjust this text, and it will be inserted when necessary.

Table 4.8 List of Parameters in the EPM – User Options Dialog Box (Cont.)

Command Display Options

The EPM – COMMAND DISPLAY OPTION screen controls what you'll see in the initial screen. This is a decision to turn on the display of each of the sections in the EPM ribbon. For example, if you don't really need to see the options in the DATA INPUT section of the EPM ribbon that have to do with planning and consolidation, then you can remove those items from the list (see Figure 4.97).

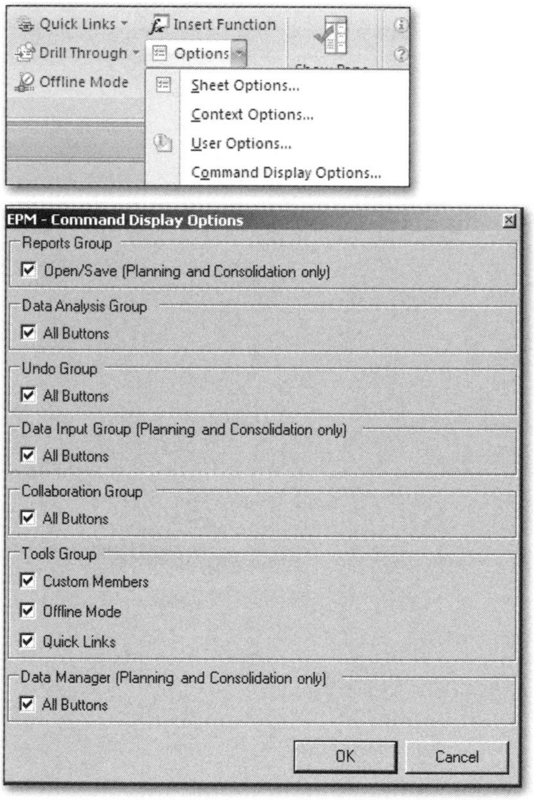

Figure 4.97 EPM – Command Display Options

More

The MORE portion of the EPM ribbon is a series of features that have more to do with extensions of the EPM add-in rather than core functionality. Some are also repeats of parameters in the USER OPTIONS or other portions of the ribbon. Figure 4.98 shows the list of options available.

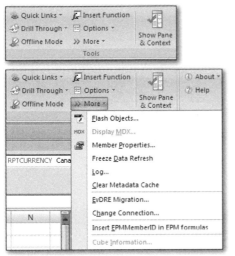

Figure 4.98 More Options in the EPM Ribbon

Flash Objects

Basically, a *Flash object* is created via the SAP BusinessObjects Dashboard Designer (hereafter, Dashboards) component. The FLASH OBJECT option enables the retrieval of information based on a graphical or visual view of the data. This also allows the graphical report to have functionality that supports what-if analysis. After you design the object using the Dashboards component and export it in the Flash format, you can retrieve it in the EPM add-in platform by using this feature. It can be inserted into any of the Microsoft Office suite components.

Display MDX

This option allows the display of the MDX (MultiDimensional eXpressions) query that is being used by the current data sheet. You can then copy and reuse this MDX query for creating other reports.

Member Properties

The MEMBER PROPERTIES option might be of interest to you in terms of displaying the properties of a dimension. This option can be executed from the MORE option, and it will show a list of the properties and members of those properties assigned to the specific dimension value. If you click on a member in the report, and then execute the MEMBER PROPERTIES option, you'll see something similar to what is displayed in Figure 4.99. This shows not only the properties but also the hierarchy links.

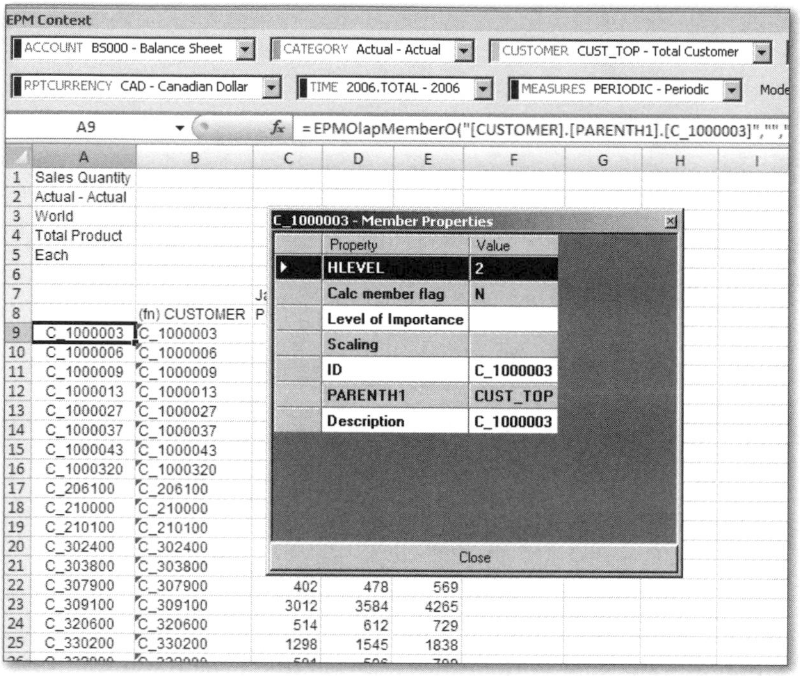

Figure 4.99 Showing Properties and Hierarchy Links

Freeze Data Refresh

This option will eliminate the refresh process as you navigate the report. If you have several changes to make and want to hold the refresh until the end of the changes, then choose this option. After completion of the changes, execute a data refresh to access the database once to realign the report with all of the changes.

Log

The log is very important in the process of analyzing errors in the processing of the EPM add-in. This LOG option generates a temporary file with all of the executable activities that have occurred in the report and will help focus your efforts to debug any issues with error messages or warnings generated by the EPM add-in.

Clear MetaData Cache

This feature is normally managed from the USER OPTIONS dialog box where you can identify a time where the metadata cache can be cleared either daily or on a specific sequence of days. If the TIME filter is set to "1", then the metadata cache is cleared once a day; if set to "2", then it's cleared twice a day; and so on. If you chose CLEAR

METADATA CACHE from this dropdown list,it will clear the Cache immediately.This is a user setting that is an immediate clear of the memory in cache. This might come in useful, for instance, when the master data has changed, and you need to clear the current metadata to get a clean update to the local cache.

EvDRE Migration

This is the link to execute the migration of the EvDRE reports to the EPM features. This is discussed and demonstrated in Chapter 10.

Change Connection

This function allows the user to switch connections to another BPC model or BW InfoProvider. This feature is available in a number of locations on the EPM ribbon, such as in the SAVE or OPEN context menus. If, for example, you require two reports in one worksheet or workbook, you'll need to change the connection to the other source of information. Using this CHANGE CONNECTION link will allow you to display all of the connections and link to a different model or InfoProvider.

Insert EPMMemberID in EPM Formulas

This option is explained in Table 4.8 and is available via USER OPTIONS • OTHER.

4.7   EPM Add-In Basics

Now that we've gone through the features you'll find on the ribbon to help with your reporting, we can start to get into the details available to create a report. You've already created a basic report using just the drag-and-drop process of incorporating some of the dimensions in the report. Now let's get into the specifics available in the EDIT REPORT and NEW REPORT components. We bypassed these two during our initial conversations about the REPORTS portion of the ribbon because these supporting components are the critical tools in the toolset. If we bypass all of the other features available, you can still create a report. Without the REPORT EDITOR and NEW REPORT components, however, you would have to create a report using the REPORT pane or the drag-and-drop methods. After you get use to the Report Editor that you access either via the NEW REPORT or EDIT REPORT links, you'll probably use the REPORT EDITOR as much as possible.

Another feature we need to cover that we passed over in the ribbon is the use of the EPM FORMAT component. This can definitely put the finishing touches on a report for you and make the whole process of formatting more focused and centralized while addressing any corporate requirements for formatting of official reports. The ability to create a workbook with multiple reports embedded that come from different source systems is also invaluable. For example, if you want to pull together a comparison process to view two different InfoCubes, and you don't have the ability to use a MultiProvider, then this just might do the trick for you.

4.7.1 Report Editor, Report Selection

The REPORT EDITOR is used by both the EDIT REPORT and NEW REPORT links. This is the primary component to help with a report after it's created. These features make moving dimensions around the report and realigning the data very easy. There are 10 different tabs in this component of the EPM add-in. Each has specific responsibilities, and you'll probably only use a few of them regularly, but understanding what all of the functions do can be useful. For example, the SORTING, FILTERING, and RANKING tabs can be used to allow the report to show specific views of the data, but you can also use the basic Excel functions to do these tasks. The business users can decide which of these approaches works best for them. Table 4.9 lists the different tabs and provides a short description of what features each has to offer.

Tab	Description
LAYOUT	This tab's features support the creation of a report—from the layout of the rows, columns, and axis to the option to "shift" the report format allowing the creation of butterfly reports as well as a basic realignment of the report.
OPTIONS	This tab's features support a combination of formatting, refreshing, data options, and display or hide options for records with zeroes. These options can also be defaulted from the OPTIONS in the TOOLS section by checking the parameter INHERIT SHEET OPTIONS in this tab.
SORTING	This offers the ability to sort the members in ascending and descending order based on specific members, first column, or last column.
FILTERING	This offers the ability to rank members by values using multiple different scenarios by amounts and by criteria based on columns or rows.

Table 4.9 EPM – Report Editor Tabs

Tab	Description
RANKING	This offers the ability to rank by member values based on TOP X or BOTTOM X values.
READ-ONLY DATA	This allows the restriction of posting values on these specific members.
LOCAL MEMBERS	This offers the option to create a formula using MDX and/or to change an existing formula. Additionally, this allows the ability to position the formula (local member) within the report.
MEMBER NAMES	This offers the ability to change the member descriptions so that they can be unique for specific reports. This doesn't change the description assigned to the members in the database but only for the report.
EXCLUDED MEMBERS	This supports the restriction of specific members from being available in the report itself.
MEMBER INSERTION FILTERING	This supports the restriction of member availability within the MEMBER SELECTION screen. This will reduce the total number of members showing within the member selection.

Table 4.9 EPM – Report Editor Tabs (Cont.)

The first tab, LAYOUT, is the most used, and it's one of the three approaches that can be used for creating a report (see Figure 4.100). To use this tab to create a report, you just drag and drop the dimensions into the appropriate sections of the LAYOUT screen, and this will help construct the report with the rows and columns. The PAGE AXIS DIMENSIONS are those that can be used as filters on the report. For example, if you want to be able to filter the report based on category, you drag and drop the dimension CATEGORY into that section of the screen. After a dimension is moved into a section, you can click on it to open the MEMBER SELECTION screen and filter and align the members of each dimension as required. You saw this earlier in the chapter in the example of setting up a basic report earlier.

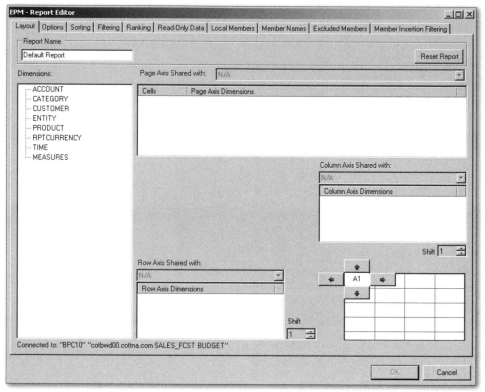

Figure 4.100 EPM – Report Editor: Layout Tab

Several other features on the LAYOUT tab can be useful during the build of your reports as well. For example, let's discuss the use of the SHIFT option beside both the ROWS and COLUMNS sections of this screen. If you notice the normal position is "1" in both SHIFT cells, then the results of a basic report using this is similar to Figure 4.101. If you go back into the LAYOUT screen and change the SHIFT to a "–1" (Figure 4.102), the final result changes as shown in Figure 4.103. This can be of significant use if you're dealing with a butterfly report where you see data on both sides of the dimension members. This is the first step, followed by creating another report with the same dimension as a connector. So this report might be something to see the data based on "Actuals" on one side and "Budget" on the other side. As you can see this, is a very easy process when you use the SHIFT feature.

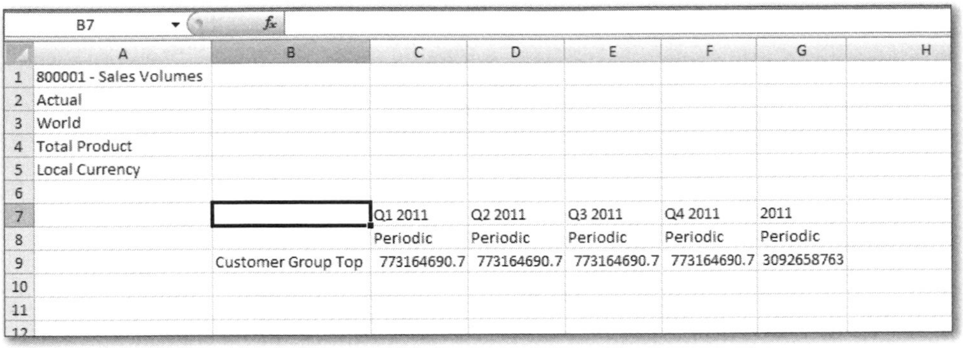

	A	B	C	D	E	F	G	H
1	800001 - Sales Volumes							
2	Actual							
3	World							
4	Total Product							
5	Local Currency							
6								
7			Q1 2011	Q2 2011	Q3 2011	Q4 2011	2011	
8			Periodic	Periodic	Periodic	Periodic	Periodic	
9		Customer Group Top	773164690.7	773164690.7	773164690.7	773164690.7	3092658763	
10								
11								
12								

Figure 4.101   Report with Shift 1 Positioning

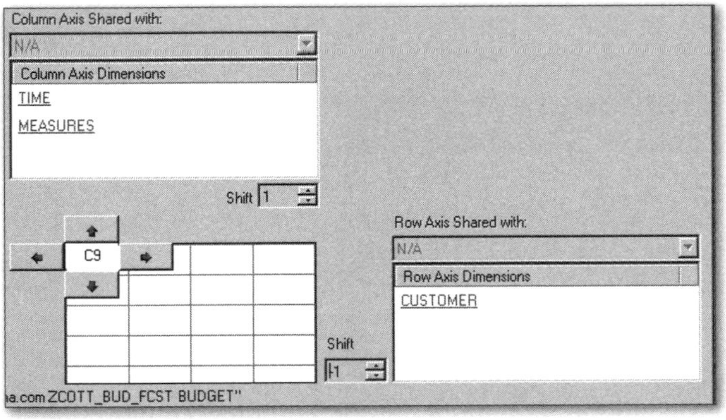

Figure 4.102   Layout Screen with Shift –1 Positioning

EPM Context

ACCOUNT Balance Sheet | CATEGORY Actual | CUSTOMER Total Customer | ENTITY Consolidation Entity | PRODUCT Total Product

MEASURES Periodic   Model:BUDGET

	A	B	C	D	E	F	G	H
1	800001 - Sales Volumes							
2	Actual							
3	World							
4	Total Product							
5	Local Currency							
6								
7			Q1 2011	Q2 2011	Q3 2011	Q4 2011	2011	
8			Periodic	Periodic	Periodic	Periodic	Periodic	
9			773164690.7	773164690.7	773164690.7	773164690.7	3092658763	Customer Group Top
10								

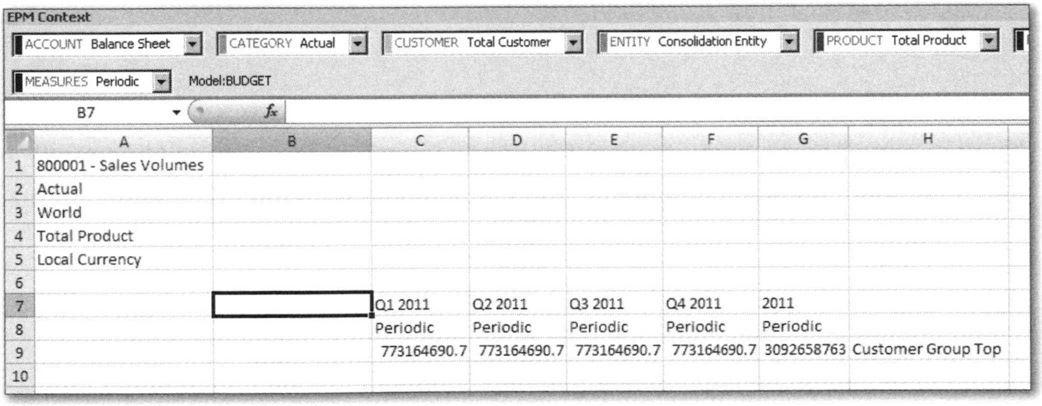

Figure 4.103   Report with Shift –1 Positioning

There are a few other features on the LAYOUT tab, such as changing the name of the report from the "default" report to a specific name and the ability to move the dimension positions around the report. However, the primary use for this tab is to develop the basics of the report.

The second tab, OPTIONS (see Figure 4.104), has very similar features as the SHEET OPTIONS and USER OPTIONS. The parameter at the /top—INHERIT SHEET OPTIONS—is usually checked, so all of the features that you use in the SHEET OPTIONS and USER OPTIONS are also used here. If you need any information on these features, refer to Section 4.6.6.

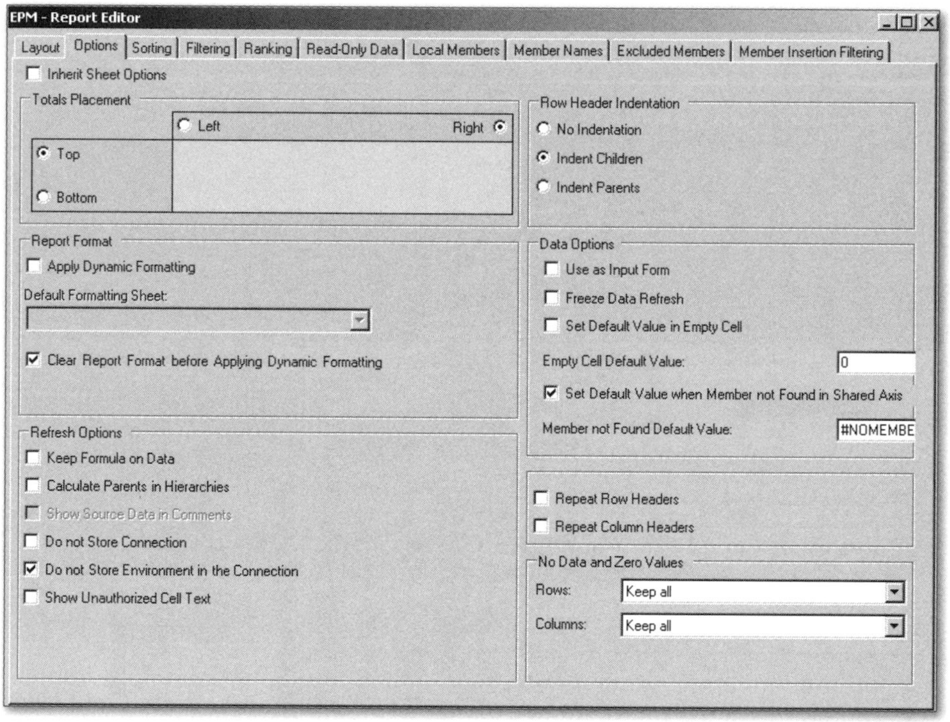

Figure 4.104 EPM – Report Editor: Options Tab

The next several tabs—SORTING, FILTERING, *and* RANKING—are used for realigning the data into specific views. For example, the SORTING tab shown in Figure 4.105 has several available parameters for sorting data.

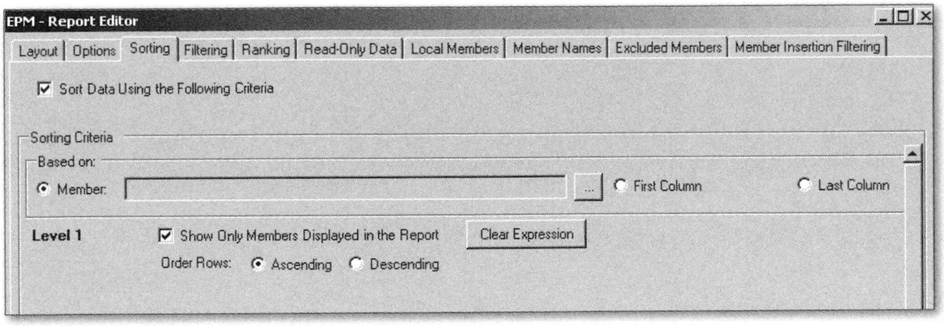

Figure 4.105   EPM – Report Editor: Sorting Tab

To use this feature, you first need to check the SORT DATA USING THE FOLLOWING CRITERIA checkbox, and then the rest of the parameters become available. For the BASED ON parameter, you can choose the actual member that you want to use as a value for either the ASCENDING or DESCENDING values. The other option is to choose the FIRST COLUMN or LAST COLUMN. In our example, we chose to use the member "Jan 2011, Periodic" and ASCENDING display as shown in Figure 4.106.

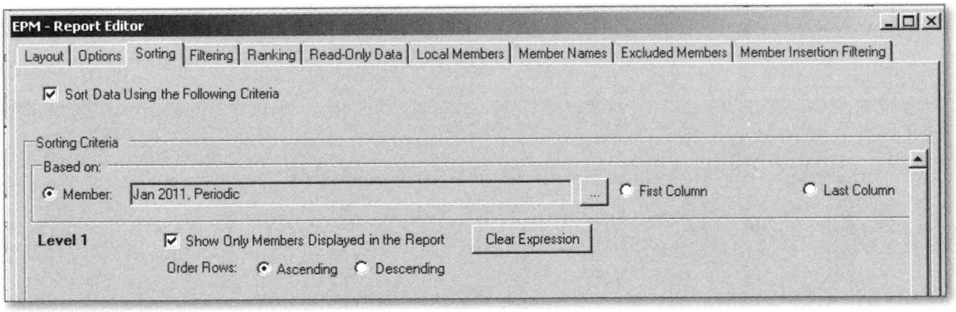

Figure 4.106   EPM – Report Editor: Sorting Tab

The results are shown in Figure 4.107. As you can see, the values in the first column were used for the ascending values. Looking closely, you can see that C_320600 (line 22) is consistent for Jan, 2011, but not for Feb, 2011 since in Jan 2011 it is properly positioned in ascending order but in Feb 2011 it is not positioned properly in ascending order. If this would be the case then it would be before C_400200.

	A	B	C	D	E
1	Sales Quantity				
2	Actual - Actual				
3	World				
4	Total Product				
5	Each				
6					
7		Jan 2011	Feb 2011	Mar 2011	
8		Periodic	Periodic	Periodic	
9	C_520000 - C_520000	59	83	116	
10	C_510000 - C_510000	62	87	122	
11	C_355100 - C_355100	116	138	164	
12	C_540000 - C_540000	226	317	443	
13	C_530000 - C_530000	262	367	514	
14	C_500000 - C_500000	361	505	707	
15	C_400500 - C_400500	398	485	592	
16	C_307900 - C_307900	402	478	569	
17	C_341000 - C_341000	409	487	579	
18	C_1000037 - C_1000037	474	569	683	
19	C_332100 - C_332100	487	580	690	
20	C_332000 - C_332000	501	596	709	
21	C_400200 - C_400200	511	624	761	
22	C_320600 - C_320600	514	612	729	
23	C_401000 - C_401000	561	685	836	
24	C_210000 - C_210000	576	685	815	
25	C_210100 - C_210100	576	685	815	
26	C_374800 - C_374800	651	774	921	
27	C_206100 - C_206100	715	851	1013	
28	C_1000006 - C_1000006	741	889	1067	

Figure 4.107 Report with Sorting Active

The RANKING option is used for a specific ranking process rather than just ascending or descending, but the parameters look very similar as shown in Figure 4.108. The difference is the use of the RANKING parameter for either the TOP or BOTTOM number of ROWS.

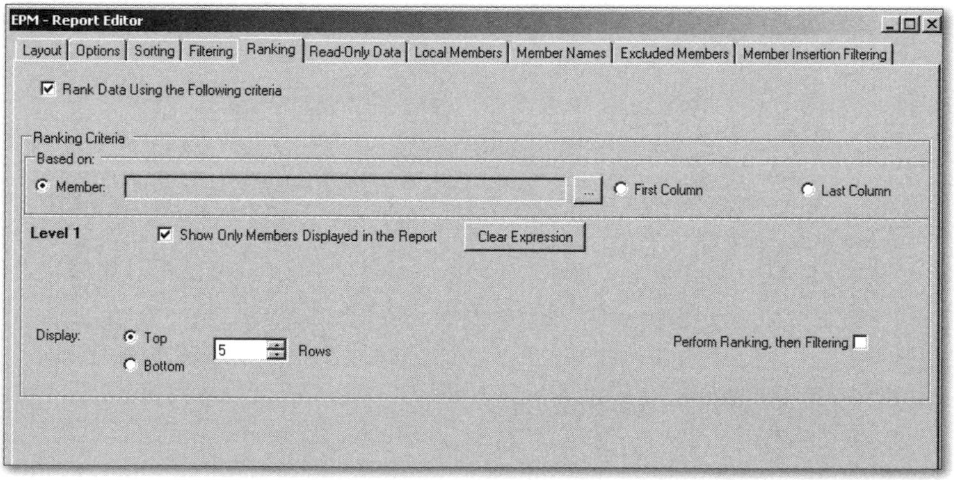

Figure 4.108 EPM – Report Editor: Ranking

The FILTERING tab offers a few additional required settings, but it has a very similar feel, as shown in Figure 4.109. The idea to remember with this feature is that you're looking to create a view of the data based on a specific value, for example, all values greater than 1,000,000.00. And, if there are a series of dimensions in the column, you can use a specific dimension to support the set of information displayed as a result.

Again, to activate this feature, check the FILTER DATA USING THE FOLLOWING CRITERIA checkbox. Then work through the following parameters to set up the view of data you are interested in:

▶ BASED ON – ROWS/COLUMNS or FILTER ON ALL COLUMNS/ROWS
If you choose ROWS, then the options that are displayed are the dimensions in the columns. For example, is if you choose ROWS here—meaning that you're looking to filter based on the customer list—then the parameter available is the time that appears across the columns. After you think about this for a bit, it makes sense because you're looking to filter the customers based on what's in the columns.

▶ IS = empty; second parameter = values; third parameter = dimension
The use of one or the other parameter depends on what is positioned in the BASED ON value. To continue the preceding example, let's assume that the BASED ON value is TIME. Then the second parameter might be a good choice, and you can then add a value such as $1,000,000. This means that you will see all customers with values in the TIME column over $1 million.

▶ ADD CRITERIA
After all parameters are filled in, this option becomes accessible and you can add your criteria to the FILTER EXPRESSIONS that appear below this option.

> **Note: Using Sorting, Filtering, Ranking**
>
> Depending on if you're looking to use more than one of these features at the same time, remember to deactivate the other features before activating another. If not, a combination of these features may not display the appropriate set of data.

The READ-ONLY DATA tab allows you to restrict certain dimension members or intersection of members to be read only. If you do, you can't post any data into that specific dimension value or intersection of values.

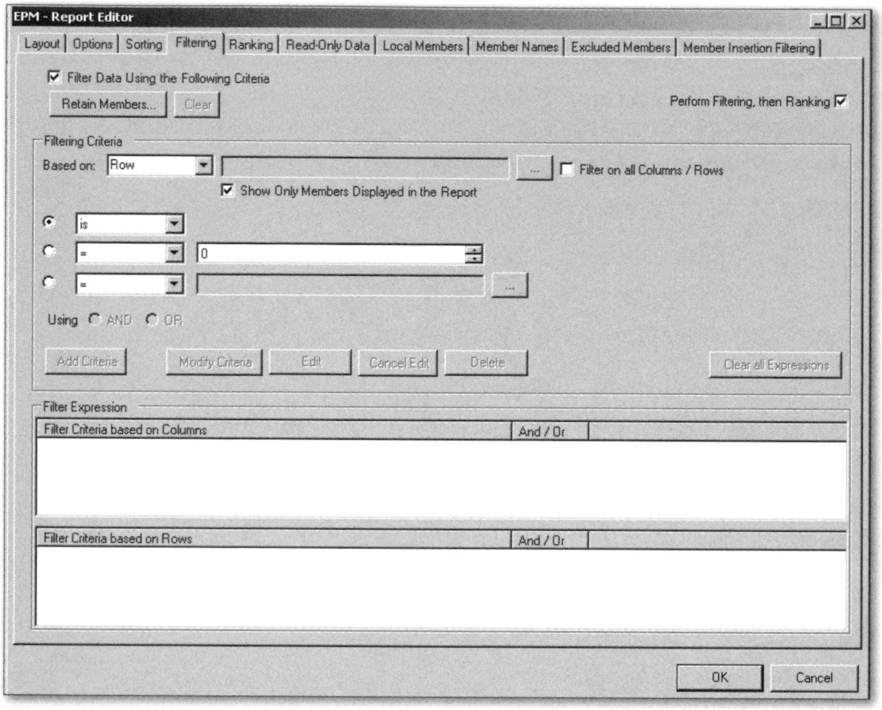

Figure 4.109 EPM – Report Editor: Filtering Tab

The LOCAL MEMBERS tab allows you to create a local member. We'll discuss the LOCAL member feature in the next section. If you're good at creating MDX statements, then you should come directly here to create a local member. A local member is a calculated value with a placeholder in that particular report. The formula is inserted in the field labeled FORMULA as shown in Figure 4.110.

There are also parameters to position the local member, such as insert before or after a specific position in the report or attach to a specific member or combination. It's normally much easier to create the local member in the report itself by creating an Excel formula with the LOCAL MEMBER RECOGNITION option turned on (this can be found in the SHEET OPTIONS, which were covered in Section 4.6.6), so that it can recognize and generate the format of the local member. This will allow all of the information required in the screen to be generated automatically. Just remember that a local member can only be created on base-level members and not on nodes. So if you have a calculation in a P&L statement, for example, and you need a local member created, you'll have to make sure to use only base-level members of the dimension and not the hierarchy node level members. If you use the hierarchy node level members, you'll create the Excel-based formula, but it won't convert to a local member. We'll show an example of this in the next section.

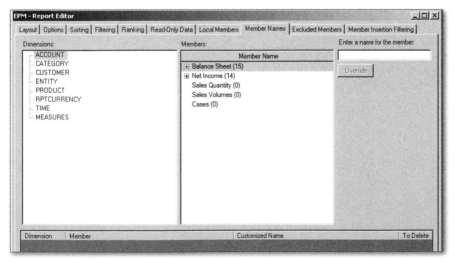

Figure 4.110   EPM – Report Editor: Local Members Tab

The next tab—MEMBER NAMES—provides another useful feature for reports. This feature comes in handy when faced with the common situation where you have standard naming conventions for the global view of the information, but a particular department needs to have a different description. Figure 4.111 shows the parameters and information required.

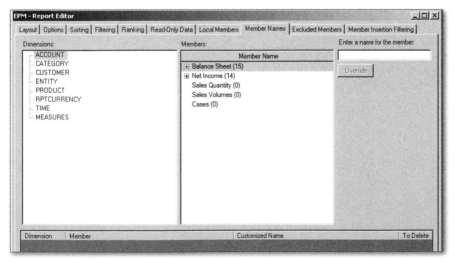

Figure 4.111   EPM – Report Editor: Member Names Tab

To use this feature, click on the appropriate member, and fill in the name or description that you want to see on your report. This will be unique to your report and not alter the standard naming convention.

The next two features—EXCLUDED MEMBERS and MEMBER INSERTION FILTERING—offer some other options to adjust the member view. EXCLUDED MEMBERS allows you to specifically select the members that you want to remove from the list of viewable members. This is a manual process, so if you want to manage this centrally, you should probably go to security and authorization to take care of this situation. In terms of the member insertion, this doesn't have an impact on the actual report, but it does allow the filtering of the MEMBER SELECTION screen. This is useful if you have a dimension with a large number of members because you can filter some members that aren't used or inactive, so that the system will display fewer members.

4.7.2 Local Members

LOCAL MEMBERS is an excellent feature that will help the end user create the calculations and formulas required to improve report results. Information that is being delivered by the basic InfoCube from either BPC or BW won't have all of the required calculations or combinations to accommodate the business user reports. This puts a toolset in the users' hands so they can create the formulas on their own. Although this can be good or bad, you can control who has access to create these formulas. With this feature, you have to remember to understand the situation where you can actually use the local members. Let's take a look at an example first. Looking at the current view of the example report in Figure 4.112, you can see that JAN, FEB, MAR appear across the columns.

If you want, you can create a quarterly calculation directly in the report. You can just add the QTD value that is available in the system, assuming that you want to use this feature. Remember; before you use this, make sure the ACTIVATE LOCAL MEMBER RECOGNITION parameter is set in the SHEET OPTIONS (see Figure 4.113). After this is confirmed, you can proceed to create a local member value. To do this within the EPM add-in, you just choose the appropriate cell and create the Excel-based formula. This can be any basic Excel-based formula that you normally see in an Excel spreadsheet.

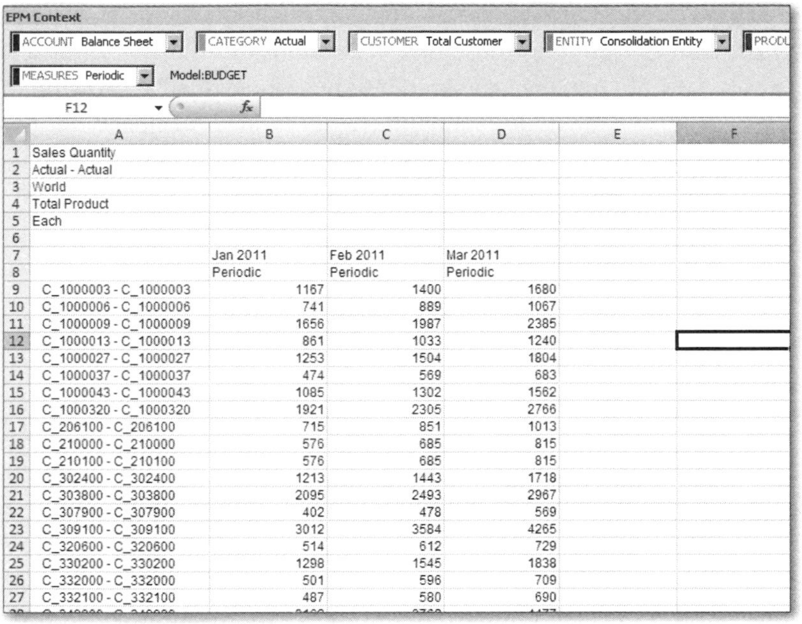

Figure 4.112 EPM add-in Report

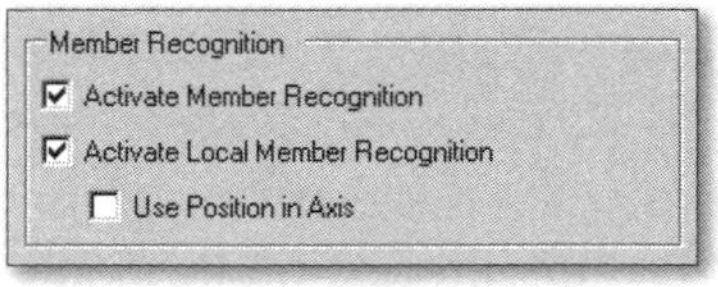

Figure 4.113 Activate Local Member Recognition Parameter in Sheet Options

In Figure 4.114, you see that a formula has been created with a summing of the three columns of data. Remember, these are base-level members, that is, months, so this is possible. After pressing ⌈Enter⌉, the results are shown in Figure 4.115.

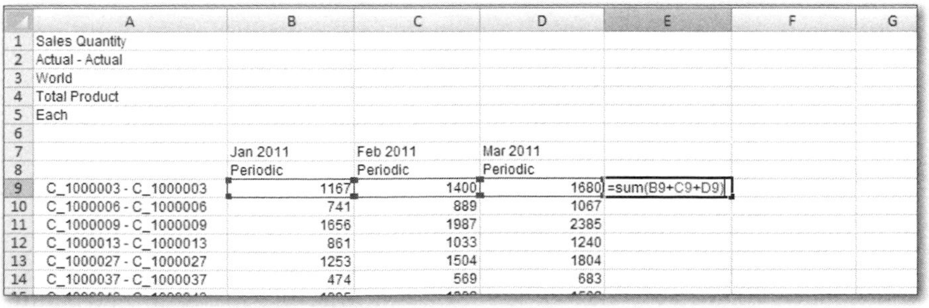

Figure 4.114 Report with SUM for Columns B+C+D

The calculation is generated all the way down the list of customers, and it will flex as the report is changed as well (see Figure 4.115). It will also be available even if you switch the axis and hold the formula. As mentioned, this will also show up in the REPORT EDITOR, and you can adjust some information on this calculation. For example, the title of the column isn't that user friendly, so you can step into the REPORT EDITOR and fix this issue.

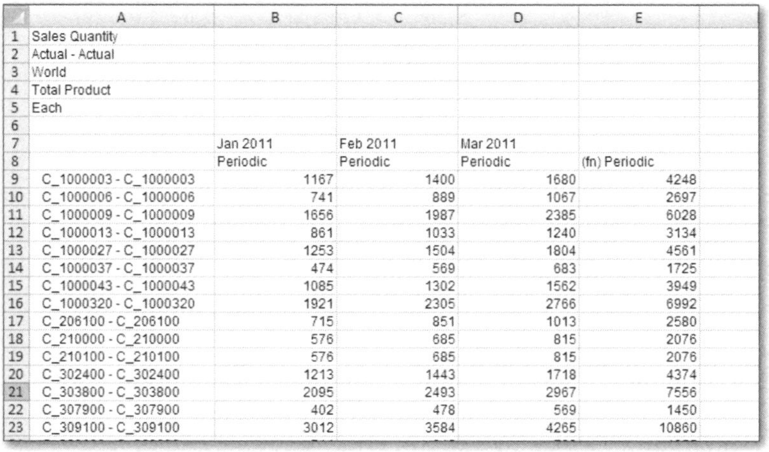

	A	B	C	D	E
1	Sales Quantity				
2	Actual - Actual				
3	World				
4	Total Product				
5	Each				
6					
7		Jan 2011	Feb 2011	Mar 2011	
8		Periodic	Periodic	Periodic	(fn) Periodic
9	C_1000003 - C_1000003	1167	1400	1680	4248
10	C_1000006 - C_1000006	741	889	1067	2697
11	C_1000009 - C_1000009	1656	1987	2385	6028
12	C_1000013 - C_1000013	861	1033	1240	3134
13	C_1000027 - C_1000027	1253	1504	1804	4561
14	C_1000037 - C_1000037	474	569	683	1725
15	C_1000043 - C_1000043	1085	1302	1562	3949
16	C_1000320 - C_1000320	1921	2305	2766	6992
17	C_206100 - C_206100	715	851	1013	2580
18	C_210000 - C_210000	576	685	815	2076
19	C_210100 - C_210100	576	685	815	2076
20	C_302400 - C_302400	1213	1443	1718	4374
21	C_303800 - C_303800	2095	2493	2967	7556
22	C_307900 - C_307900	402	478	569	1450
23	C_309100 - C_309100	3012	3584	4265	10860

Figure 4.115 Results from Local Member Calculation

If you open the REPORT EDITOR, you see that on the LOCAL MEMBERS tab, a member has been created. Now you can just type in the appropriate title for this column—"QTD 2011"—and it will be displayed on the report (see Figure 4.116).

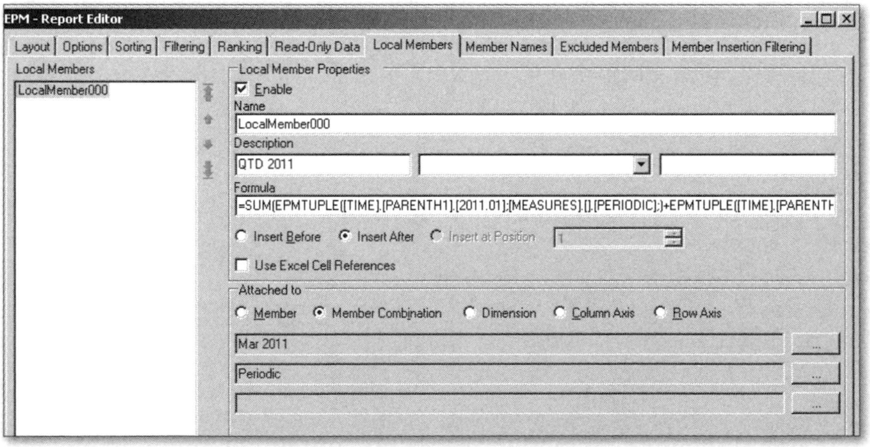

Figure 4.116 EPM – Report Editor: Local Members Tab

The results are shown in the report in Figure 4.117.

	A	B	C	D	E	
1	Sales Quantity					
2	Actual - Actual					
3	World					
4	Total Product					
5	Each					
6						
7		Jan 2011	Feb 2011	Mar 2011	QTD 2011	
8		Periodic	Periodic	Periodic		
9	C_1000003 - C_1000003	1167	1400	1680	4248	
10	C_1000006 - C_1000006	741	889	1067	2697	
11	C_1000009 - C_1000009	1656	1987	2385	6028	
12	C_1000013 - C_1000013	861	1033	1240	3134	
13	C_1000027 - C_1000027	1253	1504	1804	4561	
14	C_1000037 - C_1000037	474	569	683	1725	
15	C_1000043 - C_1000043	1085	1302	1562	3949	
16	C_1000320 - C_1000320	1921	2305	2766	6992	
17	C_206100 - C_206100	715	851	1013	2580	
18	C_210000 - C_210000	576	685	815	2076	
19	C_210100 - C_210100	576	685	815	2076	
20	C_302400 - C_302400	1213	1443	1718	4374	
21	C_303800 - C_303800	2095	2493	2967	7556	
22	C_307900 - C_307900	402	478	569	1450	
23	C_309100 - C_309100	3012	3584	4265	10860	

Figure 4.117   Report with New Column Title

This feature can be used quite nicely in a P&L report or statement to create summing levels for groups of GL accounts or to create percentage information such as Gross Margin % or Net Profit %. As the report is drilled down into or sliced and diced, these values and members will move with the report. If you use Excel-based formulas, the Excel formulas may not move as consistently with the report process if the report is expanded and collapsed.

Note: Custom Members

Custom members can also be created from a local connection and not specifically from a Web services connection. Therefore, with the connection process used for BPC cubes, this feature isn't available. If you're in a local connection, an additional link in the EPM – TOOLS section will be available to create custom members. The custom members can be shared across InfoCubes and therefore can be saved, imported, and exported as an MDX definition. You can also convert a local member to a custom member but not vice versa. With the additional feature of the custom member, you can also remove a portion of the formula from the report, and the custom member will still show the appropriate value based on the core formula even if a portion of the formula isn't present in the report.

4.7.3 Formatting of Reports

Now that we have everything in the report that we need for the data, we have to determine what the business user wants in terms of a finished report. To help with this, the very flexible formatting template delivered with the EPM add-in offers a significant number of features. If you are used to the Excel formatting process, you can use that as well. If you decide to use the Excel formatting, the report/input template that the formatting is applied to—once saved—will continue to hold the formatted applied. We recommend that you review and work with the EPM formatting features before moving directly to the Excel option. After working with this for a bit, the process becomes very straightforward and uses components you will be familiar with from working with Excel. One benefit is that it allows you to assign formats centrally and then you don't have to worry about the look and feel of the corporate reports.

The template also has some unique features specific to EPM. One of the unique features is the ability to format based on the nature of the line in the report. For example, the levels that formatting can be assigned are CUSTOM MEMBER DEFAULT FORMAT, CALCULATED MEMBERS, INPUT MEMBERS (great for input templates to show where the business user can and can't post data), LOCAL MEMBERS (the calculated values), CHANGED MEMBERS, and member-specific formatting based on a property of those members. In each of the different sections of the FORMATTING SHEET, there are parameters that are general to all areas, such as formatting for the data and the header, and what formatting should be assigned and used in the report.

The EPM FORMATTING SHEET is broken down into the following four sections:

▶ HIERARCHY LEVEL FORMATTING
This allows formatting at the different levels of the hierarchy. You can add more levels or remove levels from this list, and each level can have different formatting for display. You also can assign these formats to either the rows or columns. Figure 4.118 shows the HIERARCHY LEVEL FORMATTING section.

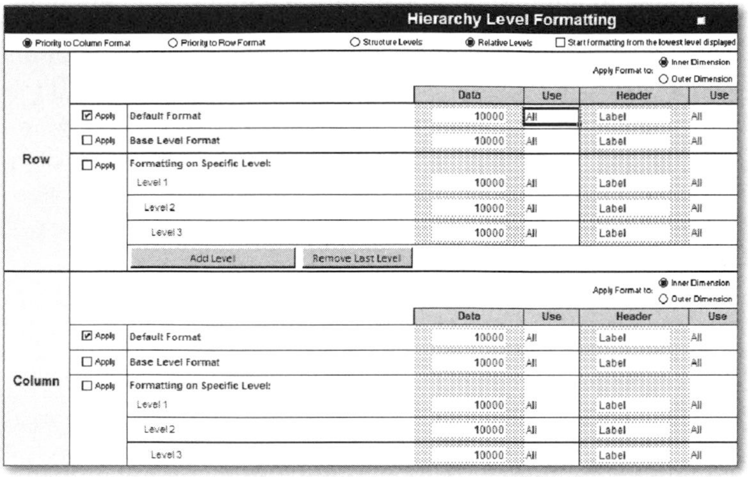

Figure 4.118 EPM Formatting Sheet – Hierarchy Level Formatting

▶ DIMENSION MEMBER/PROPERTY FORMATTING

This allows the business user to formatting the specific members on the rows and the columns. There are six different types of member values that you can format unique views for to customize the report. The options to actually create the customized formatting view are the same as the hierarchy. The only difference is the assignment to the actual members versus using the hierarchy as a formatting prompt (see Figure 4.119).

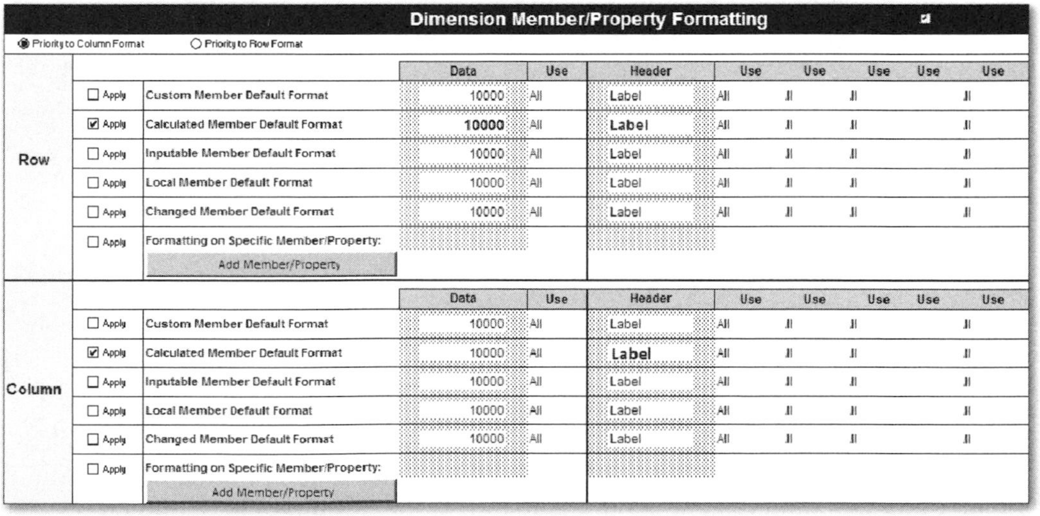

Figure 4.119 EPM Formatting Sheet – Dimension Member/Property Formatting

► ROW AND COLUMN BANDING

This option offers more of a generic approach to formatting and focuses on the structure of the report rather than the actual data. In this case, you can add formatting to the even or odd rows and columns. The approach to the actual parameters assigned is the same as the others described (see Figure 4.120).

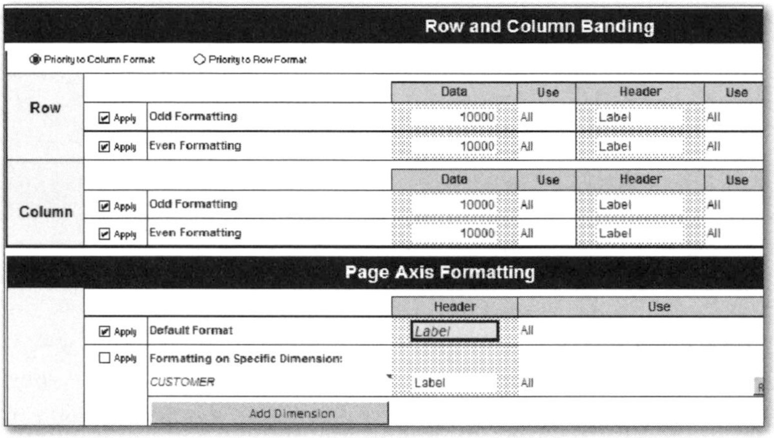

Figure 4.120 EPM Formatting Sheet – Dimension Member/Property Formatting

► PAGE AXIS FORMATTING

This focuses specifically on the PAGE AXIS section or basically the filtering dimensions to the report (refer to Figure 4.120).

Now, let's look at a basic example of these features to see how straightforward the use of this FORMATTING SHEET really is. Let's start out with the basic report shown in Figure 4.121, which is nothing more than a report generated to show the customers sales volumes by quarter in 2011.

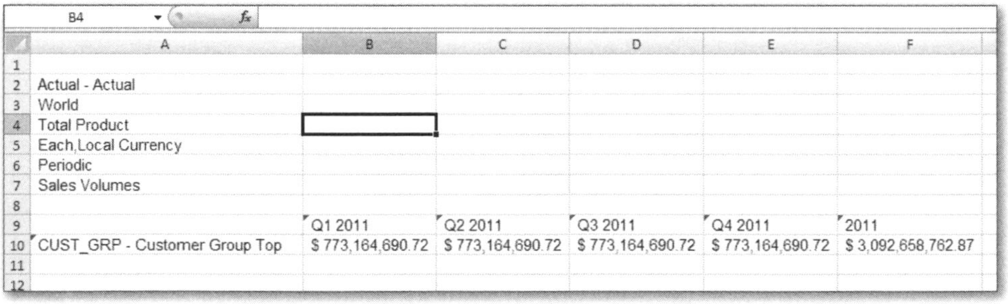

Figure 4.121 EPM add-in Report – Sales Volumes by Quarter

To open the EPM Formatting Sheet, click the View Format feature in the Report portion of the EPM ribbon. This will generate another sheet in the workbook called EPMFormattingSheet, which holds the formatting information that is directly linked to the current workbook. After you configure some formatting features, you can refresh the report to see the results. For the Page Axis Formatting portion, you need to check the box next to the Page Axis Formatting title as well as the Apply checkbox beside the Default Format line (Figure 4.122). Then right-click on the Header cell, and open the Excel formatting dialog box to make some changes to the basic setup (see Figure 4.123). This is the very familiar dialog box with the Excel formatting options to be applied to the EPM Formatting Sheet.

> **Note: EPM Formatting Parameters**
>
> Make sure that the Formatting parameters in the Sheet Options are selected appropriately for the use of dynamic formatting.

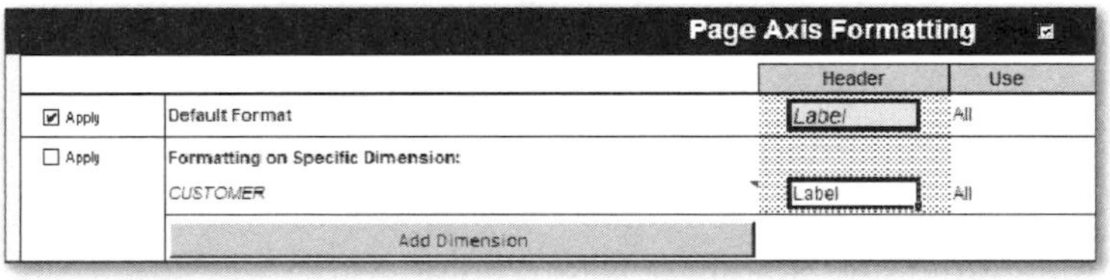

Figure 4.122   EPM Formatting Sheet – Page Axis Formatting

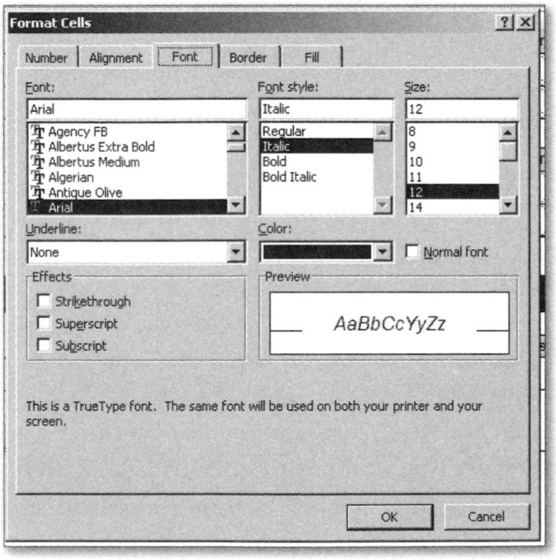

Figure 4.123   Changing Font, Color, and Size in the Format Cells Dialog Box

After these changes are made, you can go back to the report and execute a refresh to see the results shown in Figure 4.124. As you can see, the formatting for the page axis has been changed based on the adjustments in the EPM FORMATTING SHEET.

	A	B	C	D	E	F	G
1							
2	Actual - Actual						
3	World						
4	Total Product						
5	Each,Local Currency						
6	Periodic						
7	Sales Volumes						
8							
9		Q1 2011	Q2 2011	Q3 2011	Q4 2011	2011	
10	CUST_GRP - Customer Group Top	773164690.7	773164690.7	773164690.7	773164690.7	3092658763	
11							
12							

Figure 4.124 EPM add-in Report with Formatting Applied

Taking this a step further and using the DIMENSION MEMBER/PROPERTY FORMATTING section, you can adjust the format for the rows and columns to show the results of these changes. Specifically, the changes shown earlier in Figure 4.119 include checking the APPLY parameter as well as selecting the checkbox to the right of the DIMENSION MEMBER/PROPERTY FORMATTING title. With these two items checked and the changes made to the formatting, you can go back to the report and execute a refresh to see the results shown in Figure 4.125.

	A	B	C	D	E	F
1						
2	Actual - Actual					
3	World					
4	Total Product					
5	Each,Local Currency					
6	Periodic					
7	Sales Volumes					
8						
9		Q1 2011	Q2 2011	Q3 2011	Q4 2011	2011
10	CUST_GRP - Customer Group To	773164690.7	773164690.7	773164690.7	773164690.7	3092658763
11						
12						
13						

Figure 4.125 EPM add-in Report with Formatting Applied

In this case, we changed the color of the row values and adjusted the font of all of the areas in the report. As you can see, applying this formatting is a very straightforward process. This formatted template can now be saved and later applied to all of the newly created reports.

4.7.4 Multi-Reports in a Workbook

Being able to have multiple reports in one workbook from different sources is very useful. You may not use this feature much in the beginning of your experiences with the EPM add-in, but you may come to rely on it later, especially when it comes to requirements such as a comparison or validation on the fly. This feature doesn't use any specific EPM add-in functionality, but it does use multiple connections in one worksheet or multiple worksheets. For example, data might be in two different sources or different InfoCubes. In a normal BW situation, the BW technical team would have to create a MultiProvider to create the union of the data. If you have some leeway in this area, you can just create two views in one worksheet to see the information side by side from the different InfoCubes. Going back to our initial report, you would need to use the indicator on the CURRENT REPORT link to highlight the space of the current report in order to know where to position the new report (see Figure 4.126). The highlighted sections show the limits of the current report.

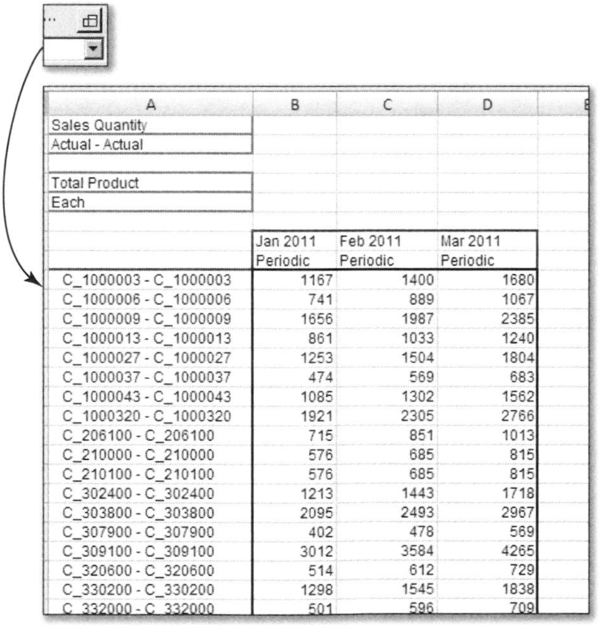

A	B	C	D
Sales Quantity			
Actual - Actual			
Total Product			
Each			
	Jan 2011	Feb 2011	Mar 2011
	Periodic	Periodic	Periodic
C_1000003 - C_1000003	1167	1400	1680
C_1000006 - C_1000006	741	889	1067
C_1000009 - C_1000009	1656	1987	2385
C_1000013 - C_1000013	861	1033	1240
C_1000027 - C_1000027	1253	1504	1804
C_1000037 - C_1000037	474	569	683
C_1000043 - C_1000043	1085	1302	1562
C_1000320 - C_1000320	1921	2305	2766
C_206100 - C_206100	715	851	1013
C_210000 - C_210000	576	685	815
C_210100 - C_210100	576	685	815
C_302400 - C_302400	1213	1443	1718
C_303800 - C_303800	2095	2493	2967
C_307900 - C_307900	402	478	569
C_309100 - C_309100	3012	3584	4265
C_320600 - C_320600	514	612	729
C_330200 - C_330200	1298	1545	1838
C_332000 - C_332000	501	596	709

Figure 4.126 Report Definition in the EPM add-in

Now you can add the report to either the side or the bottom of the report by selecting a cell and then connecting to a different source. Start by choosing a cell such as H1. From there, choose SELECT ANOTHER CONNECTION from the ACTIVE CONNECTION list as shown in Figure 4.127.

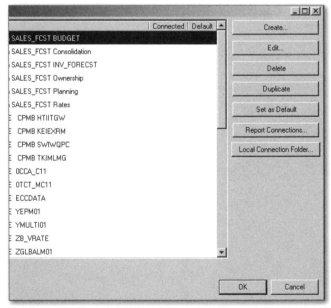

Figure 4.127 Selecting Another Connection

After you choose SELECT ANOTHER CONNECTION, you'll see a full list of all of the connections that are currently possible for you to choose from (see Figure 4.128).

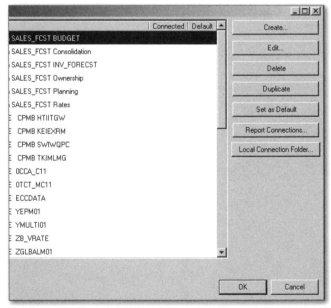

Figure 4.128 Connections Available for Source Data

Choose the CONSOLIDATION connection. The ACTIVE CONNECTION switches from the Forecast model to the Consolidation model as shown in Figure 4.129.

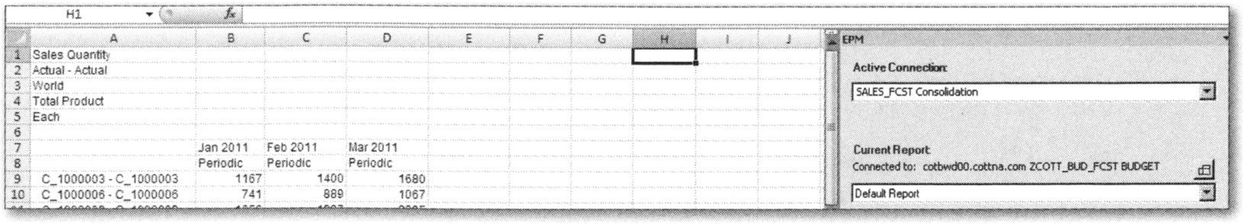

Figure 4.129 Multiple Reports in One Worksheet: Forecast and Consolidation

Notice that the Active Connection on the right side of the screen is Consolidation versus Budget. The final result is that you now have two reports on the same worksheet, and both are active and linked directly to the backend server. Clicking on each will switch the Active Connection from/to the multiple sources (see Figure 4.130).

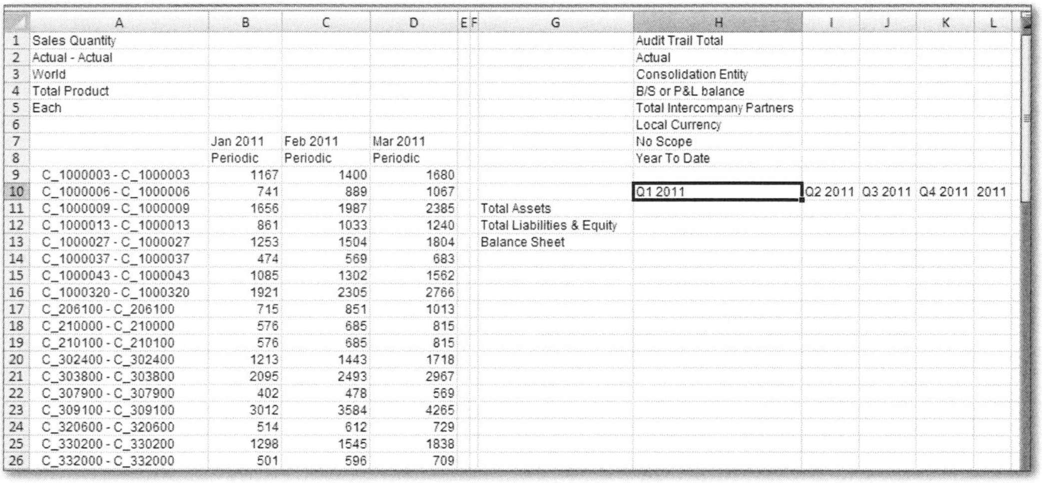

	A	B	C	D	E	F	G	H	I	J	K	L
1	Sales Quantity							Audit Trail Total				
2	Actual - Actual							Actual				
3	World							Consolidation Entity				
4	Total Product							B/S or P&L balance				
5	Each							Total Intercompany Partners				
6								Local Currency				
7		Jan 2011	Feb 2011	Mar 2011				No Scope				
8		Periodic	Periodic	Periodic				Year To Date				
9	C_1000003 - C_1000003	1167	1400	1680								
10	C_1000006 - C_1000006	741	889	1067				Q1 2011	Q2 2011	Q3 2011	Q4 2011	2011
11	C_1000009 - C_1000009	1656	1987	2385			Total Assets					
12	C_1000013 - C_1000013	861	1033	1240			Total Liabilities & Equity					
13	C_1000027 - C_1000027	1253	1504	1804			Balance Sheet					
14	C_1000037 - C_1000037	474	569	683								
15	C_1000043 - C_1000043	1085	1302	1562								
16	C_1000320 - C_1000320	1921	2305	2766								
17	C_206100 - C_206100	715	851	1013								
18	C_210000 - C_210000	576	685	815								
19	C_210100 - C_210100	576	685	815								
20	C_302400 - C_302400	1213	1443	1718								
21	C_303800 - C_303800	2095	2493	2967								
22	C_307900 - C_307900	402	478	569								
23	C_309100 - C_309100	3012	3584	4265								
24	C_320600 - C_320600	514	612	729								
25	C_330200 - C_330200	1298	1545	1838								
26	C_332000 - C_332000	501	596	709								

Figure 4.130 Multiple Reports on the Same Worksheet

This is just one approach when combining reports on the same worksheet or multiple worksheets in the same workbook. You can also use this functionality to create butterfly reports where two reports share a common dimension and can both be navigated on the same dimension. You can see now how quickly you can create a validation report, and as long as the dimensionality is consistent, you can also set up a very nice comparison report.

4.8 Excel Add-In Advanced Features

Some of the other more advanced features that are available in the EPM add-in include the ability to create asymmetric reports as well as use the new EPM and FPMXL functions. Creating asymmetric reports was not possible in either the BEX or the Analyzer (SAP BusinessObjects Suite component), but with the cell-based flexibility of the EPM add-in, you're now able to develop, save, and retrieve these types of reports with ease. You can do this in BEX, but you have to use the Local Calculations feature, which creates a more cell-based report in BEX and disconnects the OLAP feature of BEX. The result is that you won't have as much of a drilldown as you might want.

4.8.1 Asymmetric Reports

This isn't a specific feature in the EPM add-in, but this is an approach of how to use the functionality. An *asymmetric report* isn't consistent across either the rows or columns. For example, many of the reports that you use in the finance area are asymmetric in nature, where the report is showing a series of categories but not in any set order. So you might have the initial set of columns being controlled by Actual and Budget, but then a switch occurs to have a column controlled by Forecast data. Another example of an asymmetric report is a report with multiple different time frames across the columns. To contrast the asymmetric report with a symmetric report, see the symmetric report example shown in Figure 4.131. Unlike an asymmetric report, the columns are consistent across the entire symmetric report.

B5

	A	B	C	D	E	F	G	H
1	Sales Volumes							
2	United States							
3	Product A							
4	Local Currency							
5	Periodic							
6								
7								
8		Jan 2011		Feb 2011		Mar 2011		Apr 2011
9		Forecast	Actual	Forecast	Actual	Forecast	Actual	Forecast
10	C_206100	524000	524000	571160	623560	622564	742036	67
11	C_210000	513000	513000	559170	610470	609495	726459	66
12	C_210100	4035000	4035000	4398150	4801650	4793984	5713964	522
13	C_302400	2369000	2369000	2582210	2819110	2814609	3354741	306
14	C_303800	917000	917000	999530	1091230	1089488	1298564	118
15	C_307900	1178000	1178000	1284020	1401820	1399582	1668166	152
16	C_309100	2391000	2391000	2606190	2845290	2840747	3385895	309
17	C_320600	1879000	1879000	2048110	2236010	2232440	2660852	243
18	C_330200	3127000	3127000	3408430	3721130	3715189	4428145	404
19	C_332000	867000	867000	945030	1031730	1030083	1227759	112
20	C_332100	2383600	2383600	2598124	2836484	2831955	3375416	308
21	C_340000	2653000	2653000	2891770	3157070	3152029	3756913	343
22	C_341000	13232000	13232000	14422880	15746080	15720939	18737835	1713
23	C_355100	2821000	2821000	3074890	3356990	3351630	3994818	365
24	C_374800	122000	122000	132980	145180	144948	172764	15799
25	Total Customer	39011600	39011600	42522644	46423804	46349682	55244327	505211
26								
27								

Figure 4.131 Symmetric Report in EPM add-in

Now you can tweak this symmetric report to basically create an asymmetric report on the fly as shown in Figure 4.132.

	A	B	C	D	E	F	G	H
1	Sales Volumes							
2	United States							
3	Product A							
4	Local Currency							
5	Periodic							
6								
7								
8		Jan 2011	Mar 2011	Feb 2011	Feb 2011	Feb 2011	Mar 2011	Mar 2011
9		Forecast	Budget	Forecast	Actual	Budget	Forecast	Actual
10	C_206100	524000	555912	571160	623560	539720	622564	742036
11	C_210000	513000	544242	559170	610470	528390	609495	726459
12	C_210100	4035000	4280732	4398150	4801650	4156050	4793984	5713964
13	C_302400	2369000	2513272	2582210	2819110	2440070	2814609	3354741
14	C_303800	917000	972845	999530	1091230	944510	1089488	1298564
15	C_307900	1178000	1249740	1284020	1401820	1213340	1399582	1668166
16	C_309100	2391000	2536612	2606190	2845290	2462730	2840747	3385895
17	C_320600	1879000	1993431	2048110	2236010	1935370	2232440	2660852
18	C_330200	3127000	3317434	3408430	3721130	3220810	3715189	4428145
19	C_332000	867000	919800	945030	1031730	893010	1030083	1227759
20	C_332100	2383600	2528761	2598124	2836484	2455108	2831955	3375416
21	C_340000	2653000	2814568	2891770	3157070	2732590	3152029	3756913
22	C_341000	13232000	14037829	14422880	15746080	13628960	15720939	18737835
23	C_355100	2821000	2992799	3074890	3356990	2905630	3351630	3994818
24	C_374800	122000	129430	132980	145180	125660	144948	172764
25	Total Customer	39011600	41387406	42522644	46423804	40181948	46349682	55244327
26								
27								

Figure 4.132 Asymmetric Report in EPM add-in

As you can see, the columns aren't consistent at all. We have JAN, MAR, FEB, then FEB twice, and MAR twice. Also, the categories aren't consistent because we have FORECAST, BUDGET, FORECAST, then ACTUAL. This makes creating user-friendly financial reports easier and faster and without any support from the BW IT group. Think about the period-ending reports that you need to create. Faced with some of these report requirements, what might have taken a day or two to accommodate can be reduced to hours by creating a report with this method.

4.8.2 EPM and FPMXL Functions

The EPM and FPMXL functions are replacing the EV functions found in the BPC V7.5. Many of these functions are very similar in nature and configuration. There are more than 35 different EPM functions and another 30 plus FPMXL functions, which are components that use the Application Program Interface component (API). These are executed with a call from the EPMExecuteAPI function. A full list of both of these different components can be found in the User Guide for the EPM add-in v10.0. Both of these help support additional enhancements in the reporting display both for calculations as well as additional information. To access these functions, you need to click the fx INSERT FUNCTION to see a list of EPM functions (see Figure 4.133) and a list of FPMXL functions (see Figure 4.134).

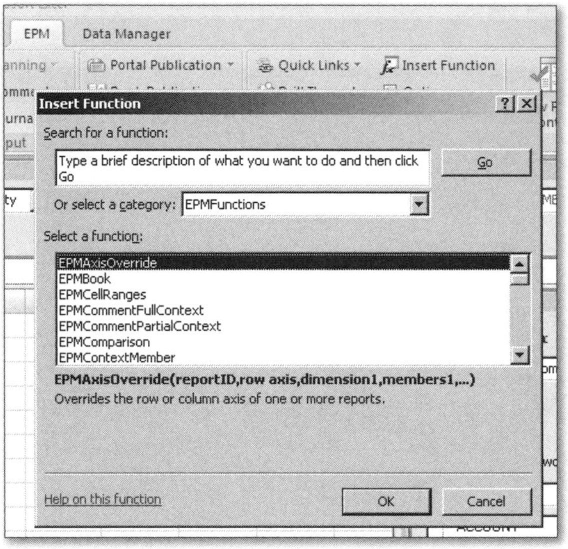

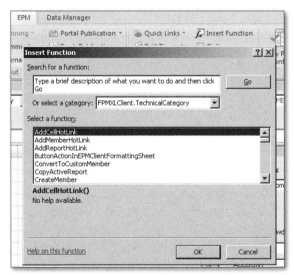

Figure 4.133   EPM Functions in the EPM add-in

Figure 4.134   FPMXL Functions in the EPM add-in

For example a very basic EPM function helps support the addition of the description for the dimension members that are being displayed in the report. To accomplish this, you need to start with a basic report as shown in Figure 4.135. As you can see, the GL account is in the row portion of the report.

	A	B	C	D	E	F	G	H
1								
2	Actual - Actual							
3	World							
4	Total Product							
5	Each,Local Currency							
6	CUST_GRP - Customer Group Top							
7	Periodic							
8								
9								
10			Q1 2011	Q2 2011	Q3 2011	Q4 2011	2011	
11		800000	120440	120440	120440	481758		
12		800001	$ 773,164,690.72	$ 773,164,690.72	$ 773,164,690.72	$ 773,164,690.72	$ 3,092,658,762.87	
13								
14								
15								
16								

Figure 4.135 EPM Report

Now insert a column in column C, click on cell C11, and then click the fx INSERT FUNCTION (found on the EPM Ribbon in the TOOLS section), then use the EPM Functions to find the EPMMEMBERDESC function for the EPM description (see Figure 4.136).

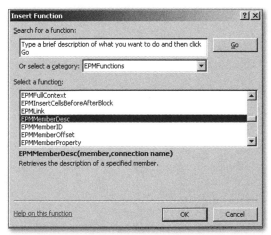

Figure 4.136 Insert Function – EPMMemberDesc

Click OK, and a dialog box is displayed for the required parameters. The only parameter required is for the MEMBER value, which is "B11" (see Figure 4.137).

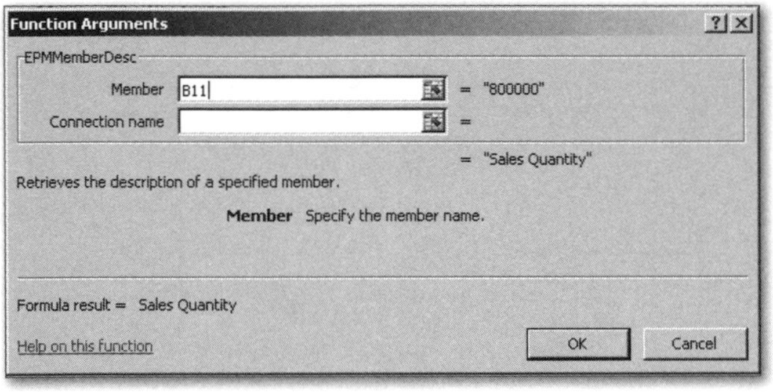

Figure 4.137 Function Arguments – B11

After you click OK, you'll see that the EPM function pulls the descriptions from the database and the dimension table for the account as shown in Figure 4.138. One of my favorite EPM functions is EPMCOMPARISON. This function allows you to create a comparison column for Actual versus Plan or one period versus another. The nice thing about this function is that when you use it with your ACCOUNT dimension it uses the ACCOUNT TYPE property and identifies the Better/Worst variance based on that signage. In this case, you don't have to worry about whether you are showing the appropriate signage for an Income versus an Expense account. If you remember this was a very detailed process with other reporting tools and you had to identify individually each account as to whether it was an Income-based or Expense-based account and what the signage would be to show the appropriate view. You should definitely review each of the EPM functions to make sure you are taking full advantage of their features.

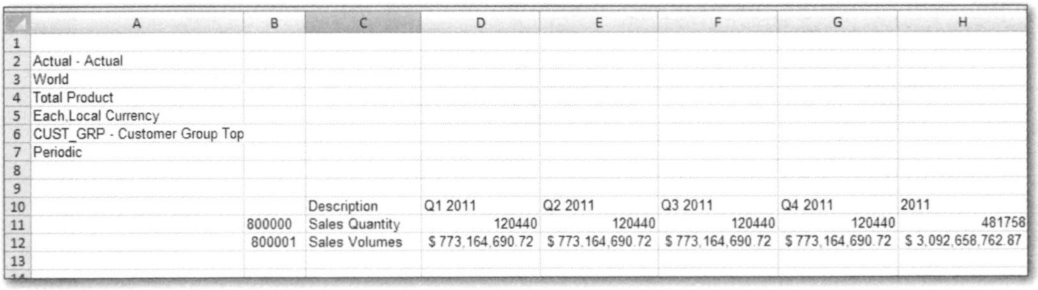

	A	B	C	D	E	F	G	H
1								
2	Actual - Actual							
3	World							
4	Total Product							
5	Each,Local Currency							
6	CUST_GRP - Customer Group Top							
7	Periodic							
8								
9								
10			Description	Q1 2011	Q2 2011	Q3 2011	Q4 2011	2011
11		800000	Sales Quantity	120440	120440	120440	120440	481758
12		800001	Sales Volumes	$ 773,164,690.72	$ 773,164,690.72	$ 773,164,690.72	$ 773,164,690.72	$ 3,092,658,762.87
13								

Figure 4.138 EPM Report with the EPM Description Assigned in Column C

In this situation, if additional accounts are added to the report, the EPM function automatically links to the other GL accounts and inserts the descriptions into the report. These features are being used on just about all reports both in BPC V7.5 (using the EvDRE features) as well as BPC V10.0. In this case the EPM Functions are used for enhancing the report with additional information such as Member ID's, Member Descriptions or additional properties of a dimension, whereas the FPMXL Functions are more specific to activities involved in processes in the report such as accessing the Data Manager Package, executing a Drill Through to another report or drilling down on a hierarchy automatically. This component can also be used in conjunction with Excel Macros as well as VBA to enhance the report features available to the end user. You should get familiar with these functions because you'll likely use a handful of them on an ongoing basis. The important takeaway is that you know they are available and can review them to see if any will be of use during your project.

4.9   Data Manager in the EPM Add-In

The DATA MANAGER tab is an integral part of the BPC process, but in terms of reporting and input forms, this feature isn't specifically involved. We'll cover this component in Chapter 5 due to the direct integration of the Data Manager component with the data loading and execution of the process chains in BPC.

4.10   PowerPoint and Word Documents in the EPM Add-In

Although this feature seems to always be of interest to business users, in the end, it's not used as much as you might think. This feature allows the use of both the Microsoft PowerPoint and Word document components of the Microsoft Office suite to integrate with the EPM add-in Excel-based features. Of course, because PowerPoint and Word don't have the Excel features, you can't use them in the same manner, but after a report is complete, you can easily copy it over to either of these two reporting components for display and use. Also the features in the EPM ribbon are limited by the functionality of the PowerPoint and Word components. The EPM ribbon for Word is shown in Figure 4.139. All of the formulas and calculations aren't available, and many of the options will be grayed out. For example, in the dropdowns available for the OPTIONS section, we will see options grayed out.

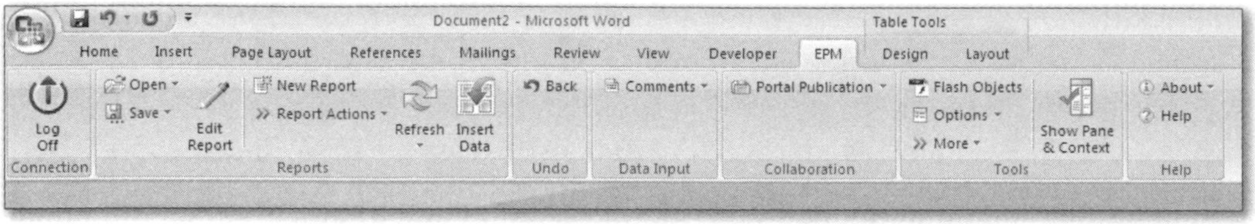

Figure 4.139 EPM Ribbon for Microsoft Word

To create a Word-based EPM report, you can either start from scratch or create the report in the EPM add-in and transfer it with the use of the COPY function. To create from scratch, you need to open a blank Word document; you'll see that the EPM tab is available. Log on and link to whatever source you like. Let's continue with the Forecast model from BPC and then work with the creation of the report in a similar fashion as we did for the Excel add-in. Figure 4.140 shows the EPM – REPORT EDITOR being used to create the report.

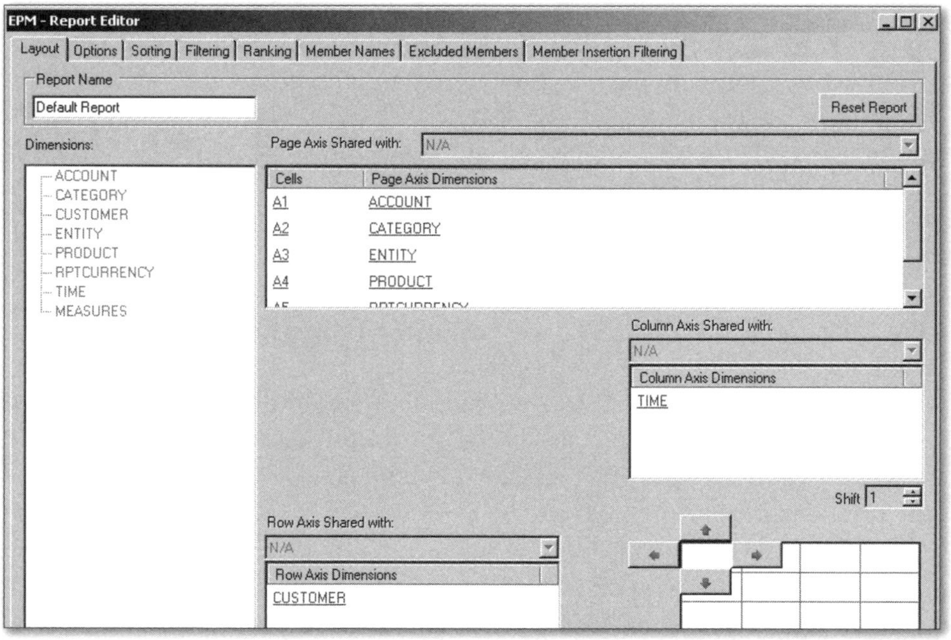

Figure 4.140 EPM – Report Editor Used to Create the Report

After the filters and dimensions are positioned correctly, you can execute the report and see it displayed in the Word document similar to Figure 4.141.

You can change the report information directly from the Word document by using the INSERT feature in the EPM ribbon, but to make any complex changes to the Word document, you should use the EDIT REPORT approach. This is the same approach when working with PowerPoint, but you need to be aware of the total amount of information you're attempting to display in the PowerPoint slide. A small amount of information displays much better as shown in Figure 4.142.

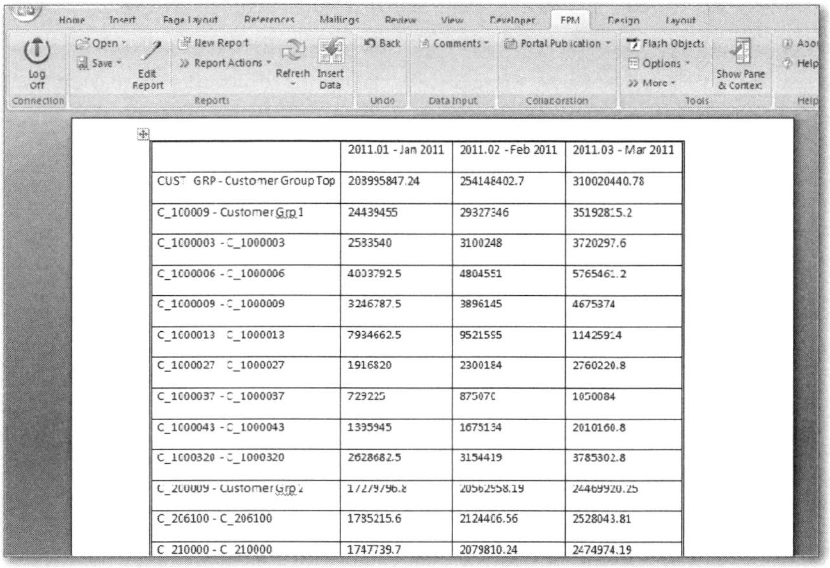

Figure 4.141 EPM Word Document

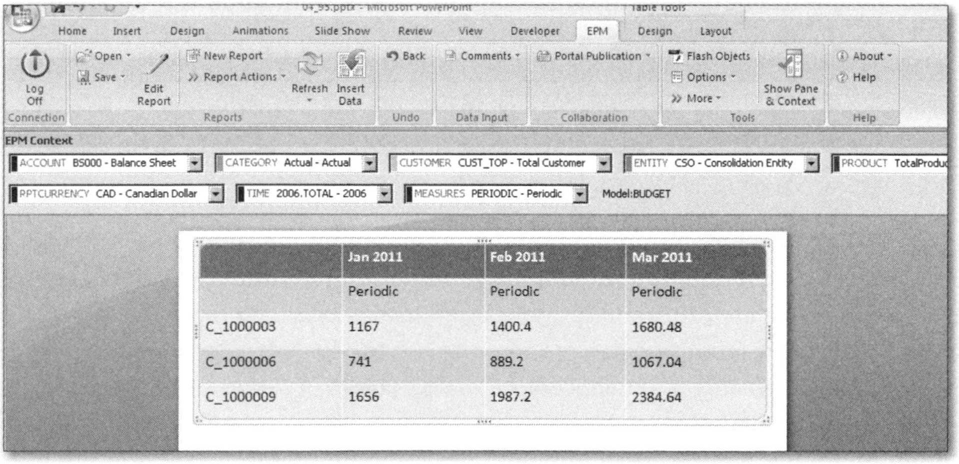

Figure 4.142 EPM Component in Microsoft PowerPoint

As you can see, this feature can be a very powerful addition to all of the features offered via the EPM add-in.

4.11 Summary

This chapter has covered quite a bit of the features and functionality of the EPM add-in, but there's a ton of features available using this frontend. We covered the basic concepts and where this reporting component is positioned in the lineup of all of the BI Suite reporting toolsets. We also discussed in detail all of the different features available using the EPM ribbon. As mentioned before, you can probably work through about 60-70% of all of your needs using some of the basic functionality available. Following are some of the highlights of the features we've discussed:

▶ The REFRESH feature
▶ Local members for supporting calculations
▶ The SHEET OPTIONS for everything from formatting to calculations
▶ The USER OPTIONS
▶ The formatting features
▶ The DRILL THROUGH options
▶ Navigational activities in the report itself

We also discussed some of the advanced features, including the EPM functions, the FPMXL functions, and the integration between the entire Microsoft suite reporting toolsets.

Being able to create asymmetric and multi-report workbooks is an excellent improvement over some of the other reporting toolsets. It's also a great feature to be able to use all of the Excel functions and integrate the EPM features with the Excel-based VBA and macros.

All in all, there's a tremendous amount of functionality available in the EPM add-in, and don't be surprised to see some of your customers looking to purchase *only* this component and integrate it into the reporting suite of the general reporting process. If you're interested in seeing an example of a fully developed report, we've included a sample in the Appendix of this book. This includes many of the different features we've discussed in this chapter.

This chapter discusses the data loading process required to start any of the activities in BPC, including consolidation, budgeting, planning, and forecasting. It starts with the basic process of uploading data from different sources of data to BW for the BPC version for SAP NetWeaver and a flat file upload for both BPC for SAP NetWeaver and for Microsoft, and then moves into a discussion of uploading from BW or any other source system into BPC for SAP NetWeaver or Microsoft.

5   Data Loading in BPC

This chapter covers the data loading activities for the BPC versions for both SAP NetWeaver and Microsoft. Because the primary method of uploading data into the BPC version for Microsoft is executing a flat file upload and this approach is used quite a bit in the version for SAP NetWeaver as well, we can cover a good portion of both approaches to getting the required data from source systems into the BPC environment. We'll cover in detail the loading process for master data members for the dimension, properties, and hierarchies. We'll also discuss the process and basic functionality as well as comment on more advanced aspects of this process. This will be followed by the configuration and processes to upload transactional data. This chapter will also look at the process of uploading currency exchange rates to the BPC Rate model for use with currency translation.

5.1   Overview of Data Loading Processes in BPC

When you think about data flow, you need to look at the entire process from start to finish—that is, from the original source of information all the way through to when it ends up in BPC objects. The reason to start the analysis at the source of the data flow for either master or transactional data is because in some situations—more so in the transactional data processing than the master data processing—how the data flows from the originating source drives the upload into BPC. We'll investigate all aspects of the uploading process, but again, as in other areas, we'll be focused on the basic processes and will highlight some advanced options that are available to help improve or enhanced the loading process. This topic could definitely cover a books worth of information based on the different approaches to data loading architecture. In this case we will cover the core features of the data loading process. Once you are familiar with the core processes the ability to use some of the advanced features will be more easily integrated into the BPC data loading process.

These activities, although not in the spotlight during a BPC project, are critical and need to be approached with as much diligences as the core configuration being assigned to the BPC development. It really doesn't matter how great the configuration or implementation of the BPC system is unless you can deliver good consistent data that has been validated and can provide a good starting point during the consolidation, budgeting, planning, or forecasting processes. There are some components that you'll be using throughout the uploading process, including the Data Manager, BW components, and flat files.

5.1.1 Data Manager

The Data Manager is a core component of the data loading process when it comes to moving data from any source system into BPC. Whether it's from a flat file, BW, Oracle, or another source system, the Data Manager is a part of this process. We ran into this topic in Chapter 4 because it's a part of the EPM add-in installation if you decide to download the SAP NetWeaver version of the EPM add-in. If you go with the Microsoft version, then you'll only see the EPM tab on the ribbon. We also deferred the conversation on this topic until it made more sense and that time is now. Figure 5.1 shows that the Data Manager is visible after you access the EPM Office add-in for Excel from your home page, you can simply open up an Excel spreadsheet and go to the Log On for the Data Manager.

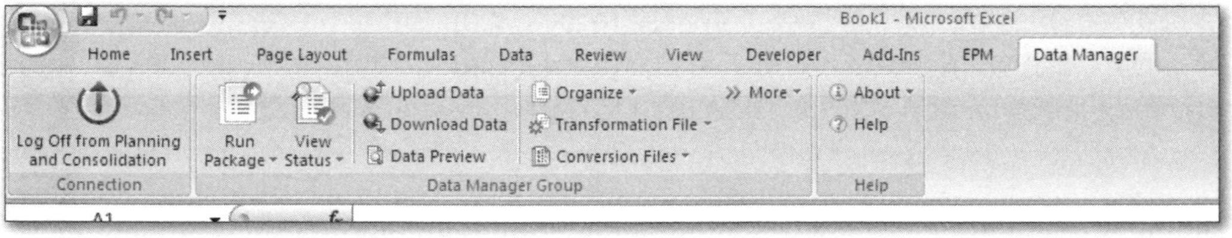

Figure 5.1 Data Manager Portion of the Ribbon

There are several portions within the DATA MANAGER GROUP section, and they all break out into different types of tasks. At a high level, the first section on the left incorporates the activities involved in both running a package and viewing the results. Figure 5.2 shows the different subtasks assigned to each of the groups. RUN PACKAGE is broken up into two other activities: RUN A PACKAGE or RUN PACKAGE LINK. A package is generally one executable process that occurs, such as COPY, CLEAR, IMPORT TRANSACTIONAL DATA, and others that are listed. A *package link* is a combination of more than one package; these packages are set in a sequence and executed one at a time. Therefore, the package is the more important object. After this is complete, it's assigned to a package link, and all of the parameters that are required to execute that package are filled in or assigned in the link and then the packages are executed.

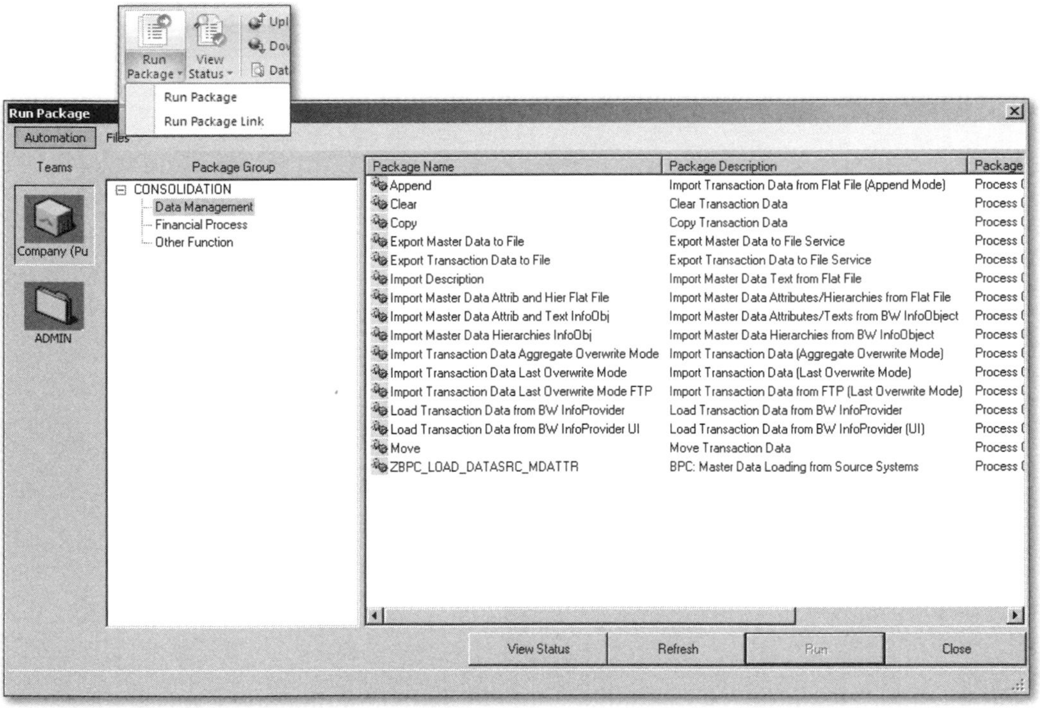

Figure 5.2 Running a Package with Some Packages That Are Available

The packages you see here are all standard content delivered with the system. We'll go over these and more once we've laid the groundwork of the different components.

As far as the other option in this group—VIEW STATUS—there is no executable activities involved, but this is a great location to view the status and progress of the process chain runs. As Figure 5.3 shows, the display of information includes everything from the user's name, date, and time, to the type of package, schedule that is assigned to the package, and all packages that are assigned to a package link.

Figure 5.3 Viewing a Schedule Status

This is a great location to both view and fine-tune the parameters and setup that you may have in the target state for uploading purposes.

Moving to the next set of tasks in the DATA MANAGER GROUP, you see that it deals with the uploading and downloading of data. Figure 5.4 shows the straightforward options available for uploading. The UPLOAD DATA and DATA PREVIEW options are self-explanatory. To upload a flat file into a BPC table in the Microsoft or SAP NetWeaver versions, you first have to upload the flat file into the server and then into the database. The UPLOAD DATA option starts that process. After you click on the link to UPLOAD DATA, you'll see a DATA MANAGER—UPLOAD dialog box similar to the one in Figure 5.4, which will allow you to BROWSE any drive available and pick the appropriate flat file to upload to the server. After the flat file has been uploaded successfully to the server, you can then use the DATA PREVIEW option to see the results and validate the file format before you attempt to execute an upload to the database or model.

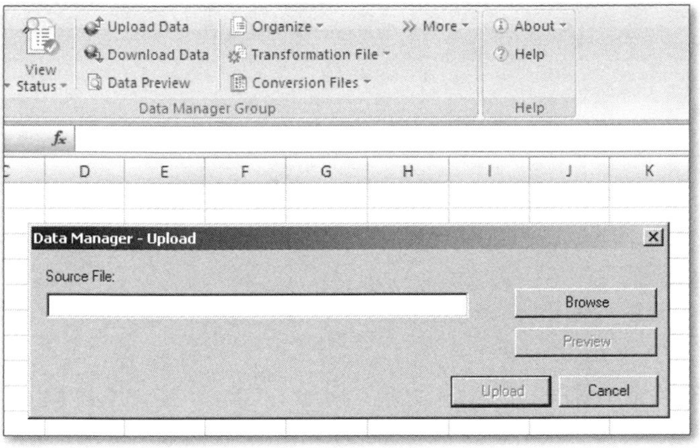

Figure 5.4 Data Manager – Upload Dialog box

As far as the DOWNLOAD DATA option, this can be used to download the files within the server to other systems or to a data directory for further processing. This can be used for the download of information that was used for a consolidation or planning process and now is required to be shared for other reporting purposes. We'll use this quite a bit later in this chapter when we work through the flat file process.

The final portion of the DATA MANAGER GROUP is the executable activities used on the uploading process from source systems into the BPC database. After the flat file is uploaded to the server, you can use a combination of activities within the transformation files and conversion files to move the file into the BPC space, whether that is a model in SAP NetWeaver or in the Microsoft platform. A breakout of the different features is shown in Figure 5.5.

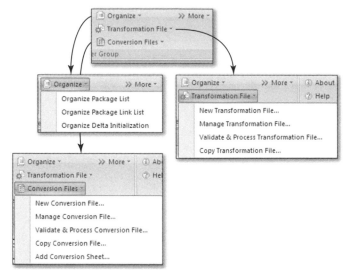

Figure 5.5 Data Manager Group: Organize, Transformation File, and Conversion File Options

These options are the most critical in the Data Manager portion of the ribbon. In the previous section, we discussed the execution of the packages, so now let's discuss the configuration of the packages or package link lists and the setup and configuration of the transformation file and the conversion file.

> **Note: Transformation Files versus Conversion Files**
>
> The *transformation file* is the only file that is required for all data loading. The *conversion file* is a very useful feature that allows you to separate the manipulation of the information from the formatting of the information into BPC, but it isn't a required file in the upload of data into BPC.

The ORGANIZE dropdown shows the list of packages that have been configured and can be executed in this feature. This is the area where you set up and configure the PACKAGE LIST or LINK LIST to be used during the uploading process. Figure 5.6 shows the dialog box that is displayed after you choose ORGANIZE • ORGANIZE PACKAGE LIST.

In this screen, you can assign a process chain to the package and then to the package group using the GROUP dropdown menu. You can also tweak the configuration of the package by changing some of the code to allow different variables to show up during the execution of the package and to enable who can see this package to execute it—those with a user view versus an administration view.

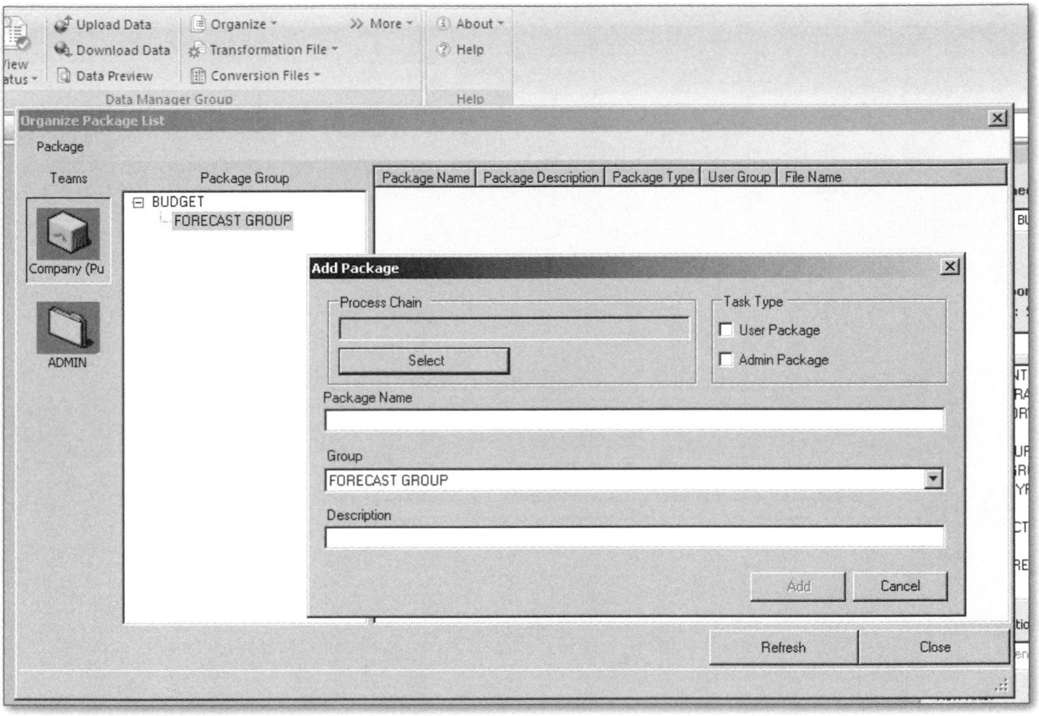

Figure 5.6 Add Package Screen

The last option on the ORGANIZE dropdown is a new feature available in BPC vV10.0 for the use of a *delta loading process* using the ORGANIZE DELTA INITIALIZATION parameters. This will help support a faster uploading process by transferring only the delta records rather than a full load or having to set up a pseudo delta uploading process. This process as well as the more detailed activities in the transformation and conversion files will be discussed later in this chapter in Section 5.4.3. The next option on this list is the TRANSFORMATION FILE, and you assign the mapping of the source objects to the BPC objects for uploading purposes in this file. In Figure 5.7, in the *MAPPING portion, you set up a link between the different objects. For example, whenever you upload master data from a source object such as a BW InfoObject or a flat file, you usually see the mapping ID = ID. This is the linking of the core master data value in the source system to the BPC system. In the master data uploading process, the mapping is from attributes (BW term) to properties (BPC term), whereas with transactional data, the mapping is from characteristics (BW term) to dimensions (BPC term) and the key figure value SIGNDATA.

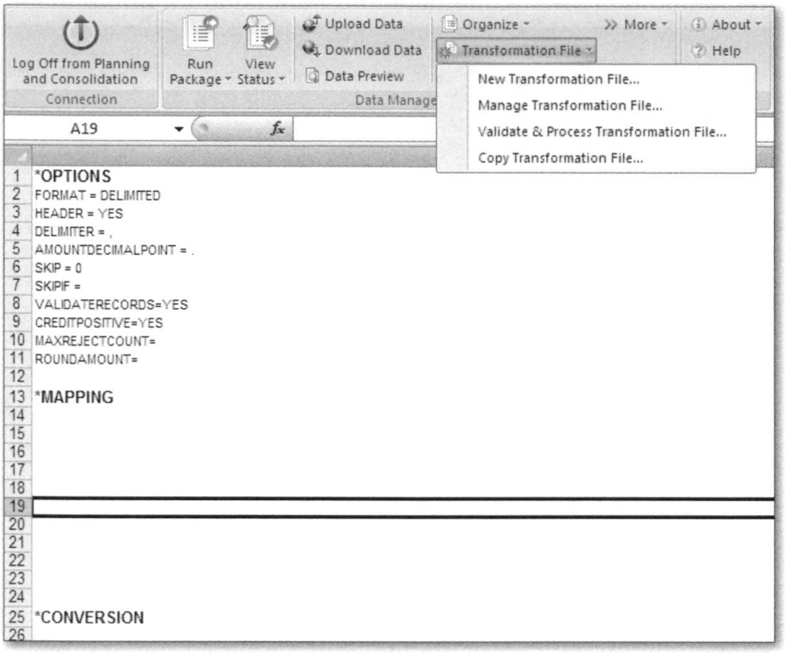

Figure 5.7 New Transformation File

In the *OPTIONS portion, there are parameters that provide header information for the upload process. For example, MAXREJECTCOUNT= reflects the number of rejected records before the uploading process is stopped. The default is 501 records and that's if you don't assign any value to this parameter. If you want everything to be uploaded and hold off the failed values, then you can assign a value of –1 to this parameter. That way, even if there's only one valid record to be uploaded, it will be uploaded, and all of the rest will be displayed as failed records. As you can see, there is also a *CONVERSION section to this file. If you want to have everything in one file, then you can assign the full conversion values to this option of the screen.

> **Note: Transformation File**
>
> Even if you don't have any parameters to enter, don't delete any of the prompts or mapping sections from this file. These headers are standard delivered and the Transformation file as well as the Conversion file use these prompts in the data loading process. If you remove them but in the future need them making sure that the programs that run against the prompts is critical.

In this case, the NEW TRANSFORMATION FILE option in the dropdown in Figure 5.7 allows the creation of the file itself, the MANAGE TRANSFORMATION FILE option allows the alteration of the existing transformation files, the VALIDATE & PROCESS TRANSFORMATION FILE allows the testing of the transformation file before using it in the actual uploading process, and the COPY TRANSFORMATION FILE allows the creation of a copy of the file to reuse in other data loading processes. Even copying and tweaking the transformation files is easier and faster than starting from scratch. This is also an easy way to see if the flat file that has been uploaded is consistent and will allow the data to be uploaded to the database. If there is an issue with the transformation file during the validate and process activity, the system will identify any issues and offer to either highlight them or attempt to fix them for you.

Finally the conversion files are used to create the mapping of the members from a source system to the BPC objects. So this level of file continues the mapping process but rather than at the dimension level (transformation file), you go to the member level to align the values.

In Figure 5.8, the *new conversion file* is shown and, in this case, the only two defined columns are the EXTERNAL and INTERNAL. These are associated with the source (EXTERNAL) and the target (INTERNAL) values. For example, a very normal mapping or conversion is for something like TIME where the source system has values such as 2012001 (JAN/2012) for its values where BPC has 2012.01 for its values. You assign these values to each of the columns, and during the uploading process, the system reads these values and interprets the data as it's loaded into the BPC object. Therefore, BPC has its own Extraction, Transformation, and Loading (ETL) process. In the same vein as the transformation files, the conversion file has a MANAGE CONVERSION FILE option, VALIDATE & PROCESS CONVERSION FILE OPTION, and a COPY CONVERSION FILE option. Each does the exact same thing for the conversion file as the corresponding options do for the transformation file. The last option in the CONVERSION FILES dropdown list is the ADD CONVERSION SHEET option. In this case, let's assume that you have two or more dimension values that are in need of being converted. You can either use the standard Excel process of adding another sheet or use the ADD CONVERSION SHEET option in the CONVERSION FILES dropdown menu. The two columns for EXTERNAL and INTERNAL mapping are created automatically in the added sheet.

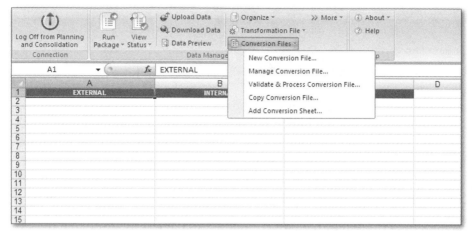

Figure 5.8 Conversion Files Options

The final option on the sheet shown in Figure 5.8 is in column C - FORMULA, and this allows formulas to be assigned to the conversion sheet. In this case, during the upload, you want to execute a formula against the data if, for example, you're uploading transactional data and want to execute a shift or realignment of the data for specific member values. For example, if a record is being uploaded, and the profit center for that record is 2000, then change it to 2020; if not, leave the profit center as is and continue the uploading process. You'll use this component constantly, so it's important that you're well aware of the features and functions available for the upload process. There are different options in terms of mapping that can be incorporated in the conversion and Transformation File.

5.1.2 Business Warehouse (BW)

In terms of the process for data loading into the BPC version for SAP NetWeaver, the source system of BW is the primary data flow used. There are many reasons for this approach. They all stem from the fact that the BW system with all of the functionality from the ETL process through to the multiple different InfoProviders that are available for supporting reporting and data loading is the most logical location to homogenize all of the data from different source systems and position it correctly for the BPC models to upload. There have been so many enhancements in the overall BW process that bypassing this layer goes against all best practice rules currently available. Sure there are situations where the question of whether to use BW as a source is appropriate, but all in all, the pros outweigh the cons by far. These exceptions to the rule need to be discussed, and a solution based on the customer's situation needs to be put forth. An example of this is with a number of dimensions in BPC where the properties that are needed in BPC don't reside within BW. In that case, you can use a flat file approach so that you can accommodate all of the properties, or you can use the BW system, add the required properties to the dimension, and find a consistent way to fill these properties before uploading into BPC. These are some of the issues we'll discuss in more detail during the course of this chapter.

The best approach to offering an overview of the BW process is with a high-level diagram of the data flow from start to finish within BW. Figure 5.9 offers a basic view of this data flow process. We'll reference this diagram during this chapter as we move the data—both master and transactional—through the system.

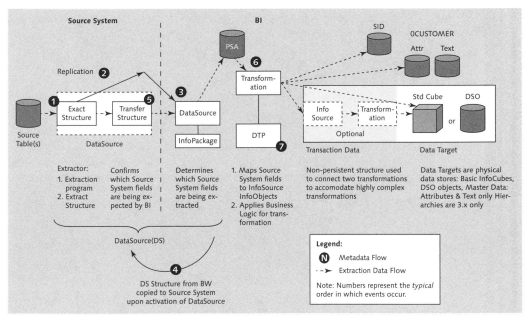

Figure 5.9 Data Flow from Source System to BW

Rather than getting too much into the details of both processes, let's look at a generic data flow from the SAP ERP source tables through to the BW InfoProviders (Std Cube and DSO) and the InfoObjects (Attr. and Text). This approach can start from any module within SAP ERP and travel into BW. We've assigned numbers to each of the different tasks involved so we can address them on an individual basis. You can see that this is a sequence of tables for storage and transformations for flexibility of the data load. Again, we won't get into the heavy details of each aspect of the data load because we'll leave that for the BPC side of the fence, but just to make you aware of some of the functionality of BW to support BPC, the process is described in Table 5.1.

Step	Description
❶	This is the process of identifying the appropriate table(s) for the required data. In our case, we are looking at data to support the consolidation process and the planning and forecasting (P&F) process. During this process, a DataSource is built on the SAP ERP side that uses the table(s) that we need the data from as sources of information. After we create the DataSource, the system automatically creates an extract structure and extraction program within the DataSource.
❷	A replication process occurs from the SAP ERP side to the BW side. During this process, an image of the DataSource is created on the BW side.
❸	This DataSource is a mirror image of the DataSource on the SAP ERP side of the system. In addition, a table called a Persistent Staging Area (PSA) is created on the BW side. This PSA is used to store a raw version of the data from the source tables to the BW side of the fence. This is for a number of reasons, one of them being the ability to have a backup version of the data available in case additional loads of the same data are required in the future.
❹	After the DataSource is activated on the BW side, the system generates a connection to the DataSource on the SAP ERP side.
❺	After the activation is complete, a transfer structure is created on the SAP ERP side of the system connections.
❻	The next structure created is the transformation rule, which links the DataSource and PSA to the next layer in the BW system. This could be either a Data Store Object (DSO) or directly to an InfoProvider. The transformation rule is the mapping link between the data moving from the PSA into the next layer. During this process, we can manipulate the data by either enhancing the record itself or changing/shifting the information. There are numerous standard function activities that can be accomplished during this process.

Table 5.1 Steps in the Data Flow in BW

Step	Description
❼	Optionally, there can be either an InfoSource or another transformation rule. An InfoSource was used primarily in the BW V3.5, but it still has value in the BW V7.3. It allows additional flexibility to move the data into multiple different presentation layer objects—InfoCubes and DSOs—using different filters and enhancements. The transformation rule at this level is no different from the one discussed at step 6, just that it now links the lower-level object to the presentation layer InfoProvider. This is basically moving the data from a DSO (detailed data) into an InfoCube (summary data) for reporting purposes. The Data Transfer Process (DTP) is used in this case to facilitate the uploading process from the lower level objects such as the DSO's to the InfoCubes. A DTP is used from any level after the initial upload into the PSA is complete. You will see a DTP at all levels of the data loading process.

Table 5.1 Steps in the Data Flow in BW (Cont.)

The final objects found on the right side of Figure 5.9 are the presentation layer objects. The top objects are listed as the Set ID (SID), Attr (attribute), Text (text tables), and the hierarchies; this is where the master data is stored to be used by as many InfoProviders as are required. The other objects—Standard InfoCubes and DSOs—are used to store the transactional data for reporting and possibly sources for other third-party data warehouses to consume. The key items here are that the data is available for you in BPC from the InfoObjects and the InfoProviders.

Now the BW purist will likely have a nervous twitch while reviewing this diagram because there is so much more behind this process that isn't shown here but may be critical for the BW developer to understand to support the BPC process. BPC consultants need to be aware of these issues and when necessary integrate the BW group into the process so that these topics can be shared and configuration can be used to proactively address these issues. For example, will the data be positioned correctly for BPC with only one key figure versus multiple key figures? This is important because based on this answer, BPC will have to do more work via its own transformation file (not rule) going from BW to BPC. Another topic mentioned previously that will have an impact on the BW architecture is whether the BW InfoObjects will supply *all* of the properties required by BPC for the processes being configured? The GL account is one of the biggest culprits of having multiple properties that aren't standard available in BW because there are about 15 different properties found in the BPC Account dimension that aren't available in the standard BW InfoObject for the GL account.

Another topic of interest is the positioning of the hierarchies as well as the need for a compound on an InfoObject to show its true definition. The movement of data within BW needs to be reviewed and understood. Normally you'll always have data loaded based on a PERIODIC view; therefore, all of the information loaded into BW is based on a periodic basis and not a YTD basis where the BPC Consolidation model prefers the data to be positioned. All of these questions and more will be critical to answer and be able to integrate into the data flow in BPC. We'll discuss and formulate a solution for each of these issues and more. In some cases, these solutions will be very similar to what you might have used, but others may be a bit different. It's always good to have and test multiple solutions for a particular problem and then use the best approach for your customer.

5.1.3 Flat Files

Now that we have an overview of the BW approach let's look at the next-best data loading process for the BPC version for SAP NetWeaver and the primary option for the BPC version for Microsoft. If you're looking for a core process to use and understand for data loading purposes, the flat file is the answer. Of any of the different methods used, this one is a primary approach for the BPC version for Microsoft. It's being used quite a bit in the BPC version for SAP NetWeaver as well, and in the older version of SAP NetWeaver, the flat file was used often due to the amount of integration that was available. So, understanding the process and approach for this uploading method not only offers you a fallback process but also a very good idea of the actual loading process into BPC. You still have to use the same components on the BPC side such as the transformation file and the conversion file. In other aspects of data requirements such as the exchange rates, the flat file uploading process is probably used a lot, especially if you have rates that are unique such as budgeting or planning rates that may not be available in SAP ERP or BW. Even if you get the exchange rates from a service, in many cases, you'll download them to a flat file and then use this as the source of information for BPC.

If this is one of the main approaches to supporting the BPC process with data, then several questions need to be considered for this to work consistently and correctly. The initial question and the easiest is how to store the different files that will be used for the uploading purposes. Normally, customers set up a directory on the corporate SharePoint to support the storage of the historic information based on a flat file. This seems to be the most consistent as long as there's some sort of business process that will align the approach to this activity, such as the timing of the storage, historical data to be stored or archived, and the format of the stored files. Basically, you must have a good and consistent process of managing the flat files being used in the uploading process.

The next question is the format of the flat file to be used. A good practice is to align everyone to use one specific template format so that no matter where the data is coming from, you always know what format it will be arriving in and how to interpret the data. The CSV format is often used during an upload into BPC. Again, the critical concern here is to make sure a template for the source data is reasonable for everyone and consistent with their approach to collecting and sending data. You don't want to add too much burden to other groups who may have difficulty aligning their information into a specific template. An example of a flat file is shown in Figure 5.10.

Figure 5.10   Flat File Example – CSV Format

As you can see, the first line is a header line with the names of the different items that are listed below it. Basically, the dimension level objects and then the members are listed. The separator of choice is the comma in this case, but others can be used, including the 'NO' separator. There should be some protection on these files due to the sensitivity of the data available in them, so make sure that you include some time to discuss the format of the template to supply flat file and the whole management process for the flat files.

Another aspect of the flat file process is the type of data that you are uploading. For example, is the data going to be delivered in a YTD format or a periodic format? This is a significant item to understand in any uploading process because it directly impacts the approach to uploading into BPC. However, because these are flat files and don't have the inherit system controls that uploading from an SAP system has, it's important to verify. In terms of consolidation, the data is normally delivered in the YTD format, and in the budgeting and planning process, a periodic approach is usually used. This is also a question in terms of the exchange rates that are being delivered via a flat file. A periodic approach is usually used for this set of data as well. After you make decisions on these topics, the use of flat files to upload will be more controlled and secure.

In the flat file uploading process, there are two generic steps: uploading and reviewing. First, you need to upload the flat file from a directory of some sort into the server level in BPC by using the functions on the Data Manager. The initial step uses the UPLOAD DATA option in the DATA MANAGER GROUP on the ribbon. After you access the DATA MANAGER – UPLOAD dialog box, you can browse to the location of the flat file for uploading. After you assign the flat file path to the dialog box, click on UPLOAD (see Figure 5.11).

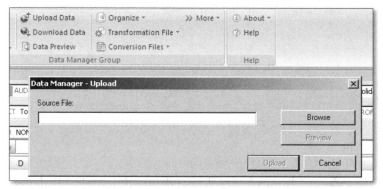

Figure 5.11   Uploading Data via the Data Manager – Upload Dialog Box

After you've uploaded the flat file information, the second step is to review the data using the DATA PREVIEW option in the DATA MANAGER GROUP. The initial step is shown in Figure 5.12. The initial screen after you select the DATA PREVIEW option shows you the list of files that have previously been uploaded to the BPC server to be used in the data loading process into the database. After you choose the flat file that you're interested in previewing, click on the OPEN *button.* As shown in Figure 5.13, you can then review the information based on a specific option, either DELIMITED or FIXED WIDTH, and then select the delimiting identifier (in this case, a comma). You can then review the information to identify any glaring issues and then move forward or reload an appropriate file that will fix any issues in the data. Notice that in this case all of the cells are filled with values as expected by BPC.

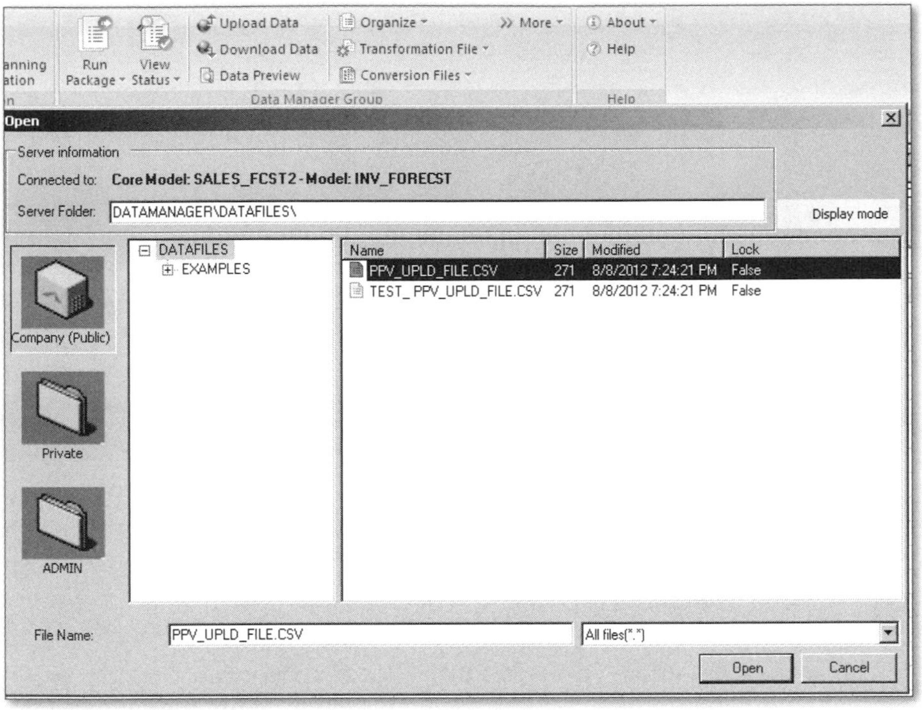

Figure 5.12 Initial Open Dialog Box for Data Preview

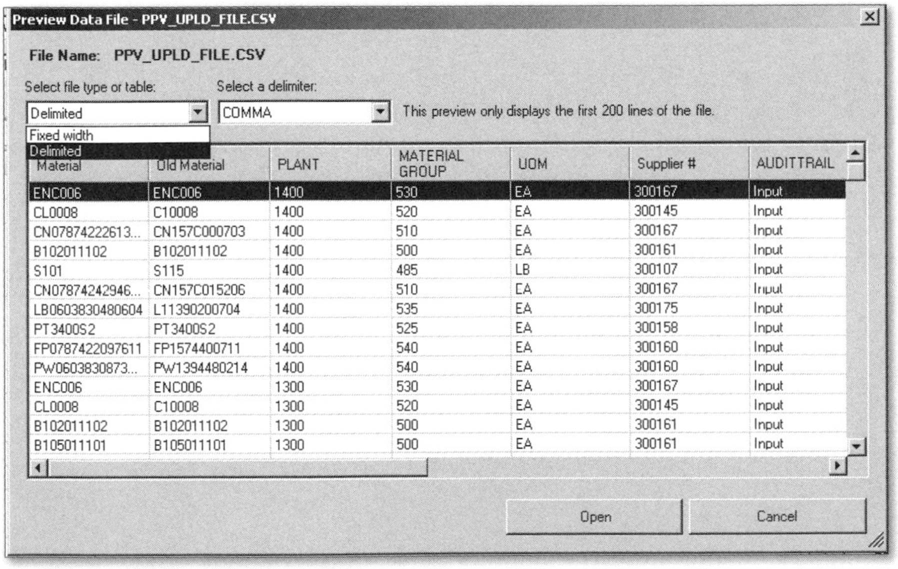

Figure 5.13 Data File Preview

After these two steps are completed, your flat file is ready to be moved into the database of the system. We'll take this scenario the rest of the way during the more detailed discussion of flat file uploads. Now that we've covered the basics, let's discuss each of these tasks in detail, starting with the initial upload into BW from SAP ERP.

5.2   Data Loading Process in BW

Before we start to upload data from any source system into the BPC version for SAP NetWeaver, you must decide whether to use the uploading process from BW into BPC as a source. This is definitely a best practice when it comes to the SAP NetWeaver, but there are questions to be answered for the master data, text, and hierarchies as well as for the transactional data. One of the driving reasons to approach the data loading this way (with BW as the source) is that you can have a central source of information for validation purposes. This provides a good platform to group together all of the data you need and homogenize it before moving it into BPC. This definitely makes sense because BW has many of the necessary toolsets to do this inherently in the ETL layer of BW. You can manipulate the data in any number of ways, including deriving additional characteristic values, expanding the information using ABAP code, and integrating data from multiple sources. This applies to both master data and transactional data. Another significant issue is that, in many cases, BW and BPC don't have the same attributes on familiar characteristics, so you'll need to decide how to get the rest of the attributes to be filled and connected to the master data. For example, a key characteristic is GL accounts. This characteristic/dimension is essential for BPC to work properly, and there are a number of attributes/properties that aren't present in the standard InfoObject in BW that are critical properties in BPC. So the question is how to fill that gap and still be able to use the BW system as the system of record for the data. Other characteristics/dimensions have this same issue such as company code/entity and category. another issue to consider is that some dimensions aren't available in BW and are needed in BPC especially for consolidation. In this instance, you either have to add them to the architecture or source them from a flat file. We'll discuss these methods in more detail later in this chapter.

> **Note: Terminology**
>
> You'll notice that we use certain terms interchangeably such as attributes and proper-ties, characteristics and dimensions, and master data and members. To make sure you're keeping these different terms in focus please reference Table 3.1 in Chapter 3, which shows the BW and BPC terms side by side.

Let's look at a typical data flow from the SAP ERP system into BW. We'll focus on this approach because it's a very common process, but don't lose sight of the fact that you can also upload a flat file into BW as well. The only difference is that the DataSource isn't connected to the SAP ERP system, but instead looks to a directory of some sort to locate the flat file to upload. In this discussion, we'll offer a view of the normal processes involved in uploading data into BW. However, much more can be accomplished and configured with the support of the BW team that is onsite or a part of the company's production support team.

5.2.1   Master Data, Text, and Hierarchies

The uploading process takes a specific approach to uploading the data into BW according to the requirements or needs of the system. In other words, you need to have the master data in the BW system first before loading the transactional data. There are parameters within BW that allow you to upload the transactional data without the necessary master data, but again, that's getting too far into the weeds for this conversation.

If we follow that same logic about having the master data available before the transactional data, then we should do the same with the three different types of metadata we have to upload. They are the actual master data, the text, and finally the hierarchies. Because the master data should already be uploaded before getting the text that links to it, the first upload is master data, then the text, and finally the hierarchy after all values/members are uploaded. This is the normal process that usually occurs during the nightly load or once a day. There are times when the master data is uploaded more often, but this is dictated by the transactional data loading process.

To start, Figure 5.14 shows that there are three processes for uploading the master data. We'll look in more detail at just one of the processes because the other two follow a similar approach and, in the case of text, a very similar setup.

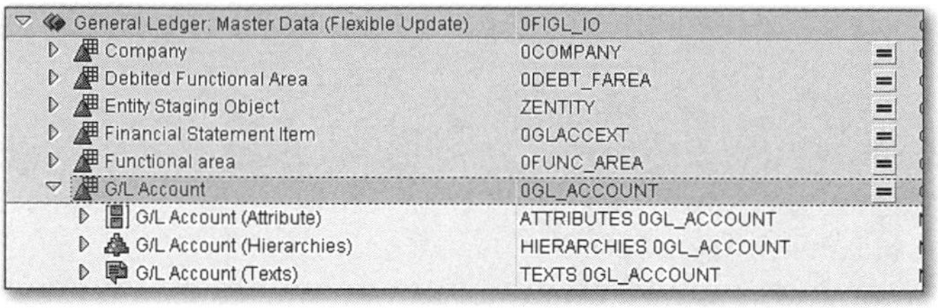

Figure 5.14 GL Account with Attributes, Texts, and Hierarchy Data Loading

If we expand on this view and look at the detailed steps involved in uploading the master data, you can see that there are several parts to the process. If you refer back to Figure 5.9, you can track these tasks via that diagram or review them via the layered approach within the BW DATA WAREHOUSING WORKBENCH.

Normally, to start this process, you build out some components, but this is a standard content object, which means much of what you need is already set up, and all you have to do is activate it and maybe create one or two objects. Figure 5.15 shows the lowest level of the process: the InfoPackage.

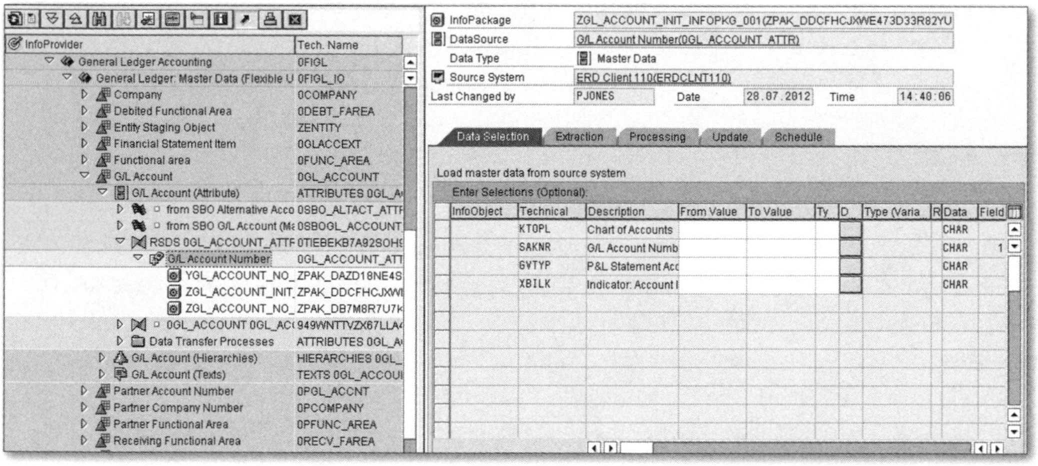

Figure 5.15 Data Selection Tab of the InfoPackage

Note: Approach

In this discussion, we'll be approaching the data loading process from the initial task through to the last level where the data resides. This isn't the configuration process because you must have the DataSource already created to configure the InfoPackage.

In this case, the InfoPackage is open to the DATA SELECTION tab where you can define the option to filter the data that is being uploaded. You can filter based on the CHART OF ACCOUNTS, GL ACCOUNTS, or either a P&L STATEMENT ACCOUNT or BALANCE SHEET(XBILK FIELD) account. You can also assign some coding at this level to offer more flexibility during the data loading process.

The next two tabs—EXTRACTION and PROCESSING—enable you to adjust the extraction adapter, which manages the link and type of uploading that occur (via service API or SOAP adapter) and the data formatting that is used (normally fixed length in this case).

The third-tab—UPDATE—shows the types of updating that are available. Figure 5.16 shows that this uploading process can use a delta uploading feature. Because this already shows the options for DELTA UPDATE, we know that this InfoPackage has already been initialized and probably has been used as a full upload as well. In any case, you now have the ability to upload only the changed or new records (master data) during the loading process. This will definitely help with the processing times of the data loading because only a handful of new GL accounts might be created on an ongoing basis. So, rather than moving thousands, you only have to move a few.

Several other options are available that are grayed out in this case, but if you choose the INITIALIZE DELTA PROCESS option, you can pick the appropriate parameters. Each parameter is responsible for a specific phase during the data loading processes; for example, the INITIALIZE WITH DATA TRANSFER or INITIALIZE WITHOUT DATA TRANS-FER options are used for the first time upload. If you choose an INITIALIZE DELTA PROCESS and also select INITIALIZE WITHOUT DATA TRANSFER, then you either have to do a very large initial delta upload or do a full upload for the historical data prior to the initialization task. After the INITIALIZE DELTA PROCESS option is executed and activated, a pointer is set that will manage the delta records coming through the system. If the INITIALIZE DELTA PROCESS is done INITIALIZE WITH DATA TRANSFER, then after the historical data is moved over, the pointer is set, and everything after that is only the changed or new records from the last data loading process.

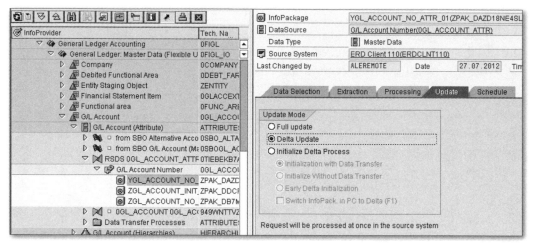

Figure 5.16 InfoPackage Component – Update Tab

Moving up the levels, the DATASOURCE component is shown in Figure 5.17. The DataSource is linked to the SAP ERP system, so you only need to confirm that the connection between the two systems is correct, and you can leave all of the settings alone.

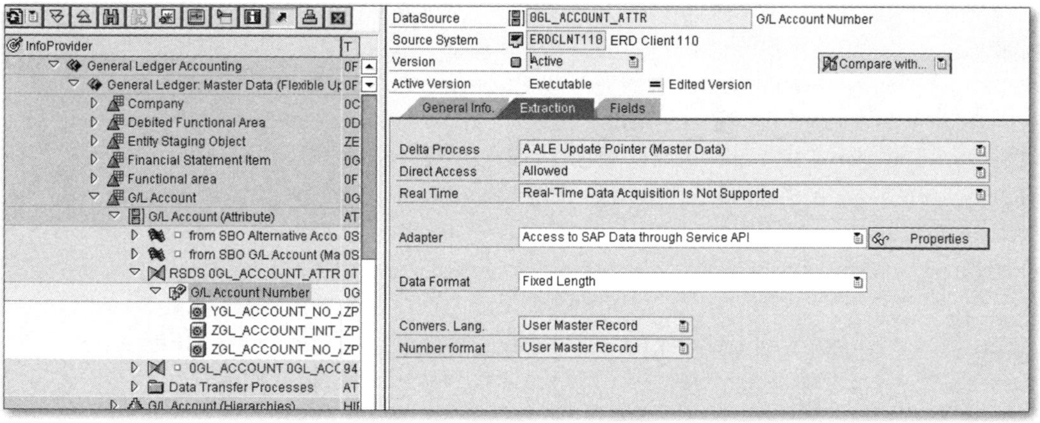

Figure 5.17 DataSource for GL Accounts – Extraction Tab

In the EXTRACTION tab, the process used to upload the data, the data format, the conversion language, and the number format have all been set. If this is standard content, much of the setup of this component is already completed. This tab shows that you'll be using a pointer to manage the delta uploads, the data format is fixed, and the language and number format settings are from the master record.

Figure 5.18 shows another view of the properties/attributes that will be filled based on this DataSource. These fields can be altered, but because this is a direct link to the SAP ERP system, you have to go back into that SAP ERP system to make the changes. This gives you all of the detailed information on the attribute values, including the length, data type, and description. If the data load fails, you can check these parameters to confirm that the data being uploaded fits the parameters.

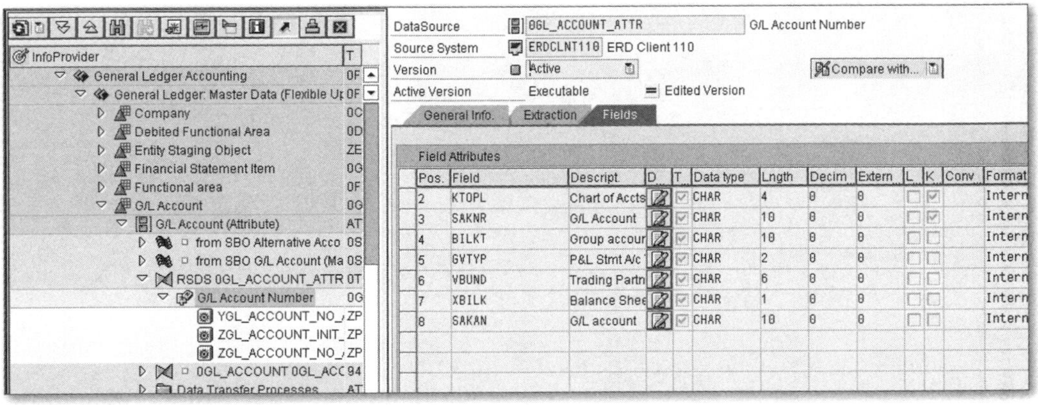

Figure 5.18 GL Account DataSource – Fields Tab

The next layer, TRANSFORMATION rule (not to be confused with the transformation file in BPC), is used to manipulate the data values during the uploading process. If there are additional properties that need to be derived, then this might be the point in the data loading process that it is addressed and configured, as shown in Figure 5.19. Notice that there are only four fields that will be filled by this transformation rule configuration: CHART OF ACCOUNTS, GL ACCOUNT, P&L STMT, or BALANCE SHEET SETTING. In most cases, the total attributes/properties from SAP ERP aren't moved to the BW system but only those that are consistent with the reporting requirements. In this case, the source system ID isn't required for any reporting and therefore not linked to allow the upload of values to occur.

Notice that in Figure 5.19, there are multiple different "connections" all linking up to the InfoObject 0GL_ACCOUNT. This shows that not just one option is available but multiple. Each of these links can be used and, depending on the configuration in the BW system, can accommodate the requirements. Notice that beside the symbol for the TRANSFORMATION option, there's a small rectangular shape. This shows that the link in this case is from BW V3.5 functionality and not BW V7.0 or even a V7.3. There are situations where using an older version of the transformation process is better fitted to the requirements, but this is something to make sure you review thoroughly before using because all of the newer features will be assigned to the BW V7.0 or V7.3 functionality rather than V3.5.

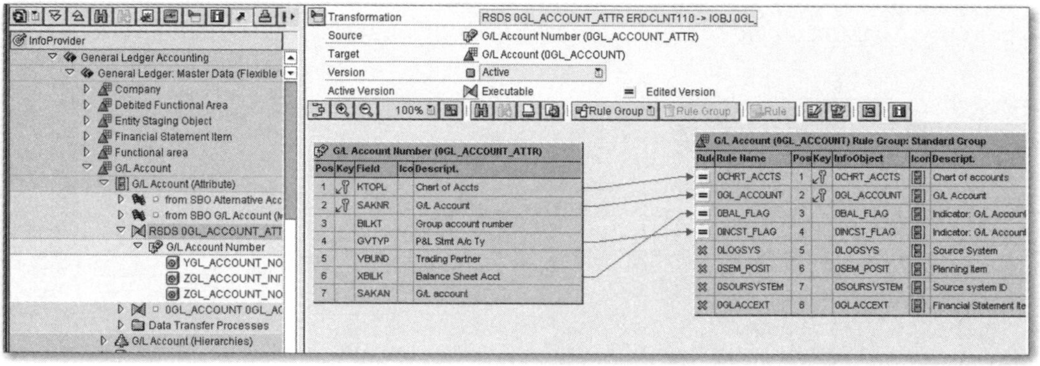

Figure 5.19 GL Account - Transformation Rule Configuration

Finally, we get to the top of the food chain and the table that will store the information after the data flow is run to upload the master data in this case.

Note: Data Flow Approach

In a fully active productive system, the process used to execute the upload is done via a process chain. A *process chain* is a component that offers the ability to create a pictorial view all of the components needed to be used during the uploading process. This way, you don't have to deal with any manual uploading process. The process chain will be described in more detail in this chapter as well as in Chapter 6 on P&F.

In Figure 5.20, you see the master data REQUEST ID list for the InfoObject 0GL_ACCOUNT. The master data has been processed on an ongoing basis. The InfoObject itself is the next object up in the diagram as we discussed earlier. As you can see, the data loading process is on a daily basis, and in this case, there have been no new or changed records for the past several data loads because the total records uploaded is zero (see Figure 5.21).

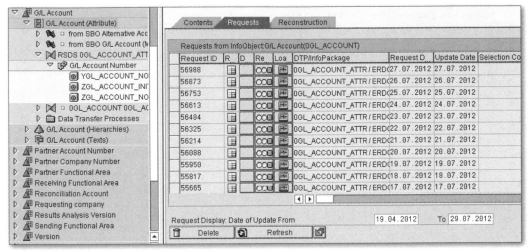

Figure 5.20 GL Account – Attributes Table Showing Data Loading Daily

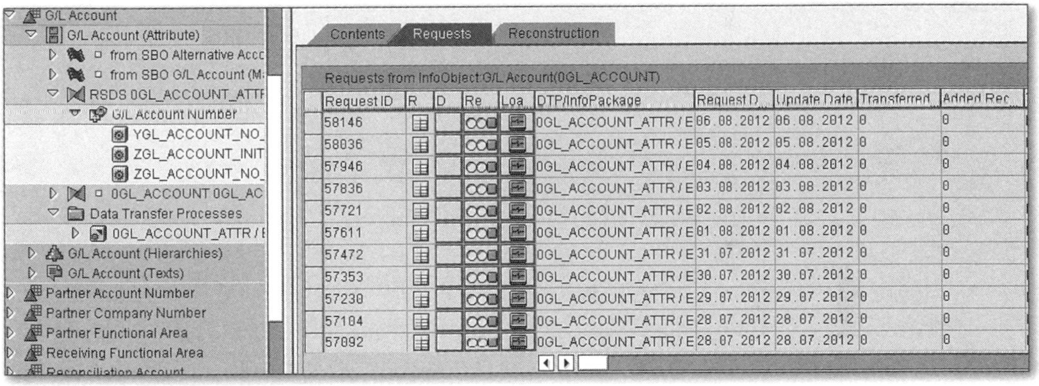

Figure 5.21 GL Account – Request Tab with Added Record Count

Upon completion of the master data upload, you can view the information that's available in the 0GL_ACCOUNT table. The GL Accounts are listed, and some additional attributes have been uploaded. Figure 5.22 shows that the text for each GL Account has also been uploaded into the text tables. The process used for the text upload is very similar to that of the master data, so a detailed explanation of this process won't be given here.

Characteristic 0GL_ACCOUNT - maintain master data: List

Data Records to be Edited

G/L Acco...	Lang.	Balance Sh	Ind.: P&L	Srce Sys.	Plannin...	SrceSys.ID	Fin. State	Short Description	Long Description
350545	EN	X						IC RE transfer-USA C	IC RE transfer-USA Corp
350550	EN	X						IC R/E transfer-Conc	IC R/E transfer-Concentrates
360000	EN	X						CTA - IC Loans / Adv	CTA - IC Loans / Advances
360010	EN	X						CTA - IC Investments	CTA - IC Investments
360020	EN	X						CTA - Translation	CTA - Translation
360030	EN	X						Unrealiz Gain/Loss C	Unrealiz Gain/Loss Cashfl Hedg
360040	EN	X						OCI -- Pension Liab	OCI -- Pension Liab
360042	EN	X						Preferred Shares Ser	Preferred Shares Series 1
360044	EN	X						Contribution Surplus	Contribution Surplus Push down
360046	EN	X						Retained Earnings -	Retained Earnings - Opening
360048	EN	X						Retained Earnings Op	Retained Earnings Open Adj.
360050	EN	X						Retained Earnings-Fi	Retained Earnings-Fin 48
390000	EN	X						FI/CO Reconciliation	FI/CO Reconciliation
399998	EN	X						BPCS Suspense Acct	BPCS Suspense Account
399999	EN	X						Legacy system load -	Legacy system load - Suspense
400000	EN		X					Sales at List Price	Sales at List Price
400002	EN		X					Sales at List Price	Sales at List Price - credit note provision (m
400004	EN		X					Resin Surcharge	Resin Surcharge
400100	EN		X					Sales Discounts	Sales Discounts
400200	EN		X					Cash Discounts	Cash Discounts
400300	EN		X					Rebates	Rebates and Incentives
400500	EN		X					Returns and Allowanc	Returns and Allowances
401000	EN		X					Sales Dedns-Off Invo	Sales Dedns-Off Invoice Allow
401010	EN		X					Sales Dedns-Price Al	Sales Dedns-Price Allowance
401020	EN		X					Sales Dedns-Cash Dis	Sales Dedns-Cash Discounts
401030	EN		X					Sales Dedns-Prepaid	Sales Dedns-Prepaid Contract
401040	EN		X					Sales Dedns-Retrns&A	Sales Dedns-Retrns&Allowances
401050	EN		X					Sales Dedns-Adjustme	Sales Dedns-Adjustments
401100	EN		X					Sales Dedns-Billback	Sales Dedns-Billbacks
401110	EN		X					Sales Dedns-Volume I	Sales Dedns-Volume Incentives

Figure 5.22 0GL_ACCOUNT Maintain Master Data: List

The hierarchy upload, on the other hand, is a bit different and having additional knowledge of this process will help you understand the BW to BPC upload. The significant difference in the process is the additional features on the DataSource that allow you to upload the different portions of the hierarchy. Figure 5.23 shows the DataSource architecture, and on the SEGMENTS/FIELDS tab, there are additional options to allow the configuration of the DataSource to upload the HIERARCHY HEADER , HEADER TEXT, HIERARCHY NODES, AND NODE TEXTS for those nodes. As you choose the different views of the data, the parameters on the screen will change to show what is available for uploading. If you're using SAP ECC for the source of the hierarchies, the DataSource for these hierarchies is normally set, and other than some minor parameters to select, the upload process is consistent. As you can see on this screen, the hierarchy that will be uploaded has time involved; that is, to and from dates will be assigned at the header level. If the hierarchy is time dependent as some are in SAP ECC (e.g., cost center and profit center), then the HIERARCHY NODE view would also have required to and from dates.

DataSource ⬣ 0GL_ACCOUNT_T011_HIER G/L account number
Source System 🖳 ERDCLNT110 ERD Client 110
Version 📀 Active
Active Version   Executable   = Edited Version

General Info. | Extraction | Segments/Fields

Segment [1 Hierarchy header] ☑ Primary Segment

| 1 Hierarchy header |
| 2 Header texts |
| 3 Hierarchy nodes |
| 4 Node texts |

Field Attributes

Pos.	Field				Lngth	Decim	Extern	L	K	Conv	Format	SS C	cur/unit
1	HIENM				30	0	0				Internal		
2	VERSION	Hierarchy vers		CHAR	3	0	0				Internal		
3	HCLASS	Hierarchy clas		CHAR	4	0	0				Internal		
4	DATEFROM	Valid from		DATS	8	0	0				Internal		
5	DATETO	To		DATS	8	0	0				Internal		
6	OBJECTID	Object ID		INT4	10	0	0				Internal		

Figure 5.23 DataSource for Hierarchy Uploads – Segment/Fields Tab

Figure 5.24 shows a view of the HIERARCHY NODES fields and the appropriate structure for the nodes to be uploaded. Many of these fields are required due to the need to position each of the values/nodes in the appropriate location in the hierarchy. Understanding what the prior and subsequent nodes and locations are in the hierarchy is critical to recreating the structure.

DataSource ⬣ 0GL_ACCOUNT_T011_HIER G/L account number
Source System 🖳 ERDCLNT110 ERD Client 110
Version 📀 Active
Active Version   Executable   = Edited Version

General Info. | Extraction | Segments/Fields

Segment [3 Hierarchy nodes] ☐ Primary Segment

Field Attributes

Pos.	Field	Descript.	D	T.	Data type	Lngth	Decim	Extern	L	K	Conv	Format	SS C	cur/unit	S	S
1	NODEID	HierNode ID		☑	NUMC	8	0	0				Internal				0
2	IOBJNM	InfoObject		☑	CHAR	30	0	0				Internal				0
3	NODENAME	Node name		☑	CHAR	32	0	0				Internal	ALPHA			0
4	TLEVEL	Node level		☑	NUMC	2	0	0				Internal				0
5	LINK	Link ID		☑	CHAR	1	0	0				Internal				0
6	PARENTID	ID superior n		☑	NUMC	8	0	0				Internal				0
7	CHILDID	ID sub. node		☑	NUMC	8	0	0				Internal				0
8	NEXTID	ID of the next		☑	NUMC	8	0	0				Internal				0
9	DATEFROM	Valid from		☑	DATS	8	0	0				Internal				0
10	DATETO	To		☑	DATS	8	0	0				Internal				0
11	INTERVL	Indicator		☑	CHAR	1	0	0				Internal				0
12	FIELDNM	Field		☑	CHAR	30	0	0				Internal				0
13	KTOPL	Chart of Accts		☑	CHAR	4	0	0				Internal				0
14	SAKNR	G/L Account		☑	CHAR	10	0	0				Internal	ALPHA			0
15	RSIGN	Chg of sign(+		☑	CHAR	1	0	0				Internal				0
16	PLUMI			☑	CHAR	1	0	0				Internal				0
17	OBJECTID	Object ID		☑	INT4	10	0	0				Internal				0

Figure 5.24 DataSource for Hierarchy Upload – Hierarchy Nodes

The other feature that makes the data loading process consistent across the systems is the InfoPackage. Figure 5.25 shows that the InfoPackage has significant integration with the SAP ECC system because each of the hierarchies that are available in SAP ECC show up as options in the HIERARCHY SELECTION tab of the InfoPackage. All that is needed is to identify the appropriate hierarchy to be uploaded and execute the process.

InfoPackage	YGL_ACCOUNT_HIER_001(ZPAK_DBRLYC721AEPRBA3RQV7V3MLI)						
DataSource	G/L account number(0GL_ACCOUNT_T011_HIER)						
Data Type	Hierarchies						
Source System	ERD Client 110(ERDCLNT110)						
Last Changed by	ALEREMOTE	Date	28.03.2012	Time	11:22:56		

Extraction | Hierarchy Selection | Processing | Update | Schedule

Hierarchy Selection

Selected	Technical Name	R	Versi	Hier	From Date	To Date
○	C001	☑		T011		
⦿	CFSV	☑		T011		
○	Z001	☑		T011		
○	Z0TB	☑		T011		

Figure 5.25 InfoPackage for Hierarchy Upload – Hierarchy Selection Tab

Using these different data loading processes allows you to position the master data in BW and be ready to create the links into the BPC objects to upload the master data and hierarchies.

5.2.2 Transactional Data

Now that the master data are available in BW, you can execute the upload of the transactional data. As noted in Figure 5.9, the data flow is very similar to uploading master data; the big difference is that rather than uploading to an InfoObject, the end result is uploading the transactional data to an InfoProvider, including an InfoCube or DSO. The data are usually manipulated more, but the overall components are the same. Figure 5.26 shows that the overall structure and architecture is similar to what you saw in the master data discussion. The list of objects, including the InfoPackage, DataSource, transformation rule, and Data Transfer Process (DTP), are the same. The difference is the InfoCube and another feature called an InfoSource. An InfoSource was used more frequently in the previous versions of

BW, but in this case, this option allows you more flexibility to transform the data during the uploading process.

▽ ◈ Financial Management & Controlling	0FMCO		Change
▷ ◈ Investment Management	0IMFA		Change
▷ ◈ Public Sector Management	0PSM		Change
▷ ◈ Accounts Receivable Accounting	0FIAR		Change
▽ ◈ Financial Accounting	0FI		Change
▷ ◈ Accounts Payable Accounting	0FIAP		Change
▽ ◈ General Ledger Accounting	0FIGL		Change
▷ ◈ General Ledger: Master Data (Flexible Update)	0FIGL_IO		Change
▽ ◈ General Ledger Accounting (New)	0FIGL_ERP		Change
▽ ◉ GL YTD Balances	ZGLBAL_01	≡	Manage
▷ ⋈ RSDS ZBPC_PLAN_UOM_001 EXTERNAL -> C	00JVWINTF93JL5N79CO8PYI...	≡	Change
▽ ⋈ TRCS ZFI_NEWGL_01 -> CUBE ZGLBAL_01	03V7INX61EKA35Q0OATBHA...	≡	Change
▽ ◎ Infosource from NEW GL to GL Cube	ZFI_NEWGL_01	≡	Change ▦ InfoSources
▽ ⋈ RSDS 0FI_GL_12 ERPCLNT300 -> TRC 07XHURG2R4MC0XCSYE4X...	≡	Change
▽ 🗐 General Ledger: Balances of Leading 0FI_GL_12	≡	Change ▦ DataSources ▦ 📋 ERPCLNT300
◉ DELT - 0FI_GL_12	ZPAK_DB7HYI004QIKFM1XP...	Execute	▦ DataSources
◉ FULL - 0FI_GL_12	ZPAK_DB7HYDKQ3O0722R...	Execute	▦ DataSources
◉ INIT - NO LOAD - 0FI_GL_12	ZPAK_DCDL76EZQKU1DXR...	Execute	▦ DataSources
▷ 🗀 Data Transfer Processes	ZGLBAL_01		Create Data Tra...

Figure 5.26 Data Flow for Transactional Data into InfoCube ZGLBAL_01

For transactional data that is needed in BW for BPC, one of our main goals is to make sure that the data are consistent with the format and structure required by BPC. We talked about the fact that the BPC model only has one key figure (account based), and many of the BW InfoCubes have more than one key figure (key figure based). So one of the main objectives is to make sure that after uploading the data into the "staging" InfoCube in BW, you're left with an account-based structure. This makes the uploading process much more consistent and reduces any alignment issues with BPC. Having this set up also helps with validation processes across the BPC and BW landscape. If you have an InfoCube architecture that's similar, then you can validate the data more effectively.

Getting into some additional detail, note that the InfoPackage also has the DELTA UPDATE capability (see Figure 5.27). The Delta Update feature is more frequently used for transactional data because of the larger amounts of records being uploaded and the frequency of the records changing. The options displayed on the UPDATE tab are exactly the same as you saw on the master data InfoPackage.

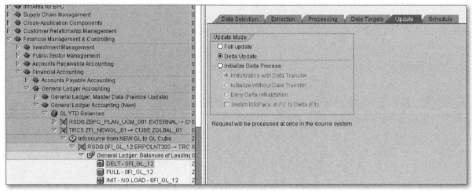

Figure 5.27 InfoPackage for Transactional Data Upload – Update Options

As you move up the layers in this case, you find the DataSource of the transactional data as well as two transformation rules that are used. Figure 5.28 shows the first transformation rule. This transformation rule is used to do the following:

▶ Fill the functional area using the combination of cost center and cost center category during the transformation process – ❶ in Figure 5.28.

▶ Derive the currency key based on the company code – ❷ in Figure 5.28. All of the other connections are direct one-to-one relationships, so they only have the line drawn between each of them.

7	RLDNR	Ledger					
8	RRCTY	Record Type		**Rul**	**Rule Name**	**Pos Key**	**InfoObject**	**Descript.**
9	RVERS	Version	=	0GL_ACCOUNT	1	0GL_ACCOUNT	G/L Account
10	LOGSYS	Logical system	=	0VERSION	2	0VERSION	Version
11	RACCT	Account Number	=	0COMP_CODE	3	0COMP_CODE	Company code
12	COST_ELEM	Cost Element		Fill functional area using cost center and cost center cat ❶	4	0FUNC_AREA	Functional area
13	RBUKRS	Company Code	=	0CURTYPE	5	0CURTYPE	Currency Type
14	RCNTR	Cost Center	⏱	0FISCPER3	6	0FISCPER3	Posting period
15	PRCTR	Profit Center	⏱	0FISCPER	7	0FISCPER	Fiscal year / period
16	RFAREA	Functional Area	⏱	0FISCVARNT	8	0FISCVARNT	Fiscal year variant
17	RBUSA	Business Area	=	0CHRT_ACCTS	9	0CHRT_ACCTS	Chart of accounts
18	KOKRS	CO Area	=	0RECORDMODE	10	0RECORDMODE	BW Delta Process: U
19	SEGMENT	Segment		master data from Company Code ❷	11	0CURRENCY	Currency key
20	SCNTR	Sender cost ctr	=	0BALANCE	12	0BALANCE	Cumulative Balance
21	PPRCTR	Partner PC	=	0DEBIT	13	0DEBIT	Total Debit Postings
22	SFAREA	Partner FArea	=	0CREDIT	14	0CREDIT	Total credit postings
23	SBUSA	Trdg Part BA	=	0SALES	15	0SALES	Sales for the Period
24	RASSC	Trading Partner	=	0SEGMENT	16	0SEGMENT	Segment for Segmen
25	PSEGMENT	Partner Segment	⏱	0FISCYEAR	17	0FISCYEAR	Fiscal year
26	QUANUNIT	Unit of Measure	=	0COMPANY	18	0COMPANY	Company
27	VALUETYPE	Value Type					

Infosource from NEW GL to GL Cube (ZFI_NEWGL_01) Rule Group: Standard Group

Figure 5.28 Transformation Rule from the DataSource to the InfoSource

Looking at the next transformation rule up the chain, you see some additional changes that are happening. In Figure 5.29, the transformation rule is being used to do the following:

► Calculate the OCALMONTH from the fiscal period – ❶ in Figure 5.29.

► Fill in any blanks (FILL IN BLANK FIELDS FOR COMPANY) for the company (trading partner) – ❷ in Figure 5.29.

► Assign a CONSTANT for the MOVEMENT TYPE upload – ❸ in Figure 5.29. All of the other fields are again a one-to-one relationship. You can create all of these changes in one transformation rule, but having the option to validate the data in two steps is a nice luxury. However, if your SLAs are very tight, then creating all of these transformations in one rule is acceptable and required.

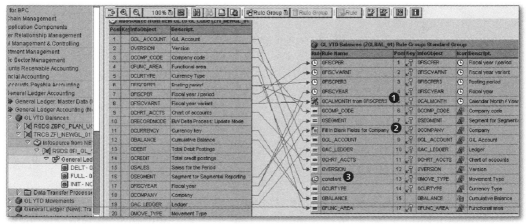

Figure 5.29 Transformation Rule from InfoSource to InfoCube

The final stop in this data flow is into an InfoCube. Figure 5.30 shows the architecture of the InfoCube that will be used as the staging InfoCube for the BPC model. Notice that, in this case, there is only one key figure available in the BW-based InfoCube, which was a primary goal for this data flow. This means that you're ready to create the connections to the BPC models and link the appropriate objects for the next step in data loading.

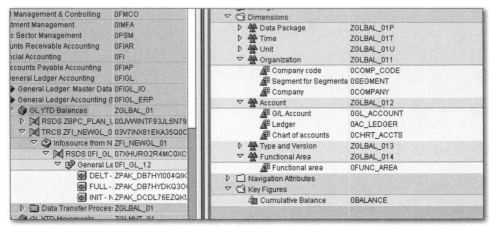

Figure 5.30 BW InfoCube Used for Staging Data into BPC Model

5.3 Data Loading Processes from BW to BPC

You're now ready to start the data loading process from source systems such as BW or a flat file into BPC. Again, you need to upload all of the master data/members to BPC objects before uploading the transactional data. In fact, in BPC, it's even more critical to make sure that all of the member values are available in the dimensions because if you upload the transactional data and don't have the appropriate member values, then you'll end up with error(s) in the uploading process. Depending on what you set up in the transformation file in the parameter about errors during the upload, a file may show the errors and the remaining transactions uploaded or the entire loading process may be stopped from going forward after a specific number of errors. You'll see that the data loading process in BPC is pretty much routine after you get used to it. Of course, there are times where you'll have to tweak the transformation files or conversion files, but overall the basic format will be consistent.

5.3.1 Master Data, Text

Let's get into all of the steps and activities involved in the first part of the uploading process and then we'll refer back to them in the subsequent uploading activities. Normally the first process in uploading is to upload the master data from the BW

InfoObject to the BPC dimension. The screens and activities are a bit different from BW, but the concepts are the same, and the end result needs to be the same. You first need to upload the members and member properties from one table to another. To start, let's look at the source object—the BW InfoObject ZMATERIAL in the BW system. Figure 5.31 shows that the ZMATERIAL InfoObject has numerous attributes available to you for processing.

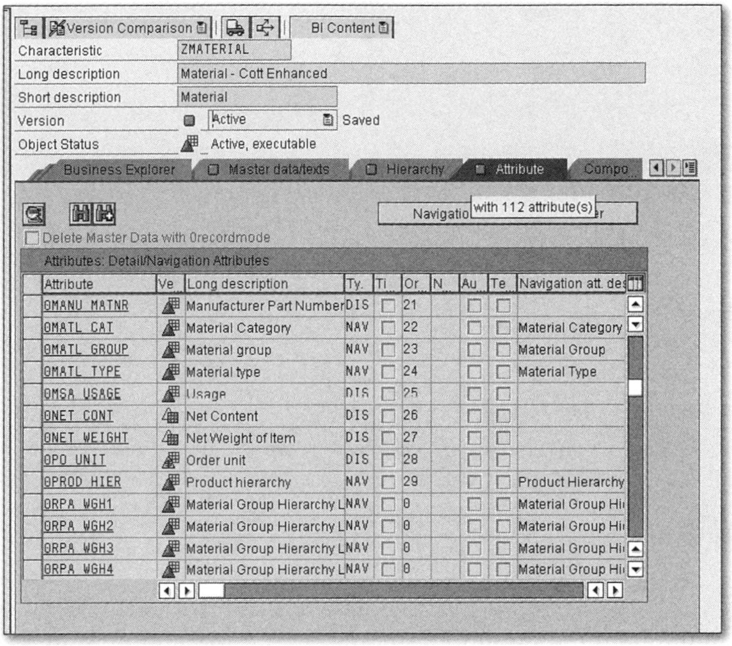

Figure 5.31 ZMATERIAL – Attribute Tab

You only need to connect a select few of these different attributes to accommodate BPC. In Figure 5.32, the PRODUCT dimension in BPC only has about six properties to fill. If you want more, you can enhance the data mapping, upload more, and also fill in the ones that you had done in the initial uploads. So adding another property to the PRODUCT dimension and filling it with members isn't a complex process. That doesn't mean you can be lax about the initial requirements, but it does mean that you don't have to go back and reengineer the entire architecture if you miss a property or two that is needed for reporting.

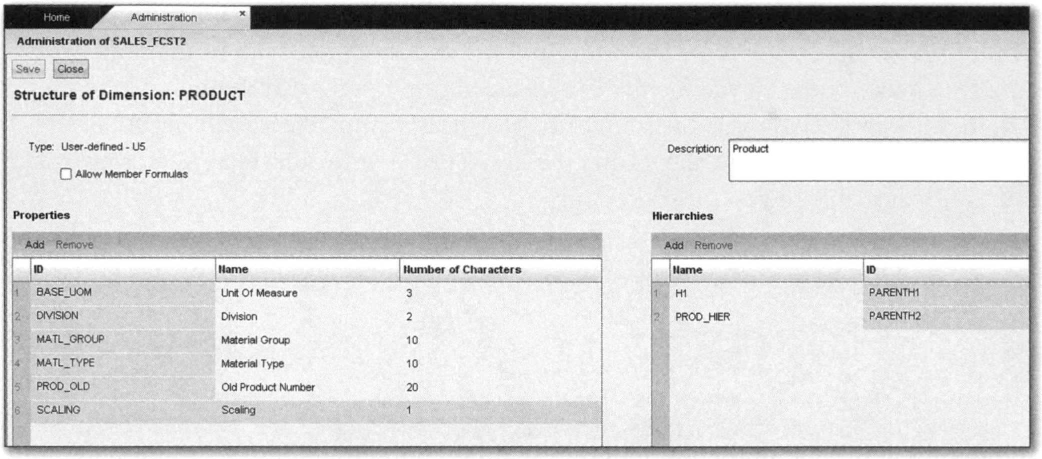

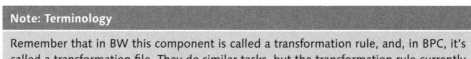

Figure 5.32 BPC PRODUCT Dimension – Properties Section

To do this, you align the transformation file to help with the mapping process. Note in Figure 5.33 that there are 293 members in the BW ZMATERIAL.

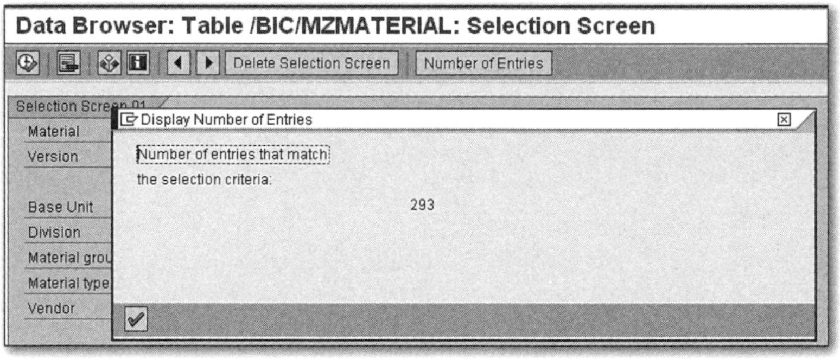

Figure 5.33 ZMATERIAL – Number of Entries in the Master Data Table

Note: Terminology
Remember that in BW this component is called a transformation rule, and, in BPC, it's called a transformation file. They do similar tasks, but the transformation rule currently has more flexibility and standard mapping components.

To start this process, go into EPM OFFICE ADD-IN EXCEL and access the DATA MANAGER tab. Using the web link for the BPC HOME page, you choose HOME • EPM OFFICE ADD-IN EXCEL. Then, pick the appropriate model, and the Excel add-in will open with that model as the current source. Use the Data Manager to access the New Transformation File option shown in Figure 5.34.

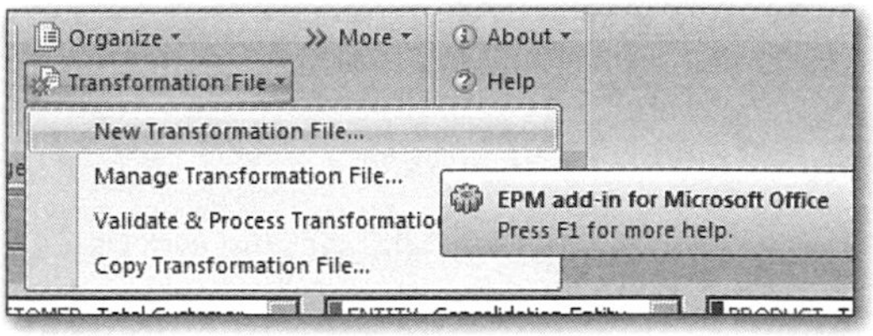

Figure 5.34   Selecting the New Transformation File Option

After the spreadsheet opens, you'll see that there are three sections of the transformation file (see Figure 5.35). We already talked about what you need to do in the *MAPPING and *CONVERSION sections (we'll see more of this in a bit as well). For now, however, let's discuss the header information available in this spreadsheet. These different parameters are very helpful in setting up the events in the upload process.

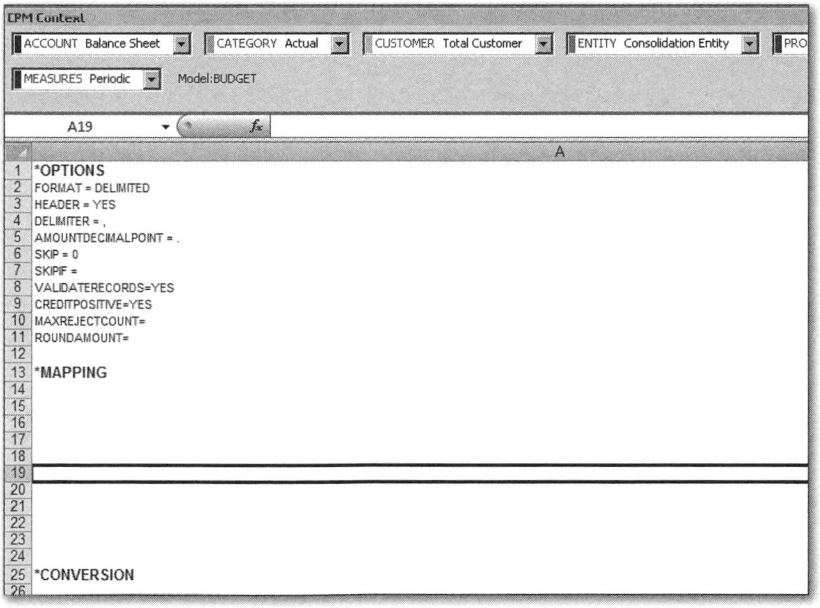

Figure 5.35   Transformation File – *OPTIONS, *MAPPING, and *CONVERSION

The parameter definitions, as shown in Figure 5.35, are each listed in Table 5.2.

Parameter	Definition
FORMAT	This option must be defined because there is no default. The DELIMITED value means that there is a special character between each column of data, defined by the delimited option. FIXED means that the data is in a fixed field format.
HEADER	If YES, then your input file contains one header row that defines the fields.
DELIMITER	This value can be a comma, space, or tab. The default value is a comma. If the FORMAT option is set to DELIMITED, this option defines the single character that is delimited between columns. Use the keywords SPACE or TAB if space or tab delimiters are used.
AMOUNTDECIMALPOINT	This will allow you to enter non-period decimal points, so a comma can be read as a decimal point.
SKIP	This is the number of lines to skip at the top of the data file. If your data file has a header, set this value so that those lines are skipped during transformation.
SKIPIF	This will skip a record if it's NULL.
VALIDATERECORDS	If YES, validate the mapping and that members exist, and map data in the proper order.
CREDITPOSITIVE	If NO, all amounts referring to an account type (LEQ, INC) will have their signs reversed.
MAXREJECTCOUNT	This is the number of bad records before the data load fails. This is only applicable to the upload of transactional data—not master data.
ROUNDAMOUNT	This indicates the amount of decimal values to round to.
SELECTION	This is an additional option (not visible in Figure 5.35) that can be inserted into the HEADER area. This allows the data to be filtered from the source. For example, SELECTION = ENTITY,1000 will only load company code 1000 from the source system.

Table 5.2 *OPTIONS in the Transformation File and Definitions

In terms of the two other sections of the transformation file, you'll insert some basic logic for the mapping process. For master data uploads, you normally don't get too much into the conversion file, but we'll cover that during the transactional data upload. Figure 5.36 shows the mapping process for the ZMATERIAL to the PRODUCT objects. Again, remember that the target object is on the left side of the equals sign, and the source is on the right side. In this case, the objects on the left side come from the technical names of the properties in the PRODUCT dimension, and the objects on the right side come from the technical names of the attributes from the ZMATERIAL characteristic. For example, 0MATL_GROUP (BW) will be mapped to and therefore upload the members into MATL_GROUP (BW/BPC). You can see that one of the mappings—SCALING—is basically feeding a constant into a property as a value. SCALING just assigns a "Y" to the member field for each of the master data items.

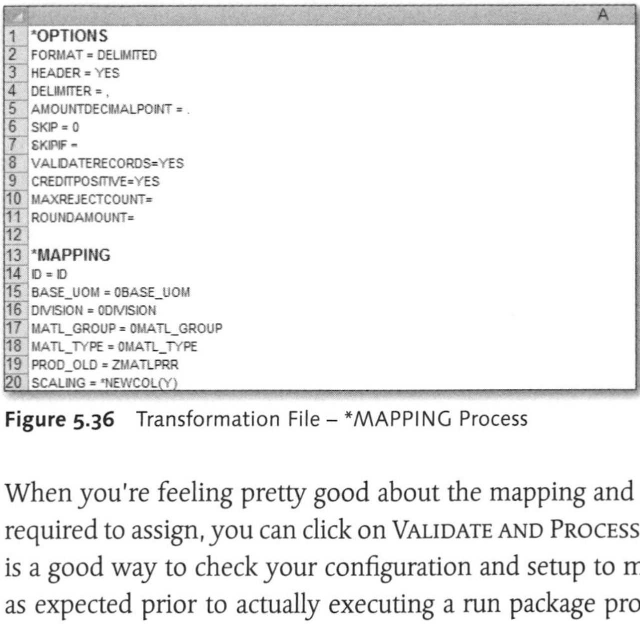

```
                                                          A
1   *OPTIONS
2   FORMAT = DELIMITED
3   HEADER = YES
4   DELIMITER = ,
5   AMOUNTDECIMALPOINT = .
6   SKIP = 0
7   SKIPIF =
8   VALIDATERECORDS=YES
9   CREDITPOSITIVE=YES
10  MAXREJECTCOUNT=
11  ROUNDAMOUNT=
12
13  *MAPPING
14  ID = ID
15  BASE_UOM = 0BASE_UOM
16  DIVISION = 0DIVISION
17  MATL_GROUP = 0MATL_GROUP
18  MATL_TYPE = 0MATL_TYPE
19  PROD_OLD = ZMATLPRR
20  SCALING = *NEWCOL(Y)
```

Figure 5.36 Transformation File – *MAPPING Process

When you're feeling pretty good about the mapping and any conversions that you're required to assign, you can click on VALIDATE AND PROCESS TRANSFORMATION FILE. This is a good way to check your configuration and setup to make sure that the results are as expected prior to actually executing a run package process. Figure 5.37 shows the dialog box that appears after you execute the validation process. In the VALIDATE AND TRANSFORMATION dialog box, you have several items to assign information to:

▶ DATA TYPE
In this case, you're uploading master data/texts from the BW InfoObject. A number of options are available in this field, including those in the following list. Depending on the option chosen, the fields will adjust to accommodate the data loading process.

- ▶ Transactional data from the BW InfoProvider

- ▶ Transactional data from a flat file

- ▶ Master data from a flat file

- ▶ Master data descriptions from a flat file

- ▶ Master data/text from the BW InfoObject

- ▶ Master data hierarchy from the BW InfoObject

- ▶ Export master data

- ▶ Export transaction data

▶ DATA – SELECT AN INFOOBJECT
This is the source InfoObject for the master data.

▶ SET SELECTION
This allows the filtering of the information that is uploaded.

▶ FORMAT
This is the internal or external format of the data being uploaded.

▶ SELECT A DIMENSION
This is the target dimension for the master data upload.

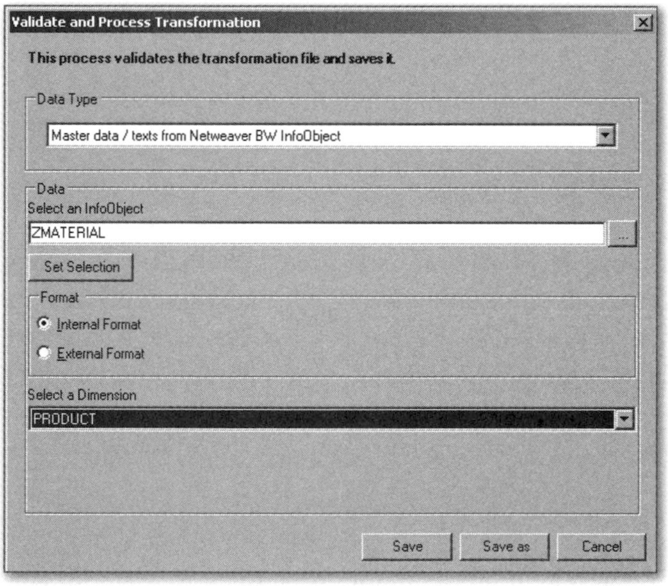

Figure 5.37 Validate and Process Transformation

When you click the SET SELECTION button, a dialog box appears with a series of tabs available (see Figure 5.38). This dialog box enables filtering based on different properties available on the BW InfoObject (source InfoObject).

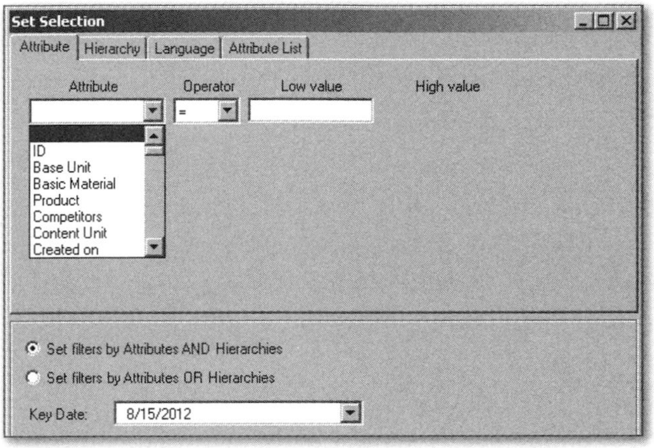

Figure 5.38   Set Selection – Attributes to Filter the Upload

In the HIERARCHY tab shown in Figure 5.39, you can upload the text nodes of a hierarchy as the master data is being uploaded. This is required so that the actual hierarchy can be uploaded. Remember that BPC hierarchies are a bit unique and different from the BW hierarchies. A BPC hierarchy needs to have all of the levels as actual members rather than having the base value as a member and the other levels and text nodes. In BPC, the concept of a hierarchy with text nodes doesn't exist. Therefore, the BW hierarchy text nodes are translated into true member values by using this option.

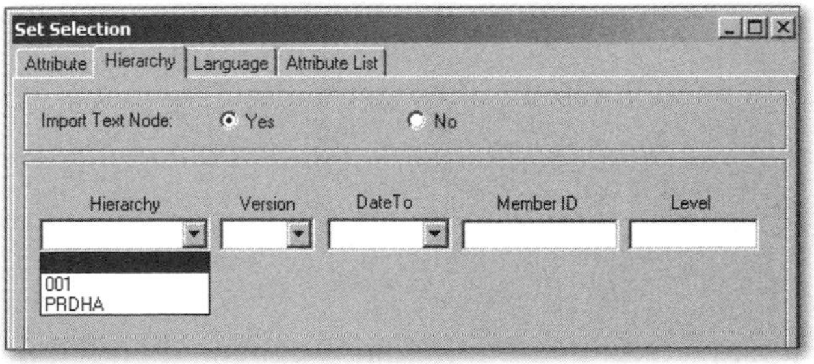

Figure 5.39   Set Selection – Hierarchy Tab

You can choose whether to import the text nodes or not by choosing YES or NO at the top of the tab. You also need to identify the hierarchy that you are uploading as well as if there's a version assignment from the BW side or a DATETO option. The hierarchy text nodes can also be uploaded from a specific level or using a member ID starting at that level.

The LANGUAGE tab only offers an option to upload based on a language; in most cases, this is EN – ENGLISH.

The final tab—ATTRIBUTE LIST—allows the filtering of the values that the system will use to base its search on during the uploading process (see Figure 5.40). No assignments or adjustments are required on this tab, but it's good to filter to the appropriate attributes required to help the performance of the data loading process. This can be done in the actual run package process, but for now, you can leave these as-is and execute the validation process.

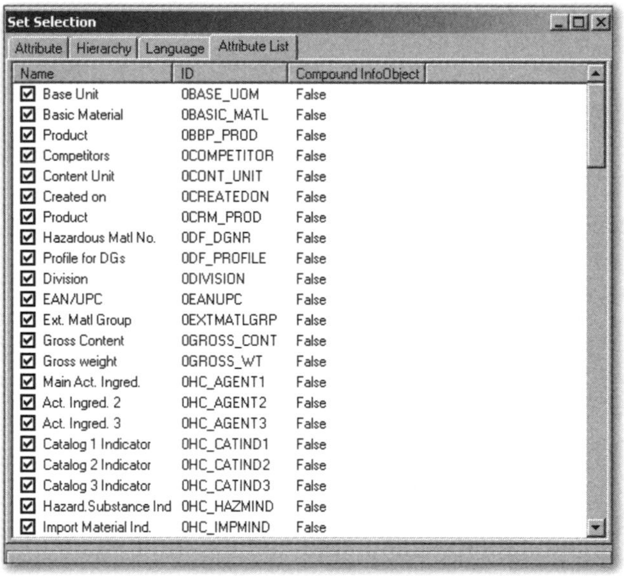

Figure 5.40 Set Selection – Attribute List Tab

After these parameters are set, you can either select SAVE or SAVE AS to assign a naming convention to the transformation file. In either case, the VALIDATION STATUS dialog box appears as shown in Figure 5.41. As you can see the results of the validation are that everything was passed with no errors. You can also see that 292 members were validated during this process. If you remember, the total number of members in the InfoObject was 293, which included a blank initial member. So the total of 292 is consistent with what is in the InfoObject. You can now move forward and execute the actual run package process to upload the master data.

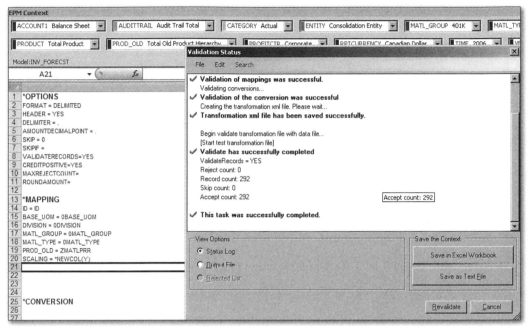

Figure 5.41 Results of the Validate and Process Transformation File

The details of the validation process show that the master data ID as well as the values of the properties were uploaded and configured. Notice that the text was also uploaded in this process. This is a difference between using a BW InfoObject and a flat file. With the BW InfoObject the attributes and text come over in a single upload process, then the hierarchy is uploaded in another. For a flat file, the master data and hierarchy are uploaded together, and the text comes in on another package. The details of the validation are given in Figure 5.42.

We'll cover the actual run package process using the hierarchy upload. The sequence of parameters is just about the same, but we'll comment on any differences.

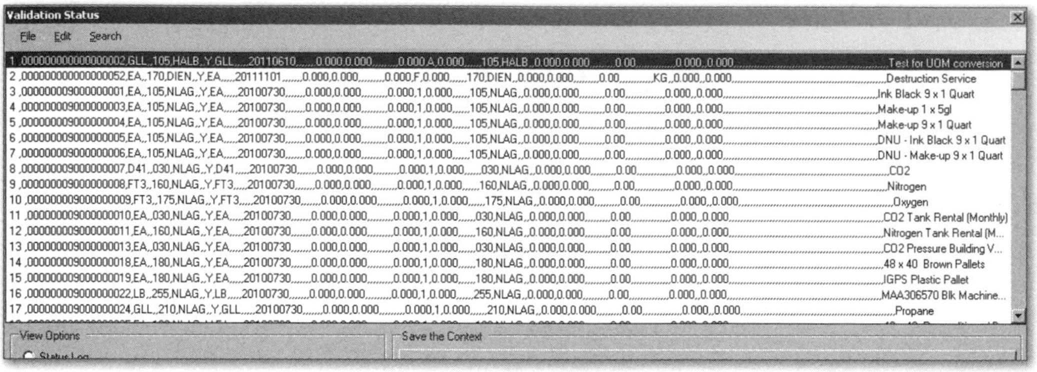

Figure 5.42 Results of the Upload Process for PRODUCT

In this straightforward view of the steps and sequence of activities to upload the master data, we mapped about 6 dimensions out of more than 100 available attributes, but the process is the same no matter the number of attributes to map. Some cases may call for a different scenario. For example, one of the common differences between a BPC dimension and a BW InfoObject is that the BPC dimension has no concept of what a compound characteristic is and also doesn't support the uploading of a compound characteristic. In these cases, you have to look to a slightly different mapping process, but the concept is the same. If you have a compound InfoObject, this means that there is a superior InfoObject that controls the core InfoObject.

> ### Note: Compound InfoObject
>
> A compound InfoObject is controlled by another InfoObject. An example of this is any city in the United States. To find the actual location of that city, we also need the state it's located in because there are many cities by the same name in the United States (e.g., there are six Philadelphia's in the United States).

There are several different approaches to uploading the master data for this example. One is to actually add a prefix to the master data value on the upload, causing the mapping to look something like this:

ID = 0PLANT+ID (example – Plant = 1000; Material = M101)

This concatenates the material number with the plant, and the result is something like 1000M101. This allows all of the material values to be unique. Of course, this mapping is followed by all of the properties that you wanted to upload to members into BPC.

5.3.2   Hierarchies

After the master data is uploaded, you can direct your attention to the hierarchy upload process. Let's discuss the process of uploading a hierarchy from the BW InfoObject to the BPC dimension. As we mentioned, the concept of a hierarchy in BW and BPC objects are similar in nature, but the result and the configuration is quite different. The BPC hierarchy is made up of all values or members, whereas the BW hierarchy has members at the lowest level, and the levels above are made up of text nodes. During the upload of the master data, you use the feature in the Set Selection dialog box to automatically upload the text nodes, which turns them into actual members for BPC to use in the hierarchy. After that occurs, you can upload the BW hierarchy. Let's look at the upload of the 0GL_ACCOUNT hierarchy in this situation. The GL account hierarchy presents a bit of a different issue when it comes to uploading the hierarchy. Unlike the upload of hierarchies attached to objects such as profit centers and cost centers, where the dimension type is more than likely to be U (user defined) and not A (account), the GL account has a requirement that the ACCTTYPE property be assigned to the member prior to the upload of that member to the BPC dimension. This presents an interesting series of questions concerning how to accomplish this, and we'll look at the details of some solutions later in this chapter. After the assignment of the ACCTTYPE to the member, the upload process for the hierarchies is very similar.

Figure 5.43 shows the BW InfoObject you'll be using as a source for the hierarchy and also the hierarchy root name – CFSV. In this example, you'll be uploading one of the financial statement version hierarchies (CFSV).

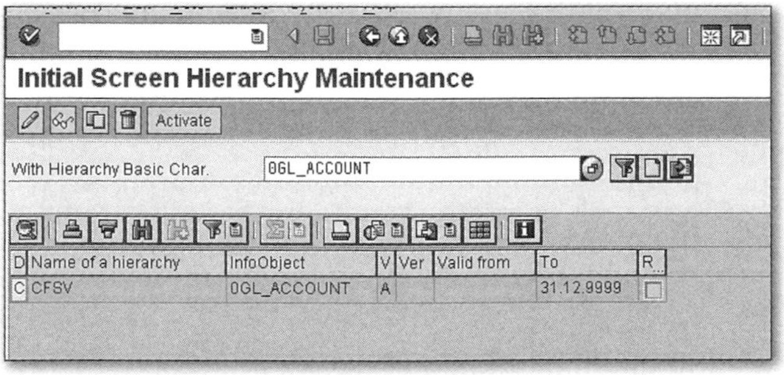

Figure 5.43   Initial Screen Hierarchy Maintenance in BW

Because we've already covered the process of accessing the Data Manager screen as well as starting a new transformation file, refer to Section 5.1.1 about the master data and text upload if you need to refresh your memory. At this point, let's look at the transformation file that will be used to upload the hierarchy into the BPC dimension. Figure 5.44 shows the transformation file with the *MAPPING and *CONVERSION already set up. In this case, a hierarchy upload requires both a transformation file and a conversion file.

The *MAPPING component is a bit different from the master data mapping (discussed earlier) to accommodate the architecture of the hierarchy within the BW system. The nodes of the hierarchy that are used for the organization and upload of the appropriate structure are listed under the title of NODE NAME in BW. If you review the structure of a hierarchy in BW, you'll see this column and the appropriate technical names of the different levels.

In this case, the initial read being done by the first line of code is directed toward the format of the technical names of the hierarchy nodes. Consider the following statement as an example, as shown in Figure 5.44, Line 14:

```
NODENAME = *IF(NODENAME (1:4) = *STR(CSFV) then NODENAME; NODENAME(9:14))
```

This reads that if the NODENAME (column in BW hierarchy with all of the technical names listed) = IF, the NODENAME has a string of characters = CFSV in the first four positions, then use the NODENAME, if not, then use the NODENAME but only the characters in positions 9 through 14. Therefore, this removes the compounding that is on the GL account members because the 0GL_ACCOUNT InfoObject is compounded with the chart of accounts. After this line of code, the rest is fairly straightforward. The next three lines of code are shown in a hierarchy *MAPPING section of the transformation file. The HIER_NAME, PARENT, and ORDER mapping move the same positioning from the BW InfoObject to the BPC dimension.

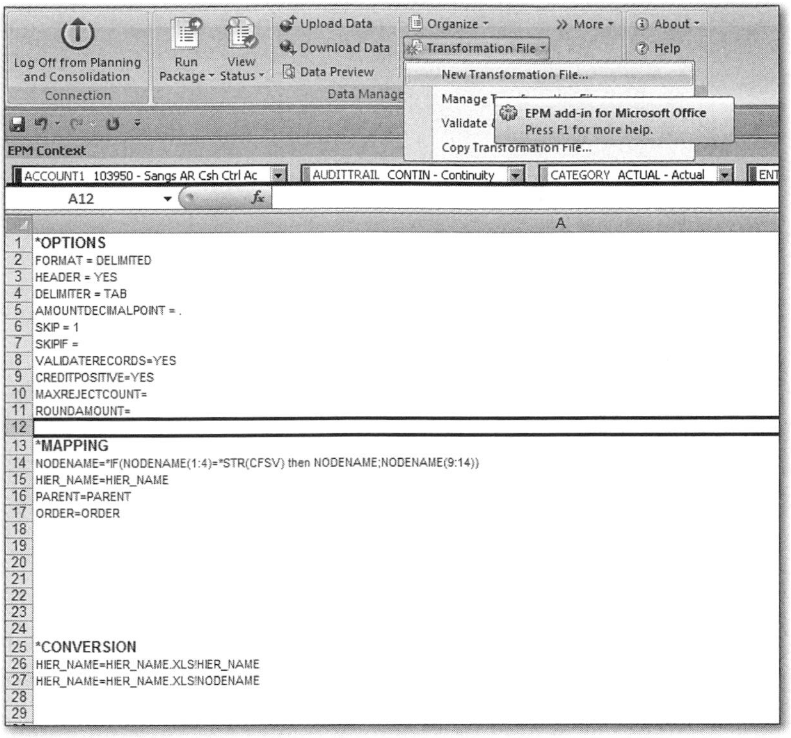

Figure 5.44 Transformation File in BPC for Uploading the GL Account Hierarchy

The conversion file in this case is required to add some additional detailed mapping to the hierarchy upload. In Figure 5.45, you see that the initial spreadsheet shows the conversion file with a single line of code in line 2, columns A and B.

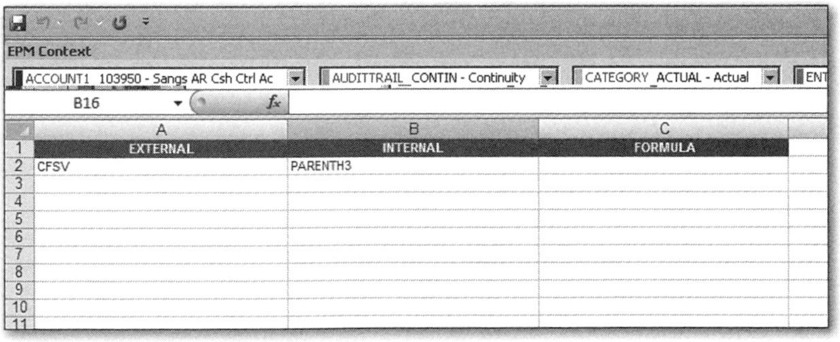

Figure 5.45 Conversion File for Hierarchy Upload

In this case, the CFSV hierarchy will be assigned to the PARENTH3 position in the BPC dimension. Figure 5.46 shows the other spreadsheet for the conversion file. In this case, you just need to make sure that any special characters in the hierarchy levels are removed and a space is inserted during the upload.

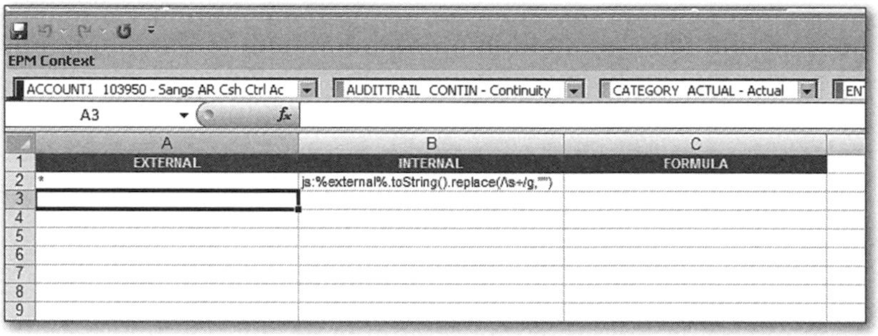

Figure 5.46 Conversion File for Hierarchy Upload – Converting Special Characters into Blanks during Upload

Again, you should execute a validate and process approach to this upload, especially for hierarchy uploads. For master data, you can feel reasonably comfortable that your code is consistent, but with hierarchies, there can be a number of issues, so executing the validate and process is a good idea. As we go through the process, you'll notice fairly similar screens as before. Figure 5.47 shows the initial dialog box for the parameters to validate and process.

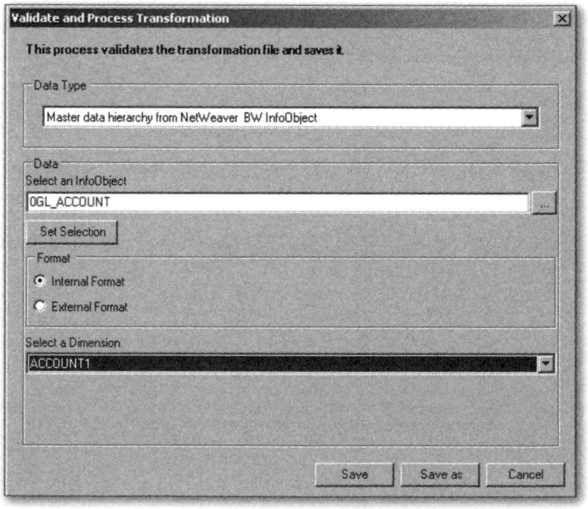

Figure 5.47 Validate and Process Transformation

These are the same options, but after the data type is set to upload the BW hierarchy, then the settings change a bit, and you notice that the format is either internal or external to be read. This references the view of the hierarchy either from the BW side or the BPC side. The SET SELECTION dialog box is very similar to what you saw before, except that you are selecting the hierarchy and possibly a version and a specific level to upload the hierarchy from (see Figure 5.48).

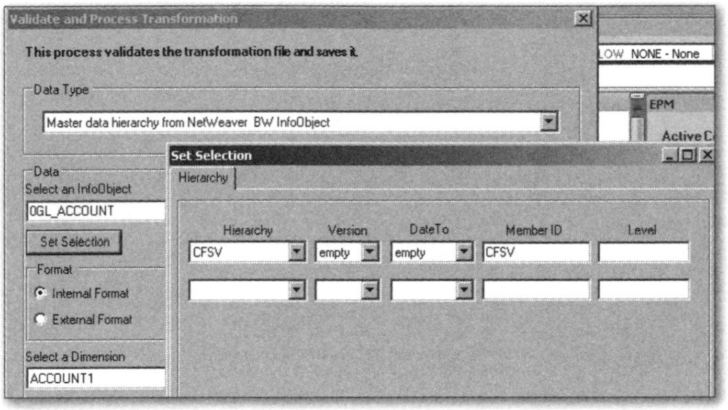

Figure 5.48 Validate and Process Transformation – Set Selection

After the dimension is assigned, then the validation process begins when you use either SAVE OR SAVE AS. The results are shown in Figure 5.49.

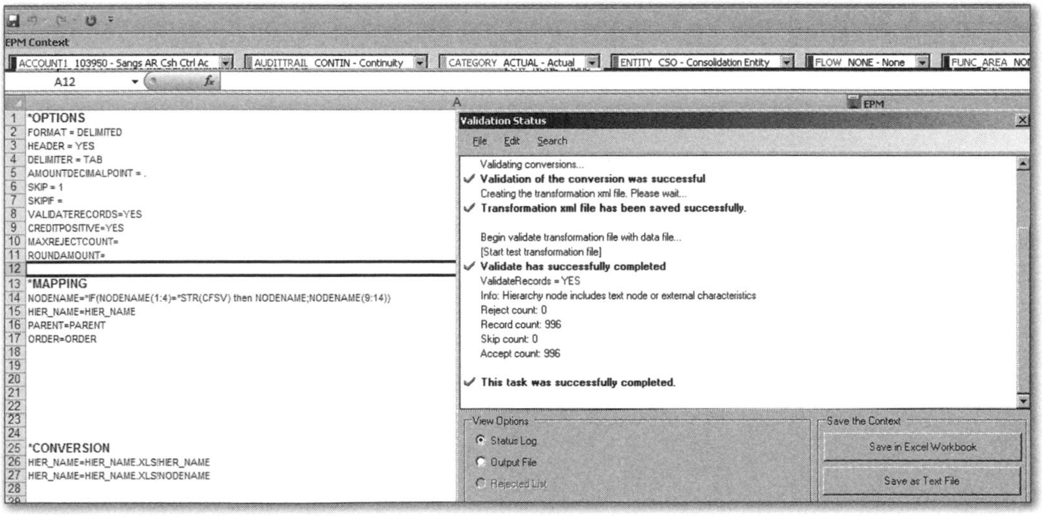

Figure 5.49 Validation Results for the GL Account Hierarchy

The results are a success, so from here, you can execute the run package process. In this case, we'll walk through these steps to see the process. In a normal production scenario, you execute these activities from a Business Process Flow screen (BPF), and the prompts you're seeing manually here are automatically available for you to view. We'll discuss BPFs in detail in Chapter 9.

To start the actual uploading process, choose RUN PACKAGE • RUN PACKAGE, and a dialog box appears as shown in Figure 5.50. Here you can see that rather than a dropdown with the specific packages to select from, this is a displayed list of packages that you can choose from. In this case, select the uploading a hierarchy from a BW InfoObject package (Import Master Data Hierarchies InfoObj).

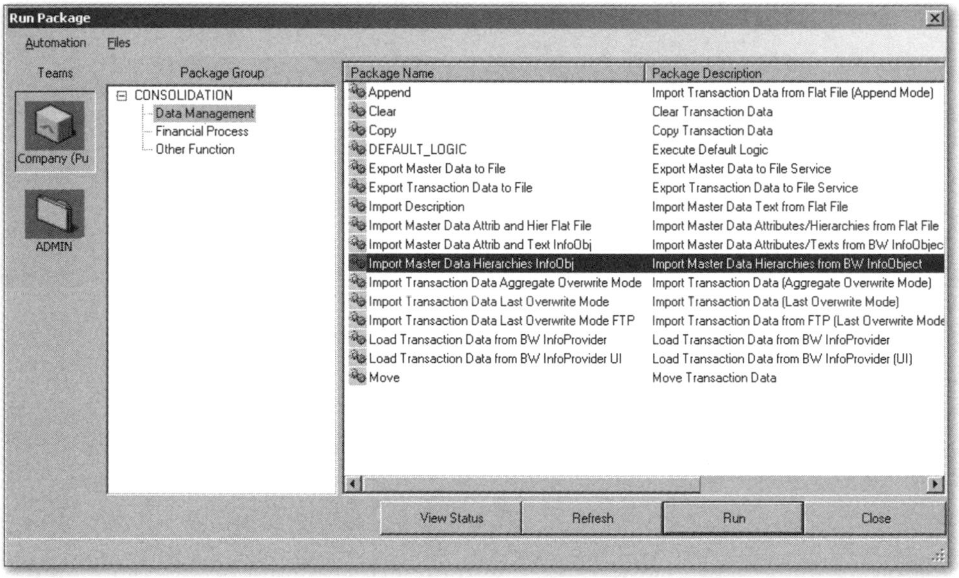

Figure 5.50 Run Package – Package Group and Package Assignment

After this, click on the RUN button to move through the next series of screens. Figure 5.51 shows the next screen, which requires an InfoObject to be assigned. Notice that the SET SELECTION button is available from this screen.

Figure 5.51 Run Package – Import Master Data Hierarchies InfoObject

Next, Figure 5.52 shows that you can either overwrite the current hierarchy if one is already assigned or update the hierarchy. The OVERWRITE option completely replaces the hierarchy with the one that is being uploaded, whereas the UPDATE option just changes the existing hierarchy. There's an important factor to consider when using these two options. If you choose to use the OVERWRITE option, then you must upload all of the hierarchies that are assigned to your dimension each time. If you don't do this, the hierarchy that you're actually overwriting will come through fine, but it will remove all of the other hierarchies. So, during this upload, you must upload all of the hierarchies each time. If you're using the UPDATE option, then you'll only have to identify the one hierarchy that you'll be uploading, and all of the others won't be impacted. So, if you can simply update the hierarchy, you might want to select that option to help improve performance and processing time.

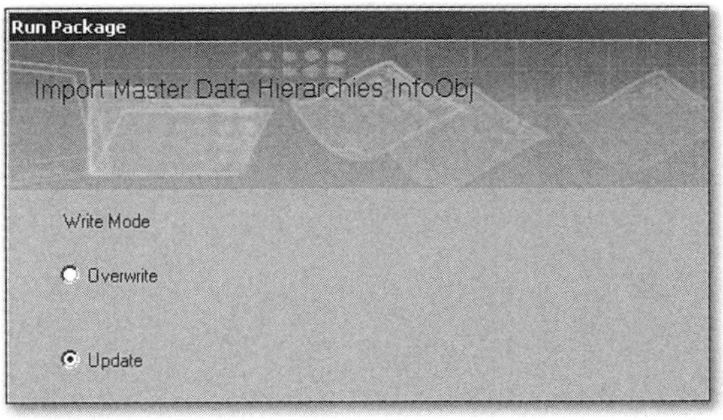

Figure 5.52 Run Package – Overwrite or Update

Figure 5.53 is the next screen with the choice of internal or external formatting,

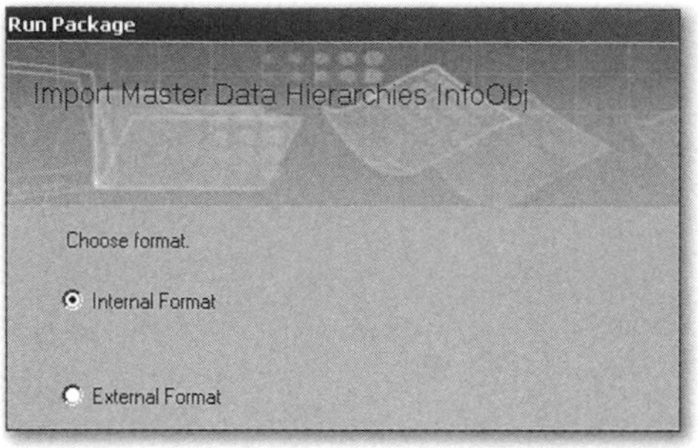

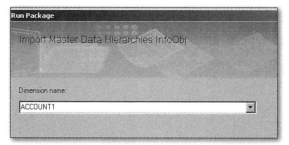

Figure 5.53 Run Package – Formatting

Next, Figure 5.54 requires the assignment of the transformation file.

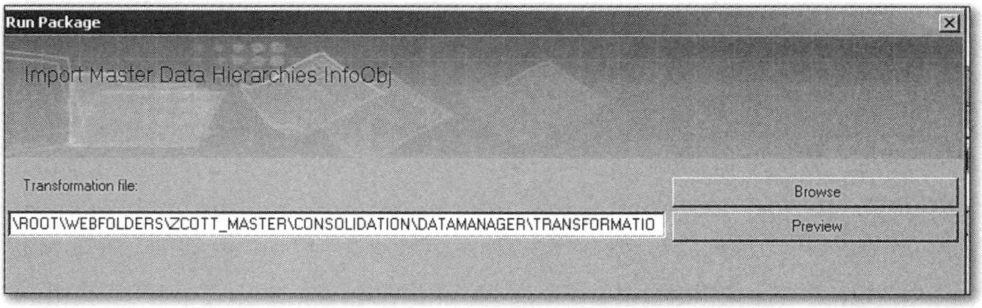

Figure 5.54 Run Package – Assignment of the Transformation File

Figure 5.55 shows the assignment of the dimension name.

Figure 5.55 Run Package – Assignment of Dimension Name

Figure 5.56 is the final step in the process—choosing whether to RUN, SCHEDULE, or RUN & SCHEDULE.

Figure 5.56 Run Package – Run or Schedule Upload

Finally, after the package is run and a success result is shown, you can review the results from the BPC side. Figure 5.57 shows the dimension you uploaded this hierarchy to so that additional reporting can be accomplished.

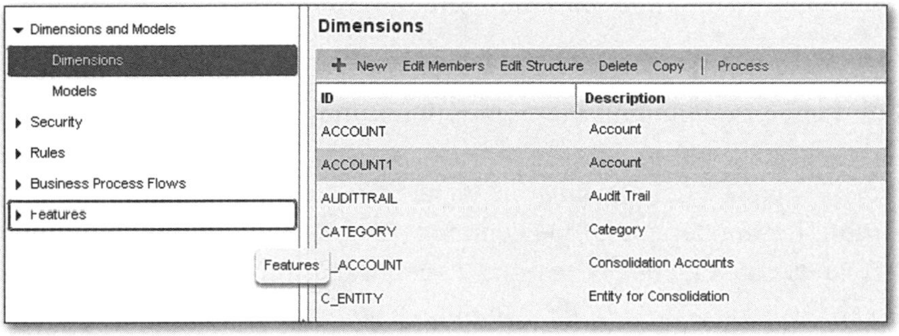

Figure 5.57 Dimension ACCOUNT1

Figure 5.58 shows the option to readjust the view from a list to a hierarchy view, so you can see the uploaded CFSV.

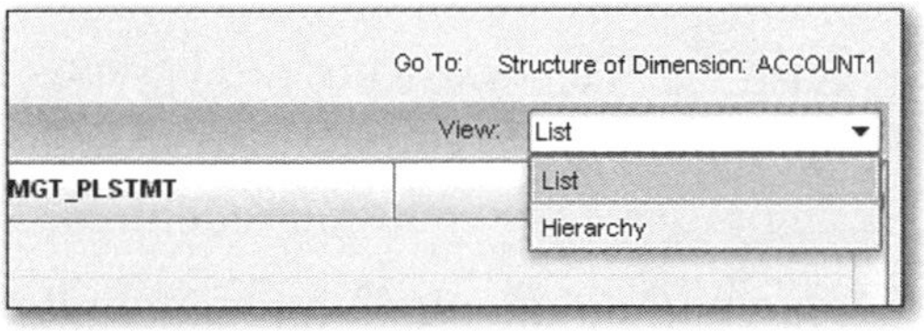

Figure 5.58 Dimension View as Hierarchy

Finally, in Figure 5.59, you see the final results of the upload of the GL account hierarchy.

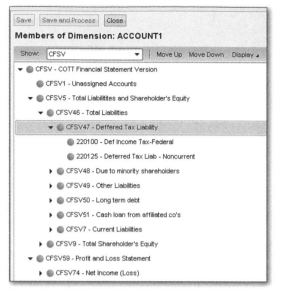

Figure 5.59 CFSV Hierarchy View from the Dimension ACCOUNT1

This is a typical approach to uploading the hierarchies from a BW InfoObject to a BPC dimension. Remember one of the common situations you might bump into is the ability to upload a hierarchy that has a compound InfoObject. In this case, you can tweak the transformation file mapping section to accommodate a concatenation of the compound to the initial ID of the hierarchy members. You can use a very similar piece of code to the one provided for uploading master data to help support this situation as well.

5.3.3 Transactional Data

You're now ready for the upload of the transactional data from a BW InfoProvider; in this case, it's the BW InfoCube ZGLBAL_01to the BPC Consolidation model . To start, you go back to the Data Manager and access a new transformation file to build out your mapping and conversion information. For transactional data, it's more common to see a conversion file used as well as the transformation file. We'll review the formatting of the conversion file in more detail during this example. To start, you can see from Figure 5.60 that some of the mapping components are already filled in the file.

Figure 5.60 Transformation File for Transaction Data

Notice that the same concept is used here where the target dimension is on the left side of the equal sign, and the source is on the right side. We're using the technical names of the dimensions from the BPC Consolidation model and the technical names of the characteristics from the BW InfoCube. There are some tweaks to the one-to-one mapping though, which are based on the types of data that might be coming through the uploading process. For example, the functional area and the intercompany (trading partner) values may not always be filled in on the record that's being uploaded, so to avoid any errors during the upload, we've added a small piece of code to help fill in the ones that are found to be empty.

```
=*IF(0FUNC_AREA = *STR()THEN *STR(NONE);FUNC_AREA
```

This is read as, if the functional area is empty, then insert the string NONE into the field; if not, then just use the functional area that is assigned to the record. This will help avoid empty fields, which will show up as errors during the upload.

This is another strategy decision that needs to be made during the course of your project: whether it's okay to allow the source system to have blanks in the records during the upload and then fix the record during the process of loading into the

BPC model. Both approaches are commonly used. In this example, we've required the source system to have everything filled in, but rather than taking a chance on an error occurring during the upload, we've inserted the code just to be sure.

You will also see some additional tweaks in the mapping process, for example, the use of *NEWCOL. This helps fill in the dimensions that aren't in the BW InfoCube but are necessary for this BPC model. In this case, we've hardcoded the values for the LEDGER = GAAP and REPORT CURRENCY TO = LC. This will depend on the consistency of the granularity between the source InfoCube and the target model.

As you can see, we decided to have a staging cube for the upload of data from the BW InfoCube to the BPC model. If you decide that the BW InfoCube that will be used for the source of data for the BPC model will have more than one key figure, then you should use the *MVAL script. This allows you to take multiple key figures and realign them into the appropriate format for the BPC model, which is one key figure and the actual key figure information transformed into a GL account. A typical format is shown here:

```
ACCOUNT = *MVAL(0BALANCE|*NEWCOL(800000)||0QUANTITY|*NEWCOL(800001)
```

In this case, the key figures 0BALANCE and 0QUANTITY are mapped into the ACCOUNT dimension and assigned the accounts 800000 and 800001, respectively. There are numerous options available for use in this mapping process, and we've incorporated a number of them in the Appendix for your review.

To complete this discussion, we'll look at the conversion file that is being referenced in this transformation file at the bottom of the sheet. As you can see, there are six different sheets in this one conversion file, and the reference process is with an exclamation point ("!") between the technical name of the conversion file and the worksheet that the information is found in. Figure 5.61 shows the initial start of building out a conversion file. Go to CONVERSION FILE • NEW CONVERSION FILE. A blank conversion file has been pulled up in the background for your review. Again, there are three columns: EXTERNAL, INTERNAL, AND FORMULA. In this example, you'll be using the EXTERNAL AND INTERNAL columns.

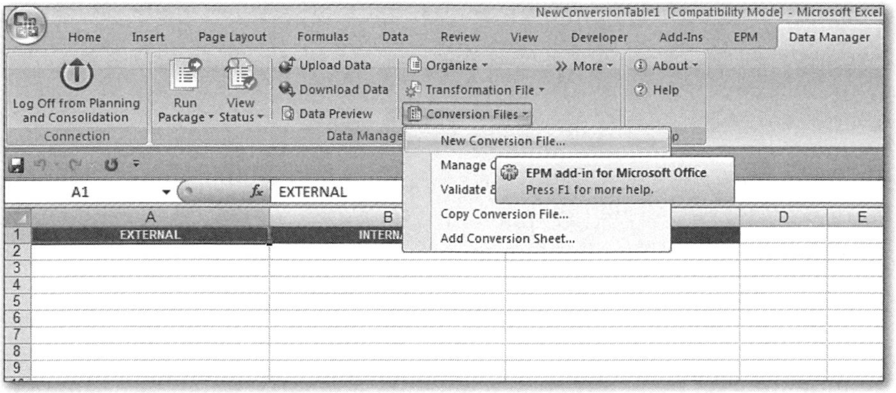

Figure 5.61 Opening a New Conversion File

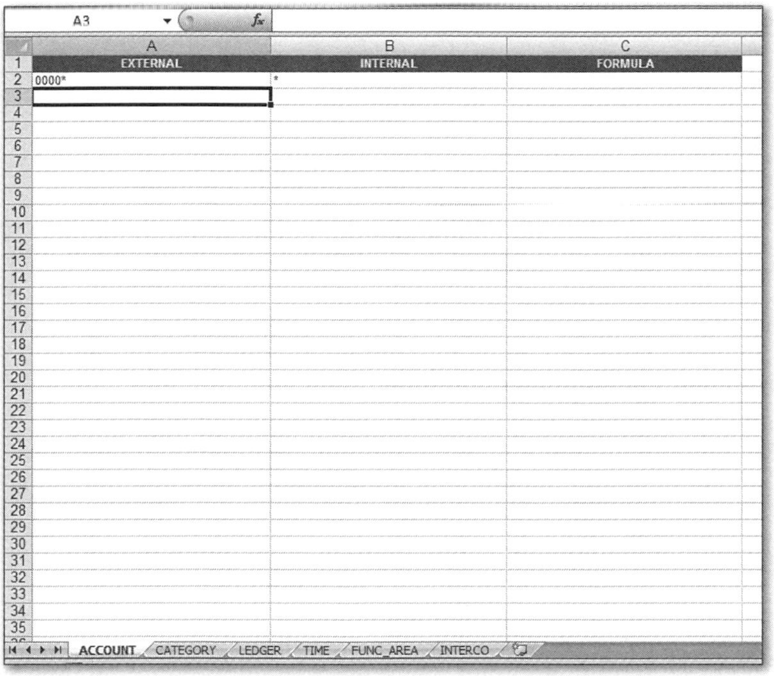

Figure 5.62 Conversion File with ACCOUNT Conversion

A perfect example of the use of a conversion file in uploading transactional data is shown in Figure 5.62. The EXTERNAL column has a parameter 0000*, and the INTERNAL column shows an inserted *. This means that in the incoming file, you'll see GL accounts (ACCOUNT is the worksheet we're using) with four zeroes in front of the actual GL account. In this case, you need to strip these out of the uploaded record and replace them with the INTERNAL member values that are shown without any lead zeroes. This spreadsheet also has six tabs or worksheets, each with a title specific to the dimension it will impact.

Figure 5.63 shows some of the more common conversions that you'll run into: CATEGORY, TIME, and INTERCO. You'll probably run into the TIME conversion most of the time where the external source has a different format than the internal target. In this case, you need to change the TIME format of YYYYMMM to YYYY. MM. The others offer similar tweaks based on the master data members that are in both objects.

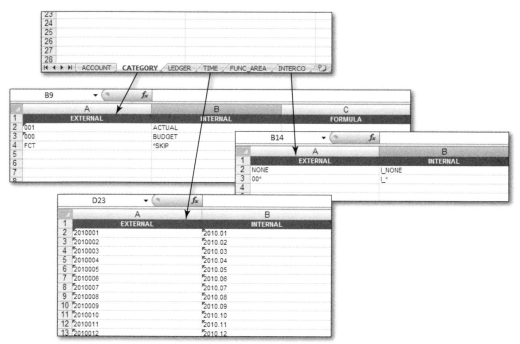

Figure 5.63 Conversion File with CATEGORY, TIME, and INTERCO Shown

After this is complete, you execute a VALIDATE AND PROCESS against the transformation file. Because we've worked through this process with the master data and hierarchy, we can review the differences that you might see during this process. Figure 5.64 shows the following steps during this process for transactional data validation:

1. Choose VALIDATE & PROCESS TRANSFORMATION FILE.

2. Enter the DATA TYPE.

3. Enter the InfoProvider required.

4. Under SET SELECTION, assign any filters based on the data to be uploaded, and also filter the dimensions that you'll be uploading based on the Target model.

5. After this is completed, you choose SAVE or SAVE AS to start the validation process.

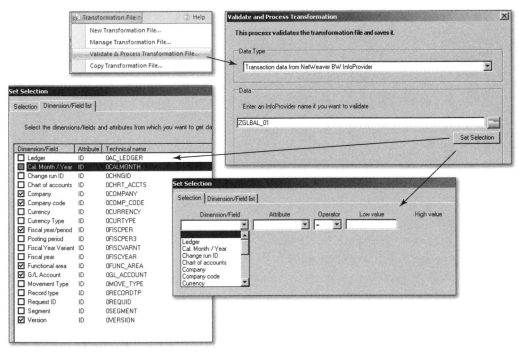

Figure 5.64 Validate and Process Transformation File

The records are validated against the conversion and transformation file, and if everything is correct, you'll receive a successful result as shown in Figure 5.65. To review additional detail you would use the Output file option on this dialog box. This will give you an example of the data that is uploaded and the format that it is received.

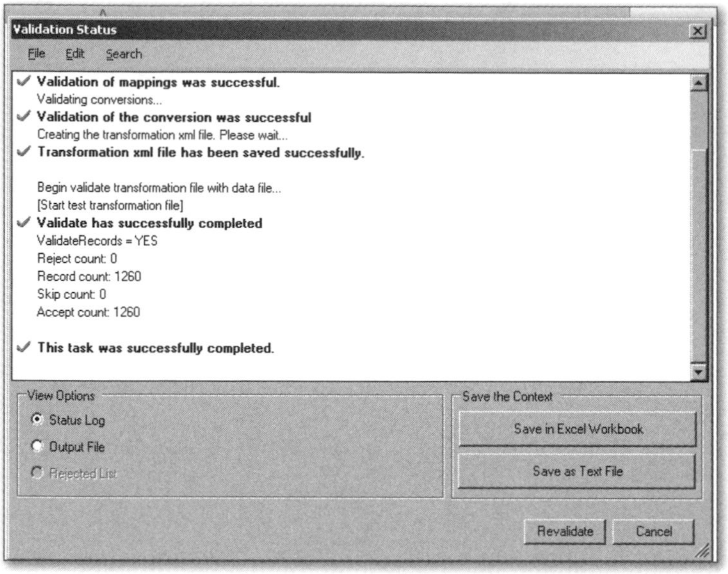

Figure 5.65 Validation Status for Transactional Data Validation

Now you're ready to execute the upload of data using the run package process. As you'll see, the process of actual executing the upload includes very similar types of tasks as used in validate and process. Figure 5.66 shows the initial screen that appears when you select RUN PACKAGE • RUN PACKAGE. Many of the standard packages are listed here because we used the approach to copy over the environment from the EnvironmentShell initially. If you choose not to copy over the environment initially, then you won't see all of these packages and you must create the package and then assign the appropriate process chain to the package for this to be available in the RUN PACKAGE screen.

In this case, select LOAD TRANSACTION DATA FROM BW INFOPROVIDER UI from the list. The difference between the package directly above this one and the one we're using is the user interface, which allows additional flexibility in terms of parameters because there is no SET SELECTION option on the other package. Numerous other packages are also available. For example, is the /CPMB/LOAD_DELTA_IP package is the new delta process chain/package that allows delta uploads of transactional data rather than having to upload full loads all of the time. You might also run into another set of package/process chains with prompts that support uploads from SAP source systems; in this case, these process chains are set up to execute an upload directly from SAP ECC and bypass BW to move the data directly into the BPC models. This is helpful for performance, but the offset is that there's no fallback system with the appropriate data that was uploaded. In any case, these four process chains are currently still under construction and won't show up in the Data Manager package screen until later. As of now (SP06), they aren't available to be used, but you can copy and adjust them to be used for your own purposes but remember you will have to enhance the parameters within the Process Chain.

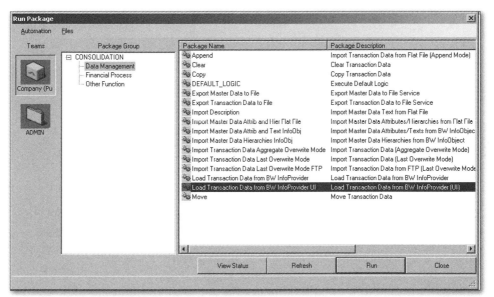

Figure 5.66 Run Package View of the Packages Available

Figure 5.67 shows the next step in this process, which is to assign the InfoProvider. Then, Figure 5.68 shows the SET SELECTION dialog box with the filter options that are available for the dimension and members.

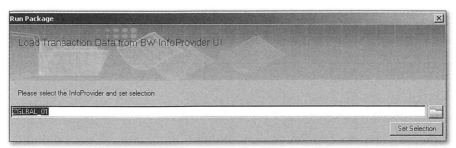

Figure 5.67 Run Package – Assign InfoProvider

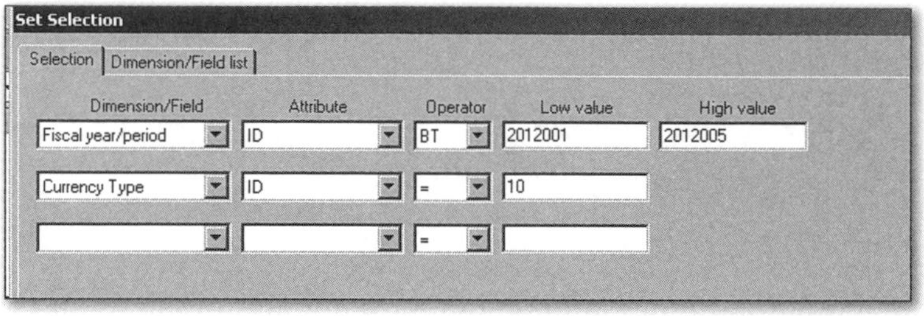

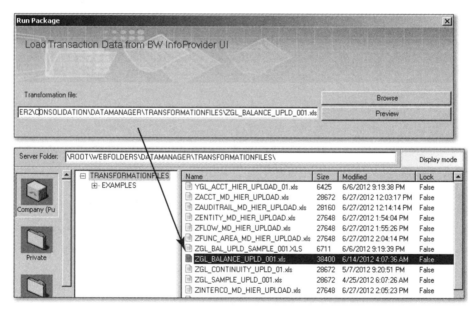

Figure 5.68 Set Selection – Filters for Dimensions and Attributes

After this is complete, click on NEXT to move to the subsequent screen. Now you choose the TRANSFORMATION FILE, which you completed earlier for transactional data uploads (see Figure 5.69).

Figure 5.69 Run Package – Transformation File Assignment

In this case, you select the ZGL_BALANCE_UPLD_001 file and default it into the TRANSFORMATION FILE field. The next series of prompts are a bit different from what we've discussed previously. Figure 5.70 shows the options to AGGREGATE OVER-WRITE or APPEND the transactional data. This will depend on how the data is being sourced into the system. If you've uploaded transactional data as a full upload, then you use the AGGREGATE OVERWRITE option to overwrite all of the data currently in the system that it finds as a match of the uploaded data. If you're bring in only the changed records, then you use the APPEND option to add the current records with the changes that occurred in the period being uploaded.

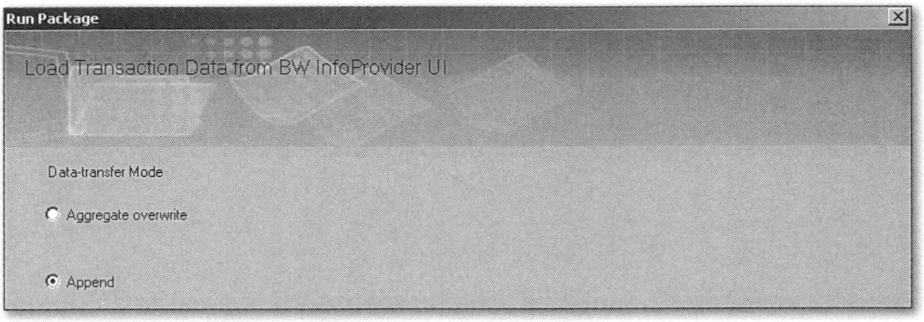

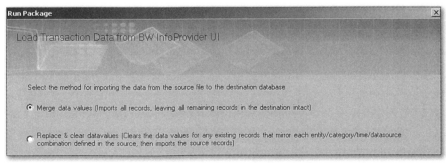

Figure 5.70   Run Package – Aggregate or Append

After this decision is made, Figure 5.71 presents further questions concerning the data loading process. Following are the two options to consider:

▶ MERGE DATA VALUES (Imports all records, leaving all remaining records in the destination intact)

▶ REPLACE & CLEAR DATAVALUES (Clears the data VALUES for any existing records that mirror each entity/category/time/datasource combination defined in the source, then imports the uploaded records).

These two options are critical in how the data will be uploaded and received into the BPC model. A little testing and validation of how the data will react to each of the options is a good proof of concept (POC) process that will pay off in the long run because you'll have confirmed with test information how the data should show up in the BPC model.

Figure 5.71   Run Package – Merge Data Values or Replace & Clear Datavalues

The next series of prompts address features that you might use during the data loading process. Figure 5.72 shows the option to check for any default logic that is run against this data load. For example, you may be executing a calculation for retained earnings on the way into the BPC model. This is something that you can prompt by using the default logic option.

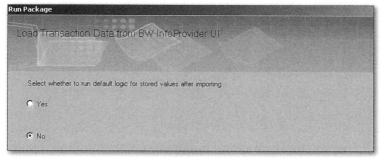

Figure 5.72   Run Package – Default Logic

Next you have the option to affect the data loading process with work status parameters that you may have set up. In this case, the system is confirming that the process of uploading data into this BPC model is still available based on the parameters set for work status (see Figure 5.73).

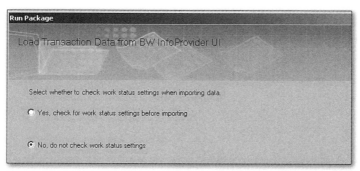

Figure 5.73   Run Package – Work Status

After this screen, you either select RUN or RUN & SCHEDULE to upload this data. If all goes well, you'll see a run package with the status of SUCCEEDED, as shown in Figure 5.74. You can then drill down on this result to see the details by choosing the DETAILS button at the bottom of the screen.

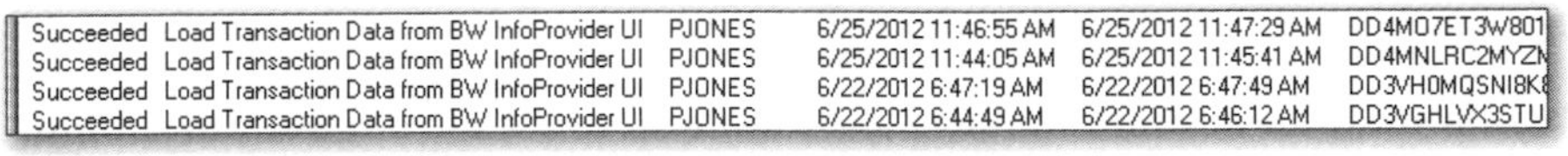

Succeeded	Load Transaction Data from BW InfoProvider UI	PJONES	6/25/2012 11:46:55 AM	6/25/2012 11:47:29 AM	DD4MO7ET3W801
Succeeded	Load Transaction Data from BW InfoProvider UI	PJONES	6/25/2012 11:44:05 AM	6/25/2012 11:45:41 AM	DD4MNLRC2MYZN
Succeeded	Load Transaction Data from BW InfoProvider UI	PJONES	6/22/2012 6:47:19 AM	6/22/2012 6:47:49 AM	DD3VH0MQSNI8K8
Succeeded	Load Transaction Data from BW InfoProvider UI	PJONES	6/22/2012 6:44:49 AM	6/22/2012 6:46:12 AM	DD3VGHLVX3STU

Figure 5.74 Succeeded Load of Transactional Data

Figure 5.75 shows you the details of the data load process. This shows that there were 32,597 records uploaded with no errors or warnings. You can then review the records either via a report from the EPM add-in, or if you have access, you can quickly go into the BW InfoProvider and display the information directly from the InfoCube.

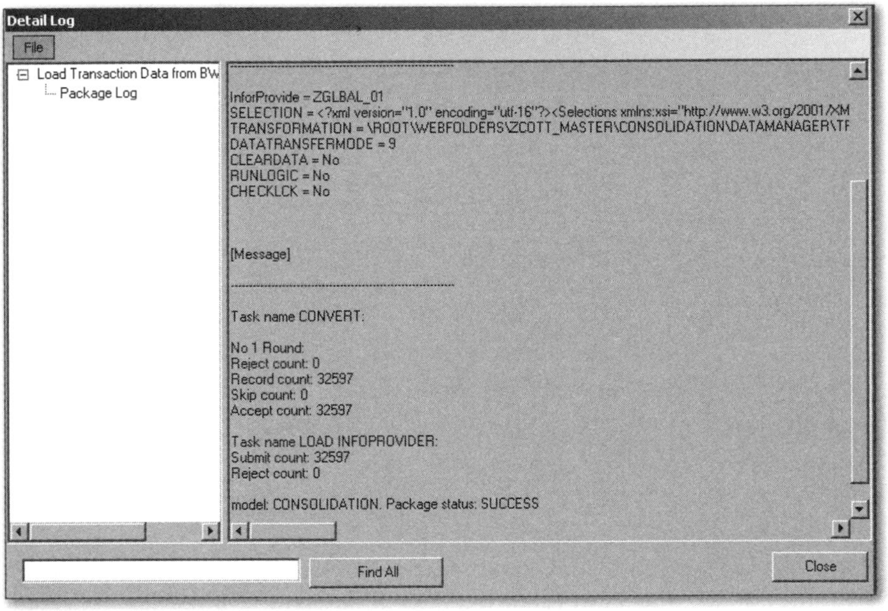

Figure 5.75 Detail Log – Results of Upload of Data

Now that we've worked our way through the process of uploading all of the different types of data into BPC via a BW object, let's look at the use of a flat file as the source of data for BPC.

5.4 Data Loading Processes from a Flat File to BPC

The use of a flat file to upload data into any of the many different systems has been around for quite some time and is a tried and true approach to moving data around.

There are some questions about using flat files because this approach generates additional touch points for the data. Also, the ability to validate is more difficult because being able to create a report that reads a flat file and also reads the target system with the ability to combine these reports is a bit more complex than you might think. In any case, this is the primary approach to uploading information into the BPC V10.0 for Microsoft. It's also a good fallback for the BPC version for SAP NetWeaver as well because you sometimes don't really want everything to come through BW and may decide to bypass BW and go directly into the BPC objects. Two aspects of using a flat file need to be discussed and agreed upon by the business users and IT. First, you need to structure a strong process to store, manage, and process the flat files. If you're working with multiple flat files coming in on a daily or weekly basis, then you'll get to a point where the sheer volume of flat files will overwhelm you, so having a strong FTP or SharePoint strategy is critical. The second issue is to agree on a template that will support the data loading requirements. If possible, this should be a template that will support multiple different data loading activities so that you can reduce the number of individual links and DataSources required for uploading the data. If you have 10 different templates, then you'll probably have 10 different uploading streams. If you can reduce this to only 5, you'll be able to manage the process much more effectively.

In the next section, we'll look at the general process used for uploading, but in terms of specific step-by-step processes, we'll only look at those features that are different from what you saw in the preceding section on the upload via the BW InfoProviders.

5.4.1 Master Data, Hierarchy

In this process, we'll use the Customer dimension as an example of the data loading process. In terms of the overall process, the biggest difference is in the initial setup and positioning of the data to be uploaded. In the BW InfoCube scenario, you created a link directly to the BW InfoCube and uploaded the information. In the flat file process, you need to first upload the flat file to the server of BPC, and then upload it from there to the database. In this example, you'll upload it to the BPC model in SAP NetWeaver and therefore into an InfoCube; however, for the Microsoft version, you execute the same process but upload into the Microsoft database for analysis and calculation. Figure 5.76 shows the CUSTOMER dimension in BPC. This is a basic dimension with only two properties, and one, SCALING, is standard. You'll supply the information for this dimension and enter the ID as well as the two properties.

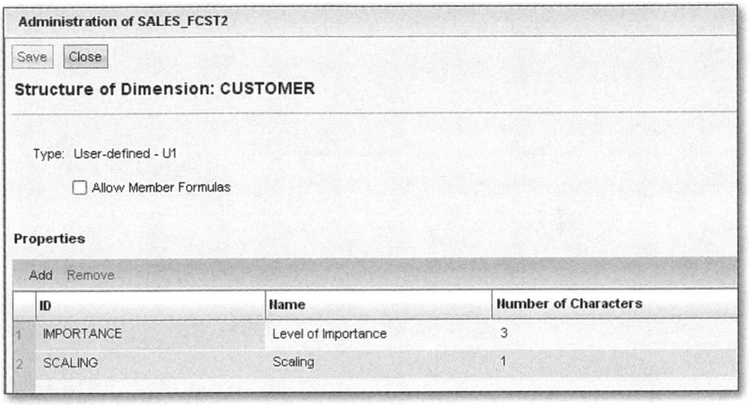

Figure 5.76 CUSTOMER Dimension with Properties

To start, you upload the flat file template with the master data into the BPC server as shown in Figure 5.77. This dialog box is displayed after you click on the UPLOAD DATA link in the DATA MANAGER GROUP portion of the ribbon.

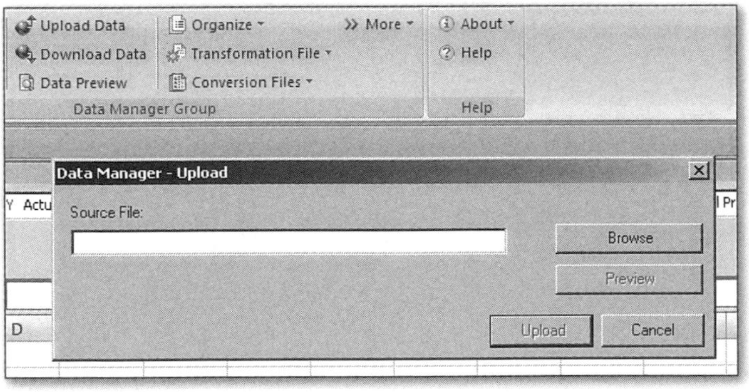

Figure 5.77 Data Manager – Upload

After you fill the field with the file path to the CSV file with the customer data, you click on the UPLOAD button. If all goes well, the successful load screen will appear as shown in Figure 5.78.

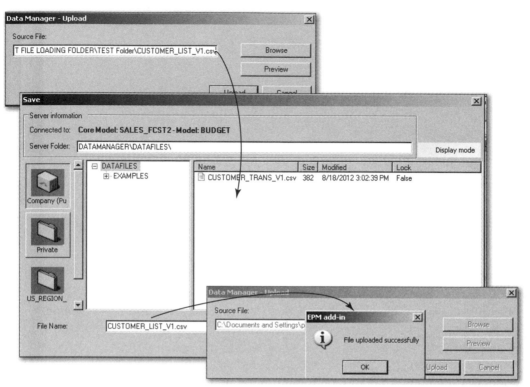

Figure 5.78 Data Manager Upload: Assign File Name and Upload Success

You can review the data just uploaded by using the DATA PREVIEW option on the ribbon and the results of the DATA PREVIEW can be seen in Figure 5.79. The uploaded file has master data, attributes, and text so that you can use the same file for both uploads and save the trouble of having multiple files for similar processes.

Now that the data are uploaded into the server, you can review the transformation file. The process of setting the transformation file up for a flat file upload is the same as for the BW InfoCube upload. Figure 5.80 shows that the transformation file has been created; it's basic, but it will do the trick. There are only two mapping lines in this case: one for the ID and the other for the IMPORTANCE property.

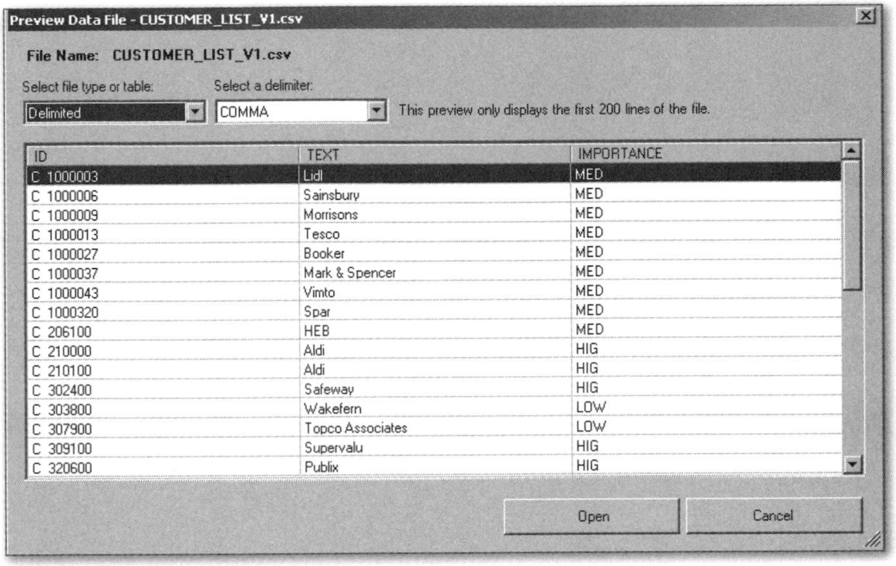

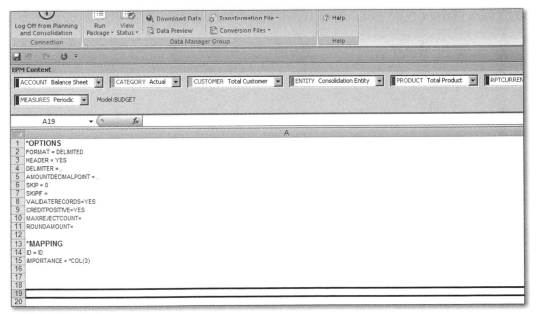

Figure 5.79 Preview of Data File for CUSTOMER

Figure 5.80 Transformation File for Customer Master Data

The validate and process execution is exactly the same as before, so select VALIDATE AND PROCESS on this transformation file to see that you have a successful test. Now you can start the actual run package to upload into the customer dimension. Figure 5.81 shows the initial screen after you start the run package process, where you choose the package—IMPORT_MD_HIER—to import from a flat file.

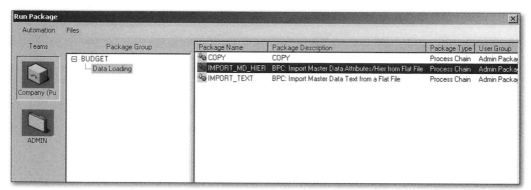

Figure 5.81 Run Package – Package Name

Notice this screen doesn't show all of the other standard packages that you've seen in the past. This is because during the creation of this model, we didn't copy from another but created it from scratch. So, everything needed for these uploads must be created. Although this isn't the best approach, sometimes it's required. At the very least, you can use the standard packages, but you have to configure them to be seen in the Data Manager. In the next series of screens, you perform the following tasks:

▶ Assign the file to be imported to the process.

▶ Assign the transformation file to the process.

▶ Choose the dimension that the members will be uploaded into—CUSTOMER.

▶ Either overwrite or update hierarchies, if any, and decide whether to upload them. In this example, however, you won't upload a hierarchy to the Customer dimension.

▶ Run the package.

Figure 5.82 shows the results of this process on the Customer dimension. A total of 36 members were uploaded.

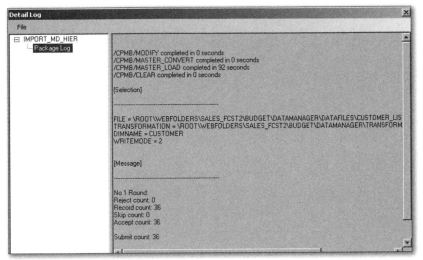

Figure 5.82 Detail Log for Member Upload into the Customer Dimension

Figure 5.83 shows a display of the members that were uploaded via the BW CUS-
TOMER object: Master Data Table.

CUSTOMER	L	Long Description
CUST_GRP	E	Customer Group Top
CUST_TOP	E	Total Customer
C_1000003	E	C_1000003
C_1000006	E	C_1000006
C_1000009	E	C_1000009
C_1000013	E	C_1000013
C_1000027	E	C_1000027
C_1000037	E	C_1000037
C_1000043	E	C_1000043
C_100009	E	Customer Grp 1
C_1000320	E	C_1000320
C_200009	E	Customer Grp 2
C_206100	E	C_206100
C_210000	E	C_210000
C_210100	E	C_210100
C_300009	E	Customer Grp 3
C_302400	E	C_302400
C_303800	E	C_303800
C_307900	E	C_307900
C_309100	E	C_309100
C_320600	E	C_320600
C_330200	E	C_330200
C_332000	E	C_332000
C_332100	E	C_332100
C_340000	E	C_340000
C_341000	E	C_341000
C_355100	E	C_355100
C_374800	E	C_374800
C_400000	E	C_400000
C_400009	E	Customer Grp 4

Figure 5.83 Customer Master Data Viewed from the BW Tables

In this case, you can see that the text isn't quite useful for the business user, so you need to fix this situation. To do so, you need to upload the text using the same file used for the members.

5.4.2 Text

By this time, the process of setting up these data uploads should be fairly routine, so we've jumped to the point of having created the transformation file and tested the process. Figure 5.84 shows the results.

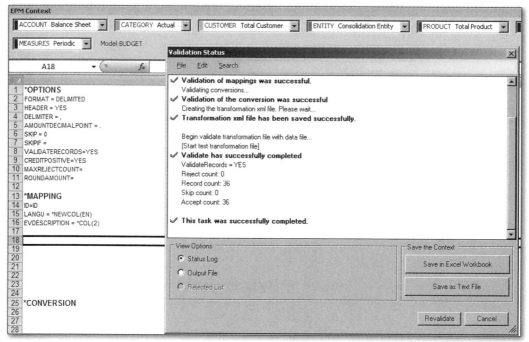

Figure 5.84 Validate Text Upload via a Flat File

A total of 36 records were tested and validated, the same as the master data, so that's a good sign that this upload will also be successful. The process of running a package for a text file upload is the same as the master data upload, except that you must make sure to assign the correct transformation file. Notice that this text transformation file has three mapping lines—one for the ID, another for the language, and the final for the descriptions. These three mapping lines are the same for all flat file text uploads. Normally there are no variations to this process. After executing the text file upload, you see that it was a success and that a total of 36 records were in fact uploaded (see Figure 5.85).

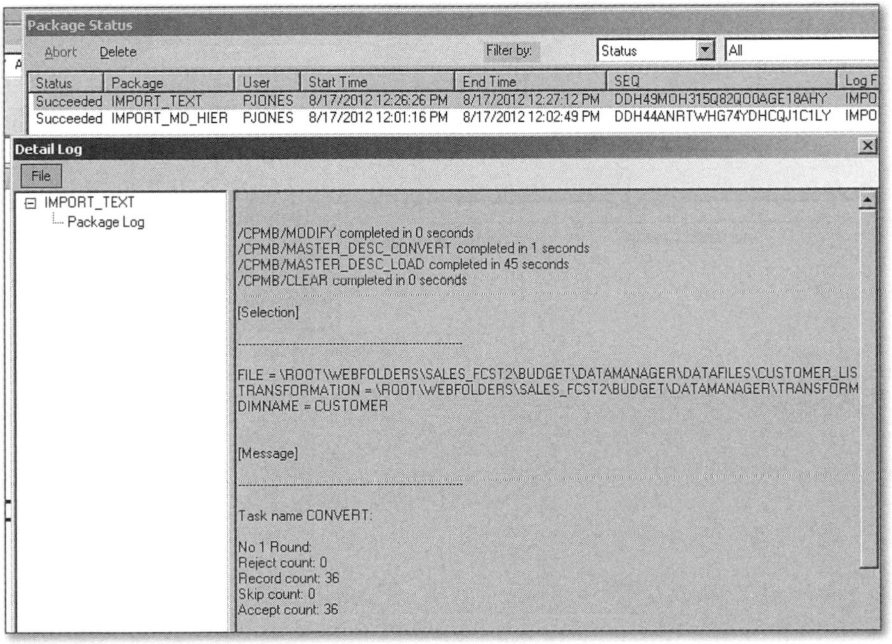

Figure 5.85 Package Status and Detail Log for Text upload from a flat file

To make sure that this has worked correctly, you can review the master data in the BW system. Looking at the master data and text from the BW side, you can see that the text has replaced the member values in the TEXT field, and the Customer dimension is now ready to be used for reporting or planning (see Figure 5.86).

With the entire dimension master data uploaded, you can now upload the transactional data without worrying about any errors due to missing master data.

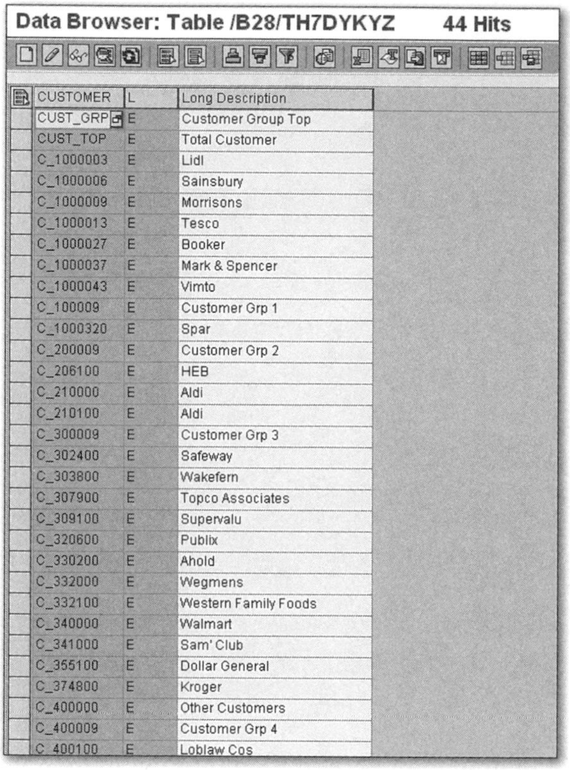

Data Browser: Table /B28/TH7DYKYZ 44 Hits

CUSTOMER	L	Long Description
CUST_GRP	E	Customer Group Top
CUST_TOP	E	Total Customer
C_1000003	E	Lidl
C_1000006	E	Sainsbury
C_1000009	E	Morrisons
C_1000013	E	Tesco
C_1000027	E	Booker
C_1000037	E	Mark & Spencer
C_1000043	E	Vimto
C_100009	E	Customer Grp 1
C_1000320	E	Spar
C_200009	E	Customer Grp 2
C_206100	E	HEB
C_210000	E	Aldi
C_210100	E	Aldi
C_300009	E	Customer Grp 3
C_302400	E	Safeway
C_303800	E	Wakefern
C_307900	E	Topco Associates
C_309100	E	Supervalu
C_320600	E	Publix
C_330200	E	Ahold
C_332000	E	Wegmens
C_332100	E	Western Family Foods
C_340000	E	Walmart
C_341000	E	Sam' Club
C_355100	E	Dollar General
C_374800	E	Kroger
C_400000	E	Other Customers
C_400009	E	Customer Grp 4
C_400100	E	Loblaw Cos

Figure 5.86 Customer Master Data after Text Upload from a Flat File

5.4.3 Transactional Data

The final common uploading process that we'll review is the use of the flat file to upload the transactional data required. We've worked through the general uploading process many times, and the step-by-step process to use a flat file for transactional data is very much the same as the others.

To start, you need the same upload of the transactional data flat file to the server. You then create the transformation file as well as the conversion files (if needed) to execute a VALIDATE AND PROCESS activity. Figure 5.87 shows the uploaded flat file of transactional data. Of course, the difference between the other files and this one is the last column that includes amounts/values.

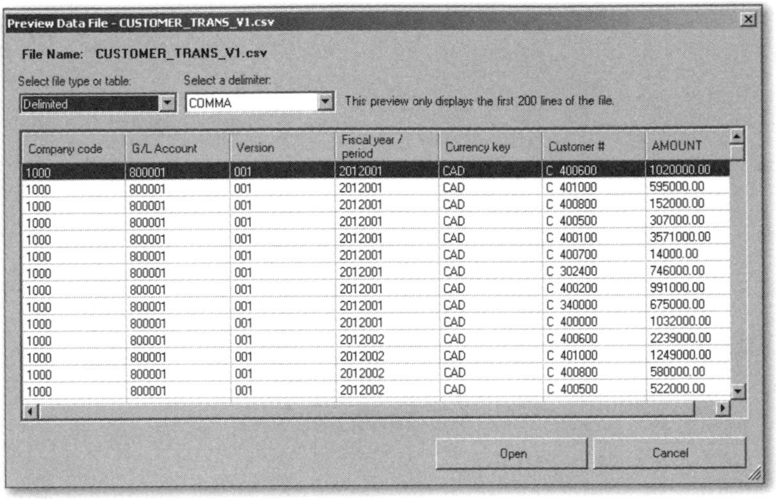

Figure 5.87 Preview of Transactional Data

In this case, you're uploading several different types of data including sales volumes, sales quantities, and cases sold. Therefore, the report currency takes on a bit of a different flavor and rather than seeing only Local Currency (LC) as a report currency we'll see Cases (CS) and Each (EA) for the quantities coming through.

Before starting the uploading process, let's look at the BPC model to which we will upload. Figure 5.88 shows that there is already some data in the BUDGET BPC model. This can be seen by the fact that we have a Request ID 58413 that shows up in the Manage/Requests tab of the BUDGET model. You'll be uploading information for the 2012 budget process.

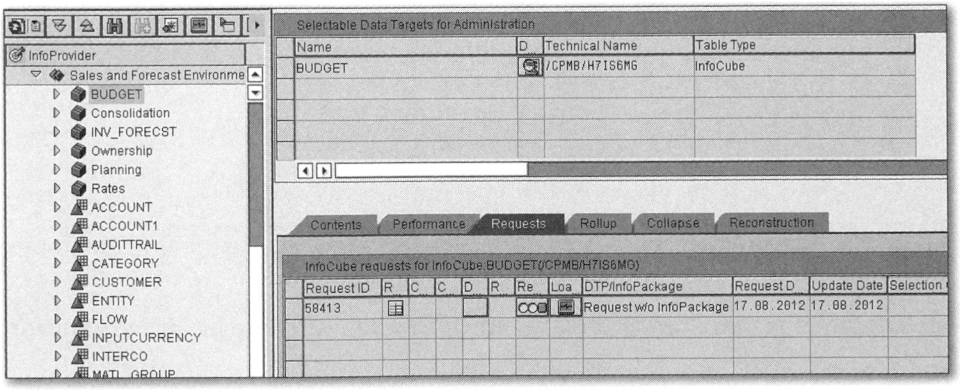

Figure 5.88 BUDGET BPC Model – View from BW

335

A transformation file is also needed, as always, for this process to occur (see Figure 5.89). The difference in this transformation file is the *MAPPING section. The mapping is using a column location process here. For example, in the case of ENTITY, the value that will fill this field can be found in column 1, ACCOUNT is found in column 2, and so forth down the line. One of the dimensions isn't found in this file, and for PRODUCT, the field is filled with NONE by using another prompt, so rather than *COL(X), you use *NEWCOL(X). This way, the system knows that it's a new column and fills it with NONE rather than looking for something in the flat file that's being uploaded. Also notice that the next dimension picks up the *COL(X) positioning and doesn't skip a column value. Finally, the two conversion files being used are the common ones—CATEGORY and TIME. The CATEGORY/VERSION has been changed from 001 (BW) to ACTUAL (BPC), and the TIME required for the normal shift has been changed from a three-digit period to a two-digit period.

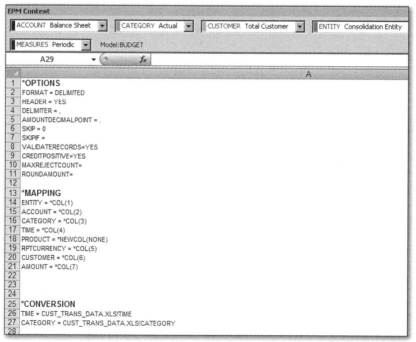

Figure 5.89 Transformation File for Transactional Data from a Flat File

Execute the VALIDATE AND PROCESS, and you see that the format for the Transformation and conversion files are correct (see Figure 5.90).

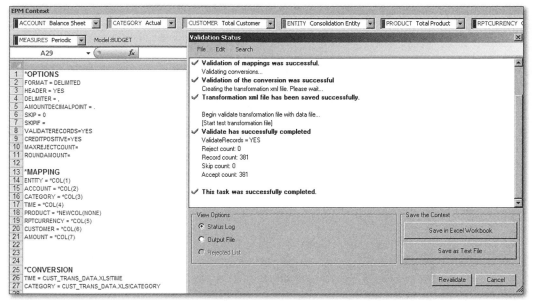

Figure 5.90 Validate and Process Flat File Transactional Data

After you have this verification, you can start the actual run package upload. In this case, you don't have the appropriate package in the Data Manager to upload transactional data from a flat file, so you need to add this package to the list. To do this, select the ORGANIZE • ORGANIZE PACKAGE LIST from the ribbon, as shown in Figure 5.91.

Figure 5.91 Selecting Organize Package List from the Ribbon

On the ORGANIZE PACKAGE LIST screen, you can add a package. Initially we could set up a separate Package Group on the left side of the screen and this would help support additional segregation of the packages. In this case, we will just add an additional package to the existing Package Group by using the Add Package from the context menu in the field Package Name. Figure 5.92 shows this screen.

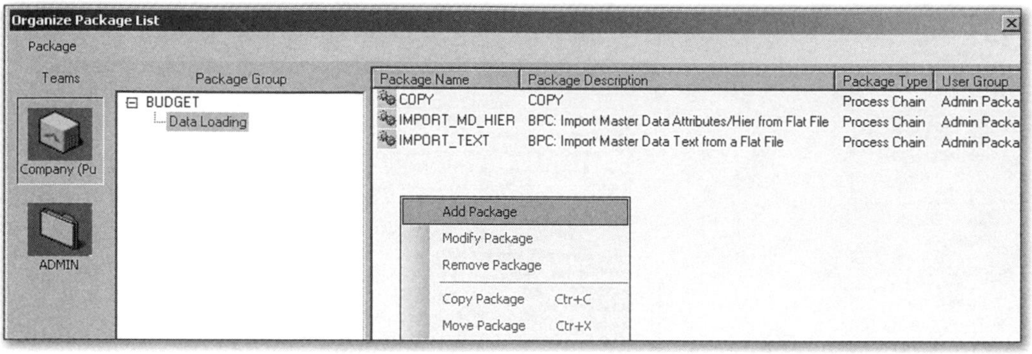

Figure 5.92 Organize Package List: Add Package

In the ORGANIZE PACKAGE LIST dialog box, click on ADD PACKAGE option so you can assign a package in the ADD PACKAGE dialog box that appears (see Figure 5.93).

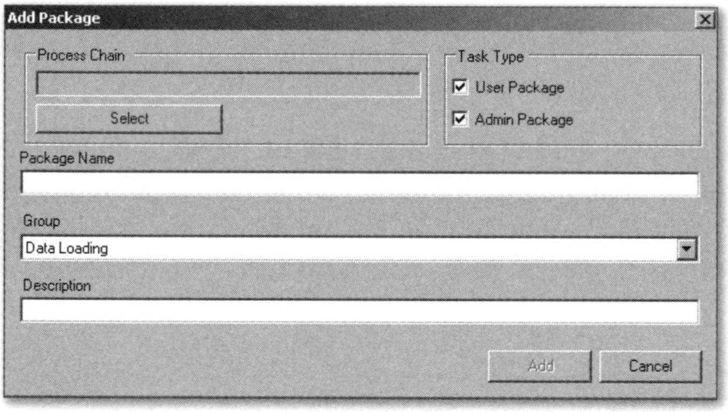

Figure 5.93 Add Package Options

In the TASK TYPE assigns the security options of the USER PACKAGE or ADMIN PACKAGE. The PACKAGE NAME and DESCRIPTION can be manually filled in with whatever makes sense based on the process chain we're adding to this package. Click on the SELECT button to see the process chains available (Figure 5.94). In this case, use the PROCESS CHAIN that will allow you to upload the transactional data via a flat file.

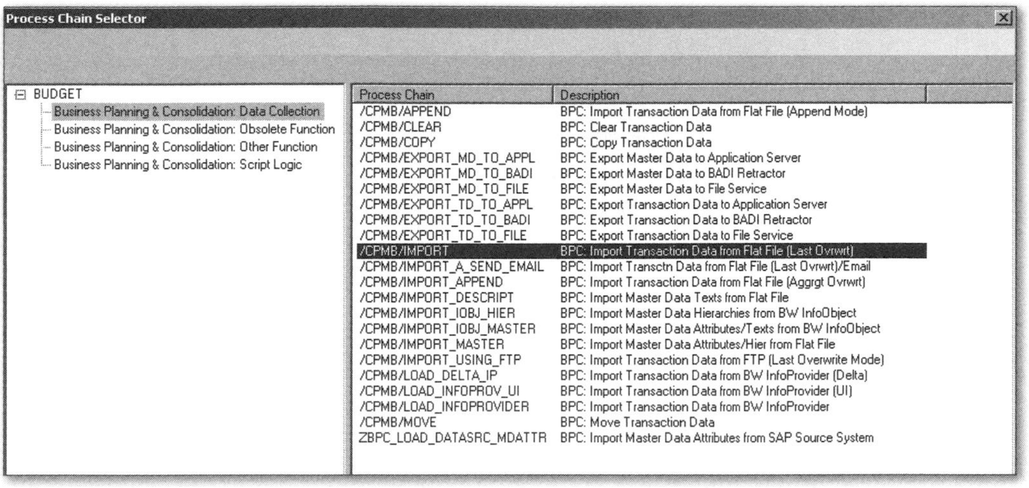

Figure 5.94 Process Chain Selector List

After we identify the process chain, click the OK button at the bottom of the screen to go back to the ADD PACKAGE screen with the PROCESS CHAIN filled in. Assign a PACKAGE NAME and a DESCRIPTION, and then click on ADD to assign this to the ORGANIZE PACKAGE LIST dialog box.

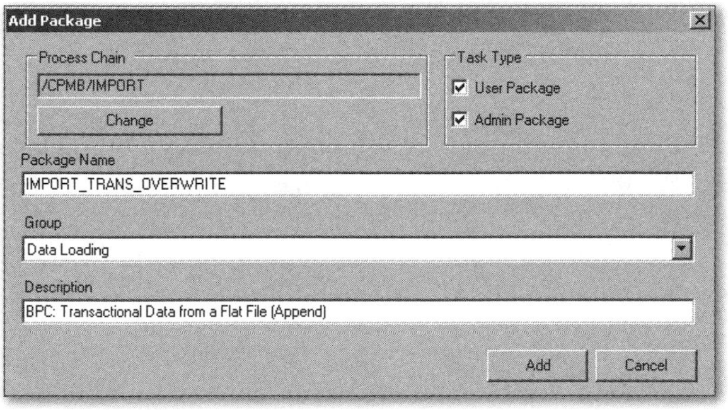

Figure 5.95 Add Package with the Process Chain

Figure 5.96 shows this package added to the list of available packages to execute.

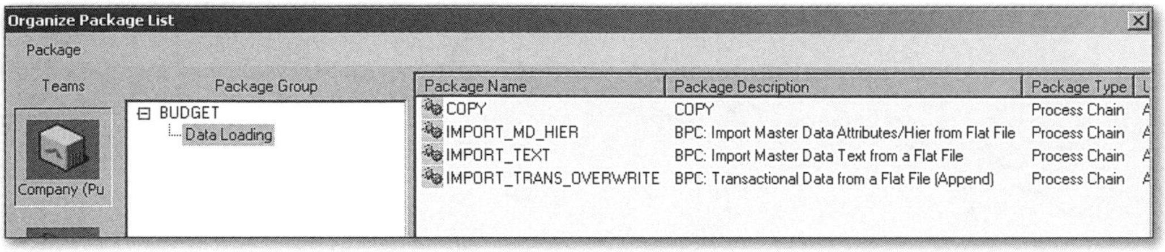

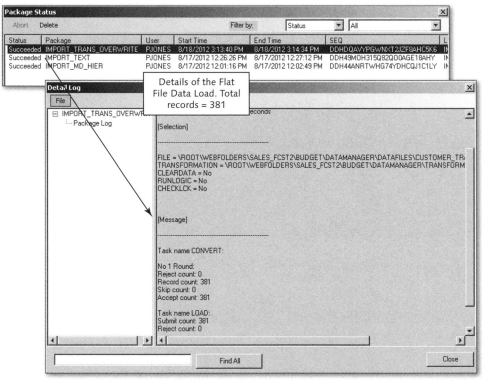

Figure 5.96 Organize Package List

Assuming that the entire configuration is correctly set up, you can execute this package and view the results. Figure 5.97 shows the final results of the data process and the PACKAGE STATUS: SUCCESS at the bottom of the screen. A total of 381 records were uploaded into the BPC model for BUDGET.

Figure 5.97 Package Status – Details

You can now look at the BPC model from the BW side to see if all of the records were uploaded correctly. Figure 5.98 shows the REQUESTS tab of the BUDGET model from the BW side, which shows that another Request ID is now displayed. Earlier, in Figure 5.88, there was only one request ID initially.

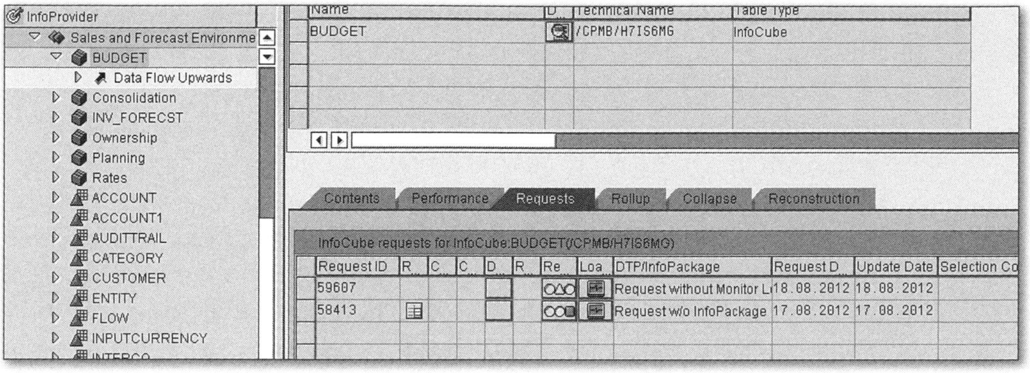

Figure 5.98 BW Requests Tab on the BPC Model BUDGET

If you readjust the request ID and close it, you'll see that exactly 381 records were uploaded into the BUDGET model. This confirms that all of the records from the flat file have been transferred to the BPC model as shown in Figure 5.99.

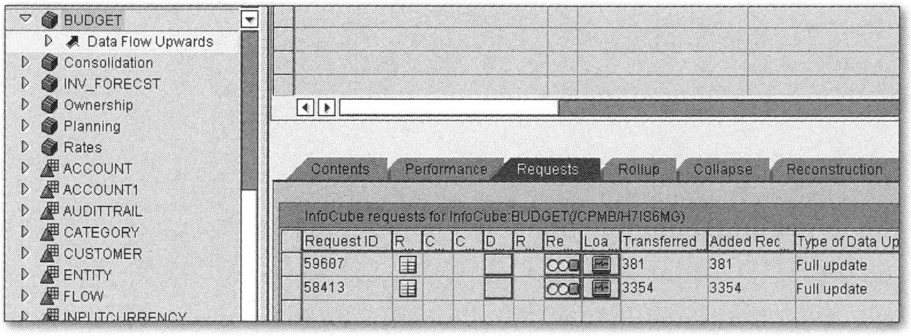

Figure 5.99 BW Requests Tab on the BPC Model BUDGET – 381 Records Loaded

You've now uploaded master data, text, and transactional data using flat files into the BPC models. The process is reasonably consistent across the different components, and after you have some hands-on experience with the creation of the transformation and conversion file mapping logic, the setup will become routine for you.

5.5   Using the Data Manager Functionality in BPC

The Data Manager is critical to the uploading process whether it's using the BW process or the flat file process. You've seen the Data Manager in action, but at this point, we need to get a better understanding of its functionality and features. So far, we've used just about all of the standard content uploading Data Manager packages, and this is normally what you'll see and experience. However, there are times when you might need to tweak the code a bit in a specific Data Manager package or add an additional process chain to the list available. For instance, you might set up a process chain to allow the BPC user to execute a package that will start the uploading process directly from SAP ECC through BW and then into BPC. This is a bit unusual because the BW team may have something to say about the execution of a data load directly from the SAP ECC source system, but it is possible. The only thing you have to be aware of to make sure the process chain can use the Data Manager process is that the process chain is assigned to one of the display components that are BPC specific (/CPMB/), as shown in Figure 5.100. If the process chain is located in one of these four components, then you should be able to select it from the Data Manager for use.

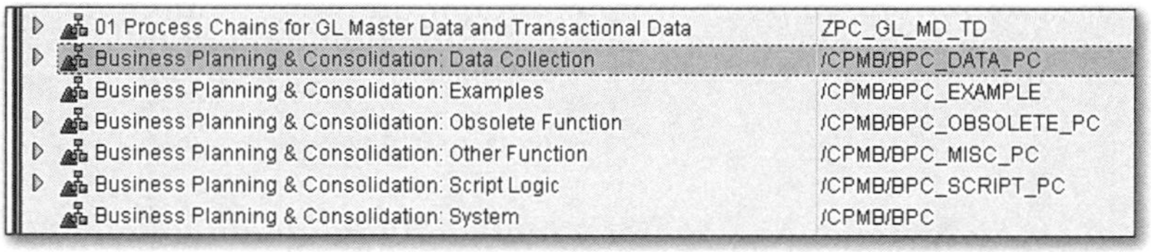

▷ 🏭 01 Process Chains for GL Master Data and Transactional Data	ZPC_GL_MD_TD
▷ 🏭 Business Planning & Consolidation: Data Collection	/CPMB/BPC_DATA_PC
🏭 Business Planning & Consolidation: Examples	/CPMB/BPC_EXAMPLE
▷ 🏭 Business Planning & Consolidation: Obsolete Function	/CPMB/BPC_OBSOLETE_PC
▷ 🏭 Business Planning & Consolidation: Other Function	/CPMB/BPC_MISC_PC
▷ 🏭 Business Planning & Consolidation: Script Logic	/CPMB/BPC_SCRIPT_PC
🏭 Business Planning & Consolidation: System	/CPMB/BPC

Figure 5.100   Display Components for the BPC Process Chains

The Data Manager process is a combination of execution of process chains from the BW side of the fence and in some cases in conjunction with Script Logic from the BPC side of the fence. You'll see this in the consolidation process in Chapter 7 where the Script Logic options are used and are more consolidation specific. During this data loading process, you didn't really run into any Script Logic as a prompt for the Data Manager package to be executed (see Figure 5.101).

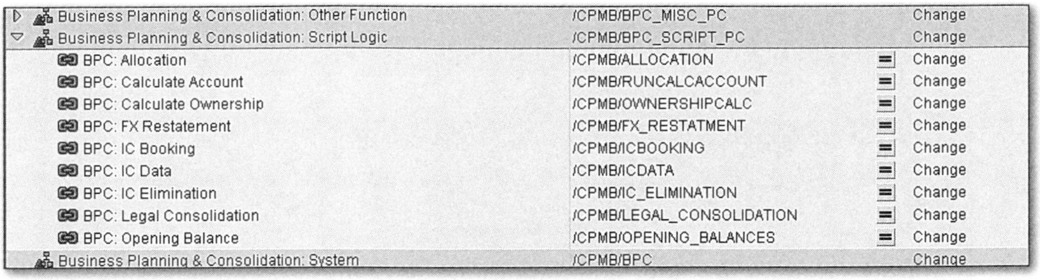

▷ ⚙ Business Planning & Consolidation: Other Function	/CPMB/BPC_MISC_PC	Change
▽ ⚙ Business Planning & Consolidation: Script Logic	/CPMB/BPC_SCRIPT_PC	Change
⚙ BPC: Allocation	/CPMB/ALLOCATION	≡ Change
⚙ BPC: Calculate Account	/CPMB/RUNCALCACCOUNT	≡ Change
⚙ BPC: Calculate Ownership	/CPMB/OWNERSHIPCALC	≡ Change
⚙ BPC: FX Restatement	/CPMB/FX_RESTATMENT	≡ Change
⚙ BPC: IC Booking	/CPMB/ICBOOKING	≡ Change
⚙ BPC: IC Data	/CPMB/ICDATA	≡ Change
⚙ BPC: IC Elimination	/CPMB/IC_ELIMINATION	≡ Change
⚙ BPC: Legal Consolidation	/CPMB/LEGAL_CONSOLIDATION	≡ Change
⚙ BPC: Opening Balance	/CPMB/OPENING_BALANCES	≡ Change
⚙ Business Planning & Consolidation: System	/CPMB/BPC	Change

Figure 5.101 Process Chains That Use Script Logic to be Executed with Parameters

5.5.1 Data Manager Configuration

To look at some of the details behind the Data Manager components, start by choosing EPM ADD-IN > DATA MANAGER > ORGANIZE > ORGANIZE PACKAGE LIST (see Figure 5.102). One item not yet discussed is the PACKAGE LINK LIST. This useful toolset allows you to assign multiple packages to one executable process. So, in this case, if you have 10 packages that need to be executed in a sequence, you can use the PACKAGE LINK LIST to string them together, and then the execution will occur automatically.

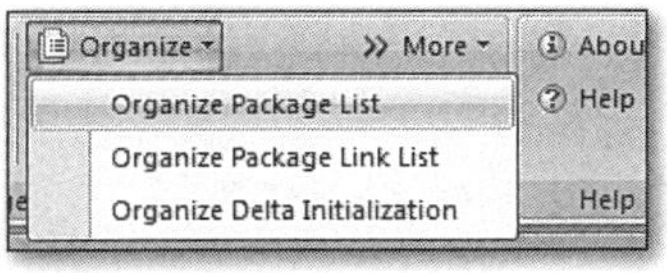

Figure 5.102 Selecting Organize Package List from the Ribbon

You've already seen how to add a package, but let's now look at the MODIFY PACKAGE function (see Figure 5.103) where you'll select the MODIFY PACKAGE option and look at the Script Logic behind the scenes.

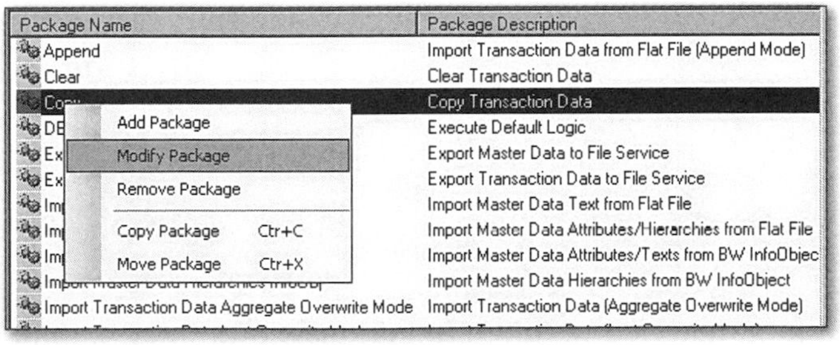

Figure 5.103 Package Name – Modify Package

After you choose MODIFY PACKAGE, the MODIFY PACKAGE dialog box opens that enables you to access and modify the Script Logic (see Figure 5.104).

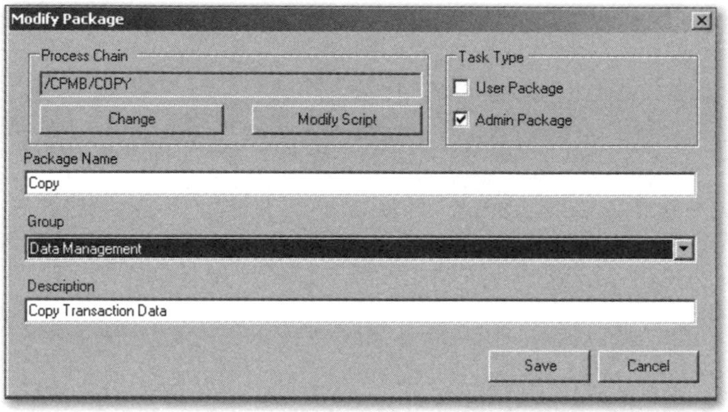

Figure 5.104 Modify Package

Clicking on the MODIFY SCRIPT button shows you the programs and logic that are executed during the COPY process. The initial screen is shown in Figure 5.105. The TASKS listed that are executed based on the parameters chosen in the Data Manager package include the CLEAR, CONVERT, and/or APPEND data tasks. Below this, you can see that the DYNAMIC PACKAGE SCRIPT is showing as modifiable script.

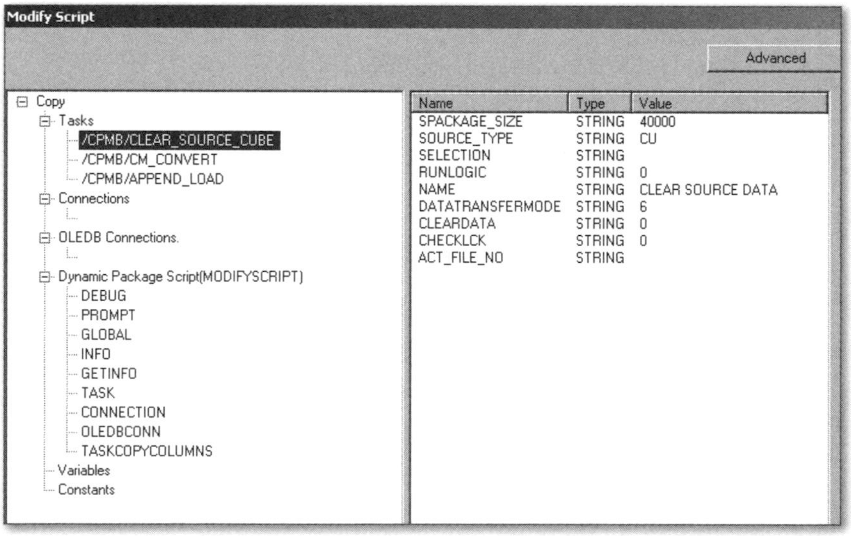

Figure 5.105 Modify Script Options

If you choose the PROMPT option in the DYNAMIC PACKAGE SCRIPT section, it shows the type of option you'll see; in this case, it's a radio button feature (you can also change that if desired with the dropdown options), the variable name that will be executed, and the description that will show up during the process (see Figure 5.106). Remember these property descriptions, and we'll point them out as we go through the copy process.

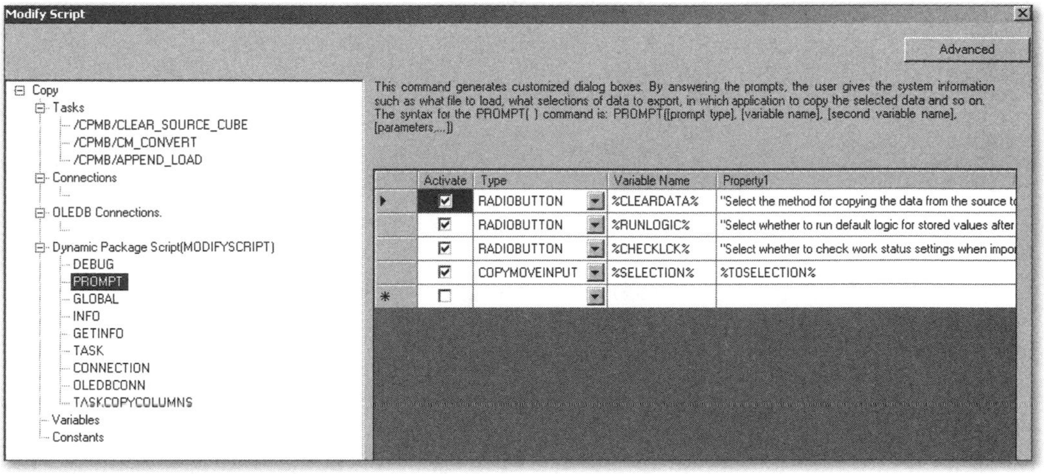

Figure 5.106 Modify Script – Prompts

Figure 5.107 shows the different tasks that are executed during the copy process. Each is used in different phases of the copy activity, but you can see that the TASK NAME is the initial program executed, and the VALUES are assigned that you fill in during the copy process.

Figure 5.108 shows the CONSTANTS that are used during this process. They are directly assigned and specific to a model, which in this case, is the Consolidation model. As you can see, the list of dimensions are belowthe constant values. They start right below the %APPBINAME% name. These dimensions will be available during the copy process to assign values.

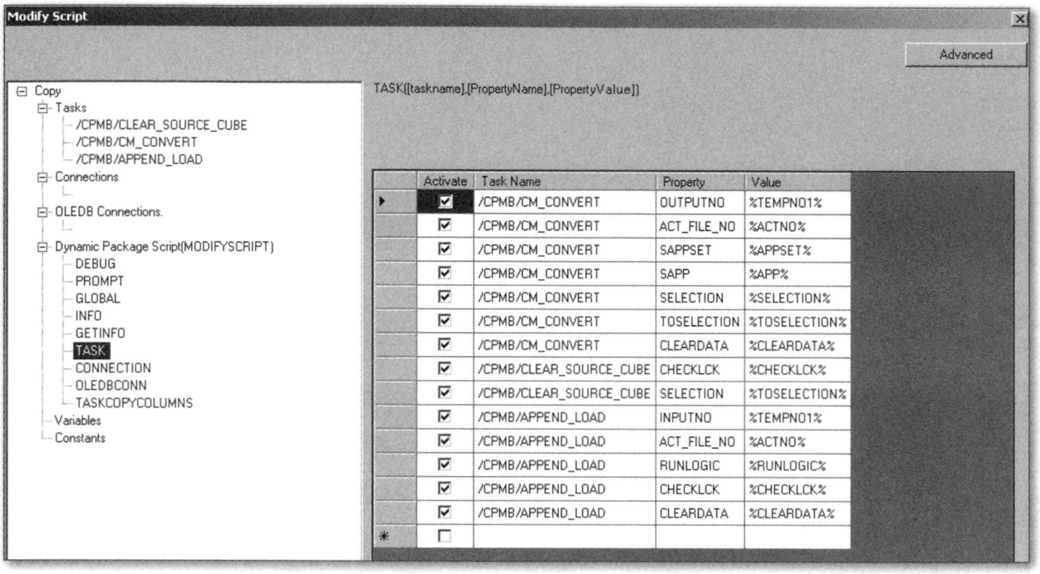

Figure 5.107 Modify Script – TASK

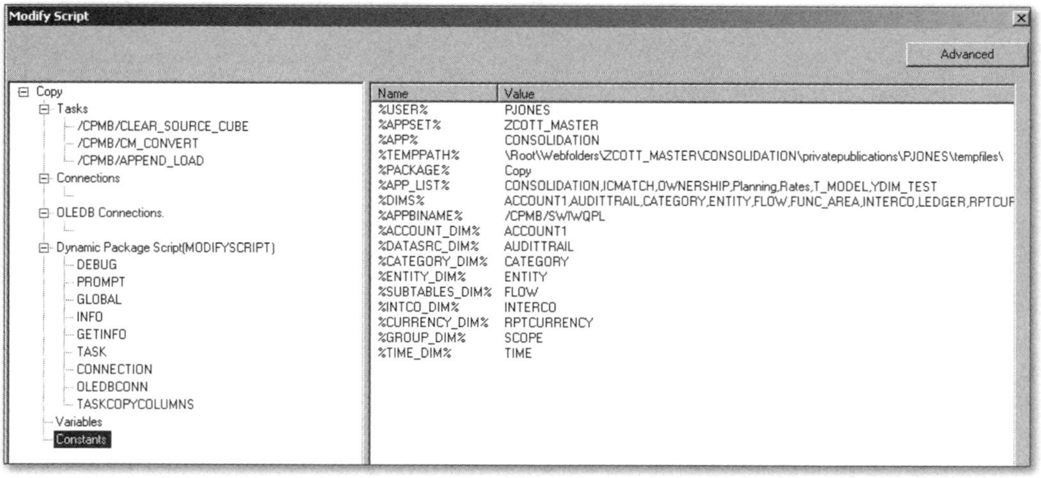

Figure 5.108 Modify Script – Constants

To see some of this script in action, let's go back to the execute dialog box that shows up when we start the process of executing the DM package and work through some of the steps in executing the copy process chain. After you choose COPY and then click on NEXT, you'll see the RUN PACKAGE screen shown in Figure 5.109.

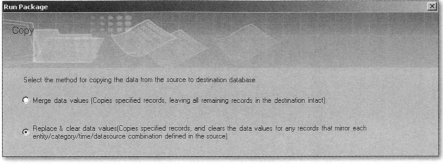

Figure 5.109 Run Package – Copy Selection Screen

Remember the initial Script Logic from Figure 5.106? This is the outcome of that Script Logic. This is also visible in Figure 5.110, which is the next screen in the copy process. This requires the assignment of whether you want the default logic to be executed during the copy process (also shown earlier in Figure 5.106). Also notice that all of the parameters are using the radio button feature, which was also configured in that Script Logic.

Figure 5.110 Run Package – Default Logic

These Script Logic prompts can be matched up with each screen that appears during the copy process or any other process. In this case, the next screen is the option to validate the copy process against the work status, which is also the last line of Script Logic in the MODIFY SCRIPT LOGIC screen. So the controls of what is shown during the execution of these different packages can be modified by adjusting the code. One of the scripts that we commonly change is for the currency exchange rate calculation. Depending on whether we're using the FX translation for consolidation or just financial information, we adjust a variable in the screen to either show the GROUP as a filter or the ENTITY. If you look at the process of executing the FX

347

translation, you can review this adjustment. The execution of the FX translation process is available in the Data Manager screen for you to use as shown in Figure 5.111.

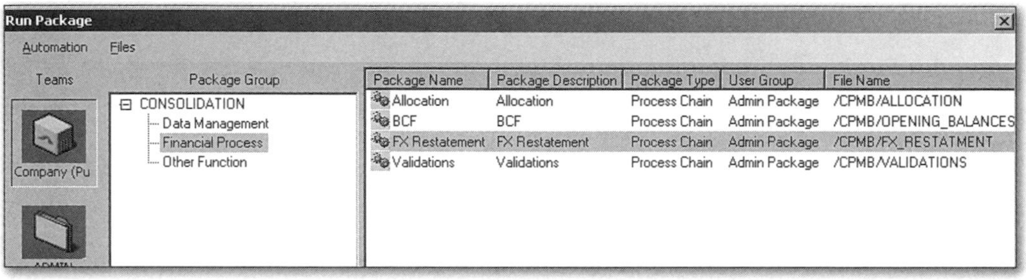

Figure 5.111 Run Package – FX Restatement

Upon execution of this package, the screen prompts you with four variables: CATEGORY, ENTITY, RPTCURRENCY, and TIME (see Figure 5.112).

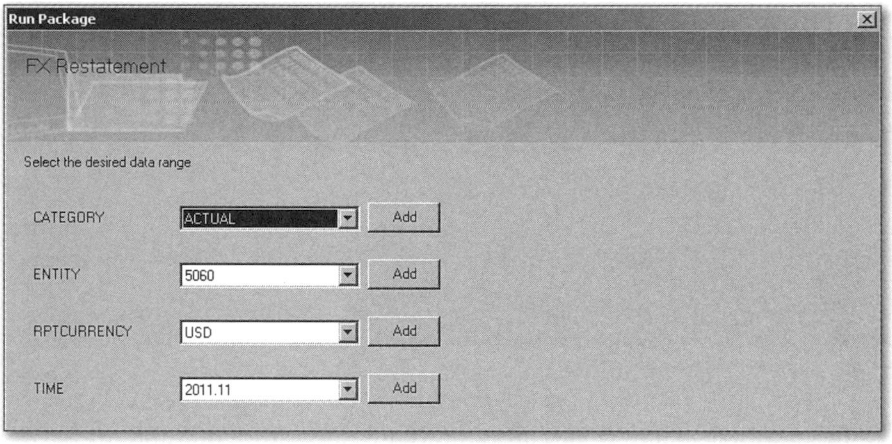

Figure 5.112 Run Package – FX Restatement Variable Screen

The Script Logic in the modify view shows that this is controlled by the assignment of the different variables. In the PROPERTY3 column of the MODIFY SCRIPT screen shown in Figure 5.113, the prompts highlighted there are the four dimensions that show up as variables.

The %ENTITY_DIM% represents a variable for the dimension, and, in this case, it's the ENTITY.

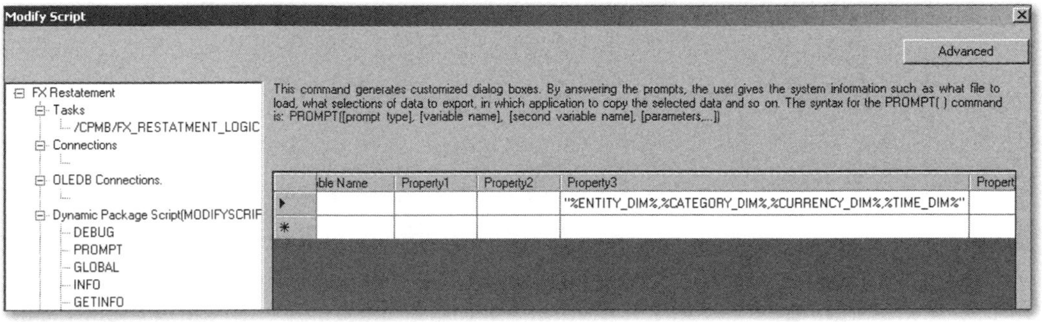

Figure 5.113 Modify Script – Dynamic Package Script – PROMPT values

Now you'll remove the %ENTITY_DIM% from this list and review the results of this change. Figure 5.114 shows the entity removed.

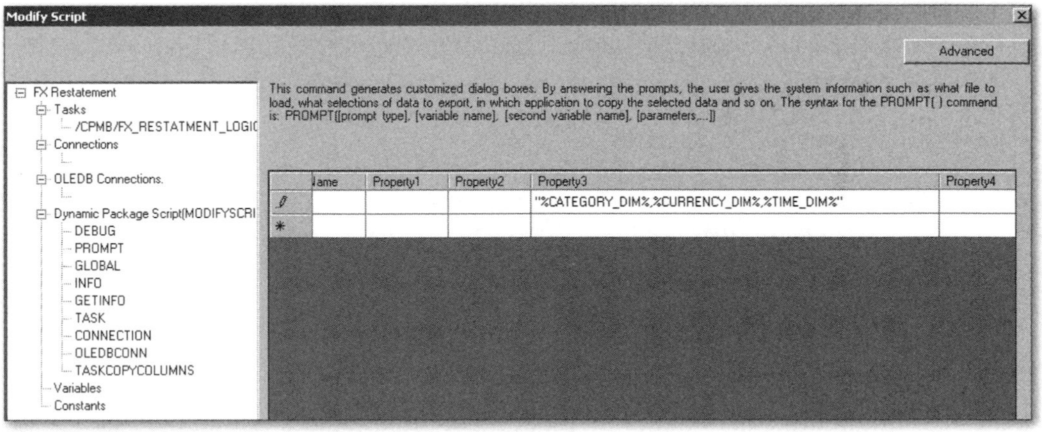

Figure 5.114 Modify Script – Removing ENTITY as a Variable

After you save this change and go back and execute the FX translation, the variable screen will appear again, but now you only see three variables without the ENTITY prompt due to the modification (see Figure 5.115).

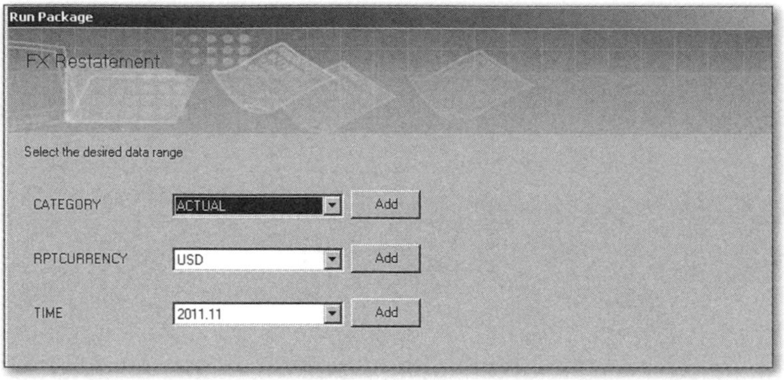

Figure 5.115 Run Package – FX Restatement with Only Three Variables

So modifying the Script Logic that is being used in the Data Manager packages can be reasonable to work with and readjust.

5.5.2 Process Chains

The core component of the Data Manager packages is the process chain. Normally, you can use the standard process chains that have been delivered with BPC and BW, but there are times when you may need to create one of your own and assign it to the Data Manager package. Most of the time, the BW team will take care of this, but the process of setting up the process chain is fairly straightforward, and you can think of it as a component used to collect and organize all of the objects configured to run a data loading process. We've been discussing and using the process chains in the data collection component, but the others are used very actively in the consolidation and P&F processes. Figure 5.116 shows the list of process chains that are available based on the BW view. In most cases, these process chains are already available in the Data Manager, but if you run into issues with one, then check that, in fact, the content has been activated correctly. If not, you'll need to reactivate the content.

Double-clicking on any of the PROCESS CHAINS in this dialog box shows the actual components of the process chain that are executed upon the run package process. In this case, the COPY process chain is displayed. Normally, a number of activities are completed during the run process; Figure 5.117 shows what occurs during the copy process. The initial START variant and the different components are linked together to run the objects assigned in the following sequence:

1. Initiate the copy process.

2. Incorporate all of the values for the variables to be executed during the process chain run.

3. Execute the copy process itself.

4. Delete the source cube of any indexing.

5. Append the data during the upload process.

6. Finally clear the temporary tables that were built to do any of the calculations or references during the execution process.

7. Save the data in the target with the appropriate dimension values and transactional data.

Process Chains	Tech. Name	M	Execute Functi
▽ Business Planning & Consolidation: Data Collection	/CPMB/BPC_DATA_PC		Change
BPC: Clear Transaction Data	/CPMB/CLEAR	=	Change
BPC: Copy Transaction Data	/CPMB/COPY	=	Change
BPC: Export Master Data to Application Server	/CPMB/EXPORT_MD_TO_APPL	=	Change
BPC: Export Master Data to BADI Retractor	/CPMB/EXPORT_MD_TO_BADI	=	Change
BPC: Export Master Data to File Service	/CPMB/EXPORT_MD_TO_FILE	=	Change
BPC: Export Transaction Data to Application Server	/CPMB/EXPORT_TD_TO_APPL	=	Change
BPC: Export Transaction Data to BADI Retractor	/CPMB/EXPORT_TD_TO_BADI	=	Change
BPC: Export Transaction Data to File Service	/CPMB/EXPORT_TD_TO_FILE	=	Change
BPC: Import Master Data Attributes from SAP Source System	/CPMB/LOAD_DATASRC_MDATTR	=	Change
BPC: Import Master Data Attributes/Hier from Flat File	/CPMB/IMPORT_MASTER	=	Change
BPC: Import Master Data Attributes/Texts from BW InfoObject	/CPMB/IMPORT_IOBJ_MASTER	=	Change
BPC: Import Master Data Hierarchies from BW InfoObject	/CPMB/IMPORT_IOBJ_HIER	=	Change
BPC: Import Master Data Texts from Flat File	/CPMB/IMPORT_DESCRIPT	=	Change
BPC: Import Master Data Texts from SAP Source System	/CPMB/LOAD_DATASRC_MDESC	=	Change
BPC: Import Master Data from SAP Source System (Generic)	/CPMB/LOAD_DATASRC_MD	=	Change
BPC: Import Transaction Data from BW InfoProvider	/CPMB/LOAD_INFOPROVIDER	=	Change
BPC: Import Transaction Data from BW InfoProvider (Delta)	/CPMB/LOAD_DELTA_IP	=	Change
BPC: Import Transaction Data from BW InfoProvider (UI)	/CPMB/LOAD_INFOPROV_UI	=	Change
BPC: Import Transaction Data from FTP (Last Overwrite Mode)	/CPMB/IMPORT_USING_FTP	=	Change
BPC: Import Transaction Data from Flat File (Aggrgt Ovrwrt)	/CPMB/IMPORT_APPEND	=	Change
BPC: Import Transaction Data from Flat File (Append Mode)	/CPMB/APPEND	=	Change
BPC: Import Transaction Data from Flat File (Last Ovrwrt)	/CPMB/IMPORT	=	Change
BPC: Import Transaction Data from SAP Source System (Full)	/CPMB/LOAD_DS_TD_FULL	=	Change
BPC: Import Transctn Data from Flat File (Last Ovrwrt)/Email	/CPMB/IMPORT_A_SEND_EMAIL	=	Change
BPC: Move Transaction Data	/CPMB/MOVE	=	Change

Figure 5.116 Standard Process Chains in BW for BPC Data Collection

As long as you create the process chain in the /CPMB/ display component, you can see and use it in BPC. An example of this might be the use of the process chain IMPORT MASTER DATA ATTRIBUTES FROM SAP SOURCE SYSTEM, which doesn't appear in the Data Manager package in this case. In Figure 5.118, you'll see that we've made a copy of this process chain just below the original.

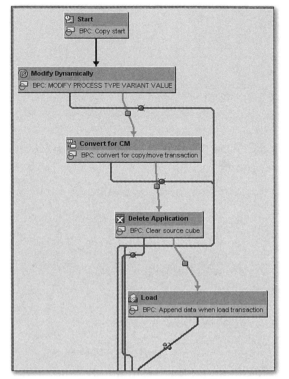

Figure 5.117 Detailed View of the Copy Process Chain

▽ 🏭 Business Planning & Consolidation: Data Collection	/CPMB/BPC_DATA_PC		Change
🔁 BPC: Clear Transaction Data	/CPMB/CLEAR	≡	Change
🔁 BPC: Copy Transaction Data	/CPMB/COPY	≡	Change
🔁 BPC: Export Master Data to Application Server	/CPMB/EXPORT_MD_TO_APPL	≡	Change
🔁 BPC: Export Master Data to BADI Retractor	/CPMB/EXPORT_MD_TO_BADI	≡	Change
🔁 BPC: Export Master Data to File Service	/CPMB/EXPORT_MD_TO_FILE	≡	Change
🔁 BPC: Export Transaction Data to Application Server	/CPMB/EXPORT_TD_TO_APPL	≡	Change
🔁 BPC: Export Transaction Data to BADI Retractor	/CPMB/EXPORT_TD_TO_BADI	≡	Change
🔁 BPC: Export Transaction Data to File Service	/CPMB/EXPORT_TD_TO_FILE	≡	Change
🔁 BPC: Import Master Data Attributes from SAP Source System	/CPMB/LOAD_DATASRC_MDATTR	≡	Change
🔁 BPC: Import Master Data Attributes from SAP Source System	ZBPC_LOAD_DATASRC_MDATTR	≡	Change
🔁 BPC: Import Master Data Attributes/Hier from Flat File	/CPMB/IMPORT_MASTER	≡	Change
🔁 BPC: Import Master Data Attributes/Texts from BW InfoObject	/CPMB/IMPORT_IOBJ_MASTER	≡	Change
🔁 BPC: Import Master Data Hierarchies from BW InfoObject	/CPMB/IMPORT_IOBJ_HIER	≡	Change
🔁 BPC: Import Master Data Texts from Flat File	/CPMB/IMPORT_DESCRIPT	≡	Change
🔁 BPC: Import Master Data Texts from SAP Source System	/CPMB/LOAD_DATASRC_MDESC	≡	Change
🔁 BPC: Import Master Data from SAP Source System (Generic)	/CPMB/LOAD_DATASRC_MD	≡	Change
🔁 BPC: Import Transaction Data from BW InfoProvider	/CPMB/LOAD_INFOPROVIDER	≡	Change
🔁 BPC: Import Transaction Data from BW InfoProvider (Delta)	/CPMB/LOAD_DELTA_IP	≡	Change
🔁 BPC: Import Transaction Data from BW InfoProvider (UI)	/CPMB/LOAD_INFOPROV_UI	≡	Change
🔁 BPC: Import Transaction Data from FTP (Last Overwrite Mode)	/CPMB/IMPORT_USING_FTP	≡	Change
🔁 BPC: Import Transaction Data from Flat File (Aggrgt Ovrwrt)	/CPMB/IMPORT_APPEND	≡	Change
🔁 BPC: Import Transaction Data from Flat File (Append Mode)	/CPMB/APPEND	≡	Change
🔁 BPC: Import Transaction Data from Flat File (Last Ovrwrt)	/CPMB/IMPORT	≡	Change
🔁 BPC: Import Transaction Data from SAP Source System (Full)	/CPMB/LOAD_DS_TD_FULL	≡	Change
🔁 BPC: Import Transctn Data from Flat File (Last Ovrwrt)/Email	/CPMB/IMPORT_A_SEND_EMAIL	≡	Change
🔁 BPC: Move Transaction Data	/CPMB/MOVE	≡	Change

Figure 5.118 Data Collection – ZBPC_LOAD_DATASRC_MDATTR

If you now go back into the Data Manager by choosing DATA MANAGER • ORGANIZE • CREATE PACKAGE, you can review the process chains that are available and notice that ZBPC_LOAD_DATASRC_MDATTR is available now for your use (see Figure 5.119).

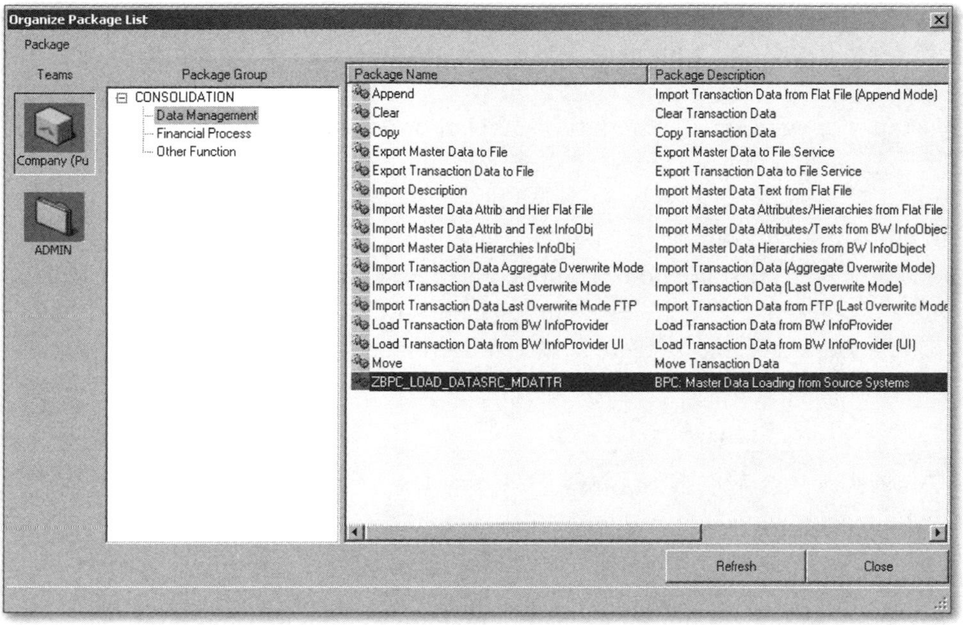

Figure 5.119 Organize Package List – ZBPC_LOAD_DATASRC_MDATTR is available

Numerous documents are available for creating a process chain, but we won't delve too deeply into this portion of the process due to the overlap with the BW teams that we'll encounter, along with the fact that the process of creating a process chain is more BW functional. If you need to understand more about the creation of a process chain, please see the SAP Help files rather than the BPC files because this is more of a core BW function than a BPC function. You can find the SAP Help files at *http://help.sap.com* and follow the links to the SAP NetWeaver Business Warehouse.

5.6   Uploading Currency Exchange Rates for BPC

For the execution of the currency exchange calculation, BPC requires that you download the exchange rates from a source system. Normally, you would look to SAP ERP for this information (in the BPC version for SAP NetWeaver), but you can upload this information from whatever service you have access to for your systems. If using SAP ECC as the source, these exchange rates are still uploaded using either a manual process via a flat file or based on a service. Therefore, you have two choices in terms of BPC: flat file them directly into BPC or use the SAP ECC system to upload them into BW and then into BPC. In SAP ECC, the exchange rates are stored in Table TCURR and are used in the calculations. This is the same approach in BW where on a periodic basis—usually nightly—the exchange rates are uploaded from the SAP ECC system into the BW system and are then available for currency conversion via a report or other approaches. In BPC, this changes a bit, and rather than rely on Table TCURR stored in BW, you need to upload the rates into a Rate model that is then used in the exchange rate calculations. This process is fairly straightforward but needs a little customization due to the difference between Table TCURR and the Rate model in BPC. For example, in Table TCURR, the exchange rates are stored as an equation. he exchange rate is shown with a To and FROM currency. Figure 5.120 shows Table TCURR in BW. As you can see, there is the TO/FROM currency translation as well as the exchange rate by rate type.

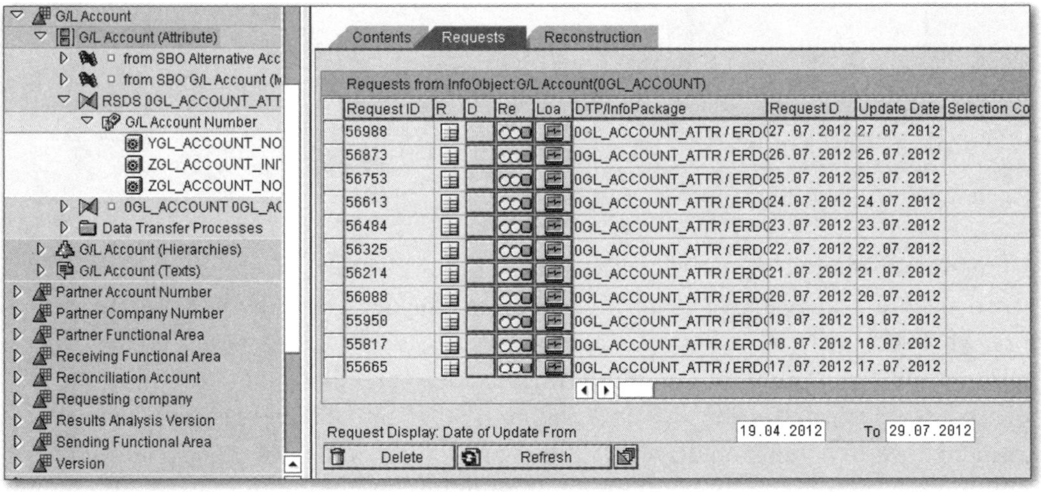

Figure 5.120 Currency Exchange Rates via the Reference IMG

Also in this process, the exchange rates are uploaded or assigned to an individual date/day. In BPC, you want a monthly or periodic rate rather than a daily rate, so there are some changes to the data that need to be made. These exchange rates can be seen either by using Transaction SE11 and then using Table TCURR to access, or by going directly into the Implementation Guide (IMG), as we just did, to see the details via the display view of Table TCURR.

If you look at the Rate model, you see that it's set up on more of a directional approach where you don't see a TO/FROM, but you see a FROM rate, and everything is basically directing to a group rate—in this case, USD. This is also due to the data model of the BPC InfoCube where there is only have one key figure to work with, and because TO/FROM rates require two key figures, this isn't possible in a BPC model. Figure 5.121 shows this an example of the data that can be found in a Rate model.

"/CPMB/SWIXX4L", List output

CATEGORY	...SWDQE	...SW	R_ENTITY	TIME	SignD
ACTUAL	BDT	AVG	GLOBAL	2011.01	0,01432
ACTUAL	BDT	AVG	GLOBAL	2011.02	0,01380
ACTUAL	BDT	AVG	GLOBAL	2011.03	0,01370
ACTUAL	BDT	AVG	GLOBAL	2011.04	0,01350
ACTUAL	BDT	AVG	GLOBAL	2011.05	0,01387
ACTUAL	BDT	AVG	GLOBAL	2011.06	0,01375
ACTUAL	BDT	AVG	GLOBAL	2011.07	0,01360
ACTUAL	BDT	AVG	GLOBAL	2011.08	0,01370
ACTUAL	BDT	AVG	GLOBAL	2011.09	0,01370
ACTUAL	BDT	AVG	GLOBAL	2011.10	0,01350
ACTUAL	BDT	AVG	GLOBAL	2011.11	0,01330
ACTUAL	BDT	AVG	GLOBAL	2011.12	0,01300
ACTUAL	BRL	AVG	GLOBAL	2011.01	0,59907
ACTUAL	BRL	AVG	GLOBAL	2011.02	0,59750
ACTUAL	BRL	AVG	GLOBAL	2011.03	0,60230
ACTUAL	BRL	AVG	GLOBAL	2011.04	0,63080

Figure 5.121 Rate Model in BPC – Stored Exchange Rates

In this case, the rates are assigned to a Category as well as showing on the one currency rather than two currencies as does Table TCURR. So during the calculation in BPC, the system reads two rates in the Rate model. The first rate and currency is the one that is being translated from, and the second is the rate and currency that is being translated to. Normally, the To rate is the one in the table that has an exchange rate of 1, and this designates that it's the group rate. In our case, it's USD. A good example of this is the use of the currency conversion applied in the consolidation process in Chapter 7, but first the exchange rates need to be uploaded to be used.

5.6.1 Data Flow of Currency Exchange Rates to the Rate Model

An overview of the process shows that most of the initial work is standard functionality and will execute without any manual intervention after it's set up. Figure 5.122 shows the initial flow of information from SAP ECC to BW via Table TCURR and then into a DSO in the BW system, which stages it for the upload into the BPC Rate model.

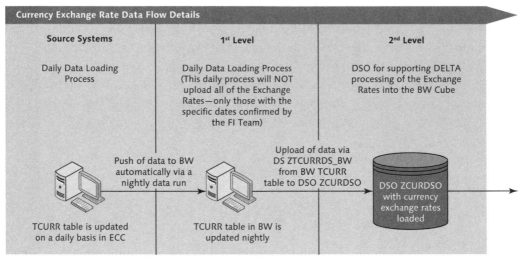

Figure 5.122 Overview of Data Flow for Exchange Rates

Some changes have to be made to the data during this uploading process, which we'll discuss in detail in the next section. Overall, however, the DSO stages the data with the BPC relationships in mind so you only have one currency assigned to the exchange rate in the DSO. From here, you then upload the exchange rates into an InfoCube and the final staging location before the upload into the BPC Rate model (see Figure 5.123).

The transformation rules from the DSO into the ZBPCCUTRN cube are also used to make the final alignments of the exchange rates to be uploaded directly into the Rate model. During the upload into the Rate model, there are also minor changes; for example, the exchange rates used in BW, such as 1001 and M, generally thought of as ending and average, are mapped to the exchange rates in BPC, such as END and AVG. The other assignment that is required is to a category in BPC. This isn't available in BW, so that additional assignment is done during the upload. In most cases, this is also straightforward because rates coming from SAP ECC to BW and then to BPC are normally for the actual data; others that are more for plan or forecast will come in under a different exchange rate or via a flat file, so you can create a different transformation file for those and single out the assignment of the correct category.

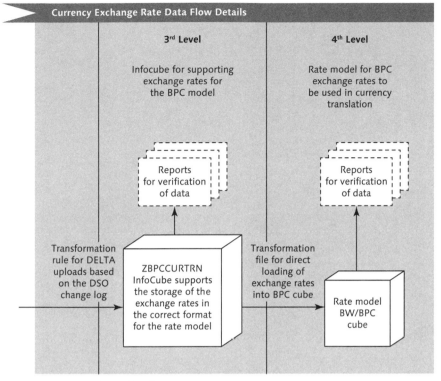

Figure 5.123 Data Flow of Exchange Rates into BPC

5.6.2 Configuration of BW and BPC for Exchange Rate Uploads

Now that discussed the data flow process at a high level, let's look at the details. In the BW system, the exchange rate upload between Table TCURR in BW and that in SAP ECC is done automatically and normally on a daily basis, as shown in Figure 5.124. This upload is set up to automatically occur so this is a standard process in BW.

After this information is available in Table TCURR, you can then upload that directly into a BW InfoProvider to stage the data correctly. Figure 5.125 shows the data flow created to execute this process.

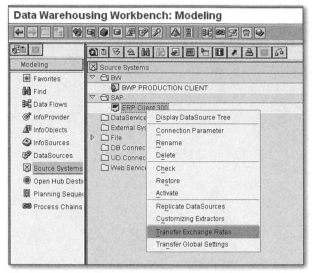

Figure 5.124 BW Transfer Exchange Rates Task

Figure 5.125 Data Flow for Uploading Table TCURR into a BW InfoProvider

At this time, the critical activities in this process flow are done in the transformation rules in BW where you align the data to allow the BPC model to upload the information directly without any further changes. Figure 5.126 shows the first transformation rule used.

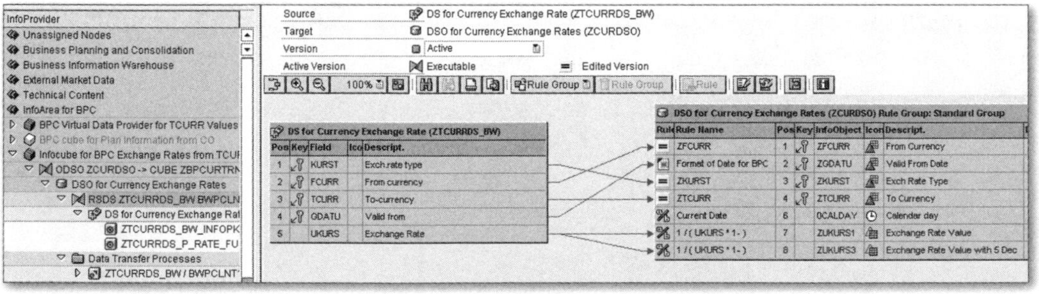

Figure 5.126 Transformation Rule from the DataSource to the DSO

During this data flow, you adjust two items. The first is the format of the date. This is due to the way that Table TCURR stores the dates as a string of information rather than the actual date. If you look at Table TCURR and look at the date field, to make sense out of the actual date, you have to subtract it from 99999999. This is what occurs in this minor program. The second change is to compensate for the field length of the exchange rates. The normal BW key figure stores only two places after the decimal point, and even if you use the FLOAT key figure type, this doesn't really support the format that is needed for the BPC Rate model. To address this, you create another DOMAIN for the key figures that supports a value with five places after the decimal point. You might also notice that we're executing the flip of the amount (1–) in this calculation. You can also do this in BPC with the property of the INPUTCURRENCY – MD, which allows the system to either multiply or divide the number to arrive at the correct rate to use in the calculation. The second transformation rule needs a few more changes, as shown in Figure 5.127.

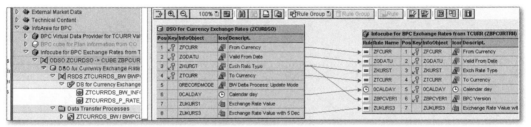

Figure 5.127 Transformation Rule for DSO to InfoCube

In this case, the exchange rate type is aligned to the BPC version to drive the assignment of the version/category to the BPC records. The final storage location for the exchange rates is the staging InfoCube, as shown in Figure 5.128. The InfoCube will support all of the exchange rates, and it still holds the rates in a To/From format so during the upload into BPC, you'll eliminate one side of that formula.

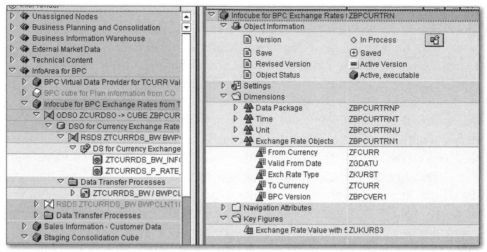

Figure 5.128 Staging InfoCube for Exchange Rates

> **Note: Staging InfoCube**
>
> The term "staging InfoCube" isn't a specific type of InfoCube in BW. "Staging" is just the label for the function that is represents.

At this point, you're now ready to go over to the BPC side of the fence to look at that configuration. In terms of the data loading process, this follows the same steps you've seen throughout this chapter. We'll highlight the unique features of this data loading process. To start, you can't do anything without a transformation file; the completed transformation file is shown in Figure 5.129.

In this case, the CATEGORY has been mapped to ZBPCVER1, and, if you remember, that field has been filled with the exchange rate values. The other fields are being mapped on a one-to-one basis except for the R_ENTITY dimension, which is getting a hardcoded value assigned of GLOBAL via the link to the *NEWCOL prompt in the *MAPPING section. This is normally the only value in the R_ENTITY dimension unless you might be using multiple global currencies, in which case, additional values might be used in this dimension.

A number of conversion files are being used as shown in Figure 5.130.

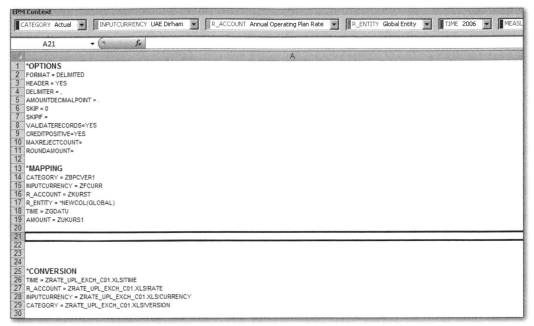

Figure 5.129 Transformation File for Currency Exchange Rate Upload

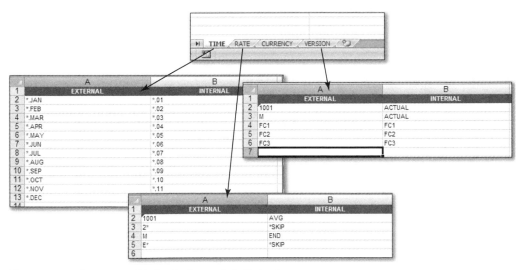

Figure 5.130 Conversion File for Exchange Rate Upload

The typical conversions are here for the TIME and CURRENCY, but the RATE and VERSION are mapped to the appropriate values available in BPC. For example, for the RATE, in BW the average rate is 1001, which is mapped to the AVG in BPC. Also, the same rates are being used in the VERSION/CATEGORY mapping, but, in this case, 1001 is mapped to the ACTUAL category as well as the M rate. For the other rate's FC1 (Forecast rate 1), the same category of data is in the BPC system so this is a one-to-one mapping.

Now that the entire configuration is complete, you can execute the run package process, and the unique tasks in the process are aligned to the appropriate TIME during the upload. This example is only uploading the rates applicable to the current period. If the closing is in MAY, then only MAY's exchange rates are uploaded. To avoid overwriting other exchange rates, you assign the TIME (MAY/2012) in the SET SELECTION dialog box as shown in Figure 5.131.

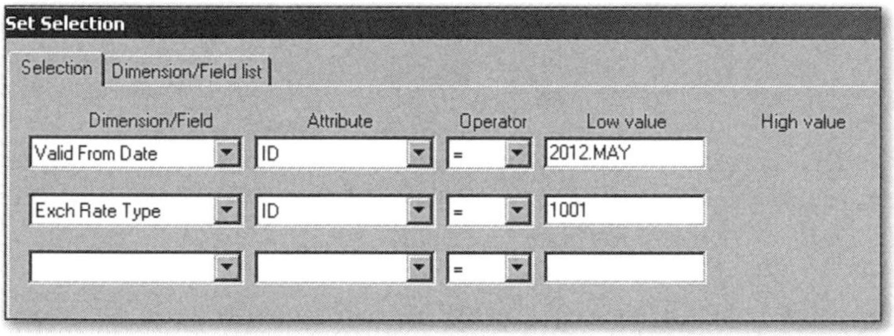

Figure 5.131 Set Selection for the Upload of Exchange Rates

After this parameter is filled in, you can execute the upload and expect to see a successful upload status as shown in Figure 5.132.

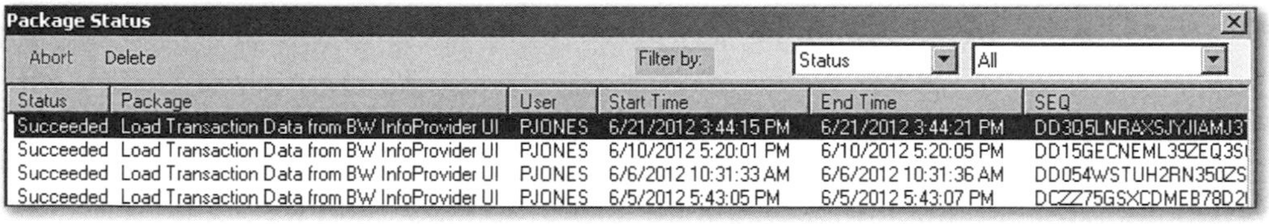

Figure 5.132 Package Status for Exchange Rate Upload

To review the results directly from the Rate model, go to the MANAGE tab of the InfoCube content and filter the information to be displayed to see the values in May, 2012 (see Figure 5.133).

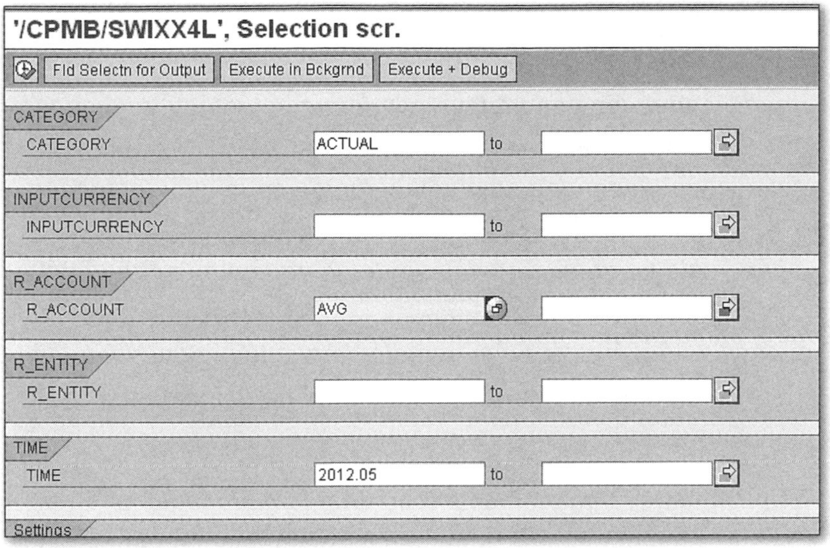

Figure 5.133 View of the Field Selection Screen of the Rate Model

You can then execute to display the results as shown in Figure 5.134. As you can see, we've successfully uploaded the exchange rates with the assignment to the appropriate CATEGORY and TIME values.

Depending on the SLA for this activity, you can see that there are aspects of this process that can be grouped together, such as the upload of the exchange rates from the DataSource to the DSO and then into the staging InfoCube. This can probably all be done in one transformation rule rather than two that we've shown here, but if there's time available in the uploading process, it can be beneficial to break up the data loading process to see and troubleshoot the information during the upload activities.

You've now uploaded the currency exchange rates from Table TCURR in SAP ECC through the entire system and into the Rate model for BPC.

"/CPMB/SWIXX4L", List output

CATEGORY	...SWDQE	...SWD	R_ENTITY	TIME	...B/SDATA
ACTUAL	BDT	AVG	GLOBAL	2012.05	0,0124000
ACTUAL		END	GLOBAL	2012.05	0,0124000
ACTUAL	BRL	AVG	GLOBAL	2012.05	0,5098000
ACTUAL		END	GLOBAL	2012.05	0,4957000
ACTUAL	CAD	AVG	GLOBAL	2012.05	0,9972000
ACTUAL		END	GLOBAL	2012.05	0,9733000
ACTUAL	CHF	AVG	GLOBAL	2012.05	1,0765000
ACTUAL		END	GLOBAL	2012.05	1,0436000
ACTUAL	CNY	AVG	GLOBAL	2012.05	0,1586000
ACTUAL		END	GLOBAL	2012.05	0,1579000
ACTUAL	CZK	AVG	GLOBAL	2012.05	0,0513000
ACTUAL		END	GLOBAL	2012.05	0,0494000
ACTUAL	DKK	AVG	GLOBAL	2012.05	0,1739000
ACTUAL		END	GLOBAL	2012.05	0,1688000
ACTUAL	EUR	AVG	GLOBAL	2012.05	1,2930900
ACTUAL		END	GLOBAL	2012.05	1,2540000
ACTUAL	GBP	AVG	GLOBAL	2012.05	1,6031000
ACTUAL		END	GLOBAL	2012.05	1,5662900
ACTUAL	GTQ	AVG	GLOBAL	2012.05	0,1313000
ACTUAL		END	GLOBAL	2012.05	0,1310000
ACTUAL	HUF	AVG	GLOBAL	2012.05	0,0044000
ACTUAL		END	GLOBAL	2012.05	0,0042000
ACTUAL	ILS	AVG	GLOBAL	2012.05	0,2629000
ACTUAL		END	GLOBAL	2012.05	0,2599000
ACTUAL	INR	AVG	GLOBAL	2012.05	0,0185000
ACTUAL		END	GLOBAL	2012.05	0,0179000

Figure 5.134 Exchange Rates in the Rate Model InfoCube

5.7 Additional Concepts in BW for BPC Data Loading

There will always be aspects of the data loading process that will require additional effort and customization. Several are very common to any BPC project, but the decisions around these topics will drive out the architecture and structures of the data modeling as well as the data loading processes. We've touched on some of them during this chapter, but they are important enough to single out and highlight a bit more.

One that will always be a concern is the solution is the existence of compounded InfoObjects in BW and none in BPC. Compounded InfoObjects can be found in most areas of BW, including Finance, Controlling, and Logistics, so this isn't something that will be unusual for you to bump into. When you encounter this situation, however, it's important to make sure that the data flow from master data, text, and hierarchies are consistent or the master data loading won't work correctly. The question here is how will this be resolved in the BPC uploading process. If we can do without compounding in BPC and, if so, then all you need to do is make sure that during the upload, you truncate the compound off of the hierarchy levels and align the master data as required. If you must have compounding, then make sure that the master data has the correct member values so that the hierarchies can be uploaded correctly. This can be accomplished by using either a prefix or suffix on the master data values to allow the unique members to be uploaded. We discussed this in section 5.3.1 in more detail.

> **Note: Compound InfoObjects**
>
> If you find members that have unique properties based on a specific filter, the compounding process will be required in BPC. An example might be the Product dimension. If the Product dimension has properties that are specific to a plant, such as standard cost, text, or size, then the compounding will need to be transferred to BPC.

Another issue that will generate quite a bit of interest is the concerns around uploading the GL accounts into the BPC Account dimension. The reason for this issue is the fact that the ACCTTYPE property is required prior to the members being uploaded. We mentioned this before, but it's important to highlight because the BPC model is an account-based view and that means you'll run into this one most if not all of the time. One of the options during the data loading of the accounts or any dimension's master data is to allow the system to automatically create members for the text nodes/levels of the hierarchy. If you decide to attempt to use this feature during the data loading of the GL accounts, you'll encounter an error stating that the text nodes of the account hierarchy do not have an ACCTTYPE assigned to them and that you need to assign ACCTTYPE values to these members before they can be uploaded. This presents two issues: getting the correct ACCT-TYPE on each of the text level nodes, and where to store that ACCTTYPE property on a hierarchy text node.

To review some thoughts on the assignment of the ACCTTYPE to the text nodes, access the standard 0GLACCEXT InfoObject is . This InfoObject was used to upload financial statement versions into BW and is still available, but the unique part of this InfoObject's hierarchy is that it supports a property assignment. This might be helpful, but because it only addresses assets and liabilities and not income and expense accounts, it doesn't go all the way to resolving this issue. You may find that using a combination of some old approaches and new approaches will do the trick. One approach is to use an older method of creating a flat file of the hierarchy values to be uploaded into a generic InfoObject. This generic InfoObject stores the flattened hierarchy node values as true master data with an attribute assignment, ACCTTYPE, which this will give you the required members with the attribute required by BPC. The only tricky part is the uploading process. A small change is required, which is that rather than uploading the members *and* text nodes for the hierarchies, you only upload the members. You then execute an upload of the generic InfoObject with the hierarchy text nodes that have already been turned into true member values with ACCTTYPE. Finally, you upload the hierarchy from the standard InfoObject to take the flattened values of the previous upload and structure them correctly into the GL account hierarchy. This may sound a bit complex, but it's really not that difficult to both configure and maintain.

The next issue that will always arises is the fact that the BW standard content InfoObjects won't have the required properties for the BPC dimensions. So the question here is do you enhance the standard BW objects with the appropriate properties and then use them as the source for the BPC objects, or do you somehow sidestep the BW issue and use a flat file upload directly into the BPC objects to enhance them and supply the required property values. There are a number of approaches to this issue, and all seem to work nicely, but need to use only one approach rather than having multiple approaches in the same environment. So a discussion of what is the most effective approach for the customer via the following questions is required:

▶ Should we use a flat file to enhance the properties, and should we upload that into the BW object or go directly to the BPC object?

▶ Should we enhance the standard BW InfoObject with the other properties or create a Z BW InfoObject and add the properties to this generic object, use the standard InfoObject to upload the members that it has available as well as properties, and then follow that upload with another to complete the master data?

▶ Should we derive the member and property values in BW or derive them during the upload into BPC objects?

▶ Do we allow the business user to manually update the BPC-specific property values after the entire data loading is over?

▶ All are viable solutions for this issue, but the correct answer is based on your architecture and structure.

▶ The final common challenge in integration between BW and BPC is the fact that there are two different data models which makes the reporting and data loading process between the two models more challenging. BW's data model is based on key figures, and BPC's is based on accounts. Where is the best place and approach to align the models? Is the best approach to realign the data models during the upload process from BW into BPC, or is it best to align them during the data loading done in BW? To address this issue, SAP has developed a very nice code option to be used in the transformation file: *MVAL. This prompt allows you to take a multi-key figure data model and switch it into an account-based data model during the process of moving data from BW to BPC. SAP has also offered some very nice DataSources that will accommodate this change during the data loading on the BW side. The answer varies in this case, but much of this depends on the SLA requirements and processing time during a period-closing process. It's helpful to have a staging cube in BW that allows you another layer to upload the data through and manipulate the data into the correct structure, but many times that's not available.

▶ The bottom line with all of these scenarios is that you have options, but the answer will vary based on the unique situations and requirements of the company.

5.8   Summary

Building on the previous chapters about BPC architecture, we moved into the data loading process in BPC. This chapter has described and outlined the processes required to configure the data flow from multiple source systems to BPC. Due to the required loading from a basic BW object (Z or 0 object) to a BPC object (/ CPMB/ object), it's important to understand the process of moving the information along from the core source all the way through to the BPC objects. In this chapter, we investigated both the upload for master data/attributes/hierarchies as well as transactional data. We also presented the differences and options to upload data into BPC from both the BW and flat file approaches. These different approaches were used for both the master data and transactional data structures. We discussed and demonstrated the use of the Data Manager component and the critical use of this component in the entire uploading process. In addition to the data flow processes for the BW and flat file sources into BPC, we also discussed the use of the direct upload from SAP ECC to BPC and other sources of data directly to BPC. In addition, one of the more important uploading processes that is required if you're using currency translation in BPC is the data flow of the FX exchange rates from SAP ECC all the way through to the BPC Rate model. The last series of topics focused on some of the aspects of data loading that will present a possible customization requirement for the system to accomplish the task.

This chapter works through the implementation and configuration of the planning, forecasting, and budgeting component of BPC. This will follow a generic planning and budgeting process from the initial upload of the data through to some typical steps within a planning process then to the final outcome of a planning and budgeting process.

6　Forecasting, Planning, and Budgeting in BPC

This chapter reviews the use of the multiple objects and processes available for the planning, budgeting, and forecasting process. We'll leverage what we have learned in previous chapters. These activities will follow a generic planning and budgeting process from the initial upload of the data through to the final reporting of the planning and budgeting results. This will include components of planning such as versioning, data transfer, top-down, bottom-up, and allocation processes. The chapter will also review and work on the use of Script Logic in BPC. Script Logic is used all throughout BPC in both the P&F and consolidation processes, but this will be a more detailed review of this component and its use in BPC. This topic will be covered here and referenced in several chapters, including Chapters 5 and 7.

6.1　Overview of Planning, Forecasting, and Budgeting in BPC

When we talk about the concept of planning, budgeting, and forecasting, this conjures up images that are very different depending on the person and company that we're talking to. So to clarify before we get started, we need to discuss these terms. Also, please note that throughout the chapter when "planning" is mentioned, it refers to all three terms—planning, budgeting, and forecasting—unless stated otherwise. For clarity, we still need to confirm the meaning of each of these concepts before moving on. The *budgeting* concept is more of a top-down process where there is a specific budget that has been assigned or allocated to each group or department, and you need to manage the budget costs to that amount. This is used in many different corporations but is very common in the public sector where governmental agencies have to align themselves to a budgeted amount.

The driver in this case could be the fact that there is a limited amount for expenses, for example. During the budgeted time frame, you've already been given an amount to drive toward, and you can analyze where you are in terms of that budgeted amount. If your budget to run a department is $200,000, then during the year, you can see exactly where you are and whether you'll "make" budget at the year end. In the case of a *planning* process, you're not necessarily assigned a "budget," but you're looking at what you can plan for in terms of expenses and revenue. This is more of a bottom-up approach to the analysis of the corporation. Taking into account all of the factors available, you then look at what is possible based on growth rates and expense programs. After all of this is taken into account, you create a plan amount and look to that amount during the year to see if you're on track. For example, if you plan to have sales of $1.5 million, and it's now August, and you only have sales of $250,000, you know that you're not trending to the plan and can review the issues/concerns to direct you back to the plan. So rather than a top-down slant where an amount is driven down the levels, you're looking at the formulation of the amounts at a lower level and then roll up to the top level for validation. Of course, in many cases, a disagreement occurs after that information is discussed at the higher levels, so to resolve these situations, you find that a change or tweak to the plan is then pushed down to the lower levels.

The concepts of *forecasting* for a corporation involve looking further out to future years rather than a closer analysis of what may be coming in the next 12–24 periods. In this case, you're attempting to forecast out 2, 5, or even 10 years of what is expected at a high level. It's not worth the effort to attempt to forecast a cost center or rate calculation out to 5 years because too much can change at that granularity level. For forecasting, the goal is to evaluate the longer term information about markets, government, competition, and product issues such as lifetime of a patent and the effect of a patent expiration on the corporate revenue stream.

6.1.1 Approaches to Planning, Forecasting, and Budgeting

Now let's look at the next level down for the planning process and the available options during the planning cycles. As you know, there are many approaches to planning based on multiple business situations. This is definitely not like a consolidation process where you can use specific guidelines for the process and steps involved. In some cases, having the government lay out a roadmap with some flexibility but the same core process is very helpful. In the case of the planning process, this can be much more flexible and tailored to the specific industry, region, and type of planning being done in the corporation. In terms of the planning process, you normally see an initial approach of looking at areas of the corporation such as sales, inventory, CAPEX, HR, logistics, financial, liquidity, and Selling, General and Administrative Expenses (SG&A) . In each of these areas, there are specific processes you can review, which will allow you to see that many of these have standard components are delivered within BPC either v7.5 or 10.0. If necessary you could migrate the standard content from the v7.5 to v10.0 and we will discuss this in Chapter 10. We looked at these planning processes in Chapter 2 when we discussed the standard content available in BPC. Even if you don't have standard content in the system for some of these planning processes, you can definitely find some initial approaches to these either based on the specific industry that you're working in or by looking at an older component of SAP planning—Strategic Enterprise Management (SEM)—for some guidance.

SEM-BPS (Business Planning and Simulation) has standard content for all of these approaches that you can use as a starting point concerning how to architect the appropriate planning process for your company. These aspects are broken out around a managerial P&L statement, and the modeling can be started with an analysis of this statement. Let's examine a typical P&L for a manufacturing corporation that is broken out into segments to see how this works. Figure 6.1 shows the SALES REVENUE, QUANTITIES & VOLUME section of the data model. We can start with this portion of the P&L and align it with possible system architecture in BPC. It's clear that there's going to be identifying information for this portion of the P&L statement, which will allow you to develop the data model architecture to include the dimensions, properties and models required for planning to take place for this section as well as the required data flow process needed to accommodate the planning process with the initial data required. In this case, the estimated data model architecture is two models—detailed and summary—for handling larger data volumes with the planning process.

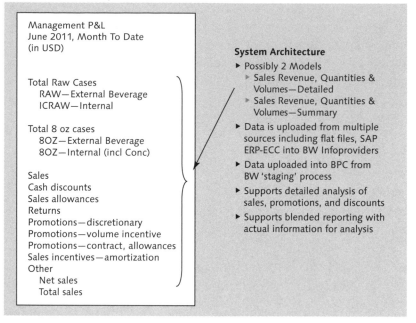

Figure 6.1 Management P&L – Sales Revenue, Quantities & Volumes

Moving down the P&L statement, you start getting into the costing aspect of the accounts. In this manufacturing business, about 80% of all costs occur in the ingredient & packaging (I&P) and manufacturing & warehousing categories. Figure 6.2 shows these two line items isolated in order to build out a sizable architecture to support all of the detailed information in these two lines of the plan. This information contributes the costs possibly down to the SKU level as well as standard cost values, variance information, and overall inventory information, including production activities and warehousing costs. Based on additional information, this requires a set of models to accommodate these components.

The next section of the P&L gets a bit lighter just due to the level of granularity that you might plan and budget costs such as freight, royalty, and depreciation/amortization. Figure 6.3 shows that the data model structure requires two models for each grouping of costs, whereas each of the two first lines require three models each. Also even though there are four line items in the final section, this can be accommodated using just one model for both summary and detailed information.

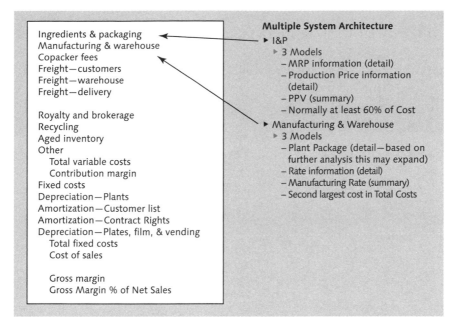

Figure 6.2 Management P&L – I&P and Manufacturing & Warehouse Costs

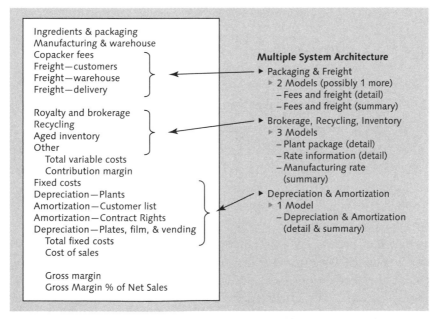

Figure 6.3 Management P&L – Freight, Additional Line Items for Cost, Depreciation, and Amortization

The final portion of the P&L statement shows the selling and marketing expenses as well as other overhead components. This area needs to be reviewed and analyzed, but, in this case, the costs are less than 10% of the total costs incurred, so you can group all of this information into two models rather than a more segregated view of the data (see Figure 6.4).

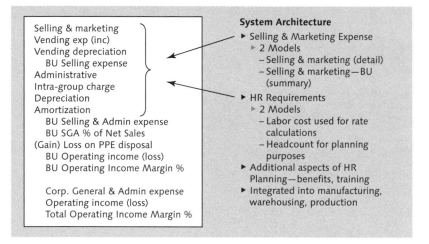

Figure 6.4 Management P&L – SG&A Expenses and Additional Selling Expenses

With these overview concepts of the planning architecture, you can see that the result will be a hub-and-spoke structure with all of the different components feeding their information into the Financial model so that you can accommodate the need for a forecast/planning financial analysis around the managerial P&L. This is depicted in Figure 6.5.

As you can see, this is working toward a fully integrated planning model with all aspects of the planning process integrated. The initial data flow might be toward the Financial model, but during an iterative planning process, the data can flow both ways and use the same functionality available in BPC to supply this approach. From this point, you can start to develop the details behind each of these areas such as the data flow required and the dimension block that you need to support the planning final result. Of course, to get to an overview diagram for the planning process, you've already developed some of the SAP dimension block. In this case, because you have *all* of the different aspects of the corporation process involved, the coding block will vary somewhat between models, but overall, the granularity levels need to be kept as close as possible.

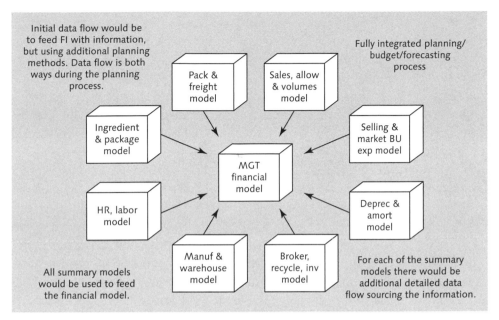

Initial data flow would be to feed FI with information, but using additional planning methods. Data flow is both ways during the planning process.

Fully integrated planning/ budget/forecasting process

Pack & freight model

Sales, allow & volumes model

Ingredient & package model

Selling & market BU exp model

MGT financial model

HR, labor model

Deprec & amort model

Manuf & warehouse model

Broker, recycle, inv model

All summary models would be used to feed the financial model.

For each of the summary models there would be additional detailed data flow sourcing the information.

Figure 6.5 Hub-and-Spoke View of the Architecture for a Corporation's Global and Strategic Planning Process

For example, in this case, manufacturing & warehousing looks to Plant as the core dimension, HR looks to Employee as the core, sales views Customer as the core, and finance relies on Company Code. This analysis allows you to flush out some of the critical architecture requirements and answer some questions around the referencing or sharing of data between models. In Figure 6.5, you can match up each of the different types of planning directly to one of the areas. For example, the straightforward ones could be the Mgt Financial Model which would use the FI planning process as well as the core dimension of Company Code, HR and Labor model would use the HR & Headcount planning process with the core dimension of employee, the multiple Manufacturing models just due to the sheer data volumes would be using some sort of Logistics planning such as Materials Requirements Planning (MRP) or other Inventory Planning processes and these would use Plant and Product as core dimensions.

Now that we've reviewed the types of planning possible via your walk through the P&L statement, you can look at some of the approaches to planning that are used by the different types of planning. There are several approaches to the whole planning process such as driver-based or non-driver-Based, top-down, and bottom-up.

Driver-Based Approach

The approach you take will depend on exactly how much time and effort you want to put into your planning processes. The most time and effort is put into a true driver-based planning process. In this approach, you identify the "drivers" that will support the growth of the corporation and use these as the foundation of the global or strategy view of the planning process. For manufacturing companies, the true drivers may be some sort of specific margin analysis or turn rates. A real-world example of this process during a planning session with an automotive company centered on the questions concerning what will help support the planning process for inventory and manufacturing. After a series of meetings and workshops to review the current drivers of the company, they found that the true driver wasn't really a core financial or manufacturing component but a survey process that would indicate the customer's satisfaction. If the customer satisfaction rating was trending downward over a certain period of time, then the total sales would drop, and inventory and production would need to be adjusted going out approximately six months. So, during your meetings and discussions of true drivers for the business, don't restrict the conversation to only those indicators that you're familiar with but expand the discussion to both soft information (i.e. surveys, customer satisfaction ratings, etc.) and nonfinancial information such as competitor information, impact of currency fluctuations, economic environment, and government restrictions. Any of these could be the true drivers of your business and therefore support the appropriate planning process.

Top-Down and Bottom-Up Approaches

Top down and bottom up take a more directional approach to the planning process. The process is more direct and usually based on financial or statistical information. For example, a top-down approach might be based on the need to generate a specific profit margin or cost reduction, so you would increase the planned sales amount by a blanket 10% across the corporation or reduce the costs by 5% in a specific section of the managerial P&L. After that decision is made, then a distribution process would occur to drive this decision down into the different divisions or departments, which, in turn, would need to incorporate these changes into their plan and then resubmit the plan for approval. The bottom-up approach is more grassroots planning where the initial plan information is developed at the detailed level or at the material level and then rolled up to the more summary dimensions for analysis and approval. As a usual result, there is always a gap between what is being developed at the bottom-up level versus the top-down level, and another solution is needed to decide on what do to with the interim gap that occurs at the mid-level of the plan. You can drive the differences back down into the detailed plan and create a revised view, or you can analyze the reasons for the gaps and either realign the values at the higher level to reconcile or offer additional solutions for the plan to work. For example, the sales requirements for 2013 can't be accommodated by the current production levels. So, you need to increase production at the current plants, open up another plant, or purchase products from another source and resell as a distributor of the products.

That's not all that you have to worry about during this process; you may still have issues with the different regions throughout the world that you need to align to a specific planning concept. We can all appreciate the fact that things aren't done around the globe in the same manner. What you do in the United States can vary significantly from what you do in the United Kingdom or Canada. So you need to look at these different regions and assimilate them into this process to get everyone on the same approach to planning.

The process of going through and identifying the planning concepts and strategies is often *more* difficult than the actual configuration of a system to support these approaches. If this is done consistently and given the appropriate amount of time, then the result will be a true global planning, forecasting, and budgeting process for the entire corporation. After these decisions are made, then you'll have a template to work from for the implementation of the BPC planning process. Now that this exhausting process is complete, let's move into the system and start the configuration process.

6.2   Script Logic in BPC

One of the main components of BPC when it comes to planning is the use of Script Logic. You've seen this component in many of the different tasks and aspects of BPC so far, but planning is where Script Logic is used most proactively. This is the core program option available for creating formulas and programs to execute calculations and manipulate the data to allow you to create additional plan data or take the plan data you currently have and realign it in some way. There are several different levels or approaches to using Script Logic. Table 6.1 lists these approaches and provides a high level definition for each.

Script Logic Type	Description
Worksheet Logic	Logic that is embedded directly into the local worksheet/workbook to create calculations. This uses standard Excel-based features to calculate the required results. The results only exist in the local worksheets.
Dimension Member Formulas	Logic that is stored directly on the dimension based on an additional parameter that can be turned on and used to support calculations at the member level. These formulas are available to any model that uses the dimension that supports the member formulas. These are also not stored in the database but are generated during the execution of the report or input template.
Script Logic	Logic that is created on the model level. This uses true members and can be used to create calculations and program calls that result in data stored in a model when the data is updated. At this level, this Script Logic is used to execute calls for the consolidation standard content.

Table 6.1 Types of Script Logic

There are a number of different scenarios where each Script Logic type could be used appropriately and although we won't discount any of the different approaches during the configuration process, we will discuss and review the configuration for each so as to ensure that we're not skewing the options to use one Script Logic approach or another. What I mean by this is that in most cases when we look at the different types of Script Logic the most commonly used is the third one – Script Logic, whereas the other two types are only used when absolutely needed. This is due to several aspects of each but the most important would be the impact on performance that they have. In both cases the stress of the calculation is placed on the frontend reporting component – EPM add-in – and we normally want to limit or eliminate entirely any additional effort on the EPM add-in since it is going to be handling the heavy work of calculations and manual data entries.

6.2.1 Worksheet Logic

The first type of Script Logic, Worksheet logic, really isn't any different from what you encounter when you add some Excel formula function to a report. This consists of using Excel and the inherent formulas used throughout Excel. This option doesn't have anything to do with BPC or features within BPC. It's actually used in conjunction with other Script Logic options. Figure 6.6 shows an example of the use of worksheet logic. As you can see, this is nothing but a standard Excel formula that you might insert into your report. Note that when we refer to worksheet logic, we're not talking about the concept of local or global members that are available via the EPM add-in frontend.

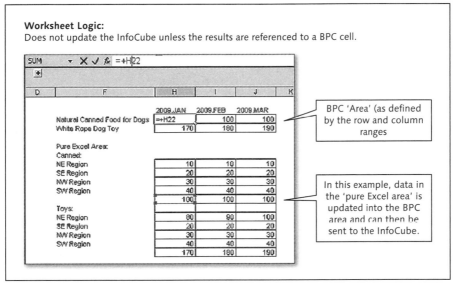

Figure 6.6 Worksheet Logic – Calculation to Support the Results Required in the Report

This particular logic is very useful for display purposes within the report, and the impact on performance is consistent with the normal Excel activities that you encounter during the execution of an Excel spreadsheet with embedded formulas and macros. This approach to script logic can also be equated with the use of either Local Members or Global Members where these are calculations but in this case we use an EPM add-in feature rather than an Excel based feature.

6.2.2 Dimension Member Logic

The first type of Script Logic that we talk about in connection to BPC is dimension logic. In this case, the configuration is done against the dimension (as the name implies) that you want to have the calculation return a result for. One of the more common dimensions you may run into this with type is the Account dimension because of the constant summing or subtotaling of the information for accounts. In this case, as in worksheet logic, the calculations are run at the time of the execution of the report. However, unlike worksheet logic, these calculations follow the dimension from report to report and aren't specific to the worksheet. This is a helpful feature, but in terms of performance and effort on the frontend, you need to be aware of the total number of dimension logic formulas you have as well as how complex they are. It can come in handy, but there are several restrictions. One is that the dimension logic will only run on base-level members. So if you have a net income GL account, which is a summary of multiple subtotals, you can't use the subtotals. Instead, you have to build the entire string of accounts within the formula editor. If you do this, you'll probably run into one of two issues: you'll run out of space because the total formula length is a maximum of about 500 characters, or you'll run into issues trying to organize all of the GL accounts in the appropriate string. Best practice is to use this if necessary but sparingly and with an eye on the performance experience.

The approach to configuration of this feature has changed since BPC V7.5. You now start in the configuration of the dimension and check off the option that ALLOW MEMBER FORMULA that appears just below the reference dimension option. Figure 6.7 shows this view.

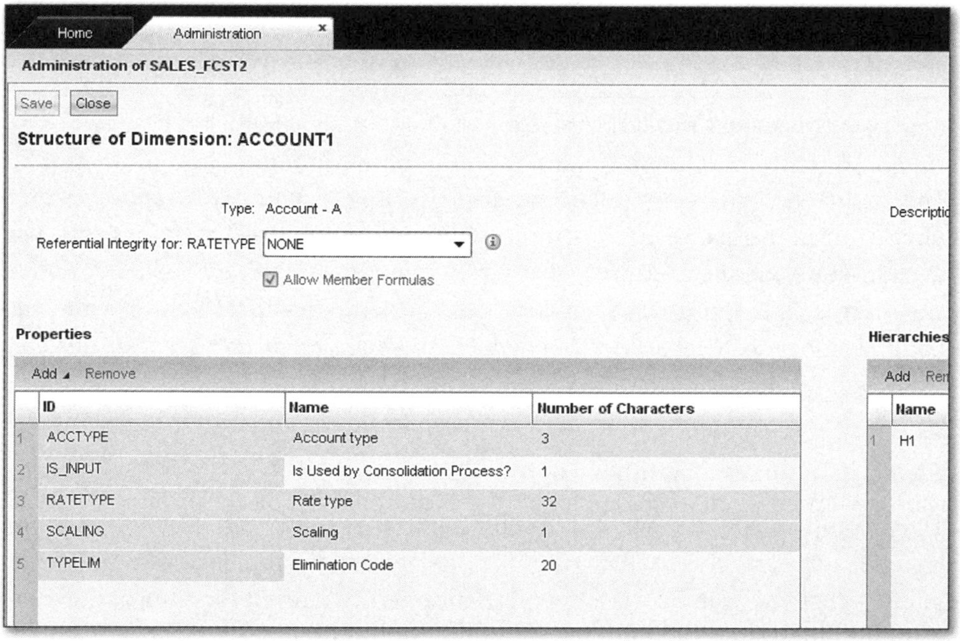

Figure 6.7 Administration Tab – Allow Member Formulas

In this case, there's no configuration of the length, so just checking off the parameter will allow the use of this feature. After this is complete, you can then choose RULES • MEMBER FORMULAS to start the configuration process. Figure 6.8 shows this information.

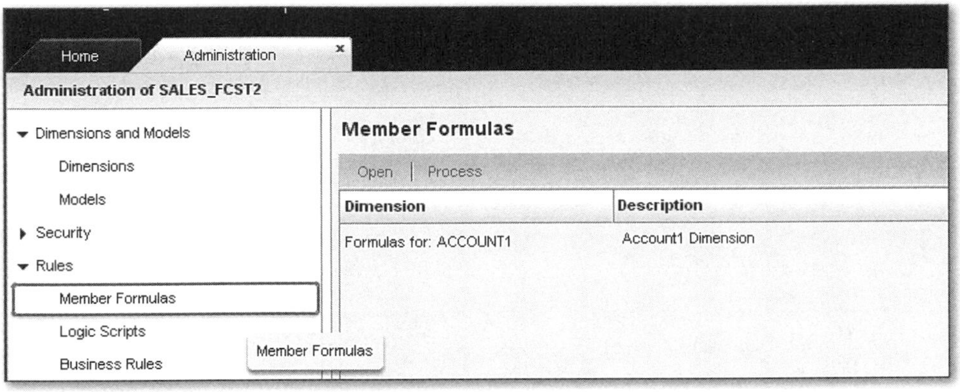

Figure 6.8 Administration – Member Formulas Configuration

After you click on the dimension that is available—ACCOUNT1—or click on the line with ACCOUNT1 assigned and then click on OPEN to be able to create a new formula. Figure 6.9 shows this screen.

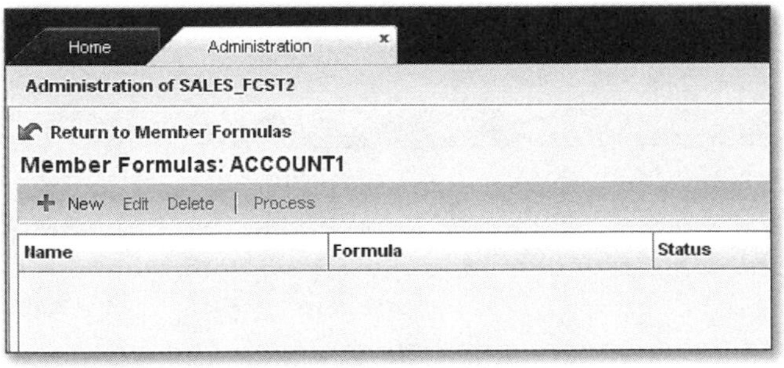

Figure 6.9 Administration – Member Formulas Creation Screen

Choose NEW to open a dialog box with the components of the formula that you can use, as shown in Figure 6.10. In the EDIT FORMULAS configuration screen, the FORMULA FOR MEMBER field is the field or Account in this case, that the formula will apply to. Fill the GL Account for Projected Price Variance (PPV), which is GL Account 800702. After you identify this required field, you can create the rest of the formula.

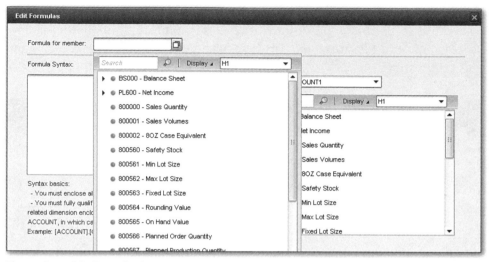

Figure 6.10 Edit Formulas Screen

The option DIMENSION, as shown in Figure 6.11, allows you to use the other dimensions to work into the formula. Again, remember that this formula will only work on base-level members, but you can use prompts for properties or other MDX-related (MultiDimentional eXpressions) options to develop a formula. We've used this type of script logic before for some reports, and the functionality is good, but we could see the difference in performance after there were a number of dimension member formulas incorporated in the report itself.

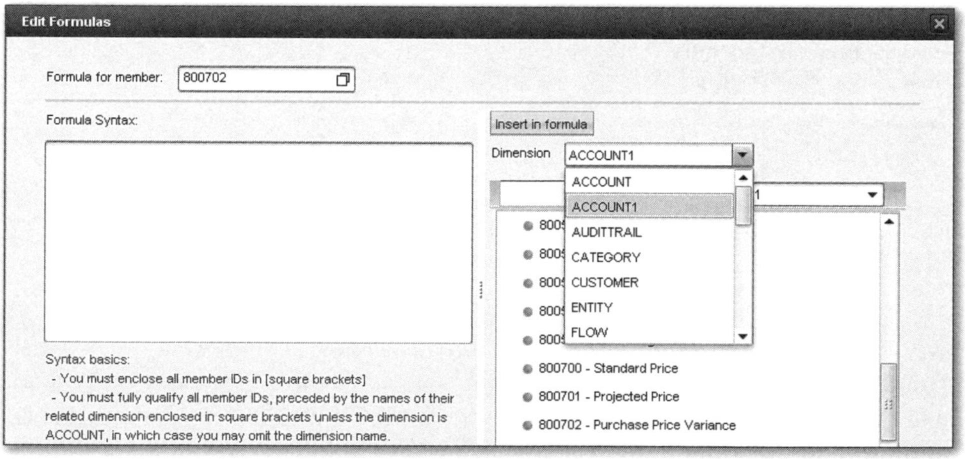

Figure 6.11 Edit Formulas – Using Other Dimensions and Members in the Formula

In this case, you're building out a formula that will fill the Project Price Variance account with information at the execution of the report (see Figure 6.12).

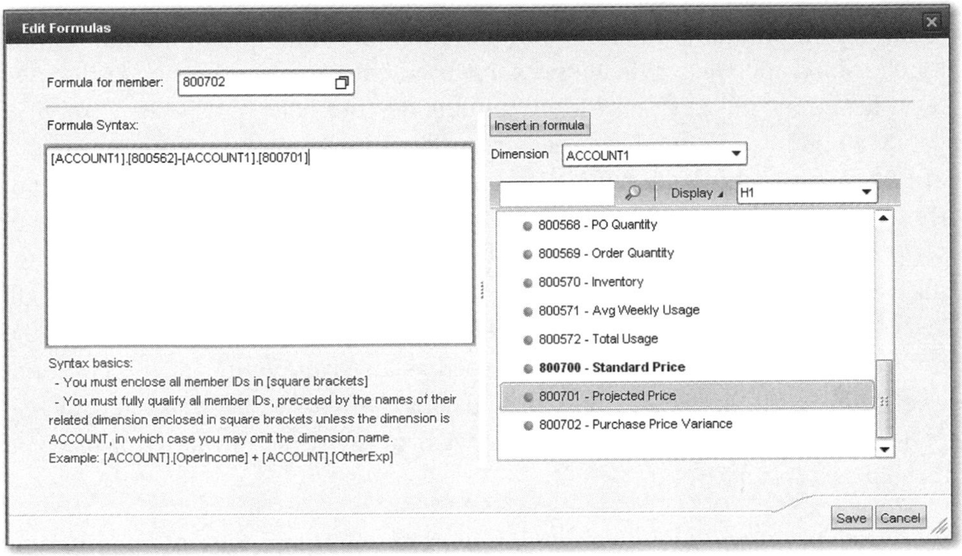

Figure 6.12 Edit Formula – Creating the Dimension Formula

You can also decide to use additional accounts just for reporting purposes rather than having to use the standard accounts that are required for the company chart of accounts. Figure 6.13 gives you the final result of the configuration of a dimension formula. In this case, you have GL account 800700 – 800701 (project price – standard price), which you then multiply by the total quantity volumes. This will create the calculation for the variance amount on the fly.

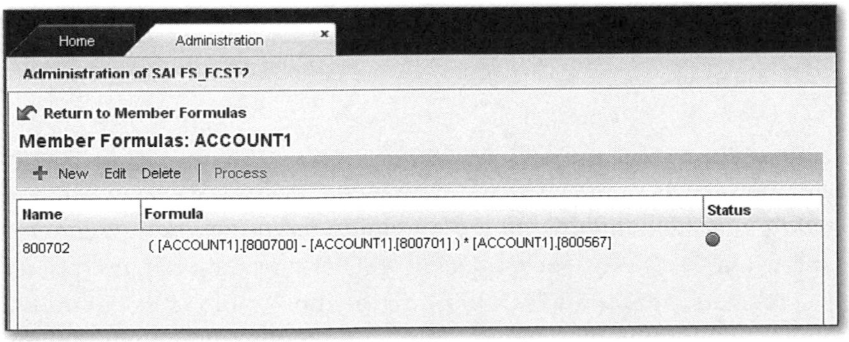

Figure 6.13 Administration – Process the Formula to Make It Available

6.2.3 Standard Script Logic Prompts for BPC

We've reviewed worksheet logic then dimension logic and finally we are now going to discuss the most commonly used script logic approach. This is used most often because of a number of reasons including performance, stability and serviceability. This final approach is the most widely used option of the three and offers the most flexibility and functionality. Depending on your level of expertise, you may very well understand and have been using the Script Logic in the former versions of BPC; fortunately, the Script Logic available in BPC V10.0 isn't much different. However, there are some new features and prompts within the configuration of Script Logic that will be helpful during the planning process. To get to the editor that you use for all of this work, you go to the ADMINISTRATION screen, click on RULES, and then choose the LOGIC SCRIPTS feature. When you do so, you'll see the different models available that can be used as a starting point for the build out (see Figure 6.14). Any logic that is created is model specific, but you can copy and paste the logic to another model if you want to use some of the script that you created as a starting point.

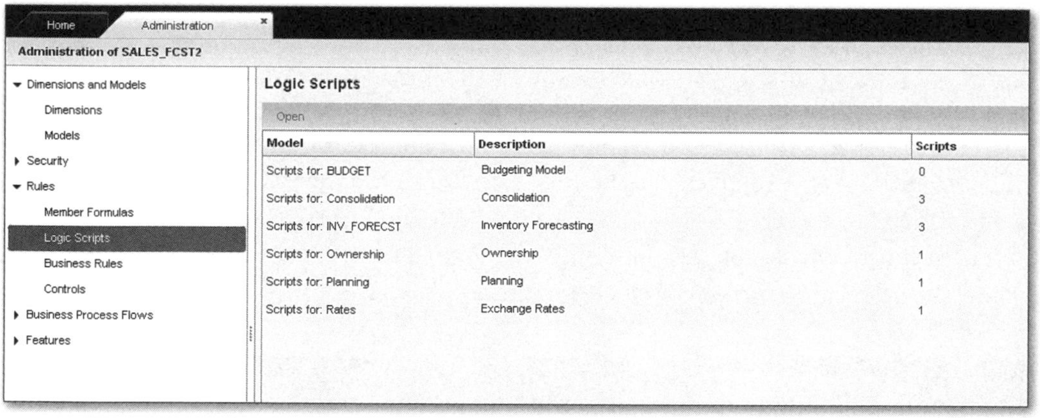

Figure 6.14 Administration – Logic Scripts by Model

After you choose the model and click on OPEN, a screen appears that lists all of the different Script Logic programs that are available. Figure 6.15 shows that in the INV_FORECST model, three Script Logic scripts have already been built. One of them, DEFAULT.LGF, is the standard default logic prompt. You can insert other Script Logic programs into the DEFAULT.LGF so that during the execution of the EPM add-in process (during the send process), the Script Logic included in the DEFAULT.LGF script will be executed and a write-back to the system will occur based on the script logic included in the DEFAULT.LGF package. Data is first committed to the model during the SAVE process, and then DEFAULT.LGF is run on the model data. In most cases, you'll develop the Script Logic as separate programs and then just insert the name of the program that you want to run in the DEFAULT logic prompt. This will avoid having all of your logic in the DEFAULT.LGF logic file which might become unmanageable. You can use the INCLUDE statement to execute specific logic in real time, such as currency translation if desired, rather than having to run a separate batch process.

You can also prompt the DEFAULT logic option by using the Data Manager during the execution of a planning process. So this one Script Logic can be used quite nicely during the execution of the planning process. When you initially access the first screen, you may find that the DEFAULT.LGF isn't available, you can create it for future use by clicking on the NEW button and typing in "DEFAULT". The system will then assign it the LGF file type during the save process.

Home	Administration	×
Administration of SALES_FCST2		
⬑ **Return to Logic Scripts**		
Scripts for: INV_FORECST		
✚ New Edit Delete Copy		
Name		
DEFAULT.LGF		
FXTRANS.LGF		
PPV_CALC.LGF		

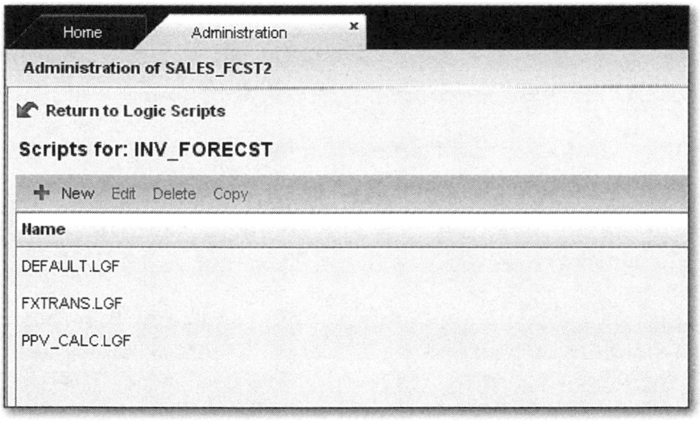

Figure 6.15 Initial Screen for Creation of Script Logic

Script Logic allows you to create files called logic scripts containing instructions for performing calculations on planning and consolidation data. Using Script Logic, you can perform calculations on base-level members only. This is not too much of an issue since there are a number of ways to identify the appropriate group of base-level members such as using a property to identify a specific group or a hierarchy node that you can point to and use the BAS() option to point the system calculation to the appropriate group of members. To help with the different prompts, BPC provides a library of MDX formulas, and the EnvironmentShell sample environment contains a number of logic functions. This is another reason why starting with the copied version of the EnvironmentShell is a good approach, it gives you all of the core standard script logic programs and you can build on them.

The following two files accompany each piece of Script Logic you create:

▶ An .LGF file, which is an ASCII file, is created once you fill in the script logic required. In this case you would prompt to access the script logic editor and then develop your logic calculations. You access the .LGF file through the logic editor.

▶ An .LGX file, which is the compiled logic file created by the system when you validate and save your logic. This is an executable version of the .LGF file that isn't stored in planning and consolidation.

In both cases, the system will create these for you, so after you create the Script Logic, save the code, and each of these file formats will be generated.

Planning and consolidation has a library of standard logic functions available for your use. The files have the extension .LGF, which can be called at validation by using the INCLUDE function in your logic file. The logic module scans the library file for the appropriate formulas to use based on the information in the .LGF file.

The following are examples of logic delivered with planning and consolidation:

NOTE: Script Naming convention

The information in the parentheses is the system assigned naming convention used in the script logic editor to integreate it into the program that is used to execute the script. For example, the script logic title used to link the script logic to the program that runs the allocation process is ALLOCATION. So if you are creating any of these script logic files you will need to use the exact script naming convention.

▶ **ALLOCATION.LGF**
Runs an allocation (ALLOCATION).

▶ **CALCACCOUNT.LGF**
Prepares cash flow; runs an account calculation business rule (CALCACCOUNT).

- **CONSOLIDATION.LGF**
  Runs a legal consolidation business rule (CONSOLIDATION).

- **COPY_OPENING.LGF**
  Runs a balance carry forward business rule (COPY_OPENING).

- **FX_TRANS.LGF**
  Runs currency conversion (FXTRANS).

- **ICBOOKING.LGF**
  Runs intercompany reconciliation and difference posting (ICBOOKING).

- **ICDATA.LGF**
  Runs intercompany reconciliation (ICDATA).

- **ICELIM.LGF**
  Runs intercompany reconciliation (ICELIM).

- **MDXLIB.LGF**
  Library of MDX financial functions.

- **SYSTEM_CONSTANTS.LGF**
  Stores constant values for use within Script Logic. See the system constants file information that follows for more details.

- **SYSTEM_LIBRARY.LGF**
  Includes basic examples of a set of keywords.

- **VALIDATION.LGF**
  Runs a validation rule (VALIDATION).

As you can see, these are focused mostly on the consolidation activities being done in the system. Again due to the consistent process that is followed in consolidation.

The system also delivers a file that supports constants in the logic file that maps your dimension names for a model to the standard planning and consolidation logic. By updating the dimension constants file with your dimensions, you avoid having to change or rewrite any of the standard functions that are included with planning and consolidation. For example, if you decide to use something like C_COMPANYCODE as the consolidation dimension for Entity, you'll need to align the system constants file to reflect that change. The system constantsfile is located in the \\ROOT\WEBFOLDERS\<ENVIRONMENT>\SYSTEMLIBRARY\LOGICLIBRARY folder. You can edit this file using download and upload functions from Transaction UJFS in SAP NetWeaver BW.

The standard Script Logic prompts provide a number of available options, and this number will expand as you continue to identify areas where something more standard can be helpful for everyone using BPC.

Note: Script Logic

The process that you used in SEM for these calculations may be an option in BPC in the future. Therefore, it's possible that the Formula extension (FOX) formulas might be available in a future SP in BPC as well. You can already see that several prompts, including TVML, are available in BPC.

The Script Logic Keyword List below features several BPC keywords and some examples of what each keyword does during the executable process in BPC. All of the keywords are prefixed with an asterisk (*), which is the prompt within the Script Logic that confirms with the system that this is an executable activity. Comments in the code are distinguished with //.

Script Logic Keyword List

▶ *ADD/*ENDADD – This structure allows you to automatically cumulate a set of members to a calculated member as specified in a comma-delimited range. The range can be dynamically derived using a *SELECT( ) instruction.

The syntax is:

```
*ADD {variable} = {set}
{formula}
*ENDADD
```

An example of this is:

```
*ADD %ACC%=[CE0004011],[CE0004021],[CE0004031][#CE0661200] = %ACC%/
[CE0652100]
*ENDADD
*COMMIT
[#CE00661200] = [CE0661000]/[CE0652100]
```

Note

The *COMMIT keyword is required so that the value for CE661000 is populated before the next calculation is completed.

▶ ***INCLUDE** – Multiple files can be combined into one logic file by using the instruction INCLUDE. During the LGX generation of the Script Logic execution step, the statements in the INCLUDE file are combined with the main file:

```
*INCLUDE FUNCTION_DEFINITIONS.LGF
[ACCOUNT].[#PER_PRICE] =
Price([ACCOUNT].[PERSONAL_COST],[ACCOUNT].[LAB_HOUR])
A FUNCTION_DEFINITIONS.LGF file can include all definitions:
*FUNCTION PERSONAL_COST = CE0004222
*FUNCTION LAB_HOUR = CE0652333
*FUNCTION PER_PRICE = CE0661560
*FUNCTION ACCOUNT = P_ACCT
Price(%COST%,%HOUR%)
%COST%/%HOUR%
*ENDFUNCTION
```

▶ ***REC** – The *REC( ) instruction tells the program what to do after the specified criteria has been met. Each REC instruction generates one new record to post to the database. Each source record can generate as many records as desired, even pointing to the same destination cell.

The parameters of the REC( ) function specify what to modify of the original record. Any dimension member can be modified using the following syntax:

```
{DimensionName}={"member"}
 *XDIM_MEMBERSET ACCOUNT = CE0004555
*WHEN CATEGORY
*IS ACTUAL *REC(FACTOR = 1.1, CATEGORY="FORECAST")
*ENDWHEN
```

The {member} must be enclosed in double quotes and can contain the name of any dimension enclosed between percent signs (e.g., ENTITY="IC_%ENTITY%"). In this case, the dimension name is replaced with the value of the current member for that dimension, not with just the dimension name.

You can use property values in the WHEN statement.

```
*XDIM_MEMBERSET CATEGORY = PLAN
*WHEN TIME.YEAR
*IS "2007"
*REC(FACTOR = 1.1, CATEGORY="FORECAST")
*ENDWHEN
```

You can write multiple REC statements within one WHEN/IS/ENDWHEN statement:

```
*XDIM_MEMBERSET TIME = 2008.AUG,2008.SEP
*XDIM_MEMBERSET ACCOUNT=CE0004232
*XDIM_MEMBERSET CATEGORY=ACTUAL
*WHEN ACCOUNT
*IS "CE0004232"
*REC(EXPRESSION=%VALUE%/1.5111, RPTCURRENCY="EUR")
*REC(EXPRESSION=%VALUE%/1.3226, RPTCURRENCY="CAD")
*REC(EXPRESSION=%VALUE%/1.6541, RPTCURRENCY="GBP")
*ENDWHEN
```

▶ ***SELECT** – The special instruction *SELECT allows the user to retrieve a list of elements from a dimension and save it in a user-defined variable for use somewhere else in the logic:

```
*SELECT ({variable}, {[What]}, {From dimension}, {Where})
```

With the following instruction, the user can retrieve the ID of all members in the CURRENCY dimension where the property CURRENCY TYPE has the value R:

```
*SELECT(%CURRSET%,"[ID]",RPTCURRENCY, [REPORTING] = 'Y'") *XDIM_MEMBERSET
RPTCURRENCY = %CURRSET%
```

The *SELECT statement fills the variable %CURRSET% with the list of reporting currencies defined in the current model. The content of the resulting variable is then used in the XDIM_MEMBERSET statement.

The SELECT instruction isn't specific to a given logic section, but it can be written once anywhere in the logic and used across multiple commit sections.

The SELECT statement is fairly limited, as it only supports the equal sign (=) and not equal to (<>) sign, and can't be used to combine multiple filter criteria with AND or OR keywords.

▶ ***WHEN/*ENDWHEN** – A WHEN / ENDWHEN structure works in the same way as the SELECTCASE / ENDSELECT structure, with *REC( ) statements that generate new records. The syntax is the following:

```
*WHEN {criteria}
*IS [=]{value1}[,{value2},…] | <>{value}
```

```
*REC(FACTOR={Real number}|EXPRESSION={Expression}
[,{dim1}={member},{dim2}=…])
[*REC(FACTOR={Real number}|EXPRESSION={Expression}
[,{dim1}={member},{dim2}=…])]
[*ELSE]
*ENDWHEN
```

{criteria} refers to what to test. Typically, this is a property of the current member of a dimension. The syntax is DimensionName.Property | DimensionName, such as *WHEN ACCOUNT.RATETYPE. If Property isn't specified, the ID property is assumed. For example, *WHEN ACCOUNT equals to *WHEN ACCOUNT.ID.

{ValidCondition} is one or more values that meet the criteria. You can enclose them in double quotes to treat them as strings. Omit the quotes if they represent numeric values. For example:

```
*IS "AVG","END"
*IS 10,20,30
```

If no operator is specified, the *IS clause assumes the presence of an equal sign (*IS = "AVG", "END").

The {value} must be literals only, not variables. Therefore, the following sample isn't supported:

```
*IS dimension.property
```

WHEN / ENDWHEN structures can be nested by as many levels as desired and in any sequence, as shown in the following sample:

```
*WHEN xxx
*IS "X"
*REC(…)
*IS "Y"
*REC(…)
*WHEN yyy
*IS "A","B","C"
*REC(…)
*ELSE
*REC(…)
*ENDWHEN
*ENDWHEN
```

▶ ***DESTINATION_APP** – This is used to cross-reference models. This will push the data from one model to another, and with the appropriate prompts, skip the dimensions that aren't available in the Target model.

For example:

```
*XDIM_MEMBERSET CATEGORY = FORECAST
*XDIM_MEMBERSET ENTITY = 1000
*XDIM_MEMBERSET ACCOUNT = 100100
*XDIM_MEMBERSET ACCT_ACTIVITY = MAINT
*XDIM_MEMBERSET DATASRC = INPUT
*XDIM_MEMBERSET TIME = BAS(2011.TOTAL)
*DESTINATION_APP = BUDGET
*SKIP_DIM = RPTCURRENCY
*SKIP_DIM = SEGMENT
```

▶ ***XDIM_MEMBERSET** – *XDIM_MEMBERSET defines the scope of the data in which subsequent business logic will be applied:

```
*XDIM_MEMBERSET {Dimension name} = {Members Set}
* XDIM_MEMBERSET {Dimension}<>{MemberSet}
```

For example:

```
*XDIM_MEMBERSET TIME = 2010.DEC
*XDIM_MEMBERSET ACCOUNT = bas(CE0008400)
[TIME].[#2011.DEC] = [TIME].[2010.DEC] * 1.1
*COMMIT
```

This example first reads all children of CE0008400 in the 2010.DEC period, increases them by 10%, and then copies them to the 2011.DEC period.

Another example follows:

```
*XDIM_MEMBERSET ACCOUNT = CE0004888, CE0004122, CE0004300
*XDIM_MEMBERSET ACCOUNT = CE0004000 //All children values are
summarized to one parent record.
*XDIM_MEMBERSET ACCOUNT <> CE0004010
```

You can't combine bas() with any other member set.

```
*XDIM_MEMBERSET ACCOUNT = bas(CE0004000), CE0004210 //This is not a
valid use case.
```

Use `*XDIM_ADDMEMBERSET` to add more members to the scope of the member set defined by `bas()` already.

▶ ***LOOKUP {MODEL}** – This prompt allows the model to reference and use the information in another for calculations or analysis. This is very useful during allocation processes.

For example:

```
*XDIM_MEMBERSET CATEGORY = FORECAST
*XDIM_MEMBERSET ENTITY = 1000
*XDIM_MEMBERSET ACCOUNT = 100100
*XDIM_MEMBERSET ACCT_ACTIVITY = MAINT
*XDIM_MEMBERSET DATASRC = INPUT
*XDIM_MEMBERSET TIME = BAS(2011.TOTAL)
*LOOKUP = BUDGET
*DIM CATEGORY = ACTUAL
*DIM ENTITY = 1000
*DIM ACCOUNT = bas(4500000)
*DIM TIME = 2012.002
```

▶ ***XDIM_ADDMEMBERSET** – With the keyword `XDIM_ADDMEMBERSET`, the logic can merge a specific set of members with the members passed in the region for which the logic should be executed. This instruction is similar to the instruction `*XDIM_MEMBERSET`. The difference is that, while `XDIM_MEMBERSET` redefines the region passed by the user, `XDIM_ADDMEMBERSET` adds the defined set to the passed region:

```
*XDIM_ADDMEMBERSET {dimension} = {members set}
```

For example :

```
*XDIM_MEMBERSET P_ACCT = bas(CE0004100)
*XDIM_ADDMEMBERSET P_ACCT = CE0004210
[TIME].[#2010.DEC] = [TIME].[2011.DEC] * 1.1
*COMMIT
```

`CE0004210` is scoped along with all children of `CE0004100`.

▶ ***COMMIT** – A logic file can contain formulas that depend on the result of calculations performed by the model, and these calculations in turn depend on the results of other formulas in the same logic.

For example:

```
[ACCOUNT].[#CE0004044]=([ACCOUNT].[CE0004055]+ [ACCOUNT ].[CE0004066] )
* 0.15
[ACCOUNT].[#CE0661000]=([ACCOUNT].[CE0004044]+ [ACCOUNT
].[CE0004020]+[ACCOUNT].[#CE0004044])/ [ACCOUNT ].[CE0652000]
```

In this example, CE0661000 depends on the first calculation, and this calculation in turn depends on the calculation of CE0004044. The logic, if written in the preceding format, doesn't work correctly because CE0004044 can't be retrieved from the model until its result has been posted to the model. To get the right results, CE0004044 must be calculated *and* stored in the model. *Then*, the calculated result can be retrieved from the model and be used to calculate CE0661000. To force a write-back of the result of the calculation of CE0004044 into the model before the calculation of CE0661000, you can insert the instruction *COMMIT between the two calculations. The logic then works when written as follows:

```
[ACCOUNT].[#CE0004044]=([ ACCOUNT].[CE0004055]+ [ACCOUNT ].[CE0004066]
) * 0.15
*COMMIT
[ACCOUNT].[#CE0661000]= ([ACCOUNT].[CE0004044]+[ ACCOUNT ].[CE0004020]+
[ACCOUNT ].[CE0004030] ) / [ACCOUNT ].[CE0652000]
```

In this case, CE0004030 in the second formula doesn't have the pound sign (#) because it's a stored amount read from the model.

▶ TMVL – This optional parameter returns a time value after taking into consideration an offset value from a given time period. This function works only with base member values.

The format for this parameter is TMVL(offset, base_period). Use this parameter by following these guidelines:

▶ Offset can be either negative or positive.

▶ Only integers are allowed.

▶ The base period can be a hardcoded value such as 2009.MAY, a time script variable such as %TIME_SET%, or a Data Manager prompt variable such as $CURPER$. Nested TMVL parameters such as TMVL(-1, TMVL(-3, 2009.JAN))) aren't supported.

▶ You can use TMVL in the following:

▶ FACTOR/EXPRESSION within REC

- FOR/NEXT loops
- IS conditions inside WHEN/ENDWHEN
- Variables, such as %TIME_SET%
- The first period of the TIME_SET is used as the base period for a negative offset, and the last period of the TIME_SET is used as the base period for a positive offset.
- Multiple separate (not nested) TMVLs can be used in one scope statement.
- When 0 is used as offset, no offset will be done for the provided time member.

In conjunction with these common Keywords, there are some differences between the Microsoft version and the SAP NetWeaver version of Script Logic. Table 6.3 lists the prompts available in both Microsoft and SAP NetWeaver as well as a couple that are specific to SAP NetWeaver. If the keyword doesn't appear in the table, then it's specific to Microsoft.

Keyword	Microsoft	SAP NetWeaver
*ADD/*ENDADD	X	X
*ADD_DIM	X	X
*ADD_TABLE	X	X
*BEGIN/*END	X	X
*LOOKUP/*ENDLOOKUP	X	X
*REC	X	X
*RENAME_DIM	X	X
*RUNALLOCATION	X	X
*SKIP_DIM	X	X
*COMMIT	X	X
*SELECT	X	X
*SELECTCASE/*ENDSELECT	X	X
*START_BADI/END_BADI		X

Table 6.2 Script Logic Prompts Specific to Microsoft and SAP NetWeaver

Keyword	Microsoft	SAP NetWeaver
*SUB/*ENDSUB	X	X
*WHEN/*ENDWHEN	X	X
*DESTINATION_APP	X	X
*XDIM_ADDMEMBERSET	X	X
*XDIM_FILTER	X	X
*FOR/*NEXT	X	X
*FUNCTION	X	X
*FUNCTION/*ENDFUNCTION	X	X
*INCLUDE	X	X
*XDIM_MAXMEMBERS	X	X
*XDIM_MEMBERSET	X	X
*DIMNAME_DIM	X	X
*DIMNAME_SET	X	X
TMVL		X

Table 6.2 Script Logic Prompts Specific to Microsoft and SAP NetWeaver (Cont.)

6.2.4 Use of Script Logic in the Planning Process

Even though there's quite a bit of standard delivered information and prompts, you still have to go through the process of setting up the Script Logic. Normally, this is the responsibility of the BPC consultant. Now, if the approach is to basically set up some generic Script Logic, then that is assigned to the BPC team. However, depending on the complexity of the Script Logic, you need to figure out if it's better to have a BW ABAP person create the code and then you execute from a BAdI or use Script Logic. If you feel that a testing process is warranted to determine this, the process is usually not that time consuming. A real-world example of this situation had to do with SKU-level information. The calculation was very basic, so in this case, the Script Logic was more on the level of A+B(XX) = D. There was nothing complex or dealing with loop issues or MDX. This was due to the high data volumes that the company was experiencing during the execution of the process. In this instance, we created the ABAP program, executed a test, and found that with the data volumes, the ABAP/BAdI approach was much faster than the basic Script Logic. So, we set up the process of calling the Business add-in (BAdI) from the Data Manager and executing from the frontend versus executing the Script Logic from the Data Manager. So make sure that you cover all aspects of the execution before deciding on one approach versus another.

To start the process of developing your Script Logic, you go to the ADMINISTRATION tab in BPC. Then you access Script Logic from the dropdown under RULES. Once in this screen, select the model name and then click NEW.

In the Create a New Logic Script dialog box that appears, enter a technical name and then choose CREATE (see Figure 6.16). This will take you to the editor screen for Script Logic, as shown in Figure 6.17.

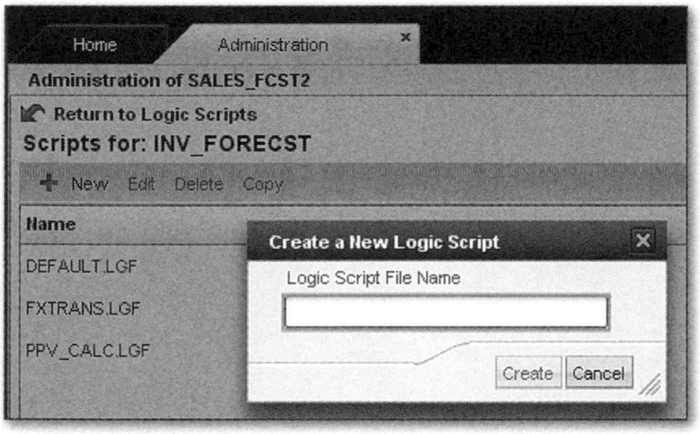

Figure 6.16 Create a New Logic Script

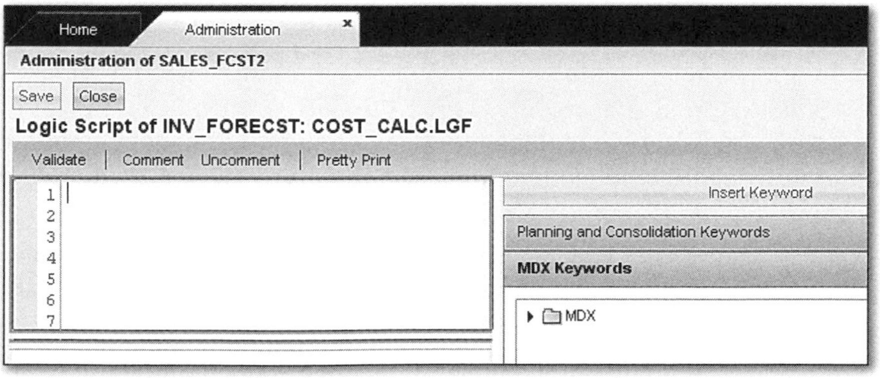

Figure 6.17 Script Logic Editor Screen

There are some improvements in this create process in terms of help with the actual script program prompts. As you type your components into the screen, you are prompted with keywords to select from instead of having to type everything into the screen. In addition, Figure 6.18 shows that there are helpful folders on the right side of the screen to offer you a view of the different keyword options. You can then drag and drop to insert them into the formulas or just start to type, and they will show up as a selection on the screen. You can see some of the keywords we talked about before in this list.

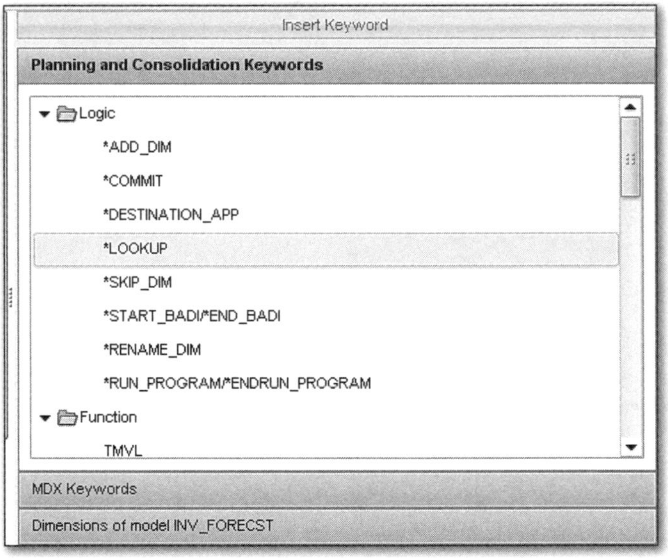

Figure 6.18   Keywords Folder with Folders for Each Group

In Figure 6.19, you see the string manipulation options with some of the XDIM_ MEMBER options available.

This is very helpful when you're focused on getting the correct spelling of these prompts into the formula. Figure 6.20 shows that there are two groups of Keywords: Planning and Consolidation Keywords and MDX Keywords. The other folders are for the model INV-FORECST that you're using in this Script Logic process and the next folder down below the folder for Dimensions of Model INV-FORECST is for the Member Selector in case you want to use a dimension that is not directly used in the Model that is assigned this Script Logic.

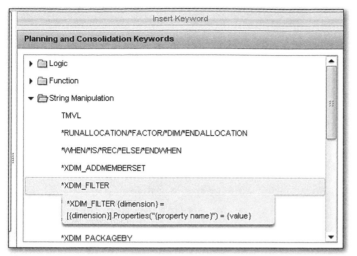

Figure 6.19 Planning and Consolidation Keywords

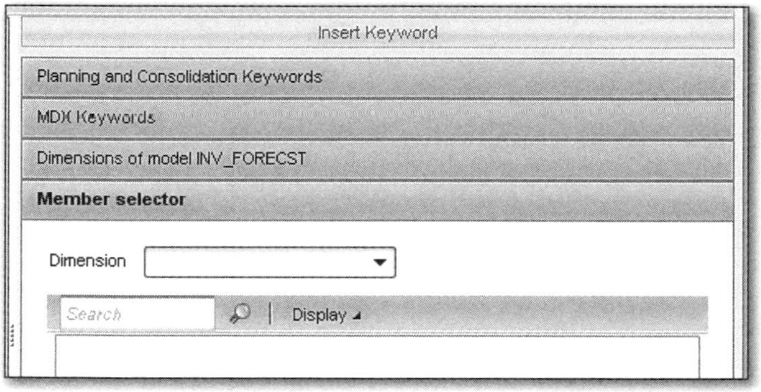

Figure 6.20 Insert Keyword Screen

On the left side of the screen, there are options for validating, adding comments, and uncommenting the information, as well as the Pretty Print option, which aligns the code in a cascading format down the editor (see Figure 6.21).

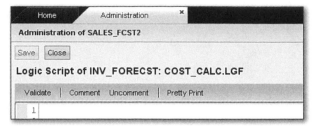

Figure 6.21 Administration – Validate, Comment, and Pretty Print Features

Now that you have a feel for how to start this process, let's review an example of a completed Script Logic. Figure 6.22 displays the calculation you created using the dimension logic as well. In this case, if you execute this from the Script Logic view, you will post the results into the BPC InfoCube.

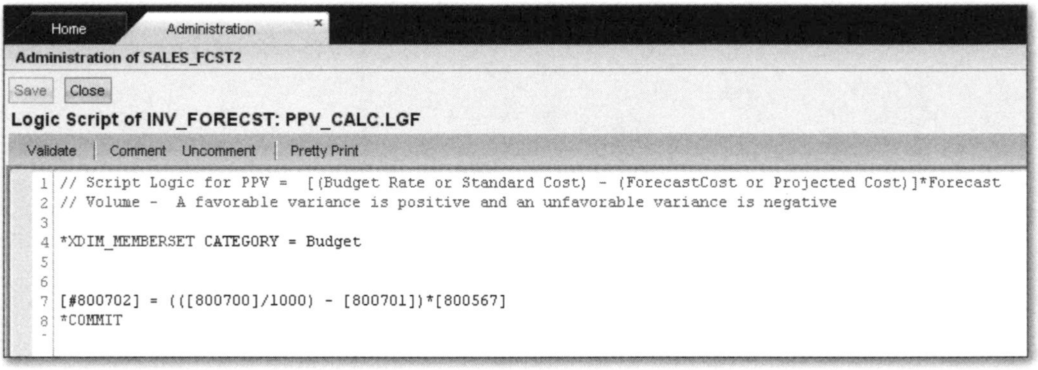

```
Home                Administration        x
Administration of SALES_FCST2
Save   Close
Logic Script of INV_FORECST: PPV_CALC.LGF
Validate  |  Comment  Uncomment  |  Pretty Print
  1  // Script Logic for PPV =  [(Budget Rate or Standard Cost) - (ForecastCost or Projected Cost)]*Forecast
  2  // Volume -  A favorable variance is positive and an unfavorable variance is negative
  3
  4  *XDIM_MEMBERSET CATEGORY = Budget
  5
  6
  7  [#800702] = (([800700]/1000) - [800701])*[800567]
  8  *COMMIT
```

Figure 6.22 Completed Script Logic View: PPV_CALC

In this case, you use the *XDIM_MEMBERSET to narrow the calculation down to the CATEGORY = Budget members. After selecting the data to execute the calculation against, you then can execute this Script Logic to populate the GL account that represents the PPV (GL account 800702). There are several items to note in this basic Script Logic formula:

▸ The executable lines all start with an asterisk (*).

▸ The XDIM_MEMBERSET is used to focus the calculation.

▸ Only one *COMMIT is used in this code.

▸ Comments,(lines starting with //), offer the next person a view of what calculation is based on.

Now the interesting part about this basic Script Logic formula is that it has a difficult time working properly because the calculation is bringing together information that has different currencies. The budget rate and any other rate has a currency of an amount, whereas the multiplication is being done with a quantity. Now you can't really see this from the actual formula but looking at the text explaining the formula you can see that it's multiplying two different currencies. If you have different currencies in the same formula, the formula won't work. To alleviate this issue, you have to use multiple activities to generate the results you actually want to achieve. For most BPC consultants this as a basic calculation, but if you look closer, you'll see the need to execute multiple Data Manager packages to get this to work. The best approach is to take the following steps:

1. Execute a copy process to move the data from a QUANTITY (EA) to the appropriate currency to allow the Script Logic to work. This would be the COPY DM package in Figure 6.23.

2. Execute the custom Script Logic to create the postings for the PPV in the system. This would be the RUN DEFAULT LOGIC DM package in Figure 6.23.

3. Execute a clear function to reverse the postings you just created. This will remove any information in the system around the copy process. This would be the CLEAR DATA DM package in Figure 6.23.

Completing this process allows you to "combine" different currencies in the same formula.

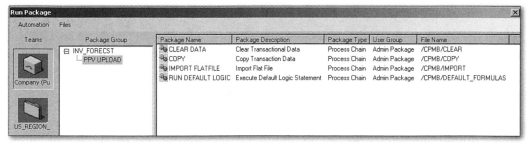

Figure 6.23 DM Packages Used for Executing a Calculation Against Different Currency Values

There are a number of these unique tweaks to the process in BPC that you need to be careful of and be ready to adopt the system calculations around these roadblocks.

During the process of creating Script Logic, you still need to be aware of the performance impact on the system and code accordingly. Following are some key rules and best practices to keep in mind during this process:

▶ Manage the amount of Script Logic that is being built. As we discussed before, make sure that you test if the use of a BAdI with an ABAP program supporting is better than developing tons of Script Logic.

▶ Use MDX as the last resort. It has been tested and validated that using MDX in a Script Logic formula will generate lower performance than using generic Script Logic.

▶ Load into memory *only* the records that are required for the calculation; any additional records will generate a poorly performing Script Logic code. This will require the proper use of the XDIM_MEMBERSET prompt.

▶ Review the Script Logic structures to make sure they are consistent and lean — reduce/eliminate any unnecessary loops that occur in the system. This is something that should be done automatically for all Script Logic that is being written. Realigning any Script Logic to make the process more effective will generate benefits in the future.

▶ Reduce the total number of COMMITS. COMMITS, in some cases, take more time than either a REFRESH or simply a READ. Although the use of a *COMMIT is required in some cases, make sure that your code is consistent and doesn't overuse the *COMMIT statement.

▶ Keep in default logic only the calculations required for real-time calculations — all others are handled by the background calculations. In other words, only use the Script Logic process for the truly required real-time calculations. Reduce the refresh after send in Excel (possible by using the Excel formulas to display a result rather than waiting for a Script Logic calculation to be executed to view the results). Do the background calculation and store, but display the result via the worksheet logic.

Another very useful toolset in BPC for helping with the validation of script logic is the Script Logic Tester. This is found directly in the BW system and can be executed using the transaction code UJKT. Once you execute this t-code you will see a screen where you can cut and paste your script logic into and insert additional parameters to filter down the set of data you will be using and execute this Tester. It will show you quite a bit of statistics on the script logic execution and whether it was successful or not as well as the amount of time it took to execute and also if there was an error what the error was. I've included this tcode into the additional material section for this book.

At this point let's walk through several example of some script logic to see the steps involved and the approach that can be taken to help support some of the calculations and realignment of data needed for your planning process. When we look at script logic we see that this component allows the development of unique calculations and data movements to occur that can be tailored for the specific business requirement. Advance programming skills are not a prerequisite, and once the basics are understood programming in script logic can be intuitive and easily accomplished. Knowledge of the basic keywords that we discussed earlier in this chapter and the data model that you are working with will support about 60% of what you need to know to work with script logic. When the logic module (.LGF) is executed the system will read a specific data selection from the model(s) based on the types of script you have created. Then applies to the data just read a set of user-defined formulas (stored in a logic file), calculate any new/modified records and their values and finally the results are written directly to the application database as base member data. If we look at the structure of script logic we see that it's broken down into three components.

▶ Scoping – What records are incorporated into my calculation and what records am I going to be interested in when I execute my script logic file? Basically this portion of the script logic filters the records that will be read during the execution process. Of course, it is important to make sure you include all necessary records but at the same time, make sure you include as few unnecessary records to be read.

▶ Body/Code – What results am I interested in calculating. What do I want to do with the scoped records?

▶ Commit – This is the act of writing the records to the data base

This can be seen in Figure 6.24.

In this case we are SCOPING the records down to the Category of ACTUAL and the TIME of 2012.01. Once the system generates an internal table with these values it will then execute the BODY of the script logic and basically this will calculate the results requested by the formula that was built. In this case, the body of the script logic is focusing even more on a specific set of data with the *WHEN statements. This can be read as When the Account is 760100 and the Entity is 3020 and the Intercompany value is I_NONE and the FLOW value is F_999 (Closing Balance) then execute a calculation that will take 49% of the value and assign it to the GL Account 760100 and Entity 2030. In the second line we are doing the same exact calculation but we are postings a credit of 49% to the 3020 entity and basically creating an offset postings. Finally we see that this is COMMITTED to the data base as a last step.

```
Logic Script of CONSOLIDATION: NRB_MIN_INT_ENT.LGF

Validate  |  Comment  Uncomment  |  Pretty Print

 1  //this will generate the offsetting entries for the minority interest calculation
 2  //calculation for NRB minority Interest Entry
 3
 4  *XDIM_MEMBERSET CATEGORY = ACTUAL
 5  *XDIM_MEMBERSET TIME = 2012.01
 6
 7  *WHEN ACCOUNT1
 8  *IS 760100
 9  *WHEN ENTITY
10  *IS 3020
11  *WHEN INTERCO
12  *IS I_NONE
13  *WHEN FLOW
14  *IS F_999
15  *REC(FACTOR=.49, ACCOUNT1 = "760100", ENTITY = "2030")
16  *REC(FACTOR=-.49, ACCOUNT1 = "760100", ENTITY = "3020")
17  *ENDWHEN
18  *ENDWHEN
19  *ENDWHEN
20  *ENDWHEN
21
22
23  *COMMIT
24
25
```

Figure 6.24   Script Logic Showing the Scoping, Body, and Commit

Scoping

When we look at the Scoping portion of the script logic process we see that there are specific keywords that are used for this purpose. This is a very critical portion of the script logic component since it will focus the calculation and in most cases generate a reasonable body of records to execute the calculations against. Scoping identifies the specific records that will be subject to processing by the main body of the script logic program. Initial scope refers to the set of all records passed to the script logic engine prior to any code execution. The executable scope consists of the initial collection of records that may be modified by the application of special key words in script logic that limit or extend the initial scope of records that will be processed by script logic code. There are two approaches to the initial scoping of the data.

▸ Calling the Script Logic from an Input Schedule via a Data Send process in which the Default Logic Script is prompted to be executed.

▸ Executing a DM package that will prompt the script logic program to be executed.

Independent from which method is used to define the initial scope, the executable scope can be overridden / modified / filtered with various keywords (i.e.: *XDIM commands). These are:

▶ *XDIM_MEMBERSET – This command allows the restriction of the initial scope to one or more specific values. For example, if the initial scope contains data including categories "PLAN" and "ACTUAL", and the command *XDIM_MEM-BERSET Category = PLAN is entered, the execution scope is restricted to only records that have a category equal to "PLAN". Data Manager Variables (see section 4) can be used as the subject of *XDIM statements, for example: *XDIM_MEMBERSET ENTITY=$SOURCE$

▶ *XDIM_ADDMEMBERSET – This command allows additional dimension values to be added over and above the values included in the initial scope. For example, if the initial scope contains data including categories "PLAN" and "ACTUAL", and the command *XDIM_ADDMEMBERSET Category = FORECAST is entered, the execution scope includes PLAN, ACTUAL, and FORECAST for the dimension Category.

▶ *XDIM_FILTER – This command allows the determination of execution scope using MDX filtering. Typically this command is used to deliver a set of dimension members that have a specific property (attribute) associated with the dimension definition.

▶ For example the command: The XDIM_FILTER command allows the determination of execution scope using MDX filtering. Typically this command is used to deliver a set of dimension members that have a specific property (attribute) associated with the dimension definition.

▶ For example the command: *XDIM_FILTER TIME = [TIME]. PROPERTIES("MONTHNUM") = "2" will restrict the execution scope to only records containing a TIME dimension for February (month number 2).

Body/Coding

Once we have defined the Scoping portion we can look at the configuration of the Body or code of the script logic program. The power of script logic is in its ability to create and modify records. There are several commands and techniques used to accomplish this action: in general, the techniques can be divided into two main categories: SQL based commands and MDX based commands. SQL based script logic commands start with an asterisk ("*") in the first column of the code line and is the most commonly used logic. MDX based commands typically use square brackets ("[ ]") to identify specific records for processing and has more of an impact on performance than SQL.

Some examples of the SQL approach to script logic are:

▶ ***REC** – instruction is used to generate a new database record, and/or it can be used to modify an existing record. The *REC statement is typically used to perform a calculation on the current value of the record being processed (using the keywords "EXPRESSION" and "FACTOR"). The *REC statement can also write calculation results to a different record that has one or more different dimension members (when compared to the original record).

Examples:

The following syntax multiplies the value of the record by 4 and writes the result back to the category FORECAST (note: all other dimensions remain the same):

*REC(FACTOR=4,CATEGORY="FORECAST")

The following statement adds 750 to the original value (represented by the variable %VALUE%) of the record being processed:

*REC(EXPRESSION=%VALUE% + 750)

The *REC command must be enclosed within a loop that selects specific records to be processed. This loop is established by the *WHEN/*IS/*ENDWHEN commands. For example:

The following syntax loops through the execution scope and selects only those records that have the dimension ACCOUNT equal to the value "CE0004220". When this specific ACCOUNT value is found, the record is processed by the *REC command (the original value of the record is multiplied by two and the result is stored with a new CATEGORY dimension, FORECAST. The original record is not modified.

*WHEN ACCOUNT

*IS CE0004220

*REC(FACTOR=2,CATEGORY="FORECAST")

*ENDWHEN

You can use BPC variables to accomplish concatenation within a REC statement. In the following example, two script variables (%ABC% and %DEF%) are defined prior to execution of the REC statement. During the execution of the REC statement, the system will replace the variables with their current values. The net result is the concatenation of the two variables into the dimension "ABCDEF" during the execution of the *REC statement:

*FOR %ABC% = 40110

*FOR %DEF% = CC1000550

*WHEN ACCOUNT

*IS CE0004220

*REC(FACTOR=1,ABCDEF=%ABC%%DEF%)

*ENDWHEN

*NEXT

*NEXT

▶ Conditional logic can also be incorporated within the *REC statement. An example would be the following IIF statement can be used within a *REC command to provide conditional processing:

*WHEN CATEGORY

*IS FORECAST

*REC(EXPRESSION=IIF([ACCOUNT].[A]<0,[ACCOUNT].[A], [ACCOUNT].[B]))

*ENDWHEN

There are restrictions when using the *REC statement and these are:

▶ You can't use MDX keywords in the expression

▶ You can't use the GET() function

▶ You can't use the NOADD function

▶ You can't use the SIGNEDDATA key figure

▶ You can only use the base level members so hierarchy levels are not supported

When we look at MDX statements we see a more detailed option for creating script logic. MDX commands allow the programmer to specify a specific record by indicating its dimension value, for example in the formula below: [ACCOUNT].[CE0004020] this MDX structure points to only one value of the dimension ACCOUNT, that value is CE0004020. Note that this structure consist of two parts, the dimension

[ACCOUNT] and the specific dimension member [CE0004020], a decimal point ties the two components together to uniquely specify a dimension and specific value. Note: the ACCOUNT dimension is an exception in that it is not necessary to specify the dimension name. In other words, [CE0004020] will have the same effect as [ACCOUNT].[CE0004020] as long as ACCOUNT is an account dimension. The hash sign, #, identifies a receiving record for a calculated result. For example in [#CE0004020] = [CE0004050]+[CE0004060], the calculated member is prefixed with a "#".

▶ ***WHEN_REF_DATA** – This key word allows control over the records that are looped through (based on Master Data values or Transactional Data values) in a WHEN/ENDWHEN loop. The WHEN_REF_DATA code line is used to switch the calculation mode of subsequent WHEN/ENDWHEN loops. For example:

*WHEN_REF_DATA=MASTER_DATA will enable master data mode.

*WHEN_REF_DATA=TRANS_DATA will enable transaction data mode

An example of this would be:

*WHEN_REF_DATA=MASTER_DATA

*WHEN ACCOUNT

*IS *

*REC(FACTOR=4,CATEGORY="FORECAST")

*ENDWHEN

▶ ***FOR / *NEXT** – Script logic variables can consist of one or more dimension member values in a reference list. In the following example, the variable %Q5% is defined in the *FOR statement as consisting of the three dimension members: 2012.JAN, 2012.FEB, 2012.MAR:

*FOR %Q5% = 2012.JAN, 2012.FEB, 2012.MAR

The *FOR command is followed by a *NEXT command to establish a process loop. The intent when using a *FOR/*NEXT is to define a variable with one or more values, then cycle through each member of the variable list one at a time. In the following example the logic will execute the specified *allocation* function three times, once for each value of the %Q5% variable defined within the *FOR statement:

*FOR %Q5% = 2012.JAN, 2012.FEB, 2012.MAR

*RUNALLOCATION

*FACTOR=1/3

*DIM TIME WHAT = 2012.JAN; WHERE = %Q5%;

*DIM CATEGORY WHAT=ACTUAL; WHERE=<<<;

*ENDALLOCATION

*NEXT

▶ ***SELECT** – The *SELECT statement allows the dynamic programming of a variable typically based upon properties of the dimension. The resulting variable definition can be used to dynamically define scoping commands (such as *XDIM_ MEMBERSET) and/or included in subsequent *FOR/*NEXT loops.

In the following example, the *SELECT statement is defining the variable "%ACCTSET%" by populating it with dimension member IDs from the dimension ACCOUNT where the property CALC has a value of "N". The variable is then being used to dynamically define the execution scope of the dimension ACCOUNT in the subsequent *XIM_MEMBERSET command:

*SELECT(%ACCTSET%,"[ID]",ACCOUNT,"[CALC]='N'")

*XDIM_MEMBERSET ACCOUNT = %ACCTSET%

▶ ***ADD /*ENDADD** – *ADD command allows the specification of a variable list. This variable can be incorporated into a MDX statement and allow the execution of the MDX statement for all values of the define variable. In the following example, the *ADD statement defines a variable %ACCT% which consists of three values. When the MDX statement is executed, the logic will loop through each value in the variable list and execute the MDX statement three times:

*ADD %ACCT%=[CE0004020],[CE0004030],[CE0004040]

[#CE0661000] = %ACC%/[CE0652111]

*ENDADD

The equivalent logic without the *ADD/*ENDADD loop:

[#CE0661000] = [CE0004020]/[CE0652111]

[#CE0661000] = [CE0004030]/[CE0652111]

[#CE0661000] = [CE0004040]/[CE0652111]

In addition to program defined variables, the system has several predefined variables that are always available such as:

%USER% - Returns current Planning and Consolidation User

%APPSET% - Returns current Planning and Consolidation AppSet

%APPLICATION% - Returns current Planning and Consolidation Application

%YEAR% - Returns current calendar year

We saw these in the script logic within the Data Manager package as well.

For example: *XDIM_MEMBERSET MONTH = BAS(%YEAR%.TOTAL)

Tip: %YEAR% will always return only the current calendar year, if the execution scope is for a year other than the current calendar year, %YEAR% will still return the current calendar year.

Some of the more advanced options that we have with script logic might be:

▶ **Boolean Expressions** – Boolean (or yes/no logic) can be incorporated in script logic. By enclosing a Boolean expression in parenthesis the formula will be evaluated as a true or false condition, returning a value of 1 for the expression if TRUE, and 0 if FALSE. An example of this would be:

*BEGIN

*REC (EXPRESSION=((%VALUE% > 11200) * 110) + ((%VALUE% < 12000) * (%VALUE% * LOOKUP(LR_RATE))),ACCOUNT="TEMP")

*END

This *REC statement is evaluated as follows:

If the original record's value (%VALUE%) is greater than 11,200

(%VALUE% > 12000) is interpreted as a logical "1", then the original value of the record is multiplied by 110 and the expression (%VALUE% < 10000) is interpreted as a logical "0". A new record is created with the original recordÐs ACCOUNT dimension value is replaced with a new member id: "TEMP".

If the original record's value (%VALUE%) is less than 12,000.

(%VALUE% > 12000) is interpreted as a logical "0": 0 multiplied by 110 = 0. (%VALUE% < 12000) is interpreted as a logical "1" and the original value of the record is multiplied by the Look Up rate "LR_RATE". A new record is created with the original recordÐs ACCOUNT dimension value is replaced with a new member id: "TEMP".

▸ **Conditional logic** can also be incorporated into a MDX statement, similar to the option in SQL, using new key symbols. In the following example:

[ACCOUNT].[#CE0001010]=([ACCOUNT].[CE0001020]>0? [ACCOUNT].[CE0001020] : 0)

The "?" performs a conditional test, if the test is true then the left hand side of the equation is set equal to [ACCOUNT].[CE0001020], if the test is false, then the left hand side of the equation is set equal to 0. The special character ":" separates the two TRUE/FALSE outcomes.

▸ ***IIF** – The IIF statement allows a conditional IF/Then/Else statement to be defined. Objects of the IIF statements can include *REC commands:

The following example line executes as follows: If the variable %VAR210% is blank, then execute the first *REC statement, if the conditional statement is false, then execute the second REC statement:

*IIF(%VAR210%="",*REC(DATA_SOURCE="CALC", MEASUREID="A100"), *REC(DATA_SOURCE = "INPUT", MEASUREID="A200"))

These are just some of the different keywords and formulas that can be created with script logic. Again, there are a number of documents available either on the help.sap.com/epm site or at BI Expert.com. As you read through these different keyword functions we can easily see where each would be useful during a planning cycle whether it be in a Copy process, or a Top Down distribution or even a calculation to execute the population of a Trending report for planning purposes.

6.2.5 Allocation Script Logic

Now that you're feeling more comfortable with the concept of Script Logic, let's discuss the use of Allocation in Script Logic. The prompts are a bit different from the other Script Logic that we've discussed. The Allocation process executes a distribution of the values based on a specific basis. This functionality doesn't require any additional business rules to function. All of the required processes are incorporated into the Script Logic code. There are two options when running allocations: *RUNALLOCATION is use when the allocation is only executed with one process to run, and *RUN_ALLOCATION is used if there are multiple cycles of the allocations to occur. The following is some sample Script Logic code:

```
*RUNALLOCATION
*FACTOR=<driver>
*DIM ACCOUNT WHAT=<source>; WHERE=<target>; USING=<distribution key>;
[TOTAL=<distribution key>]
*DIM <other dimensions>
*ENDALLOCATION
```

To read this, you can look at each of the different prompts within the code:

▶ FACTOR
The initial parameter is the driver to use for the calculation. This can be a fixed amount, a mathematical expression, or an expression with the prompt USING/ with TOTAL or some factor. This is the total amount to be allocated.

▶ WHAT
This is the sender for the allocation.

▶ WHERE
This is the target for the allocation.

▶ USING
This points to what is to be used for the allocation key or factor.

▶ TOTAL
This is the sum of the driver or USING amounts.

▶ DIM
This refers to additional dimensions for the allocation values that are involved in the allocation process.

Here's an example:

```
*ALLOCATION DIST2
*FACTOR=USING/TOTAL
*DIM ACCOUNT WHAT= 104010; WHERE= 104020; USING= 104030; TOTAL=<<<
*DIM ENTITY WHAT=1000; WHERE=<<<; USING=<<<; TOTAL=<<<
*DIM TIME WHAT=2011.JAN; WHERE=>>>; USING=BAS(2011.TOTAL); TOTAL=<<<
```

```
*ENDALLOCATION
*RUN_ALLOCATION DIST2
```

The result is the TOTAL amount of the dimensions ACCOUNT = 104010, ENTITY = 1000, TIME = JAN.2011 will be used to allocate to ACCOUNT = 104020, ENTITY = 1000, TIME = BAS (base members) of 2011, using ACCOUNT = 104030, ENTITY = 1000, TIME = BAS (base members) of 2011 as the factor, and the TOTAL is consistent with the source of the data.

6.2.6 Script Logic in the Automation of Data Loading

Script Logic also shows up in the process of executing different functions in BPC. The majority of the standard automated data processing is used by the consolidation process, but there are a couple of standard Script Logic prompts that you use in the planning process: allocations and currency translation. In any case, the positioning of the Script Logic is very similar. This type of Script Logic allows the calculation process to start, so the Script Logic is used as a trigger point for the data processing. In these situations the Script Logic is executed based on the Data Manager package, and then it feeds the parameters into the ABAP program that is assigned to the process chain to be executed during the calculation. Let's consider an example of this based on the currency translation process. The Script Logic is found in the ADMINISTRATION tab. Choose RULES • SCRIPT LOGIC, as shown in Figure 6.25.

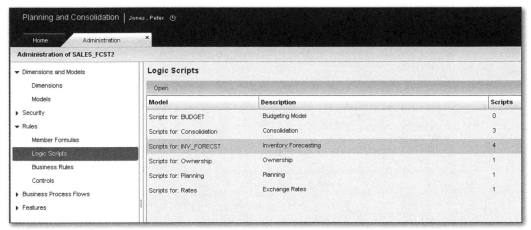

Figure 6.25 Administration Tab – Logic Scripts

Using the OPEN link, you can see several available logic scripts; in this case, we're interested in reviewing the FXTRANS script, shown in Figure 6.26.

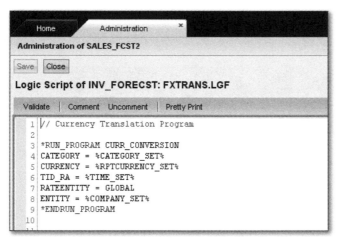

Figure 6.26 FXTRANS Logic Scripts

Click on the EDIT link to see that this is a standard script delivered by SAP with the variables of CATEGORY, CURRENCY, TIME, and ENTITY (see Figure 6.27).

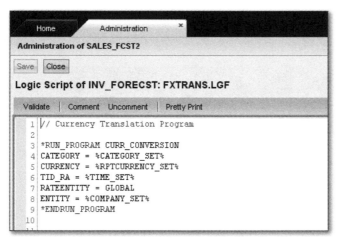

Figure 6.27 FXTRANS Currency Translation Script

After the Data Manager package is executed, the values you use in the variables are assigned to the ABAP program that is executed in the process chain. To review the additional links in this process, you need to view the FXTRANS Data Manager package and process chain. To do so, access the EPM add-in, go to the Data Manager tab, select ORGANIZE • ORGANIZE PACKAGE LIST, and view the FXTRANS package (see Figure 6.28).

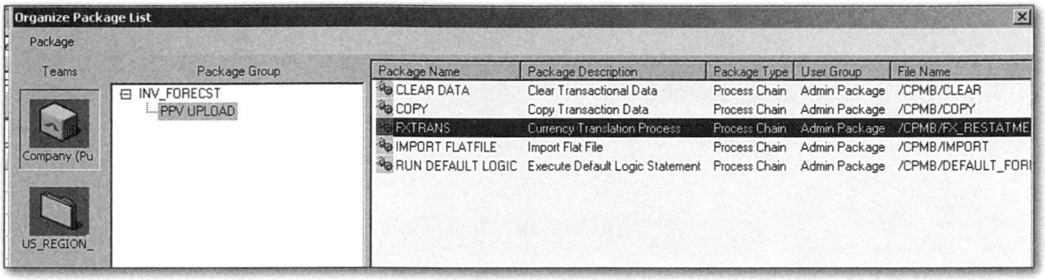

Figure 6.28 Organize Package List – FXTRANS Package

From here, right-click on the FXTRANS package, and select the MODIFY SCRIPT option to see the additional code. Figure 6.29 shows the PROMPT details, and, as expected, there is a series of variables that will take the information you enter via the FXTRANS logic script and use that information in the calculations.

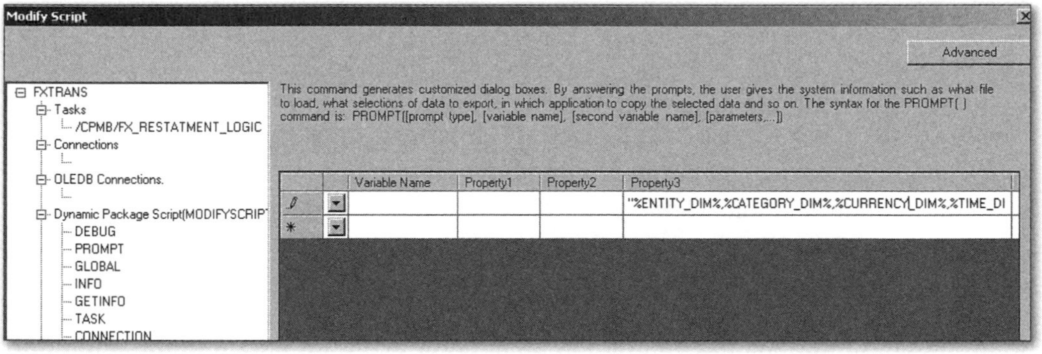

Figure 6.29 Modify Script for FXTRANS with Variables for ENTITY, CATEGORY, CURRENCY, and TIME

Look down the list and select the TASK option to see that it has the FXTRANS standard program in the VALUE column (see Figure 6.30). This will be executed after the Data Manager runs.

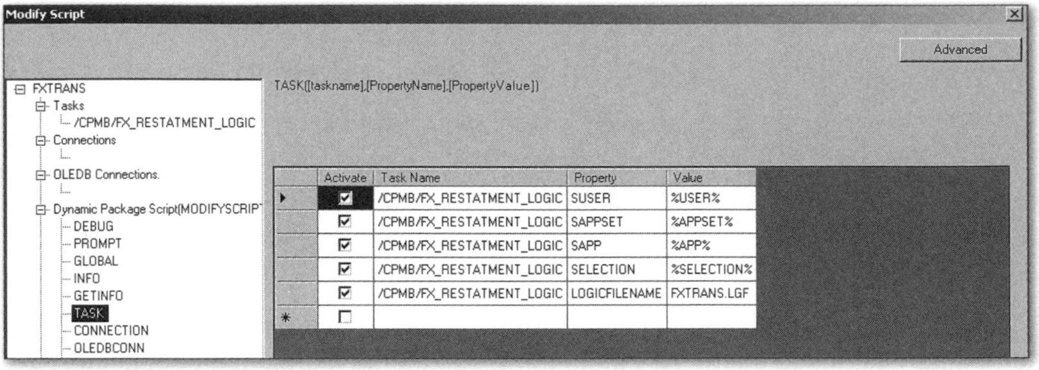

Figure 6.30 Modify Script – TASK

This automated use of Script Logic is the primary option to execute the Data Manager packages in consolidation. You'll see this much more about this in Chapter 7.

6.2.7 BAdIs and the ABAP Program

In addition to all of the other options that are available for using Script Logic, you can also insert a BAdI into the Data Manager package and execute this to further enhance capabilities. In this case, the BAdIs can be executed from the Data Manager package, or they can be directly inserted into the transformation file and be executed during the uploading process. In any case, the BAdIs are built within the BW component, and the initial location to create BAdIs is Transaction SE19. They can be inserted into a SAP system to accommodate user requirements that are too specific to be included in the standard delivery using the basic Script Logic. BAdIs can be called from within Script Logic to perform an endless variety of functions. The enhancement spot UJ_CUSTOM_LOGIC forms the initial framework for the development of the customization. Figure 6.31 shows the initial screen via Transaction SE19. To start the process of creating a new BAdI, you use the ENHANCEMENT SPOT field shown in the figure.

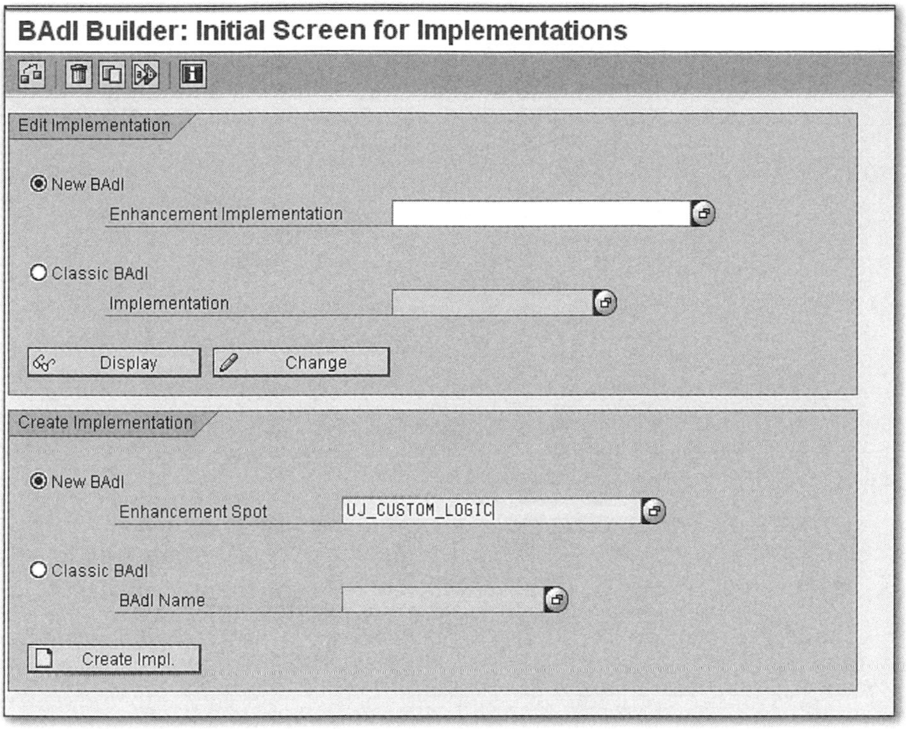

BAdI Builder: Initial Screen for Implementations

Edit Implementation

⦿ New BAdI
    Enhancement Implementation

○ Classic BAdI
    Implementation

[👓 Display] [✏ Change]

Create Implementation

⦿ New BAdI
    Enhancement Spot   UJ_CUSTOM_LOGIC

○ Classic BAdI
    BAdI Name

[🗋 Create Impl.]

Figure 6.31 Transaction SE19 – New BAdI with the Enhancement Spot

After this is created, you then click on CREATE IMPL. and work through the process of configuration for the new BAdI (see Figure 6.32).

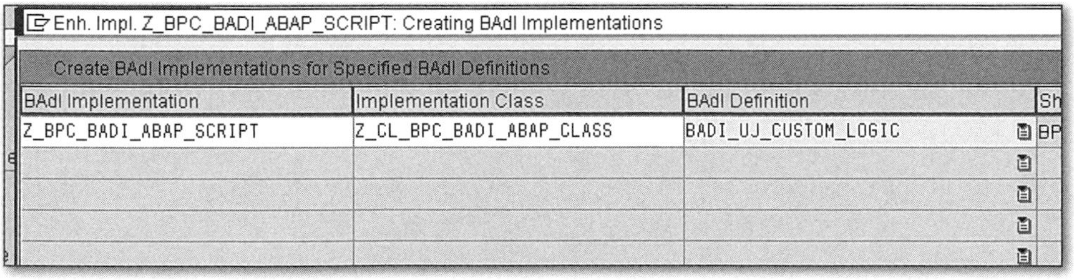

Enh. Impl. Z_BPC_BADI_ABAP_SCRIPT: Creating BAdI Implementations

Create BAdI Implementations for Specified BAdI Definitions

BAdI Implementation	Implementation Class	BAdI Definition	Sh
Z_BPC_BADI_ABAP_SCRIPT	Z_CL_BPC_BADI_ABAP_CLASS	BADI_UJ_CUSTOM_LOGIC	🗎 BP
			🗎
			🗎
			🗎
			🗎

Figure 6.32 Enhancement Implementation for BAdI Creation

After you've filled in the appropriate technical IDs, you then can start the process of inserting the code into the enhancement. Figure 6.33 shows this initial screen.

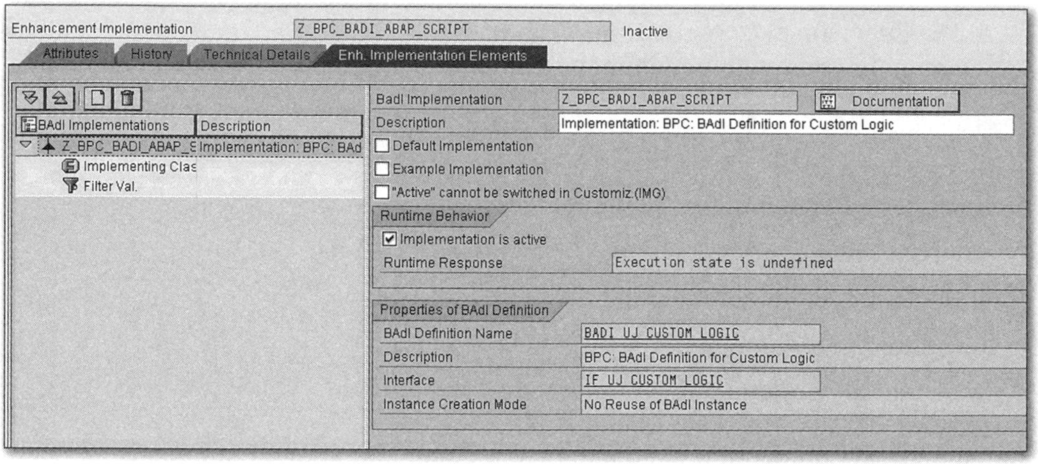

Figure 6.33 Enhancement Implementation Elements

After this is complete, you can insert this into the Data Manager package and work through the process of executing the BAdI. Figure 6.34 shows an overview of the process the system goes through after the execution of the Data Manager package. This is from the EPM add-in frontend. All of the Data Manager packages use a very similar process for the execution of the process chains. Following is the sequence shown in Figure 6.34:

❶ The BUSINESS USER clicks on the RUN PACK button, which is set up to execute the prompt to the Data Manager package.

❷ After this is executed, the system links to the Data Manager package prompts, which then execute the Script Logic that reads the Script Logic and starts the execution of the BAdI.

❸ The Data Manager package then displays a prompt to execute the Script Logic file.

❹ This in turn executes the process chain, which executes the actual BAdI and the ABAP program associated with it.

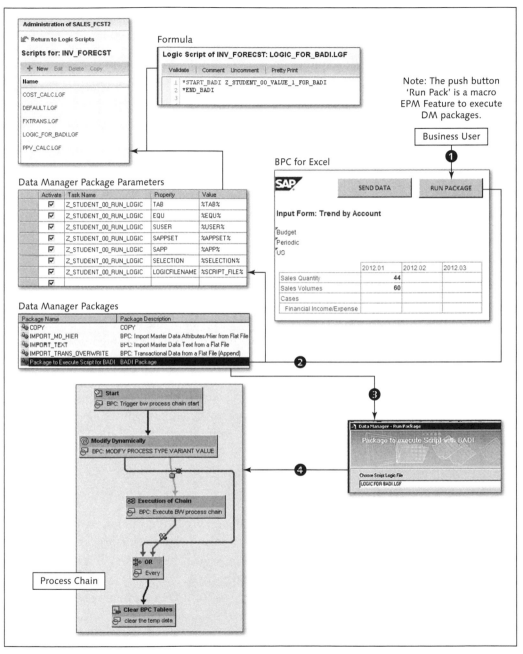

Figure 6.34 Integrated BADI and User Interface Features

As you can see, there are quite a few moving parts to this process, but as long as the appropriate technical information is passed from program to program, the process will execute. Again, the use of a BAdI is integrated into the process when all of the other standard options aren't able to support the customer request. That being said, this is becoming a more commonly used option due to the flexibility available by creating the required ABAP program.

6.3 Generic Planning Process

Now that we've covered all of the different Script Logic options, let's discuss a generic planning cycle. In each of these processes, some sort of Script Logic is probably used to help facilitate the execution of the calculations. A number of documents are available on the SAP websites such as *help.sap.com/epm* and the SDN websites under the search name of BPC Script Logic, that go into multiple scenarios around the use and configuration of Script Logic. There are many different options are available in Script Logic to accommodate the process of manipulating data for planning from basic calculations to allocations. This is one of those instances where normally you'll probably remember only those prompts and keywords that you use consistently. However, if needed, you can always reference the online documents or go to *http://help.sap.com/saphelp_bpc10_nw/helpdata/en/bpc_nw_index.htm* to obtain the necessary components of Script Logic to create the appropriate program. These are topics that could again fill another book with material but we have highlighted some of the functions and features so that you can get started and understand the concepts and approaches.

6.3.1 Initial Planned Data

The initial process of planning or budgeting requires the corporation to identify the specific set of data that it wants to use for this purpose. This process is normally consistent from planning cycle to planning cycle, but the key is to identify the appropriate data set to help facilitate the process. You can use just about any of the data sets available whether it's the actuals from the previous year, the planned or budgeted data from last year, or something more involved such as using the data set for the previous two years and executing a smoothing process to get to the correct initial data set. This can be as time consuming as you want or fairly straightforward, but the important thing is to make this initial starting point as accurate as possible. If you start with data that isn't a good sample set, then the entire planning process will generate information that is not of much use. For example, if year after year a particular department is always beating their planned revenues and expenses, then the problem may be that the initial planned data being used didn't reflect a true view of the planned amounts, so it was fairly easy to beat the estimated numbers. The same situation can occur in a budgeting scenario. A particular division has a budget that seems to always be achievable year after year. Now, I'm not saying that we need to make the budgeting process so difficult that it is unachievable but it would be a consistent budgeting process if the division doesn't hit the budget all of the time and you notice that with three periods left in the budget year they have over 50% of their budget left. This means that either a) the total consumption of the budget occurs at the very end of the year or b) that the division has not started with a fair estimate of the true budget for the year. In BPC, you can stage the identified set of data in the BPC model and possible tag it with a unique version (INIT_PLAN), so that you can identify the information in a report or input template. Normally you would like to have a pristine copy of the original plan so that if you need to you can revert back to that original raw plan and start the process over.

6.3.2 Copy Process

After the initial planned data has been specified, you execute the initial copy process from the INIT_PLAN to the WORK_PLAN version. The concept of versioning is very important during the planning process. Versions are used for a number of different reasons. The most common is for storing multiple versions of the plan for various reasons, such as versions for a WORK_PLAN_VER (the initial working version for planning activities), FINAL_VER (the final version that will be submitted to management), OPTIM_VER (the most optimistic view of the plan), PESSIM_VER (the most pessimistic view of the plan), and others. This means that each of the planners have approximately five to eight versions assigned to them for their use, but only one FINAL_VER is used to upload the set of data for final approval. In other situations, the versioning is used for simply tagging sets of data based on time. Rather than having a series of activities to freeze the information, you might decide to use versions for JAN.20XX, MARCH.20XX, etc., rather than using something like FSCT1 (for Q1 of the year), FSCT2 (for Q2 of the year), to identify a set of data. Versions are also one of those dimensions that can be offered to the business user to create as needed using the functionality available in BPC V10.0 to create master data on the fly. This way, users can generate whatever versions are required to accommodate their plan process.

> **NOTE: Master Data on the Fly**
>
> This option to create master data on the fly is a combination of the use of script logic, several BAdIs, a new process type, a new Process Chain, two Classes required to implement to align the new process type feature, a class specifically for the master data on the fly functionality, and some additional dictionary objects. This will allow the user to create their own master data directly from the EPM add-in screen while you are executing the planning process.

Generally, at this point in the copy process, you might see a system process where additional Script Logic is created, and rather than using the generic copy process to move the data from one version to another, you can add to this other features that might be required during the corporate planning process. For example, the business requirement might be to increase revenues by 10% and decrease expenses by 5%. You can incorporate this into a Script Logic sequence, and rather than having multiple steps, you can use the package link to accommodate the sequence of scripts and have everything done at the same time. This was discussed in chapter 5 with the Data Manager information. Other normal processes that might be executed during the initial copy process include the calculation of depreciation, currency translation, and additional promotional items.

During the planning process, there will be multiple times where the process of copying the data from one version to another is required. This will depend on the length of the planning process as well as the multiple iterations involved. One question which will need an answer is how many and when do I copy my planning work? If you have a very long planning process with multiple iterations or calculations going on during the process then you might want to copy a snapshot of your planning data at given times during the planning cycle. This way you will have some sort of timeline and milestone to fall back on if you have a situation where your data becomes corrupt or you end up having to redo some of the planning steps in the process. It would be difficult if after 10 steps in the planning process you find out that step number 4 was wrong or the assumptions that were made are incorrect and you have to go back to that step in the cycle and start over again. It would be better to be able to retrace your activities rather than having to start from scratch.

6.3.3   Data Transfer Processes

As you move through the planning process, you'll need to segregate the data for a number of reasons. One of the most critical reasons is for the sake of granularity and data volumes. Partitioning of data is almost always a reason for data segregation in projects. In the area of Logistics, it isn't uncommon to have multiple detailed models that roll up to a summary model. At this level, you can support the final financial statement results. The movement of data between the different levels of models is classified as a data transfer activity. In P&F, you need to have links between multiple models, and the ability to transfer information between them is critical to having one integrated view of the data. Always remember that it's much easier to go from a more detailed or granular view of the data to a summary view. To accommodate this, you'll probably see some sort of derivation process. For example, to move from a SKU level of detailed planning to a more summary level such as material groups, you need to understand how to aggregate the data by a mapping process between the base material and the material group. You can also have basic data transfers due to reporting or planning requirements. Because you can reference data from one model to another for calculations and processing, you don't have to physically move the data. One of the reasons you might need to move the data is for reporting purposes. In this case, you can perform a direct data transfer without any manipulation of the data. There's also a fine line between using the option for referencing data versus moving the data; as in other situations, you have to test the process to see if having the data actually in the model would improve the performance of the processes in the target model. In terms of actual script logic options to help support this process we saw two of them in section 1.2.3 where we could either REFERENCE (Lookup) the data from one model to another or we could COPY (Destination_App) the data from one model to another.

6.3.4 Executing Calculations in Planning

As we mentioned in the preceding discussion, you will always use some sort of calculation process in the planning, budgeting, and forecasting activities. Further calculations or realignment of the data are almost always necessary. Numerous components are available to accommodate this need to change the data (as highlighted earlier in this chapter). Some of the situations where you might use these features include the following:

▶ Trending analysis across periods (static 12 months)

▶ Rolling Trend analysis across 12 months

▶ Executing the calculation to adjust plan data for increases or decreases in revenues based on planning assumptions

- ▶ Calculating the variance between plan and actual values and then creating a plan to analyze the variances

- ▶ Extrapolating out the data across years for forecasting purposes

- ▶ Executing a top-down planning process

- ▶ Allocating plan information to reflect the appropriate assignment of revenue or expenses to departments or regions

- ▶ Enhancing the data to reflect additional derived dimension values, for example, enhancing the records to reflect a plan-specific set of values

- ▶ Performing what-if analysis on plan data

- ▶ Enhancing the plan data based on economic or competitor information

- ▶ Running iterative cycles of planning based on changes made by different groups, for example, movement of production from one plant to another requiring changes to the inventory valuation and allocation of expenses and cost

These calculations, using script logic and the DM packages, can be either dynamically or manually executed, which is left up to the business user to confirm. After the approach is confirmed, you can then either create a button in the EPM add-in for the business user to execute or have the process scheduled to be executed at a given time during the planning cycles.

6.3.5 Top-Down Planning

Another generally used option is a top-down process in the planning cycle. This concept suggests that at a given time during the planning activities, the corporation identifies changes that are confirmed from the corporate management, and these amounts are required to filter down from a very high level of granularity to the lower levels. This can be done via either an allocation process or a user-built Script Logic code. In either case, there are a number of options to confirm, such as during the allocation process, do you want the amounts to be evenly divided among the different groups or use some sort of factor to allocate the amounts based on a pro-rata basis? For example, if you're going to require that sales revenue increase by $10 million, and there are four regions to allocate this amount down to—NA, SA, EUR, and ASIA—would you want to divide this amount evenly across all of the regions or divide this amount across the regions based on a factor associated to their actual revenue from the previous year? This is a significant decision that will impact the ability to achieve the sales revenue goals for the slower growth areas. That being said, you need to identify the specific factor that will divide the amounts appropriately and fairly. You can also set this up to allocate based on a process where the total amount that needs to be divided can't be divided across the regions evenly even with a factor of the previous year's sales taking differences into account. In this case, you can allocate only a portion to all of the regions and then surcharge one region with the remaining amounts. For example, only allocate $8 million, and then charge the other $2 million to the SA area due to predictions that the growth rate of South America is much higher in the coming year than previously expected. If necessary, you can also create unique allocation options by using the core Script Logic rather than relying on the standard BPC delivered allocation Script Logic.

6.3.6 Bottom-Up Planning

Bottom-up planning doesn't involve calculations, but if planned correctly, the ability to execute bottom-up planning will be available based on the dimensions within the records. A bottom-up planning process includes the aggregation of the data records to higher level dimension member values. This process is done inherently based on the member combinations. For example, if you've designed the data model correctly, you should be able to do a bottom-up plan view from SKU-level products or materials to the material group or material types. A similar bottom-up example is from a country to a region or vice versa. These links are created directly in the records as they are uploaded into the system or are created based on some sort of derivation process. This is a critical component of the planning process because you'll always have to aggregate the data up to a higher level. This can also be accomplished in a report based on the use of hierarchies. In the Logistics area, the product hierarchy has three standard levels—material, material type, and material group. If the data model has been defined correctly, the bottom-up display from material to material type to material group is inherent in the design.

6.4 Summary

In this chapter, we reviewed different approaches to planning, forecasting, and budgeting, with a focus on both the global and regional views and challenges. We discussed some of the challenges that you will face during the planning process in terms of types of planning and areas of planning. We also reviewed the use of Script Logic during the planning process and how the use of BAdIs will help enhance the functionality and features available for planners and analysts. We listed some of the commonly used Script Logic keywords as well as the different keywords used in MS BPC and NW BPC. We also reviewed and discussed allocations, top-down planning, bottom-up processes, and other data transfer features. We also discussed some of the basic planning processes used during the different cycles of planning, budgeting, and forecasting and in the final portion of the chapter we followed a series of generic planning steps and activities that might be encountered during the planning process.

In this chapter, we'll discuss why companies need to consolidate their books and how we do it in SAP Business Planning and Consolidation (BPC) version for SAP NetWeaver. We'll explain how to maintain ownership data, use journals, configure business rules, and set up Script Logic, as well as how to configure Data Manager packages. You'll learn how to use balancing logic as well as how to set up and use the Consolidation Monitor.

7 Consolidation in BPC

Those of you who have worked in corporate accounting or implemented consolidation systems may already have a really good idea of what the month-end process entails. For those of you without that background, we'll touch on a few of the basic concepts in the overview of consolidation. And then, we'll discuss how consolidation is performed in BPC.

7.1 Overview of Consolidation

In this section, we'll go over some of the fundamentals of consolidations. After that we'll discuss the four major steps in the process: prepare, collect, consolidate, and report. Then we'll introduce the business rules.

7.1.1 What Consolidation Is All About

The primary reason corporations need to consolidate their financials at month end is that they are made up of multiple legal subsidiaries in one or more countries. As way of example, Figure 7.1 outlines an ownership investment structure. In this example, the corporate holding company is C9000, and it is based in the United States.

This corporation operates in a few different countries in the Americas, Europe, and Asia Pacific, and, therefore, it uses a few different local currencies and may also use multiple accounting standards such as US GAAP (Generally Accepted Accounting Principles) and IFRS (International Financial Reporting Standards).

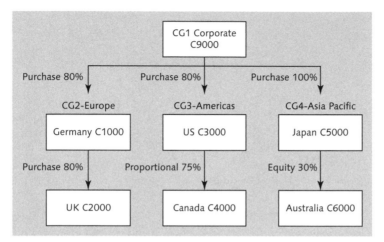

Figure 7.1 Ownership Investment Structure

In addition, subsidiaries can have a variety of ownership relationships such as a total ownership like Japan pictured in Figure 7.1 (C9000 owns 100% of C5000) or the UK subsidiary, which has 80% of its shares owned by Germany. In the Europe group, for example, the financial statements at the group level must reflect the fact that Germany has an ownership interest in UK's equity.

Also, there are usually transactions between the subsidiaries, so each company can have intercompany sales, cost of goods sold (COGS), intercompany accounts payable (IC AP) and receivables (IC AR), and so on, on its books.

Using the prior example as a backdrop, the goal of the consolidation process is to generate a set of group financial statements in the group currency with values that reflect the group accounting standards.

Because this corporation is based in the United States, the group currency will be USD, and US GAAP will be the set of standards to go by.

The consolidated financial statements also need to only reflect third-party transactions and not intercompany, so all intercompany sales, COGS, IC AP, IC AR, and so on, need to be eliminated.

Next, let's go over a typical month-end close from a functional perspective (we'll get into the technical configuration steps later in this chapter).

7.1.2 Performing Consolidations with Planning and Consolidation

From a broad perspective, there are four key steps when preparing for and executing consolidation (see Figure 7.2):

▶ **Prepare**
The prepare step includes the setup of the dimensions, loading the master data, creating the business rules, and configuring the security to support the process of consolidation.

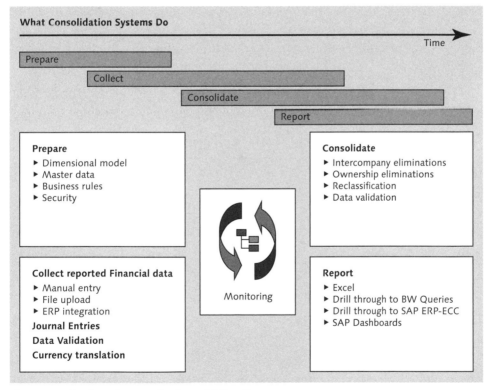

Figure 7.2 The Four Steps in the Consolidation Process

▶ **Collect**
The collect step involves collecting data via manual entry, file uploads, SAP ERP integration, and journal entries. Then the data is validated, and currency translation is performed.

▶ **Consolidate**
The consolidate step involves running the eliminations, reclassification, and data validation.

▶ **Report**
The report step involves analyzing the data via Excel, drilling through to SAP NetWeaver Business Warehouse (BW) queries and SAP-ERPECC, and SAP BusinessObjects Dashboard Designer (Dashboards, for short).

Now, let's walk through a more detailed set of month-end activities. A sample list of steps can be viewed from the business process flow in Figure 7.3. This list represents a typical Consolidation Business Process Flow.

▶ BALANCE CARRY FORWARD
The classic first step is to carry forward the prior year balance sheet closing balances into the current year opening balances.

▶ IMPORT ACTUALS
Then the current month's financial data from the local subsidiaries is imported into planning and consolidation.

▶ DATA VALIDATION
A data validation to perform integrity checks such as Assets = Liabilities and Owners Equity can be run at this point as well as later in the process.

▶ RECLASSIFICATIONS
Automated adjustments can be run at this point in the process as well as later.

▶ JOURNALS
Manual adjusting entries to meet the group standards can be entered at this point in the process as well as later.

▶ OWNERSHIP DATA
The ownership methods and percentages are entered into the Ownership model.

▶ CURRENCY TRANSLATION
Local currency is translated into other reporting currencies if necessary.

- IC Matching

  IC AP/AR differences must be identified and booked.

- IC Eliminations – US Method

  IC revenue and COGS, for example, are eliminated.

- Consolidation Monitor

  The Consolidation Monitor is used to run group currency translation and ownership eliminations, for example.

- Publish the Group Financials

  The final set of financial statements is published.

The steps in your month-end closing process may vary from this example. For instance, you may not use the IC Eliminations – US Method. Also the sequence of the steps may vary; for example, you might update the ownership data in the very first step.

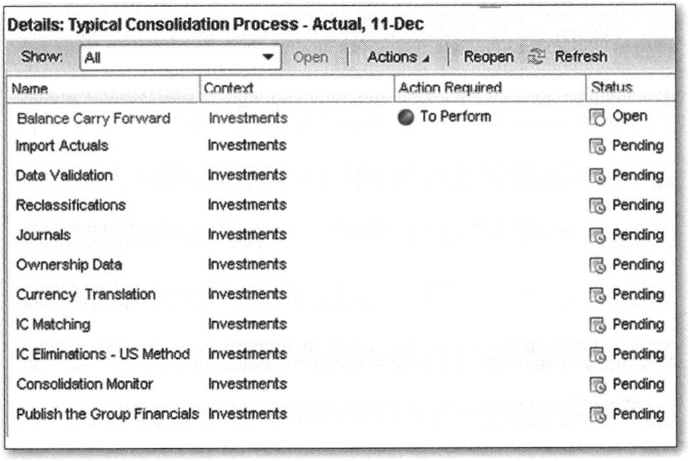

Details: Typical Consolidation Process - Actual, 11-Dec			
Show: All ▼ Open | Actions ◢ | Reopen ⇄ Refresh			
Name	Context	Action Required	Status
Balance Carry Forward	Investments	● To Perform	▣ Open
Import Actuals	Investments		▣ Pending
Data Validation	Investments		▣ Pending
Reclassifications	Investments		▣ Pending
Journals	Investments		▣ Pending
Ownership Data	Investments		▣ Pending
Currency Translation	Investments		▣ Pending
IC Matching	Investments		▣ Pending
IC Eliminations - US Method	Investments		▣ Pending
Consolidation Monitor	Investments		▣ Pending
Publish the Group Financials	Investments		▣ Pending

Figure 7.3 A Typical Consolidation Business Process Flow

At this point, you should have a better understanding of the reasons for consolidation and what the process entails. Because the business rules are the center of attention when it comes to consolidating financial statements, let's discuss those next.

7.1.3   Introducing Business Rules

First, let's define business rules and discuss how to turn them on. At the 50,000 foot level, *business rules* are defined as the planning and consolidation user interfaces to enter metadata into database tables.

The metadata includes, for example, source dimension members, target dimension members, filtering criteria, and settings that are used to control the calculations.

The system uses ABAP code to read the business rules to perform calculations and ultimately write data records into the InfoCube.

Business rules are defined at the environment level, grouped under the GLOBAL DEFINITIONS, and also at the model level.

There are two environment-level business rules:

▶ **Methods**
These are different types of consolidation methods such as the 86-Purchase Method, 70-Proportional Method, 90-Holding Method, and 30-Equity Method.

▶ **Method-based Multipliers**
This table contains rules that are used to select entity source values and apply percentages to those values to ultimately book new data records.

On the ADMINISTRATION tab, the METHODS and METHOD-BASED MULTIPLIERS are grouped under GLOBAL DEFINITIONS as shown in Figure 7.4.

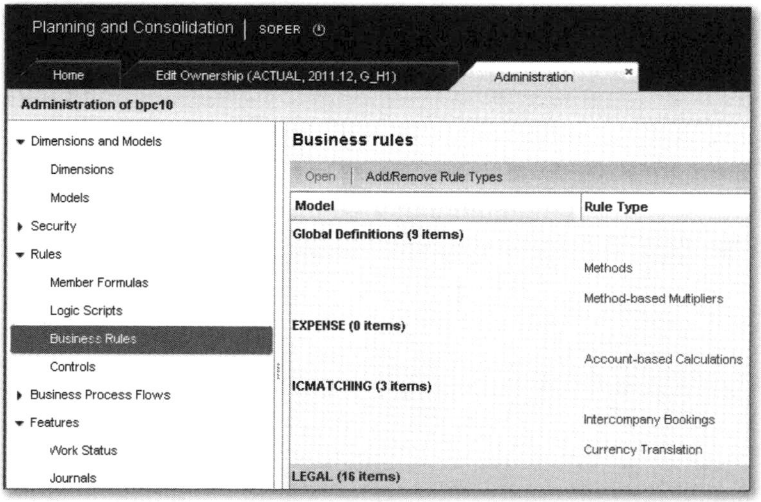

Figure 7.4   Global Definitions of Business Rules

There are six business rule types for consolidation type models as listed here and shown in Figure 7.5:

▶ INTERCOMPANY BOOKINGS
This rule is used to book IC differences as mentioned previously in the IC Matching step.

▶ CURRENCY TRANSLATION
This rule is used to translate local currency values into reporting and group currency.

▶ ELIMINATIONS AND ADJUSTMENTS
This rule is used to eliminate ownership as well as other intercompany activities.

▶ US ELIMINATIONS
This is used to perform simpler IC activity such as revenue and COGS.

▶ CARRY-FORWARD
This is used to carry prior period closing balances.

▶ ACCOUNT-BASED CALCULATIONS
This is used to perform reclassifications.

To use a business rule for a model, you must activate it by going to the Web Client and choosing PLANNING AND CONSOLIDATION ADMINISTRATION • RULES • BUSINESS RULES • SELECT ADD/REMOVE RULE TYPES.

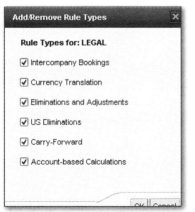

Figure 7.5 Add/Remove Types for the Consolidation Model

So now with this general background on business rules, let's head toward the setup of ownership data and elimination methods.

7.2 Ownership Data and Elimination Methods

Because the majority of corporations who use BPC for consolidations own multiple legal subsidiaries, let's discuss the ownership process, and how ownership data is recorded into the Ownership model. This data will be used later to perform intercompany and ownership interest elimination entries. We'll also delve into the differences among the purchase, proportional, and equity methods.

7.2.1 The Ownership Process

The ownership process comes into play in scenarios in which a corporation has many legal subsidiaries with a wide variety of ownership interests and complex relationships that require you to automate the month-end accounting entries.

First let's go over some of the key terms and then get right into the Ownership Manager to set up the investment structure and input the ownership percentages and methods.

We'll also discuss the requirements to use the Ownership Manager, including the Ownership model, the methods business rule table, the Group type and Account type dimensions.

After that, we'll use the ownership data to run the purchase, equity, and proportional eliminations. In Section 7.4, we'll go through the business rules configuration for the first time.

Now, let's review some of the key terms.

- **Investor**
  The buyer. For example, company C9000 buys company C1000. C9000 is therefore the investor.

- **Investee**
  The company being purchased, such as C1000 in the example just mentioned.

- **Direct share**
  The % ownership between the investor and the investee. For example, C9000 owns 80% of C1000's nonvoting shares.

- **Indirect share**
  The % ownership between the higher level parent and the investee. For example,

C1000 owns 80% of C2000. Therefore, C9000's indirect share of C2000 is 64% (.8 × .8). Indirect share is also referred to as group share.

▶ **Minority interest**

The % portion of the investee not owned by the parent. For example, C2000's minority interest is 20%.

▶ **Goodwill**

The difference between the purchase price and the book value of the investee's equity.

▶ **Method**

The consolidation method such as purchase, proportional, or equity.

▶ **POWN**

The percentage of ownership (how much they are owned by the group). This represents the percentage of an entity's nonvoting shares that other entities own, directly or indirectly. Direct percent ownership is the percentage of regular non-voting shares of stock owned by each entity.

▶ **PCON**

The percentage of consolidation. This represents the percentage of an entity's values that consolidates to its group.

▶ **PCTRL**

The percentage of control (how much they are controlled by the group). This represents the percentage of an entity's voting shares that other entities own directly or indirectly. It can also be used to determine the consolidation method.

The corporate consolidation group will be referred to as CG1 (consolidation group 1), and it represents the corporate level with C9000 as the corporate holding company. This corporation includes the three consolidation groups: Europe-CG2, America-CG3, and Asia Pacific-CG4.

Planning and consolidation uses customer-defined integers to designate method assignments. We'll use 86 for the purchase method, 70 for proportional, and 30 for equity. Also, parents will use a method of 90. We'll see how to set these up shortly in the Methods table.

The data that forms the investment structure is stored as transaction data in the Ownership model and can be input manually via the Ownership Manager or planning and consolidation input forms, or you can do a flat file import.

7.2.2   Setting Up Ownership Data

To record ownership data, there are two required settings in the Ownership model:

▶ Non-interco Member in Ownership
This setting contains the intercompany member that is used for external, third-party transactions.

▶ Parent/child property used for the hierarchy of groups
Contains the property in the group dimension used to form the ownership hierarchy (PARENT_GROUP in this case).

These settings are displayed in Figure 7.6.

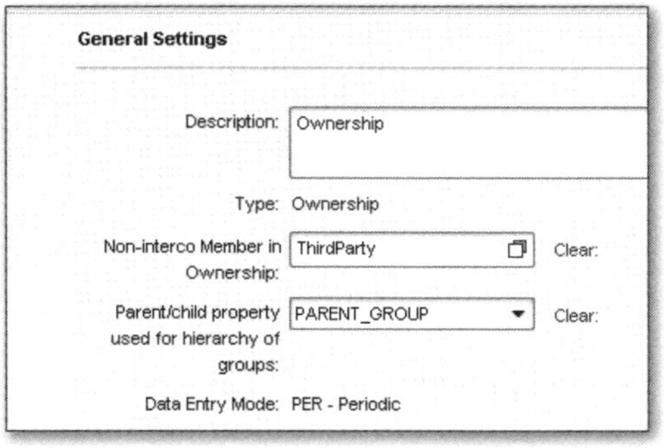

Figure 7.6   General Settings for the Ownership Type Model

In addition, Ownership models can use a Data Entry Mode of either PER-Periodic or YTD-Year to Data basis.

To access the Ownership Manager, go to the Web Client, and click on the new Consolidation Central. In Figure 7.7, you can see the Ownership Manager (in read mode) from the Home tab.

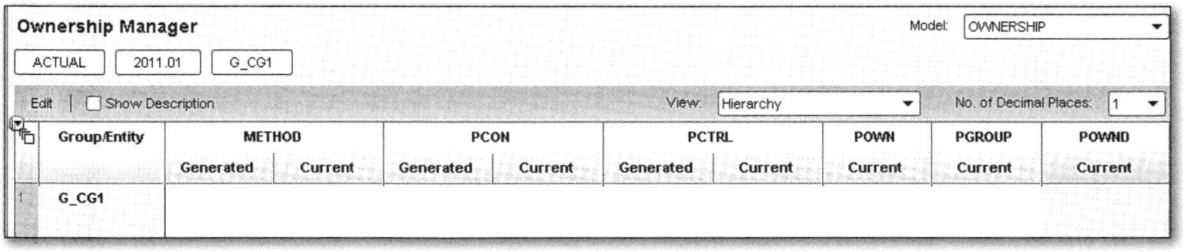

Figure 7.7   Initial Ownership Manager Screen in Display Model

When you first go into the OWNERSHIP MANAGER, select the OWNERSHIP model, and set your VIEW to HIERARCHY.

The data is stored by category, year/period, and consolidation group, so you'll need to make those data selections when you work with the Ownership Manager.

In the columns, you'll see the Ownership model account member IDs such as METHOD, PCON, and PCTRL for CURRENT, which is based on data you enter, and GENERATED, which is based on system-generated values.

To maintain the ownership data, choose EDIT, and a new tab opens up called EDIT OWNERSHIP with the context members for the category, group, and time dimensions as shown in Figure 7.8. Now you'll be able to read and write data back to the Ownership model.

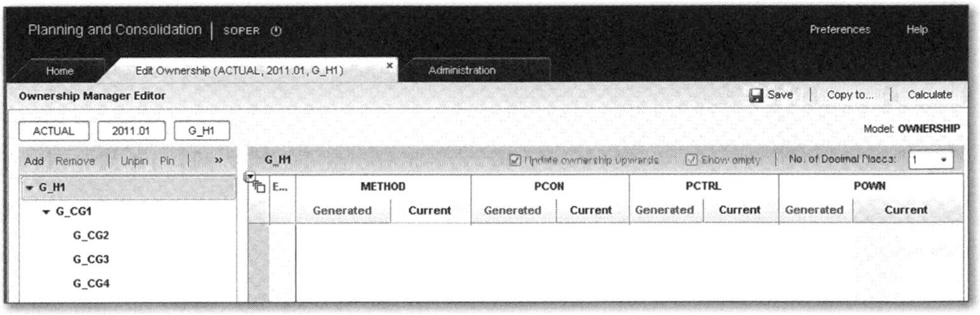

Figure 7.8 Initial Ownership Manager Editor Screen

The rows are made up of the PARENT_GROUP property values in the CONSGROUP dimension.

In the CONSGROUP dimension shown in Figure 7.9, the PARENT_GROUP column is being used to assign G_H1 as the parent for G_CG1, and G_CG1 is the parent for the C_CG2-4 members.

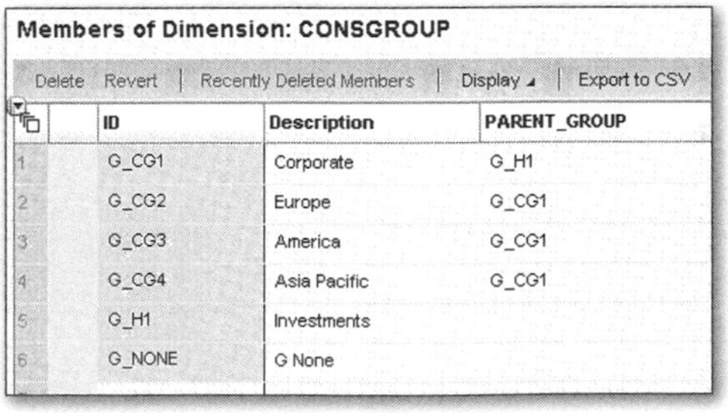
Members of Dimension: CONSGROUP

Delete Revert | Recently Deleted Members | Display | Export to CSV

	ID	Description	PARENT_GROUP
1	G_CG1	Corporate	G_H1
2	G_CG2	Europe	G_CG1
3	G_CG3	America	G_CG1
4	G_CG4	Asia Pacific	G_CG1
5	G_H1	Investments	
6	G_NONE	G None	

Figure 7.9 Group Dimension Members

The next activity will be to set up the initial parent child relationships. By selecting each group and using the ADD button, you can set up the initial ownership structure based on Figure 7.1, shown earlier. Remember that we said that C9000 is the corporate holding company, and in the Europe group, we have C1000 and C2000 and so forth. That ownership structure in the system appears as shown in Figure 7.10.

Figure 7.10   Initial Ownership Structure

Next, we'll assign the methods for each group and input the percentage data. If you select the G_CG2 group and then double-click the intersection of C1000 and CURRENT METHOD, you can select the method from a dropdown list to make the selections.

In the G_CG2 group shown in Figure 7.11, you can see that a METHOD of 90-HOLDING has been assigned to C1000 because it is the parent of the group. C2000 is assigned the 86-PURCHASE method because we own over 50% of its shares. The investee C2000 is incorporated fully into the group, so the PCON percentage is 100%, and the group owns 80% of their shares. Because C1000 is the parent, it is therefore 100% incorporated (PCON) and 100% owned (POWN).

This same approach is used for G_CG3 and G_CG4 except that the PCON for C4000 is 70% because the proportional method doesn't call for having all of the investee's financials incorporated into the group. Likewise, C6000 will have a PCON of 30% for the same reason.

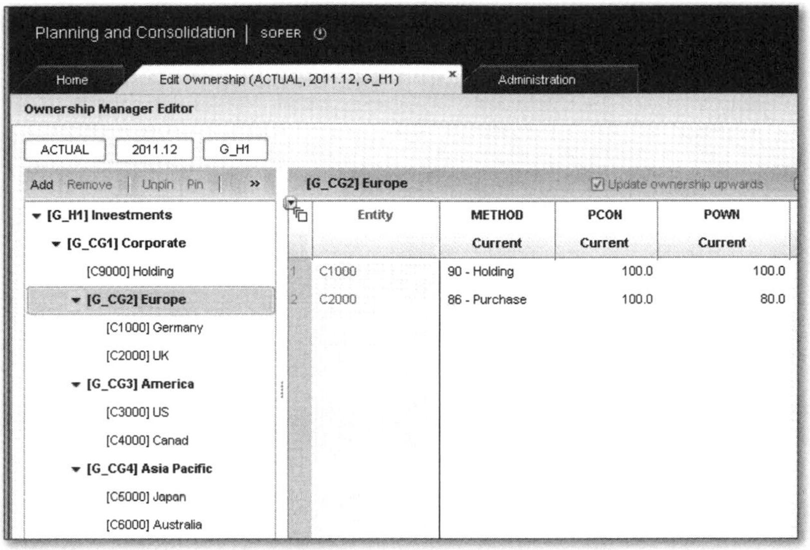

Figure 7.11 Ownership Data for Europe

Now that the method assignments are complete for the three consolidation groups G_CG2 – G-CG4, the ownership methods can be set up for the top group G_CG1 as displayed in Figure 7.12.

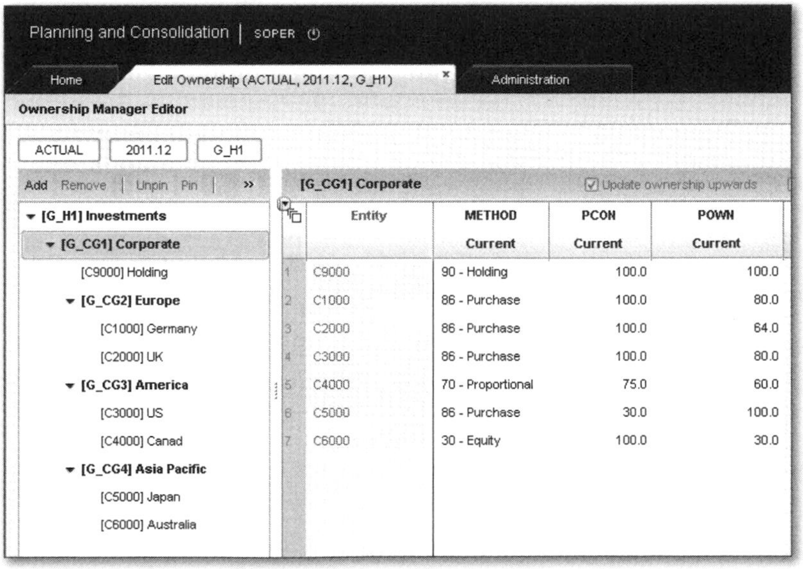

Figure 7.12 Ownership Manager Editor – Ownership Data for the Corporation

This ownership data will be used to book elimination entries at each group level. The example in Figure 7.12 is relatively straightforward. Planning and consolidation can certainly handle more complex ownership structures with hundreds of entities as well as entities with multiple parents.

The UPDATE OWNERSHIP UPWARDS checkbox can be used to populate the ownership data into the G_CG1 group because it is further up in the hierarchy. Selecting SHOW EMPTY will display IDs with no PCON and POWN, for example.

By saving this data to the Ownership model, you can record the ownership structure and method assignments into the database.

You can easily copy this data from one month into several months at once via the Ownership Manager COPY TO button at the top of the screen.

Also, the CALCULATE button can be used to generate proposed methods and PCON values.

The methods used, such as 90–HOLDING and 86–PURCHASE, are set up in the GLOBAL DEFINITION METHODS business rule table shown in Figure 7.13.

> **Note: Method Codes**
>
> You can use two- or three-digit method codes; however, 99 is a reserved method that represents all intercompany IDs.

The METHODS table values also include percent control (PCTRL) threshold values (in the SHARE RANGE column) that the system can use to propose the method and the percent consolidation (PCON). In the example shown in Figure 7.13, an integer of 90 is used for the PARENT method with a METHOD TYPE of H (HOLDING).

The PURCHASE method is set up as 86 with METHOD TYPE of G (GLOBAL, i.e., 100% incorporated), and so on.

The SHARE RANGE 0.75<,<=1.00 is interpreted as follows: if PCTRL is greater than 75% and less than or equal to 100%, the system will generate a proposed method of G–Purchase and will generate a proposed PCON value of 100% when ownership calculation is executed.

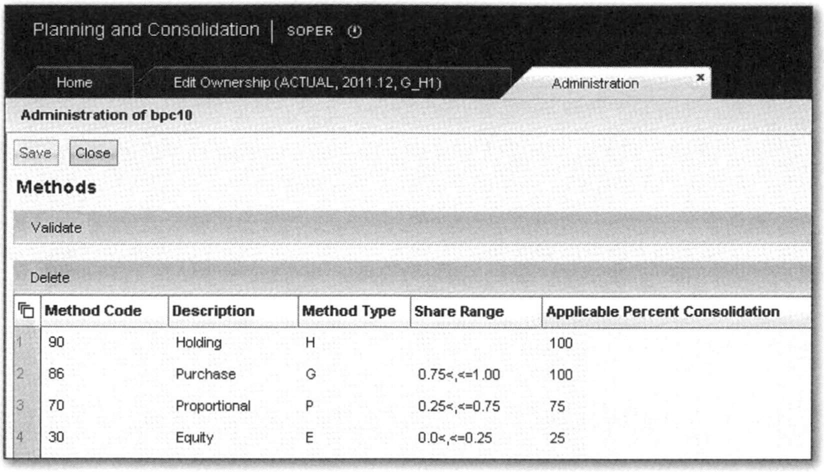

	Method Code	Description	Method Type	Share Range	Applicable Percent Consolidation
1	90	Holding	H		100
2	86	Purchase	G	0.75<,<=1.00	100
3	70	Proportional	P	0.25<,<=0.75	75
4	30	Equity	E	0.0<,<=0.25	25

Figure 7.13 The Methods Business Rule Table

In static scenarios, there isn't a big need to run the ownership calculation on a frequent basis. The best application might be to perform a check when the ownership data is a little more fluid.

Now we're ready to use this ownership data to perform the purchase method elimination.

7.2.3 The Purchase Method Concept

The purchase method is typically used when the investor owns over 50% of the investee's shares. The investee is completely incorporated into the group's financial statements. If the percent ownership isn't 100%, the remainder is booked as minority interest. Any difference between the purchase price and the investee book value is captured as goodwill.

The purchase method is the method of choice for companies following US GAAP with ownership of over 50%.

In Figure 7.14, C1000 acquired C2000 for an investment of 80,000. The aggregated amounts can't be reported because they include values for both the parent and the subsidiary. Therefore, the values that are in common are eliminated to produce the group results.

Only 80% of the subsidiary is owned in this example, so there was a premium paid, which is booked as goodwill of 40,000, and minority interest of 10,000 is also booked for the remaining 20%.

Goodwill of 40,000 is based on the parent's share of the subsidiary equity, which is 40,000 (.8 × 50,000) for which the parent paid 80,000.

	Germany C1000	France C2000	Aggregated	Elimination Entries	Group
Goodwill				40,000	40,000
Cash	70,000	50,000	120,000		120,000
Investments	80,000		80,000	-80,000	0
Total Assets	**150,000**	**50,000**	**200,000**	**-40,000**	**160,000**
Common Stock	100,000	50,000	150,000	-50,000	100,000
Retained Earnings	50,000		50,000		50,000
Minority Interest			0	10,000	10,000
Total Liabilities and Owners Equity	**150,000**	**50,000**	**200,000**	**-40,000**	**160,000**

Figure 7.14 A Purchase Method Example

The elimination entries described in Figure 7.14 take place when a company is first acquired by an investor. This is referred to as the *first consolidation* entries.

In periods after the initial acquisition, the accounting entries are referred to as *subsequent consolidation* entries. For example, if you own 80% of a subsidiary, you can only claim 80% of their annual net income while the minority share is 20%. Therefore, the subsequent consolidation eliminates net income from the investee.

7.2.4   The Proportional and Equity Method Concepts

The proportional method is similar to the purchase method in that the investor usually owns over 50% of the investee's shares; however, the investee isn't completely incorporated into the group financials, and minority interest isn't booked.

When using the proportional method, any difference between the purchase price and the investee book value is captured as goodwill. The proportional method isn't used as often as the purchase method when ownership is over 50%. The equity method is used in cases where ownership is less than 50%.

When using the equity method, the investee's financial statements aren't completely included in the group statements. Goodwill is booked in the equity method as well if there is a difference between the purchase price and the book value of the investee's shares. The equity method is applicable for companies following US GAAP, for example, and ownership is less than 50%.

In summary, we've discussed how to record an investment structure as transaction data into the Ownership model, and we've also reviewed the differences among the purchase, proportional, and equity methods.

To help prepare the data to run the ownership eliminations, you may need to adjust the raw data via journal entries.

7.3   Setting Up Journal Entries

In this section, we'll discuss how to configure and use journal entries in planning and consolidation. In general, manual journal entries are necessary to make adjusting entries to your financial statements. Conceptually these are the same as journal entries in OLTP systems except that these are being used to adjust the data in BPC that came from your OLTP systems.

7.3.1   The Business Scenario for Using Journal Entries

After the raw data is imported into the Consolidation model or even after eliminations have been executed, there are group-level adjusting entries that typically need to be made. Most of these are in cases that can't be automated in the reclassification business rule or Script Logic. For example, a one-time adjustment to depreciation and accumulated depreciation might be required if the local subsidiary was more aggressive in its depreciation calculation versus the group accounting standard.

7.3.2   Creating Journal Templates

A journal template must be built to use journals. The template is used to identify whether dimensions are located in the line items (rows) or in the header of the journal. Journal templates can be built and maintained from the Web Client in ADMINISTRATION under FEATURES. A model can only have one journal template.

When configuring journals, the journal parameters are used to force debits to equal credits and also to allow journals to be reopened. The term "reopen" is misleading in this case. It actually means that an existing journal can be copied into another new journal ID with the signs reversed, for example. The REOPEN RULES tab in the JOURNAL TEMPLATE contains the sign reversal setting as well as SOURCE and DESTINATION dimension members if you want to copy a journal into different members.

When configuring the REOPEN RULES tab, accounts are selected initially by the ACCOUNT TYPE property such as AST (assets). The FILTERING PROPERTY dropdown can be used to further select accounts based on properties such as DIMLIST.

In Figure 7.15, when a journal has accounts 11112000 and 1211000 that are reopened, their values will be reversed because the SIGN is "-".

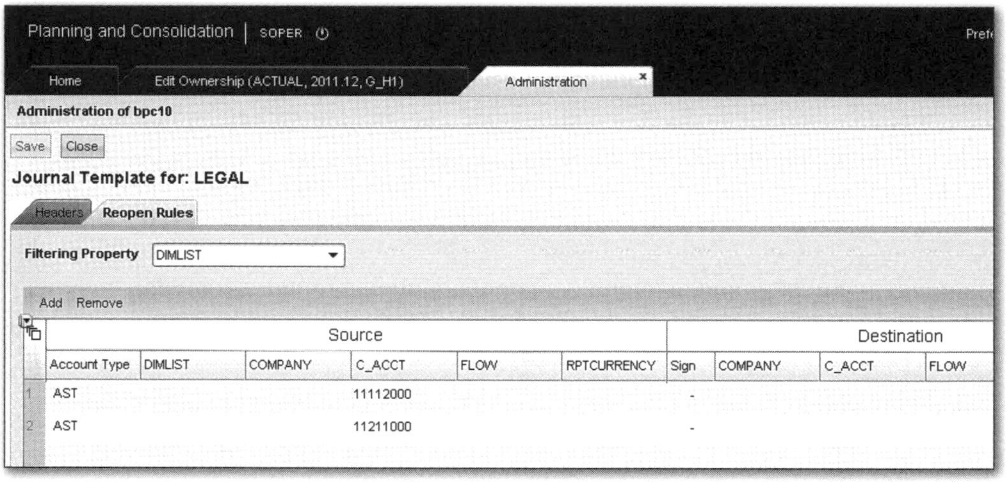

			Source			Sign	Destination		
	Account Type	DIMLIST	COMPANY	C_ACCT	FLOW	RPTCURRENCY	Sign	COMPANY	C_ACCT	FLOW
1	AST			11112000			-			
2	AST			11211000			-			

Figure 7.15 Journal Reopen Rules

Because the DESTINATION C_ACCT dimension is blank, the same accounts as shown in the SOURCE field in Figure 7.15 will be reversed. All remaining dimensions will have the same members as the original journal ID.

When creating a new template, you can decide whether dimensions are to be used in the header versus the rows. This is a key decision point because after some journals have been posted, the dimensions in the rows can't be moved to the header without deleting the journal detail table entries.

If you create journal entries across companies and currencies, you should turn on the settings BALANCED BY ENTITY and BALANCED BY CURRENCY.

ADDITIONAL HEADERS are used to categorize journal entries similar to document types in SAP ECC. For example a journal entry for CLOSING can be assigned a value of Finished Goods Inventory (FGI) for that type of adjusting entry. You can also use an additional header with a date field to do cash flow forecasting.

7.3.3 How to Control Journal Activity

Because journal entries are manually entered, you need to know how to control that activity. To maintain journal templates and create journal entries, the following security journal tasks are required.

- ▶ MANAGE
    - ▶ Create and maintain journal templates
    - ▶ Clear journal tables
    - ▶ Create journals
- ▶ EDIT
  Create or modify journal entries.
- ▶ POST
  Post journal entries.
- ▶ VIEW
  View journal entries.
- ▶ UNPOST
  Unpost journal entries. This will change the journal status to Unposted and will also reverse the values in the database.
- ▶ LOCK/UNLOCK
  Lock and unlock journal entries.
- ▶ REOPEN
  Reopen journal entries.

Based on the this list, you can see that there are quite a few tasks related to journals, including a separate task for creating versus posting journals, which provides for separation of duties.

In addition to security, work status can be used control who can post a journal entry based on various work states. For example, if the work state is approved for period 6 2012, then no journal postings are allowed for that time frame.

A popular journal control feature is the idea of limiting which dimension members can be used in journal postings by using the ENABLEJRN property. You can use this property in any dimension type, but it's best used with the DataSource type dimension on members used exclusively for journals such as MJ_Group (manual journal, group adjusting entries). As a result, only the MJ_Group member can be used to create a journal.

7.3.4 Creating Journal Entries

From consolidation central, users create new journals by selecting the NEW button to open a new tab called NEW JOURNAL, as shown in Figure 7.16.

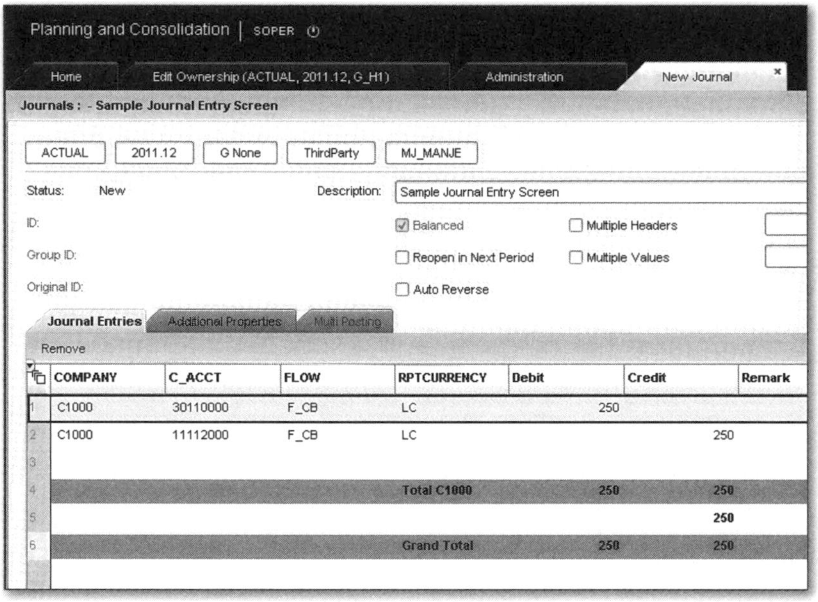

Figure 7.16 New Journal Tab

The header of the journal is automatically populated with the user's context members, which results in quicker journal creation. The DESCRIPTION field is used to describe the purpose of the entry and add other important textual information. As you can see there a quite few options when creating journals. Let's take a look at the definition of each option:

▶ BALANCED
This option allows you to require that journals are balanced upon posting. In Figure 7.16, it's grayed out because we set journals to balance in the journal template.

446

- ▶ REOPEN IN NEXT PERIOD
  This option allows you to reopen (copy) the journal entry to another account in a subsequent time period.

- ▶ AUTO REVERSE
  This option allows you to automatically reverse the journal entry in the next time period.

- ▶ MULTIPLE HEADERS
  This option enables you to post multiple periods at once. For example, a journal for three months will actually generate three new journal IDs, and the first ID will also be identified as the group ID.

- ▶ MULTIPLE VALUES
  This option enables you to post different values per month, for example.

In summary, we've seen how to create a journal template for a model, how to control journal activities, and how to create new journal entries.

Next, we'll discuss how to set up and execute other consolidation tasks.

7.4   Setting Up and Executing Consolidation Tasks

In this section, we'll configure and execute a typical set of month-end consolidation tasks, including the following:

- ▶ Balance carry forward
- ▶ Reclassification
- ▶ Currency translation
- ▶ Purchase method elimination
- ▶ Proportional method elimination
- ▶ Equity method elimination
- ▶ Intercompany matching
- ▶ Intercompany eliminations
- ▶ US eliminations

We'll dive into ownership eliminations and also discuss how to use balancing logic.

Now let's turn our attention to the tasks that are performed during the close. Let's get into balance carry forward (BCF) first because that's usually the first task of a fiscal year.

7.4.1 Balance Carry Forward

If you're an accountant, this certainly won't be a new topic for you because almost every accounting system has a way to perform BCF. I think you'll start to see how flexible BPC is as we go through the set up for BCF.

Balance Carry Forward Business Scenario

BCF traditionally is used to carry forward closing balances from the prior year end to opening balances for the next fiscal year for balance sheet accounts. Most accounts are copied into the same accounts for the new year except for current year retained earnings, which is carried forward into the prior year retained earnings account.

Balance Carry Forward Components

For BCF to work properly, the FLOW dimension must have one member with a FLOW_TYPE property value of OPENING and one with a value of CLOSING. In Figure 7.17, the ID F_OB has a FLOW_TYPE property value of OPENING and so forth.

In addition, the DataSource dimension has a property called COPYOPENING which must contain a value of Y for members to be included in the BCF job, as you can see in Figure 7.17.

Next, you need to configure the BCF business rule. This rule basically copies records from the source members into the destination members. You can also reverse the sign if needed and filter by audit type.

The CARRY-FORWARD business rule has the following fields and settings:

▶ SOURCE ACCOUNT
The source account base level, parent, or DIMLIST property value is selected.

▶ SOURCE FLOW
The source flow base level, parent, or DIMLIST property value is selected.

▶ SOURCE AUDIT (DataSource)
The source DataSource base level, parent, or DIMLIST property value is selected.

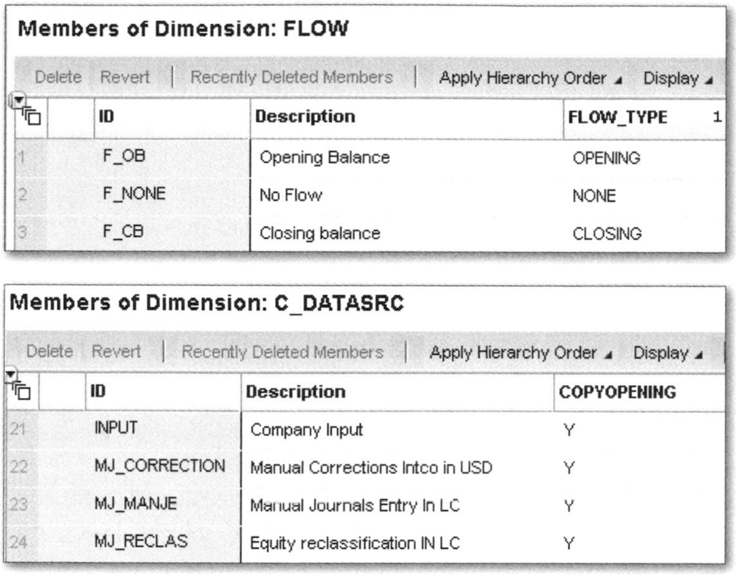

Members of Dimension: FLOW

Delete   Revert | Recently Deleted Members | Apply Hierarchy Order ◢   Display ◢

	ID	Description	FLOW_TYPE	1
1	F_OB	Opening Balance	OPENING	
2	F_NONE	No Flow	NONE	
3	F_CB	Closing balance	CLOSING	

Members of Dimension: C_DATASRC

Delete   Revert | Recently Deleted Members | Apply Hierarchy Order ◢   Display ◢

	ID	Description	COPYOPENING
21	INPUT	Company Input	Y
22	MJ_CORRECTION	Manual Corrections Intco in USD	Y
23	MJ_MANJE	Manual Journals Entry In LC	Y
24	MJ_RECLAS	Equity reclassification IN LC	Y

Figure 7.17   Important Flow and DataSource dimension members and Properties for BCF

▶ DESTINATION ACCOUNT
The destination account base level or parent is selected. If blank, it will inherit the account from the source data records.

▶ DESTINATION FLOW
The destination flow base level or parent. If blank, it will inherit the flow member from the source data records.

▶ DESTINATION AUDIT (DataSource)
The destination DataSource base level or parent. If blank, it will inherit from the source data records.

▶ REVERSE SIGN
Reverse the sign of the source value.

▶ AUDIT TYPE
Select the audit type to include:

  ▶ A: ALL

  ▶ I: INPUT

  ▶ M: MANUAL

> **Note: Automatic Audit Type**
>
> You can't select the automatic audit type because the BCF rule doesn't carry those values forward; the eliminations and adjustments rule does that.

- SAME PERIOD
  If selected, the source time period is the same as the destination. Otherwise, the source data is the last period of the prior year.
- APPLY TO YTD
  In a periodic model, select to calculate the YTD value to copy into the next year for example.

Figure 7.18 shows a BCF rule with the following three rows:

- In the first row, the entire balance sheet (1) closing balance is carried forward into the same accounts using the opening balance flow and a unique Destination Audit ID of AJ_BCF. Using a unique audit ID such as AJ_BCF allows for easy identification of the values carried forward.
- In the second row, the current year retaining earnings (25712000) that is carried forward in row 1 is negated.
- In the third row, the current year retained earnings is written into prior year retained earnings (25714000).

Carry-Forward

Validate

Delete

	Source Account	Source Flow	Source Audit	Destination Account	Destination Flow	Destination Audit	Reverse Sign	Audit Type	Same Period	Apply To YTD
1	1	F_CB	INPUT		F_OB	AJ_BCF	☐	A	☐	☐
2	25712000	F_CB	INPUT	25712000	F_OB	AJ_BCF	☑	A	☐	☐
3	25712000	F_CB	INPUT	25714000	F_OB	AJ_BCF	☐	A	☐	☐

Figure 7.18 Carry-Forward Business Rule Example

If a destination is left blank, the system will use the same members as the source. For example, the SOURCE ACCOUNT for the balance sheet parent (1) will be used as the DESTINATION ACCOUNT because it's blank.

The business rule is called by the program included in the logic file. The copy opening logic file calls the standard COPYOPENING program. The logic file also includes the dimension member prompts, that is, %<DIMENSION NAME>_SET%, as shown in Figure 7.19.

```
Logic Script of LEGAL: COPY_OPENING.LGF

  Validate  |  Comment  Uncomment  |  Pretty Print

  1  // For running balance carry forward rule (copy opeining)
  2
  3  *RUN_PROGRAM COPYOPENING
  4  CATEGORY = %C_CATEGORY_SET%
  5  CURRENCY = %RPTCURRENCY_SET%
  6  TID_RA = %TIME_SET%
  7  ENTITY = %COMPANY_SET%
  8  *ENDRUN_PROGRAM
  9
```

Figure 7.19 BCF Script Logic File

The Data Manager package passes the dimension members to the Script Logic. This delivered Data Manager package runs the COPY_OPENING.LGF balance Script Logic file. When the user executes the package, he is prompted for members of the COMPANY, C_CATEGORY, and RPTCURRENCY.

If the 2011.12 values are being carried forward to 2012.01, for example, then 2012.01 will be selected as the time member.

There are a fair number of components, so let's take a look at a graphical view. In Figure 7.20, you can see how the BCF components are used as described here:

1. The business user runs the BCF package.

2. The Data Manager prompts for the CATEGORY, CURRENCY, TIME, and ENTITY members and then calls the associated process chain.

3. The dimension members are passed to the logic file.

4. The COPYOPENING program is called, which then reads the dimensions, reads the business rule, and runs the COPYOPENING program.

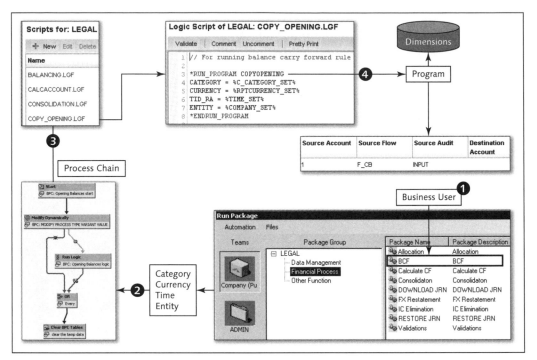

Figure 7.20 BCF Components

Balance Carry Forward Results

In Figure 7.21, you can see that the 2011.12 values have been copied into 2012.01 after executing the Data Manager BCF package. In addition, the RETAINED EARNINGS – CURRENT YEAR values have been carried forward to RETAINED EARNINGS – PRIOR YEAR.

		2011.12	2011.12	2012.01	2012.01
		AJ_BCF	INPUT	AJ_BCF	INPUT
Cash	F_CB		436,923		
	F_OB			436,923	
Trade Receivables | Gross	F_CB		22,000		
	F_OB			22,000	
Machinery & Equipment	F_CB		200,000		
	F_OB		120,000	200,000	
Acc. Depr. - Machinery & Equipment	F_CB		7,000		
	F_OB			7,000	
Retained Earnings - Current Year	F_CB		40,000		
	F_OB			0	
Retained Earnings - Prior Year	F_OB			40,000	

Figure 7.21 BCF Results for 2012.01

If you're using a YTD model for consolidations, then you need to run the BCF package for each period of the new year. This is necessary to record the opening balance for each period because in a YTD model, the opening balance isn't summed up from the prior periods.

In Figure 7.22, you can see the results of running the BCF package for several periods. The values are the same for each period because from a YTD perspective, the opening balance represents the opening balance for the entire year.

AJ_BCF - BCF Target			
F_OB - Opening Balance			
	2012.01	2012.02	2012.03
11112000 - Cash	436,923	436,923	436,923
11211000 - Trade Receivables| Gross	22,000	22,000	22,000
11301100 - IC Trade Receivables	21,000	21,000	21,000

Figure 7.22 Results of the BCF Package for Three Months

Now that the beginning balances are recorded, we can move to the next month-end task of reclassification.

7.4.2   Reclassification

As we work our way through reclassification, you'll see a similar look and feel to BCF. You'll also notice more options with the reclassification business rule, which makes it a possible solution for a wider variety of calculations. As a matter of fact, some companies use the reclassification business rule to perform BCF.

Reclassification Business Scenarios

In general, reclassification is a way to automate manual journal entries and perform cash flow calculations. Also, in situations when the corporation imports raw data from SAP ECC, reclassification can be used to calculate annual net income and post it to retained earnings. This is necessary because SAP ECC doesn't store annual net income, therefore it must be calculated in BPC.

Reclassification can also be used to book subsidiary finished goods inventory (FGI) into corporate work in process inventory (WIP).

This may be necessary in cases where a company (let's refer to them as Company A) produces semi-finished goods for another company in the same corporation.

453

At the end of the month, Company A has completed units in its FGI. However, from a group perspective, the corporation doesn't sell semi-finished goods, so the corporation reclassifies Company A's FGI into WIP.

Reclassification Components

Let's use the business scenario of a cash flow calculation as a backdrop for examining the reclassification components. The reclassification business rule is similar to the BCF business rule except that it has four source and target dimensions instead of three. Also it has an ID, which is used to create multiple business rules for different purposes.

> **Note: Reclassification Business Rule**
>
> The reclassification business rule is referred to as the ACCOUNT-BASED CALCULATION in the system.

In general, the reclassification business rule reads and aggregates the values posted to specific combinations of accounts, category, flow types, and audit IDs, and posts the aggregated amount under an alternate destination account, category, flow, and audit ID combination.

The example in Figure 7.23 is using an ID of CF (short for cash flow). You can easily have another reclassification business rule with an ID such as ANI_RE to reclassify annual net income to retained earnings, for example.

Just as you saw with the BCF business rule, you can copy from the source dimension members into the destination members.

In Figure 7.23, the rows are performing the following three functions:

The first row copies annual net income (39000000) into the CF001 cash flow account.

The second row copies the depreciation account (30527140) into the CF002 cash flow account.

The third row (copies) the depreciation account (30527150) into the CF002 cash flow account.

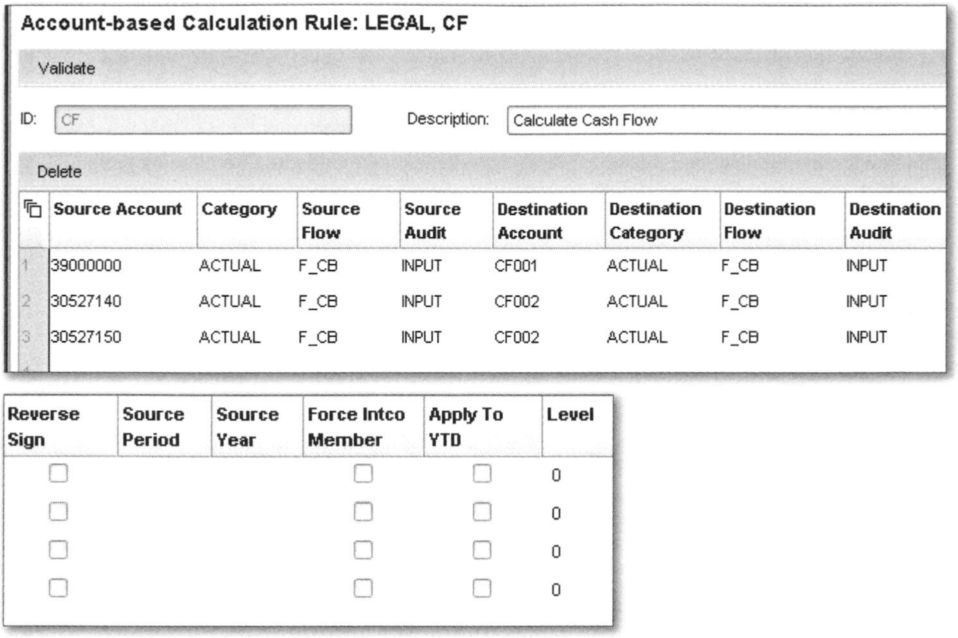

Account-based Calculation Rule: LEGAL, CF

Validate

ID: CF   Description: Calculate Cash Flow

Delete

	Source Account	Category	Source Flow	Source Audit	Destination Account	Destination Category	Destination Flow	Destination Audit
1	39000000	ACTUAL	F_CB	INPUT	CF001	ACTUAL	F_CB	INPUT
2	30527140	ACTUAL	F_CB	INPUT	CF002	ACTUAL	F_CB	INPUT
3	30527150	ACTUAL	F_CB	INPUT	CF002	ACTUAL	F_CB	INPUT
4								

Reverse Sign	Source Period	Source Year	Force Intco Member	Apply To YTD	Level
☐			☐	☐	0
☐			☐	☐	0
☐			☐	☐	0
☐			☐	☐	0

Figure 7.23 Account-Based Calculation Business Rule for Cash Flow

The fields in the reclassification business rule are defined as follows:

▶ ID
Identifier used in the logic file to call the business rule.

▶ SOURCE ACCOUNT
The source account base level, parent, or DIMLIST property value.

▶ CATEGORY
The source category base level, parent, or DIMLIST property value.

▶ SOURCE FLOW
The source flow base level, parent, or DIMLIST property value.

▶ SOURCE AUDIT
The source audit base level, parent, or DIMLIST property value.

▶ DESTINATION ACCOUNT
The destination account base level or parent. If blank, inherit from source.

▶ DESTINATION CATEGORY
The destination category base level, parent, or property value. If blank, inherit from source.

▶ Destination Flow
The destination flow base level or parent. If blank, inherit from source.

▶ Destination Audit
The destination DataSource base level or parent. If blank, inherit from source.

▶ Reverse Sign
Reverse the sign of the source value.

▶ Source Period
If not specified, the source time period is the same as the destination. This can also be used in planning scenarios.

▶ Source Year
If not specified, the source year is the same as the destination. This can also be used in planning scenarios.

▶ Force Intco Member
Use an intercompany member different from the source data record.

▶ Apply to YTD
In a periodic model, select to calculate the YTD value to copy. This can also be used in planning scenarios.

▶ Level
This controls the sequence of execution for each row.

The reclassification Script Logic file is just like the one for BCF except it has a keyword CALC, which is used to call the business rule ID (see Figure 7.24).

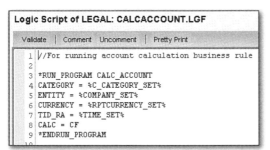

Figure 7.24 Logic Script for Reclassification

The delivered Data Manager package for reclassification is referenced to the CALCACCOUNT.LGF file name, so if you want to use a different logic file name, all you have to do is change the Data Manager package.

To run different reclassification business rules at different points in time, you can have multiple IDs with a separate logic file and Data Manager package for each one.

Reclassification Results

In our simple cash calculation scenario, you can see in Figure 7.25 that the amounts for DEPRECIATION – MACHINERY and ANI TRANSFER ACCOUNT were copied into the corresponding CF001 and CF002 cash flow accounts when the Data Manager package was executed.

	C1000	C2000
30527140 - Depreciation - Machinery	5,000	2,000
39000000 - ANI Transfer Account	20,000	20,000
CF001 - Net Icome	20,000	20,000
CF002 - Add Back Depreciation	5,000	2,000

Figure 7.25 Cash Flow Reclassification Result

Reclassification is typically run before currency translation, so now we'll move into the currency discussion.

7.4.3 Currency Translation for Consolidations

In this section, we'll discuss how to perform currency translation for consolidation, that is, FASB52.

If you're new to the concept of currency translation, it's helpful to think about it in terms of an asset account because most of the accounting concepts for currency translation come into play when you deal with the asset's opening balance, changes, and closing balance. So in the next few pages, the example used is for a machinery account.

The goal is to translate the machinery opening balance, changes, and closing balances from local to group currency and do it in a way that explains the differences that are due to changes in the base values versus rate changes.

Currency Translation Business Scenario

Financial data reported by subsidiaries is usually transferred to corporate headquarters in local currency. You need to translate this data to group currency before you can run eliminations and create consolidated financial statements. Correspondingly, if you already have group currency values coming in from the source system, you can easily choose not to re-translate those values.

Currency Translation Components

Before we get into the business rule and Script Logic, let's review the most important dimension members and their properties:

▸ **Entity dimension**
Entity members have the CURRENCY property which contains the local currency for each company. For example, company C1000 (Germany) has a local currency of EUR.

When transaction data records for C1000, for example, are imported into planning and consolidation, the report currency ID in the data record is usually LC, which represents EUR for Germany.

The system then refers to the entity dimension to look up the EUR CURRENCY.

▸ **Account dimension**
The Account dimension has the RATETYPE property that is used to select accounts in the currency translation business rules thereby acting as an account grouping mechanism. For example, a PL account has a rate type of AVG, and a balance sheet account has a rate type of END (a month-end rate).

The exchange rates are stored in the Rate model. In Figure 7.26, you can see the AVG-AVERAGE RATE and END-END OF MONTH RATE by currency for 2010.12 and 2011.12. All of the rates reference the group currency, which is USD in this example.

		2010.12	2011.12
EUR	AVG - Average Rate	1.00	1.50
	END - End of Month Rate	1.20	1.30
GBP	AVG - Average Rate	1.00	1.50
	END - End of Month Rate	1.20	1.30
JPY	AVG - Average Rate	1.00	1.50
	END - End of Month Rate	1.20	1.30
USD	AVG - Average Rate	1.00	1.00
	END - End of Month Rate	1.00	1.00

Figure 7.26 Exchange Rates

The currency translation business rule is used to select the appropriate exchange rate from the Rate model.

To create a currency translation rule, you first select an ID. The IDs are the RATE TYPE property values in the Account dimension. Then, the fields of the rule need to be configured based on the desired translation. But first, let's go over the definition for each field:

- ▶ ID

  This is the rate type used to select accounts for translation.

- ▶ DESCRIPTION

  Description of the rule.

- ▶ SOURCE FLOW

  This can be a base level or parent member ID from the Flow dimension or several flow members as identified by their DIMLIST properties.

- ▶ DESTINATION ACCOUNT

  The account that stores the converted value. If empty, it's the same as the source account member.

- ▶ DESTINATION FLOW

  The flow member that stores the converted value. If empty, then it's the same as the source member.

- ▶ FORMULA

  The factor to apply to the source value. This field can contain any arithmetic expression, including members in the account dimension of the Rate model. All members in the Rate model's Account dimension with the rate type property value of FX can be used.

- ▶ FORCE CLOSING

  If checked, the system will also write a value into the closing balance in an additional record.

- ▶ PERIODIC CALC

  This field should only be used in a YTD model when the currency translation is performed on the monthly value only. If the box is checked, the difference between the current period and prior period amounts is applied to the rate specified in the FORMULA column.

- ▶ ENTITY FX TYPE

  This field can be used to enforce a given set of rules for specific entities. If this field has a value, the rule will only be applied to the entities having a matching value in the property named FX_TYPE.

The FORMULA field contains the currency keywords that are used to select rates for the calculation.

▶ END
Uses the current end of month rate.

▶ AVG
Uses the current average rate.

▶ COPYLC
Translates the local currency to group currency with a factor of 1.

▶ OPEEND
The end rate of the last period of the prior year.

▶ AS_IS
Leave values already in the target currency untouched.

▶ OPEAVG
Reflects the average rate of the last period of the prior year.

In Figure 7.27, you can see a completed rule for the ENDFLOW rate type.

ENDFLOW has been selected, which effectively selects all accounts with the END-FLOW property value. In reality, you also need to have business rules for other rate types such as average for income statement and historical for equity accounts.

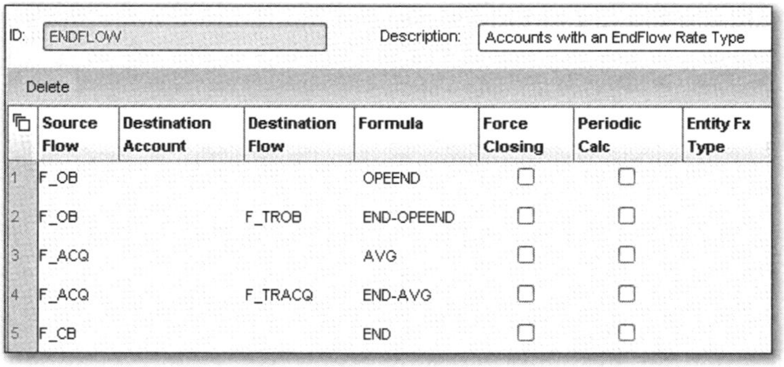

ID: ENDFLOW				Description: Accounts with an EndFlow Rate Type		
Delete						
Source Flow	Destination Account	Destination Flow	Formula	Force Closing	Periodic Calc	Entity Fx Type
1 F_OB			OPEEND	☐	☐	
2 F_OB		F_TROB	END-OPEEND	☐	☐	
3 F_ACQ			AVG	☐	☐	
4 F_ACQ		F_TRACQ	END-AVG	☐	☐	
5 F_CB			END	☐	☐	

Figure 7.27 Currency Business Rule for Accounts with the ENDFLOW Rate Type

Let's go over what each row in Figure 7.27 does for accounts that have a rate type of ENDLFOW:

▶ **Row 1**

Multiply the opening balance by the ending rate from the last period of the prior year, and write the result to the same account and flow using the target currency.

▶ **Row 2**

Multiply the opening balance by the current end rate minus the rate from the last period of the prior year, and write the result to the same account and to the F_TROB (Translation Opening Balance) flow using the target currency.

▶ **Row 3**

Multiply the acquisition value by the average rate, and write the result to the same account and flow using the target currency.

▶ **Row 4**

Multiply the acquisition value by the current end rate minus the current average rate, and write it to the same account and to the F_TRACQ (Translation Acquisition) flow using the target currency.

▶ **Row 5**

Multiply the closing balance by the current end rate, and write the result to the same account and flow using the target currency.

If currency translation is executed with the FX restatement package and the standard logic file, the results can be used for reporting scenarios. When you run currency translation from the Consolidation Monitor, those results will be used to generate the group financial statements.

The FXTRANS.LGF logic file is similar to the one for BCF. Therefore, let's focus on what is different about this one shown in Figure 7.28. This logic file has three unique characteristics:

▶ In row 3, the target currency of the translation is determined.

▶ In row 5, the GLOBAL entity member of the Rate model is hard coded.

▶ In row 7, the INCREMENTAL MODE=___(blank) is used to run in Incremental Translation mode so that only new or changed data records will be processed and the runtime will be shorter.

▶ If INCREMENTAL MODE = X, then the system will translate all data records whether they have been previously processed or not.

Logic Script of LEGAL: FXTRANS.LGF

Validate | Comment Uncomment | Pretty Print

```
*RUN_PROGRAM CURR_CONVERSION
CATEGORY      = %C_CATEGORY_SET%
CURRENCY = %RPTCURRENCY_SET%
TID_RA = %TIME_SET%
RATEENTITY = GLOBAL
ENTITY=%COMPANY_SET%
INCREMENTAL_MODE =
*ENDRUN_PROGRAM
```

Figure 7.28 FXTRANS.LGF Script Logic File

Currency Translation Results

To understand the business rule entries in Figure 7.28, we'll first review a small number of data records before and then after the Data Manager package is executed.

The sample data records for a Machinery & Equipment account (12110300) can be seen in Figure 7.29 both before and after currency translation.

Before:

Account	Intco	Company	Time	Flow	DataSrc	RptCurrency	Group	Category	Amount
12110300	I_NONE	C1000	2011.12	F_OB	INPUT	LC	G_NONE	ACTUAL	100,000
12110300	I_NONE	C1000	2011.12	F_ACQ	INPUT	LC	G_NONE	ACTUAL	20,000
12110300	I_NONE	C1000	2011.12	F_CB	INPUT	LC	G_NONE	ACTUAL	120,000

After:

Account	Intco	Company	Time	Flow	DataSrc	RptCurrency	Group	Category	Amount
12110300	I_NONE	C1000	2011.12	F_OB	INPUT	USD	G_NONE	ACTUAL	120,000
12110300	I_NONE	C1000	2011.12	F_ACQ	INPUT	USD	G_NONE	ACTUAL	30,000
12110300	I_NONE	C1000	2011.12	F_CB	INPUT	USD	G_NONE	ACTUAL	156,000
12110300	I_NONE	C1000	2011.12	F_TROB	INPUT	USD	G_NONE	ACTUAL	10,000
12110300	I_NONE	C1000	2011.12	F_TRACQ	INPUT	USD	G_NONE	ACTUAL	-4,000

Figure 7.29 Before and After View of the Data Records in Currency Translation

Note: The Group ID of G_NONE

The group ID of G_NONE will stay the same in reporting currency scenarios, however, it will ultimately be replaced with other valid group IDs such as G_CG2-4 when you do group currency translation from the Consolidation Monitor.

In Figure 7.30, you can see a report with the original values in LOCAL CURRENCY, which represents EUR in this case and translation into US DOLLARS. We're using different flow IDs to capture the currency translation differences however you can easily use account IDs as well.

		Local Currency	US Dollar
Machinery & Equipment	F_OB - Opening Balance	100,000	120,000
	F_ACQ - Acquisition	20,000	30,000
	F_TROB - Transl Diff OB		10,000
	F_TRACQ - Transl Diff ACQ		-4,000
	F_CB - Closing balance	120,000	156,000

Figure 7.30 Machinery & Equipment Local Currency and US Dollars

Now let's identify the mechanics of how each US Dollar value was calculated.

Figure 7.31 is the business rule to translate F_OB –(Opening Balance) for accounts that have a rate type of ENDFLOW.

Accounts with *ENDFLOW*

	Source Flow	Destination Account	Destination Flow	Formula	Force Closing
1.	F_OB			OPEEND	☐
2.	F_OB		F_TROB	END-OPEEND	☐
	F_ACQ			AVG	☐
	F_ACQ		F_TRACQ	END-AVG	☐
	F_CB			END	☐

	End	Avg
EUR Rate 2010.Dec	1.2 (OPEND)	
EUR Rate 2011.Dec	1.3	1.5

		Local Currency	US Dollar
Machinery & Equipment	F_OB - Opening Balance	100,000	120,000
(Rate Type = EndFlow)	F_ACQ - Acquisition	20,000	
	F_TROB - Transl Diff OB		10,000
	F_TRACQ - Transl Diff ACQ		
	F_CB - Closing balance	120,000	

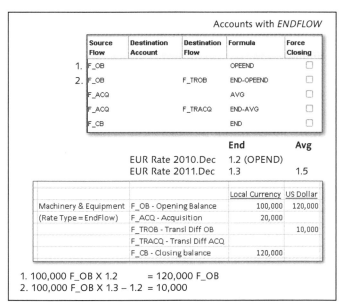

1. 100,000 F_OB X 1.2 = 120,000 F_OB
2. 100,000 F_OB X 1.3 – 1.2 = 10,000

Figure 7.31 Business Rule and Results for the Opening Balance Translation

The first row in the business rule selects the opening balance of 100,000 and multiplies it by the OPEEND 1.2 rate, which is the prior year-ending rate. The product of 120,000 is posted to the same account and flow as the source because the DESTINATION ACCOUNT and DESTINATION FLOW are blank.

The second row selects the opening balance of 100,000 and multiplies it by (END 1.3 – OPEEND 1.2). The product of 10.000 is posted to the same account but to flow F_TROB.

Figure 7.32 shows the business rule to translate F_ACQ-ACQUISITION amounts.

The third row selects the acquisition amount of 20,000 and multiplies it by the AVG 1.5 rate. The product of 30.000 is posted to the same account and flow.

The fourth row selects the acquisition amount of 20,000 and multiplies it by (END 1.3 – AVG 1.5). The product of -4.000 is posted to the same account but to flow F_TRACQ.

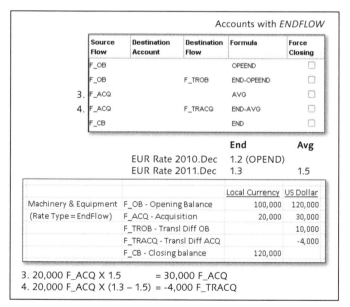

Figure 7.32 Business Rule and Results for the Acquisition Translation

Figure 7.33 is the business rule to translate F_CB-CLOSING BALANCE:

The fifth row selects the closing balance of 120,000 and multiplies it by 1.3 and posts the 156,000 to the same account and flow member.

Accounts with *ENDFLOW*

	Source Flow	Destination Account	Destination Flow	Formula	Force Closing
	F_OB			OPEEND	☐
	F_OB		F_TROB	END-OPEEND	☐
	F_ACQ			AVG	☐
	F_ACQ		F_TRACQ	END-AVG	☐
5.	F_CB			END	☐

	End	Avg
EUR Rate 2010.Dec	1.2 (OPEND)	
EUR Rate 2011.Dec	1.3	1.5

		Local Currency	US Dollar
Machinery & Equipment	F_OB - Opening Balance	100,000	120,000
(Rate Type = EndFlow)	F_ACQ - Acquisition	20,000	30,000
	F_TROB - Transl Diff OB		10,000
	F_TRACQ - Transl Diff ACQ		-4,000
	F_CB - Closing balance	120,000	156,000

5. 120,000 F_CB X 1.3 = 156,000 F_CB

Figure 7.33 Business Rule and Results for the Closing Balance Translation

Now that we've gone through the mechanics of the currency translation business rules, let's review the business rationale:

- The 120,000 is the opening balance translated using the prior year-end rate.
- The 30,000 is the acquisition translated at the current month average rate. Typically, on acquisitions of long-term assets, accountants will use the average rate for a transaction that occurred during the month because it's a current value.
- The 10,000 is the product of the current month-end rate minus the prior year-end rate for the opening balance. This is the currency translation effect on opening balance amounts for the change in the end rates. This is useful for cash flow analysis.
- The 4,000 is the product of the current month-end rate minus the current period average rate for acquisitions. This is the currency translation effect on acquisition amounts. This is also useful for cash flow analysis.
- The 156,000 is the closing balance translated at the current month-end rate. This should equal the sum of the detailed movements in Figure 7.33.

We've therefore accomplished our goal of translating an asset account's opening balance, closing balance, and changes, along with understanding the differences.

This is an example of a reporting currency scenario. We'll use the same business rules to translate into the group currency in the purchase method elimination coming up next.

7.4.4 Purchase Method Elimination

We'll use the purchase method to gain an understanding of how to perform ownership elimination in this section. After that, we'll then see how the same components can be used for the proportional and equity eliminations.

> **Note: Elimination and Adjustment for Financial Institutions**
>
> Due to some differences between the consolidation processes occurring for financial institutions, there will be some enhancements available in SP07 to accommodate the Equity Pick Up (EPU) differences.

Purchase Method Business Scenario

The business scenario is to perform ownership eliminations using the purchase method. The Europe group is being used as an example in this case. In the Europe group, Germany (C1000) purchased 80% of the UK (C2000) subsidiary's shares using the purchase method.

In Figure 7.34, you can see a combined data set from the ownership and legal models for the Europe group (values in USD).

Group	Entity	Method	POWN	12311000 Investment	25110000 Treasury Stock
G_CG2 - Europe	C1000 - Germany	90-Parent	100%	80,000	
G_CG2 - Europe	C2000 - UK	86-Purchase	80%		100,000

Figure 7.34 Europe Group Data Used for Eliminations

The objective is to use the purchase method to eliminate the investment and equity (TREASURY STOCK), and to book minority interest for the Europe group.

Purchase Method Components

Several dimensions are integral to the ownership elimination:

- **Account**
  In the Account dimension, the `DIMLIST` and `TYPELIM` properties are used to group accounts for business rule selections.

- **DataSource**
  In the DataSource dimension, members with the `Datasrc_Type` property value `A` (automatic) can be used in the eliminations and adjustments business rule.

  Also the `IS_Translated` property requires a value of `Y` to include it in the currency translation run. And the `IS_Consol` property requires a value of `Y` to include it in the consolidation run.

- **Entity**
  In the Entity dimension, the supporting property is `Intco`, which links entities to the intercompany members.

- **Group**
  In the Group dimension, the supporting property is `Entity`, which will store the consolidated results. The required member is G_NONE, which is for third-party data.

- **InterCompany**
  In the InterCompany dimension, the supporting property is `Entity`, which links the intercompany member to the entity member.

Of key importance is the integration between the COMPANY, InterCompany (INTCO), and the CONSGROUP dimensions. Figure 7.35 illustrates how the COMPANY and INTCO members are linked (i.e., C1000 to I_C1000). Also, the COMPANY E_CG2 is linked to the CONSGROUP member G_CG2 via the CONSGROUP `Entity` property. As a reminder, each group ID is assigned to a GROUP_CURRENCY in the CONSGROUP dimension as well.

To perform ownership eliminations, three business rule tables are used:

- **Methods**
  Environment level.

- **Method-based Multipliers**
  Environment level.

- **Eliminations and Adjustments**
  Model level.

Members of Dimension: COMPANY

Delete	Revert	Recently Deleted Members	Apply Hierarchy Order ▲	Display ▲

	I.	Descri...	Interco...	(	Investment
1	E_H1	Investments Elim ..		EUR	
2	H1	Investments		USD	
3	CG1	Corporate		USD	H1
4	C9000	Holding	I_C9000	USD	CG1
5	CG2	Europe		EUR	CG1
6	C1000	Germany	I_C1000	EUR	CG2
7	C2000	UK	I_C2000	GBP	CG2
8	E_CG2	Europe Elim Entity		EUR	CG2

Members of Dimension: INTCO

Delete	Revert	Recently Deleted Members	Apply Hierarchy Or

	ID	Description	Entity
1	TOTAL	Total	
2	ALL_INTERCO	All Inter-company	
3	I_C1000	Germany	C1000
4	I_C2000	UK	C2000
5	I_C3000	US	C3000
6	I_C4000	Canada	C4000
7	I_C5000	Japan	C5000
8	I_C9000	Holding Company	C9000
9	I_C6000	Australia	C6000
10	ThirdParty	ThirdParty	

Members of Dimension: CONSGROUP   Go

Delete	Revert	Recently Deleted Members	Display ▲	Export to CSV

	ID	Descr...	ENTITY	CURRENCY_TYPE	GROUP_CURRENCY	PARENT GROUP
1	G_CG1	Corporate	E_CG1	G	USD	G_H1
2	G_CG2	Europe	E_CG2	G	USD	G_CG1
3	G_CG3	America	E_CG3	G	USD	G_CG1
4	G_CG4	Asia Pacific	E_CG4	G	USD	G_CG1
5	G_H1	Investments	E_H1	G	USD	
6	G_NONE	G None		N		

Figure 7.35 Integration between the CONSGROUP, COMPANY, and INTCO Dimensions

Because we've already discussed the Methods table in the Section 7.2, now we'll go over the Method-based Multipliers table.

The METHOD-BASED MULTIPLIERS table, shown in Figure 7.36, performs the following two tasks:

- Identifies the percentage to use in the ELIMINATIONS AND ADJUSTMENTS RULE screen.

- Selects the entities and intercompany members based on their assigned method codes.

When you create a new multiplier, you provide your own ID and DESCRIPTION. In Figure 7.36, we're using "RULE010".

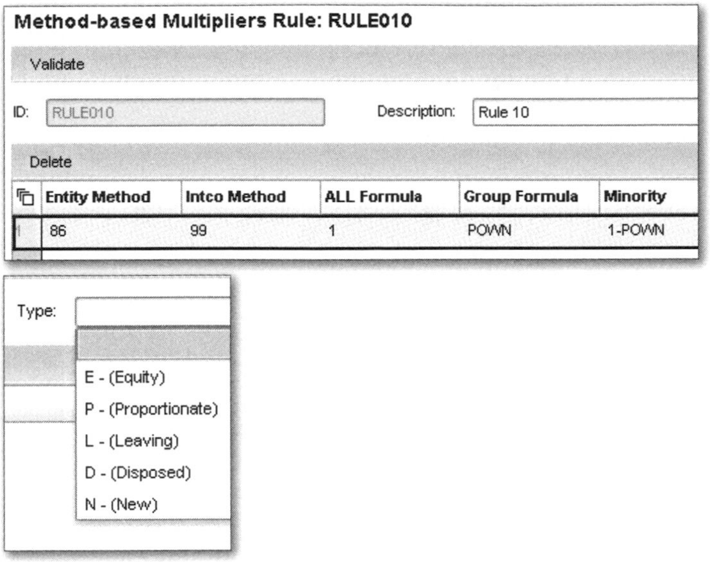

Figure 7.36 Method-Based Multipliers Rule for the Purchase Method

The METHOD-BASED MULTIPLIERS table fields are defined as follows:

▶ ID
  Logical ID.

▶ DESCRIPTION
  Description of the rule.

▶ TYPE (select one of the following):

  ▶ BLANK OR NEW
    Purchase method.

  ▶ EQUITY
    Equity method.

  ▶ PROPORTIONATE
    Proportional method.

  ▶ LEAVING
    For subsidiaries divested in current month.

  ▶ DISPOSED
    For subsidiaries divested in last month of last year.

► ENTITY METHOD

Enter a method code to select entities. You can use one method code or multiple comma-separated method code values.

► INTCO METHOD

Enter a method code to select intercompany members. Use one method code or multiple comma-separated values, or use "99" to select intercompany members with any method code.

► ALL FORMULA

The percentage or formula to apply to the DESTINATION ALL ACCOUNT in the ELIMINATIONS AND ADJUSTMENTS RULE screen.

► GROUP FORMULA

The percentage or formula to apply to the GROUP ACCOUNT in the ELIMINATIONS AND ADJUSTMENTS RULE screen.

► MINORITY FORMULA

The percentage or formula to apply to the DESTINATION MINORITY ACCOUNT in the ELIMINATIONS AND ADJUSTMENTS RULE screen.

The selections in row 1 in Figure 7.36 will do the following:

► ENTITY METHOD AND INTCO METHOD

Select the source value of entities with an ENTITY METHOD of 86 and any (99) other INTCO METHOD (99 is a system generated wildcard that is used to include investees with any method code assignment).

► ALL FORMULA

Write -1 times the source value to the account specified in the ELIMINATIONS AND ADJUSTMENTS RULE screen. Values in the ALL FORMULA field reverse the sign of the source value.

► GROUP FORMULA

Write POWN % times the source value to the group account specified in the ELIMINATIONS AND ADJUSTMENTS RULE screen.

► MINORITY

Write the source value times 1 minus POWN (.80) to the minority account specified in the ELIMINATIONS AND ADJUSTMENTS RULE screen.

When you create a new rule, at a minimum, you'll need to enter an ID and a DESCRIPTION, and you'll need to select the DESTINATION AUDIT ID on the GENERAL tab as shown in Figure 7.37.

The ID used in this example, "ELCOI1", stands for Elimination Consolidations of Investments 1. Also, the DESTINATION AUDIT ID of "AJ_COI1" stands for Automatic Journal – Consolidation of Investments 1.

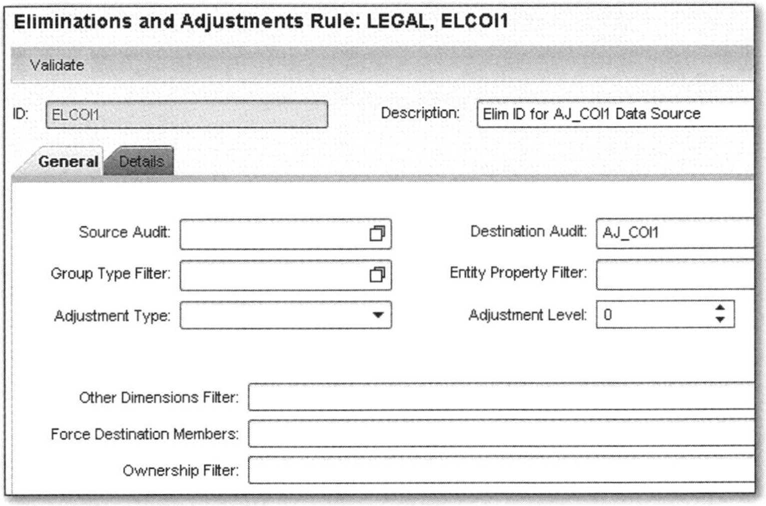

Figure 7.37 Eliminations and Adjustments Rule General Tab

The fields on the GENERAL tab are defined as follows:

► ID
Logical ID.

► DESCRIPTION
Description of the rule ID.

► SOURCE AUDIT
Select the source audit member to include.

► DESTINATION AUDIT
Select the target audit member.

► GROUP TYPE FILTER
Select the target group dimension members based on their `Conso_Type` property value.

► ENTITY PROPERTY FILTER
Select entities to include based on any property.

- ▶ ADJUSTMENT TYPE:

  - ▶ BLANK
    Purchase method.

  - ▶ EQUITY
    Equity method.

  - ▶ PROPORTIONAL
    Proportional method.

  - ▶ LEAVING
    Divestitures.

- ▶ ADJUSTMENT LEVEL
  Used to control the sequence of execution of the rule.

- ▶ OTHER DIMENSIONS FILTER
  Select the source data region for other dimensions.

- ▶ FORCE DESTINATION MEMBERS
  Used to hard-code target members in additional data records.

- ▶ OWNERSHIP FILTER
  Used to restrict the rule to members that existed in the prior year, for example. To do that, enter "PPCON <> 0".

On the DETAILS tab, make your account assignments and select the MULTIPLIER.

To eliminate the investment, for example, see the ID "ELCOI1" in Figure 7.38. In row 1, the inverse value in the SOURCE ACCOUNT 12311000 will be written to the DESTINATION ALL ACCOUNT 12311000 based on RULE060 (ENTITY METHOD code = 90, and ALL FORMULA = 100%).

In Figure 7.38, the ELCOI2 rule is eliminating the equity by taking the value in the SOURCE ACCOUNT 25110000 and writing it to the DESTINATION ALL ACCOUNT 25110000 based on RULE010 (Entity = ENTITY METHOD code 86 and GROUP FORMULA = 100%).

Figure 7.39 shows the booking of the minority interest. In rule ID ELCOI3, the value in the SOURCE ACCOUNT 25110000 will be written to the DESTINATION MINORITY ACCOUNT 24111000 based on RULE010 (Entity = ENTITY METHOD code 86 and MINORITY FORMULA 1 minus POWN).

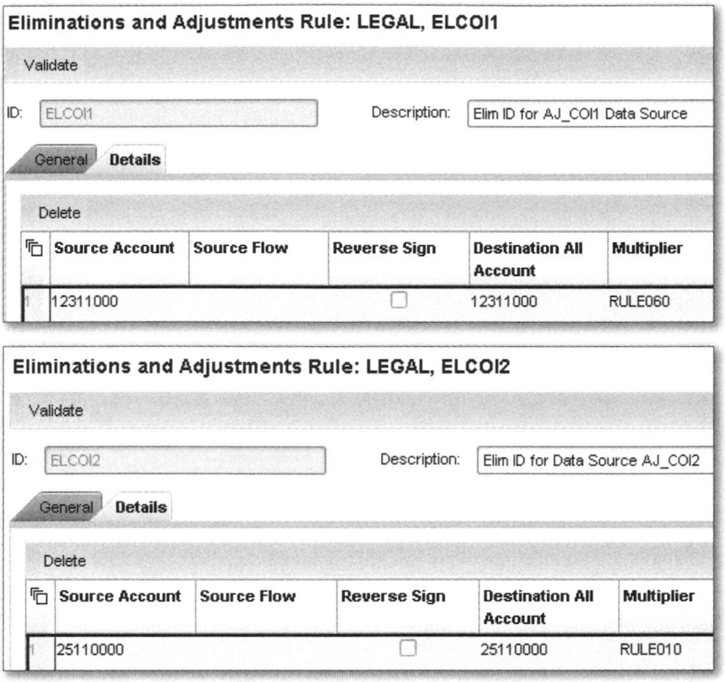

Figure 7.38 Investment Elimination Business Rule Details

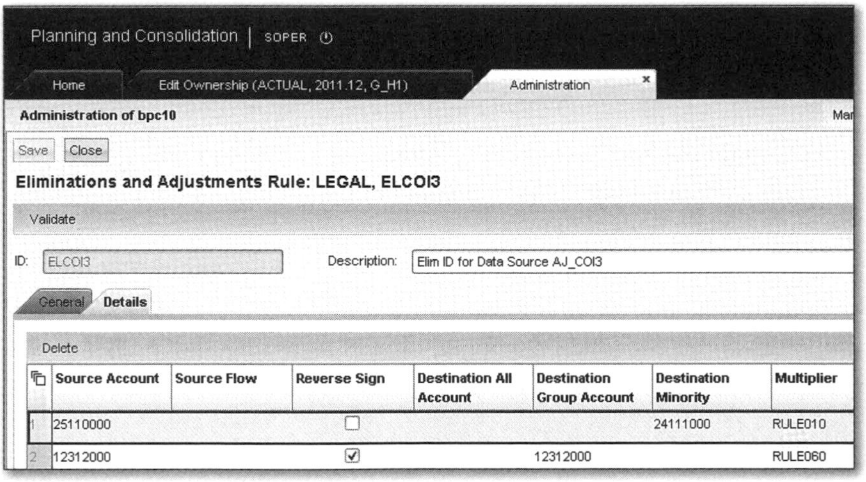

Figure 7.39 Minority Interest Business Rule Details

Each field on the DETAILS tab is defined as follows. Please note that not all fields are represented in Figure 7.39. These fields have been identified.

▶ SOURCE ACCOUNT
Select accounts to include. Use a base or parent member, or a TYPELIM or DIM-LIST property value.

▶ SOURCE FLOW
Select flow members to include. Use a base or parent member, or a TYPELIM or DIMLIST property value.

▶ REVERSE SIGN
If Y, the value is reversed; otherwise, leave blank.

▶ DESTINATION ALL ACCOUNT
Target account for the ALL FORMULA percentage in the Methodbased Multiplier table. Use a base or parent member, or a TYPELIM or DIMLIST property value

▶ DESTINATION GROUP ACCOUNT
Target account for the GROUP FORMULA percentage in the Methodbased Multiplier table. Use a base or parent account, or a TYPELIM or DIMLIST property value in the Account dimension

▶ DESTINATION MINORITY ACCOUNT
Target account for MINORITY FORMULA percentage in the Method-based Multiplier table. Use a base or parent account, or a TYPELIM or DIMLIST property value in the Account dimension.

▶ DESTINATION EQUITY ACCOUNT
Target account for the ALL FORMULA percentage in the Method-based Multiplier table for the equity method. Use a base or parent account, or a TYPELIM or DIM-LIST property value in the Account dimension.

▶ DESTINATION FLOW
Target base level member.

▶ MULTIPLIER
The rule ID from the Method-based Multiplier table.

▶ FORCE CLOSING
If Y, it generates an extra record on the closing flow; otherwise, leave blank. (not shown in Figure 7.39)

▶ SWAP ENTITY-INTCO

If Y, it will swap the member of the Entity dimension with the intercompany member. (not shown in Figure 7.39)

▶ FORCE INTCO

Member to hard-code the target intercompany member instead of using the source. (not shown in Figure 7.39)

▶ PERIODIC CALC

Can be used in a YTD model when the ownership percentage should be applied on the periodic values. (not shown in Figure 7.39)

The next component we need to discuss is the CONSOLIDATION Script Logic file.

In the CONSOLIDATION Script Logic file in Figure 7.40, you can see that CURR_CON-VERSION will be executed first and CONSOLIDATION will run second.

Also, because this currency translation is run by group ID, there is a line in the code GROUP = %CONSGROUP_SET%, which means that the group ID is determined at runtime.

In addition, there is no reference to the Currency dimension because the currency will be read from the Consgroup dimension (remember that each group ID is assigned a group currency).

This Script Logic will only run when the consolidation package is executed. When consolidation is run from the Consolidation Monitor, the ABAP code is read directly, and no Script Logic is used at all.

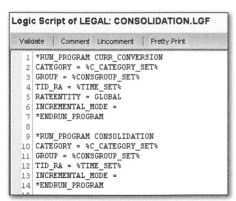

```
Logic Script of LEGAL: CONSOLIDATION.LGF

  Validate  |  Comment  Uncomment  |  Pretty Print

 1  *RUN_PROGRAM CURR_CONVERSION
 2  CATEGORY = %C_CATEGORY_SET%
 3  GROUP = %CONSGROUP_SET%
 4  TID_RA = %TIME_SET%
 5  RATEENTITY = GLOBAL
 6  INCREMENTAL_MODE =
 7  *ENDRUN_PROGRAM
 8
 9  *RUN_PROGRAM CONSOLIDATION
10  CATEGORY = %C_CATEGORY_SET%
11  GROUP = %CONSGROUP_SET%
12  TID_RA = %TIME_SET%
13  INCREMENTAL_MODE =
14  *ENDRUN_PROGRAM
15
```

Figure 7.40 Logic Script for Group Currency Translation and Consolidation

When the consolidation Data Manager package is executed, there are prompts for three dimensions: Consgroup, Category, and Time. Note that those are the same three dimension member prompts in the Script Logic in Figure 7.40.

This completes a run-through of the components for the purchase method, so now it's time to see the results.

Purchase Method Results

If you focus solely on the data set for C1000 and C2000, you can see the following expected results in an Excel report in Figure 7.41:

- ▸ The investment of 80,000 is eliminated.
- ▸ The minority interest of 20,000 is booked.
- ▸ The equity of 100,000 is eliminated.

> **Note: Journal IDs**
>
> Ownership eliminations do not create any journal IDs. Only BPC journals generate journal IDs.

		INPUT	AJ_COI1	AJ_COI2	AJ_COI3	TOTALADJ
12311000 - Investments in Subs - Purchase	C1000	80,000	-80,000			0
24111000 - Min Int - Purchase	C2000				20,000	20,000
25110000 - Treasury Stock - Purchase	C2000	100,000		-100,000		0

Figure 7.41 Consolidation – Purchase Method Results.

Next we'll break down how the system generated each entry. In Figure 7.42, you can see the source data, the business rule selections, and the results for the investment elimination.

When consolidation is run, it will perform three key steps.

❶ For the SOURCE ACCOUNT-12311000, a value of 80,000 is read into memory for C1000.

❷ For the associated DESTINATION ALL ACCOUNT 12311000 and MULTIPLIER RULE060, the percentage of 100% (1=100%) is read from the METHOD-BASED

MULTIPLIERS for C1000 because it is assigned ENTITY METHOD code 90. DESTINA-
TION ALL ACCOUNTS post with the opposite sign.

❸ For the associated RULE ID-ELCOI1, the DESTINATION DATASOURCE-AJ_COI1 is
posted -80,000(100% of the 12311000 value).

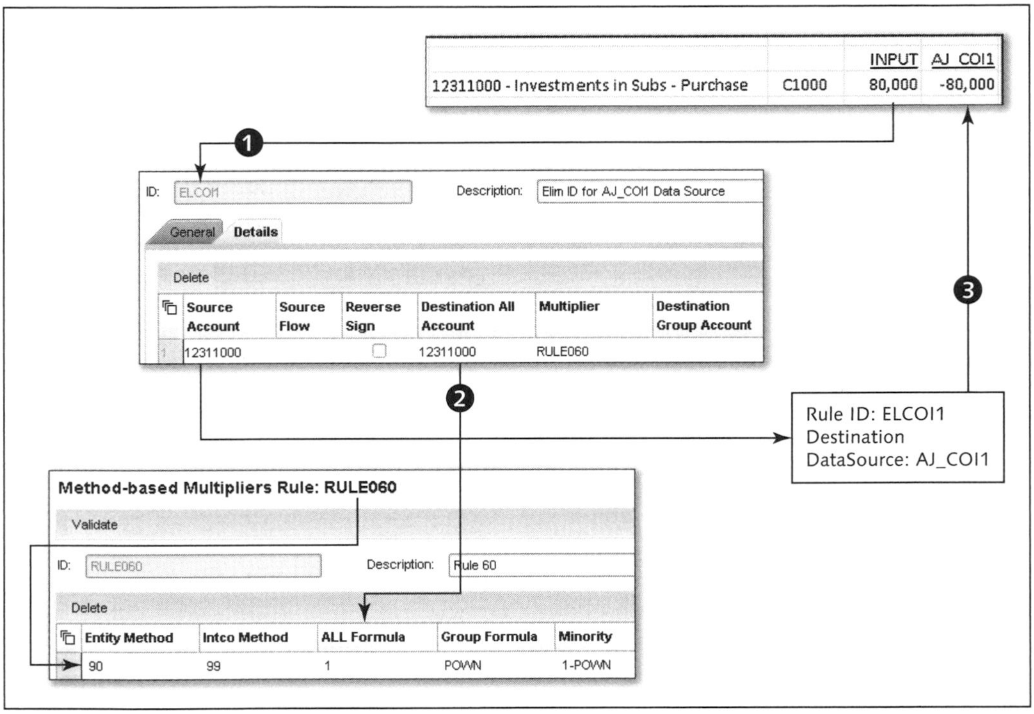

Figure 7.42 Investment Elimination for the Purchase Method

In Figure 7.43 you can see how the Equity Elimination was booked.

❶ For the SOURCE ACCOUNT-25110000, a value of 100,000 is read into memory
for C2000.

❷ For the associated DESTINATION ALL ACCOUNT-25110000 and MULTIPLIER
RULE010, the percentage of 100% is read from the METHOD-BASED MULTIPLIERS
for C2000 because it is assigned METHOD CODE 86.

❸ For the associated RULE ID ELCOI2, the DESTINATION DATA SOURCE AJ_COI2 is posted for –100,000 (100% of the 25110000 account value).

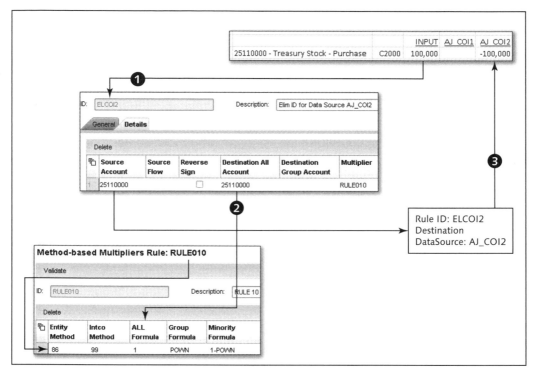

Figure 7.43 Equity Elimination for the Purchase Method

In Figure 7.44, you can see how the minority interest was booked:

❶ For the SOURCE ACCOUNT-25110000, a value of 100,000 is read into memory for C2000.

❷ For the associated DESTINATION MINORITY ACCOUNT 24111000 and MULTIPLIER RULE010, the percentage of 1.00 minus .80 (POWN) is read from the METHOD-BASED MULTIPLIERS table for C2000 because it is assigned ENTITY METHOD code 86.

❸ For the associated RULE ID ELCOI3, the DESTINATION AUDIT AJ_COI3 is used to post a value of 20,000 with the same sign (80% of the 25110000 value).

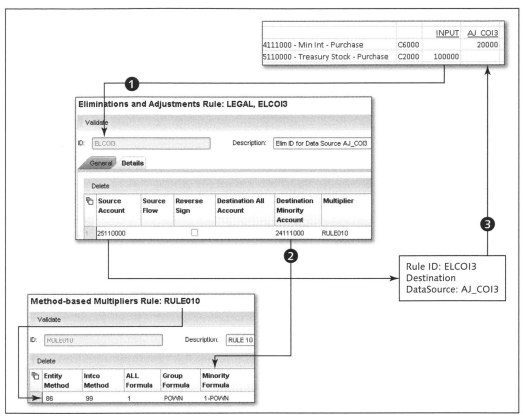

Figure 7.44 Minority Interest Calculation for the Purchase Method

Now that we've gone through the business scenario, components, and results for the purchase method, we can do the same for the proportional method.

7.4.5 Proportional Method Elimination

Because the components are the same as in the purchase method, we'll consequently focus on what is different in the configuration when using the proportional method.

Proportional Method Business Scenario

We'll use the Americas group for this example. In the Americas group, C3000 (US) is the parent who owns 80% of C4000 (Canada). In Figure 7.45, you can see a combined data set from the ownership and legal models for the Americas group (values in USD).

Group	Entity	Method	POWN	12311000 Investment	25110000 Treasury Stock	11112000 Cash
G_CG3 - America	C3000 - US	90-Parent	100%	80,000		
G_CG3 - America	C4000 - Canada	86-Proporti	80%		65,000	65,000

Figure 7.45 Europe Group Data for the Proportional Elimination

The objective is to use the proportional method to generate the following four entries:

1. Eliminate the investment.

2. Eliminate the equity (TREASURY STOCK).

3. Eliminate the nongroup share of the CASH.

4. Book goodwill for the Europe group.

In booking these entries, the Method-based Multipliers must be configured first.

Proportional Method Components

Let's take a look at the METHOD-BASED MULTIPLIERS rule screen for the proportional method. In Figure 7.46, you can see RULE210 with a TYPE of P-PROPORTIONAL.

Proportional rule types will eliminate balance sheet values automatically without any detailed account assignments in the ELIMINATIONS AND ADJUSTMENTS RULE screen IDs. Also, the system ID is actually PROPORTIONATE; however, in the trade, the term "Proportional" is used.

In this rule, entities with the method of 70 will be eliminated with a percentage of 1-POWN for the DESTINATION ALL ACCOUNTS.

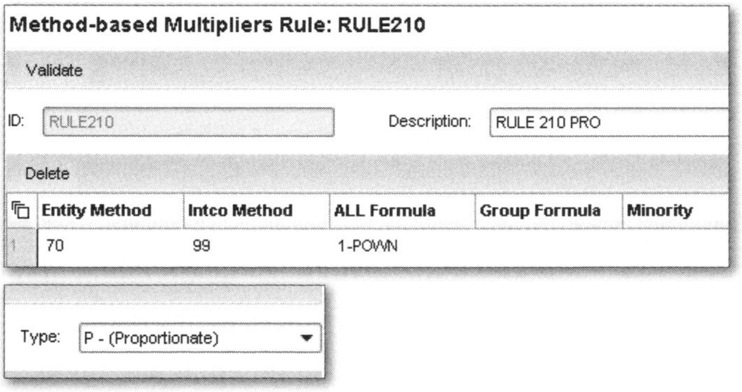

Method-based Multipliers Rule: RULE210

Validate

ID: RULE210   Description: RULE 210 PRO

Delete

	Entity Method	Intco Method	ALL Formula	Group Formula	Minority
1	70	99	1-POWN		

Type: P - (Proportionate) ▼

Figure 7.46 Method-Based Multipliers Rule for the Proportional Method

This example also needs a rule ID that has an ALL FORMULA value of POWN and a rule that has an ALL FORMULA value of 1.

Now let's go to the eliminations and adjustments business rules.

We'll need three rules in our example that are merely variations of what you saw for the purchase method. The first two rules will eliminate the investment and the equity and book the goodwill entries.

The third rule shown in Figure 7.47 will eliminate C4000's balance sheet values that should not be included in the group. The ELPRO ID has the ADJUSTMENT TYPE P-PROPORTIONATE selected, which is known as a global rule. As a consequence, there are no detailed account assignments necessary on the DETAILS tab.

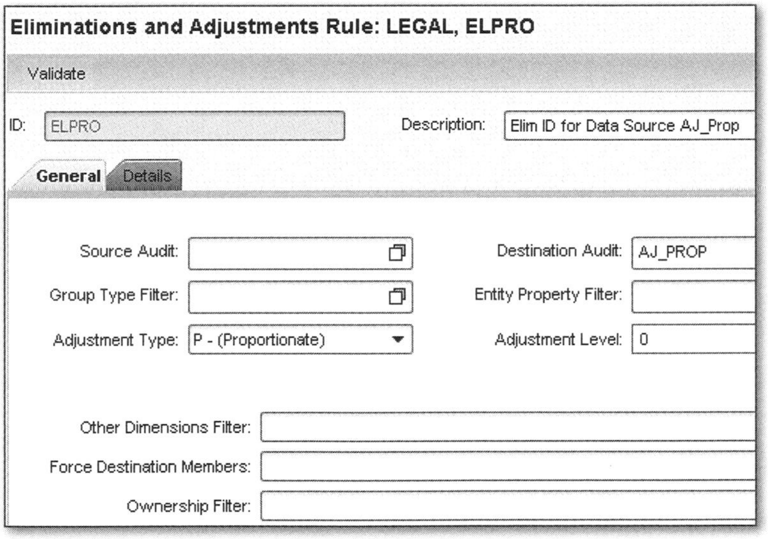

Figure 7.47 Eliminations and Adjustments General Rule for the Proportional Method

Now that the components are in place, you can check the results.

Proportional Method Results

If you focus solely on the data set for C3000 and C4000, you can see the results in an Excel report in Figure 7.48 after the consolidation package has been executed. Remember, there is no minority interest with the proportional method.

Account	Company	Intco	INPUT	AJ_PROP	AJ_COI1	AJ_COI2	AJ_COI3	TOTALADJ
11112000 - Cash	C3000	ThirdParty	70,000					70,000
11112000 - Cash	C4000	ThirdParty	65,000	-16,250				48,750
12313000 - Investments in Subs - Proportional	C3000	I_C4000	80,000		-80,000			0
12413000 - Goodwill - Proportional	C3000	I_C4000				80,000		80,000
12413000 - Goodwill - Proportional	C4000	I_C3000					-48,750	-48,750
25130000 - Treasury Stock - Proportional	C4000	I_C3000	65,000	-16,250	-48,750			0

Figure 7.48 Proportional Elimination Results

The following entries were created

▸ A credit of 16,250 to eliminate the cash not owned (AJ_PROP).

▸ A credit of 80,000 to clear the investment (AJ_COI1).

▸ A debit of 80,000 for the GOODWILL account (AJ_COI2).

▸ A credit of 48,750 for the GOODWILL account (AJ_COI3).

▸ A debit of 16,250 (AJ_PROP) and 48,750 (AJ_COI1) for the equity.

However, the goodwill entries do not show up against the correct entity and inter-company members. (This was intentional).

To fix this, you can turn on the SWAP ENTITY-INTCO option in the ELCOI3 ELIMINA-TIONS AND ADJUSTMENTS RULE screen show in Figure 7.49. The SWAP ENTITY-INTCO feature can be used for any method, not just proportional.

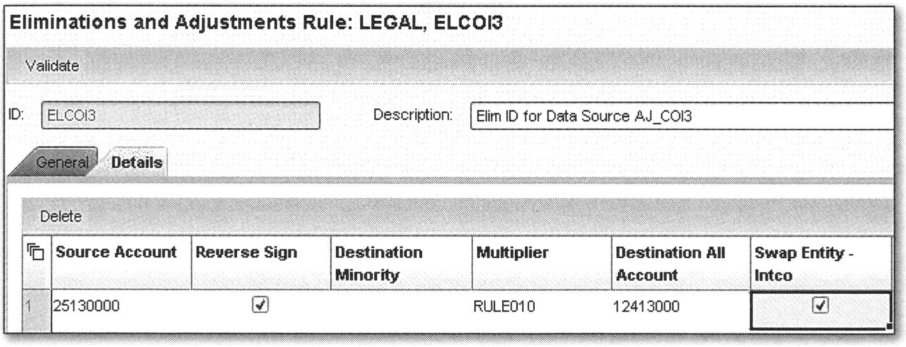

Figure 7.49 Eliminations and Adjustments Rule with Swap Entity

When the consolidation package is executed again, the two GOODWILL entries now appear on the same row because they have the same COMPANY (C3000) and INTCO (I_C4000) (see Figure 7.50).

Account	Company	Intco	INPUT	AJ PROP	AJ COI1	AJ COI2	AJ COI3
11112000 - Cash	C3000	ThirdParty	70,000				
11112000 - Cash	C4000	ThirdParty	65,000	-16,250			
12313000 - Investments - Proportional	C3000	I_C4000	80,000		-80,000		
12413000 - Goodwill - Proportional	C3000	I_C4000				80,000	-48,750
12413000 - Goodwill - Proportional	C4000	I_C3000					0
25130000 - Treasury Stock - Proportional	C4000	I_C3000	65,000	-16,250	-48,750		

Figure 7.50 Proportional Results with Goodwill Posted to C3000

In summary, following are the key points of the proportional method:

▶ You can use the proportional Method-based Multiplier to eliminate general balance sheet accounts for the investee without any detailed account assignment.

▶ You can use the SWAP ENTITY INTCO option to switch the entity and Intco members in postings.

▶ Now let's move on to a review of the equity method.

Because the components are the same as in the purchase method, we'll consequently focus on what is different in the configuration when using the equity method.

7.4.6 Equity Method Business Scenario

In this case, we'll use the Asia Pacific group as an example. In this group, C5000 is the parent, which owns 30% of C6000. Because the % ownership is less than 50%, the parent wants to use the equity method.

In Figure 7.51, you can see a combined data set from the ownership and legal models for the Asia Pacific group (values in USD).

				12311000	25110000	11112000
Group	Entity	Method	POWN	Investment	Treasury Stock	Cash
G_CG4 - Asia Pacific	C5000 - Japan	90-Parent	100%	26,000		
G_CG4 - Asia Pacific	C6000 - Australia	30-Equity	30%		65,000	65,000

Figure 7.51 Europe Group Data for the Equity Elimination

The objective is to use the equity method to book the goodwill, adjust the investment down by the goodwill amount, and eliminate the cash.

Equity Method Components

In the METHOD BASED MULTIPLIERS RULE screen for the EQUITY method, you want to eliminate 100% of entity values for those entities that are assigned METHOD 30 (see Figure 7.52).

Just like the proportional rule type, the E-EQUITY Type is a global type rule in that it will eliminate balance sheet values automatically without any detailed account assignments in the ELIMINATIONS AND ADJUSTMENTS RULE screen IDs.

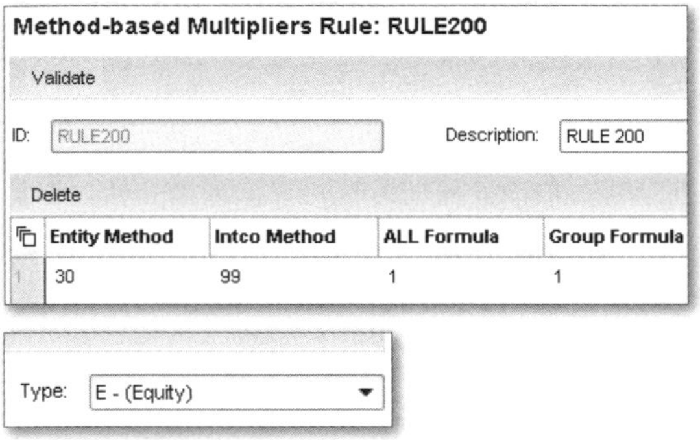

Method-based Multipliers Rule: RULE200

Validate

ID: RULE200   Description: RULE 200

Delete

	Entity Method	Intco Method	ALL Formula	Group Formula
1	30	99	1	1

Type: E - (Equity) ▼

Figure 7.52 Method-Based Multipliers Rule for the Equity Method

In the ELIMINATIONS AND ADJUSTMENTS RULE screen shown in Figure 7.53, the ADJUSTMENT TYPE E - (EQUITY) has been selected along with the DESTINATION AUDIT of AJ_EQUMETH.

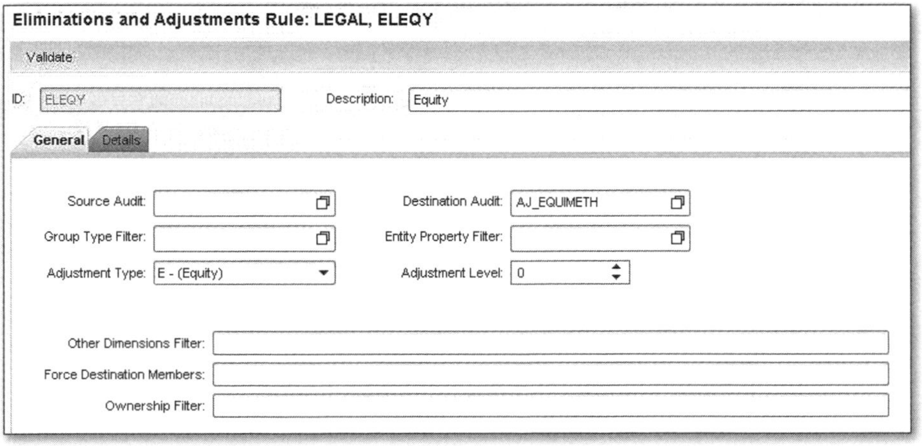

Eliminations and Adjustments Rule: LEGAL, ELEQY

Validate

ID: ELEQY   Description: Equity

General Details

Source Audit:	Destination Audit:	AJ_EQUIMETH
Group Type Filter:	Entity Property Filter:	
Adjustment Type: E - (Equity) ▼	Adjustment Level: 0	

Other Dimensions Filter:

Force Destination Members:

Ownership Filter:

Figure 7.53 Eliminations and Adjustments General Rule for the Equity Method

In this example, there are also rules needed to adjust the investment and book the goodwill.

Now that we've discussed the equity elimination components, you can check the results.

Equity Method Results

Again, if we focus solely on the data set for C5000 and C6000, you can see the expected results in an Excel report in Figure 7.54 after the consolidation package has been executed.

It's important to point out the flexibility of the business rules in the example. For both the INVESTMENTS and the GOODWILL entries, two values were used to achieve the desired net results. Also, there is no minority interest with the equity method.

Account	Company	Intco	INPUT	AJ_EQUIMETH	AJ_COI1	AJ_COI2	AJ_COI3	TOTALADJ
11112000 - Cash	C6000	ThirdParty	65,000	-65,000				0
12312000 - Investments - Equity	C5000	I_C6000	26,000			19,500	-26,000	19,500
12412000 - Goodwill - Equity	C5000	I_C6000			26000	-19500		6500
25120000 - Treasury Stock - Equity	C6000	I_C5000	65000	-65000				0

Figure 7.54 Equity Results in Excel

The following entries were created:

▸ A credit of 65,000 for cash (AJ_EQUIMETH).

▸ A credit of 26,000 for the investment (AJ_COI3).

▸ A debit of 19,500 for the investment (AJ_COI2). Therefore, a net credit of 6,500 for the investment account.

▸ A credit of 19,500 in the goodwill account (AJ_COI2).

▸ A debit of 26,000 in the goodwill account (AJ_COI1). Therefore, a net debit of 6,500 in the goodwill account.

▸ A debit of 65,000 in the subsidiary equity account to clear it (AJ_EQUIMETH).

In summary, the following are the key points of the equity method:

▸ You can use the equity type method-based multiplier to eliminate general balance sheet accounts for the investee without any detailed account assignments.

▶ Business rules in general are flexible in that they can easily be used to generate multiple values to achieve the required accounting entries.

That completes our initial pass through the method-based multiplier and eliminations and adjustments business rules. Now let's extend our understanding with a deep dive into the details.

7.4.7 Ownership Eliminations

For this detailed discussion, the purchase scenario is used as an example, however, the concepts apply to the proportional and equity methods as well.

One-Sided versus Double-Sided Entries.

The previous example took a very straightforward approach with the intent of making the first time through the eliminations and adjustments business rules easier to digest. In effect, we generated two one-sided bookings (❷ and ❸) as you can see in Figure 7.55. Entry ❶ occurred during the data import.

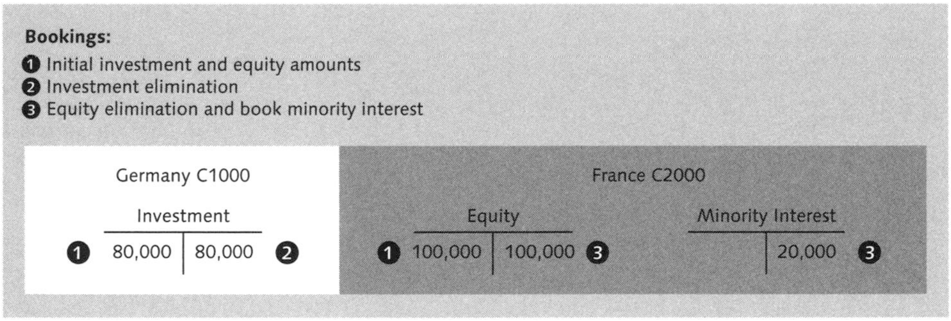

Bookings:
❶ Initial investment and equity amounts
❷ Investment elimination
❸ Equity elimination and book minority interest

Germany C1000			France C2000			
Investment			Equity		Minority Interest	
❶ 80,000	80,000 ❷		❶ 100,000	100,000 ❸		20,000 ❸

Figure 7.55 Purchase Method Initial Bookings

Although the entries ❷ and ❸ balance in total, the companies are now out of balance. So, you need to take an alternative approach by using offsetting entries into the INVESTMENT OFFSET and CONSOLIDATION RESERVES accounts, as shown in Figure 7.56.

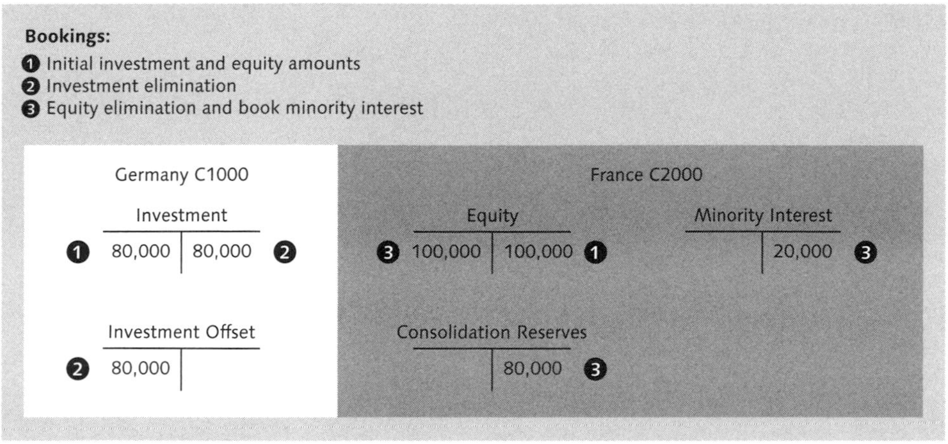

Figure 7.56 Purchase Method with Offsetting Entries

So now, not only are you in balance in total but the companies are also in balance.

A debit entry of 80,000 to the INVESTMENT OFFSET account has been added to offset the credit entry to the INVESTMENT account and that balances company C1000.

A credit entry of 80,000 to CONSOLIDATION RESERVES has been added to offset the 100,000 debit entry to EQUITY and the 20,000 credit entry to MINORITY INTEREST for company C2000.

To carry this out with the business rules, you need to use a new rule called ELCOI4 that uses a destination audit of AJ_COI1.

While you're changing the configuration, you can also try to generate all of the postings with only one rule. In the DETAILS tab in Figure 7.57, you can see there are two rows:

▶ **Row 1**
The value in the SOURCE ACCOUNT 12311000 will be written to the DESTINATION GROUP ACCOUNT 12311100 and the DESTINATION ALL ACCOUNT 12311000 based on RULE060.

▶ **Row 2**
The value in the SOURCE ACCOUNT 25110000 will be written to the DESTINATION GROUP ACCOUNT 25111000, DESTINATION ALL ACCOUNT 25110000, and DESTINATION MINORITY ACCOUNT 24111000 based on RULE010.

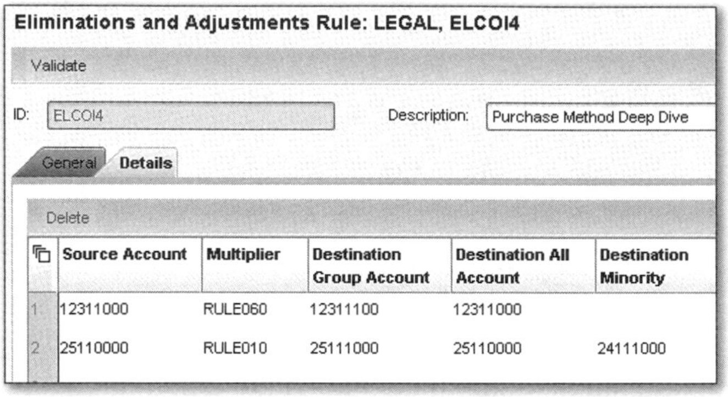

Eliminations and Adjustments Rule: LEGAL, ELCOI4

Validate

ID: ELCOI4   Description: Purchase Method Deep Dive

General **Details**

Delete

	Source Account	Multiplier	Destination Group Account	Destination All Account	Destination Minority
1	12311000	RULE060	12311100	12311000	
2	25110000	RULE010	25111000	25110000	24111000

Figure 7.57 Eliminations and Adjustments Rule for Additional Offsetting Entries

In Figure 7.58, you can see that the desired results are generated. Because only used one rule was used, only one DataSource (AJ_COI1) was used.

		INPUT	AJ_COI1	AJ_COI2	AJ_COI3	TOTALADJ
12311000 - Investments - Purchase	C1000	80,000	-80,000			0
12311100 - Investments - Offset	C1000		80,000			80,000
24111000 - Min Int - Purchase	C2000		20,000			20,000
25110000 - Treasury Stock - Purchase	C2000	100,000	-100,000			0
25111000 - Consolidation Reserves	C2000		80,000			80,000

Figure 7.58 Detailed Results

Now that we've talked about how to generate offsetting entries and how to efficiently create the business rules, let's discuss how to use the group dimension properties to provide more flexibility for reporting.

Group Dimension Properties.

In cases where there is a need to run reports by elimination entity, there are two group dimension properties that need to be used:

▶ STORE ENTITY

▶ STORE_GROUP_CURR

These two properties control the number of records generated when consolidation is executed. In the CONSGROUP dimension shown in Figure 7.59, the STORE ENTITY and STORE_GROUP_CURR properties are blank.

Members of Dimension: CONSGROUP

Delete | Revert | Recently Deleted Members | Display ⊿ | Export to CSV

ID 1 ≜	Descr...	STORE ENTITY	STORE_GROUP_CURR
1	G_CG1	Corporate		
2	G_CG2	Europe		
3	G_CG3	America		
4	G_CG4	Asia Pacific		
5	G_H1	Investments		
6	G_NONE	G None		

Figure 7.59 CONSGROUP with Blank Store Entity and Store_Group_Curr

When you run consolidation using the CONSGROUP property values in Figure 7.59, the report results appear as follows in Figure 7.60.

To completely understand the entries created by the system, the database records related to the data load, currency translation, and consolidation run are shown in Figure 7.60 as well. The values are exactly the same as in the previous report in Figure 7.58 except that the first two records in LC are also displayed.

Report View: (in USD)

		INPUT	AJ_COI1	AJ_COI2	AJ_COI3	TOTALADJ
12311000 - Investments - Purchase	C1000	80,000	-80,000			0
12311100 - Investments - Offset	C1000		80,000			80,000
24111000 - Min Int - Purchase	C2000		20,000			20,000
25110000 - Treasury Stock - Purchase	C2000	100,000	-100,000			0
25111000 - Consolidation Reserves	C2000		80,000			80,000

Data Base View:

	Entity	Group	Account	Category	D.Source	Flow	Intco	Rpt Cur	Time	Amount
1	C1000	G_NONE	12311000	ACTUAL	INPUT	F_CB	I_C2000	LC	2011.12	61,538.4615385
	C2000	G_NONE	25110000	ACTUAL	INPUT	F_CB	ThirdParty	LC	2011.12	76,923.0769231-
2	C1000	G_CG2	12311000	ACTUAL	INPUT	F_CB	I_C2000	USD	2011.12	80,000.0000001
	C2000	G_CG2	25110000	ACTUAL	INPUT	F_CB	ThirdParty	USD	2011.12	100,000.0000000-
	C1000	G_CG2	12311000	ACTUAL	AJ_COI1	F_CB	I_C2000	USD	2011.12	80,000.0000001-
	C1000	G_CG2	12311100	ACTUAL	AJ_COI1	F_CB	I_C2000	USD	2011.12	80,000.0000001
3	C2000	G_CG2	24111000	ACTUAL	AJ_COI1	F_CB	ThirdParty	USD	2011.12	20,000.0000000-
	C2000	G_CG2	25110000	ACTUAL	AJ_COI1	F_CB	ThirdParty	USD	2011.12	100,000.0000000
	C2000	G_CG2	25111000	ACTUAL	AJ_COI1	F_CB	ThirdParty	USD	2011.12	80,000.0000000-

Legend:
1 Data Load   **2** Currency Translation   **3** Run Consolidation

Figure 7.60 Results with One DataSource

In Figure 7.61, you can see that the STORE ENTITY and STORE_GROUP_CURR properties have been turned on in the CONSGROUP dimension via the "Y" value.

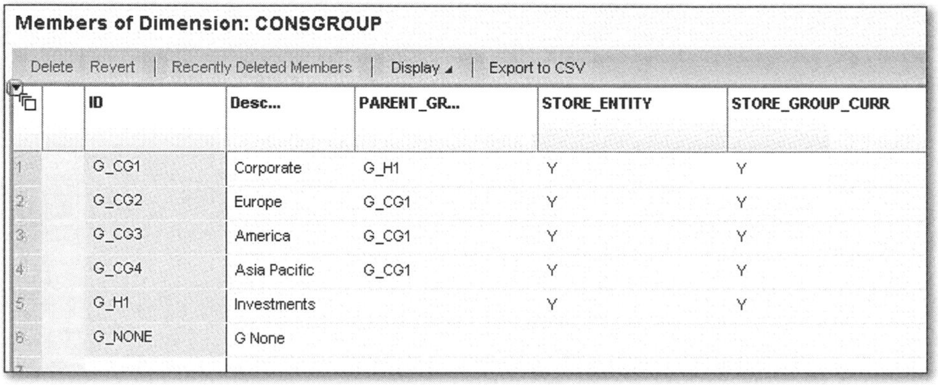

Members of Dimension: CONSGROUP

Delete | Revert | Recently Deleted Members | Display ◢ | Export to CSV

	ID	Desc...	PARENT_GR...	STORE_ENTITY	STORE_GROUP_CURR
1	G_CG1	Corporate	G_H1	Y	Y
2	G_CG2	Europe	G_CG1	Y	Y
3	G_CG3	America	G_CG1	Y	Y
4	G_CG4	Asia Pacific	G_CG1	Y	Y
5	G_H1	Investments		Y	Y
6	G_NONE	G None			

Figure 7.61 Members of Dimension CONGROUP (with STORE ENTITY and STORE_GROUP_ CURR Turned On)

By generating more records in the database, you now have more reporting options. As a consequence, this allows you to run reports at the elimination entity level as shown in the report view in Figure 7.62. Notice that the COMPANY column is now reporting on the E_CG2 entity. Now, you'll see quite a few more records generated in the database after consolidation is run. In the database view in Figure 7.62, the entities now include additional entries for the E_CG2 member.

In summary, the CONSGROUP dimension STORE ENTITY and STORE_GROUP_CURR properties are required to do reporting at the elimination entity level.

Some corporations may need to report in multiple group currencies so we'll discuss that topic next.

Setting Up Multiple Group Currencies

In some cases, corporations need to report in multiple group currencies. For example, a German-based company with a significant number of operating units in the United States may need to report in both EUR and USD.

In that case, all you need to do aside from populating the Rate model with the associated exchange rates is to add the second GROUP_CURRENCY to the group dimension as shown in Figure 7.63.

Report View: (in USD)

	Company	INPUT	AJ_COI1	AJ_COI2	AJ_COI3	TOTALADJ
12311000 - Investments - Purchase	E_CG2	80,000	-80,000			0
12311100 - Investments - Offset	E_CG2		80,000			80,000
24111000 - Min Int - Purchase	E_CG2		20,000			20,000
25110000 - Treasury Stock - Purchase	E_CG2	100,000	-100,000			0
25111000 - Consolidation Reserves	E_CG2		80,000			80,000

Data Base View:

Entity	Group	Account	Category	D.Source	Flow	Intco	Rpt Cur	Time	Amount
C1000 ⊞	G_NONE	12311000	ACTUAL	INPUT	F_CB	I_C2000	LC	2011.12	61,538.
C2000	G_NONE	25110000	ACTUAL	INPUT	F_CB	ThirdParty	LC	2011.12	76,923.
C1000	G_CG2	12311000	ACTUAL	INPUT	F_CB	I_C2000	USD	2011.12	80,000.
C1000	G_NONE	12311000	ACTUAL	INPUT	F_CB	I_C2000	USD	2011.12	80,000.
C2000	G_CG2	25110000	ACTUAL	INPUT	F_CB	ThirdParty	USD	2011.12	100,000.
C2000	G_NONE	25110000	ACTUAL	INPUT	F_CB	ThirdParty	USD	2011.12	100,000.
E_CG2	G_CG2	12311000	ACTUAL	INPUT	F_CB	I_C2000	USD	2011.12	80,000.
E_CG2	G_CG2	25110000	ACTUAL	INPUT	F_CB	ThirdParty	USD	2011.12	100,000.
C1000	G_CG2	12311000	ACTUAL	AJ_COI1	F_CB	I_C2000	USD	2011.12	80,000.
C1000	G_CG2	12311100	ACTUAL	AJ_COI1	F_CB	I_C2000	USD	2011.12	80,000.
C2000	G_CG2	24111000	ACTUAL	AJ_COI1	F_CB	ThirdParty	USD	2011.12	20,000.
C2000	G_CG2	25110000	ACTUAL	AJ_COI1	F_CB	ThirdParty	USD	2011.12	100,000.
C2000	G_CG2	25111000	ACTUAL	AJ_COI1	F_CB	ThirdParty	USD	2011.12	80,000.
E_CG2	G_CG2	12311000	ACTUAL	AJ_COI1	F_CB	I_C2000	USD	2011.12	80,000.
E_CG2	G_CG2	24111000	ACTUAL	AJ_COI1	F_CB	ThirdParty	USD	2011.12	20,000.
E_CG2	G_CG2	25110000	ACTUAL	AJ_COI1	F_CB	ThirdParty	USD	2011.12	100,000.
E_CG2	G_CG2	12311100	ACTUAL	AJ_COI1	F_CB	I_C2000	USD	2011.12	80,000.
E_CG2	G_CG2	25111000	ACTUAL	AJ_COI1	F_CB	ThirdParty	USD	2011.12	80,000.

Legend:

❶ Data Load ❷ Currency Translation ❸ Run Consolidation

Figure 7.62 Results with Store Entity and Store_Group_Curr Turned On

Members of Dimension: CONSGROUP

Delete Revert | Recently Deleted Members | Display ▲ Export to CSV

	ID	Desc...	PARENT_GR...	STORE_ENTITY	STORE_GROUP_...	GROUP...
1	G_CG1	Corporate	G_H1	Y	Y	EUR,USD
2	G_CG2	Europe	G_CG1	Y	Y	EUR,USD
3	G_CG3	America	G_CG1	Y	Y	EUR,USD
4	G_CG4	Asia Pacific	G_CG1	Y	Y	EUR,USD
5	G_H1	Investments		Y	Y	EUR,USD
6	G_NONE	G None				

Figure 7.63 CONSGROUP Dimension with Multiple Group Currencies

When you run the consolidation package, both currencies are automatically translated and consolidated as shown in Figure 7.64.

Entity	Group	Account	Category	D.Source	Flow	Intco	Rpt Cur	Time	Amount
C1000	G_NONE	12311000	ACTUAL	INPUT	F_CB	I_C2000	LC	2011.12	61,538
C2000	G_NONE	25110000	ACTUAL	INPUT	F_CB	ThirdParty	LC	2011.12	76,923
C1000	G_CG2	12311000	ACTUAL	INPUT	F_CB	I_C2000	EUR	2011.12	61,538
C1000	G_CG2	12311000	ACTUAL	INPUT	F_CB	I_C2000	USD	2011.12	80,000
C2000	G_CG2	25110000	ACTUAL	INPUT	F_CB	ThirdParty	EUR	2011.12	76,923
C2000	G_CG2	25110000	ACTUAL	INPUT	F_CB	ThirdParty	USD	2011.12	100,000
C1000	G_CG2	12311000	ACTUAL	AJ_COI1	F_CB	I_C2000	EUR	2011.12	61,538
C1000	G_CG2	12311000	ACTUAL	AJ_COI1	F_CB	I_C2000	USD	2011.12	80,000
C1000	G_CG2	12311100	ACTUAL	AJ_COI1	F_CB	I_C2000	EUR	2011.12	61,538
C1000	G_CG2	12311100	ACTUAL	AJ_COI1	F_CB	I_C2000	USD	2011.12	80,000
C2000	G_CG2	24111000	ACTUAL	AJ_COI1	F_CB	ThirdParty	EUR	2011.12	15,384
C2000	G_CG2	24111000	ACTUAL	AJ_COI1	F_CB	ThirdParty	USD	2011.12	20,000
C2000	G_CG2	25110000	ACTUAL	AJ_COI1	F_CB	ThirdParty	EUR	2011.12	76,923
C2000	G_CG2	25110000	ACTUAL	AJ_COI1	F_CB	ThirdParty	USD	2011.12	100,000
C2000	G_CG2	25111000	ACTUAL	AJ_COI1	F_CB	ThirdParty	EUR	2011.12	61,538
C2000	G_CG2	25111000	ACTUAL	AJ_COI1	F_CB	ThirdParty	USD	2011.12	80,000

Legend:
❶ Data Load ❷ Currency Translation ❸ Run Consolidation

Figure 7.64 Database Records with Multiple Group Currencies

As a result, you can now generate group-level reports in multiple currencies.

Now, let's discuss some of the new features coming out in later service packs.

Support Pack Enhancements

In SP06, there is a new model setting called Integration Rules. This is required to account for subsidiary transfers between groups within the fiscal year.

Also, the consolidation engine will be enhanced in SP07 to include additional functionality to accommodate the banking-related financial nuances of consolidation (referred to as Equity Pick Up, EPU).

In addition, in SP07, you can partition the data during consolidation to improve performance.

Currently, the consolidation process works as a single thread calculation, but in the SP07, you can identify a dimension to partition the data for faster processing.

In the next section, you'll match intercompany (IC) AP to AR to prepare the data for eliminations.

7.4.8 Intercompany Matching

Intercompany matching is typically needed for IC AP and IC AR but can also be required for IC Interest and Loans, for example. Matching must precede IC eliminations in the closing process.

Intercompany Matching Business Scenario

Before eliminating IC AP to IC AR, you need to compare the balances, take corrective action on the differences, and book the remaining differences. Following are the main reasons there are differences:

▶ Errors

▶ Timing differences

▶ Foreign exchange differences

Ideally, if these differences can be resolved in the source system before the data is imported into the planning and consolidation InfoCube, the matching process would not be needed.

In the matching process, there are two main activities:

▶ First, the data for each entity is concentrated into unique DataSources to facilitate data reconciliation (using the ICData package).

▶ Second, after the reconciliation process, the differences are booked (using the ICBooking package).

> **Note: Intercompany Matching versus SAP BusinessObjects InterCompany**
>
> By the way, planning and consolidation intercompany matching isn't to be confused with one of the other SAP products called SAP BusinessObjects InterCompany, which also performs intercompany matching except at a much more granular level.

Intercompany Matching Components

The DataSource dimension has a unique property as well as members that are used in the matching process. In Figure 7.65, you can see the DEBIT# and CREDIT# members. These are used to collect the IC data for reconciliation purposes.

The IC_ORIGINE property is used to identify which members will be written to by the IC Data package.

In Figure 7.65, the DataSource dimension is named ICDATASRC, however, you can use other names such as Audit or DataSource since dimension names are determined by the customer.

Members of Dimension: ICDATASRC

Delete Revert | Recently Deleted Members | Apply Hierarchy Order Display | Export to CSV

	ID	Desc...	IC_ORIGINE	Is Translated ?	PARENTH1
1	INPUT	Company Input	I	Y	
2	CREDIT1	Their Liab / Exp...	C1	N	TOTAL1
3	CREDIT2	My Liab / Expen...	C2	N	TOTAL2
4	DEBIT1	My Assets / Inc...	D1	N	TOTAL1
5	DEBIT2	Their Assets / I...	D2	N	TOTAL2
6	ICDIFF	IC Difference		G	
7	TOTAL1	Total 1			
8	TOTAL2	Total 2			

Figure 7.65 Members of Dimension: ICDATASRC

IC Matching uses just one business rule. To create the intercompany bookings business rule, an ID is selected. The ID is a parent in the account dimension, which contains the relevant IC accounts.

In Figure 7.66, you can see a sample INTERCOMPANY BOOKINGS RULE screen with an ID of CTLICENDOO (a parent IC account).

The fields in this business rule are defined as follows:

- ID
  The parent of the accounts to include in the processing.
- DESCRIPTION
  Description of the rule.

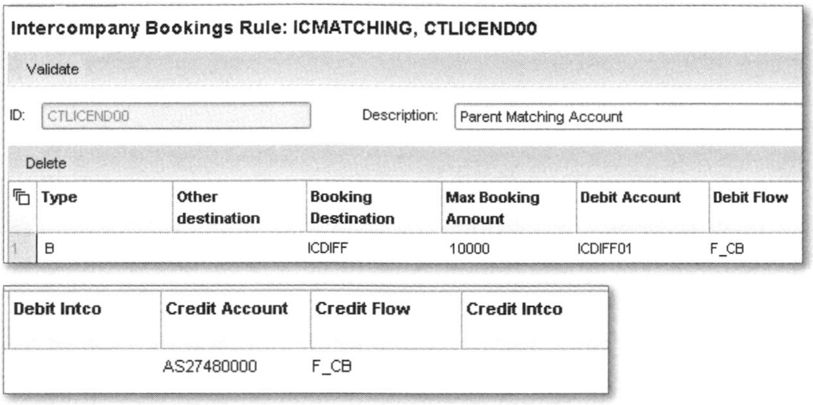

Figure 7.66 Intercompany Bookings Rule

▶ TYPE
Determines whether the buyer or seller receives the difference. The following options are available:

  ▶ S
  SELLER: The seller is correct, so the buyer receives the difference.

  ▶ B
  BUYER: The buyer is correct, so the seller receives the difference.

  ▶ G
  GREATEST: Entity with the greatest amount receives the difference.

▶ OTHER DESTINATION
Target dimension member other than account, flow, and intercompany.

▶ BOOKING DESTINATION
The target DataSource dimension member.

▶ MAX BOOKING AMOUNT
The limit of the balancing entry. Differences above this amount won't post.

▶ DEBIT ACCOUNT
Debit account for the difference.

▶ DEBIT FLOW
Debit flow for the difference.

▶ DEBIT INTCO
Debit intercompany for the difference.

▶ CREDIT ACCOUNT
Credit account for the difference.

▶ CREDIT FLOW
Credit flow for the difference.

▶ CREDIT INTCO
Credit intercompany for the difference.

IC Matching uses two logic files. The ICDATA Script Logic file is used by the ICData package as shown in Figure 7.67.

The ICDATA Script Logic file doesn't use a business rule because the DataSource dimension contains the required parameters, that is, the Ic_Origine property.

The second logic file is ICBOOKING, which is used by the ICBooking package.

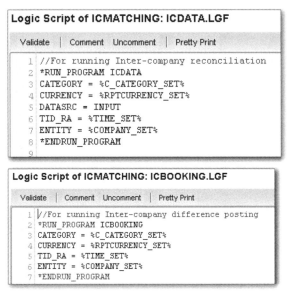

Figure 7.67 Logic Script of ICMATCHING: ICDATA.LGF

The ICBOOKING logic file is used in conjunction with the intercompany bookings business rule.

Intercompany Matching Results

In Figure 7.68, you can see the data before and after running the ICData package. C1000 is the seller and C2000 is the buyer.

Before:								
			LC	USD	USD	USD	USD	USD
			INPUT	INPUT	CREDIT1	DEBIT1	CREDIT2	DEBIT2
LI16870000	I_C1000	C2000	378.0	491.4				
LI16870000	I_C2000	C1000						
AS27480000	I_C1000	C2000						
AS27480000	I_C2000	C1000	375.0	487.5				

After:								
			LC	USD	USD	USD	USD	USD
			INPUT	INPUT	CREDIT1	DEBIT1	CREDIT2	DEBIT2
LI16870000	I_C1000	C2000	378.0	491.4			491.4	
LI16870000	I_C2000	C1000			491.4			
AS27480000	I_C1000	C2000						487.5
AS27480000	I_C2000	C1000	375.0	487.5		487.5		
ICDIFF01	I_C2000	C1000						

Figure 7.68 Results Before and After Running ICData

After running the ICData package, Figure 7.68 shows that the data was copied into the DEBIT and CREDIT DataSource members, but the ICDIFF01 account is still blank.

If needed, you can secure the access to the appropriate accountants using the DEBIT and CREDIT member IDs. Also, the key point of the ICData task is to facilitate the reconciliation process by capturing the data into the CREDIT# and DEBIT# Data-Source IDs.

At this point in the process, there would be plenty of analysis to determine what caused the differences and what action needs to be taken if necessary. In the example in Figure 7.69, the difference is small enough (3.9 USD) so that it's okay to book the difference.

After running the ICBooking package, the ICDIFF01 account for the seller (C1000) now contains the difference posting as shown in Figure 7.69.

The seller is charged the difference because we chose the B-BUYER rule which is interpreted as The buyer is correct, so the seller receives the difference.

			LC	USD	USD	USD	USD	USD	USD
			INPUT	INPUT	CREDIT1	DEBIT1	CREDIT2	DEBIT2	ICDIFF
LI16870000	I_C1000	C2000	378.0	491.4			491.4		
LI16870000	I_C2000	C1000			491.4				
AS27480000	I_C1000	C2000						487.5	
AS27480000	I_C2000	C1000	375.0	487.5		487.5			-3.9
ICDIFF01	I_C2000	C1000							3.9

Figure 7.69 Results after Running ICBooking

Now that we've balanced the IC AP AR, we can proceed to intercompany eliminations.

7.4.9 Intercompany Eliminations

To eliminate IC AP and IC AR, you can use the same components used for the purchase, proportional, and equity method eliminations. The only difference will be the account assignments in the ELIMINATIONS AND ADJUSTMENTS RULE screen. In other words, after the components are set up, they can be used for a variety of eliminations.

Intercompany Eliminations Business Scenario

A consolidated balance sheet shows only payables and receivables that relate to third-party transactions. Payables and receivables resulting from the exchange of goods and services within the corporate group must be eliminated; otherwise, they will be double-counted.

Intercompany activities that require elimination include the following:

► Intercompany AP and AR
► Intercompany loans and interest
► Intercompany profit on fixed asset transfers
► Intercompany royalties
► Intercompany revenue and COGS
► Intercompany dividends

In the following example, you need to eliminate the IC AP and IC AR between C1000 and C2000 in the Europe group.

In Figure 7.70, you can see a combined data set from the Ownership and Legal models for the Europe group (values in USD).

Group	Entity	Method	POWN	11301100 IC Trade Receivables	21171000 IC Trade Payables
G_CG2 - Europe	C1000 - Germany	90-Parent	100%	487.5	
G_CG2 - Europe	C2000 - UK	86-Purchase	80%		487.5

Figure 7.70 Europe Group IC AP and IC AR and Ownership Data

Now let's see what components you need to use for this elimination.

Intercompany Elimination Components

In the ELIMINATIONS AND ADJUSTMENTS RULE screen in Figure 7.71, the SOURCE and DESTINATION ALL ACCOUNTS contain a DIMLIST property called ARAP, which is being used to select both the source and target IC AP and IC AR accounts. In addition, the DESTINATION GROUP ACCOUNT is the APAROFFSET account, which will be used as the offsetting account. RULE040 will select the parent member along with any other trading partner and will eliminate 100%. The ELPAR rule is assigned to the AJ_ELIM audit ID.

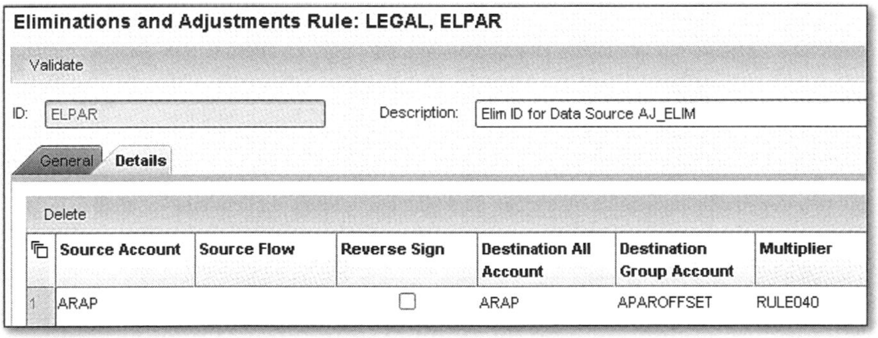

Eliminations and Adjustments Rule: LEGAL, ELPAR

Validate

ID: ELPAR   Description: Elim ID for Data Source AJ_ELIM

General | **Details**

Delete

	Source Account	Source Flow	Reverse Sign	Destination All Account	Destination Group Account	Multiplier
1	ARAP		☐	ARAP	APAROFFSET	RULE040

Figure 7.71 Eliminations and Adjustments Rule: LEGAL, ELPAR

In Figure 7.72, you can see a graphical representation of the components and processing steps.

These are the processing steps when consolidation is executed for G_CG2:

❶ The source values of $27,300 for the AR-11301100 and the AP-21171000 accounts are read into memory. The accounts are being selected via the ARAP DIMLIST property value in the Account dimension.

❷ The formula values are looked up. In this case, 1(100%) is used to eliminate all IC AP and IC AR.

❸ Of the $487.5 source values, 100% are posted to the destination accounts and AJ_ELIM DataSource.

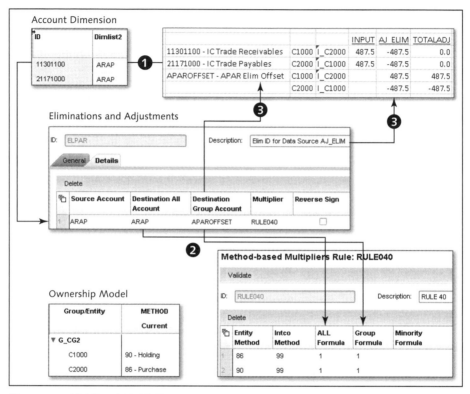

Figure 7.72 IC AP and IC AR Elimination Components

The diagram in Figure 7.72 might come in handy if you need to investigate why you aren't getting the results you expected.

Intercompany Eliminations Results

The results of the consolidation package for G_CG2-Europe are displayed in Figure 7.73. The IC AP and IC AR values in the INPUT audit ID are eliminated in the AJ_ELIM audit ID with the offset going to the APAROFFSET account.

			INPUT	AJ ELIM	TOTALADJ
11301100 - IC Trade Receivables	C1000	I_C2000	487.5	-487.5	0.0
21171000 - IC Trade Payables	C2000	I_C1000	487.5	-487.5	0.0
APAROFFSET - APAR Elim Offset	C1000	I_C2000		487.5	487.5
	C2000	I_C1000		-487.5	-487.5

Figure 7.73 IC AP and IC AR Elimination Results

In summary, IC AP and IC AR eliminations use the same components as the ownership eliminations, including the consolidations Data Manager package.

Next, we'll head into the simpler US eliminations method to perform IC eliminations.

7.4.10 US Eliminations

First of all, the US eliminations business rule isn't only for US corporations. It was named US eliminations because a US company wanted this functionality first.

This business rule is used in simpler cases, for example, when no ownership eliminations are required. However, it can also be used in conjunction with the elimination and adjustments business rules.

Before we delve into the US eliminations setup and so forth, let's compare it to the elimination and adjustments business rules.

Figure 7.74 shows a comparison of the US versus the elimination and adjustments business rules. There are six key points that distinguish the two options:

▶ The US eliminations business rule is standalone, whereas the elimination and adjustments business rules require the methods and method-based multipliers business rules.

▶ The US eliminations business rule can be used in a Financial or Consolidation type model while the elimination and adjustments business rules can only be used in a Consolidation type model.

▶ The offset account determination takes place in the account dimension for US eliminations whereas the elimination and adjustments business rules includes offset account determination.

▶ US eliminations requires a Data Manager package and Script Logic.

▶ US eliminations can only be run from a package (not from the Consolidation Monitor).

▶ Eliminations and adjustment business rules do not require a Data Manager package and Script Logic because they can be executed via the Consolidation Monitor.

Option	Business Rule Tables	Model Type	Offset Accounts Determination	Data Manager Package and Script Logic
US Eliminations	US Eliminations	Financial or Consolidation	Account Dimension	Required
Eliminations and Adjustments	Methods, Method Based Multipliers, Eliminations and Adjustments	Consolidation only	Eliminations and Adjustments, Business Rules	Not Required

Figure 7.74 US Eliminations Compared to Elimination and Adjustment Business Rules

Now let's move into the details of the US elimination option. The following example is an IC revenue and COGS elimination.

US Eliminations Components

The Account dimension has a property that is used exclusively for US eliminations called ELIMACC, which is used to assign the offset account to the IC accounts. In Figure 7.75, you can see the two IC accounts with the USELIMOFFSET account assigned in the ELIMACC column.

In addition, the Entity dimension also has a property that is used exclusively for US eliminations called ELIM.

In the COMPANY dimension shown in Figure 7.75, the E_CG# members each have a value of Y for the ELIM property, which means that they will be included when the US elimination package is run.

Now that you've seen the unique dimension properties for US eliminations, let's move on to the business rule.

The US elimination business rule can be used for both a Consolidation and Finance type model. In addition, it's only one business rule as opposed to the three that are used for ownership and IC AP and IC AR eliminations.

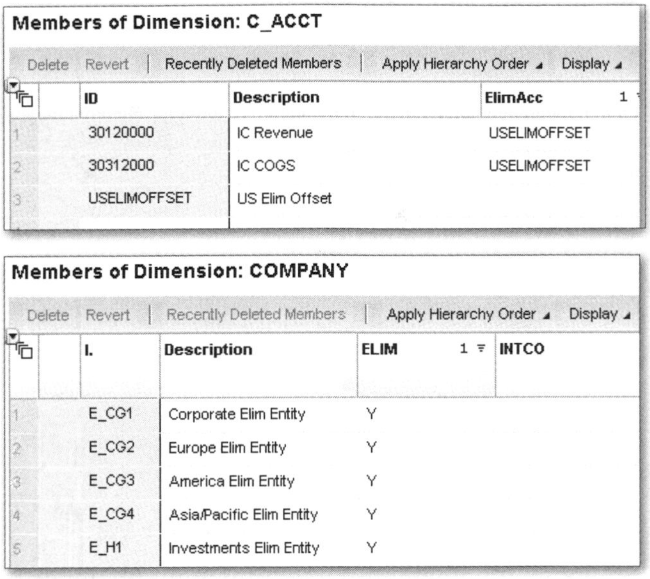

Members of Dimension: C_ACCT

Delete　Revert　| Recently Deleted Members　| Apply Hierarchy Order ◢　Display ◢

	ID	Description	ElimAcc	1
1	30120000	IC Revenue	USELIMOFFSET	
2	30312000	IC COGS	USELIMOFFSET	
3	USELIMOFFSET	US Elim Offset		

Members of Dimension: COMPANY

Delete　Revert　| Recently Deleted Members　| Apply Hierarchy Order ◢　Display ◢

	I.	Description	ELIM	1	INTCO
1	E_CG1	Corporate Elim Entity	Y		
2	E_CG2	Europe Elim Entity	Y		
3	E_CG3	America Elim Entity	Y		
4	E_CG4	Asia/Pacific Elim Entity	Y		
5	E_H1	Investments Elim Entity	Y		

Figure 7.75　Entity and Account Dimension Properties for US Eliminations

The US ELIMINATIONS screen consists of three fields.

▶ ELIMINATION ID
This is a user defined logical ID.

▶ SOURCE AUDIT
This can be a base level or parent member. You can also filter via the DIMLIST property.

▶ DESTINATION
This can be a base level or parent member.

As you can see, this business rule is very straightforward. The number of rows depends on the number of combinations of SOURCE and DESTINATION audit members.

The script in Figure 7.76 will generate entries for the G_NONE group as opposed to other valid group IDs. To book elimination entries against intercompany group IDs, just replace CURRENCY=%RPTCURRENCY_SET% with GROUP=%CONSGROUP_SET% in the Script Logic file and replace CURRENCY with GROUP in the Data Manager package parameters.

US Eliminations

	Elimination ID	Source Audit	Destination	Remark
	ICELIM	INPUT	US_ELIM	Eliminate IC Revenue and COGS

Validate

Delete

Logic Script of LEGAL: ICELIM.LGF

Validate | Comment | Uncomment | Pretty Print

```
1  *RUN_PROGRAM US_ELIM
2  CATEGORY = %C_CATEGORY_SET%
3  CURRENCY = %RPTCURRENCY_SET%
4  TID_RA = %TIME_SET%
5  ENTITY = %COMPANY_SET%
6  *ENDRUN_PROGRAM
7
```

Figure 7.76 US Eliminations Business Rule and Script Logic

US Eliminations Results

The delivered IC elimination package runs this business rule. You can see the results of this package in Figure 7.77. The elimination and offsetting entries are only generated for the elimination entity E_CG2.

Report View:

			INPUT	US_ELIM
C1000	I_C2000	30120000 - IC Revenue	36,347	
C2000	I_C1000	30312000 - IC COGS	36,347	
E_CG2	I_C1000	30312000 - IC COGS		-36,347
E_CG2	I_C1000	USELIMOFFSET - US Elim Offset		36,347
E_CG2	I_C2000	30120000 - IC Revenue		-36,347
E_CG2	I_C2000	USELIMOFFSET - US Elim Offset		-36,347

Data Base View:

	Entity	Group	Account	Category	D.Source	Flow	Intco	Rpt Cur	Time	Amount
1	C1000	G_NONE	30120000	ACTUAL	INPUT	F_CB	I_C2000	LC	2011.12	24,231.0000000-
	C2000	G_NONE	30312000	ACTUAL	INPUT	F_CB	I_C1000	LC	2011.12	24,231.0000000
2	C1000	G_NONE	30120000	ACTUAL	INPUT	F_CB	I_C2000	USD	2011.12	36,346.5000000-
	C2000	G_NONE	30312000	ACTUAL	INPUT	F_CB	I_C1000	USD	2011.12	36,346.5000000
3	E_CG2	G_NONE	30120000	ACTUAL	US_ELIM	F_CB	I_C2000	USD	2011.12	36,346.5000000
	E_CG2	G_NONE	30312000	ACTUAL	US_ELIM	F_CB	I_C1000	USD	2011.12	36,346.5000000-
	E_CG2	G_NONE	USELIMOFFSET	ACTUAL	US_ELIM	F_CB	I_C1000	USD	2011.12	36,346.5000000
	E_CG2	G_NONE	USELIMOFFSET	ACTUAL	US_ELIM	F_CB	I_C2000	USD	2011.12	36,346.5000000-

Legend:
1 Data Load   **2** Currency Translation   **3** Run Consolidation

Figure 7.77 US Elimination Results

The report in Figure 7.77 can be deceiving at first glance because the 30120000 account value has the sign switched due to an account type property of INC. To avoid any confusion, you can see from the database view that the bottom four records generated by the US elimination package do in fact offset each other.

In summary, the US elimination business rule is very easy to use and is applicable to less complex cases where ownership eliminations aren't required.

Next we'll discuss balancing logic.

7.5   Setting Up Balancing Script Logic for Consolidation

As you've seen, every consolidation task uses a Script Logic file to call the standard programs. However, Script Logic is also used to perform balancing of your financial statements.

7.5.1   Balancing Logic Business Scenario

Script logic in general has two main roles in the consolidation process:

▸ Script Logic calls standard programs such as currency translation and reclassification for example.

▸ Script Logic performs financial statement balancing.

As data is imported into the Legal model, there is usually a need to automatically keep the income statement and balance sheet in balance. For example, ANNUAL NET INCOME (ANI) should equal CURRENT YEAR RETAINED EARNINGS (CYRE). In Figure 7.78, the ANI is transferred to the CYRE via the P&L CLEARING ACCOUNT. The main point is that ANI results in CYRE in the balance sheet.

Income Statement		Balance Sheet	
Revenue	-125	Assets	200
COGS	90	Liabilities	-100
Gross Margin	-35	Owners' Equity	
Other Expense	5	Current Year Retained Earnings	-30
Annual Net Income	-30	Prior Year Retained Earnings	-65
		Common Stock	-5
P&L Clearing Account	30	Total Balance Sheet	0

Figure 7.78 Income Statement and Balance Sheet

Balancing Logic Components

To perform balancing, you can use the following logic in Listing 7.1.

```
*XDIM_MEMBERSET FLOW=BAS(F_TOT)
//This reads the opening balance plus changes(children of the F_TOT
parent) values into memory.
*XDIM_ADDMEMBERSET FLOW=F_CB
//This reads the F_CB closing balance values into memory.
*XDIM_MEMBERSET INTCO=ThirdParty
//This reads the ThirdParty member values into memory.
*WHEN C_ACCT.GROUP
//When accounts with a GROUP property value of ...
*IS PL
// PL (Profit and Loss), Sum those account values.
*WHEN FLOW
//When the Flow dimension
*IS F_CB
//Is F_CB (Closing Balance)
*WHEN INTCO
//When the INTCO dimension
*IS ThirdParty
//Is ThirdParty
*REC(C_ACCT=25712000,FLOW=F_RES,INTCO= ThirdParty)
//Record the value into 25712000 for F_RES and ThirdParty
*REC(C_ACCT=25712000,FLOW=F_CB,INTCO= ThirdParty)
//Also Record the value into 25712000 for F_CB and ThirdParty
*ENDWHEN
*ENDWHEN
*ENDWHEN
```

Listing 7.1 Sample Script Logic for Balancing

Now let's test the code by using an input form in Excel. In this case, the balancing logic has been referenced in the default logic file so that any data sends will trigger it.

Balancing Logic Results

You can see an example in Figure 7.79 where 550 is being sent to the database. During the data send, the balancing logic is triggered, and two values are booked: one for CYRE account/CLOSING BALANCE flow and another for CYRE account/CUR PER NET INCOME flow.

Before:

	Error	Closing balance	Opening Balance	Acquisition	Cur Per Net Income
Revenue		550			
Retained Earnings - Current Year					
Machinery & Equipment					
Third Party Payables					

After:

	Error	Closing balance	Opening Balance	Acquisition	Cur Per Net Income
Revenue		550			
Retained Earnings - Current Year		550			550
Machinery & Equipment					
Third Party Payables					

Figure 7.79   Balancing Logic: 550 Revenue Adjustment is Offset in Retained Earnings

In the next example, the balancing logic will check the Closing Balance = Opening Balance + Changes equation. In Figure 7.80, out of balance data is being sent to the MACHINERY & EQUIPMENT and THIRD PARTY PAYABLES accounts. After the data is sent, MACHINERY & EQUIPMENT had its out of balance of 580 booked to the error flow whereas the THIRD PARTY PAYABLES had its out of balance of 580 booked to the variation flow.

Before:

	Error	Closing balance	Opening Balance	Acquisition	Variation
Revenue		550			
Retained Earnings - Current Year		550			
Machinery & Equipment		880	200	100	
Third Party Payables		880	200	100	

After:

	Error	Closing balance	Opening Balance	Acquisition	Variation
Revenue		550			
Retained Earnings - Current Year		550			
Machinery & Equipment	580	880	200	100	
Third Party Payables		880	200	100	580

Figure 7.80   Balancing Logic – Sending Data to Test Closing Balance

Again, this is just an example to point out that you can easily direct the system to generate values in the error flow, for example, or you can force the difference into a variation flow member depending on the situation.

The balancing logic is using the DIMLIST1 property value to create a different result for MACHINERY & EQUIPMENT versus THIRD PARTY PAYABLES.

The logic used to generate the values in Figure 7.80 is detailed in Listing 7.2.

```
[FLOW].[#F_VAR]=IIF([C_ACCT].CURRENTMEMBER.PROPERTIES
("DIMLIST1")="L1_V",[FLOW].[F_CB]-[FLOW].[F_OB]-
[FLOW].[F_ACQ]+[FLOW].[F_RET],0)
// The F_VAR flow = If the DIMLIST property is L1_V then
Closing Balance - Opening Balance - Acquisitions + Returns, otherwise
it is zero.
*COMMIT
[FLOW].[#F_ERR] =IIF([C_ACCT].CURRENTMEMBER.PROPERTIES
("DIMLIST1")="L1_E",[FLOW].[F_CB]-[FLOW].[F_OB]-
[FLOW].[F_ACQ]+[FLOW].[F_RET],0)
// The F_ERR flow = If the DIMLIST property is L1_E then
Closing Balance - Opening Balance - Acquisitions + Returns, otherwise
it is zero.
*COMMIT
```
Note: The *COMMIT statement also writes data to the database.

Listing 7.2 Listing 7.2 Balancing Logic for CB = OB + Changes

You've just seen two examples of how you can apply balancing logic, one to keep the income statement consistent with the balance sheet and another to check closing balances.

7.6 The Consolidation Monitor

The Consolidation Monitor is a workspace for monitoring and executing the month-end closing tasks for a specific category, period, group, or subgroup. Up to now we've run all of the month-end closing tasks without using the Consolidation Monitor. Because the Consolidation Monitor is the primary UI for accountants to close the books, now you'll see what life is like for an end user.

7.6.1 Prerequisites to Use the Consolidation Monitor

There are four main prerequisites for using the Consolidation Monitor:

▶ The Consolidation Monitor can only be used for Consolidation type models.

▶ The investment structure data must be recorded into the Ownership model because the Consolidation Monitor uses the group/entity ownership hierarchy in the rows.

▶ Work status must be configured for the Consolidation model.

▶ The user needs to have the View Consolidation Monitor and Run Consolidation task profiles.

7.6.2 Using the Consolidation Monitor

When you enter the Consolidation Monitor from Consolidation Central, you must first set your context for the same Category, Group, and Time dimensions members that you've recorded the Ownership model. In addition, the Consolidation model must be selected.

In Figure 7.81, the Consolidation Monitor is displayed before any tasks have been performed. On the left-hand side, the investment structure from the Ownership model is displayed.

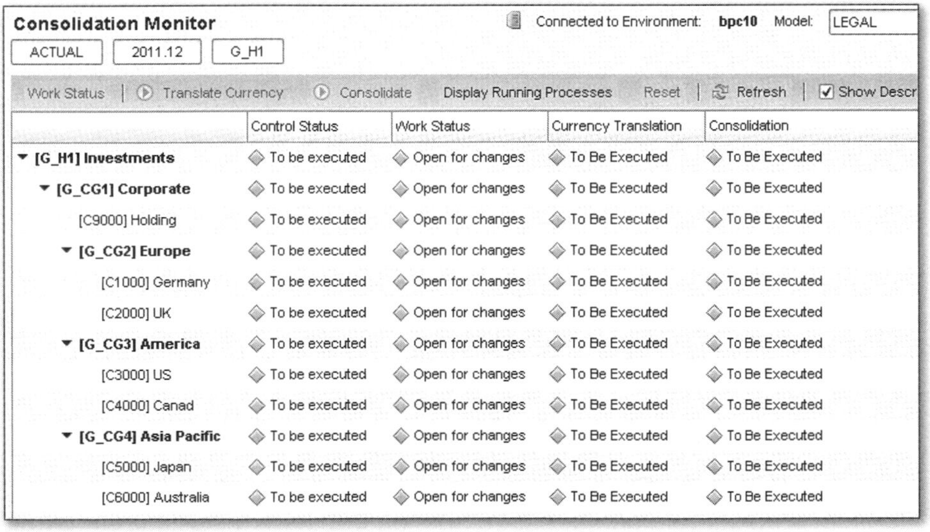

Figure 7.81 Initial Consolidation Monitor

The following list defines each of the buttons in the gray toolbar:

► WORK STATUS
Set the work status.

► TRANSLATE CURRENCY
Execute incremental or full translation.

► CONSOLIDATE
Execute incremental or full consolidation.

► DISPLAY RUNNING PROCESSES
Display the running processes with percent completion.

► RESET
Reset the currency and consolidation status.

► REFRESH
Refresh the statuses.

► MORE
Turn on the group member descriptions, and set the view to either list or hierarchy.

The four columns in the Consolidation Monitor consist of the following:

► CONTROL STATUS
The status of controls.

► WORK STATUS
The current work state.

► CURRENCY TRANSLATION
The status of currency translation.

► CONSOLIDATION
The status of consolidation.

Parent members will inherit the lowest status from their children. Using currency translation status as an example, if C1000 has a translation status of DONE, and C2000 has a status of ERROR, G_CG2 (the parent of C1000 and C2000) will inherit the ERROR status.

Now that you're familiar with the CONSOLIDATION MONITOR screen, let's use it just like you would during the month-end close.

To execute currency translation, choose the group member on the left, such as G_H1, and select TRANSLATE CURRENCY. The resulting splash screen is shown in Figure 7.82. This will perform the exact same translation as the FX restatement package however the FX restatement package doesn't update the Consolidation Monitor status.

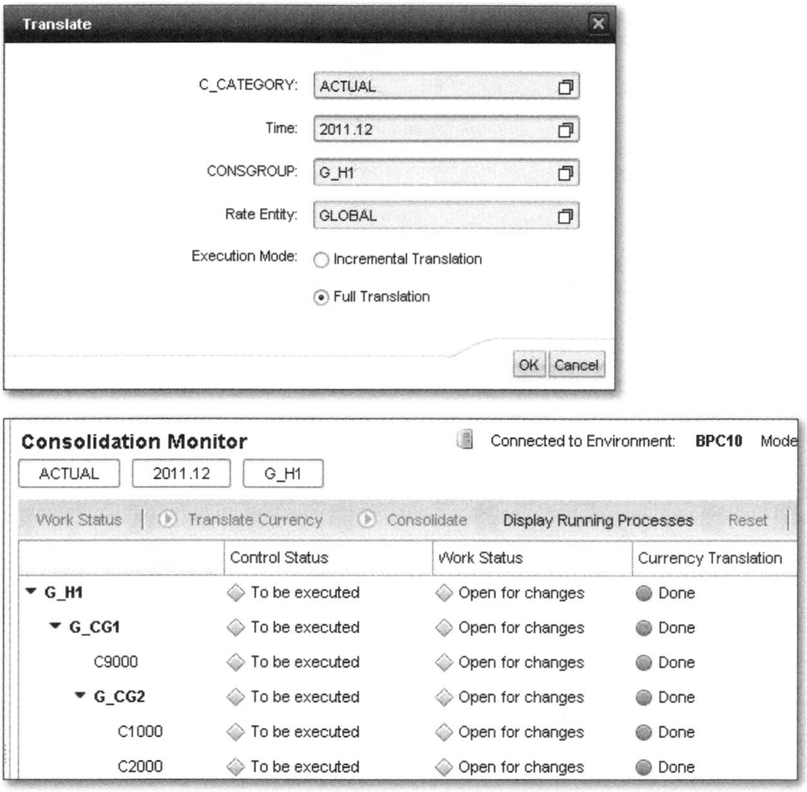

Figure 7.82 Running Translation from the Consolidation Monitor

For the EXECUTION MODE, you have two options:

▶ INCREMENTAL TRANSLATION
Use this option if running for the first time or if there are new or changed records in the Consolidation model. There is a timestamp that tracks new and changed transaction data records.

▶ FULL TRANSLATION
Use this option if the ownership or rate data has changed or if the business rules have changed.

After choosing OK, the CURRENCY TRANSLATION status should appear as DONE.

After running the currency translation, there may be some reporting needed to check the calculations and analyze the results. Assuming that is complete, you can carry out the eliminations.

If you want to do pair-wise eliminations for all entities, select the G_H1 top row (which includes all entities) and click on the CONSOLIDATE button. This executes the eliminations and adjustments business rule and runs the currency translation if it wasn't run previously. Again, a splash screen will appear as shown in Figure 7.83. After running consolidation, the updated CONSOLIDATION status of DONE is recorded.

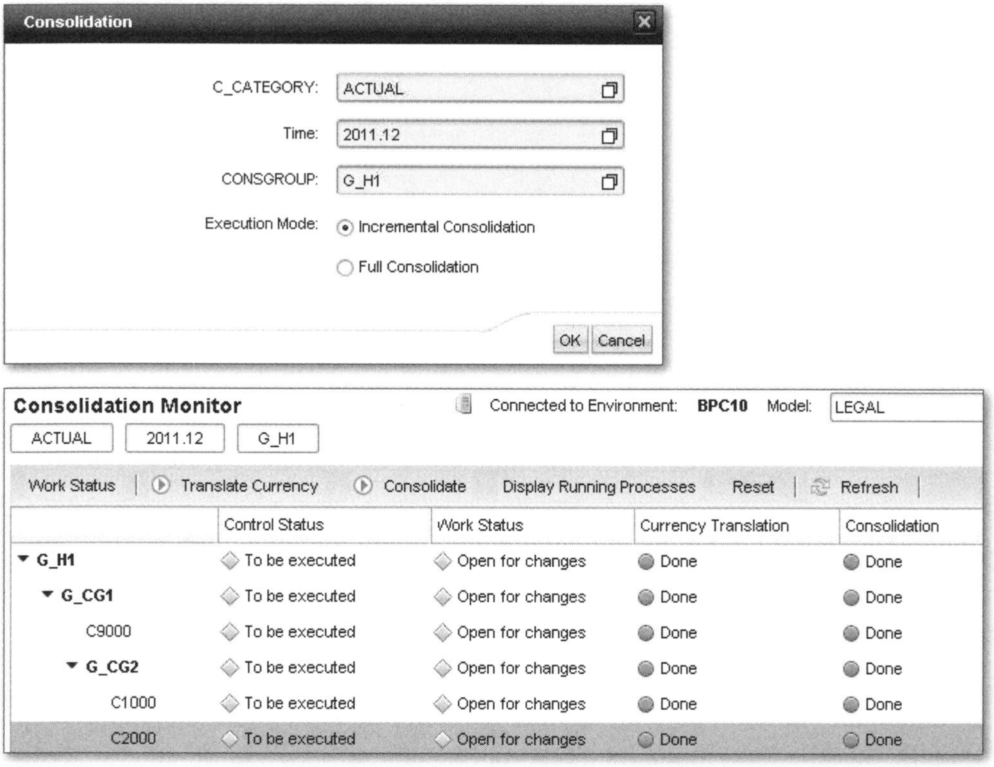

Figure 7.83 Running Consolidation from the Consolidation Monitor

At this point, controls can be executed (from the Controls Monitor). We'll discuss how to run controls in Chapter 8. After running controls successfully and assuming all other monthly closing tasks have been performed, the work status can now be set to "approved".

After the work state is set to "approved," if anyone tries to change the data in the Consolidation model, the user will receive an error message. However, the work status can easily be switched back to "in process" to allow data changes if necessary.

In Figure 7.84, you can see the Consolidation Monitor after work status has been updated.

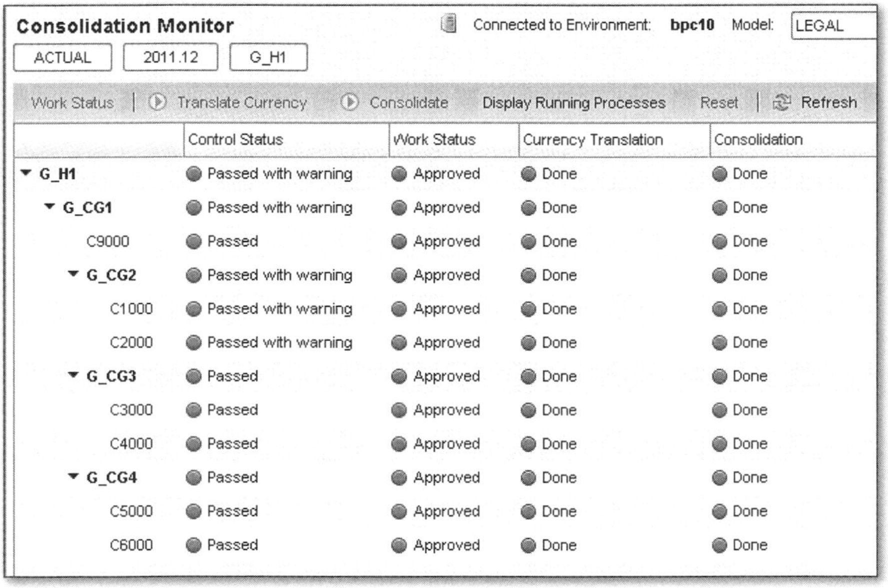

Figure 7.84 Consolidation Monitor with All Activities Completed

In summary, the Consolidation Monitor provides an all-in-one screen where end users can complete the bulk of the monthly close tasks and also view the status of the tasks.

7.7 Summary

In this chapter, you learned some of the theory involved in the consolidation process. You learned how to maintain ownership data for the purchase, proportional, and equity methods. You saw how journals are set up and managed.

We discussed the business scenario, important dimensions, components, and results for every task in the month-end close process. We worked our way through all of the business rules and even did a deep dive on generating double-sided entries, for example, which included the different types of consolidation: equity, proportional, and purchase.

You learned how to perform matching in BPC and how to do IC eliminations with not only the eliminations and adjustments business rule but also US eliminations. In additional, we discussed and showed examples of the different balance logic options that are available in BPC. Finally you learned how to set up and use the Consolidation Monitor.

This chapter covers the aspects of BPC that are consistent with the administration portion of the component but still have an impact on the configuration and functionality of BPC. The chapter will start with a discussion about security for BPC as well as security in the EPM add-in. We'll also work through the configuration and use of work status, controls, and auditing in BPC, and then we'll finish up with a review of transports.

8   Management of the BPC Process

This chapter covers the process of configuration and concepts behind security. In conjunction with security, we'll review the work status component and analyze the integration between work status and security. With the need to validate different activities that are occurring in the system as well as manage the data flow, BPC offers the controls component. This takes the place of the validation process in BPC V7.5. The activities and calculations that occur in BPC are critical especially because many deal with data that is being submitted to the stakeholders for their use. For this reason, we'll discuss the auditing options that are available in BPC. Finally we'll review the approach to transports that BPC offers and the differences in process that we'll encounter with transports in BPC versus BW.

8.1   Security

One of the areas in BPC that has been evolving into a more consistent and integrated component in the SAP NetWeaver environment is security. In BPC V10.0, many of the processes in the security area now rely more on the SAP NetWeaver security than before. The hope is that this trend will continue, and a full integration of the SAP NetWeaver concepts of security will be used for BPC. For the Microsoft version of security in BPC, the approach is very similar to the V7.5 offering, which seems consistent due to the standalone architecture of the Microsoft version. For the SAP NetWeaver version, the integration of security is critical because you want to be able to leverage some or the entire configuration you can in the BW system against BPC. The security in BPC includes four components:

- ▶ Users (who)

- ▶ Teams (optional)

- ▶ Task profile (what)

- ▶ Data access profile (where)

Figure 8.1 shows these components with a basic idea of the activities in each area.

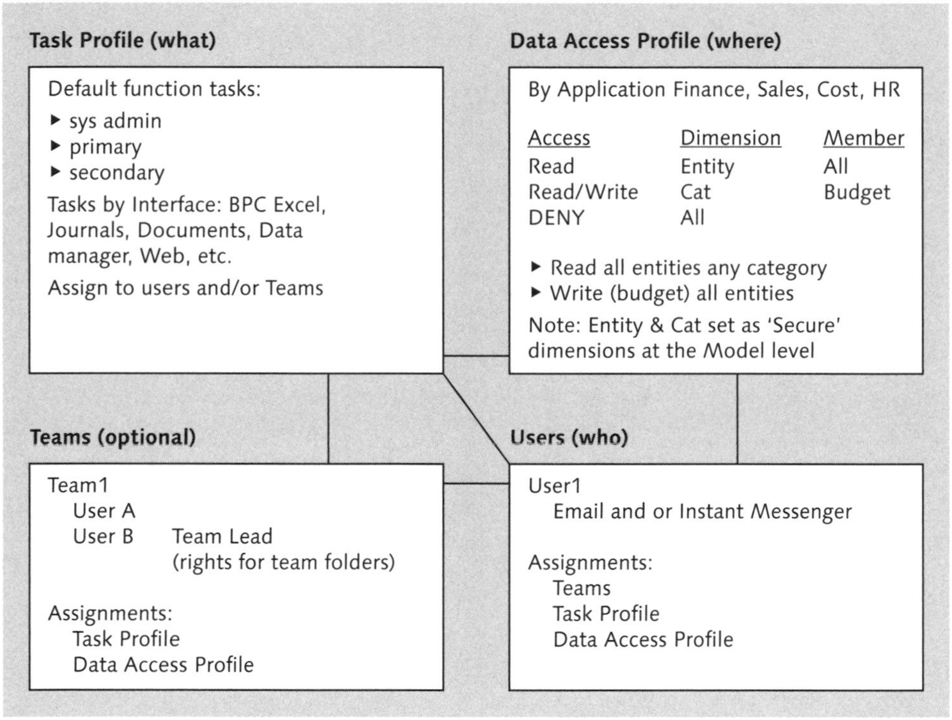

Task Profile (what)	Data Access Profile (where)
Default function tasks: ▶ sys admin ▶ primary ▶ secondary Tasks by Interface: BPC Excel, Journals, Documents, Data manager, Web, etc. Assign to users and/or Teams	By Application Finance, Sales, Cost, HR Access Dimension Member Read Entity All Read/Write Cat Budget DENY All ▶ Read all entities any category ▶ Write (budget) all entities Note: Entity & Cat set as 'Secure' dimensions at the Model level
Teams (optional)	Users (who)

Team1
  User A
  User B Team Lead
      (rights for team folders)
 	
Assignments:
  Task Profile
  Data Access Profile
	User1
	  Email and or Instant Messenger
	
	Assignments:
	  Teams
	  Task Profile
	  Data Access Profile

Figure 8.1 Security Summary for BPC

Figure 8.1 illustrates that the security process in BPC is fairly straightforward, but depending on the requirements of your company, this may be challenged in covering all of your needs. There have been a number of additional components added to the data access profile to make the filtering of the specific activities much better than in BPC V7.0 and V7.5. Knowing that the teams are optional is good, but definitely realize that you'll need to use them quite a bit to make security as streamlined as possible. You need a strategy before setting up the security for the corporation. You have to remember that in the normal responsibilities of BPC, you're looking at consolidation, planning and forecasting (P&F), and reporting. So as we work through the setup of security, you're looking at a smaller portion of the business users unless you start to use the SAP Enterprise Performance Management (EPM) frontend for more than just BPC activities and move into the more mainstream reporting activities. At this point, the current security has been working well for most corporations. The only time issues seem to come up is if the required security is very granular in nature and more like a BW-based security rather than a BPC-based approach.

For example, if you have 10000 cost centers that you want to secure at the cost center level, you'll probably encounter performance issues with the EPM process and possibly the process of saving data via an input template or executing a report. The goal in the process of setting up security is to minimize the number of profiles that you're required to create and maintain. There's really no maximum or minimum for the total number of data access profiles, task profiles, or teams, but make sure that you review and focus on grouping together as many objects as possible to try and accommodate the goal of as few objects as possible. For a basic example, let's say you have several groups of users:

▶ **Business users**
Normally only run reports and analyze the data

▶ **Consolidation accountants**
Execute the consolidation process and validate the data

▶ **P&F analysts**
Executes and validates the P&F data and activities incorporated into this area.

In this case, you start with three task profiles to cover each of the levels of activities: basic reporting, consolidation process, and the P&F analysis.

There are also five regions—United States, Canada, Germany, Japan and Mexico—and the company codes are consistent across all three countries. You can develop the security model to group together five teams—US, CAN, JPN, MEX, and GER—and have them combine with the three task profiles to create approximately 15 intersections of the task profiles with the data access profiles. This is a great start to the management of your security strategy because it reduces the maintenance and effort required to keep security up to date.

The one situation we want to stay away from would be to have individual users have their own security and basically have a task profile and a data access profile just for one person. In this case, the maintenance and overall strategy are missing, and you end up with hundreds of profiles that require a full-time job to try to keep track of them.

After you draw out your approach to security, you'll then start to build out the components. After the users, then teams, and finally the task profile and data access profile are complete, you can link them together and execute some testing to identify any gaps.

8.1.1 Users

One of the aspects of security that has really improved integration in BPC V10.0 with BW is the creation and assignment of the user. In the current version, you have to set up the user in BW to make the user available for BPC. Figure 8.2 shows a user being set up in BW. With the security and authorization provided, you can make a copy of the user with all of the required BPC roles.

Figure 8.2 User Maintenance: Initial Screen – Copy Users

In this case, user BPC_USER99 is being created. You need to assign three basic BPC roles for the user in BW based on the user's responsibilities. Others are also available, but these three are the core roles: SAP_BPC_ADMIN, SYSADMIN, and USER. We found these by using Transaction PFCG with a wildcard search of "SAP_BPC*".

Figure 8.3 shows the entire standard delivered roles that are required in other more specific situations.

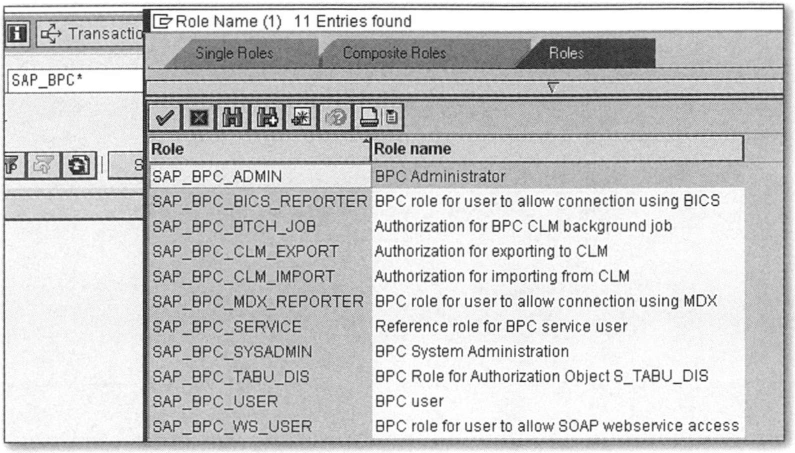

Figure 8.3 Standard BPC Roles

After the user is set up, you can then go back into BPC to see what has happened. From the HOME page, you need to access the ADMINISTRATION tab, as shown in Figure 8.4.

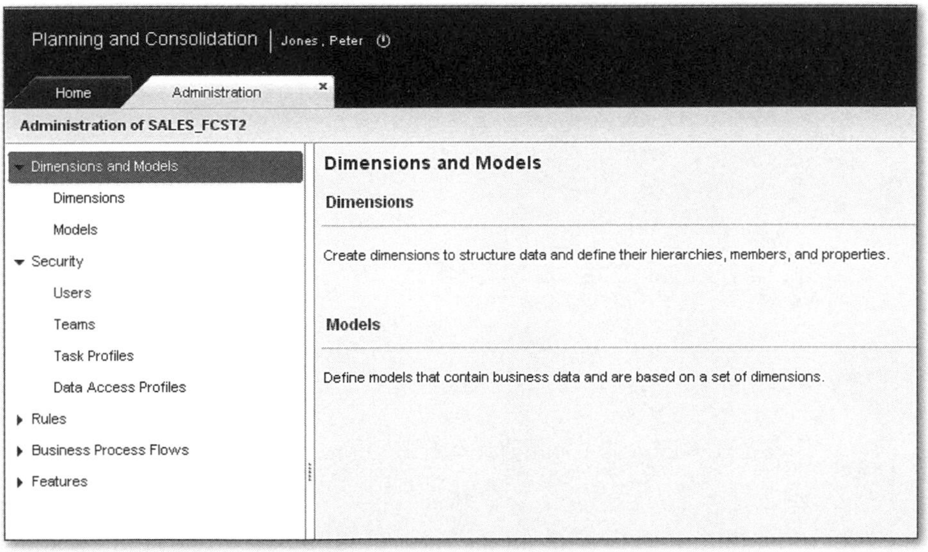

Figure 8.4 The Users Link on the Administration Tab

Next, you click the USERS link to display the users (see Figure 8.5). In this case, you can see that the new user BPC_USER99 is now available in BPC for configuration. So for BPC V10.0 for SAP NetWeaver, you'll need to have some integration with BW security to help support the setup of the users at the very least.

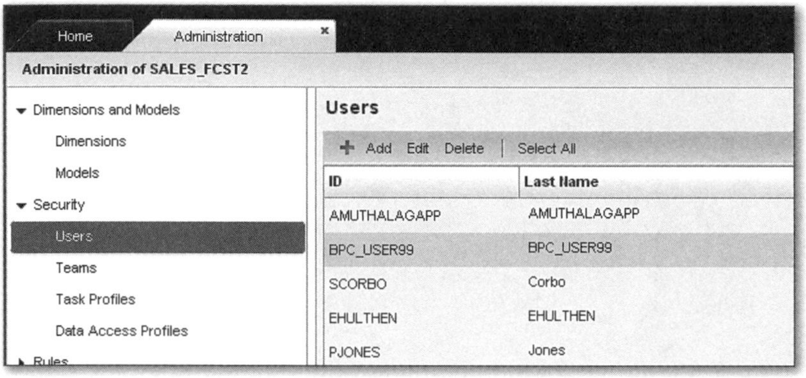

Figure 8.5 Users in the BPC Security Screen

After the user is set up, then you can add the user to the teams and, from there, the team is assigned to the task profile as well as the data access profile. Figure 8.6 shows the assignment of the user to the team.

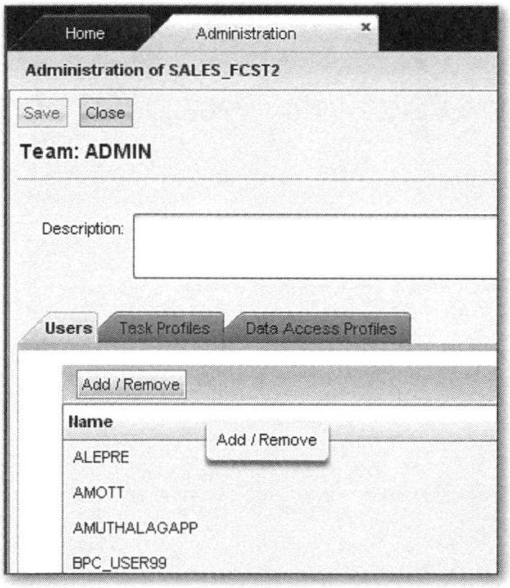

Figure 8.6 Assigning a User to a Team

Figure 8.7 shows the total user count that is assigned to the team, which is then assigned to the data access profile.

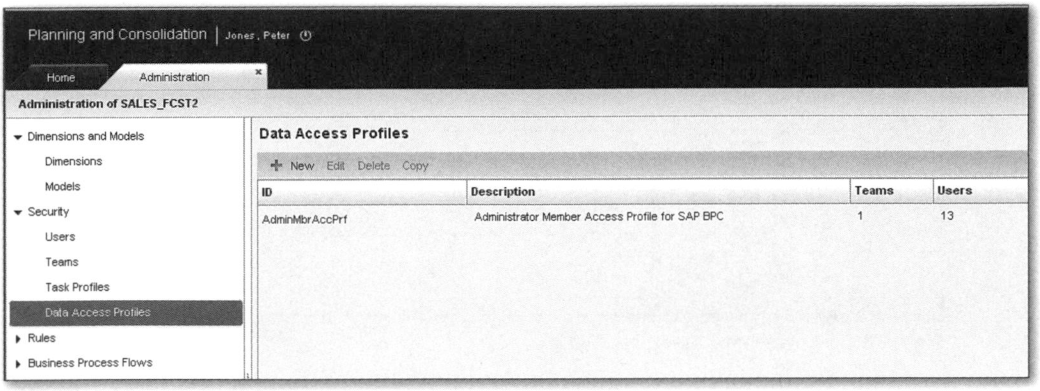

Figure 8.7 Total Number of Users Assigned

8.1.2 Teams

Next, you need to set up the structure of the team as shown in Figure 8.8. There are three basic steps in this wizard-based process.

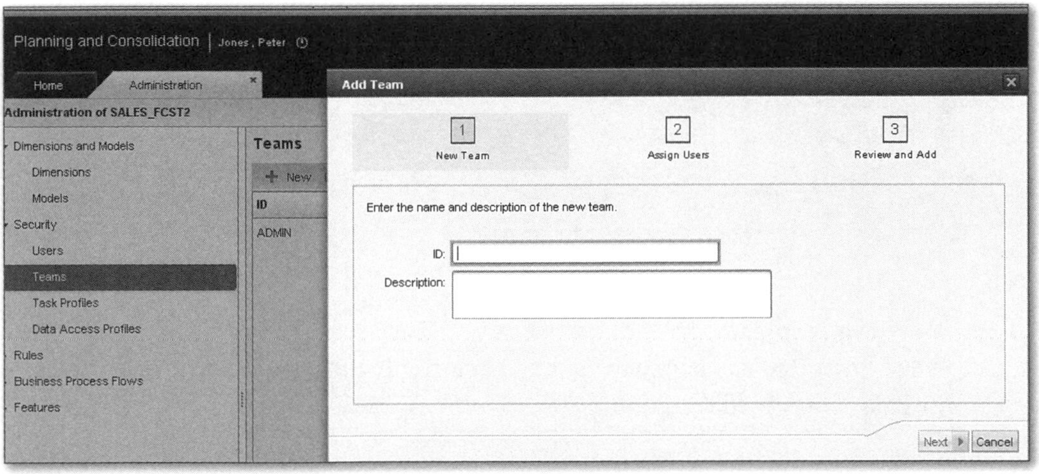

Figure 8.8 Add a Team – ID and Description

First, you assign an ID and a DESCRIPTION to the team. Figure 8.9 shows that this team is focused on the US region.

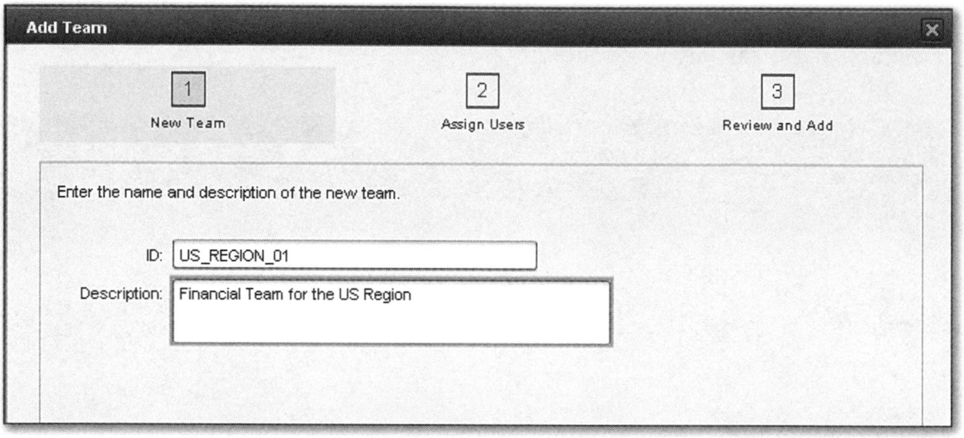

Figure 8.9 Add Team – Completed ID and Description Fields

Next, assign the users to the team as shown in Figure 8.10.

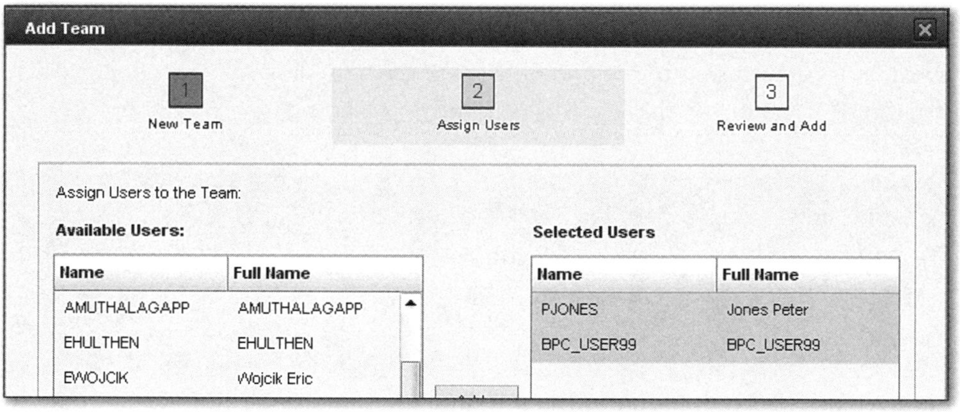

Figure 8.10 Add Team – Assignment of Users to Team

Now you should review and, if necessary, go back and add additional users. Figure 8.11 shows that you have a team, but it's currently not assigned to any task profiles or data access profiles.

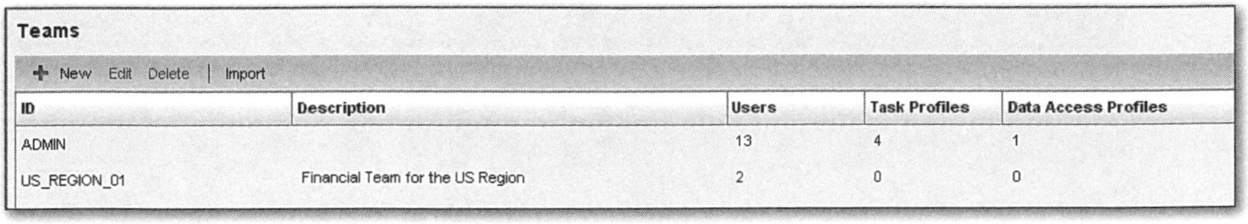

ID	Description	Users	Task Profiles	Data Access Profiles
ADMIN		13	4	1
US_REGION_01	Financial Team for the US Region	2	0	0

Figure 8.11 Teams – Displaying the Number of Users and Task/Data Access Profiles

When you're finished here, you can begin developing the task profile.

8.1.3 Task Profiles

Now you need to link the user and team with activities and tasks that they can access and execute — basically establishing a task profile for users and teams. Again, setting up the task profile is an easy wizard approach. Figure 8.12 shows the first step of setting up the ID and DESCRIPTION.

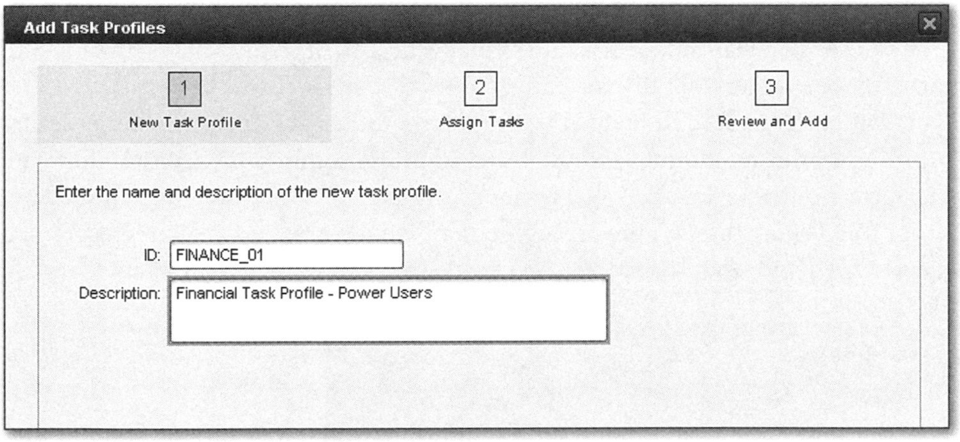

Figure 8.12 Add Task Profiles – New Task Profile

Again, this is more administrative, but it's required. After you set up the ID and DESCRIPTION, you can begin adding the tasks that you want to assign to a team. In this general case, you'll assign just about all of the tasks to this task profile, but in reality, this is the critical step in defining what a user can and can't do in the system (see Figure 8.13).

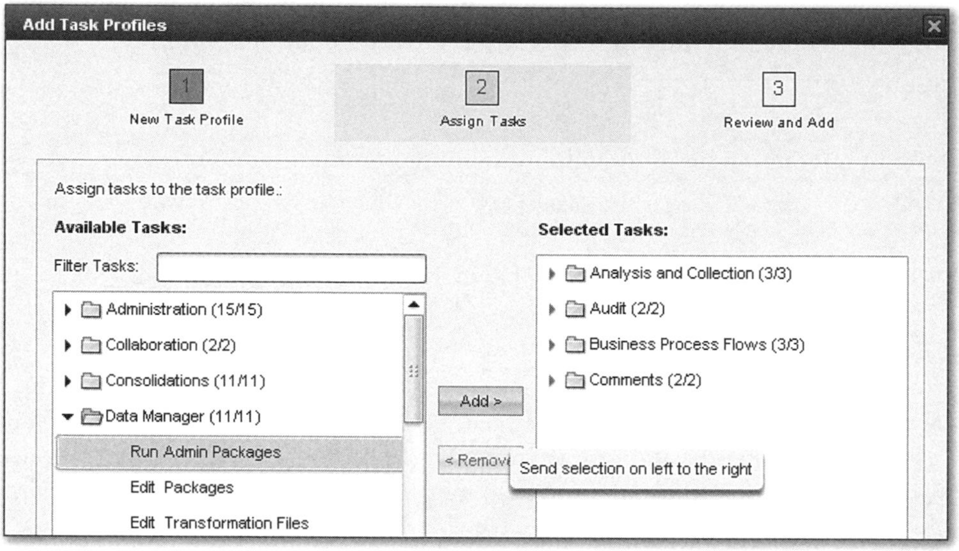

Figure 8.13 Add Task Profile – Assign Tasks

You can see that many more tasks are available here than were available in BPC V7.0 or V7.5. The folders identify specific activities that are available to be assigned, and you can either choose individual tasks under a folder or choose the entire folder to be used during the REVIEW AND ADD step. After this is completed, then you perform a quick review, and you're done. This step should be all diagrammed out prior to working through the process so that you have a good idea of what should be assigned and what should not. The final step is shown in Figure 8.14.

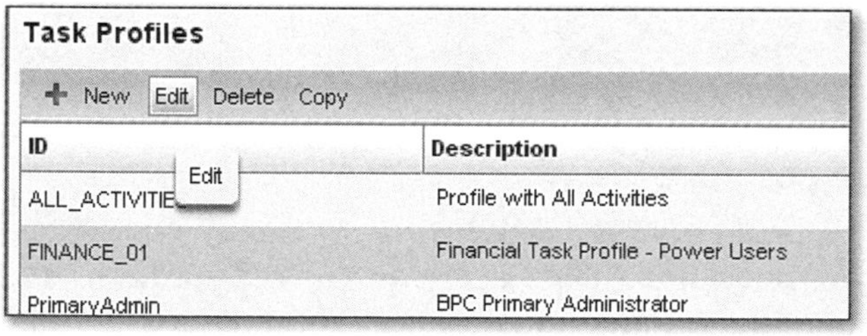

Figure 8.14 Add Task Profile – Review and Add

After you've reviewed everything, you can link the task profile to the team. Figure 8.15 shows that the FINANCE_01 team has been assigned to the task profile you just created.

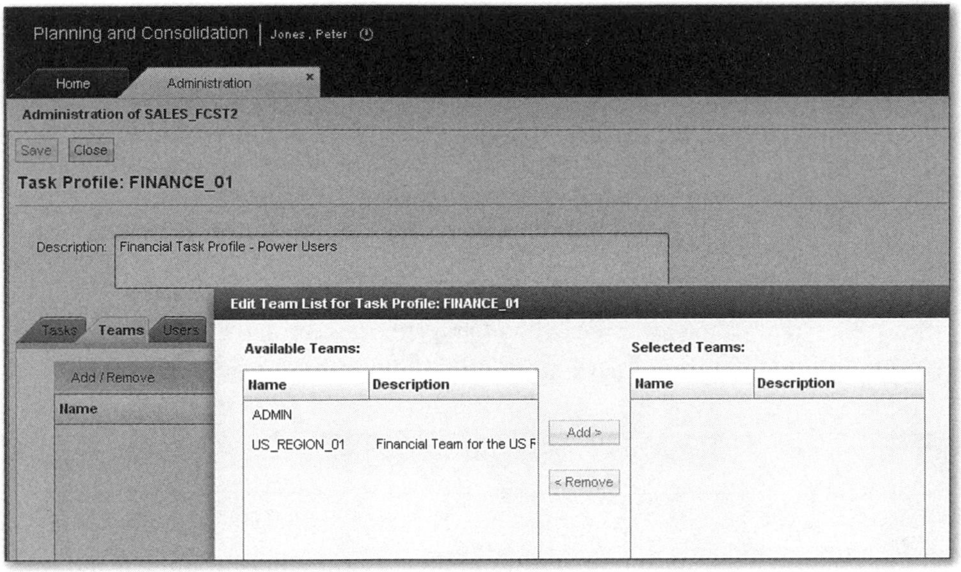

Figure 8.15 Edit Team List for Task Profile

You can now confirm that the two have been configured correctly by saving as shown in Figure 8.16.

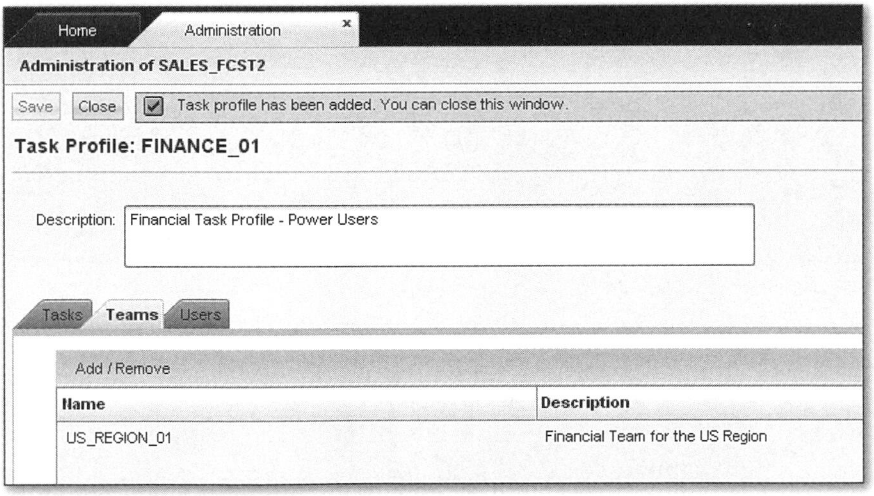

Figure 8.16 Task Profile Added Successfully

8.1.4 Data Access Profiles

Now that the user, team, and task profiles are set up, the last link is setting up what the user has access to via the data access profile. Basically this requires just one step of assigning the different models and the access levels to the security dimensions. If you remember, you identified specific dimensions as Security dimensions in the configuration of the Data model in Chapter 3. Now, you'll use these to control the access levels and what can and can't be viewed by specific users or teams. In Figure 8.17, you see the initial screen or actually the only screen other than the Team and Users screens. On this screen, when you choose a model, the dimensions that you've secured appear on the right-hand side of the screen.

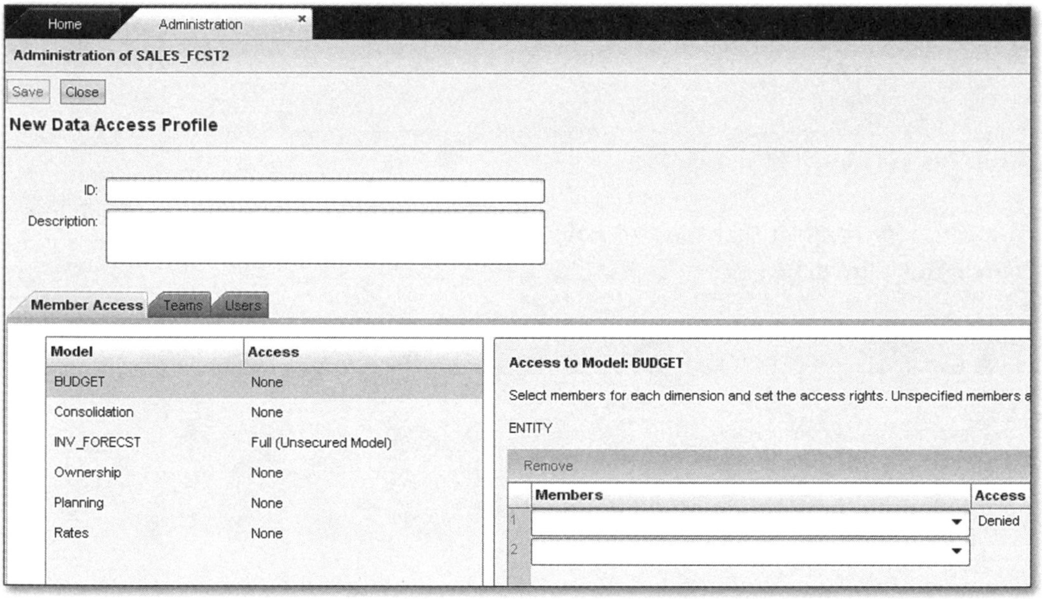

Figure 8.17 New Data Access Profile

Pick the Model on the left (i.e., Budget) to see the dimension(s) (i.e. Entity) that are used for securing the information. You can choose individual members or all members, and you can also use a hierarchical node to select them. This will help with making security a bit easier to manage. When you select the field, a pop up of the members in that dimension appears that you can select from (see Figure 8.18). In this case, the NAmerica - North America node and all of the lower level nodes are selected.

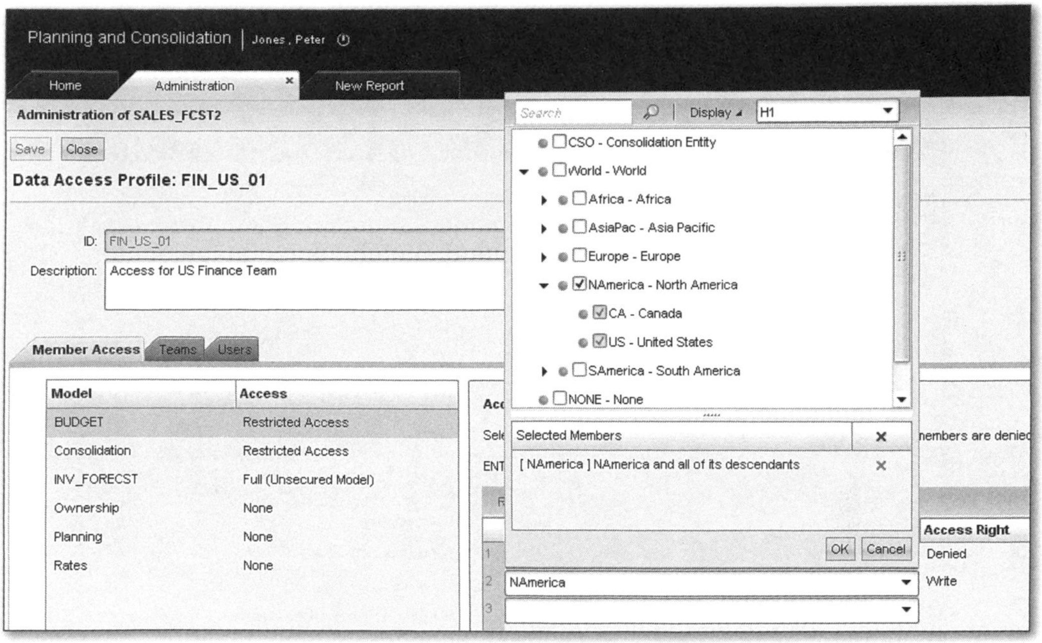

Figure 8.18 Data Access Profile – Selecting the Members to Restrict

On the right side of this list, you can identify the ACCESS RIGHT for this set of members. There are three choices:

▶ DENIED
Denied access to display/write or read will completely deny the user access to the information available against that dimension and more specific members.

▶ READ
Access to display/read will allow the user to view the information only.

▶ WRITE
Access to display/read/write will allow the user to view and post to the specific combinations of members or the whole dimension.

This is fairly straightforward based on security and authorization that you might see in the case of BW where there are more than 15 different activities that you might have to select and restrict. In this example, we tweaked this access profile to show that you can allow full access at the hierarchy node level and DENY access at one of the lower level values. Therefore, we have set up CA (base-level member) with NO access rights (DENIED), and CA (base-level member) has the DENIED access right, and the NAMERICA (node level) has the WRITE.

You can now confirm that the team and the data access profile are linked correctly, as shown in Figure 8.19.

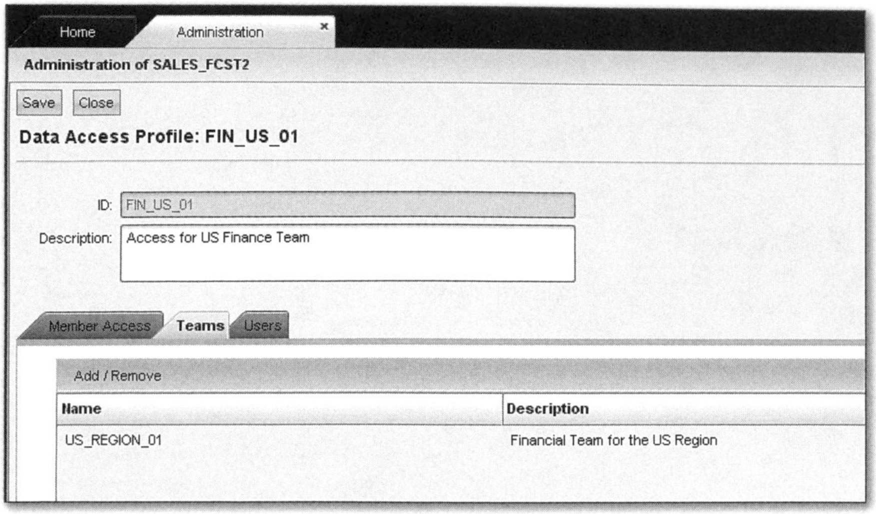

Figure 8.19 Data Access Profile – US_REGION_01 Team

Let's do a basic test to confirm that these settings will provide the required results — that you see *only* the North America level and the US member — by executing a web report. From the HOME page screen, click on the NEW REPORT option to generate a sample report. If you move the ENTITY to the header just to validate the security, you see that when click on the dropdown on the entity to show the hierarchy, only NORTH AMERICA appears and below that, only UNITED STATES, and not (CA) Canada (see Figure 8.20).

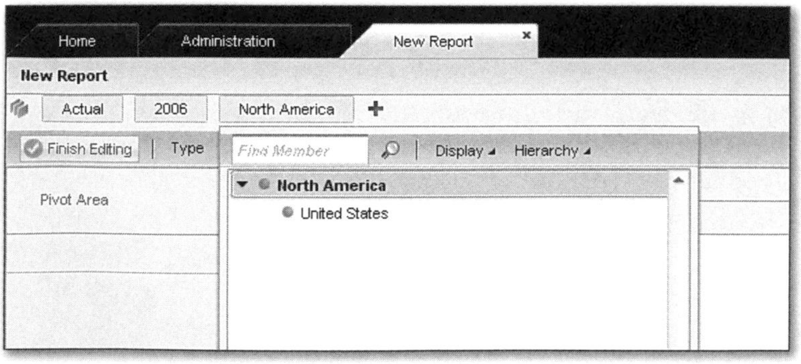

Figure 8.20 New Report – View of the Entity Hierarchy

Finally, you move the ENTITY to the rows and TIME to the columns to display a basic report that is restricted to only seeing the UNITED STATES member of the NORTH AMERICA hierarchy (see Figure 8.21).

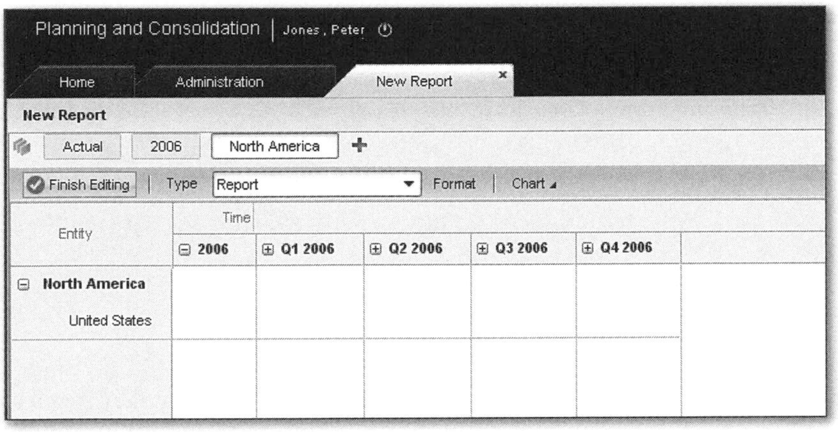

Figure 8.21 New Report Showing the Entity in the Rows and Time in the Columns

You can now do additional testing with this security combination. As we mentioned, always try and reduce the number of profiles and organize as much as possible in groups of tasks and/or access to develop a strong and consistent security process.

8.1.5   Security in the EPM Add-In

It's important to note that the security in the EPM add-in when linked to a BPC model via the Web services link is quite different from going through the OLE DB for OLAP (ODBO) connection. The Web services approach will be supported by BPC-specific security so that everything discussed here will apply. For example, a number of the task profiles that are available will focus specifically on the report folders that will be available based on whether you have an admin profile or a reporting profile. Remember that after access to the EPM add-in is given, then it's very difficult to manage the actual functions available in the EPM add-in. For example, you can't easily control whether a person can turn on or off the ability to use specific functions such as the creation of local members. So the rule of thumb here is manage the folder structure and decide who has access to the company folders and local folders. It's possible to approach the process of managing reports in a very similar way as you do in BW in terms of the path that a report might travel to go from a personal report to validation and then to a standard report. In the EPM add-in case, you have to approach this by way of having multiple folders, which a business user assigns a report to. Then submit that report for review to the "power user" and, from there, after due diligence, move the report to the company folder for use by everyone.

When it comes to using the EPM add-in on the ODBO link, you need to rely on the core BW security and not the Analysis Authorization (AA) but BW security at the object level. Because the EPM add-in doesn't support BW variables or filters, the AA can't be read by the EPM add-in. If you're going to use the EPM add-in for more reporting outside of BPC, then you should take into account this aspect and plan for additional security requirements to support the reporting security required.

8.2   Work Status

When we talk about work status, we need to make sure we're aware that it works in conjunction with security. Where security addresses the overall management of user activities and what they can gain access to, work status deals with the timing of when they can get access to the data and when they can get access to execute specific activities. So work status is very much a matrix type of component that slices across the security activities. It allows you to lock a set of data or basically a region of data in a specific model. Work status also overrides the user data access profile because it removes the ability of a user to change the data after a given time frame. Following are some examples of the use of work status mainly around the period-end closing activities:

▶ During period-end activities, having everyone aware of the specific times where activities have to be completed

▶ Having a hard stop for different activities such as data loading activities for period-ending transactions

▶ Top-side adjusting entries that are required at a certain time to accommodate any difference in the consolidation results

▶ Calculations of the FX translations because this has to run first prior to the actual consolidation process

▶ Validation activities during the window of time after specific activities

▶ Entering comments during a P&F process

▶ Executing input template activities during a P&F process

▶ After consolidation is executed so that the external reports for the stakeholders can be generated without the financial information changing

Many more can be listed because work status is an excellent component to support these types of activities.

8.2.1 Configuration of Work Status

The configuration of work status can be found in the ADMINISTRATION tab of the BPC Web Client. Choose FEATURES • WORK STATUS, as shown in Figure 8.22.

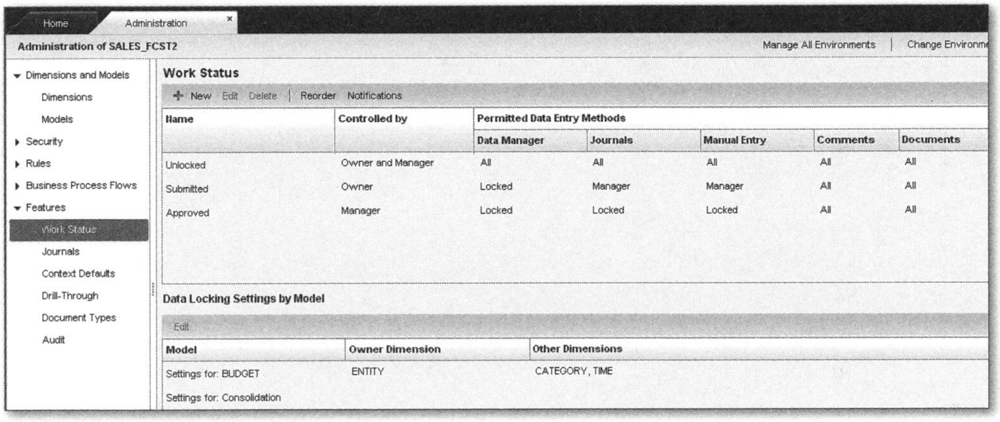

Figure 8.22 Administration – Work Status Configuration

There are two sections to this configuration screen: the WORK STATUS values and the DATA LOCKING SETTINGS BY MODEL. To edit the settings in the DATA LOCKING SETTINGS BY MODEL section, you need to choose the model and then click on the EDIT option to access the dialog box to make changes or add addition dimension values to the work status process. Figure 8.23 shows the BUDGET work status settings about to be edited.

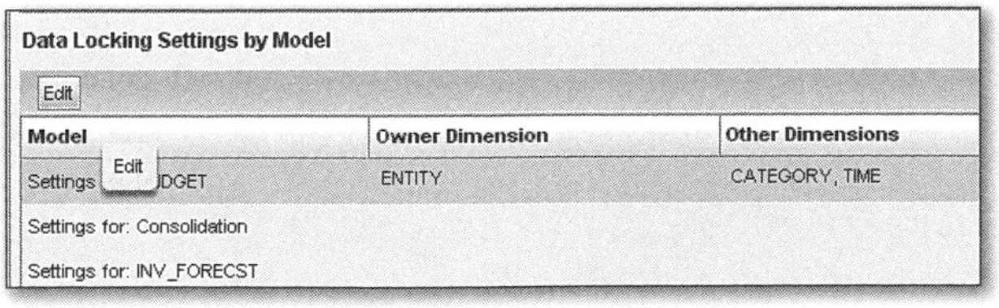

Figure 8.23 Data Locking Settings by Model – Edit

The dialog box that appears is shown in Figure 8.24. This screen lists the different dimensions that are eligible for the settings for work status in this model. These settings control the slice of data to be impacted by work status.

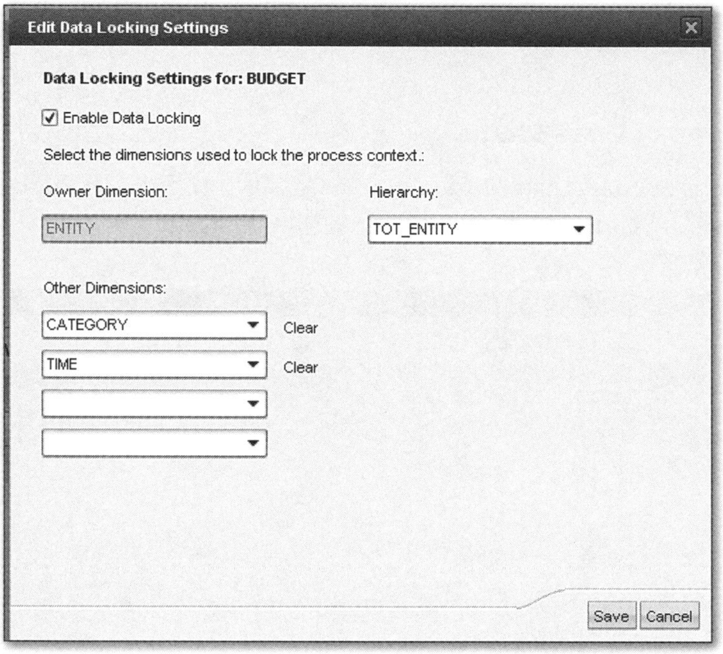

Figure 8.24 Edit Data Locking Settings

As you can see there is an option for four additional dimensions to control the data. These dimensions can be any four from the BPC model. The OWNER DIMENSION field requires a dimension to be assigned, which in this case, is ENTITY. You also have to identify a hierarchy that can be used for managing the work status process. In a number of situations, this hierarchy is specifically built for this purpose. You also don't have to use all of the dimension options, but normally anywhere from three to five dimensions are used. When you're finished, you can save your settings and move to the WORK STATUS section. Figure 8.25 shows the initial screen to set up work status.

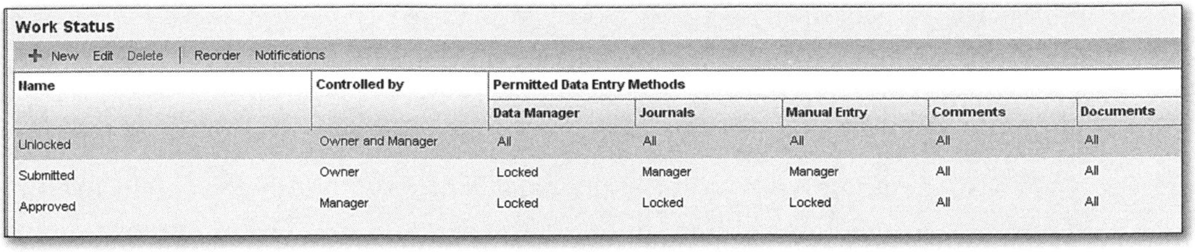
Work Status

+ New Edit Delete | Reorder Notifications

Name	Controlled by	Permitted Data Entry Methods				
		Data Manager	Journals	Manual Entry	Comments	Documents
Unlocked	Owner and Manager	All	All	All	All	All
Submitted	Owner	Locked	Manager	Manager	All	All
Approved	Manager	Locked	Locked	Locked	All	All

Figure 8.25 Work Status Settings

To review a set of parameters, you can review the SUBMITTED portion of the table as shown in Figure 8.26. In the CONTROLLED BY section, you see that this is managed by the OWNER. The OWNER parameter is integrated with the OWNER property in the Owner dimension.

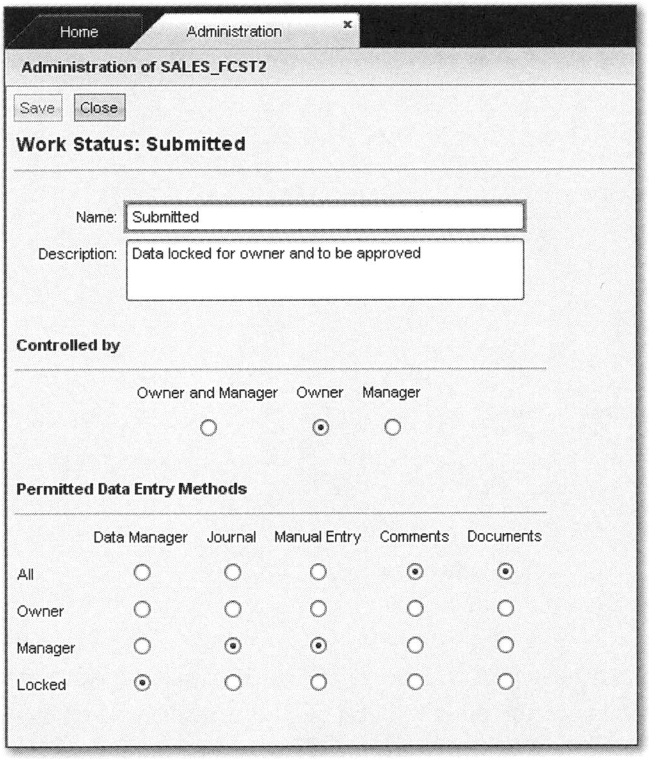

Figure 8.26 Work Status: Submitted Layout

As for the PERMITTED DATA ENTRY METHODS section, you see that the DATA MANAGER is LOCKED for all, the JOURNALS and MANUAL ENTRIES can be posted to by the MANAGER, and the COMMENTS and DOCUMENTS are open to everyone. In each case, this is a similar step for the other two different work statuses (UNLOCK and APPROVED). You can add more work statuses to the list. For example, if you need to lock down a set of data during the period close, and there's a group of business users that shouldn't have access to the data during that time, you might need to create a new work status, but you can't create additional entry methods. Some companies might want another work status such as Open or Ready for Approval, for example. You can do this directly from this screen by filling in the NAME and DESCRIPTION, and then choosing the settings at the bottom based on what you want to have available or not available. You can also set up an email notification process using work status. Figure 8.27 shows the settings for the email to be enabled.

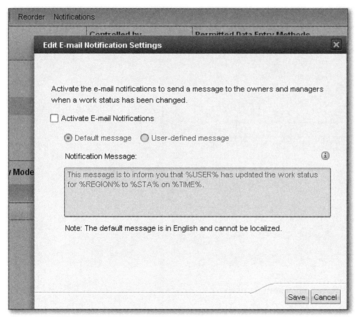

Figure 8.27 Edit E-Mail Notification Settings

In the EDIT E-MAIL NOTIFICATION SETTINGS dialog box, you can choose ACTIVATE E-MAIL NOTIFICATIONS and then decide on whether a default or user-defined message will be used. As you can see, the default message is finding the parameters for user, region, status, and time and uses those in the message that is generated. If you decide that you need email notification, you'll have to set up two parameters in the IMG as well. They are for the management of the emails as well as the customized message. The email notification BPC parameter is shown in Figure 8.28.

Environment	SALES_FCST2	
Field Name	Value
ALLOW_EXTENSIONS	ALL
ALLOW_FILE_SIZE	104857600
DEFAULT_EXTENSIONS	XLS,XLT,DOC,DOT,PPT,POT,XML,MHT,MHTML,XLSX,XLSM,XLSB,ZIP,PDF,PPTX,PPTM,POTX,P(
LOGLEVEL	3
APPROVALSTATUSMSG	This is the message that will be seen by the Business User for Work Status
APPROVALSTATUSMAIL	Y

Figure 8.28 E-Mail Notification Parameter Settings

The APPROVALSTATUSMSG and APPROVALSTATUSMAIL are the parameters to use for this customization. After these settings are completed, then you can use both reporting and managing the work status email process options.

8.2.2 Reporting and Managing of Work Status

There are several approaches for reviewing the work status settings and results of the work status activities. If you look at the auditing process for work status, you'll see a report for work status in the list of standard delivered reports, provided in the AUDIT REPORT section of the BPC HOME page. This report offers information on changes made to the work status at each of the levels. In terms of using work status, you only need to look at the current frontend of BPC, and, in most cases, you'll see a link to management of the work status. In the EPM add-in, you can choose SAVE DATA • CHANGE WORK STATUS as shown in Figure 8.29.

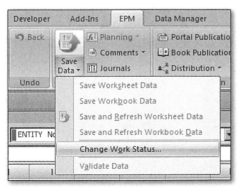

Figure 8.29 Selecting Change Work Status

Next you'll see the EPM – CHANGE WORK STATUS dialog box shown in Figure 8.30, which allows you to switch the work status settings.

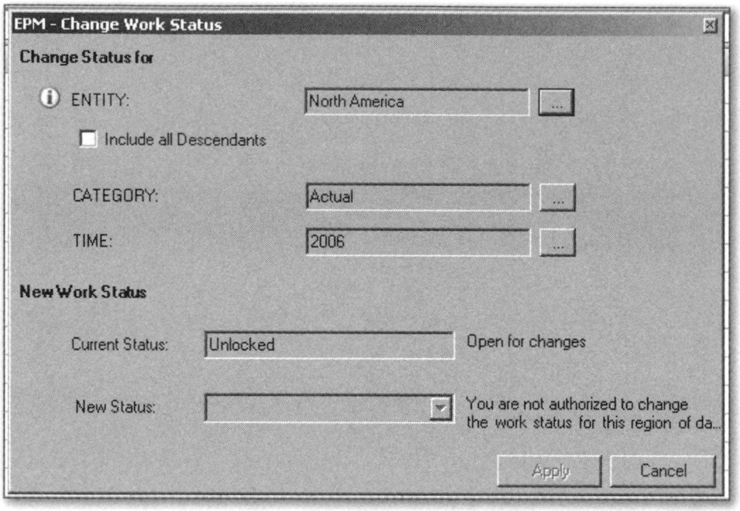

Figure 8.30 EPM – Change Work Status

Another approach is directly from the ACTIVITIES monitor, which allows you to drill-down on the link to see the details as well as change the settings (see Figure 8.31).

Figure 8.31 Activities – Work Status Task

From here, you drill down and view the actual task and make any changes that are necessary, as shown in Figure 8.32.

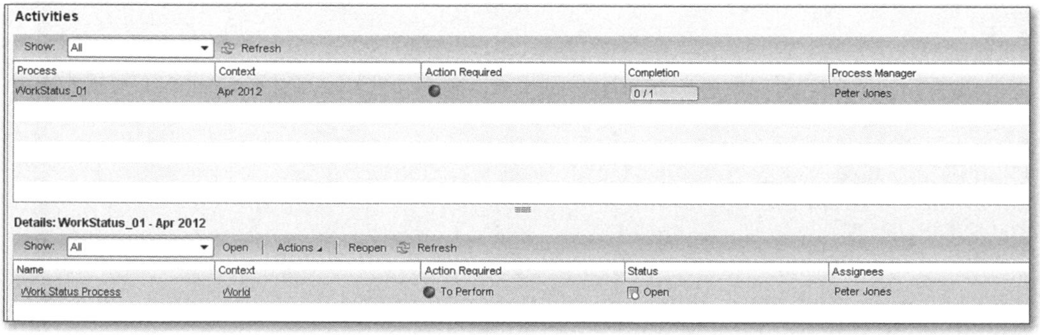

Figure 8.32 Activities and Details: Work Status

Next, click on the LINK (APPLY) in the lower section of the report to show the settings for the work status activities, as shown in Figure 8.33.

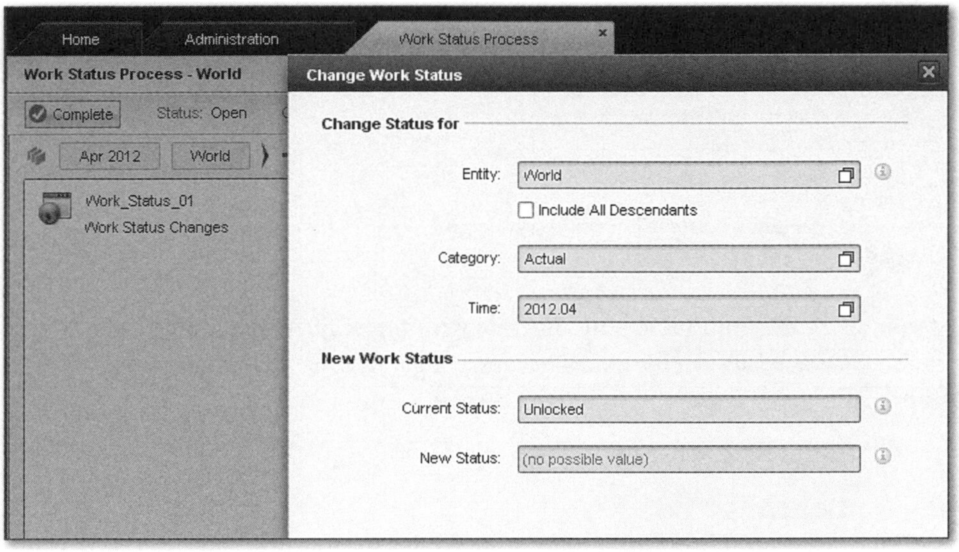

Figure 8.33 Change Work Status

You can also go to the PROCESS MONITOR to access the specific work status task and then view the information from there (see Figure 8.34).

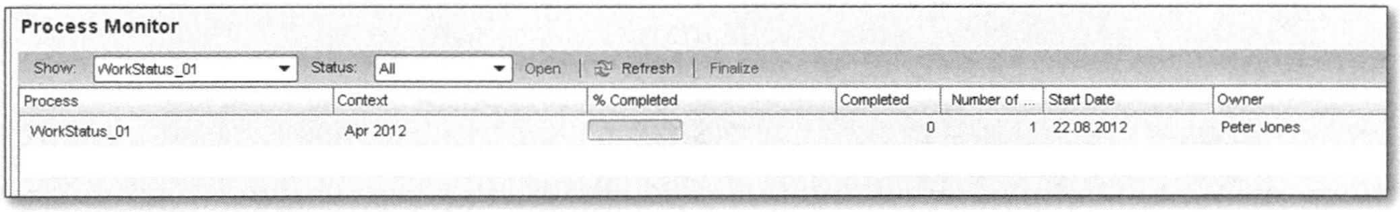

Figure 8.34 Process Monitor with Work Status Task

After these activities have been executed, you'll receive an email notification that the PROCESS MONITOR is available and that the work status is active. An example of the emails is shown in Figure 8.35. The one shown is from the ACTIVITIES process, another that you would receive would be from the PROCESS MONITOR point of view and the email would look very similar to the one shown only that it would reference the PROCESS MONITOR.

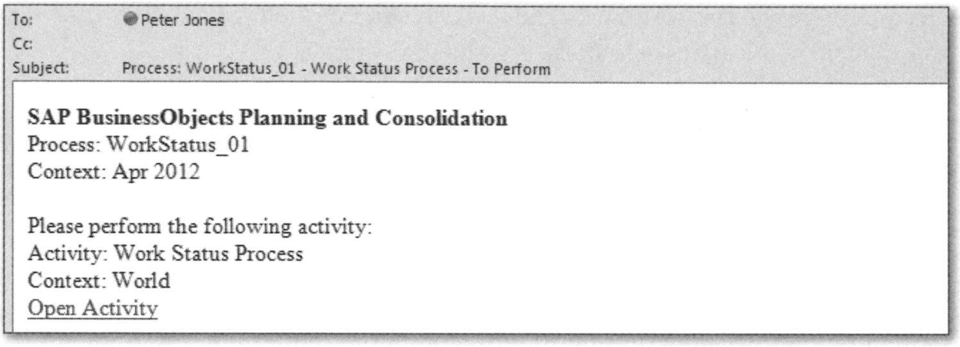
To: Peter Jones
Cc:
Subject: Process: WorkStatus_01 - Work Status Process - To Perform

SAP BusinessObjects Planning and Consolidation
Process: WorkStatus_01
Context: Apr 2012

Please perform the following activity:
Activity: Work Status Process
Context: World
Open Activity

Figure 8.35 Email Notification

If you take this component and integrate with the security and authorization, you can lock down the systems and activities at a given time during the month as well as monitor all of the activities from a central location in BPC.

8.3 Controls

Controls make up the final component that helps with data management. Controls are the processes whereby you control the consistency of financial data as it flows through the BPC system. Controls have the options for being a block for specific activities or a warning to inform users of a possible issue or concern. Controls in this situation are more about transactional data rather than master data. In this process, you can create a calculation or validation process in the control. For example, you can check if the financial statements are in balance by creating a formula in the controls to generate a result. If the result isn't as expected, then a warning or error is generated, and the user will get an email notification or view the issue directly in the Process Monitor or ACTIVITIES component of the HOME page. In BPC V7.5, this was called validation and used Transaction UJ_VALIDATION to set this up directly in the BW system. That option is still available, but this is more flexible and available to the business user who can either create the controls or at least contact a power user—instead of IT—to access and adjust these formulas and adjust.

8.3.1 Configuration

Before you get started with configuration you have to check on a couple of items. Without these items, controls won't be possible. The first is that the Entity dimension has two additional properties on the dimension:

▶ CONTROL_LEVEL

Allows a setting of 1 through 4 to manage the level of control. Level 1 is the basics, and Level 4 is the comprehensive. The levels are only components that group all of the controls together so, for example, if you wanted to you could make the controls in Level 4 very reasonable and those in Level 1 very complex. Just a reminder, that if you choose to use Level 3, then all of the controls in Levels 1 and 2 are incorporated into that level and applied to the posting process.

▶ CTRL_CURRENCY_NOT_LC

Controls whether controls should be executed in the reporting currency instead of the local currency (LC). There are two values for this: N or Y. If the setting is N, then the controls are executed in the LC; if Y, then the controls are executed based on the currency found in the currency property assigned to the entity. You also need to make sure that WORK STATUS is turned on, or you'll get an error message during the configuration process.

To start this process, go to the ADMINISTRATION tab and choose RULES • CONTROLS as shown in Figure 8.36.

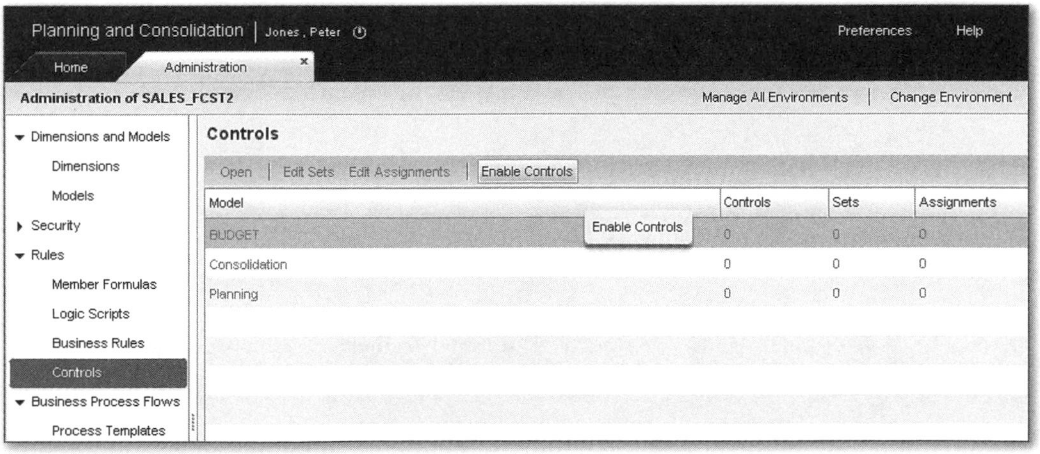

Figure 8.36 Starting the Controls Configuration

Initially you want to access the ENABLE CONTROLS checkbox (see Figure 8.37).

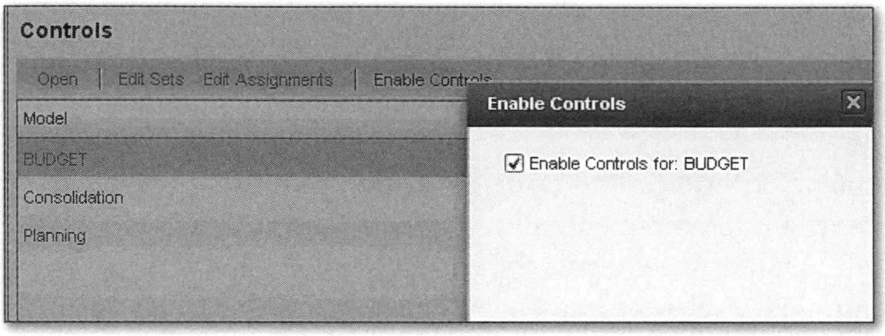

Figure 8.37 Enable Controls Checkbox

Now that you've enabled the controls, you can look at their configuration. Click on OPEN, and then in the ADMINISTRATION tab, followed and in the CONTROLS Screen, choose NEW and the initial configuration screen will display. The initial screen for configuration can be seen in Figure 8.38.

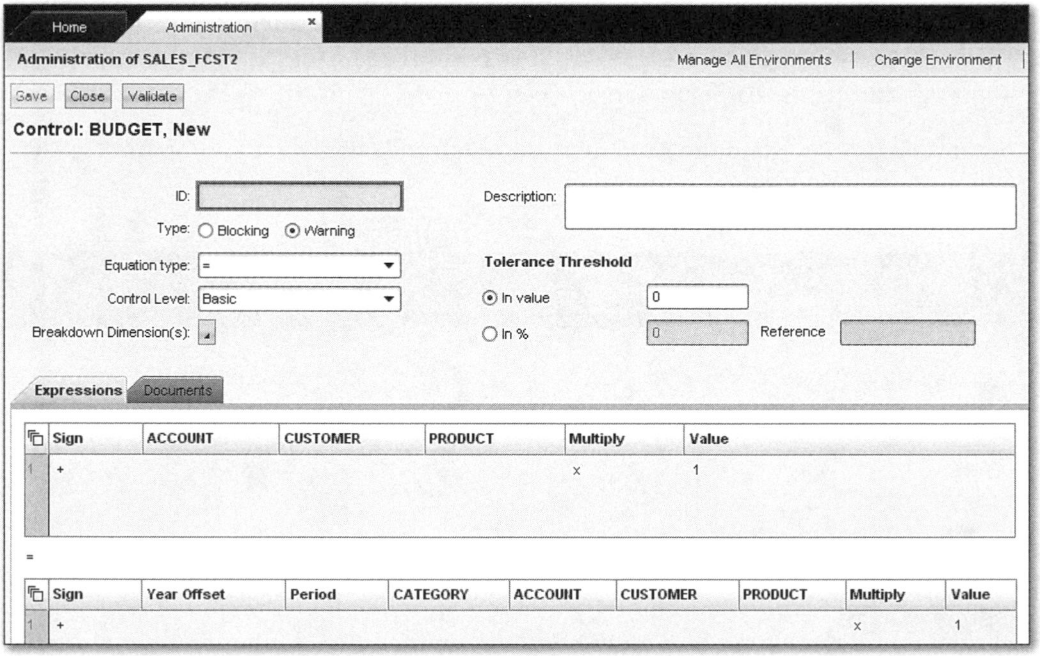

Figure 8.38 Controls Configuration at the Model Level

You're dealing with the BUDGET model, so the control will be validating the budget data quantity against the actual data quantity. Figure 8.39 shows that the control creates a formula in two parts.

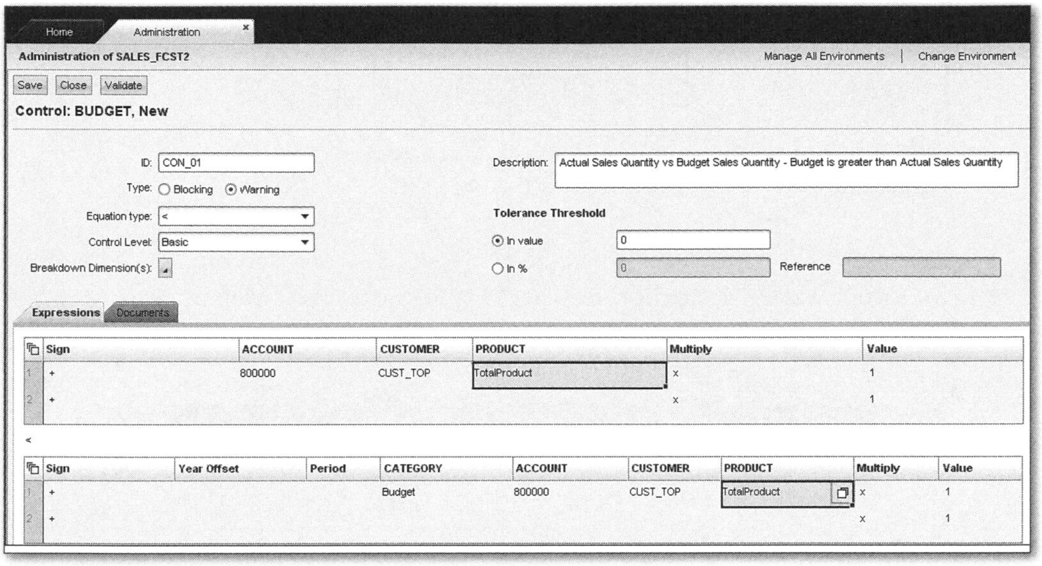

Figure 8.39   Control for the BUDGET Model

In this case, the two formulas are just being multiplied by 1, but the EQUATION TYPE field is showing that the comparison is based on a (<) less than factor. Therefore, if ACTUAL SALES QUANTITY is less than BUDGET SALES QUANTITY, then this is a successful outcome. Basically, the budgeted was created correctly and matched and/or didn't fall short of the actual requirement. This can be created with fairly complex formulas such as checking that the income and balance sheets are in balance, using specific tolerance levels in the formulas, or using a percentage in the formula, but the only calculations available are multiplication and division. After the formulas and the control itself are completed, you can also assign a document to the control. If the control shows an error, then you can access the document or report to validate (see Figure 8.40).

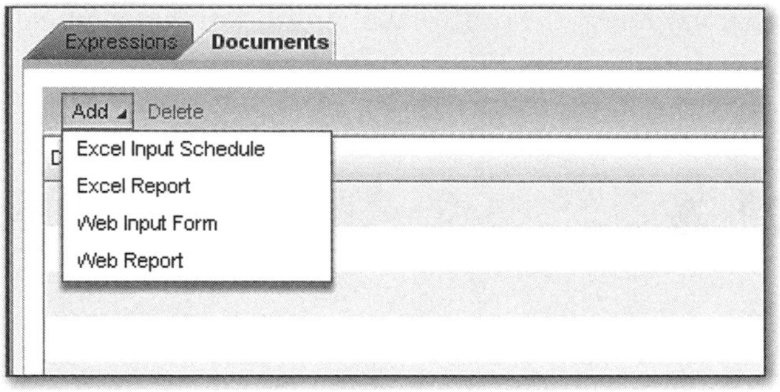

Figure 8.40 Options for Adding Documents to the Controls

After you select one of these parameters, you'll find that you can attach anything from your workspace to the control (see Figure 8.41). This is definitely useful when trying to troubleshoot a control result..

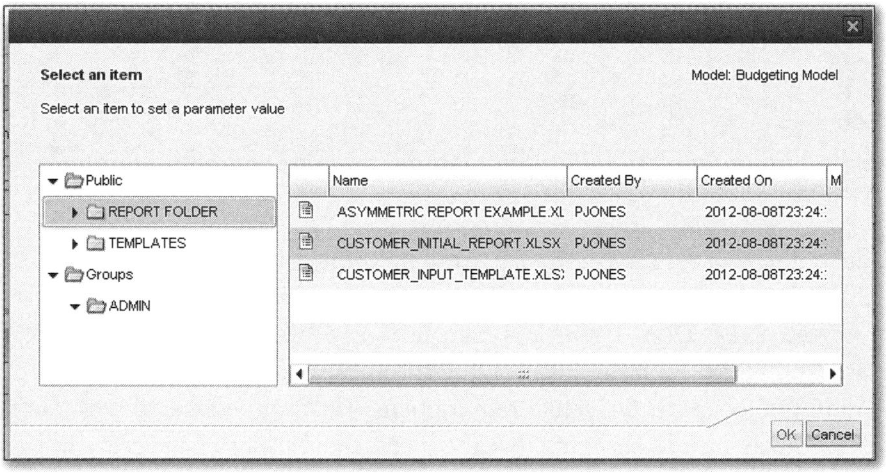

Figure 8.41 Accessing Documents to Attach to the Control

After the assignment is complete, a quick validation of the configuration helps confirm that everything is working, as shown in Figure 8.42.

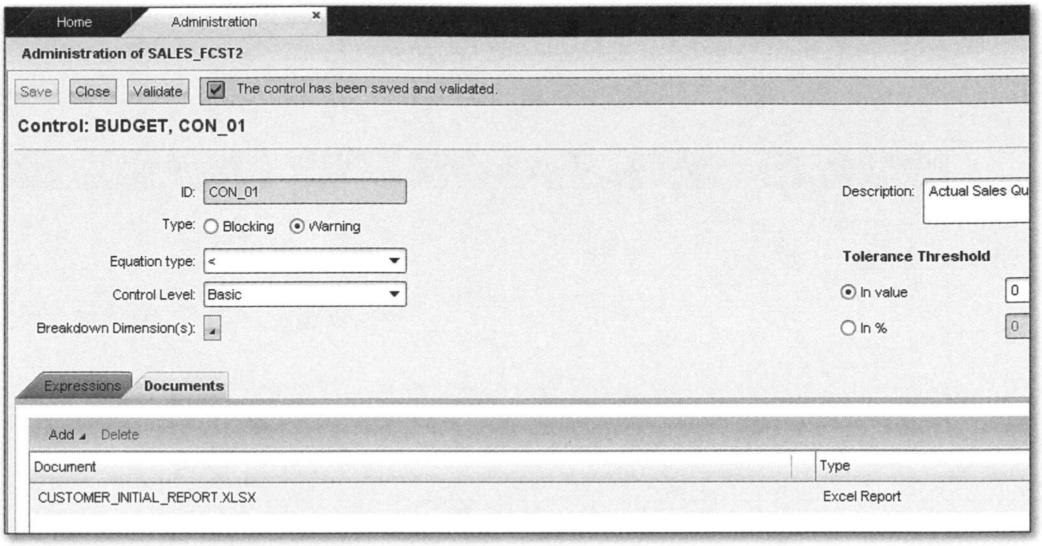

Figure 8.42 Validate the Results of the Control on BUDGET

Now that the control has been built, you need to assign it to a control set. The control set allows you to execute multiple controls in a sequence to test several formulas at the same time. To start setting up the control set, choose a MODEL and then click on EDIT SETS, as shown in Figure 8.43.

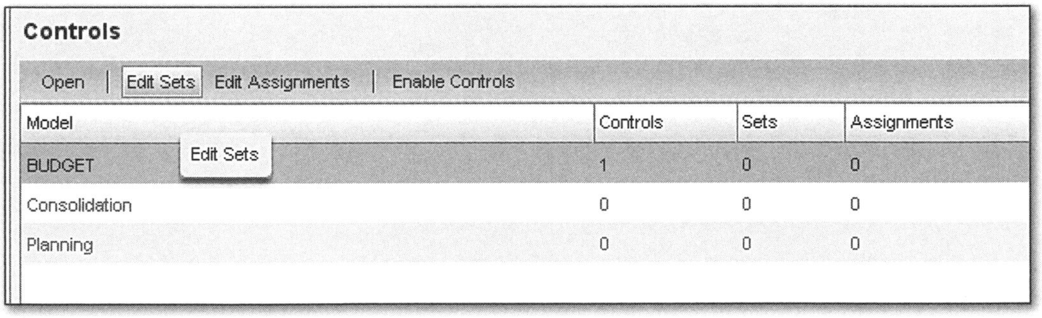

Figure 8.43 Controls – Edit Sets

In the dialog box, assign an ID and DESCRIPTION, and then use the ADD/REMOVE button to choose the controls you want to assign. Choose the controls to execute from left to right in this screen, as shown in Figure 8.44.

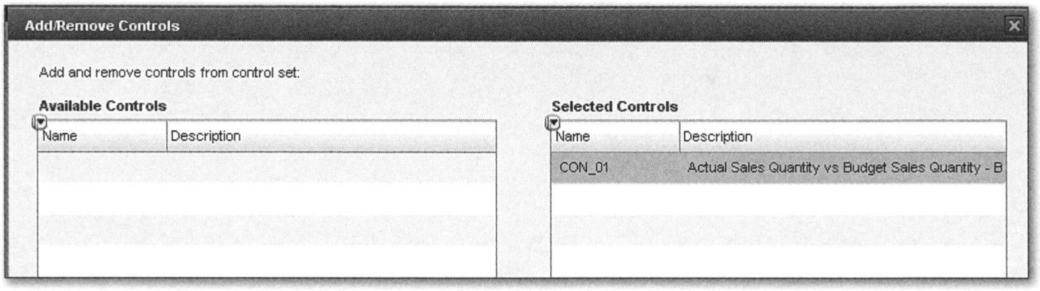

Figure 8.44 Add/Remove Controls

After a final confirmation that the control is consistent, you can then review the results in the Control Monitor (see Figure 8.45).

Next, you need to set up the assignments of the control set. This allows you to assign the sets to the dimensions you identified earlier so that you can execute the controls on a specific slice of data. The initial screen is shown in Figure 8.46.

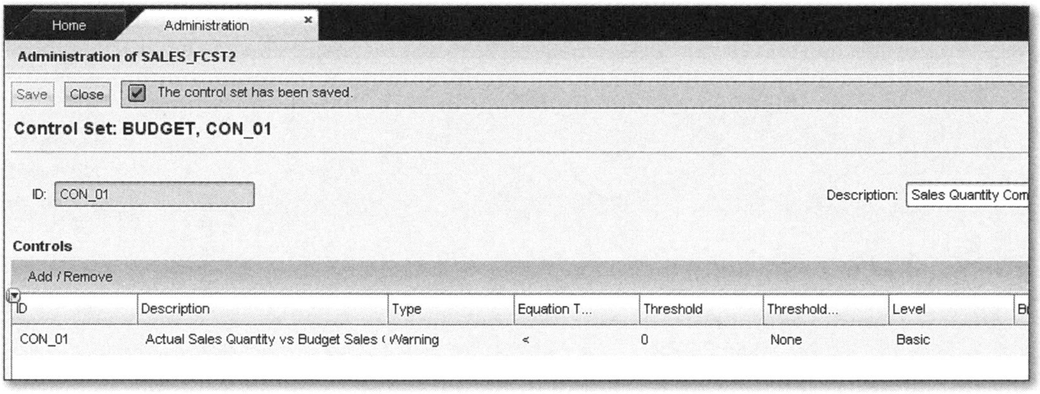

Figure 8.45 Validation of the Control Set

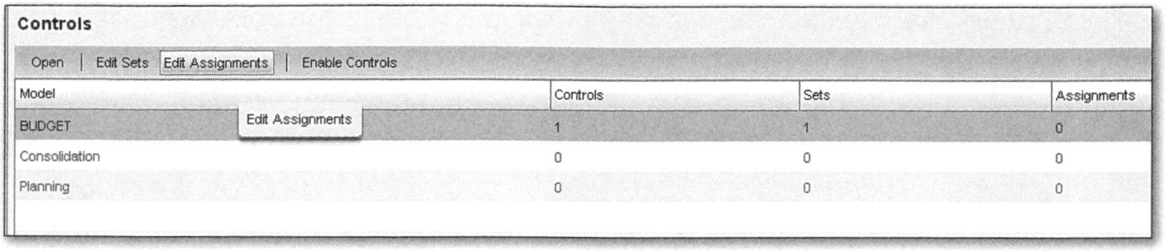

Figure 8.46 Edit Assignments in Controls

In this case, you'll be assigning the controls to the members of CATEGORY and TIME. With the category in the ROWS, and TIME in the columns, you can see that the controls are linked to the intersection of the data based on these two dimensions (see Figure 8.47).

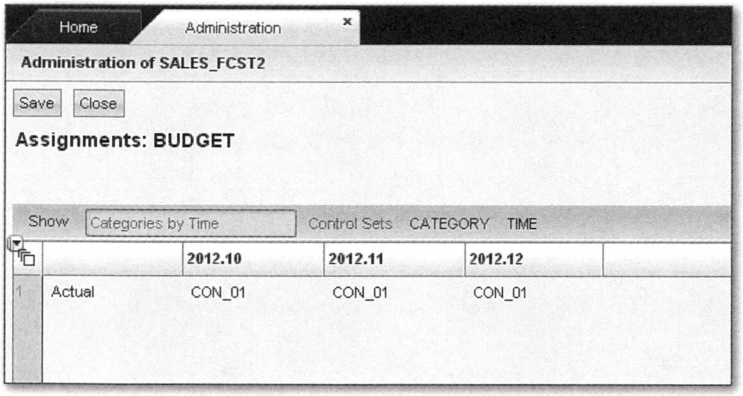

Figure 8.47 Assignments: BUDGET – CON_01 and Category/Time

Click on SAVE when you're done, and you can review the results in the Control Monitor.

8.3.2 Control Monitor

The Control Monitor is specifically used to view and manage the controls you've assigned to each of the models. This gives you an all-in-one spot to analyze and review the controls for each model. You don't really do much to set up the Control

Monitor. It's based on the hierarchy you defined in the CONTROLS MONITOR screen (see Figure 8.48).

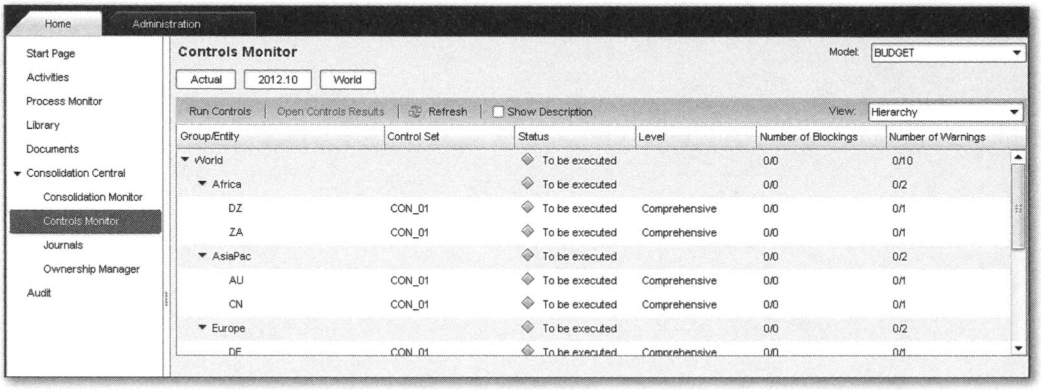

Figure 8.48 Controls Monitor Screen

When you go to RUN Controls, you get a dialog box showing you the parameters, which are standard drivers for the controls (see Figure 8.49). These parameters are standard; only the members can be changed.

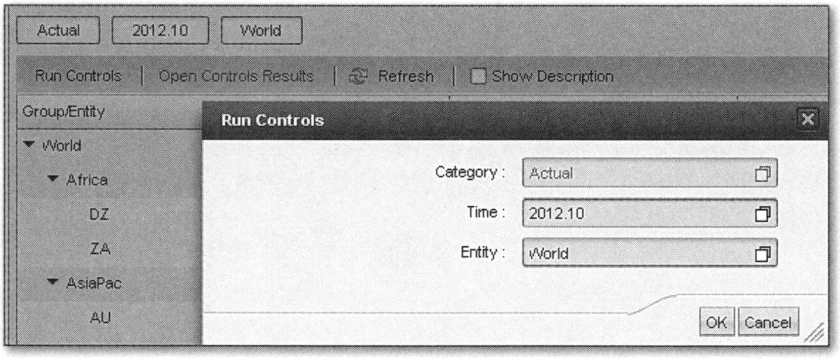

Figure 8.49 Run Controls – Parameter Screen

After you execute the controls, you should see something similar to what is shown in Figure 8.50. In this situation, you can see that all of the controls passed with a warning. You can also see that a level of COMPREHENSIVE has been assigned to the entity. This way, you can have the formula validate against data at the entity level.

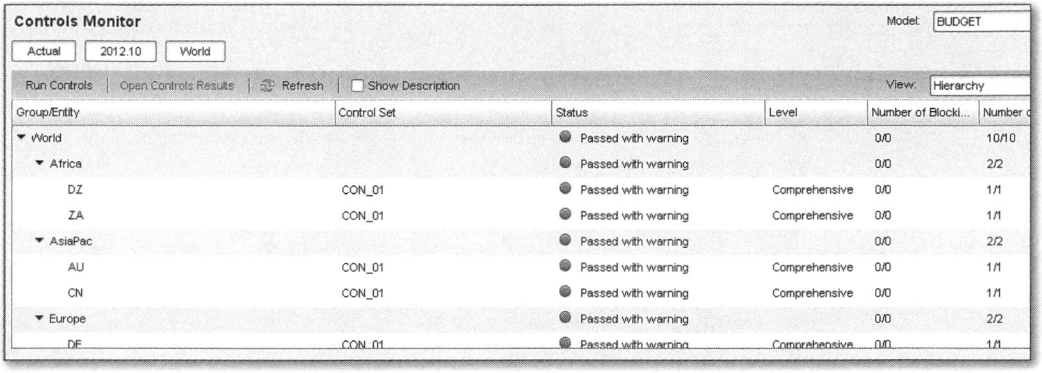

Figure 8.50 Controls Monitor – Results

Finally, you can drill down even further if you choose the OPEN CONTROLS RESULTS button and display the details of the individual control (see Figure 8.51).

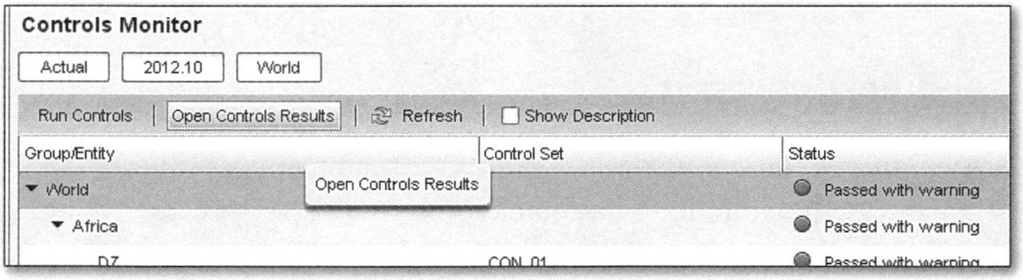

Figure 8.51 Controls Monitor – Open Controls Results

As you can see in Figure 8.52, you can now execute the report that you assigned to the to the control component: CUSTOMER INITIAL REPORT.XLSX.

The process of executing the controls is normally done during the closing process to catch any inconsistencies during the data load. This is a very useful component and should be integrated with the overall data management strategy.

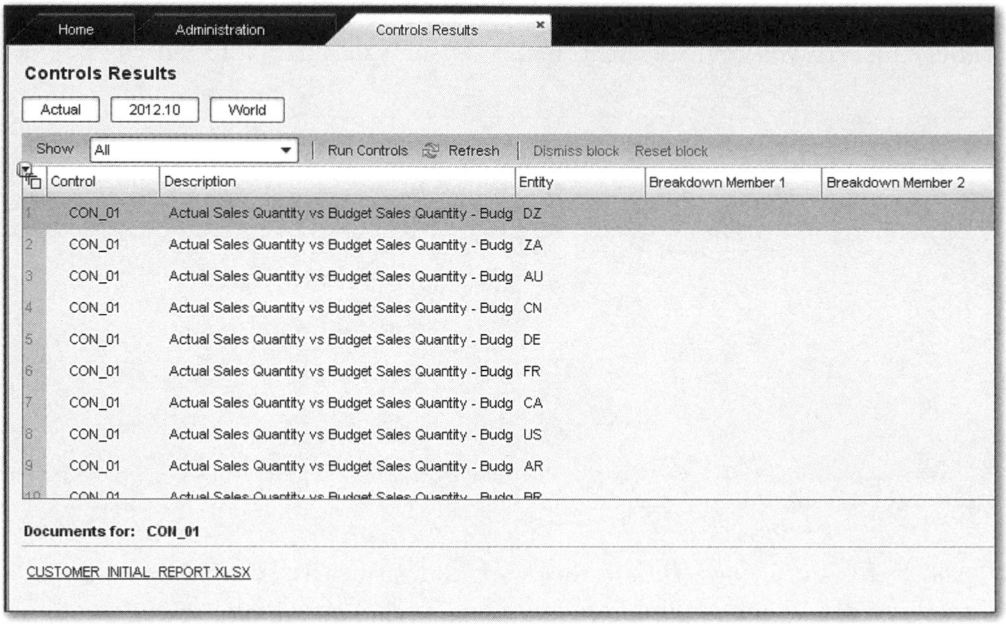

Figure 8.52 Control Results via the Control Monitor

8.4 Auditing Processes

Another component of the overall security and authorization process is *auditing*. This series of activities helps with the management of the entire BPC process. Auditing is used on all of the BPC reviews, scoping, and projects we've been involved with. The process of setting up the auditing tasks in BPC is also very straightforward and is very much part of the standard content that is delivered with the BPC system. We'll review this process shortly but before you start to turn on everything that auditing allows, you have to make sure you really know what is required for the customer. In many cases, the customer may want to turn on too many of the auditing options and therefore have an impact on the system as a whole. You have to remember that whatever you activate related to accounting for different activities in the BPC system will impact the performance. For example, if you turn on DATA AUDITING to track everything all of the time, you'll encounter a performance impact on the overall process. Anywhere from 20-25% of the time spent during a save process may be used up with the generation of the records for the audit tables. This means that something that takes about 60 seconds to run will now take about 80 seconds to run. You can see this impact if you turn on the statistics in BW for BPC

(Transaction UJSTAT) and execute the BPC process whether it's a calculation or just saving the data in an input template. Then run the statistics report and analyze the effect of the audit collection on the entire process.

The audit process is a key component in the analysis of what's going on in the system and is very helpful to both the internal and external auditors. It needs to be used, but it's very important to manage the use of this aspect of BPC. In Figure 8.53, you can see the audit statistics via the UJSTAT report.

🔔 Convert from Business	ORDER_PLANNING	36 03/20/2012	17:27:18		0.000785	0.000785	2.896235
🔔 Obtain Concurrency Loc	ORDER_PLANNING	37 03/20/2012	17:27:18		0.041285	0.041285	2.937520
🔔 Write Records to InfoCt	ORDER_PLANNING	38 03/20/2012	17:27:18		0.861634	0.861634	3.799154
🔔 Release Concurrency L	ORDER_PLANNING	39 03/20/2012	17:27:19		0.042053	0.042053	3.841207
🔔 Convert from Technical	ORDER_PLANNING	40 03/20/2012	17:27:19		0.001012	0.001012	3.842219
▷ 🔔 Update Audit	ORDER_PLANNING	41 03/20/2012	17:27:19		0.056178	6.848467	10.690686
🔔 Update Audit	ORDER_PLANNING	112 03/20/2012	17:27:28		0.058621	0.058621	10.690686
▷ ⚠ Shared Query Engine Read	ORDER_PLANNING	0 03/20/2012	17:17:17		0.766105	0.766105	0.766105
▷ ⚠ Shared Query Engine Read	ORDER_PLANNING	0 03/20/2012	17:17:16		0.685679	0.685679	0.685679

Figure 8.53 UJSTAT Report with Update Audit Information

Auditing in BPC is comprised of two areas, the ACTIVITY AUDIT and the DATA AUDIT INFORMATION. Activities meaning that we'll be able to track all of the different objects that have changed, created, adjusted, fixed, and so on throughout the system by user, Business Process Flow (BPF) creation, business rules, and administrative activities such as changing the BPC parameters in the IMG. This is definitely a portion of the audit process that is critical for the entire corporation. This will allow the auditors to view the time, date, and user that have made any changes in the system. The other area is the DATA AUDITING component, which can have a performance impact. Turning on this component will allow the collection of information on every record that has changed or created with the accompanying time, date, user, and amount of the change. For example, if you were to be executing a consolidation process for an entire company, and the consolidation process generates 20,000 records, then the DATA AUDIT process would also generate at least 20,000 records with the changed amount. As you can see, this can become a very large table very quickly, and depending on how much data you're collecting for the audit process, you would have to set up an archiving and/or deletion strategy as soon as possible.

To start the process of activating the audit component, you need to use the ADMINISTRATION screen in BPC. Then choose FEATURES • AUDIT to open the screen shown in Figure 8.54.

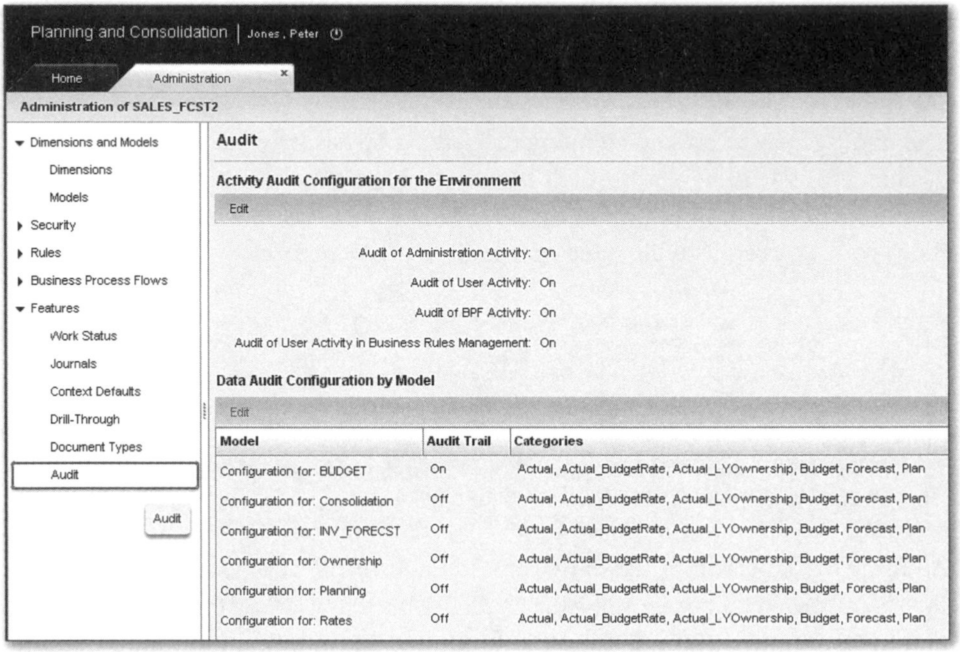

Figure 8.54 Initial Activation of Audit Component

The different activity audit areas have been turned on, including ADMINISTRATION ACTIVITY, USER ACTIVITY, BPF ACTIVITY, AND BUSINESS RULES MANAGEMENT. In Figure 8.55, you can see this more clearly. To activate these areas, you need to click on the EDIT option and then check off the aspects of auditing you want to turn on.

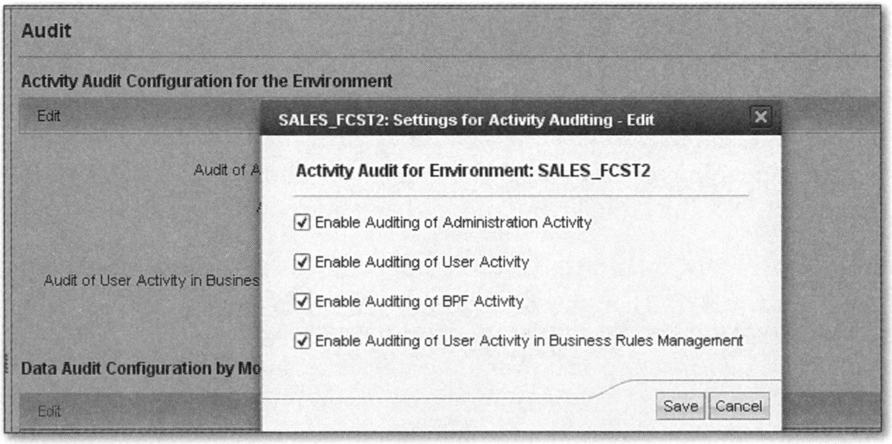

Figure 8.55 Settings for Activity Auditing

In this case, all of the different components for the activity audit have been turned on. To turn on the DATA AUDIT portion, you pick a MODEL from the list at the bottom of the page and then click on the EDIT button (see Figure 8.56). The activation in this case is model specific, so rather than activating all of the different models, you only turn on those that are critical to you such as the Consolidation model, although this is definitely a company-specific decision.

Data Audit Configuration by Model		
Edit		
Model	**Audit Trail**	**Categories**
Configuration for: BUDGET	On	Actual, Actual_BudgetRate, Actual_LYOwnership, Budget, Forecast, Plan
Configuration for: Consolidation	Off	Actual, Actual_BudgetRate, Actual_LYOwnership, Budget, Forecast, Plan

Figure 8.56 Data Audit Configuration by Model

This takes you to a detailed screen where you can identify what tasks you want the AUDIT component to collect records on (see Figure 8.57). Notice that the DATA AUDIT is controlled by the Category dimension and then decide what activities or tasks is critical for the collection of audit information. Again, it's important that you only activate what is required rather than all of the components.

	Audited Tasks								
Categories	**EPM Add-in Input**	**Data Manager Im...**	**Data Manager Cle...**	**Script Logic Exec...**	**Web Report Input**	**Journal Input**	**Business Rules E...**	**Ownership**	**FIM Import**
Actual	Yes	Yes	Yes	Yes	Yes	Yes	Yes	Yes	No
Actual_BudgetRate	No	No	No	No	No	No	No	No	No
Actual_LYOwnership	No	No	No	No	No	No	No	No	No
Budget	Yes	Yes	Yes	Yes	Yes	No	Yes	No	No
Forecast	Yes	No	No	No	No	No	No	No	No
Plan	No	No	No	No	No	No	No	No	No

Figure 8.57 Data Audit Configuration for the Model

For example, if you're not using the data management component FIM with your BPC system, you don't have to turn that on (see Figure 8.58). In this screen, to the far right, you see that there is an option to assign a time to purge the audit data. Purging the audit tables is very important in the data management process because these tables can be collecting data over a month's time and end up with millions of records. If you need to hold the data for a longer time, you can set up a process to move the audit data from the original tables to a series of BW InfoCubes to continue to be available for reporting purposes. We'll discuss this later in this section.

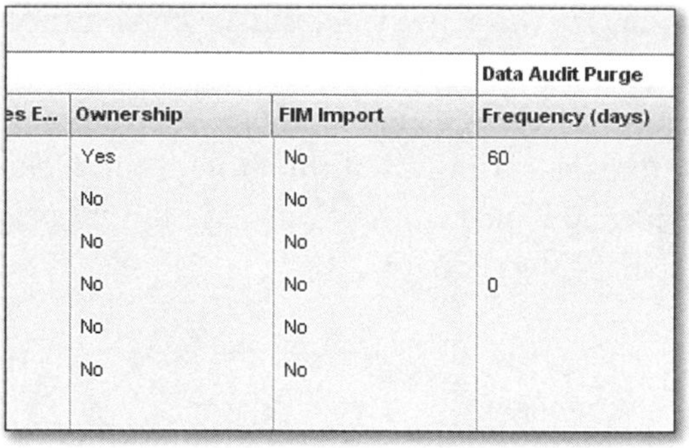

			Data Audit Purge
es E...	Ownership	FIM Import	Frequency (days)
	Yes	No	60
	No	No	
	No	No	
	No	No	0
	No	No	
	No	No	

Figure 8.58 Data Audit Purge Frequency

After these steps are taken, the audit tables will start to collect the requested data for either activities or data in the system.

8.4.1 Audit Reporting

In terms of reporting on the collected information, go to the HOME tab of the BPC Web Client screen, and at the bottom of the list, there will be a link for the AUDIT REPORTS. Click on this link, and three groups of reports appear that can be executed for the analysis of the data (see Figure 8.59). The three groups of reports are BPF, SECURITY, and GENERAL, which includes the data audit information and reports.

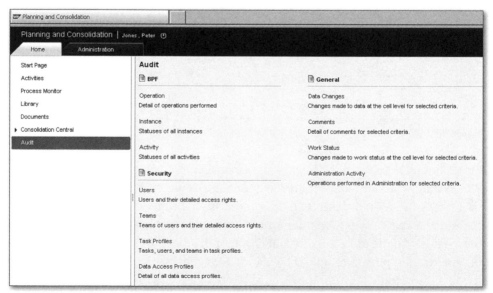

Figure 8.59 Audit Initial Screen –BPF, Security, General Report Groups

Depending on the different components that were activated during the short configuration time frame just discussed, you can use these different links to access the information. These are all standard content delivered with the BPC system.

BPF Reporting

The first section you find is for the BPF REPORTS. These three standard reports will allow you to review the processes that are ongoing for anyone using the BPF components:

▶ OPERATION reports

▶ INSTANCE reports

▶ ACTIVITY reports

Each uses a component of the BPF to show the different statuses, activities, and processes that are being executed. The OPERATION report offers the BPF AUDIT REPORT, which can deliver information for the TEMPLATES, INSTANCES, and ACTIVITIES all in one report. The display, which is static, allows some high-level filters for templates that are VALID or INVALID, and the versions that are in DRAFT, DEPLOYED, or INACTIVE status. This report also allows the filtering based on time. Of all of the reports in this BPF section, the operation reportis the critical one with most of the information that you'll need (see Figure 8.60).

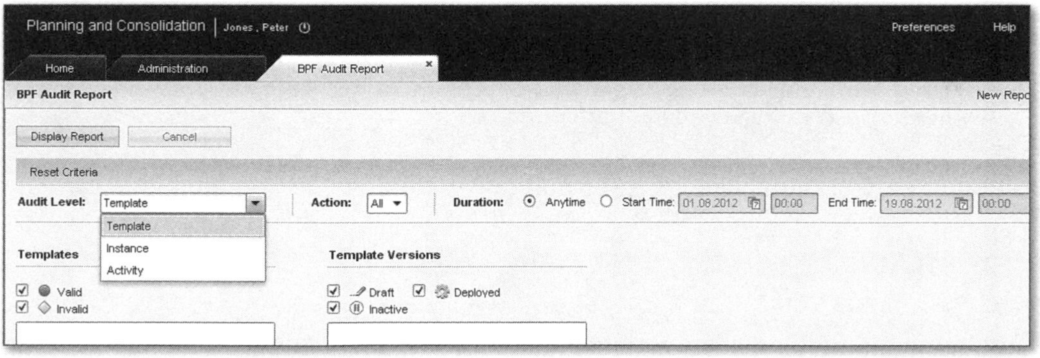

Figure 8.60 BPF Audit Report

The other two reports focus on the specifics by INSTANCE or by ACTIVITY. If you look at the ACTIVITY REPORT in Figure 8.61, you see that it changes the display of the details and has the three different components of TEMPLATES, VERSIONS, and INSTANCES in the body of the report rather than as a dropdown. In this case, the report doesn't have a filter for the time, so you'll see all of the processing that's going on with the BPFs. In the case of the INSTANCES reports in BPF, the display is similar to this and generates information only for the instances available.

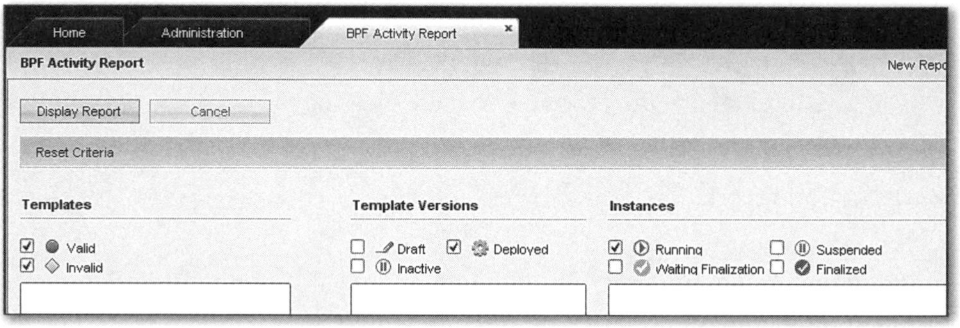

Figure 8.61 BPF Activity Report

Security Reporting

The next report group in the AUDIT report screen is SECURITY, which offers reports based on the four different components you just saw in Section 8.1of this chapter: USERS, TEAMS, TASK PROFILES and DATA ACCESS PROFILES. In Figure 8.62, you see the initial screen. The interesting element of these reports is that you can drill down directly to the security settings to view them based on a link within the report.

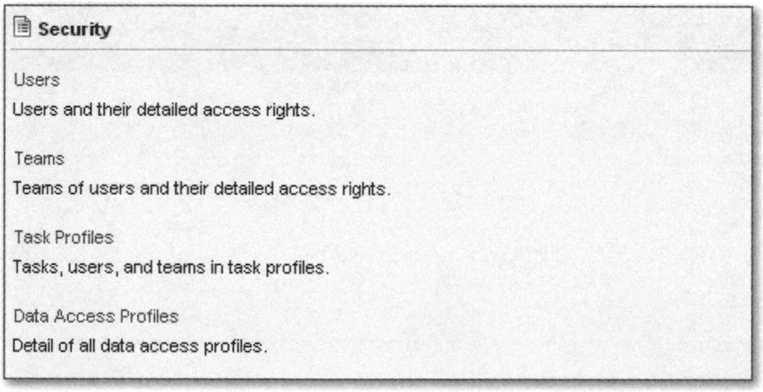

Figure 8.62 Audit Security Reports

If you look at the USERS reports, you see that each of the users shows up in a list, and you can use the user name as a link to drill down to the actual settings (see

Figure 8.63). Notice the user, BPC_USER99, that you created earlier in Section 8.1 of this chapter.

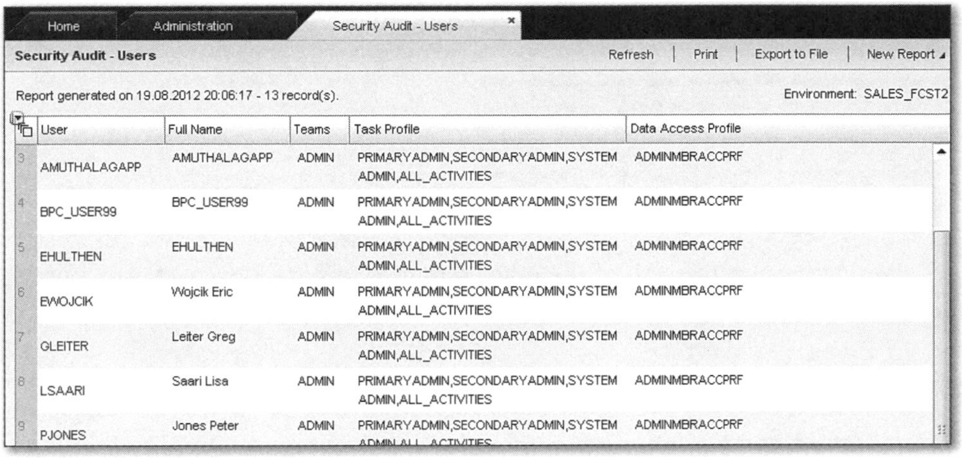

Figure 8.63   Security Audit – Users Report

This report offers the USER, TEAM, FULL NAME, TASK PROFILES, and DATA ACCESS PROFILES that the user is assigned. This is an excellent tool for the security team to be able to manage the different components assigned to the user in BPC. If you click on the link for BPC_USER99, it takes you to the actual setup, in display view only, and allows you to view all of the setup assigned to this user. Figure 8.64 shows this information. You can then just tab from TEAM to TASK PROFILES to DATA ACCESS PROFILES to review the current settings.

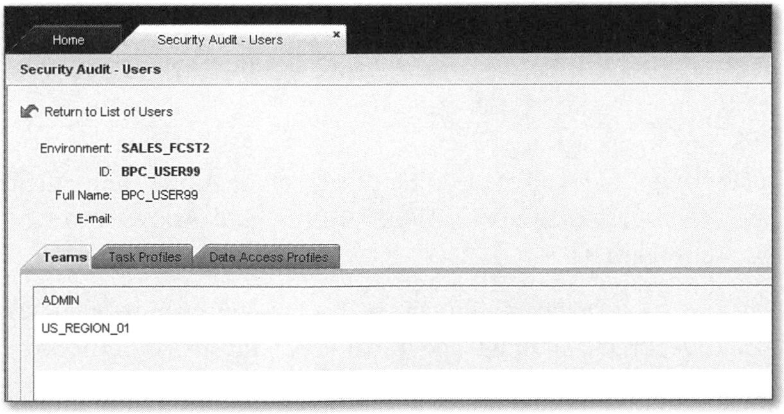

Figure 8.64   Security Audit - Users –Teams, Task Profiles, and Data Access Profiles

On the far right of this screen and on all of the security reports, you'll see a toggle option that allows you to move from report to report in the security group. It allows you to execute multiple tasks such as exporting the information or just navigating to another report. Figure 8.65 shows you this information.

Figure 8.65 Security Report – Refresh, Print, Export to File, and New Report

The reports available are all of the other activities in security as well as all of the other audit reports in each of the different areas (see Figure 8.66).

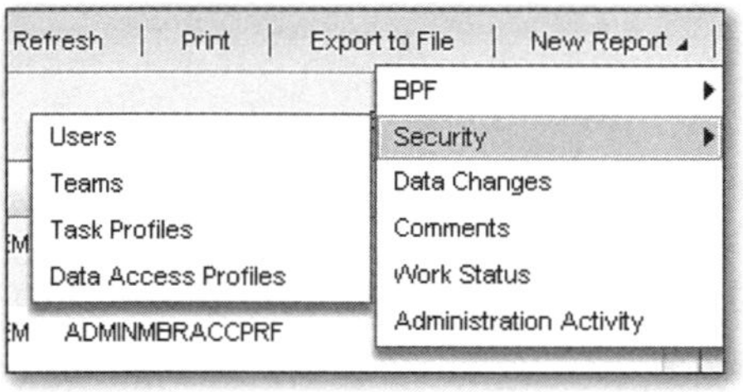

Figure 8.66 Reports Available within Audit Reporting

This is a quick and easy approach to moving from screen or report to report. The other reports in the SECURITY area work in a very similar manner as the one you just reviewed, and the ability to drill down to the lowest level of information is available in all of the reports as well. There are no filters or parameters that are needed to execute these reports, so this is more of a display and analysis process for the auditors and security team.

General Reporting

The GENERAL report group- covers all of the other aspects of the AUDIT component. It consists of DATA CHANGES, COMMENTS, WORK STATUS, and ADMINISTRATION ACTIVITIES reports (see Figure 8.67).

If you look at the DATA CHANGES report, you can see that the same sort of details are delivered as the other reports in auditing. The initial screen for the DATA CHANGES report is broken up into two sections: what you'll be viewing for the data changes and what types of data changes you want to review. Figure 8.68 shows the initial portion of the screen for the DATA CHANGES reports.

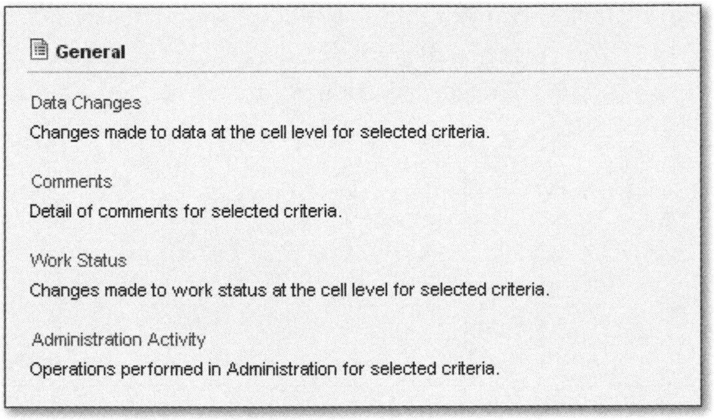

Figure 8.67 Audit General Reports – Data Changes, Comments, Work Status, and Administration Activities

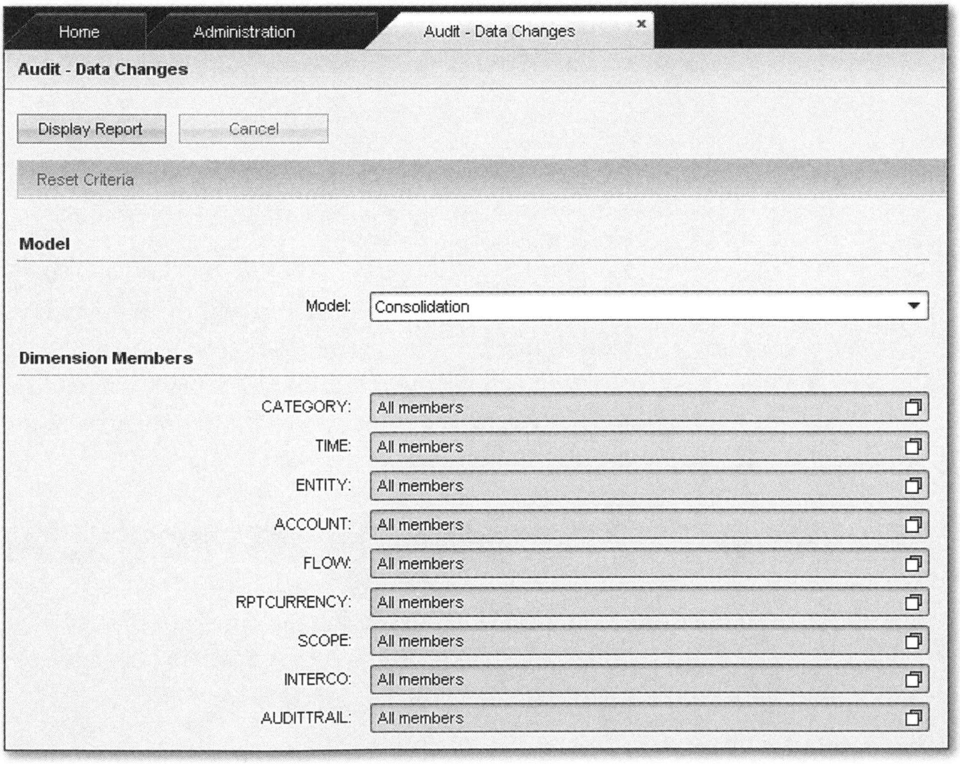

Figure 8.68 Audit – Data Changes

In the AUDIT – DATA CHANGES screen, you identify the model and all of the dimension members you want to use as an intersection of data for the report. The filters for TIME, TASK, USERS and IP SERVER are available. This can be seen in Figure 8.69 below the list of Tasks available. This will help focus the information you'll see on this report. Remember, if you've been collecting the data for some time now, you'll have millions of records and will need to minimize your display for a better view of the data (see Figure 8.69).

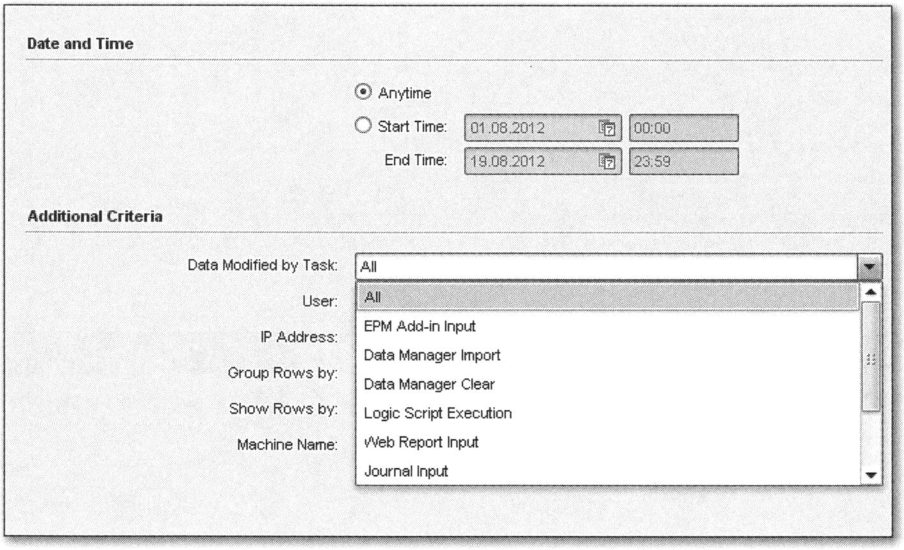

Figure 8.69 Data Audit – Date and Time; Additional Criteria

After you execute this report, you'll see a list of records that will show everything about the posting as well as the amount of the change made (see Figure 8.70). In this case, you find that the amount of information might be a bit too much; for example, having the IP address of the machine that executed the postings might not be critical information during your analysis of the data changes.

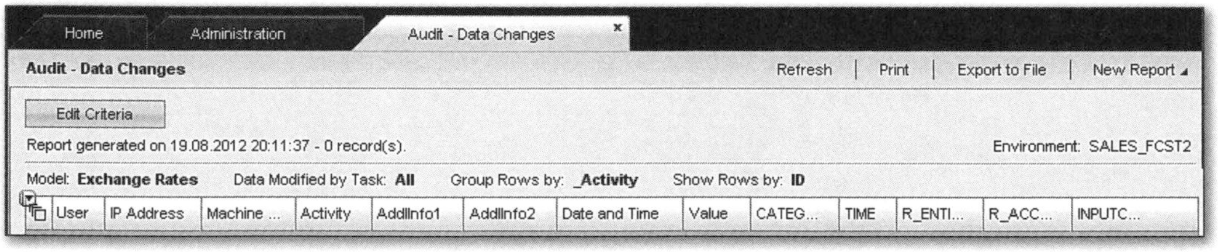

Figure 8.70 Audit – Data Change Report

Each of the other reporting components in this report group offer very similar functions for analysis of the data if you want to view the comments, work status, or administrative activities being changed.

8.4.2 Audit Tables Reports

With all of this data being collected, we need to discuss the tables in BW that are storing this information. As mentioned, the audit data is being stored in a series of tables in BW and not in other objects such as InfoCubes or DSOs. To see these tables, you can use Transaction SE12 to get to a screen similar to the one in Figure 8.71.

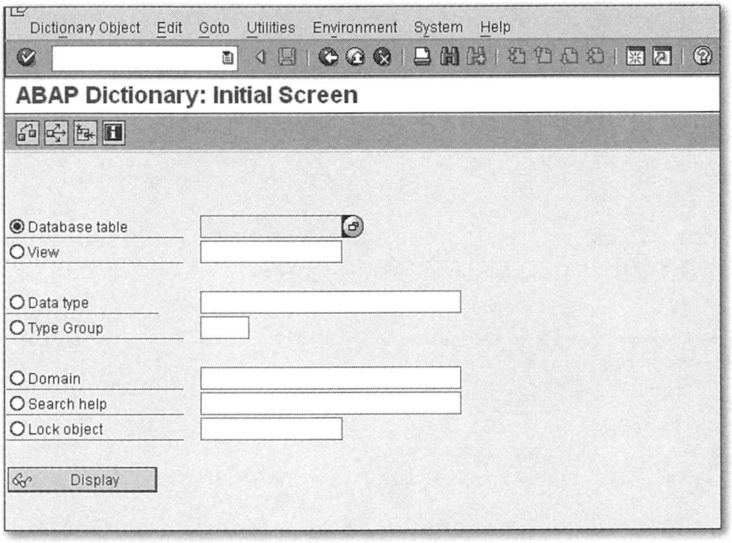

Figure 8.71 Transaction SE12 – View a Database Table

You can now use a wildcard to search for the audit tables. Remember that all tables related to BPC start with a UJ*. If you use this as well as the AUD filter, you can see the set of audit tables that support all of the activity information (see Figure 6.72). Notice that each of the tables is set up to support both current information stored in the audit tables as well as archived audit information in another table. Other tables support the header information as well as the audit settings you've configured.

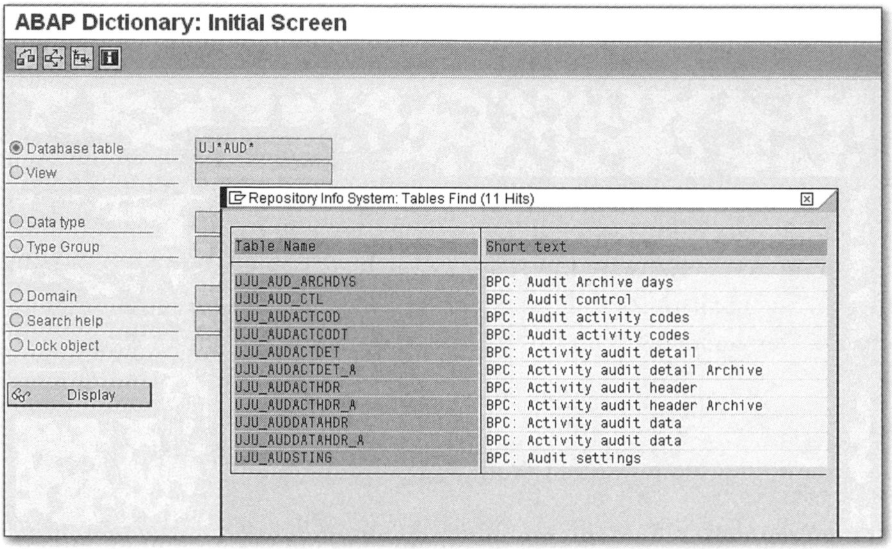

Figure 8.72 Audit Tables via the BW SAP GUI

If you review one of the tables, you see that the audit activity details has the technical name of UJU_AUDACTDET as shown in Figure 8.73.

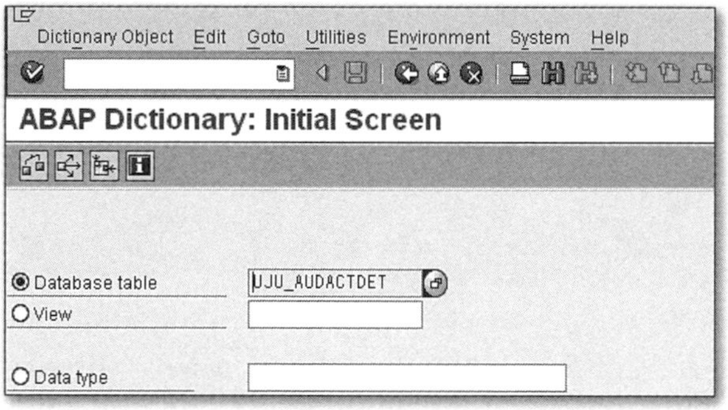

Figure 8.73 ABAP Dictionary: Initial Screen for Viewing the Database Table

This particular table includes the information on the activity details (see Figure 8.74), the different components of the audit configuration for the SALES_FCST2 environment and all of the ADDs have been turned on to show the components such as the EPM ADD-IN INPUT, DATA MANAGER IMPORT, and so on. The object that is the glue between the detailed tables and the header tables is the UNIQUE ID or the 22-character technically generated value in this table. With that piece of information, you can easily find additional activities about the process that occurred. If you cut and paste this UNIQUE ID into any of the header tables, you can find out additional details.

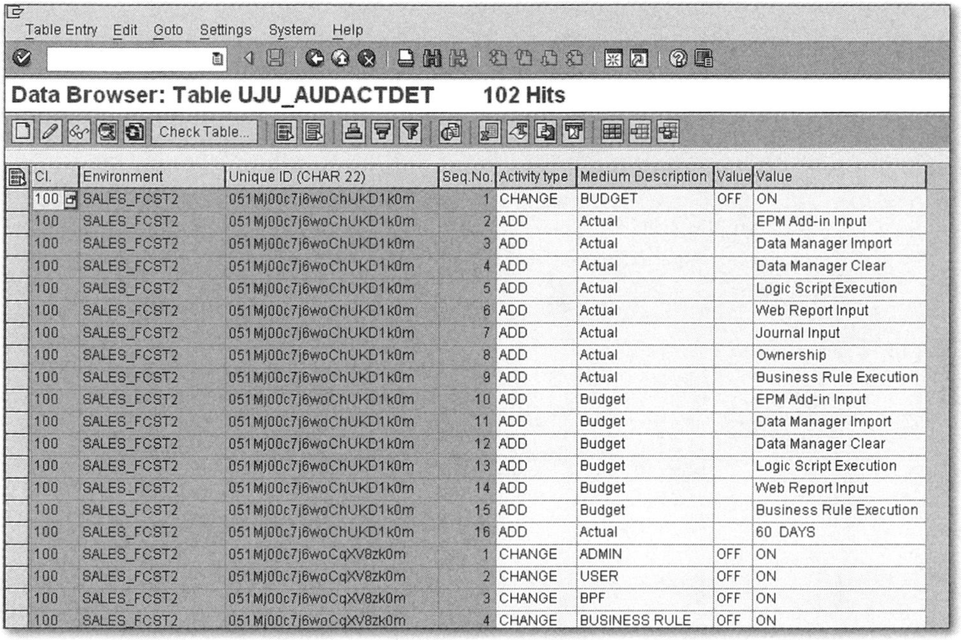

Cl.	Environment	Unique ID (CHAR 22)	Seq.No.	Activity type	Medium Description	Value	Value
100	SALES_FCST2	051Mj00c7j6woChUKD1k0m	1	CHANGE	BUDGET	OFF	ON
100	SALES_FCST2	051Mj00c7j6woChUKD1k0m	2	ADD	Actual		EPM Add-in Input
100	SALES_FCST2	051Mj00c7j6woChUKD1k0m	3	ADD	Actual		Data Manager Import
100	SALES_FCST2	051Mj00c7j6woChUKD1k0m	4	ADD	Actual		Data Manager Clear
100	SALES_FCST2	051Mj00c7j6woChUKD1k0m	5	ADD	Actual		Logic Script Execution
100	SALES_FCST2	051Mj00c7j6woChUKD1k0m	6	ADD	Actual		Web Report Input
100	SALES_FCST2	051Mj00c7j6woChUKD1k0m	7	ADD	Actual		Journal Input
100	SALES_FCST2	051Mj00c7j6woChUKD1k0m	8	ADD	Actual		Ownership
100	SALES_FCST2	051Mj00c7j6woChUKD1k0m	9	ADD	Actual		Business Rule Execution
100	SALES_FCST2	051Mj00c7j6woChUKD1k0m	10	ADD	Budget		EPM Add-in Input
100	SALES_FCST2	051Mj00c7j6woChUKD1k0m	11	ADD	Budget		Data Manager Import
100	SALES_FCST2	051Mj00c7j6woChUKD1k0m	12	ADD	Budget		Data Manager Clear
100	SALES_FCST2	051Mj00c7j6woChUKD1k0m	13	ADD	Budget		Logic Script Execution
100	SALES_FCST2	051Mj00c7j6woChUKD1k0m	14	ADD	Budget		Web Report Input
100	SALES_FCST2	051Mj00c7j6woChUKD1k0m	15	ADD	Budget		Business Rule Execution
100	SALES_FCST2	051Mj00c7j6woChUKD1k0m	16	ADD	Actual		60 DAYS
100	SALES_FCST2	051Mj00c7j6woCqXV8zk0m	1	CHANGE	ADMIN	OFF	ON
100	SALES_FCST2	051Mj00c7j6woCqXV8zk0m	2	CHANGE	USER	OFF	ON
100	SALES_FCST2	051Mj00c7j6woCqXV8zk0m	3	CHANGE	BPF	OFF	ON
100	SALES_FCST2	051Mj00c7j6woCqXV8zk0m	4	CHANGE	BUSINESS RULE	OFF	ON

Figure 8.74 Content of the Table UJU_AUDACTDET

The tables that hold the data change information are not included in this list. These tables, as you might expect, are linked directly with the core InfoCubes that are being audited. To find that information, you have to use another approach. To keep from having to remember the exact information to fill in and find the tables, you can do a search using "/1CPMB/*AD". This will get you all of the tables associated with the data change information. Figure 8.75 shows the wildcard search that will show all of the data auditing tables.

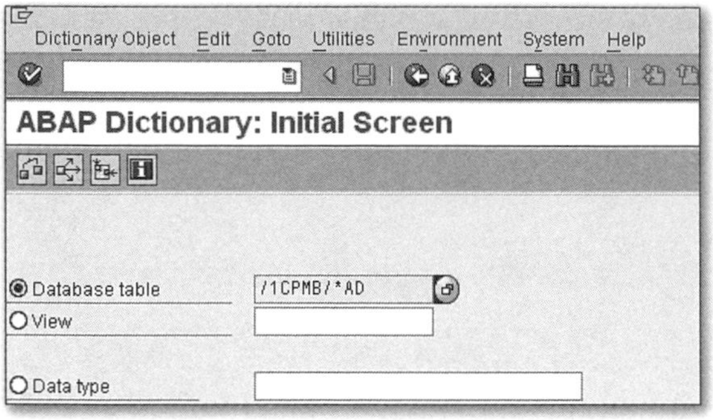

Figure 8.75 ABAP Dictionary: Initial Screen – Search for the Audit Tables

In the full list of tables, look at the technical name of the model in the system to find the one you want. Figure 8.76 shows the technical name that you need from the BW WORKBENCH screen.

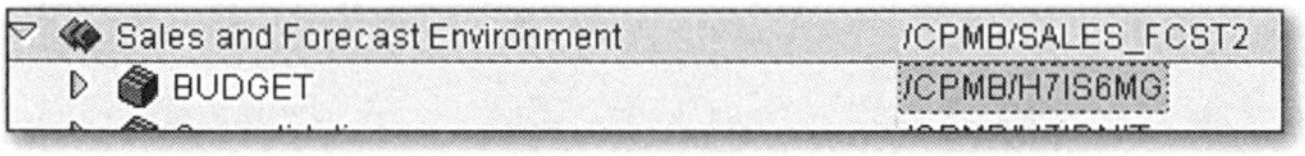

Figure 8.76 BUDGET Model and Technical Name

With that information, you can look through the table generated to find the concatenated portion of the string (see Figure 8.77). Basically, it's the first two positions (H7) after the / along with the other three characters in the string – S6M.

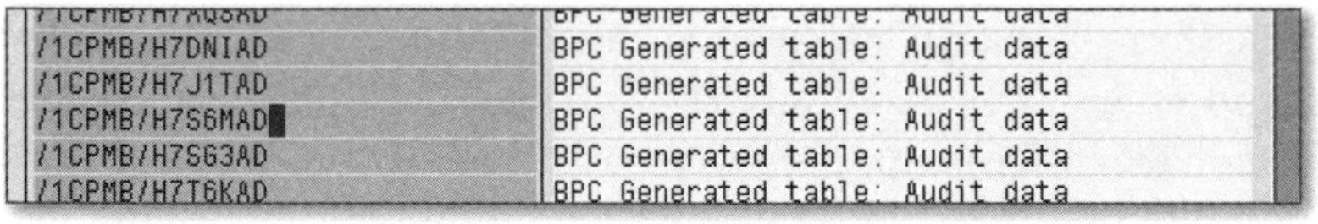

Figure 8.77 Technical Name of the BUDGET Data Audit Table

With this information, you can now see the data change values being stored by the audit tables, as shown in Figure 8.78.

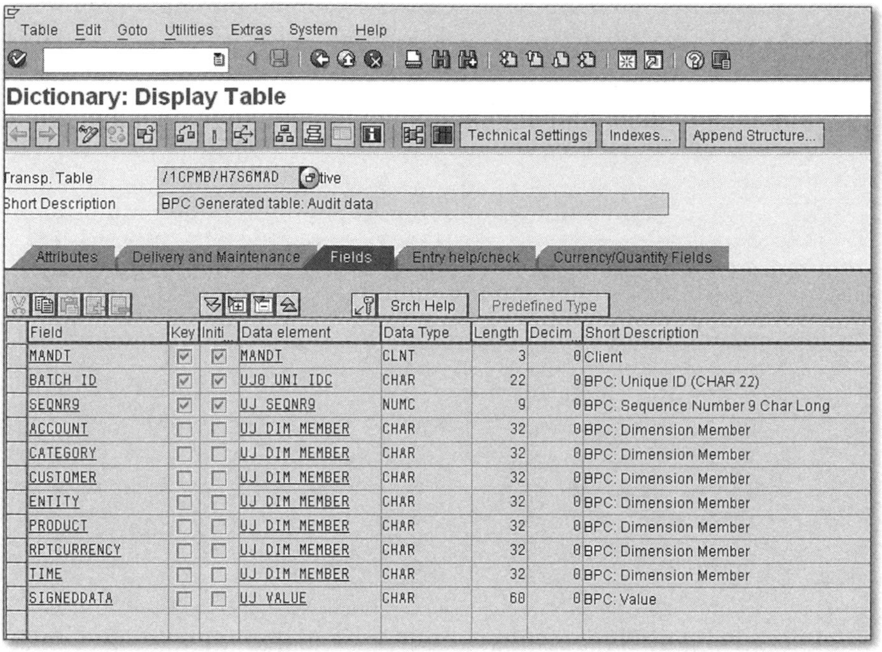

Field	Key	Initi...	Data element	Data Type	Length	Decim...	Short Description
MANDT	☑	☑	MANDT	CLNT	3	0	Client
BATCH_ID	☑	☑	UJ0_UNI_IDC	CHAR	22	0	BPC: Unique ID (CHAR 22)
SEQNR9	☑	☑	UJ_SEQNR9	NUMC	9	0	BPC: Sequence Number 9 Char Long
ACCOUNT	☐	☐	UJ_DIM_MEMBER	CHAR	32	0	BPC: Dimension Member
CATEGORY	☐	☐	UJ_DIM_MEMBER	CHAR	32	0	BPC: Dimension Member
CUSTOMER	☐	☐	UJ_DIM_MEMBER	CHAR	32	0	BPC: Dimension Member
ENTITY	☐	☐	UJ_DIM_MEMBER	CHAR	32	0	BPC: Dimension Member
PRODUCT	☐	☐	UJ_DIM_MEMBER	CHAR	32	0	BPC: Dimension Member
RPTCURRENCY	☐	☐	UJ_DIM_MEMBER	CHAR	32	0	BPC: Dimension Member
TIME	☐	☐	UJ_DIM_MEMBER	CHAR	32	0	BPC: Dimension Member
SIGNEDDATA	☐	☐	UJ_VALUE	CHAR	60	0	BPC: Value

Figure 8.78 Data Audit Change Table for BPC Model BUDGET

We mentioned that after about 90-120 days, you should be looking to purge this information just for the sake of keeping as little data as possible in the system. However, you may find that this isn't feasible and that the auditors want the information to be stored for much longer than that. In this case, you need to move the data into some other set of tables that is more suited for reporting on the audit information. This is very doable in BW and basically you have to use all of the tables involved in the audit process and link the information based on the SAP ID that we talked about earlier. This will allow you to link all of the tables together and have the entire set of information available for reporting directly out of an InfoCube or MultiProvider. The process isn't too complex, but the architecture is extensive, and remember that you have to do it for all of the different models that are being documented using the Data Audit process. In Figure 8.79, you can see that this involves multiple data loading activities, but the nice thing about this is that everything is available, and the creation of the required standard InfoObjects in BW to support isn't complex. In this case, you move the information from the audit tables in BW, to a series of DSOs, and finally into the report cubes for the queries.

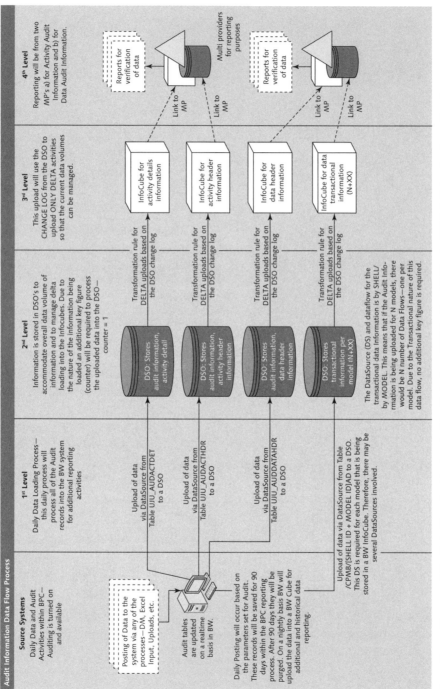

Figure 8.79 Diagram of the Data Flow for Moving Archive Data from BPC Archived Tables to BW InfoCubes for Reporting Purposes

Figure 8.79 is a rather extensive diagram of the process but it's important to get a full view of the different data layers and the data flow required. Remember that after all of the data is uploaded the key object is the SAPGUID and this needs to be used to link all of the different tables and information together in the reports. So make sure that you bring that GUID ID all the way through the data flow and in some cases you will have to 'hide' it and use it as a linking object to create the appropriate union or join of all of the data.

All in all, the audit process component of BPC is a very straightforward component to access and turn on but not to leave on throughout the monthly activities. We can definitely understand the issues that will arise with the overall data flow and volumes of records, so it's important to create processes to both store information and support the information.

8.5 Transports

Transports are critical to the uniformity of the different landscapes in any system. In BPC V10.0, this component has changed quite a bit from the former look and feel in BPC V7.5. The process, configuration, and use of transports has moved closer to the standard transport process in BW, and, in fact, you can definitely incorporate BPC transports into the generic transport strategy that you have for any SAP NetWeaver system. In the previous version, the transport process was a bit unique and was a process that had its own approach as well as strategy. Now, with the changes that have been made, it fits right into the norm and can be as flexible as BW transports in terms of being able to transport all of the objects in an environment or just the specific objects that were changed. Basically, transports are used to move objects from client to client, so you'll normally hear the comment that objects are being transported from DEV to QA, DEV to PROD, or even QA to PROD. This all occurs based on the links and connections between the different system landscapes. The setup of the systems and connections between them is handled by the Basis team and isn't something that we'll discuss in detail here. What we're focused on is the flexibility of the transports and also the process of transporting in BPC V10.0.

Figure 8.80 shows the normal approach to transports in a BW or SAP ERP system. Notice that the transports always source directly from DEV into both QA and PROD. This avoids any differences that might have happened in QA with objects that are changeable. Therefore, you're forced to do any development in the source system for the transports—meaning DEV.

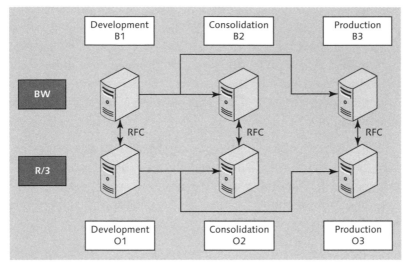

Figure 8.80 Transport Landscape

8.5.1 Configuration and Process of Transports for BPC

In BPC, there's no difference in the approach when you talk about transports for BPC versus BW. In the BPC version for Microsoft , you don't have the concept of transports available, so in that case, you need to use more of the copy process between the multiple systems of DEV, QA, and PROD. One of the new approaches to doing back up and restore - Transaction UJBR in NW BPC - is sometimes thought to replace transports, but these two concepts are quite different, and it isn't best practice to use Transaction UJBR in place of standard transports. We discussed the approach and use of UJBR in Chapter 2.

For those who use transports in BW, this discussion will sound very familiar. To start let's work through this process as though you are executing the transport process from scratch for BPC. Initially, you create and configure the SAP NetWeaver BPC objects in DEV. Then, when the transport of the currently finished configuration is needed in QA for testing, you go to the BW transport screens and start the process. From the initial screen in the SAP BW GUI, you can use Transaction RSA1 to get access to the BW DATA WAREHOUSING WORKBENCH. On the navigation pane on the left side of the screen, click on the TRANSPORT CONNECTION option to access the transport screens (see Figure 8.81). You'll see that there are a number of different objects that are transported. In most cases, there is a specific approach in terms of what objects to transport first, second, and so on. For example, if you were transporting basic BW objects, the initial transport would be for the standard content objects that are the core objects of any of the standard delivered components, and then the InfoProvider that needs the InfoObjects to be generated. Then following the process of transporting objects that are before the InfoProvider, such as the data flow objects transformation rules, DTP, DataSources, and so on, you transport all objects after the InfoProvider such as queries, MultiProviders, variables, and other objects.

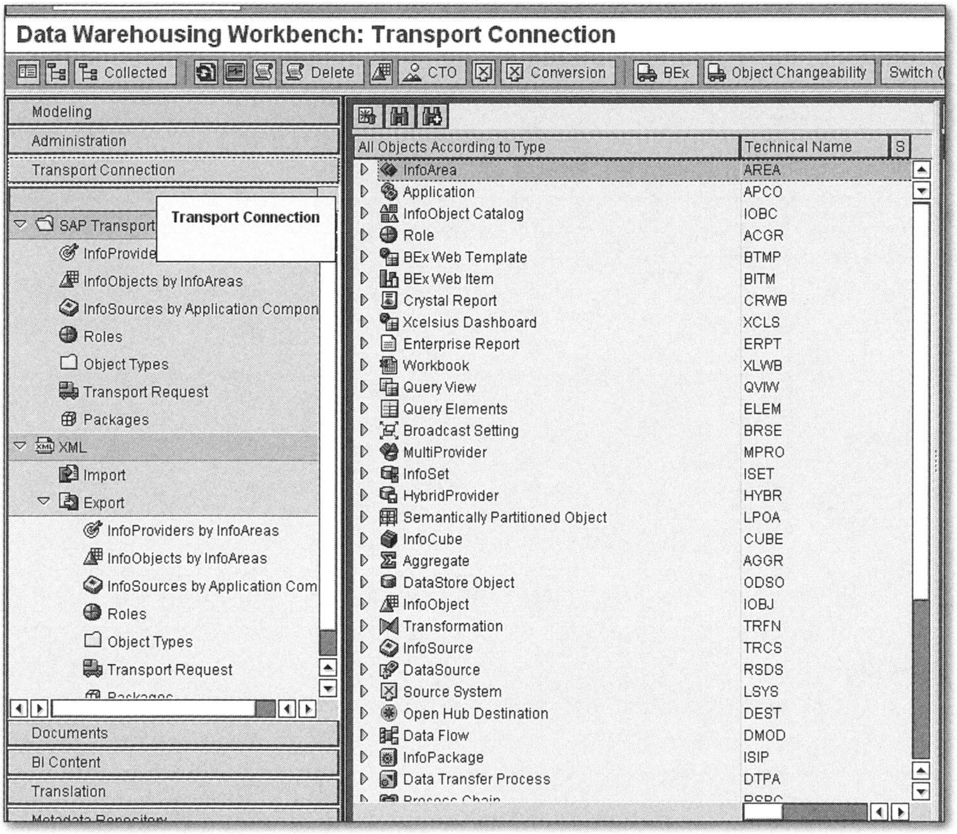

Figure 8.81 BW Data Warehousing Workbench: Transport Connection

In the BPC approach, you only need to look for the folder ALL OBJECTS ACCORDING TO TYPE, and then select MORE TYPES • ENVIRONMENT • SELECT OBJECTS (see Figure 8.82).

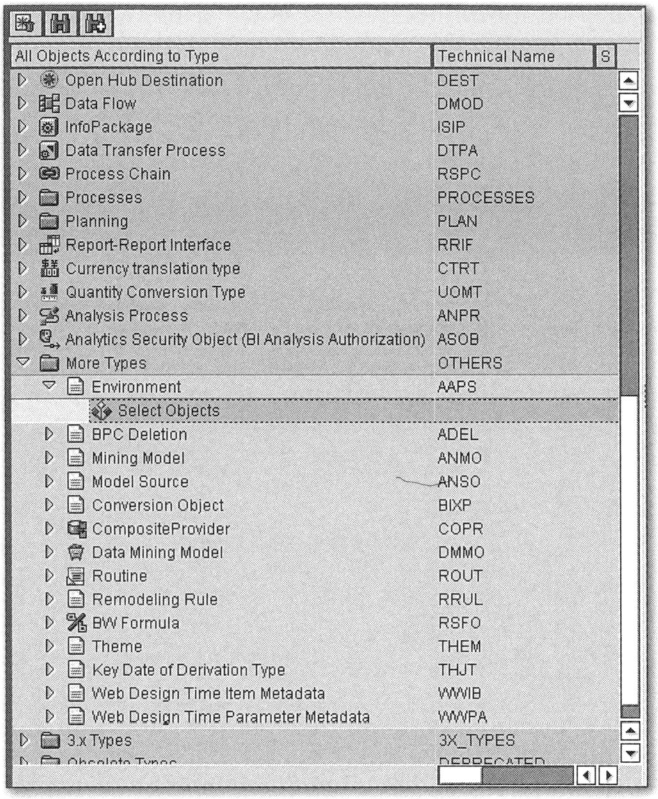

Figure 8.82 All Objects According to Types Folder

Next, you'll see a list of ENVIRONMENTS that are available to be transported. Choose the ENVIRONMENT that you want to transport for the first time, for example, ZSALES_FCST2. Figure 8.83 shows this view. Then select the TRANSFER button at the lower portion of the dialog box.

Figure 8.83 Data Warehousing Workbench: Transport Connection

After this is selected and is displayed in the COLLECTION portion of the screen, you can then either turn on or off different objects to be transported. This is a new feature for BPC V10.0. On the first transport, you want all of the objects you configured to be transported to another client (see Figure 8.84).

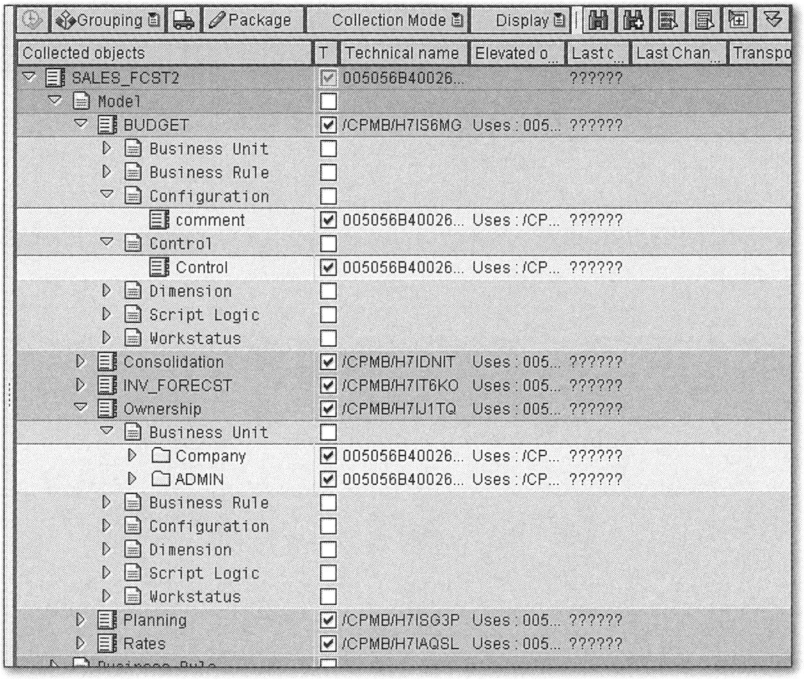

Figure 8.84 Collected Objects: Transport Option to Turn Off for Specific Objects in Environment

Again, this is collected and assigned a transport in the process. As the screen view shows, you can deactivate any of the components.

The next step is to assign them to a transport. Figure 8.85 shows the initial step in this process.

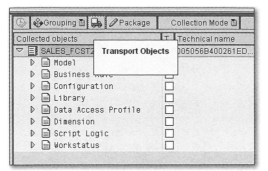

Figure 8.85 Collected Objects – Transport Objects

This, in turn activates the transport process, and you'll have to assign a transport to your objects to move them (see Figure 8.86).

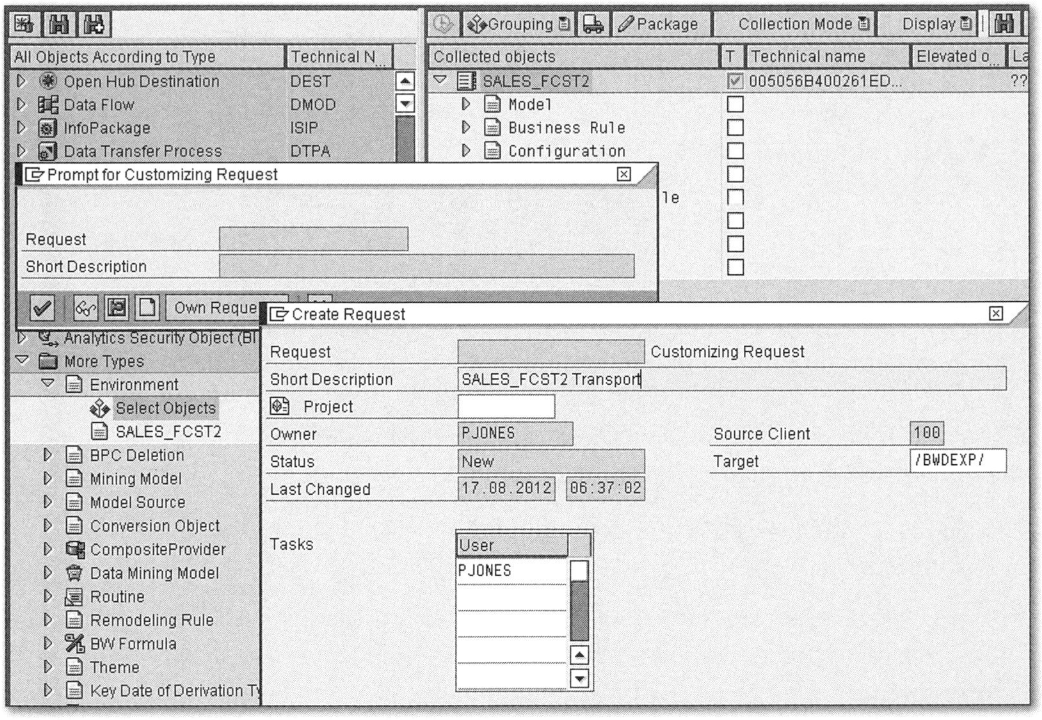

Figure 8.86 Prompt for the Creation and Assignment of the Transport

The approach to managing the actual creation of a transport to assign in this case is up to the company. Normally, you find that the transport is created by someone in BW to be assigned to the BPC objects. After this is complete, you should see a display similar to Figure 8.87 where everything is green and available to "release" the transport.

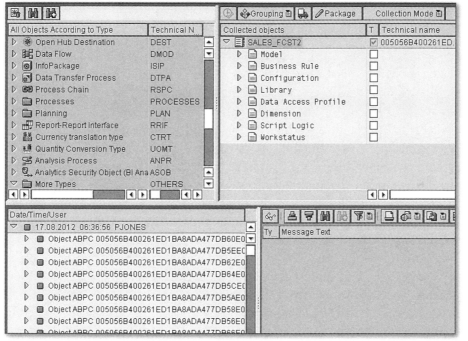

Figure 8.87 Completion of the Collection of a Transport with BPC Objects

Again, you've collected everything for this environment for the first time. After the first transport goes through, the next one you move only needs to deliver the changed or new objects and not the whole environment. This is the enhanced feature in BPC V10.0 where you can turn off the objects that you don't want to transport again unless you've done some changes or they are new objects. This is exactly the same concept as you have for BW or SAP ERP-ECC objects in the current environments.

The approach used for transporting will also depend on if you will be moving the master data over with the rest of the configuration. If this is not the case, then you will have to sequence the transport since much of the configuration in BPC around Script Logic, business rules, and other objects rely on master data to be complete. If you decide to move the environment or objects without master data then move the core objects first, then you will have to execute an upload of the master data in the target system. Once this is complete you can then transport all of the other configuration that relies on the master data being available for use.

Before you release the transport and position it for the move to the other client, you need to switch the status of the environment to OFFLINE, and, for the first time, this is done in DEV only because the environment you're moving is only found in DEV. After the first time, whatever environment you're transporting will be available in both landscapes. In that case, or the next transport for this environment, you have to switch the status to OFFLINE in both the DEV and QA. Always remember that the difference is the fact that you'll have to manage the status of the environment to allow the transport to move to the status of release and then switch the status of the environment being transported to OFFLINE for both the source and target systems. Normally, after the process has been set up, if you plan to move the transport through the entire landscape, you can initially switch the status for all of the different clients—for DEV, QA, and PROD—and not have to worry about going back and switching these environments offline one at a time. Figure 8.88 shows where to switch the environments. In the BPC Web Client, you go to the ADMINISTRATION tab and then choose MANAGE ALL ENVIRONMENTS.

Figure 8.88 Manage All Environments

Then you choose the appropriate environment, and click on the CHANGE STATUS button. In the dialog box that appears, you can just click on the OFFLINE radio button (see Figure 8.89).

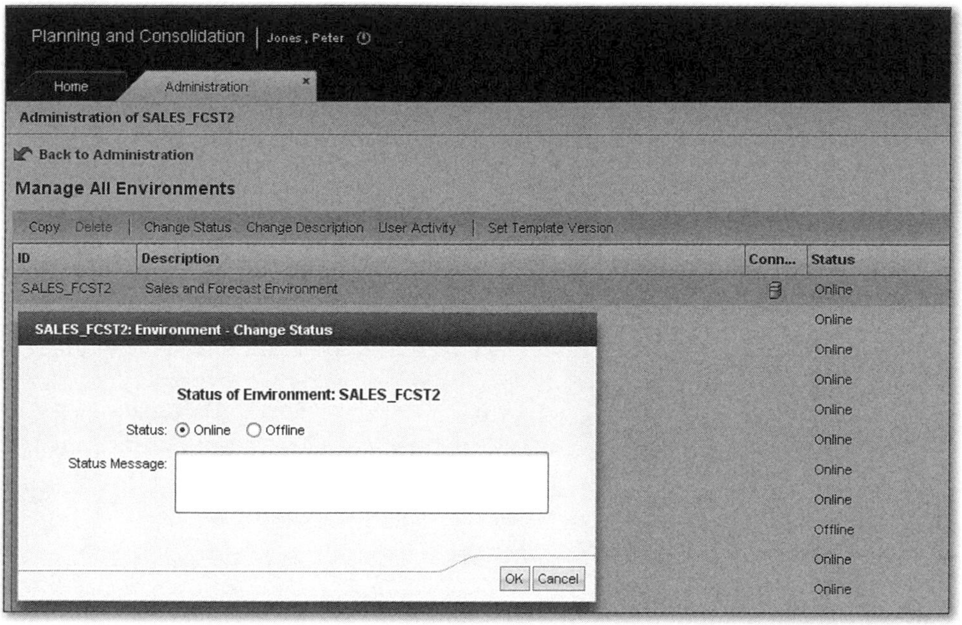

Figure 8.89 Administration – Change Status Option

Now you're ready to release the transports. So using Transaction SE01, you can see the transport and then execute the release of the transport. Normally, there is a set process for these activities and someone that is in charge of managing the transports as they are released. Remember, you can't switch the status of the environments on either source or target systems while doing this process. Figure 8.90 shows the initial screen of the TRANSPORT ORGANIZER. Choose the DISPLAY button to will show all of the transports that are available for release and, in this case, all of the other transports that are in the system. This will help you identify the exact transport that you want to release.

After you have set this up the process of transporting objects, then the objects should be available. Figure 8.91 shows that the transport is being released. Once released, you can then execute the actual move of the transport from DEV to whatever the target system is at this point in time—normally, it's QA. From this point, you can then check the transport after it's completed and validate that all of the changed and new objects have been transported correctly.

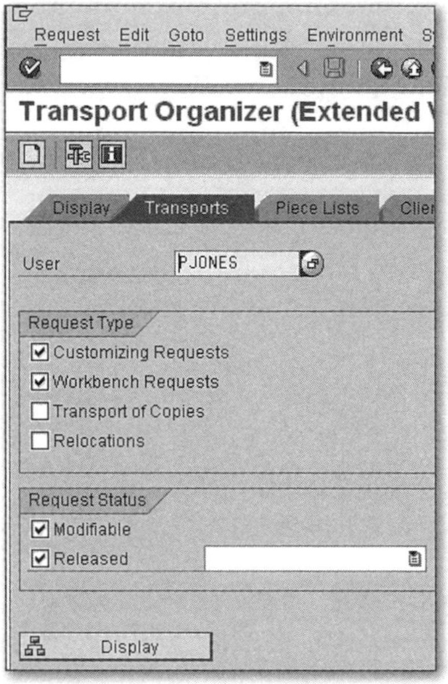

Request   Edit   Goto   Settings   Environment   S

Transport Organizer (Extended

Display   Transports   Piece Lists   Clie

User   PJONES

Request Type
☑ Customizing Requests
☑ Workbench Requests
☐ Transport of Copies
☐ Relocations

Request Status
☑ Modifiable
☑ Released

Display

Figure 8.90   Transport Organizer in BW

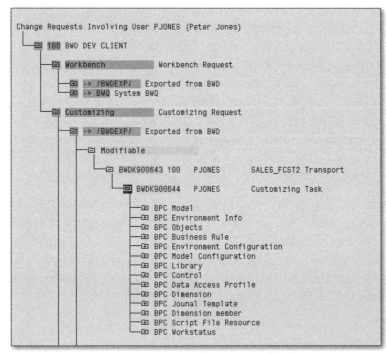

Figure 8.91   Transaction SE01 – Available Transports for the Environment

After the transport is released and moved, you can go into the system and confirm that the objects have, in fact, been transported successfully and that you can then use these objects during the BPC process. You continue to repeat this process of transporting objects whenever the development of the BPC components have gotten to a point where testing with consistent data is required. Following are the basic steps:

1. Go into BW and collect all of the objects using the environment as a starting point.

2. Use this opportunity to deactivate the objects that you don't want to be moved again in the list of BPC components.

3. Execute the collection of the objects remaining, and assign them to a transport.

4. Turn the Environment to OFFLINE (both source and target) so that the transports can be released.

5. Release the transport(s), and then execute the transport of the objects.

6. Turn the environments back ONLINE for validation purposes.

The only unique additional activity for the BPC transports is to make sure that the environments are offline both in the source and target before releasing the transports and subsequent execution of the transport. For those of you who have worked with BPC, this is a more flexible approach to transports and has come a long way to integration with the SAP NetWeaver systems.

8.6   Summary

In this chapter, we've reviewed a number of activities that are very important to the implementation of BPC. In some cases, the components aren't required, such as the controls and auditing, but in others, such as security, they are critical to the management of the different processes in BPC. As we've mentioned, it's definitely a very high priority on every corporation's plate to make sure that the data is secure, especially at the consolidation and P&F levels of information. This is required to at least the level of compliance with Sarbanes-Oxley (SOX) even though the governance requirements of this Act have been realigned several times.

In conjunction with security, we discussed, reviewed, and configured the use of work status in the overall context of activities and process controls. In addition to these components, we also reviewed and configured the controls features of BPC and how they rely on work status as well as other parameters required by security and work status. Finally, in this vein of the conversation, we looked at and reviewed the use of the auditing component. As we mentioned, this is one option in the BPC management process that requires a closer look as to what the business needs for the auditing process. The internal and external auditing department or company must make sure that the required information is collected and stored but also limited to that information only and not overwhelm the system with the collection of massive amounts of audit data. We also discussed the need to have an archiving strategy for the audit information and institute it at the go live stage rather than later.

We concluded this chapter with a discussion around transports and the improved features of BPC transports, including the fact that you can now integrate the transport process of BPC objects with the normal BW objects. Also the flexibility of transporting just specific portions of the configuration is an added benefit.

This chapter discusses the basic concept of Business Process Flows (BPFs), their pros and cons, and the integration with work status and security. You'll learn how to use a typical BPF, both from a planning and consolidation perspective. We'll review the build screens, configuration settings, and best practices for design.

9 Business Process Flows (BPF)

In this chapter, we'll review and discuss the concepts and uses of Business Process Flows (BPFs) in a SAP Business Planning and Consolidation (BPC) process. There are many reasons for using BPFs, and one that we'll discuss in detail is how it offers the business users more flexibility and flow to their processes. The integration among BPFs, work status, and security will also be discussed, along with a step-by-step process of setting these components up by either the business user or the functional department.

9.1 BPF Overview

One of the main objectives of this overview is to explain enough about BPFs so that you have the knowledge to decide whether to use them or not. A BPF is a web-based user interface (UI) that is used to guide users through a sequence of activities in a process. For example, during the monthly close, the activities include data collection, running eliminations, and then reporting and analysis. If a BPF is used for planning, for example, the activities include loading actual data, running planning functions, performing manual data input, and reporting.

The activities of the BPF are contained in a template that can be used repeatedly in instances. For example, a planning BPF template can be executed once each month for the plan category, therefore, requiring 12 instances of the BPF, one for each month, all for the same plan category in this case.

Users can access their activities from the Web Client and use the workspaces with hyperlinks to jump into other workspaces or into Excel. In other words, the BPF UI is a cockpit from which they can launch web reports or run Data Manager packages.

9.1.1 The Basic Idea

As the users complete or submit their activities for review, the status of each activity is recorded and is thereby available for other process participants and managers to see. In addition, as activities are completed, emails can be automatically generated to notify users assigned to the next sequential activity that they need to perform their activity.

9.1.2 Pros and Cons of BPFs

BPFs are used mostly by larger companies with complex processes that involve numerous users and therefore need a tool to help with coordination and tracking status. The decision of whether or not to use BPFs is an important one, so you need to know the pros as well as the cons.

Following are the pros for BPFs:

▶ Coordination

▶ Status and tracking

▶ Guided navigation

▶ Email notifications

▶ Steps reviewable by higher authorities

▶ System-generated monitor

▶ Delivered detailed reports

▶ Work status integration

▶ Real-time simulations available in design mode

▶ Used to access consolidation central tasks

Following are the cons for BPFs:

▶ BPFs must be designed, configured, and maintained just like other tools.

▶ The help desk must be trained to support BPFs.

▸ Users have to be trained.

▸ Users can't be forced to use the BPF UI.

Most of these pros and cons are fairly straightforward and don't require any additional explanation. However, we should discuss the pro of having access to consolidation central tasks, as well as the con of not being able to force users to use the BPF UI.

Because the BPF can be used as an access point for consolidation central, they can therefore be used to provide a holistic tool to manage the month-end close. Remember in Chapter 7 when we discussed how the Consolidation Monitor doesn't include all closing tasks such as balance carry forward and reclassification? BPFs resolve that issue because they can be used as an umbrella over the entire set of month-end tasks. This is one of the main reasons that you'll see a lot more companies use BPFs in BPC V10.0.

As mentioned before, a BPF is a cockpit used to get to the ultimate UI, but users can simply go to Excel or the Web Client directly as well. If users get in the habit of bypassing BPFs, they will certainly be less inclined to set activity statuses, which is one of the main reasons to use BPFs.

When you consider using BPFs, you need to take into account how it integrates with work status. In addition, whenever you work with BPFs, you must also make sure your security settings permit the users to do what you lay out for them in the BPF activities. Therefore, in this next section, we'll discuss one of the pros of BPFs: the integration with work status as well as why security must be part of the conversation.

9.1.3 Integration with Work Status and Security

Of course, the reason why users can bypass the BPF is that they have the security to perform their activities and the work status to change the data. Users' activities in the BPF guide them to tasks that need to be performed and data that needs to be viewed or changed. Therefore, the users need to have the relevant task profile to carry out their assigned activities. They also need access to the relevant data via data access profiles (discussed in Chapter 8).

In addition, by including work status in the BPF, users will be able to flexibly control data access at appropriate points in the process.

Figure 9.1 shows a conceptual example that includes the Entity dimension, BPF, work status, and security components, which use the owner, reviewer, and implied manager in the following capacities:

▶ **Owner:** This is a property in the Entity type dimension that contains users or teams.

    ▶ BPFs use this property to determine performers who can complete or submit activities.

    ▶ Work status uses this property to determine who can set the work state and enter transaction data for that member (such as Store1).

▶ **Reviewer:** This is a property in the entity Type dimension that contains users or teams.

    ▶ BPFs use this property to determine who can approve or reject submitted activities.

▶ **Implied manager:** The implied manager is determined by the system (implied) as the owner of the parent. In Figure 9.1, Pete is the implied manager for Store1 because he is the owner of US, which is Store1's parent.

    ▶ The implied manager is used by work status to control who can change transaction data.

    ▶ The implied manager is also used by work status to control who can change the work state.

In the example for Store1, Joe is the owner, Nicole is the reviewer, and Pete is the implied manager.

Moving to the security components, Joe is assigned a task profile that allows him to run an input template and also to execute a Data Manager copy and import package. He also has been assigned to a data access profile that provides him read/write access to budget data in finance along with read access to actual data.

The USER ACTIONS are the sequence of activities in this example. When Joe submits Step 4 of the BPF, Nicole is notified via email, and she approves it. Because Pete is the manager of Store1, he can set the work state to "Reviewed" and then "Approved." If the work state is reviewed no one can run a Data Manager package for that data region because it's locked.

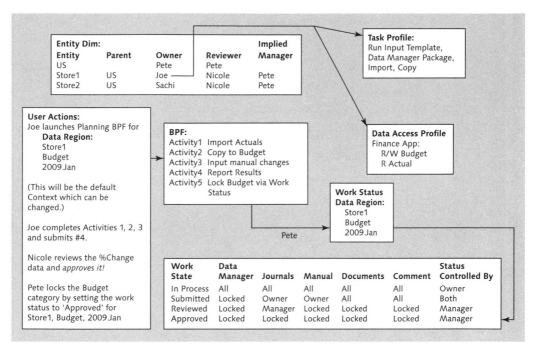

Figure 9.1 Security, Work Status, and BPF Integration

Now that you understand the basic concepts, the pros and cons, and the integration with work status and security, let's take a look at a typical planning BPF.

9.1.4   A Typical Planning BPF

In this section, let's discuss how a BPF can be used in a typical expense planning scenario. In this example, the BPF is being executed for the plan category for the year 2014.

In Figure 9.2, you can see the IMPORT ACTUALS, MANUAL PLANNING, and AUTOMATIC PLANNING activities for the EXPENSE PLANNING BPF for 2014 and the PLAN category.

In this initial activity screen, the options in the toolbar are defined as follows:

▶ SHOW: Filter activities using the following criteria:

  ▶ ALL: Display all activities.

  ▶ ACTION REQUIRED: Display activities with action required.

  ▶ NOT COMPLETED: Display activities that aren't completed.

- Open: Open an activity.
- Actions: Perform one of the four possible actions listed as follows:
    - Complete: Set the status to complete for an activity that doesn't require a reviewer.
    - Submit: Set the status to submitted for an activity that does require a reviewer.
    - Approve: Approve an activity that has been submitted.
    - Reject: Reject an activity that has been submitted.
- Reopen: Reopen a previously completed or approved activity.
- Refresh: Refresh the Status of the activities.

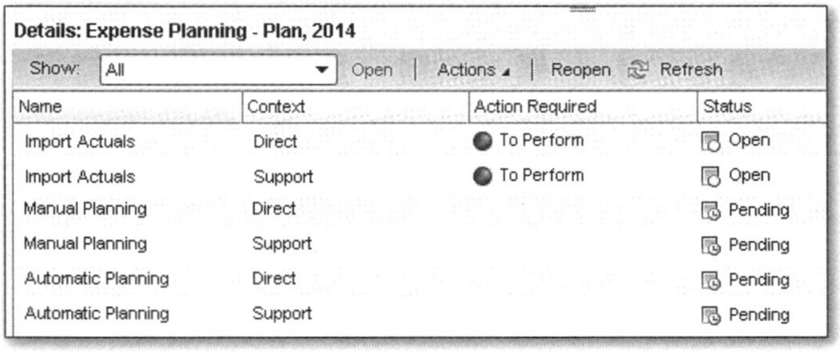
Details: Expense Planning - Plan, 2014

Show: All | Open | Actions | Reopen | Refresh

Name	Context	Action Required	Status
Import Actuals	Direct	To Perform	Open
Import Actuals	Support	To Perform	Open
Manual Planning	Direct		Pending
Manual Planning	Support		Pending
Automatic Planning	Direct		Pending
Automatic Planning	Support		Pending

Figure 9.2 Activities in a Planning BPF

Activities in a BPF can only be performed sequentially. Import Actuals for the Direct member (cost center group) must be completed before Manual Planning for the Direct member can begin and so forth. That is why only the Import Actuals activity has an Action Required of To Perform and a status of Open while the remaining activities are Pending.

Note: Cost Center Groups Using BPF

This BPF has been constructed so that each activity is tracked for both the Direct and Support Context (Direct and Support are cost center groups).

When the planner chooses the Import Actuals for Direct, the planner is taken to a new tab (workspace) called Import Actuals with a context of Plan 2014, and the Direct cost center member. The system automatically derives the cost center member context from the BPF activity (Direct). The Plan category and 2014 time member are derived from the user's workspace context.

Under OVERVIEW, the planner has two hyperlink groups, one to UPLOAD and one to IMPORT & VALIDATE DATA. If the planner selects UPLOAD, the hyperlinks assigned to UPLOAD appear (in this case, UPLOAD FLAT FILE) as shown in Figure 9.3.

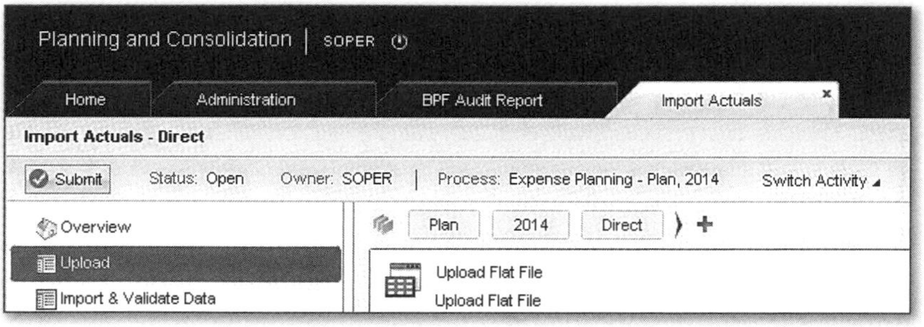

Figure 9.3 Import Actuals Tab with Upload Selected

Similarly, if the planner chooses IMPORT & VALIDATE DATA, he can IMPORT data and then RUN REPORTS.

At this point, the planner chooses UPLOAD FLAT FILE and, after a few seconds, is taken to Excel with the DATA MANAGER – UPLOAD splash screen (see Figure 9.4).

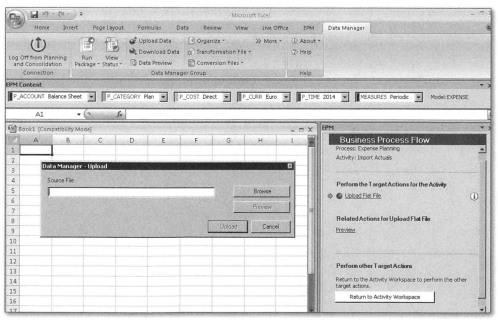

Figure 9.4 The Data Manager – Upload Dialog Box

On the right side, you can see the BUSINESS PROCESS FLOW action pane, which displays the current UPLOAD FLAT FILE activity, as well as the RELATED ACTIONS FOR UPLOAD FLAT FILE: PREVIEW and a button to RETURN TO ACTIVITY WORKSPACE.

At this point, the planner can BROWSE for the file and upload it.

Because we have explained the data loading process in Chapter 5, we'll move on to the import step in the planning process. After uploading the files and previewing, the planner can select RETURN TO ACTIVITY WORKSPACE. After selecting the IMPORT AND VALIDATE DATA hyperlink and then the IMPORT link, the planner is taken to Excel again.

In this case, the user has the import Data Manager package opened for him, and in the BUSINESS PROCESS FLOW pane on the right, the user has the IMPORT and VALIDATE DATA links as well as the RELATED ACTIONS FOR IMPORT: CHECK STATUS.

The planner (owner) then proceeds to import the flat file, check the status, and run reports to make sure the data was imported properly. The planner then returns to the Web Client and selects the SUBMIT button.

In the activities, the ACTION REQUIRED is now set TO REVIEW for the IMPORT ACTUALS and DIRECT cost center group, and the STATUS is set to SUBMITTED.

The reviewer for the direct member then receives an email as shown in Figure 9.5. The screen shot in Figure 9.5 is taken from the SAP Inbox as opposed to Outlook. (The SAP NetWeaver BW server we're using isn't connected to an Outlook server.) Also, the reviewer normally is a different user than the performer.

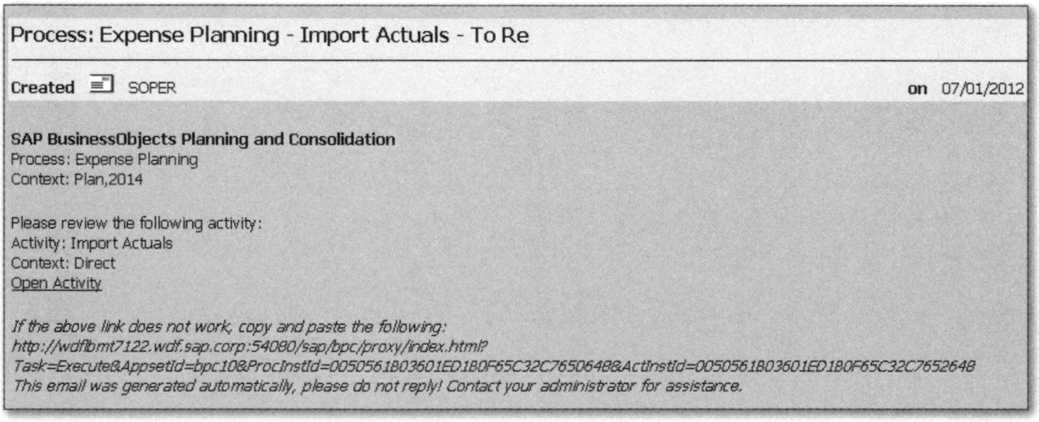
Process: Expense Planning - Import Actuals - To Re

Created SOPER **on** 07/01/2012

SAP BusinessObjects Planning and Consolidation
Process: Expense Planning
Context: Plan,2014

Please review the following activity:
Activity: Import Actuals
Context: Direct
Open Activity

If the above link does not work, copy and paste the following:
http://wdflbmt7122.wdf.sap.corp:54080/sap/bpc/proxy/index.html?
Task=Execute&AppsetId=bpc10&ProcInstId=0050561B03601ED1B0F65C32C7650648&ActInstId=0050561B03601ED1B0F65C32C7652648
This email was generated automatically, please do not reply! Contact your administrator for assistance.

Figure 9.5 A Sample Reviewer's Email

The reviewer then chooses OPEN ACTIVITY and is taken to the BPC Web Client on the IMPORT ACTUALS tab.

The reviewer can choose VALIDATE DATA, which takes the reviewer to the linked report as shown in Figure 9.6. In addition, the RELATED ACTIONS FOR VALIDATE DATA has a link to DRILL THROUGH TO ECC.

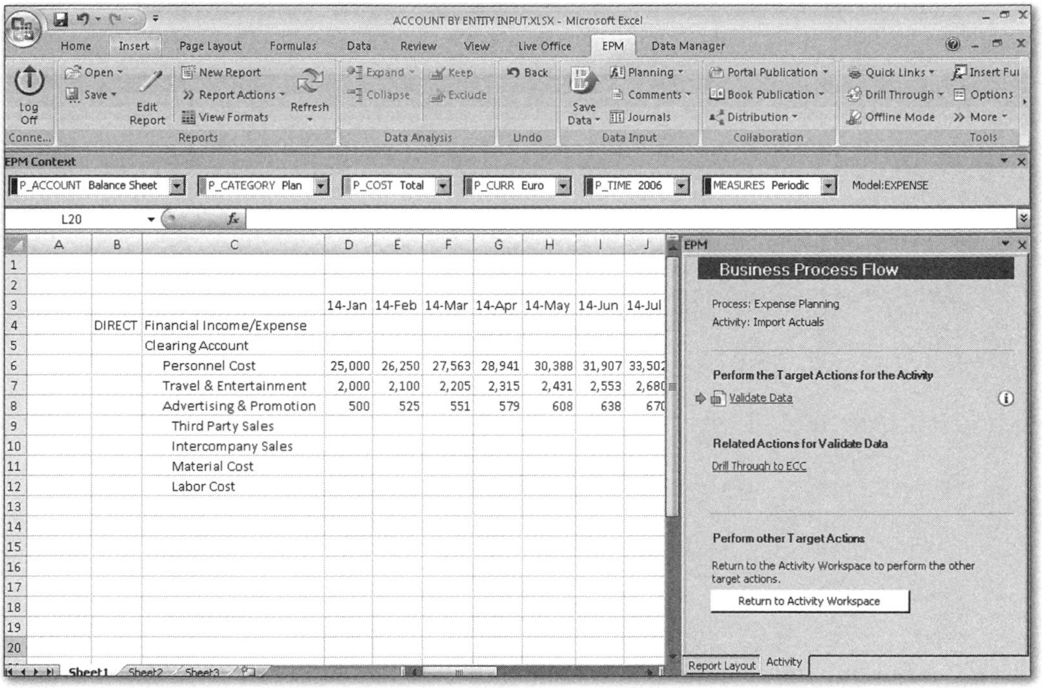

Figure 9.6 The Reviewer's Report with an Option to Drill Through to ECC

After the reviewer validates the data, he returns to the Web Client and can then either APPROVE or REJECT the activity.

If the reviewer chooses APPROVE, the activity status will be changed to COMPLETED, and the planner (owner) receives an email informing the planner that the activity has been approved.

When the planner chooses OPEN ACTIVITY, he is taken to the activities and can see the COMPLETED STATUS.

Note: BPF Process

The IMPORT ACTUALS activity has to be completed for both DIRECT and SUPPORT before the planners can proceed to MANUAL PLANNING. This is a design decision that is based on the business requirement that everyone must complete the IMPORT ACTUALS activity before anyone can proceed.

If by chance IMPORT ACTUALS for SUPPORT fails, but the planner overlooks the error, then the reviewer can reject the activity. The IMPORT ACTUALS activity will then have a status of REJECTED.

Assuming the planner takes the corrective action and submits the activity, and the reviewer approves it, then the MANUAL PLANNING activity can be performed (see Figure 9.7).

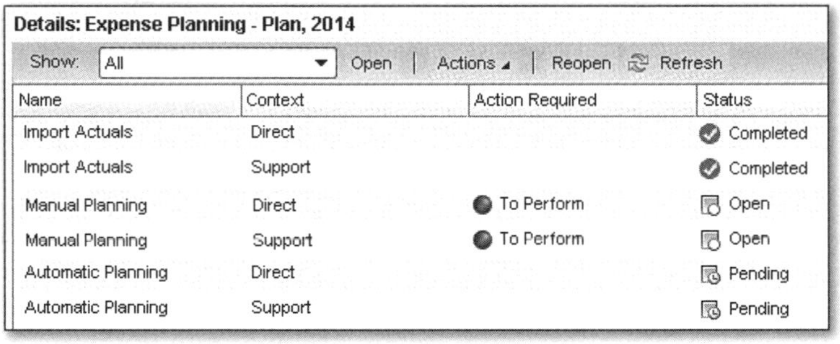
Details: Expense Planning - Plan, 2014

Show: All | Open | Actions | Reopen | Refresh

Name	Context	Action Required	Status
Import Actuals	Direct		Completed
Import Actuals	Support		Completed
Manual Planning	Direct	To Perform	Open
Manual Planning	Support	To Perform	Open
Automatic Planning	Direct		Pending
Automatic Planning	Support		Pending

Figure 9.7 Activities List with Import Actuals Completed

When the planner chooses the MANUAL PLANNING link for DIRECT, a tab called MANUAL PLANNING opens with DIRECT in the context. When the planner chooses the ENTER COST DRIVERS link, there are three input forms as shown in Figure 9.8:

- HEADCOUNTS
- PAY RATES
- BENEFIT RATES

After modifying or validating the data for the relevant planning time frame, the RUN COMPARISONS link can then be used to perform analysis, which may include the prior year's data, for example (see Figure 9.8).

Figure 9.8 The Enter Cost Drivers and Run Comparisons Hyperlinks

After the planner is satisfied with the comparisons, he can choose Lock Manual Input. This hyperlink group has two hyperlinks: one to set the work state and another to run a work status report.

If Set Work State is chosen, the planner can set a new work state. If the planner chooses Work Status Sys Report, the WS Report Widget workspace opens, and the report can be viewed as shown in Figure 9.9.

Note: Widgets

Widgets in BPC are preconfigured workspaces.

The work status report in Figure 9.9 displays the following data:

▶ STATE
The current work state.

▶ USER
Who set the current work state.

▶ DATE AND TIME
When the current work state was set.

▶ P_CATEGORY
The category dimension member.

The remaining dimensions and their values are also displayed.

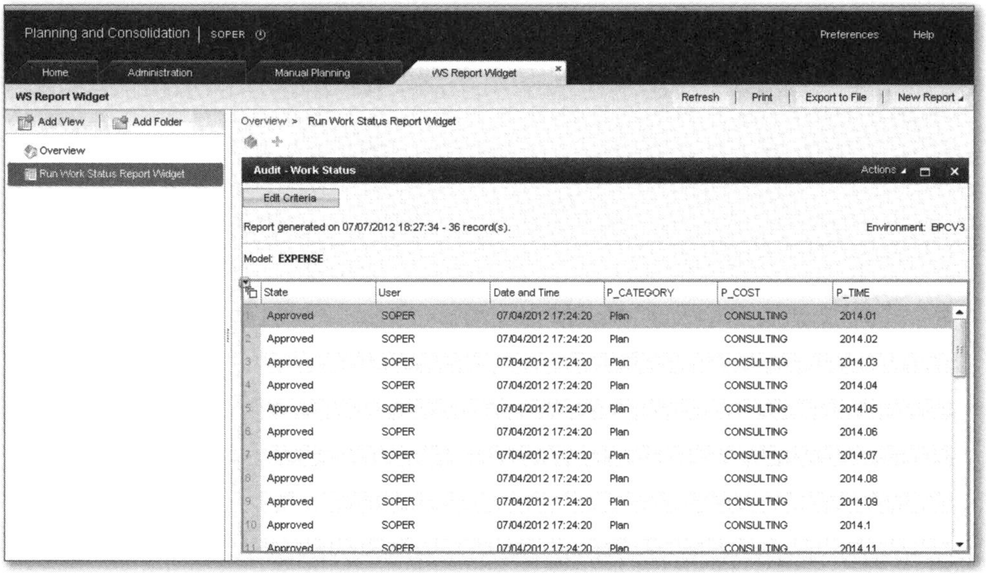

Figure 9.9 WS Report Widget Tab

When using widgets, additional hyperlink groups can be added by choosing ADD VIEW (on the upper left). In addition, folders can also be added via the ADD FOLDER option to organize the hyperlinks.

Now, let's get back to the planning BPF. After the work statuses are viewed and the activity is COMPLETE for the DIRECT member, the planner's activities reflect the COMPLETED STATUS for MANUAL PLANNING – DIRECT and OPEN for AUTOMATIC PLANNING – DIRECT (see Figure 9.10).

> **Note: Prerequisite for Open Status**
>
> In BPF configuration, the AUTOMATIC PLANNING activity is set to allow it to be performed but only for those members that have a completed status for the preceding activity(DIRECT, in this example).

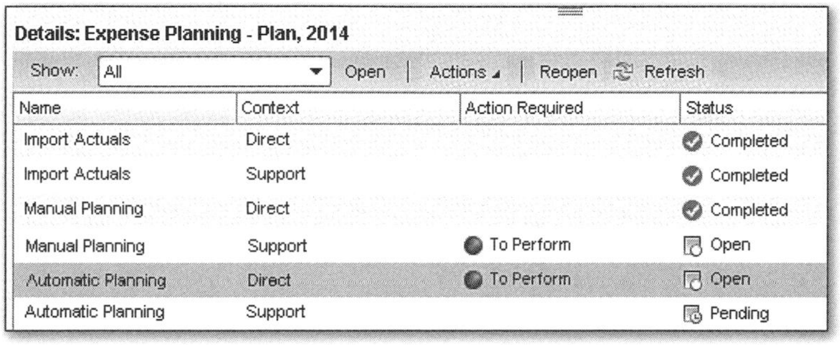

Details: Expense Planning - Plan, 2014

Name	Context	Action Required	Status
Show: All ▼	Open	Actions ◢	Reopen ⟳ Refresh
Import Actuals	Direct		✅ Completed
Import Actuals	Support		✅ Completed
Manual Planning	Direct		✅ Completed
Manual Planning	Support	● To Perform	▥ Open
Automatic Planning	Direct	● To Perform	▥ Open
Automatic Planning	Support		▥ Pending

Figure 9.10 Open Status for Automatic Planning

Now let's discuss the links in the AUTOMATIC PLANNING activity. In the COPY hyperlink group, the COPY ACTUAL TO PLAN Data Manager package and the RUN COMPARISON REPORT hyperlinks. The REVALUE and CALCULATE SALARIES hyperlinks contain similar workspaces as COPY. When the LOCK DATA MANAGER hyperlink group is opened, the SET WORK STATUS link appears for the user. The work status can then be set to a work state called LOCK DATA MANAGER, for example, which is configured to prevent any more data changes via Data Manager packages. After all activities are COMPLETED, the EXPENSE PLANNING BPF appears as shown in Figure 9.11.

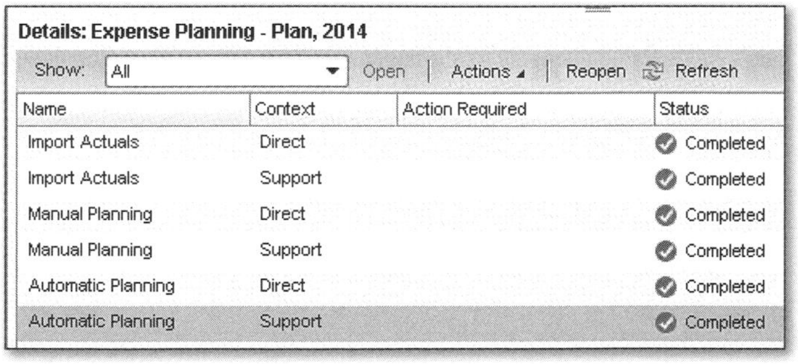

Details: Expense Planning - Plan, 2014

Name	Context	Action Required	Status
Show: All ▼	Open	Actions ◢	Reopen ⟳ Refresh
Import Actuals	Direct		✅ Completed
Import Actuals	Support		✅ Completed
Manual Planning	Direct		✅ Completed
Manual Planning	Support		✅ Completed
Automatic Planning	Direct		✅ Completed
Automatic Planning	Support		✅ Completed

Figure 9.11 Expense Planning BPF with all Activities Completed

Activities can be reopened if the planner needs to repeat them. For example, perhaps the assumed labor inflation rate changes. If an activity is reopened, the STATUS is changed to REOPEN and that status is available for others to see. Activities must be reopened in sequence. For example, AUTOMATIC PLANNING must be reopened before MANUAL PLANNING and so forth.

The planner then needs to perform the activity and then either submit it or complete it as explained before.

Before we move on to the consolidation BPF, let's review a summary of all the components for the expense planning BPF. In Table 9.1, you can see the activities, hyperlink groups, hyperlinks, and related actions for the planning BPF.

Activity	Hyperlink Group	Hyperlink	Related Action
IMPORT ACTUALS	UPLOAD	UPLOAD FLAT FILE	DATA PREVIEW
	IMPORT AND VALIDATE DATA	IMPORT FLAT FILE	CHECK STATUS
		RUN VALIDATION REPORT	
	REVIEWER ACTION	RUN VALIDATION REPORT	DRILL THROUGH TO ECC
MANUAL PLANNING	EDIT COST DRIVERS	ENTER HEADCOUNTS	RUN ACTUAL REPORTS
		ENTER PAY RATES	
		ENTER BENEFIT RATES	
	RUN COMPARISONS	COMPARISON REPORTS:	
		– HEADCOUNTS	DRILL THROUGH TO BW

Table 9.1 Planning BPF Activities, Hyperlink Groups, Hyperlinks, and Related Actions

Activity	Hyperlink Group	Hyperlink	Related Action
		– Pay Rates	
		– Benefit Rates	
	Lock Manual Input	Run Specific Workspace	
		Run Work Status Report Widget	
Automatic Planning	Copy	Copy Actual to Plan	Check Status
		Run Comparison Report	Drill Through to BW
	Revaluate	Revalue Plan Data	Check Status
		Run Comparison Report	Drill Through to BW
	Calculations	Calculate Labor	Check Status
		Calculate Benefits	Check Status
		Run Comparison Report	Drill Through to BW
	Lock Data Manager	Run Specific Workspace	
		Run Work Status Report Widget	

Table 9.1 Planning BPF Activities, Hyperlink Groups, Hyperlinks, and Related Actions (Cont.)

The condensed BPF components in Table 9.1 should give you a very clear picture of the components in the sample planning BPF.

Now that you've seen how to use a typical planning BPF, let's do the same for a consolidation BPF.

9.1.5 A Typical Consolidation BPF

In this section, you'll learn about a typical consolidation BPF from an end user perspective. Because you just learned a lot of the concepts and navigation in the planning example, we'll stress the uniqueness of the consolidation activities. Also, we'll go through a summary listing of how the BPF is put together so you have a clear overview of its components.

In this example, the activities will be performed only for the investments (corporate holding company) member of the Company dimension. The key assumption is that the process is centralized in this case, and the activities therefore don't need to be performed at a more granular level as you saw in the planning example (in that case, the activities were performed for both the direct and support cost center group members).

For our review of the consolidation BPF, we'll look at four activities in the consolidation template:

▸ Data collection

▸ Data preparation

▸ Eliminations

▸ Reporting and analysis

Figure 9.12 shows the hyperlinks for the DATA COLLECTION activity. At this point the accountant typically starts with the BALANCE CARRY FORWARD hyperlink group and then proceeds to IMPORT TRIAL BALANCES, and so on.

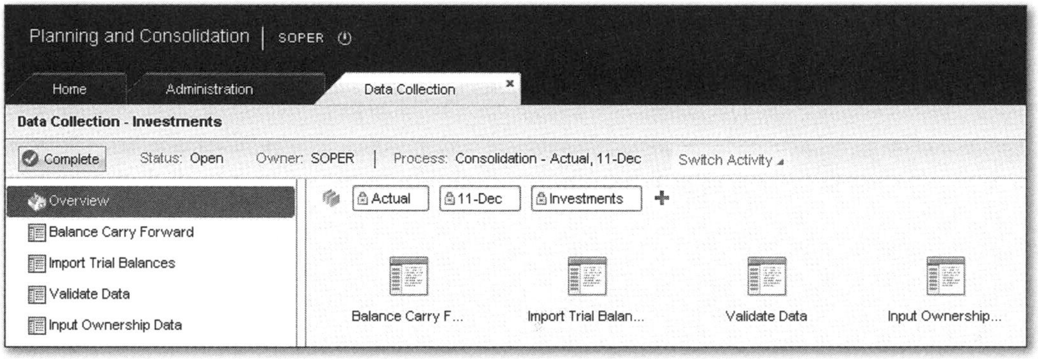

Figure 9.12 Data Collection Hyperlinks

However, to provide flexibility, the system won't force any particular sequence of the hyperlink groups (or their links) to provide for normal variation in how the process is performed. And, of course, the accountant should have a very good idea of the sequence of activities that are required in the first place.

After BALANCE CARRY FORWARD is executed, the IMPORT TRIAL BALANCES link can then be used to upload/import flat file and InfoProvider data and then RUN TRIAL BALANCE REPORT as you can see in Figure 9.13.

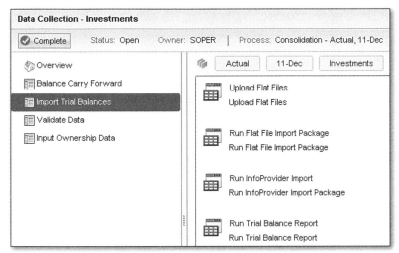

Figure 9.13 Data Collection with Import Trial Balances Opened

Most of what you've seen so far is very similar to the planning BPF, however, now you'll see a little variety when you launch the consolidation central components from a BPF.

In the VALIDATE DATA hyperlink group, there are two hyperlinks: OPEN CONTROLS SUMMARY and OPEN CONTROLS DETAIL.

When the OPEN CONTROLS SUMMARY is chosen, a new tab called OPEN CONTROLS SUMMARY is generated as shown in Figure 9.14. On the left, you can see the CONTROLS MONITOR, and on the right are four tabs that we'll detail next.

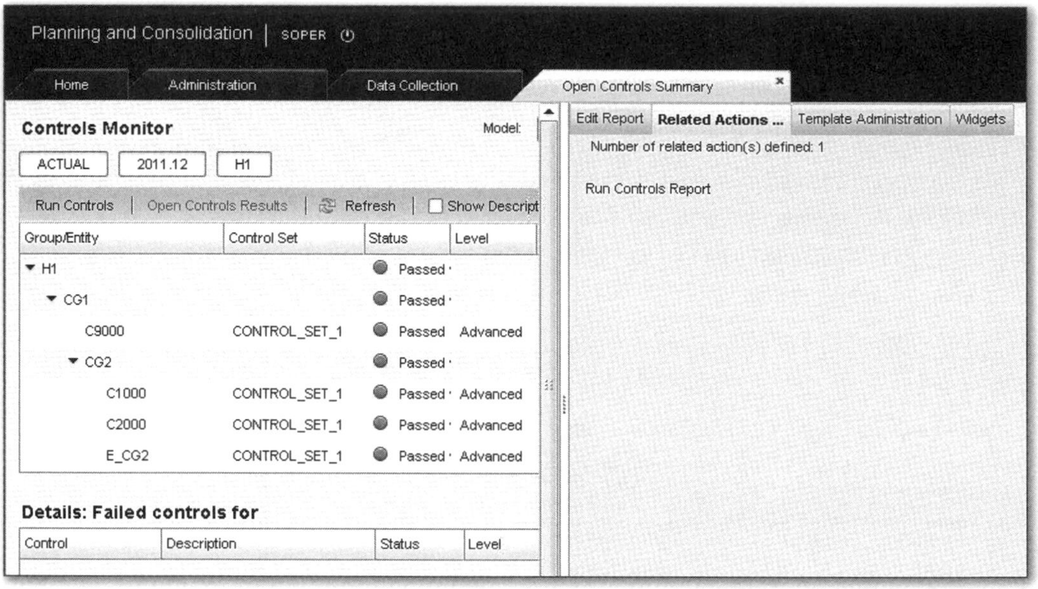

Figure 9.14 Open Controls Summary Tab

Following are the four tabs available on the right side of the screen:

▸ EDIT REPORT
Create a new web report.

▸ RELATED ACTIONS LINK
Jump to relevant reports, consolidation central components, and Data Manager functions.

▸ TEMPLATE ADMINISTRATION
Upload and view dashboards.

▸ WIDGETS
Create workspaces for web reports, input forms, and links to BPF reports, comments, controls configuration, security reports, consolidation central components, and journal reports.

As mentioned earlier, WIDGETS can be used to create workspaces that can then be added very easily as a specific workspace to RELATED ACTIONS.

Now let's get back to the consolidation process. At this point, the accountant can proceed to RUN CONTROLS as discussed in Chapter 8. If a control fails, a more detailed query is necessary.

When OPEN CONTROLS DETAIL is selected from the VALIDATE DATA hyperlink group, it will display control results based on the user's context. For example, a context of Actual, 2011.12, and C1000 will only show control results for those members. Figure 9.15 shows the OPEN CONTROLS DETAIL tab, where the accountant can easily see the results of tests that the system is performing.

For example, in row 3, the VALID_030 CONTROL is checking for cases where AP is more than 10% of the cash balance. In the EQUATION column, the 10000 represents 10% of the cash balance. The 8900 is the AP balance. In the RESULT column, you can see that the system is calculating a difference of 1100. In other words, this control passed.

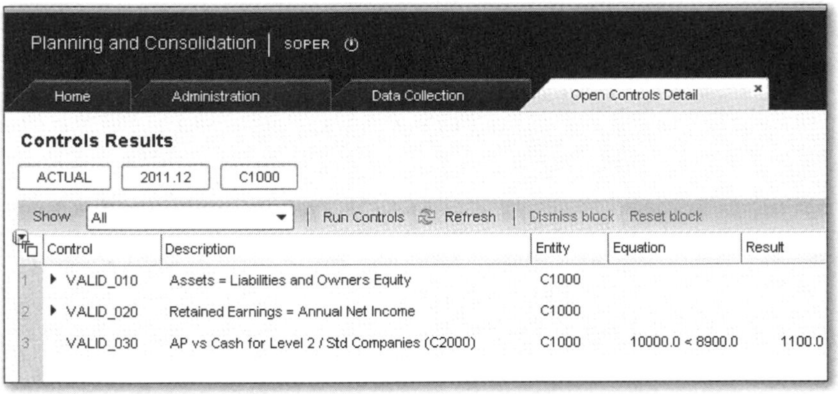

Planning and Consolidation	SOPER ⏻				
Home	Administration	Data Collection	Open Controls Detail ✕		

Controls Results

ACTUAL	2011.12	C1000

Show | All ▼ | Run Controls ⟳ Refresh | Dismiss block Reset block

	Control	Description	Entity	Equation	Result
1	▶ VALID_010	Assets = Liabilities and Owners Equity	C1000		
2	▶ VALID_020	Retained Earnings = Annual Net Income	C1000		
3	VALID_030	AP vs Cash for Level 2 / Std Companies (C2000)	C1000	10000.0 < 8900.0	1100.0

Figure 9.15 Open Controls Detail Tab

After validating the data, the accountant works his way through the remaining activities to close the books.

That should give you a feel for the unique nature of BPFs when they are used for consolidations.

Now, let's review a summary of all of the components for the DATA COLLECTION activity. In Table 9.2, you can see the four hyperlink groups with the hyperlink names for each one and their related actions.

Activity	Hyperlink Group	Hyperlink	Related Action
DATA COLLECTION	BALANCE CARRY FORWARD	RUN BCF PACKAGE	CHECK STATUS
		RUN BCF REPORT	
	IMPORT TRIAL BALANCES	UPLOAD FLAT FILES	DATA PREVIEW
		RUN FLAT FILE IMPORT PACKAGE	CHECK STATUS
		RUN INFOPROVIDER IMPORT PACKAGE	CHECK STATUS
		RUN TRIAL BALANCE REPORT	DRILL THROUGH TO ECC
	VALIDATE DATA	OPEN CONTROLS SUMMARY, RUN CONTROLS	RUN REPORT
		OPEN CONTROLS DETAIL	
	INPUT OWNERSHIP DATA	OPEN OWNERSHIP MANAGER, EDIT	SPECIFIC WORKSPACE: OWNERSHIP MANAGER EDITOR WIDGET
		RUN REPORT	

Table 9.2 Components of the Data Collection Activity

By way of example, the BALANCE CARRY FORWARD hyperlink group has two hyperlinks:

► RUN BCF PACKAGE
Carry forward prior year closing to new year opening balances.

► RUN BCF REPORT
Compare prior year closing to new year opening balances.

CHECK STATUS is the related action in this example. IMPORT TRIAL BALANCES is discussed in Chapter 5, VALIDATE DATA is covered in Chapter 8, and INPUT OWNERSHIP DATA is included in Chapter 7, so we won't go into any more detail on these right now.

Now let's use the same technique to review the remaining components of the consolidation BPF.

In Table 9.3, you can see the four hyperlink groups in the DATA PREPARATION activity. For an example, the RECLASSIFICATIONS hyperlink group includes three hyperlinks that we discussed in Chapter 7:

▶ WORK IN PROCESS TO FINISHED GOODS INVENTORY

▶ ANNUAL NET INCOME TO CURRENT YEAR RETAINED EARNINGS

▶ RUN RECLASS REPORT

In the MANUAL JOURNAL ENTRIES hyperlink group, two journal reports are included. The journal reports by account and by user are only available via widgets in a workspace. CURRENCY TRANSLATION and INTERCOMPANY MATCHING are discussed in Chapter 7.

Activity	Hyperlink Group	Hyperlink	Related Action
DATA PREPARATION	RECLASSIFICATIONS	WORK IN PROCESS TO FINISHED GOODS INVENTORY	CHECK STATUS
		ANNUAL NET INCOME TO CURRENT YEAR RETAINED EARNINGS	CHECK STATUS
		RUN RECLASS REPORT	
	MANUAL JOURNAL ENTRIES	OPEN JOURNAL LIST	SPECIFIC WORKSPACE:
		CREATE A NEW JOURNAL	JOURNAL REPORT BY ACCOUNT WIDGET

Table 9.3 Components of the Data Preparation Activity

Activity	Hyperlink Group	Hyperlink	Related Action
		RUN ADJUSTING ENTRY REPORT	JOURNAL REPORT BY USER WIDGET
	CURRENCY TRANSLATION	OPEN CONSOLIDATION MONITOR, TRANSLATE CURRENCY	SPECIFIC WORKSPACE: WEB REPORT ON EXCHANGE RATES WIDGET
		RUN CURRENCY TRANSLATION REPORT	
	INTERCOMPANY MATCHING	RUN IC DATA PACKAGE	CHECK STATUS
		RUN IC MATCHING REPORT	
		RUN IC BOOKING PACKAGE	CHECK STATUS
		RUN IC BOOKING REPORT	

Table 9.3 Components of the Data Preparation Activity (Cont.)

In Table 9.4, you can see the ELIMINATION activity with three hyperlink groups:

▶ US ELIMINATIONS is used to execute the simpler business rule for intercompany AR/AP, for example, that is explained in Chapter 7.

▶ GROUP ELIMINATIONS is used to execute the more complex eliminations and adjustments business rules for ownership eliminations, for example. A convenient widget is included in the related actions to open the Ownership Manager in edit mode.

▶ SET WORK STATUS is used to lock the data region from the Consolidation Monitor. A widget is also included to open the work status report.

Activity	Hyperlink Group	Hyperlink	Related Action
ELIMINATIONS	US ELIMINATIONS	RUN US ELIMINATION PACKAGE	CHECK STATUS
		RUN US ELIMINATION REPORT	
	GROUP ELIMINATIONS	OPEN CONSOLIDATION MONITOR: CONSOLIDATE	SPECIFIC WORKSPACE: OWNERSHIP MANAGER EDITOR WIDGET
		RUN CONSOLIDATION REPORT	
	SET WORK STATUS	OPEN CONSOLIDATION MONITOR: WORK STATUS	SPECIFIC WORKSPACE: WORK STATUS SYSTEM REPORT WIDGET

Table 9.4 Components of the Elimination Activity

In Table 9.5, the REPORTING & PUBLISHING activity is used to access reports and also to publish books to the content library. The DRILL THROUGH TO BW QUERY is used to look up detailed data in another BW InfoCube, for example.

Activity	Hyperlink Group	Hyperlink	Related Action
REPORTING & PUBLISHING	P&L AND BS REPORTS	TREND REPORT	ADD COMMENTS
		ACCOUNT BY ENTITY REPORT	DRILL THROUGH TO BW QUERY
		INTERCOMPANY ACTIVITY REPORT	
		PUBLISH BOOKS	

Table 9.5 Components of the Reporting & Publishing Activity

That wraps up the review of the features of BPFs in both a planning and consolidation business scenario.

9.2   Setting up BPFs

Now let's see how to design and configure a BPF. In these next few sections, we'll discuss design best practices, the components of BPFs, process settings, activities, workspaces, and instances.

9.2.1   BPF Design Best Practices

After you've collected the business requirements, here are some rules of thumb as you spec out your BPF:

▸ Document the end result in a design document that includes assumptions and reasoning for the design as well as detail on the components of the BPF.

▸ Consider the integration with security and work status.

▸ Organize related actions into activities to minimize the need to jump between activities.

▸ Use separate activities for actions that need to be tracked. For example, it's very important to know when data imports are complete, so that should be called out as a separate activity.

▸ Create activities flexible enough to handle normal process variations. For example, include links in an activity even if they aren't used every month so the link will be there when needed.

9.2.2   BPF Components

Before we start building a BPF in the system, let's get an overview of its components. In Figure 9.16, you can see a conceptual illustration of the BPF components. Since we'll go through all of the components in Figure 9.16 when we discuss the build screens, this section only provides some high-level comments for now.

The PROCESS TEMPLATE is assigned a MODEL, which is used to determine the DIMENSIONS that will be used to look up activity owners. The PROCESS MONITORS are users or teams of users who can view the BPF in the BPF monitor. The illustration in

Figure 9.16 only has 2 activities, however, in real life, you're more likely to see 6 to 10 activities. Again that will depend on what needs to be tracked in the process.

The HYPERLINK GROUPS are used to collect the HYPERLINKS. The HYPERLINKS contain the TARGET ACTIONS and RELATED ACTIONS. For example, a TARGET ACTION can be to UPLOAD a data file and the RELATED ACTION can be to preview it. A HYPERLINK can have several TARGET ACTIONS.

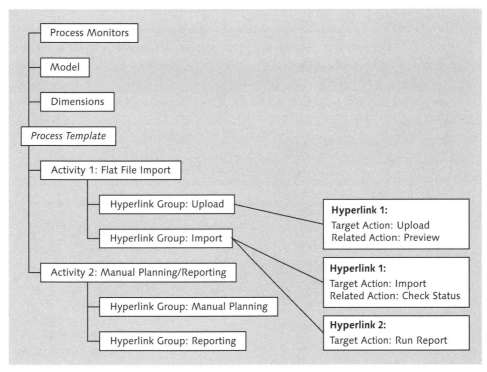

Figure 9.16 BPF Component Illustration

Now let's get into the construction of a BPF in the system. Using the design document we discussed earlier, the build phase is purely mechanical by design because that document should contain a complete set of specifications. Of course, to create such a document, you need to understand how a BPF is constructed, which we'll cover next.

When a PROCESS TEMPLATE is created, the process settings must be provided first, and then the activities are created.

9.2.3 BPF Process Settings

Process settings control the overall behavior of the process template. When you create a process template, these are the fields in the process settings that you need to configure:

▶ MODEL

Select a model that is the focal point of the process. The selected model determines which dimensions you'll use in the rest of the template.

▶ DIMENSIONS

Select the dimensions upon which you want to track the status of the activities. This will typically be Category, Time, and Entity. You might recall that the sample planning BPF included activities by DIRECT and SUPPORT, which are parent members of the Entity type dimension of the Expense model. Therefore, the Entity dimension isn't included in the DIMENSIONS in Figure 9.17 because it will be used at the activity level.

▶ USERS

Select the users or teams who not only monitor the BPF instances but also finalize them.

In Figure 9.17, you can see the PROCESS SETTINGS tab with its associated fields.

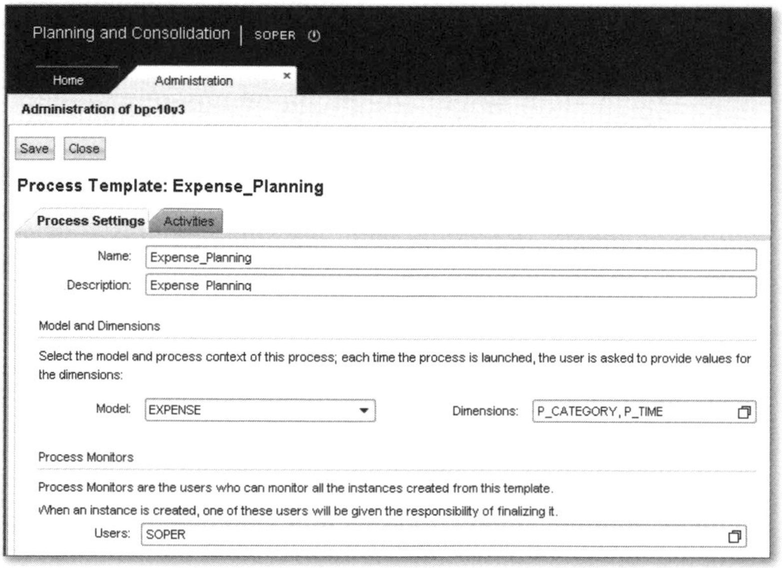

Figure 9.17 Configuring the Process Settings

The process settings can also be thought of as the header of the process template, and after it's complete, the activities can be constructed.

9.2.4 BPF Activities

The activities of the BPF represent the main steps of the planning process. The status of each activity will be recorded and that's how you'll know how you're proceeding in the planning process. Activities are also used as collectors of hyperlinks or actions to complete a task. Activities need to be somewhat generic so that users don't have to continually jump back and forth between them to do their jobs.

An activity is created by choosing the ACTIVITIES tab and selecting the NEW button. The IMPORT ACTUALS activity is shown Figure 9.18.

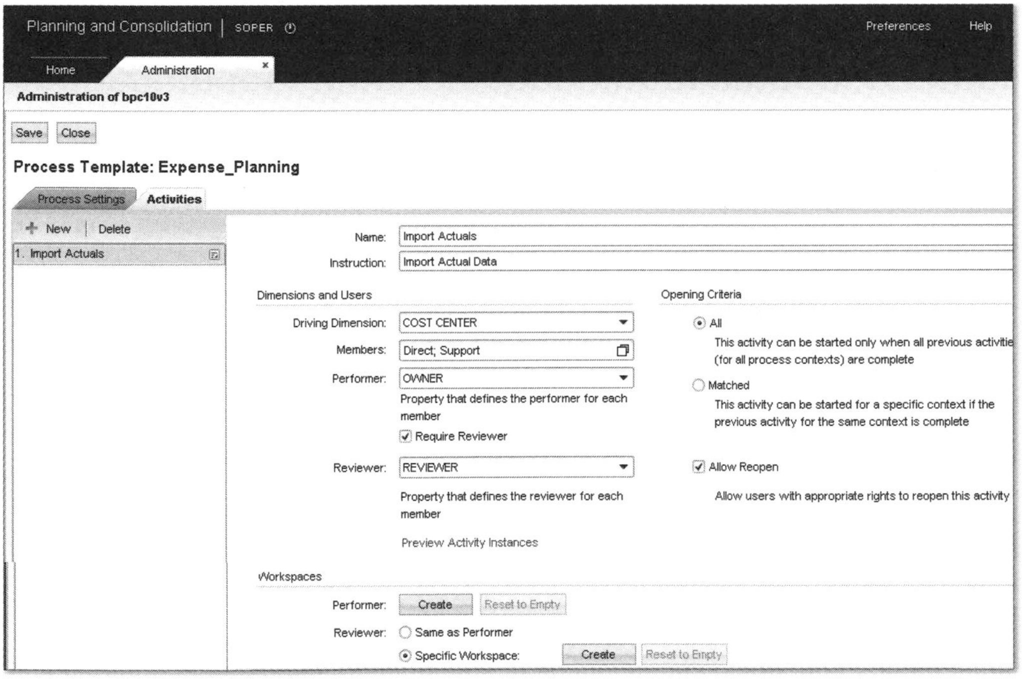

Figure 9.18 Creating a New Activity

The ACTIVITIES fields in Figure 9.18 are defined as follows:

▶ NAME
Provide a title for the activity.

- ▶ INSTRUCTION

  Provide a description of what is to be done in the activity. This is the instruction that is displayed to a user performing an activity.

- ▶ DIMENSIONS AND USERS

  - ▶ DRIVING DIMENSION: This dimension is used to determine the granularity of the activity and also to determine the performers. For example, if you want to run an activity once per cost center group, use the Entity (cost center, in this example) dimension.

  - ▶ MEMBERS: Select the members of the DRIVING DIMENSION. In the preceding example, DIRECT and SUPPORT have been selected, so that means that the IMPORT ACTUALS activity will be executed and tracked by the DIRECT cost center group and also by SUPPORT.

  - ▶ PERFORMER: Select the property that defines the performer for each member of the DRIVING DIMENSION. You can select the OWNER property or any other property for this, but OWNER is typically used.

  - ▶ REQUIRE REVIEWER: Require that a reviewer must approve or reject the activity. Turn this on for critical activities.

  - ▶ REVIEWER: Select the property that defines the reviewer for each member of the DRIVING DIMENSION. You can select the REVIEWER property or any other property, but REVIEWER is typically used.

  - ▶ PREVIEW ACTIVITY INSTANCES: Use this hyperlink to simulate the activity instance. The system will display the PERFORMER and REVIEWER DIRECT and SUPPORT MEMBERS (in this case).

- ▶ OPENING CRITERIA: Choose ALL or MATCHED activity contexts.

  - ▶ ALL: All activity regions must be complete before anyone can perform the next activity. The activity regions are DIRECT and SUPPORT in this example.

  - ▶ MATCHED: Only those completed activity regions can perform the next activity. For example, if IMPORT ACTUALS for DIRECT is complete, then MANUAL PLANNING for DIRECT can be performed. This setting is irrelevant for the first activity because it's open by default for a new instance.

  - ▶ ALLOW REOPEN: Check the box to allow authorized users to reopen an activity.

- ▶ WORKSPACES

  - ▶ PERFORMER: Use the CREATE button to build the performer workspace.

▶ REVIEWER

  – SAME AS PERFORMER: Use the same workspace as the performer.

  – SPECIFIC WORKSPACE: Use the CREATE button to build a unique workspace exclusively for the reviewer.

After creating the first activity, you can copy it by using the DUPLICATE context menu option as shown in Figure 9.19. The context menu is the actual icon in the square box to the right of the activity.

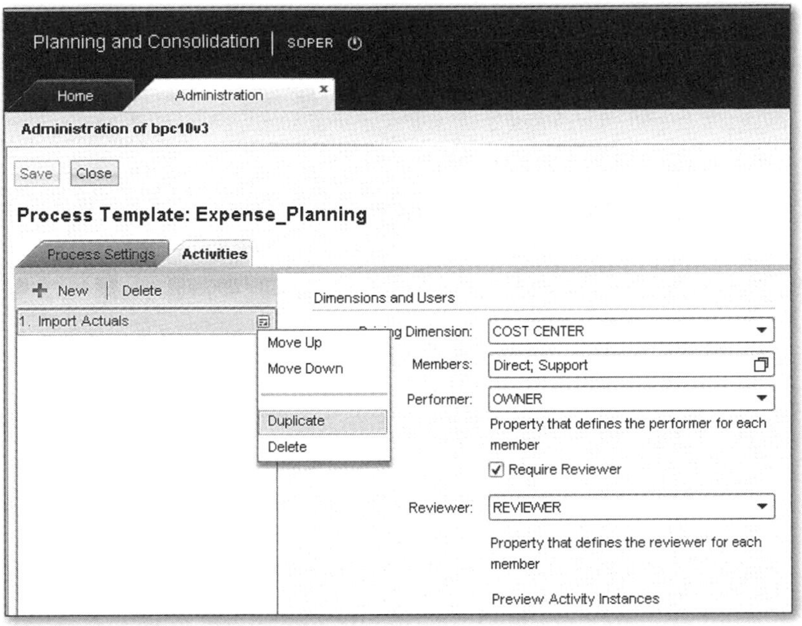

Figure 9.19 Using the Context Menu for an Activity

By selecting DUPLICATE, you'll then have the choice to either DUPLICATE ACTIVITY DEFINITION AND CONTENT or DUPLICATE ACTIVITY DEFINITION ONLY.

After duplicating and renaming the new activities, you now have three activities as shown in Figure 9.20. Also, the workspace setting SAME AS PERFORMER is selected for both MANUAL PLANNING and AUTOMATIC PLANNING because the reviewer can use the same reports to validate the performers work. The OPENING CRITERIA is set to MATCHED for AUTOMATIC PLANNING because this activity can be carried out independently for DIRECT versus SUPPORT.

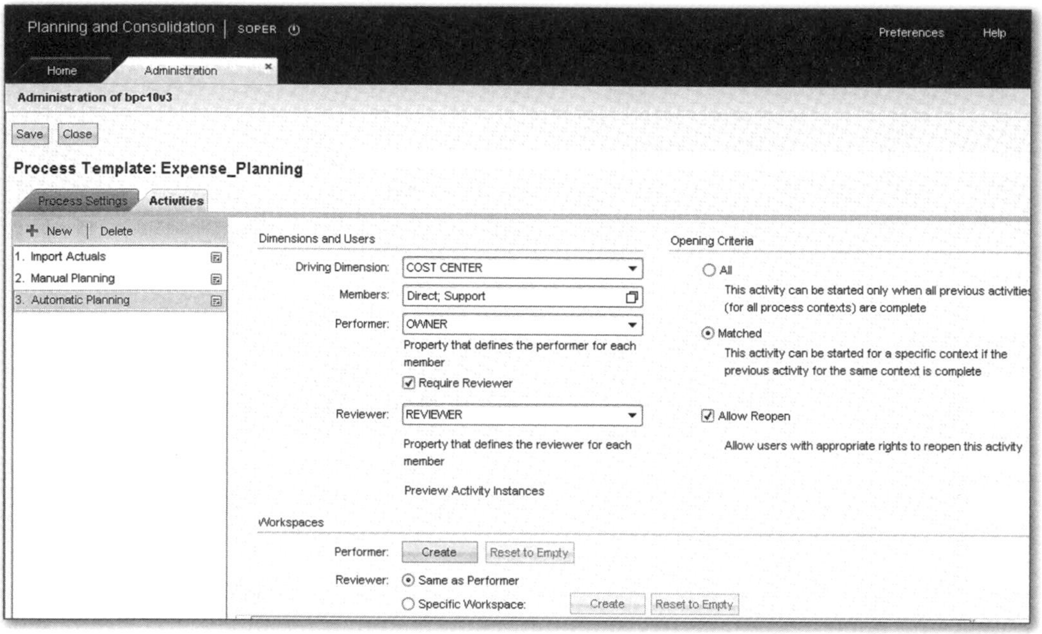

Figure 9.20 Process Template with Three Planning Activities

The three high-level activities in Figure 9.20 are part of almost every planning process. Typically, you import actual data from a source system; perform some manual input of cost drivers, for example; and then run the automatic planning functions. The sequence of the activities might vary depending on the process, and there lies the art of designing a BPF.

Now that the sample activities are in place, you can create the workspaces.

9.2.5 BPF Workspaces

Workspaces are tabs in the Web Client with a homogeneous set of hyperlinks. The workspace for the IMPORT ACTUALS activity will therefore have related hyperlinks that will be used to perform that activity.

You'll create the performer workspace for IMPORT ACTUALS by choosing the CREATE button next to PERFORMER. A new tab called IMPORT ACTUALS is created. In Figure 9.21, you can see the configured result for the UPLOAD hyperlink group.

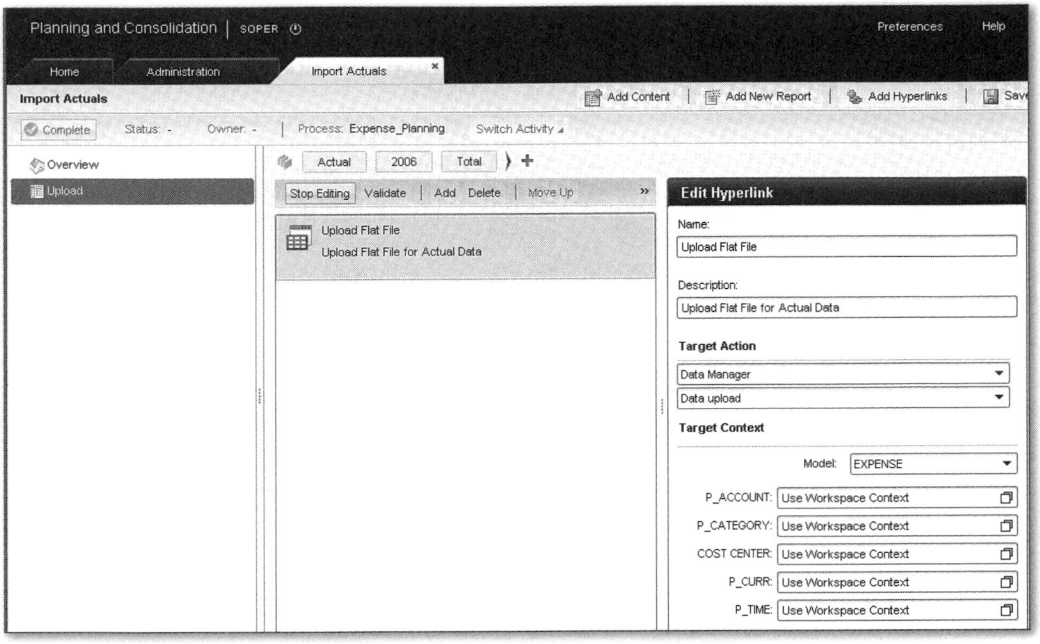

Figure 9.21 The Import Actuals Workspace

Note: BPF Toolbar

The toolbar options COMPLETE, STATUS, OWNER, PROCESS, and SWITCH ACTIVITY aren't available in design mode so they are grayed out.

In the IMPORT ACTUALS toolbar at the top right of Figure 9.21, you have the following four options:

▶ ADD CONTENT
Add an existing web report or web input form from the library.

▶ ADD NEW REPORT
Create a new web report or web input form.

▶ ADD HYPERLINK
Create a new hyperlink group.

▶ SAVE
Save the workspace.

On the upper-left side, the UPLOAD hyperlink group has several context menu options as shown in Figure 9.22. The SET AS DEFAULT option is used to select that hyperlink group as the default when this workspace is opened.

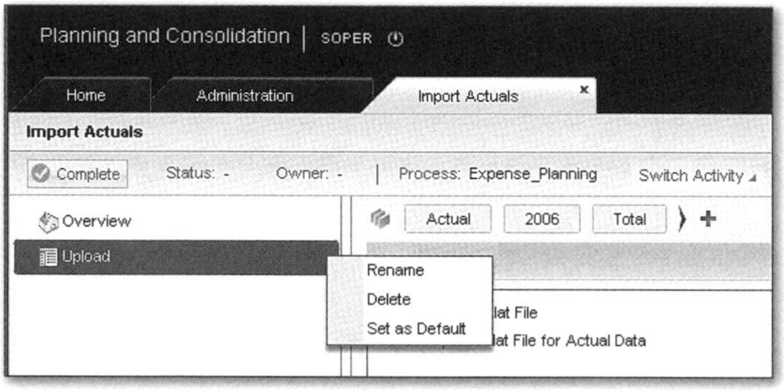

Figure 9.22 The Hyperlink Group Context Menu

Underneath PROCESS: EXPENSE_PLANNING in Figure 9.23, you'll see the model and context selection buttons. When the CUBE icon is selected, the current model for the workspace is displayed (EXPENSE, in this case). Also, CHANGE MODEL can be used to select a different model when using web reports and input forms in the workspace. In addition, there are the DISPLAY DIMENSION NAMES options.

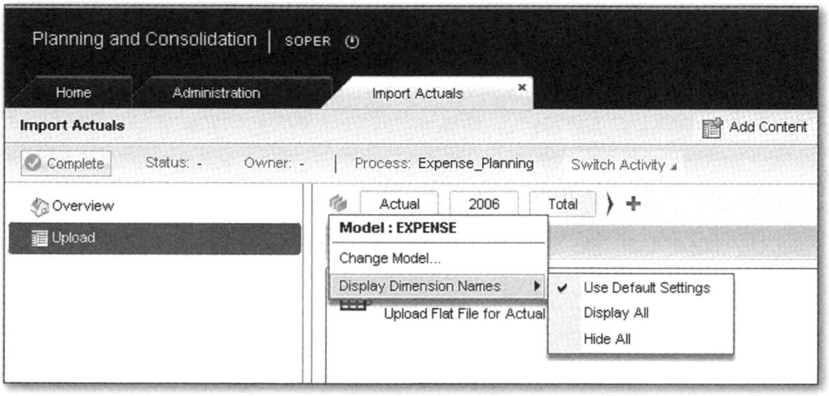

Figure 9.23 Model and Dimension Settings in a Workspace

The DISPLAY DIMENSION NAMES options are defined as follows:

▶ USE DEFAULT SETTINGS
This controls whether the dimension names appear in the context fields per the user's context menu defaults.

▶ DISPLAY ALL
This displays all dimension names in the context fields.

▶ HIDE ALL
This hides all dimension names in the context fields.

For example, if DISPLAY ALL is selected, the dimension name and current member are displayed as shown is Figure 9.24.

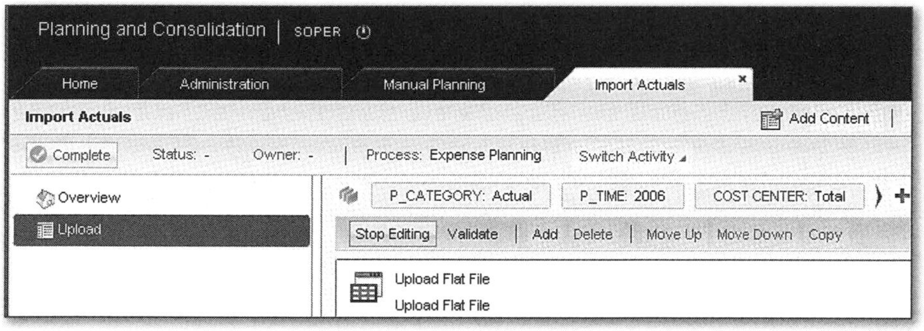

Figure 9.24 Import Actuals with Display All Dimension Names on

Note: Workspace Use in BPF

The workspace context members can be used to generate the default selections when running hyperlinks. For example, if a hyperlink for a specific report in Excel is chosen, the default selections will include the workspace context members shown in Figure 9.24 (ACTUAL, 2006, and TOTAL).

You can use the plus sign under SWITCH ACTIVITY to display selected dimensions, or you can use the ADD ALL DIMENSIONS option to display all dimensions.

The workspace toolbar options are used as follows:

▶ STOP EDITING
Perform a simulation of the hyperlink.

▶ VALIDATE
Validate the hyperlink's target actions for completeness.

▶ ADD
Add a new hyperlink into the hyperlink group.

▶ DELETE
Delete a hyperlink from the hyperlink group.

▶ MOVE UP
Move an existing hyperlink up.

▶ MOVE DOWN
Move an existing hyperlink down.

▶ COPY
Copy an existing hyperlink.

Now let's shift our attention to EDIT HYPERLINK shown on the right-hand side of Figure 9.25. The DESCRIPTION will appear as a tooltip when the user runs the hyperlink.

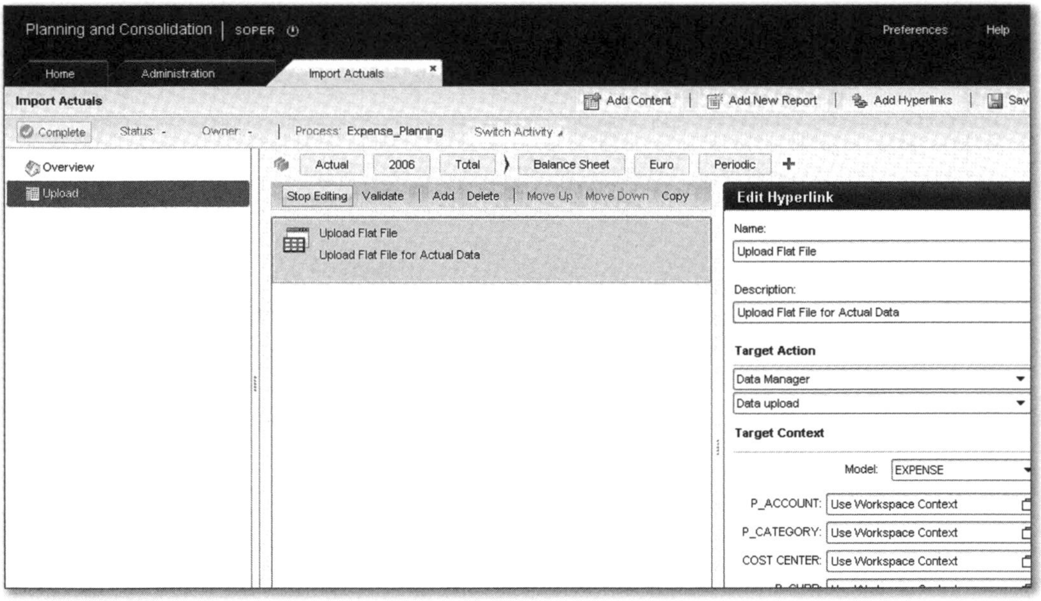

Figure 9.25 Hyperlink Settings

Under TARGET ACTION, the first dropdown is used to select the interface such as DATA MANAGER, and the second dropdown is used to select the action in that interface such as DATA UPLOAD.

As you create these hyperlinks, remember that they are basically pre-built selections for the users that allow them to perform an action at the touch of a button (or link in this case). So at this point, you're putting together a path for the user to follow by creating these hypertexts with TARGET ACTION interfaces and corresponding actions.

Following is the complete list of the TARGET ACTION interfaces and actions, along with the chapter where the actions were discussed:

▶ MICROSOFT EXCEL **(Chapter 4)**
OPEN SPECIFIC REPORT; OPEN SPECIFIC INPUT FORM; OPEN SPECIFIC TEMPLATE; OFFLINE DISTRIBUTION WIZARD; PUBLISH BOOK WIZARD; PUBLISH SPECIFIC BOOK; OPEN REPORT LIBRARY; OPEN INPUT FORM LIBRARY.

▶ DATA MANAGER **(Chapter 5)**
DATA MANAGER; DATA DOWNLOAD; DATE UPLOAD; RUN SPECIFIC PACKAGE; RUN USER PACKAGE; VIEW PACKAGE STATUS; VIEW SCHEDULE STATUS; RUN PACKAGE LINK; RUN SPECIFIC PACKAGE LINK.

▶ MICROSOFT WORD **(Chapter 4)**
OPEN SPECIFIC WORD DOCUMENT.

▶ MICROSOFT POWERPOINT **(Chapter 4)**
OPEN SPECIFIC POWERPOINT DOCUMENT.

▶ LIBRARY AND DOCUMENTS **(Chapter 2)**
ADD DOCUMENT; OPEN LIBRARY; OPEN SPECIFIC WEB INPUT FORM; OPEN SPECIFIC REPORT; OPEN SPECIFIC BOOK; OPEN SPECIFIC WORKSPACE.

▶ WORK STATUS AND COMMENTS **(Chapter 8)**
ADD COMMENTS; MANAGE COMMENTS; SET WORK STATUS.

▶ AUDIT **(Chapter 8)**
OPEN COMMENTS AUDIT REPORT; OPEN ACTIVITY AUDIT REPORT; OPEN DATA AUDIT REPORT; OPEN USER SECURITY REPORT; OPEN TEAM SECURITY REPORT; OPEN TASK SECURITY REPORT; OPEN DATA ACCESS SECURITY REPORT; OPEN AUDIT REPORT WORK STATUS.

▶ CONSOLIDATION **(Chapter 7)**
OPEN JOURNAL LIST; CREATE A NEW JOURNAL; OPEN CONSOLIDATION MONITOR; OPEN OWNERSHIP MANAGER; OPEN CONTROLS SUMMARY; OPEN CONTROLS DETAILS.

After the TARGET ACTION interface and action are selected, the TARGET CONTEXT is determined. In the TARGET CONTEXT, the MODEL is selected first.

Then, for each dimension in that model, either the WORKSPACE CONTEXT can be used as the default, or you can hard-code a default such as NET INCOME for the P_ACCOUNT dimension as shown in Figure 9.26.

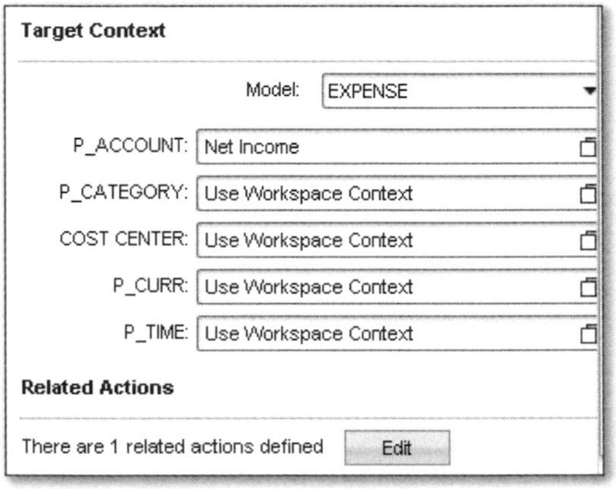

Figure 9.26 Target Context

Below the TARGET CONTEXT are the RELATED ACTIONS, which are corresponding links that appear when the hyperlink is used. To add a RELATED ACTION, you choose the EDIT button, and two dropdowns appear: one for the interface such as DATA MANAGER and also one for actions such as DATA PREVIEW (see Figure 9.27). RELATED ACTIONS are only available for the DATA MANAGER, EXCEL, and CONSOLIDATION interfaces.

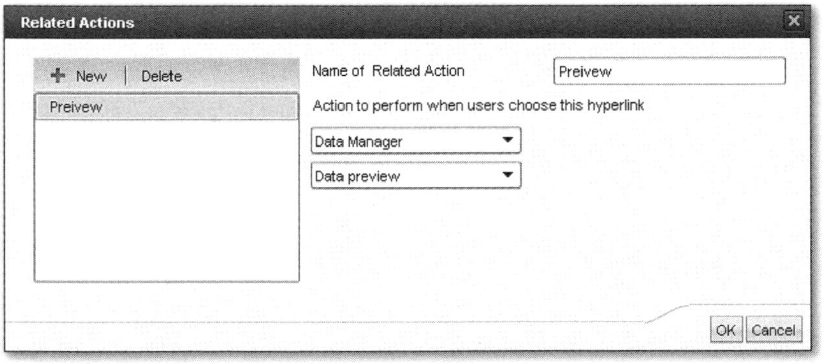

Figure 9.27 Related Actions Configuration Screen

After the workspace is complete, save and close it, and then save the process template.

After the process template is completed, its CURRENT VERSION is DRAFT as you can see in Figure 9.28. The template must be deployed before you can create an instance for it. This allows you to prevent anyone from using the template before it's complete. After a template is deployed, you must create a new version to change it; otherwise, you can only display it.

In the PROCESS TEMPLATES screen, the toolbar options are defined as follows:

▶ NEW
Create a new process template.

▶ OPEN
Open an existing process template.

▶ COPY
Copy an existing process template.

▶ DELETE
Delete an existing process template.

▶ DEPLOY
Deploy an existing process template.

▶ NEWVERSION
Create a new version of a process template.

▶ VALIDATE
Validate an existing process template for completeness. For example, you must specify a property to look up the performer.

▶ UNLOCK
Unlock a process template in draft mode to allow changes.

▶ VERSIONS
Review the version history log of a process template.

▶ REFRESH
Refresh the process template view.

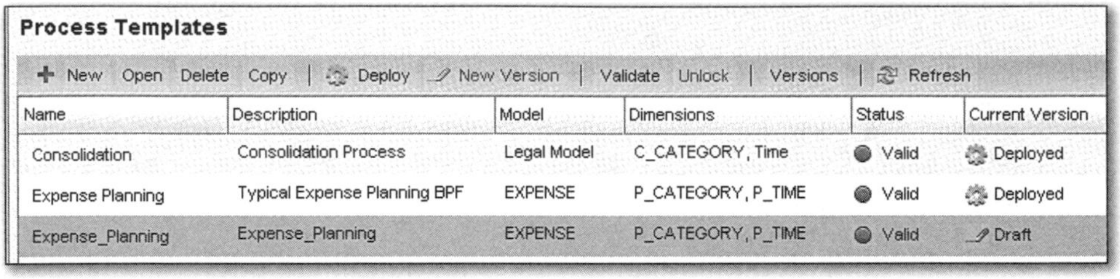

Process Templates						
✚ New Open Delete Copy | ⚙ Deploy ✎ New Version | Validate Unlock | Versions | ⟳ Refresh						
Name	Description	Model	Dimensions	Status	Current Version	
Consolidation	Consolidation Process	Legal Model	C_CATEGORY, Time	● Valid	⚙ Deployed	
Expense Planning	Typical Expense Planning BPF	EXPENSE	P_CATEGORY, P_TIME	● Valid	⚙ Deployed	
Expense_Planning	Expense_Planning	EXPENSE	P_CATEGORY, P_TIME	● Valid	✎ Draft	

Figure 9.28   Process Templates Status

9.2.6   BPF Instances

After deploying the process template, it's then made available for use by creating process instances. If the template is to be used once per month, then 12 instances need to be created, for example.

When the process instance is created, it takes a snapshot of the process template. Therefore, if the process template is changed, a new instance needs to be created.

In the PROCESS INSTANCE screen, the toolbar options are defined as follows:

▶ SHOW
Display ALL TEMPLATES instances or only those from selected process templates.

▶ NEW
Create a new instance.

▶ START
Activate a new instance.

▶ SUSPEND
Remove that instance from the users' activities list. When an instance is suspended, a RESUME option will appear.

▶ CHANGE ASSIGNMENT

   ▶ Change the owner who can finalize the instance.

   ▶ Change the performer and/or reviewers for the activities.

▶ RESET
Set a process template's activities back to the initial open and pending status.

▶ ARCHIVE
Delete a finalized or suspended instance.

▶ In Figure 9.29, you can see two RUNNING instances.

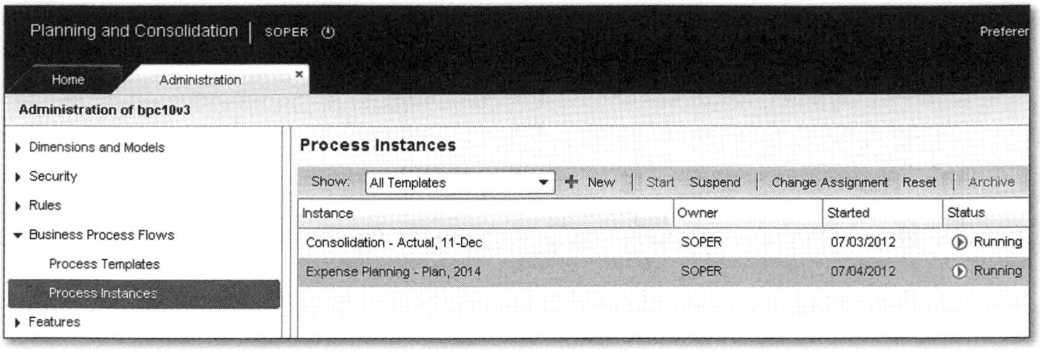

Figure 9.29 Process Instances

To create a new instance, choose the NEW button, and a wizard splash screen pops up with five steps. The activity for each step of the instance wizard is as follows:

1. SELECT PROCESS: Select a process template.

2. SELECT OWNER: Select a user who can finalize the instance.

3. SELECT CONTEXT: Select members for the dimensions chosen in the process settings (Category and Time, in this example).

4. CHECK ASSIGNMENTS: Change the performers or reviewers.

5. REVIEW AND START: Review the instance selections, and check START THE PROCESS INSTANCE to create it in RUNNING status.

With the instance in RUNNING status, the users can access their activities.

9.3   Execution of BPFs

Now let's see how to use a BPF. In these next few sections, we'll discuss how to access your activities, how to use the monitor, and how to run BPF reports.

9.3.1   Accessing Your Activities

After an instance is created and in RUNNING status, users can access their activities in the Web Client by selecting ACTIVITIES from the HOME tab. The process instances they are involved in appear, and when they select one, they can access their activities as shown in Figure 9.30.

Users will only see activities in which they are owners. For example, the owner of the DIRECT cost center group in the Entity dimension is User1, and the owner of the SUPPORT cost center group is User2. When User1 goes to his activities, he will only see activities for DIRECT, and User2 will only see activities for SUPPORT.

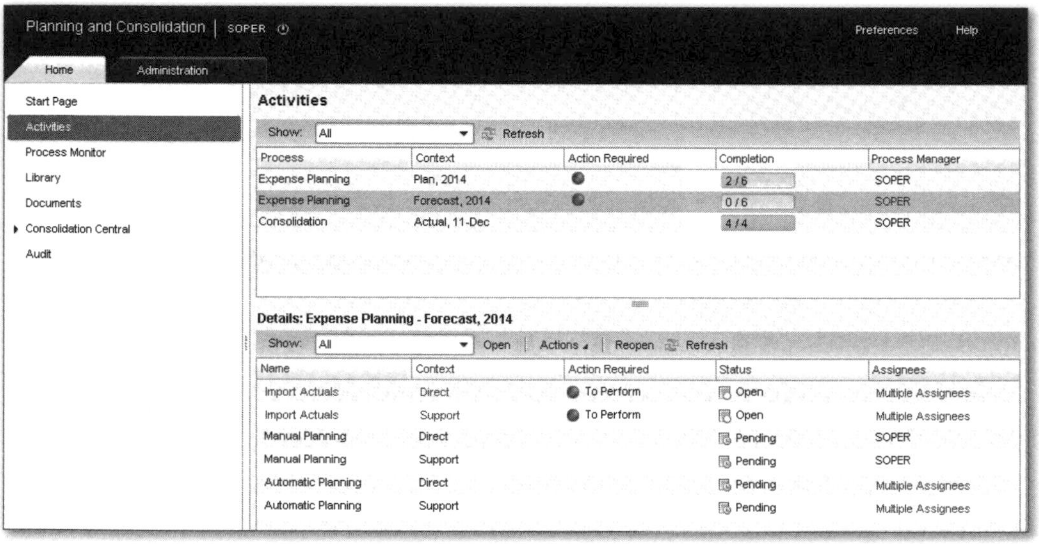

Figure 9.30 Activities from the Home Tab

In Figure 9.30, the logged-in user is the owner for both DIRECT and SUPPORT so they both appear.

Because you've already seen how to navigate in the expense planning example, let's discuss the PROCESS MONITOR, which is used to check the status of BPFs. For example, a manager can run the monitor to see how all of his divisions are progressing with the planning process. The process monitor is executed from the Web Client and delivers one of the most important benefits of the BPFs—visibility of the statuses of a process.

9.3.2 Using the Process Monitor

By choosing the PROCESS MONITOR under ACTIVITIES, users will see a listing of all of the process instances they are involved in. The toolbar options for the PROCESS MONITOR are as follows:

▶ SHOW
Display ALL instances or only those for a specific process template.

▶ STATUS
Display instances with for ALL statuses or filter by ACTIVE or FINALIZED.

▶ OPEN
Open an instance in a new tab.

▶ REFRESH
Refresh the process monitor.

▶ FINALIZE
Finalize a completed instance. Finalized instances can't be reopened or reset.

By choosing an instance and selecting OPEN, a new tab with the name of the process template is created as you can see in Figure 9.31.

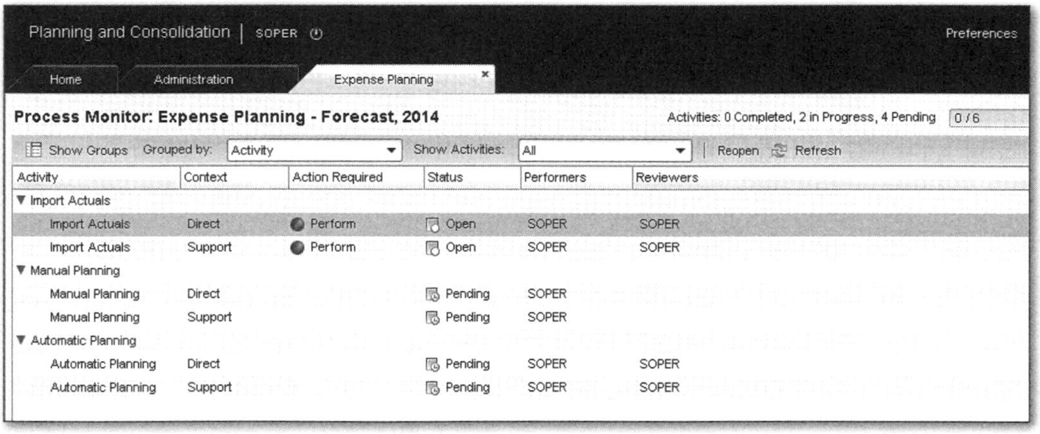

Figure 9.31 Process Monitor for the Expense Planning Template

If you choose SHOW GROUPS on the left, you can view by ACTIVITY, CONTEXT, ACTION REQUIRED, or STATUS. You can also use SHOW ACTIVITIES to filter by the following criteria:

▶ ALL

▶ ACTION REQUIRED

▶ NOT COMPLETE

In addition, you can REOPEN activities from this screen.

As you can see, the process monitor is very useful to track statuses. In addition there are also BPF audit reports in the Web Client that can be used to track runtime status information as well as configuration changes to templates, instances, and activities.

9.3.3 Using BPF Reports

You can access three BPF reports from the HOME tab in the AUDIT area:

- **Operations**
  This will display design activities that occurred on templates, instances, and activities. For example, you can find out what changes were made to a template or when an instance was activated.

- **Instance**
  This displays runtime status data on instances, including the number of complete, in process, and pending steps along with the percent of completion.

- **Activity**
  This displays runtime status data on activities by template, including their statuses, performers, and reviewers. The BPF reports require that the BPF activity audit is activated.

By way of example, let's use the OPERATIONS report because it has the most options. In the OPERATION report as seen in Figure 9.32, there are three AUDIT LEVELS to pick from:

- TEMPLATE

- INSTANCE

- ACTIVITY

When Instance and Activity are selected, an additional instance and activity selection box dynamically appears on the right.

Let's assume that you want to find out when an instance was activated for example. In Figure 9.32, the Audit Level is set to Instance, and the Expense Planning template has been highlighted. In addition, the deployed version of the template has also been highlighted along with the Forecast, 2014 instance.

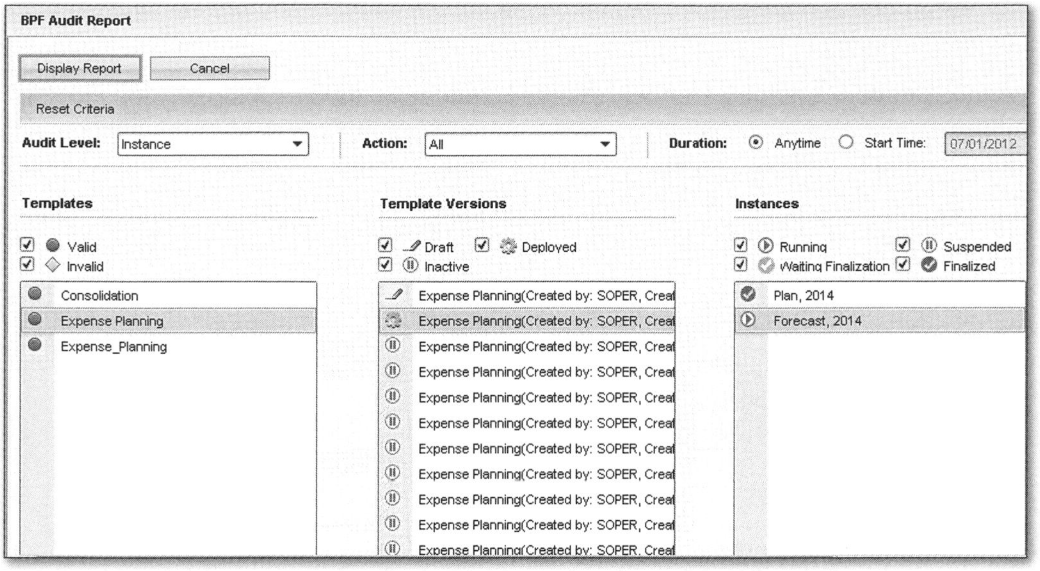

Figure 9.32 BPF Audit Report Selections

The results will show that the instance was activated along with the template, the instance selections such as the PLAN category and the time member, who did it, and when.

9.4 Summary

In this chapter, you learned all of the pros and cons of BPFs, which will help you decide whether to use them or not on your projects. We explained how to use both a planning-related and consolidation-related BPF by accessing owner activities from the Web Client and launching the workspaces and then Excel. We walked through the entire live cycle of an instance by submitting, approving, and completing its activities, and ultimately finalizing the instance. You learned how to configure a process template and then how to activate an instance for it. From a visibility perspective, you had a chance to see how the BPF monitor can be used very effectively to check the status of a process.

This chapter will analyze the option of migrating to BPC V10.0. First, we'll highlight aspects of the migration strategy and then review the actual process. This process, in terms of functional activities, can be broken down into migrating the functionality of BPC, including the objects involved with the architecture and structure, and migrating the reporting component.

10 Migration Process to BPC V10.0

You've now reviewed and experienced all of the different features and functions available in SAP Business Processing and Consolidation V10.0 (BPC), and you're now ready to investigate moving to this version. In this chapter, we'll be working through the process of migration and the different issues to be aware of during this process. We'll cover the approach from both the backend setup/implementation and the frontend process. Each has a sequence of steps involved to make everything work properly. It's important to review all of the business reasons and technical reasons for migration and base this decision on some good return on investment (ROI) results.

10.1 Migration to BPC V10.0 – A Strategy

When you think about the option of migration from a previous version of a software application to the most current, there are a number of aspects to understand and review to decide if this is right for your corporation. Besides the issues around the software itself and the compatibility concerns, you also have to look at all of the soft issues as well, which is the most critical process in the migration project. After these decisions are made, the path forward should be very clear. Every migration requires obtaining something significant from this activity for the corporation after the migration is complete. You don't want to migrate from a consistently working process and system that satisfies all your needs to another system just to have the latest and greatest version. You have to understand the ROI on a move like this, especially if the migration process is going to impact both the technical side and the function or business user side of the fence. The worst scenario is to having a migration process at the starting gate or already be underway, and the business user is wondering why this change is even happening. You want to avoid hearing users say, "I'm not getting the same functionality I had before," which normally is interpreted as the business user losing some functionality in the translation from one version to another.

> **Note: Terminology Definition**
>
> *Migration* is used when we're talking about system-to-system processes, whereas *upgrading* is used when we're talking about activities directly on an existing system.

In the case of BPC, a migration impacts both the technical and functional side of the business, so everyone will need to be onboard with the migration, which is a result of presenting a consistent and valid case for the move. Because a BPC consultant in this process is someone with experience and understanding of the system functionality and enhancements, it's critical to be sure to cover the important aspects of a migration from both the system process as well as from the business user side.

Let's assume that the corporation has the resources and budget to do any of the options that we discuss. That way we can remove the political and budgetary restrictions and talk more freely about the business and system side of the migration process. The initial process isn't to identify the system approach for migration but to identify the expected results, resources, and the overall system architecture you're looking for as an end state. If, for example, the SAP NetWeaver Business Warehouse (BW) system that is currently supporting BPC isn't just for BPC but is also used for the entire SAP BusinessObjects (BI) enterprise and supports the numerous activities that a BI system does for reporting and data loading, then you may not want to migrate at all because the BW system with all its functionality will also have to be migrated to BPC V7.3 from either V3.x or V7.x. This process may be too disruptive and impossible for all of the different groups that are being supported by your current BI environment. That being said, you need to go with an option to have a standalone BW system at the V7.3 level to use with BPC V10.0. So, one of the first concerns is how much of the company will be impacted by this move and is there time to either realign all of the architecture or very carefully transport everything over to the new V7.3 system. This makes the option of a particular system approach a matter of fact rather than a decision point.

Another question is about the by-product of upgrading to BPC V10.0, that is, for the SAP NetWeaver version, a migration to BW V7.3. A number of enhancements can be gained by just this aspect of the migration. We haven't discussed any of these improvements in BW V7.3, but much has to do with the performance of the system for both reporting as well as uploading. There are a number of new Info-Providers that can be used for the company's reporting and that support improved performance. One such improvement is the ability to use the SAP NetWeaver BW Accelerator (BWA) V7.2 (which is the application of BWA that integrates with BW V7.3) to affect the use of restricted and calculated key figures in a report situation. BWA helps support the execution of these report components. Also, the integration with SAP HANA is more available with BW V7.3 as well as other improvements around Data Store Objects (DSOs) and hierarchy uploads, to name a few.

One of the areas of BPC V10.0 that is a significant shift is in the reporting process. Even though EvDRE functions are supported in the SAP Enterprise Performance Management (EPM) add-in, we suggest the new approach of using the Excel frontend supplied by the EPM suite. This offers a cleaner version of Excel to be used, and anyone with an Excel background will be comfortable with this version quickly. Of course, the features are a bit different from the EvDRE functions, but the shift to the EPM add-in is being well-received. It also helps that the training on the EPM add-in is more natural to anyone who has used other reporting tools such as the BEX Analyzer, BEX Web, or Essbase. So this can well be one of the significant decision points in the process. You've seen many features and functions of the EPM add-in in Chapter 4 already. This might be an area that the business users will be interested in exploring; in fact, these features may help them support the migration of an existing system.

Of course, all of the new features found in BPC V10.0 make up the key reason for the migration from a previous version. These "delta" features haven't been presented in this book as such because we haven't made it a rule to compare the V10.0 to other versions, but this natural tendency to do the comparison between versions has certainly inserted itself in this book. Those of you who have worked with versions from 5.0 and up can easily pick out the enhanced features, but for those that haven't, the changes have been significant, and a number of documents have been published listing the differences if this is critical to your decision on migration. Not only has the entire frontend of the BPC system changed as mentioned in Chapter 4 but also many enhancements to the consolidation process as well as more integration with the SAP NetWeaver platform has occurred, which has affected all aspects of the BW links with the BPC environment, including security, data loading, dimensions, properties, and members. The following are some of the specific features that have changed:

In the Consolidation Process

▶ Incremental consolidation

▶ Consolidation Monitor and all of its features (SAP NetWeaver)

▶ Control Monitor (SAP NetWeaver)

▶ Journal Entry functionality and web screen

▶ Ownership Management

▶ BPC configuration of the Global, Environment, and Application (model) parameters in the IMG

In the integration with SAP NetWeaver, these features have changed:

▶ Delta uploading, which is available between BW objects and BPC models

▶ Elimination of the .NET layer, which affords more integration between the SAP NetWeaver platform and BPC

▶ Web Client start page

▶ Additional options in the creation process of dimensions, models, and properties

▶ Security linking the BW user to the BPC user and the SAP NetWeaver roles and functionality

▶ More enhanced control features

▶ Enhanced features of the Script Logic editor

▶ Start page with the enhanced use of folders for user activities

▶ Enhanced Data Manager functions and standard packages, for example, direct uploading from SAP ERP (standard)

▶ Books and the publishing/distribution

10.2 Upgrading to BPC V10.0 for SAP NetWeaver

Now that the business users and/or the technical group have pursued the decision makers to back the migration, we can start to get into the details of what it takes to actually complete this undertaking. The first thing to note about this migration process is that the migration path is only from V7.5 to V10.0. So if your current BPC system is anything previous to V7.5, you'll have to first do an upgrade/migration to V7.5 and then proceed with the current migration. This process will probably add additional tasks and time to your project plan. Also, if you've supported BW with BWA, you should review and possibly incorporate a migration of the BWA from the current version (probably V7.0) to BWA V7.2, which is the suggested version to integrate with BW V7.3. Now that you're ready to do the actual migration, you can choose from one of the three options outlined in the following subsections. Remember that the difference in these scenarios is the beginning of the process. After the initial steps, you'll see that the remaining steps including the migration program are the same.

10.2.1 Option #1 – Direct Migration on the Current System

In this scenario, you migrate directly on the current system, which means an upgrade of the BW to V7.3 and then an upgrade to BPC V10.0. After the systems have been upgraded, you then execute the migration program to migrate the information in your previous V7.5 into the V10.0 format. This requires no additional hardware or system enhancements.

> **Note: Migration Program**
>
> We'll discuss the migration program in the next section, but the execution of the program applies to all three of the different migration options.

On face value, this looks to be the most straightforward as well as the easiest approach, but the best approach is probably not the easiest, and, in this case, you expose yourself to quite a bit of risk going about the migration in this manner. In this situation, you'll need whatever quiet time necessary to complete the full migration process. This means that the system won't be available for any activities until this full migration is complete. This might be a significant amount of time, and depending on your planning cycles or consolidation process, it might be prohibitive. After you start this process, you'll be hard-pressed if issues or problems crop up during the migration activities. With all of this in mind, we don't suggest this approach as the best and caution that it might be very disruptive to the ongoing activities of the corporation.

10.2.2 Option #2 – Migration via a Copy of the System

The next option is to alter the preceding scenario by making a copy of the existing system and then executing the migration on the copy. This scenario helps reduce the risk quite a bit due to the fact that you're not impacting the production system of BPC. This means no break in the activities planned on BPC in production. The migration of the database and the operating systems are done during the copy process, and you're then ready for the subsequent steps of migration. After the copy is complete, you'll have a SAP NetWeaver 7.3 system with BPC V10.0 assigned. Again, this copy will be from a SAP NetWeaver V7.01 to a V7.3 and a BPC copy from V7.5 to V10.0.

The next step is similar in all scenarios and that is to run the migration program. This program is executed via Transaction SE38, and the standard program name is UJT_MIGRATE_75_TO_10. After this transaction is executed, you'll see a screen similar to the one in Figure 10.1. Again notice that this program starts with a UJ as do all of the programs available in BW for BPC activities.

After this program is executed, you'll see a series of parameters to select by clicking on their check boxes (see Figure 10.2). These are all of the components and tables that will be migrated from the BPC V7.5 to V10.0 after the process is executed.

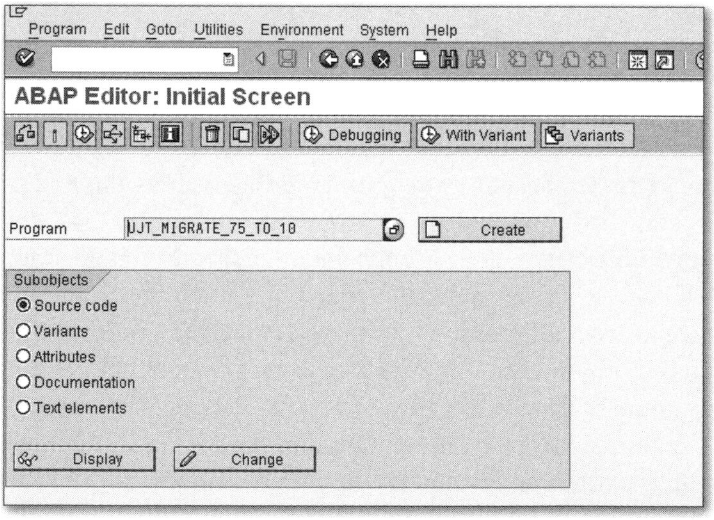

Figure 10.1 Initial Screen of Migration Program UJT_MIGRATE_75_TO_10

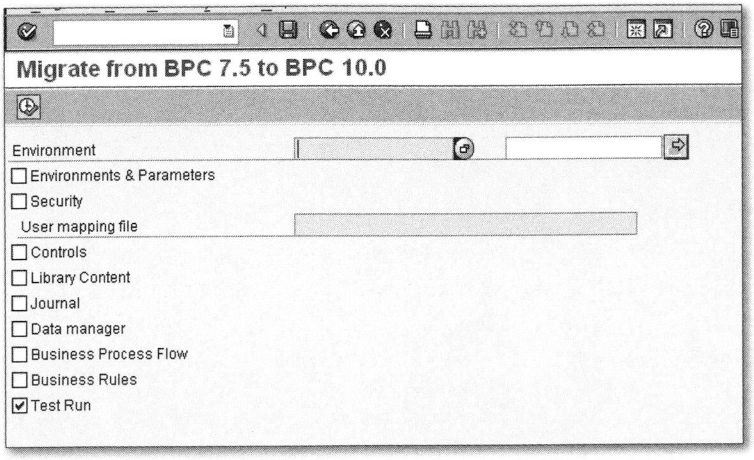

Figure 10.2 Parameters for the Migration Program

There are a number of objects, data, and programs migrated using this program. Table 10.1 shows the list of objects that are migrated and not migrated to give you an idea of the amount of manual activities required after this is complete.

Objects, Tasks, Processes	Migrated	Not Migrated
All of the administrative settings	X	
All of the applications/models	X	
All of the dimensions	X	
All terminology adjusted based on the current naming conventions	X	
User IDs	X	
User IDs in the owner and reviewer properties of the dimensions	X	
In security: teams, task profiles, and member access profiles	X	
Journals	X	
Business rules	X	
Validation rules, now called controls	X	

Table 10.1 Features in BPC That Migrate from V7.5 to V10.0

Objects, Tasks, Processes	Migrated	Not Migrated
Data Manager features, including process chains, Script Logic, prompts, and all other features	X	
Log files from the Data Manager		X
Live Reports (these are required to be rebuilt in the workspace area of the new version		X
Content Library (generally all aspects of the Content Library are migrated – please check after the migration is complete)	X	
Custom web pages and reports (these need to be rebuilt using the new web reporting and input template features)		X
Business Process Flows (BPFs)	X	
Xcelsius dashboards		X

Table 10.1　Features in BPC That Migrate from V7.5 to V10.0 (Cont.)

There is an additional step in this process to be able to migrate the user management and security. Because BPC V7.5 uses the Active Directory or the Content Management Service (CMS) accounts, you need to shift them over to the SAP NetWeaver version, which uses BW user accounts. You have to create the user accounts in the SAP NetWeaver system, and any new security roles or authorizations need to be assigned to the users. After that is all set up, a mapping file needs to be available for the migration program to use so that it can map the old users to the new users. This file will be assigned to the migration program shown earlier in Figure 10.2 in the labeled USER MAPPING FILE. This file should be tab-delimited and look something like the example in Figure 10.3.

AD User_ID for BPC 7.5	NW User_ID for BPC 10.0
<Domain>\<AD User_ID>	<ABAP User_ID>

Figure 10.3　Example of the User Mapping File required for the Migration Program

10.2.3　Option #3 – Installation of a New System

This final option is the most controlled and manageable. Because you're setting up an entirely new system with SAP NetWeaver V7.3 and BPC V10.0, you can start from scratch, and there's no interference with the production systems. This process will take the normal installation approach that can be found in the BPC V10.0 Master Installation Guide on the SAP Service Marketplace site. The difference in this scenario is that you'll have to use Transaction UJBR to back up the Appsets from the V7.5 system and then restore them in the V10.0 system as Environments. This process uses the same transaction but uses the backup process in V7.5 and the restore process in V10.0. This will install the Appsets (now called environments) and everything that comes along into the V10.0 environment and realign the objects to the V10.0 features and functionality. Figure 10.4 shows you the view of Transaction UJBR.

BPC: Backup & Restore Tool

Execution
- ◉ Execute Backup
- ○ Execute Restore

Execute in...
- ○ Background
- ◉ Foreground

Parameters & Procedures
Environment ID
Download Directory Name

Backup Metadata Tables	☑		
DM Data Files	☑	Log Files	☐
Audit Data	☑	Archived Audit Data	☐
Backup Master Data	☐		
Backup Transaction Data	☐	Record Count (0 = All Records)	200

Figure 10.4 Initial Screen for BPC: Backup & Restore Tool

As you can see, in the first section labeled EXECUTION, you have the option to EXECUTE BACKUP (take a copy) or EXECUTE RESTORE (install a copy).

10.3 Upgrading to BPC V10.0 for the Microsoft Platform

There are significant differences in the migration approach between the SAP NetWeaver and the Microsoft versions, so you need to look at the Microsoft approach to make sure you're aware of the shift required for migration. That being said, the BPC V10.0 for Microsoft is a bit of a unique situation. You can't execute a migration from any version of Microsoft to BPC V10.0. In this case, you have to install a new environment for BPC and then migrate the objects from V7.5 to V10.0 because there is no migration path from an older version of Microsoft BPC to V10.0. If you're currently on V5.x, you have to migrate the functionality and objects to V7.x and then go through the process of copying the objects to the V10.0 server. This is due to the differences between the two systems and the operating system level as well as the SQL used. Therefore, there is basically one approach to this process.

As in the case of the migration process of SAP NetWeaver, a similar situation occurs during the Microsoft process. Some of the objects can't be migrated. In this process, the administration settings and configuration are migrated automatically. During the process, a validation of all of the properties is executed to insure consistency. Also, because some of the task profiles were changed, removed, or replaced, additional manual activities are required to make sure these objects perform correctly in the new V10.0 system. Other functions that are automatically migrated include the following:

▶ Transformation and conversion files in the Data Manager (depending on the amount of customization that's been done)

▶ Dynamic scripts

▶ Package authorizations

▶ SSIS 2008 packages

▶ Content Library as well as stored documents and URLs

▶ BPFs, but must confirm that they have all moved successfully due to some BPFs being removed and/or changed

▶ Published books

▶ Transactional data

▶ Journals

▶ Comments

Custom menus aren't migrated; instead, they are replaced with the workspaces and activities options in BPC V10.0.

To start the migration process, you restore the Appset backups to the BPC V10.0 environment using the Server Manager, as shown in Figure 10.5. After you access the SERVER MANAGER, choose ENVIRONMENT • RESTORE. Then identify the backup folders in the ENVIRONMENT FOLDER SECTION, and click on NEXT (see Figure 10.6).

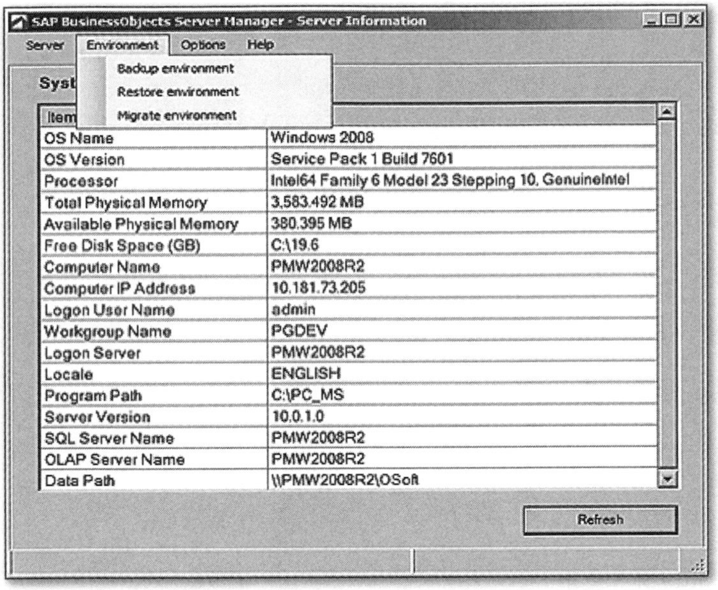

Figure 10.5 Initial Step Using the Server Manager to Restore Environment

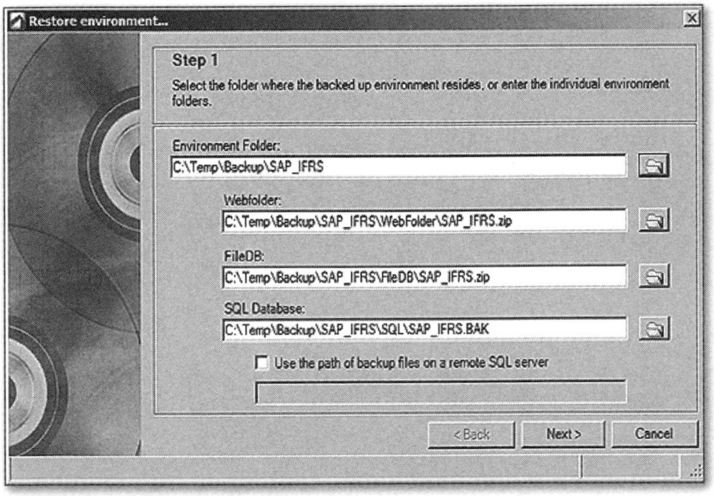

Figure 10.6 Restore Environment Backup Folders Screen

Then select the appropriate server names for each of the environment components (see Figure 10.7).

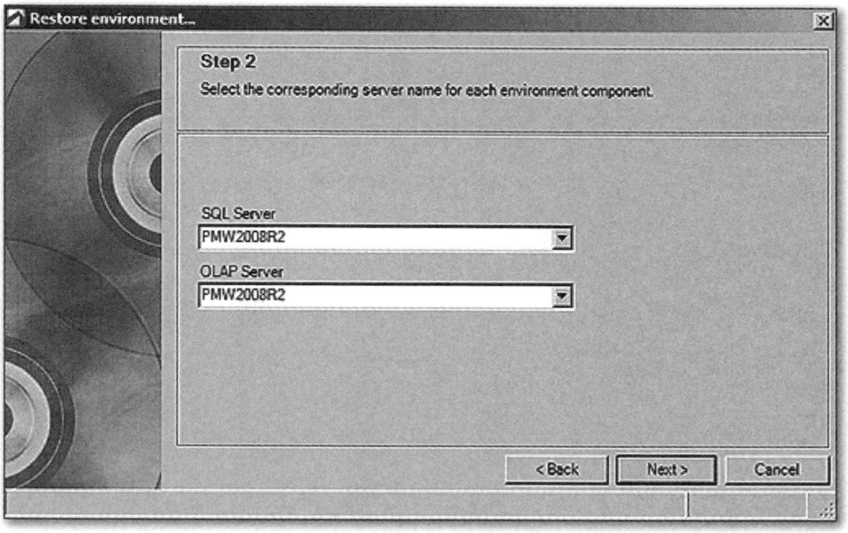

Figure 10.7 Server Names for Each of the Environments

This is a wizard approach so choose NEXT and then YES to restart the system (see Figure 10.8).

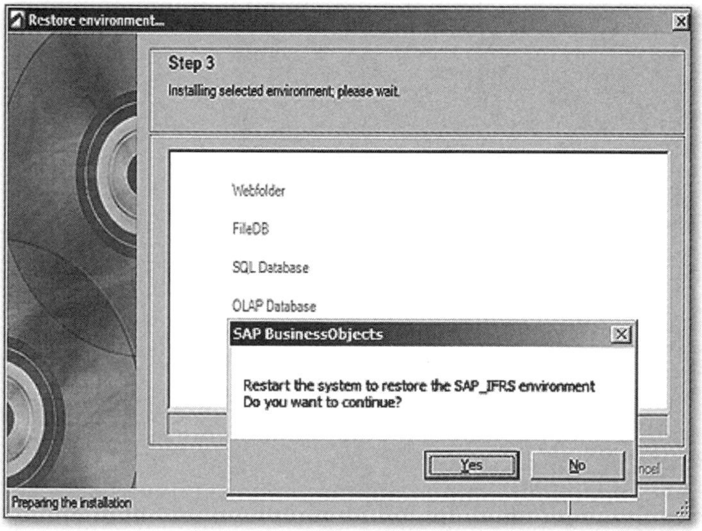

Figure 10.8 Restart the System to Restore Environment

After the system has been restored, you can migrate the different environments. Go back to the SERVER MANAGER and choose MIGRATE ENVIRONMENT to execute this process, as shown in Figure 10.9.

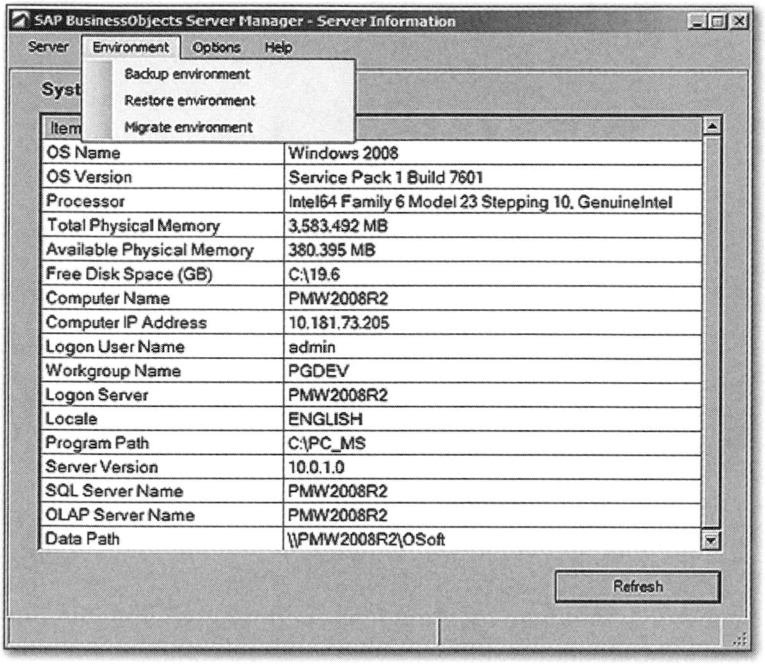

Figure 10.9 Server Manager – Migrate Environment

In the several popups that appear, fill in the appropriate parameter for each prompt. The initial one is the identity of the environment that is to be migrated. Then the next several are informational and hopefully showing messages of successful migration steps, as shown in Figure 10.10. After these steps are complete, you'll be able to access the migration logs and see what components need to be supported manually after the transition to BPC V10.0. An example of these logs is shown in Figure 10.11.

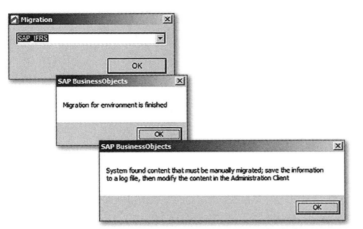

Figure 10.10 Migration steps in BPC for the Microsoft Platform

Figure 10.11 Log List of Items That Need to Be Redefined

10.4 Report Migration to BPC V10.0

This section discusses the report migration for both the Microsoft and SAP NetWeaver versions because it's the same process. In this process, there are some aspects that you have to be careful of while migrating the reports. For example, if you have a number of very complex EvDRE reports in BPC V7.5, you'll need to make sure that all of the EV functions being used will, in fact, migrate. If not, then you need to make some decisions on whether to execute the migration or keep these reports as is until you have the appropriate resources to allow you to do the migration.

10.4.1 Upgrading EV Functions

Most of the EV functions have been made available to migrate to the EPM functions, but if you really want to keep specific reports as EV reports, then that option is also available. You just migrate the reports you need. Figure 10.12 shows the location of the EV and EPM functions in the EPM add-in.

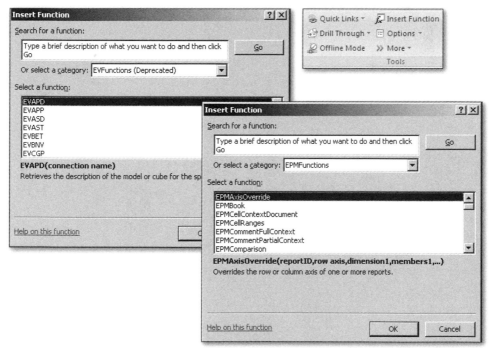

Figure 10.12 Insert Function Showing the EV and EPM Function List

Some functions are slightly different in V10.0 versus V7.5; in these cases, you have to handle these yourself and realign manually. Pay specific attention to the EV functions that relate to the portal due to the changes in the integration layer (such as EVHNV). The EV functions you have to definitely watch are those that aren't supported in BPC V10.0, such as EVHOT, EVEXP, EVENE, EVNXP, EVSET, EVLST, and EVPXR.

For some of the additional features available, there is no migration path either. For example, due to the change in the prompt to EPMXX for the EPM functions, the API is different, so many of the macros that you might have created won't be available and will have to be recreated. Another popular EV functions—EVMNU—is supported but with a new macro name, so it will have to be manually synced up.

10.4.2 Upgrading EvDRE Reports

After you've decided on the number of reports to be migrated, the process is fairly straightforward. There is an EvDRE migration tool that resides in the EPM frontend. This can be used to migrate individual reports, workbooks, or an entire folder of reports all at once. This tool can be found in the menu item MORE on the EPM ribbon. Figure 10.13 shows the location to access this component.

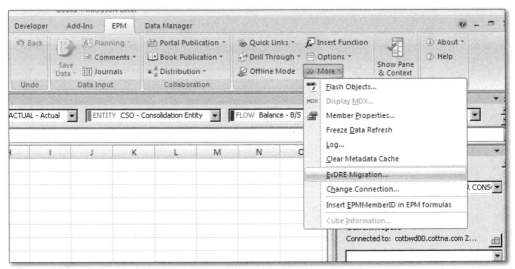

Figure 10.13 Menu Path to the EvDRE Migration Toolset

From this link, you'll see a dialog box with a number of options and parameters offered for migrating reports. Figure 10.14 shows the next screen.

The following options are available:

▶ Migrate the active worksheet

▶ Migrate the active workbook

▶ Migrate the entire folder of workbooks stored on the BPC server

▶ Migrate the local folder

When you choose a folder of workbooks to migrate, the existing workbooks are automatically duplicated in the system. The decision can then be made whether those copies can be stored in the same folder or in a subfolder of the initial folder. This is what the option at the very bottom of the dialog box is referencing: Do NOT MOVE ORIGINAL WORKBOOKS IN A DIFFERENT FOLDER.

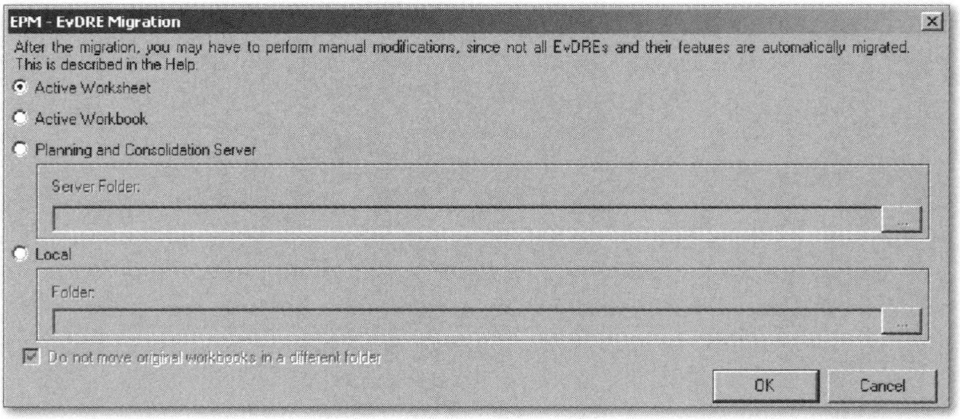

Figure 10.14 EPM – EvDRE Migration Component

After the migration is complete, you can review the items that require additional changes or manual activities to have the V10.0 system recognize the whole report. These items can be found in the LOG, which is shown in Figure 10.15.

After you execute the LOG feature, you'll see something similar to Figure 10.11 in the previous section. You can see and address the objects that require additional manual migration. Most of the objects that are used currently in BPC V7.5 will be migrated, but other items that may have issues during migration might be the SORTING, RANKING, SUPPRESSING, and INSERT options. Rule of thumb, of course, is to always check and do regression testing against all of the objects that have been migrated to validate that they work and are still functionally consistent.

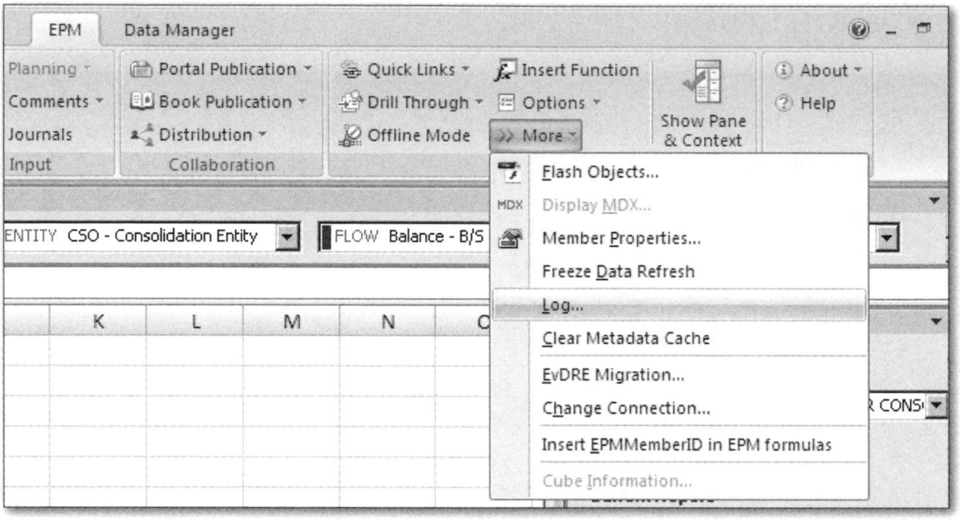

Figure 10.15 Accessing the Log for Details on Migrated Objects

10.5 Summary

Upgrading to BPC V10.0 isn't something to take lightly. There are definitely significant numbers of reasons why you may want to or need to migrate to this version, but it's something to review and develop as a project rather than as a "lift and shift" process. The features available in BPC V10.0 from a technical as well as a functional point of view definitely make the move well worthwhile, and the impact of these features offers the ROI that your corporation is looking for in BPC.

We've discussed the different approaches to upgrading to BPC V10.0 for both the SAP NetWeaver and Microsoft versions. We've looked at the functional migration process and the options possible form a system point of view. We then reviewed the migration of the reporting components of BPC. There are some concerns during the migration to take into account with both functionality that might be used currently that aren't being supported, such as complex macros or VBA in excel, as well as the reporting and input template components that have changed. You should always check and confirm what EvDRE features are supported in v10 since the support and integration for these features are changing with every SP that SAP provides.

The Author

Mr. Peter Jones is a BI/BPC Sr. Application Consultant with MI6 Solutions LLC specializing in the areas of CO (Controlling), Enterprise Controlling (EC), Business Intelligence/Business Objects (BI/BOBJ), Strategic Enterprise Management (SEM) and Business Planning and Consolidation (BPC). He has over fourteen years of consulting and educational experience in a variety of strategic and leadership roles, focused on global architecture and strategies for BI, ECC and BPC. Peter's diverse professional background includes not only consulting experience but academic experience in the areas of Finance, Controlling, Data Warehousing, Enterprise Management and Corporate Governance. He has been involved with numerous implementations for SAP in the areas of CO, SEM, BI, EPM and ECC, from the blueprint phase through to the Go-Live Process. His responsibilities include all aspects from Strategic BI/BPC analysts to the core configuration in all areas. Peter has experience with many industry-specific, cross application areas such as automotive, utilities, entertainment, consumer, banking, and public sector.

Previous to MI6 Solutions, he was a Principal/Platinum Business Application Consultant with SAP Professional Services specializing in all of the areas noted above. As a Subject Matter Expert (SME), Peter was involved in the review, configuration, and analysis for many projects with global and local requirements. Peter has completed work on the development of the course curriculum for CO, SEM, BW, BI, BPC, APO and the Auditing Application for Sarbanes-Oxley Compliance. Further to his technical background, Peter has developed and presented numerous topics for the University Alliance such as Data Mining, SEM Enterprise Performance Management, Business Intelligence and SOX (Sarbanes-Oxley Act). A speaker at ASUG, SAPPHIRE, and BI conferences, Peter has spoken on the topics of CO, SOX, SEM and BW. He is also an editor/writer for FICO Expert and BI Expert and has written several books on BI data modeling and reporting and FI/CO configuration for SAP.

He has a BA and MBA from Drexel University in Finance and is SAP certified in the areas of FI, CO, BI/BOBJ, SEM and BPC. Prior to SAP he owned his own business for 15 years and worked in the area of accounting and finance.

The Contributor

Mr. Charles (Tim) Soper is a Sr. SAP Educational Consultant and has been with SAP for over 15 years in the Educational area. His areas of expertise are FI, CO, BI, SEM, and BPC. He has been involved with the development of numerous courses including CO, BI, SEM and BPC and is a course owner of multiple courses. As an instructor he has taught courses at all levels from novice to advanced workshops. He has been involved in a number of review and customer assignments in the BI and BPC areas. He is an SME in the areas of BI and BPC and is routinely requested to offer advice and expertise on specific aspects of BPC and BI projects. Tim has written articles in the areas of BI and BPC for the BI Expert and has been a contributing author on other books in the BI area.

He has a BA and MBA from the University of Rochester in Finance and is SAP certified in the areas of FI, CO, BI, and BPC. Previous to SAP he worked for Eastman Kodak Company in various positions in the Finance and Accounting areas.

Index

- Understand the complete planning and consolidation solution from SAP

- Master features, functions, and integration with other SAP components and applications

- Completely updated for release 7.5

Sridhar Srinivasan, Kumar Srinivasan

SAP BusinessObjects Planning and Consolidation

This new edition covers the major features, functions, implementation, and integration of SAP BusinessObjects Planning and Consolidation 7.5 for NetWeaver. Beyond the product functionality, you'll find best practices for budgeting, planning, forecasting, and consolidations, and master consolidation and business planning topics. With numerous screenshots and walkthroughs, this is the one-stop overview to understand what BPC is and what it can do for you.

446 pp., 2. edition 2011, ./., 79,95 Euro / US$ 79.95
ISBN 978-1-59229-397-1

www.sap-press.com

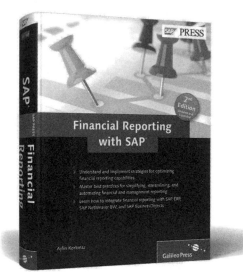

- Understand and implement strategies for optimizing financial reporting capabilities

- Master best practices for simplifying, streamlining, and automating financial and management reporting

- Learn how to integrate financial reporting with SAP ERP, SAP NetWeaver BW, and SAP

Aylin Korkmaz

Financial Reporting with SAP

This book provides finance and IT teams with best practices for delivering financial reports faster, more accurately, and in compliance with various international accounting standards. Featuring step-by-step coverage of all major FI reporting functions, this new edition helps you streamline and simplify financial business processes and automate reporting in SAP ERP Financials. This new edition includes updated content on statutory and segment reporting, AP and AR reports in SAP ERP, Consolidated Financial Reporting, SAP BusinessObjects, and much more.

745 pp., 2. edition 2011, ./., 79,95 Euro / US$ 79.95
ISBN 978-1-59229-391-9

www.sap-press.com

- Explore the entire financial close process from financial accounting to entity and corporate closing

- Maximize the potential of SAP Financial Solutions like FI, CO, and Disclosure Management for the financial close process

- Meet the latest regulatory and reporting requirements with ease

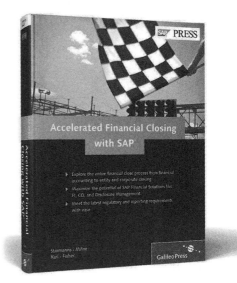

Birgit Starmanns, Elizabeth Milne, Stefan Karl, James Fisher

Accelerated Financial Closing with SAP

Navigate the complex last mile of finance with speed, efficiency, and ease with this end to end process guide for closing your books books. Address regulatory requirements, manage disclosure management and report results to key stake holders. Develop a single financial close workflow and maximize the potential of SAP's financial solutions. Close your books faster with this one-stop resource for all your financial closing needs!

approx. 300 pp., ./., 69,95 Euro / US$ 69.95
ISBN 978-1-59229-446-6, Jan 2013

www.sap-press.com

Galileo Press

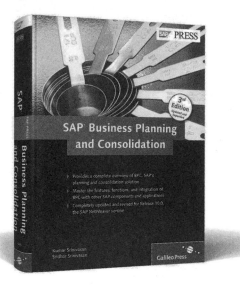

■ A complete overview of BPC, SAP's planning and consolidation solution

■ Master the features, functions, and integration of BPC with other SAP components and applications

■ Completely updated and revised for release 10.0, the SAP NetWeaver version

Kumar Srinivasan, Sridhar Srinivasan

SAP Business Planning and Consolidation

Master the expanded and new functionality of BPC 10.0 and leverage its improvements for your own workflows and planning. This comprehensive overview covers the features, functionality, and best practices for SAP Planning and Consolidation, SAP NetWeaver version. Revised for release 10.0, this edition explores the changes to BPC's technical architecture, user experience, and reporting functionality. Maximize the potential of BPC with this updated edition.

approx. 500 pp., 3. edition, ./., 79,95 Euro / US$ 79.95
ISBN 978-1-59229-445-9, Dec 2012

www.sap-press.com

■ Understand the CO component and how to make it work for you

■ Connect the CO subcomponents in SAP ERP and integrate them in your implementation

■ Master the customizing of CO in SAP ERP Financials to meet your business needs

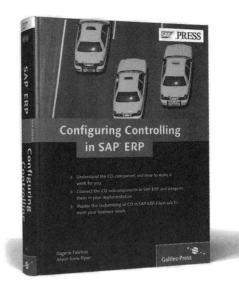

Rogerio Faleiros, Alison Kreis Ryan

Configuring Controlling in SAP ERP

This is a complete guide to SAP ERP Financials Controlling that teaches you the best way to implement and customize CO for your business. You'll master information on the various submodules and tools encountered in a CO implementation, and learn the step-by-step instructions with concrete, real-world examples. This is a comprehensive guide for anyone interested in customizing Controlling.

547 pp., 2012, ./., 79,95 Euro / US$ 79.95
ISBN 978-1-59229-401-5

www.sap-press.com

■ Learn to easily navigate the SAP system

■ Work with SAP modules step-by-step

■ Includes many examples and detailed SAP illustrations

Olaf Schulz

Using SAP

A Guide for Beginners and End Users

This book helps end users and beginners get started in SAP ERP and provides readers with the basic knowledge they need for their daily work. Readers will get to know the essentials of working with the SAP system, learn about the SAP systems' structures and functions, and discover how SAP connects to critical business processes. Whether this book is used as an exercise book or as a reference book, readers will find what they need to help them become more comfortable with SAP ERP.

388 pp., 2012, ./., 39,95 Euro / US$ 39.95
ISBN 978-1-59229-408-4

www.sap-press.com